Dies Irae

A Guide to Requiem Music

Robert Chase

The Scarecrow Press, Inc.
Lanham, Maryland, and Plymouth, UK
2003

SCARECROW PRESS, INC.

Published in the United States of America
by Scarecrow Press, Inc.
A wholly owned subsidiary of
The Rowman & Littlefield Publishing Group, Inc.
4501 Forbes Boulevard, Suite 200, Lanham, Maryland 20706
www.scarecrowpress.com

Eastover Road
Plymouth PL6 7PY
United Kingdom

British Library Cataloguing in Publication Information Available

Library of Congress Cataloging-in-Publication Data

Chase, Robert, 1938–
    Dies irae : a guide to requiem music / Robert Chase.
        p.   cm.
    Includes bibliographical references (p.   ) and index.
    ISBN 0-8108-4664-0 (hardcover : alk. paper)
    1. Requiems—History and criticism.   I. Title.
ML3088 .C43   2003
782.32'38—dc21   2002152105

In memory of my parents,
Edna Avis Chase
Robert Henry Chase

Contents

Foreword

For musicians, music lovers, choral directors, and anyone interested in music, *Dies Irae: A Guide to Requiem Music* provides a look into the numerous settings of a musical-poetic form that has been composed from the Middle Ages to the present. Not only does this guide take the reader through the better-known requiems by Mozart, Brahms, Cherubini, and Verdi, but also lesser-known settings by James DeMars, Friedrich Kiel, Théodore Gouvy, and Sir George Henschel.

Included are a number of contemporary requiems, such as Gerard Victory's *Ultima Rerum* and Britten's *War Requiem*. Dr. Chase has included a significant selection of works from the Eastern Orthodox Rites, works that are an important part of the Christian musical and spiritual heritage. Furthermore, there are also selections from the German Requiem, the Anglican Requiem, the War Requiem, and the secular requiem. It is a well-known fact that many composers have written a setting of their requiem, but I do not recall any source that puts information about them under one cover. Of special interest to me are the pieces by Gouvy, Rivier, Tomasi, Bomtempo, and the Messa per Rossini.

I have conducted many requiems with The Cleveland Orchestra and other orchestras, including Berlioz, Brahms, Faure, Mozart, and Verdi. Every time I conduct a requiem, it is an emotional experience for me and always serves to enlighten. Even though each composer has its own characteristic setting of the requiem, I always feel the same message in the music: et lux perpetua. "May the eternal light shine upon you." It is a message of hope and comfort knowing that eternal life is waiting for those who depart. No other form of music can convey this meaning so vividly except for the requiem. This book will be a welcome addition to any musical library.

Jahja Ling, Associate Conductor, Cleveland Orchestra

Acknowledgments

Few books are the product of a singular mind and a great many people have helped on this musical journey. I would like to express here my heartfelt thanks and appreciation for that assistance.

To composers, James Bingham, Thomas Beveridge, Daniel Pinkham, Edgar Grana, Anthony Newman, and James DeMars-Michel Sarda for scores and tapes of their works. Baronet Lionel Sawkins, for his sharing of his transcription of the virtually impossible-to-find score of De la Lande's grand motet, *Dies Irae*. Nikolai Kachanov, for scores of the monophonic Russian chants, Sviridov and Copytsko scores. Vladimir Morosan of Musica Russica, for various Panikhida scores, and full scores of Taniev's, *St. John of Damascus* and Kastalsy's *Commeration Fraternelle*, as well as many other valuable insights. Long-time friend and classmate, Eugene Pelletier, *titulaire du grande-orgue de L'eglise Saint Joseph des Carmes* (Paris), for reading the manuscript as well as alerting me to the Calmel, De Ranse, and Le Francois works and for sending full scores of the Rivier and Gagneux requiems. Long-time friend and classmate, Dr. Peter Bayerdörfer, for locating the Hasse, Kiel, and Gouvy scores. My friend, Shiela Hu, librarian, who located and obtained several dozen hard-to-get scores.

To the conductor, Christopher Dawes for a taped performance of Willan's *Requiem*. Fathers Oshagan Minassian, Mammigon Kiledjian, and Daniel Findikyan for musical scores and assistance with the Armenian Rite. Milos Raikovich for a copy of his setting of the *Parastasos* and help with the Serbian *Opelo*. Brother Cyril Cavet for his Latin motet translations. Eugene Mohr for reading my translations of the German requiems and, most especially, his work with the poetry of Hermann Heiss. Arlene Stadler for her preparations of the musical examples found in the Guide.

Dr. Christopher Chang, Professor of Music (Dong-Wu University, Taipei), for his support and encouragement in preparing this study.

Grateful thanks and appreciation is also extended to: Metropolitan Philip of the Antiochian Orthodox Christian Archdiocese of North America for use of the Panikhida texts. Father Spenceri Kezios for his translations of the requiem texts in the *Sacraments and Services Music Book* and tapes for the Greek service. Professor Sandro Gorli for use of his poetry. Kurt Vonnegut for use of his text, *Stones, Time and Elements: A Humanist Requiem*. Boosey & Hawkes, Inc., for the use of the Heinrich Simon poetry (Delius Requiem, © 1920, 1921, 1922 by Hawkes & Son [London] Ltd.). Chatto and Windus for use of Wilfrid Owen's *War Poems*. Elis Pehkonen and Max Hayward and Manya Harari in the translation of *Dr. Zhivago* (1965 edition) and published by Collins/Hamill in Fontana Books. Michel Sarda for the use of his Native American poetry in James De Mars' *American Requiem*. Huub Oosterhuis, *Im Vorübergehen* © Verlag Herder, Freiburg 2, Auflage 1971. Paul Celan, *Die Posaunenstelle*, Paul Celan, *Zeitgehöft. Späte Gedichte aus dem Nachlass*. © Suhrkamp Verlag, Frankfurt am Main, 1976. Dr. Johannes Graulich of Carus-Verlag for allowing me to use Dr. Robert Scandrett's English translation of the Dresden Requiem.

Finally, I want to thank my wife, Jenny, and son, Wayne, for their patience and support during the five years that have elapsed since this project was begun.

Abbreviations

VOICES & INSTRUMENTS

SATB = soprano, alto, tenor, bass. [appears in numerous combinations]
Bar = baritone
v(vv) = voice(s)
v(vv) = verse(s)
STR, WW, PERC = strings, woodwinds, percussion
vn [violin], vla [viola], vc [cello], db [double bass]
pic [piccolo], fl [flute], ob [oboe], cl [clarinet], bcl [bass clarinet] Eh [English horn],
   bsn [bassoon], cbsn [contrabassoon], Fh [French horn], tpt [trumpet], tbn
   [trombone]
org [organ], timp [timpani]

GENERAL

b.c. = basso continuo
c. = circa
[CM] = C major, [fm] = f minor [other keys follow similar pattern]
mm. = measures
perf. = performance time

COUNTRIES [ONLY IN APPENDIX I]

ARG = Argentina
AUS = Austria
BELG = Belgium
BOH = Bohemia
BRAZ = Brazil
BUL = Bulgaria
CAN = Canada
COL = Columbia
CZE = Czech Republic
DEN = Denmark
ENG = England
FIN = Finland
FRA = France
GER = Germany
HUN = Hungary

ICE = Iceland
ITA = Italy
JAP = Japan
MEX = Mexico
NETH = Netherlands
POL = Poland
PORT = Portugal
RUS = Russia
SPA = Spain
SWED = Sweden
SWIS = Switzerland
URUG = Uruguay
USA = United States
VENEZ = Venezuela
YUGO = Yugoslavia

Introduction

Meeting the final moments of existence within the physical realm of life is the one common experience fated for all mortal beings. Since time immemorial, the response of the living to this natural occurrence is to commemorate the life of the departed through ceremonies and rituals, both formal and informal, as fitting to the circumstances. Throughout history, music has played a significant role in the various rites of passages observed to sanctify this journey from life to death. For nearly two millennia, the Christian quest for eternal peace in a more perfect form of existence has been expressed in a poetic-musical structure known as the requiem. Accompanying this optimistic pursuit for everlasting bliss is its quintessential antithesis—eternal damnation, a concept spelled out so clearly in the medieval text *Dies irae*. Although the threat of such horrific consequences is muted in the prayers of the Orthodox rites, this terrifying facet of death had vividly announced its presence in the Roman rite, at least until the arrival of the Second Vatican Council, when the voice of *Dies irae* was greatly softened, or, in some cases, virtually eradicated.

Traditional requiem texts, often referred to as canonical prayers, have served as an abundant source of inspiration for an untold number of composers, many of whom have bequeathed to future generations their expert musical witness and testimony. In the present day, these works reside in both oft-used scores, performed for international audiences, and nearly forgotten manuscripts with dusty covers and yellowed pages. This book shall shed the light of recognition on a significantly extensive, but often neglected, musical repertory.

Why a book on the music and history of the requiem? Has such a topic not been thoroughly researched in many past volumes? In truth, the last English-language book on the subject, the excellent monograph *Requiem:*

Music of Mourning and Consolation, was written by Alec Robertson more than thirty years ago. Apart from this ground-breaking work, there has actually been no comprehensive study of the requiem and its music that details its evolution from its earliest beginnings to the present day. A number of doctoral dissertations, of course, have detailed the significance of specific works, such as Biber's *Requiem for Fifteen Voices* or Mozart's *Requiem*, yet there appear, until now, to be no inclusive books that recognize and examine this prominent, influential musical form and its vast, impressive history. Other musical forms—mass ordinary, motet, or vocal song—possess an equally long tradition, and, in the case of the latter two, there exists a significant anthology of literature published on the subjects. Even the mass has not served as the focus of a specific outstanding English language reference work. Published in 1913, Peter Wagner's *Geschichte der Messe* ["History of the Mass"] continues to be the most substantial work of its kind. Regarding the requiem, a most recent and valuable, albeit quite short, account of the form was written by Professor Christopher Chang of Dong Wu University (Taiwan) in Chinese.

Furthermore, in an attempt to discover which particular requiems remain in the active concert repertory, we find that there are only a handful performed with notable regularity, and as it turns out, almost to a point of redundancy. Among those are the compositions of Mozart, Britten, Fauré, Duruflé, Verdi, Brahms, and occasionally Cherubini. These, of course, qualify as outstanding works, more often than not received with great accolades from audiences, yet hundreds of other resplendent settings continue to languish in undue obscurity, merely awaiting a performance worthy of their excellence. Such a dilemma can only be described as lamentable at best.

In 1941, the American musicologist Charles Warren Fox had composed a list of more than 1,000 requiem settings, while simultaneously stating that his catalogue was far from complete. More likely, the number of works in existence is between 2,000 and 2,500. Just imagine a similar situation involving operas, orchestral symphonies, or concertos in which only five or six of the very best compositions remained in the active symphonic repertory. The dismissal and eventual loss of so many other great works of music would certainly be a tragedy, not just in the area of music history, but in human history as well.

Regarding church performance, the virtual abolition of the use of Latin from the daily liturgy has adeptly brought an end to the careers of many substantial pieces, including those inspired and nurtured by the Caecilian reform movement of the nineteenth century. There are, however, some signs of encouragement. The Schwann Catalogue of CD recordings contains a wider range of available requiem repertory, citing approximately seventy-five works. This is hopefully an indication that there is much greater interest in this musical form than had been previously suspected.

Consider the concerto, symphony, string quartet, and piano sonata. These musical forms can be traced to a much more recent origin, yet they have served as the subjects of a plethora of books, papers, dissertations, and articles, celebrating their places within musical history. At the same time, no major source work has been composed on the requiem, leaving its origin and history to be told merely through scattered bits and pieces of writing. Part of the challenge in devising this guide has been to gather and culminate a vast wealth of widely dispersed information under one title in order to make it easily accessible to the general public.

This, perhaps, serves as a partial answer to the questions posed at the outset. Another portion rests in the notion that the requiem is, in fact, an integral musical topic, laden with genuine historical significance and worthy of diligent exploration. How a profound musical form with such an extensive history could be overlooked for so long remains something of a mystery. Throughout the process of devising this guide there arose an impression within that the composers who had vehemently struggled to set the familiar, oft-used words had made sincere attempts to cast a light upon the twinned emotions of sorrow and hope. It is true that funeral music does tend to be quite pensive and serious, yet it should be noted that all of the requiems mentioned within these pages also contain passages that express great joy, passion, and spiritual ecstasy. This is only natural considering the fact that these composers had attempted not only to console sorrow and bereavement, but also to nurture and inspire happiness, optimism, and hope for resurrection. Thus, the requiem is truly a bittersweet work of art.

The name requiem is derived from the first words of the opening introit, *Requiem aeternam*. The liturgical form, requiem mass, is recognized under a host of names: *Missa pro defunctis* (Latin), *Missa de defunti* (Italian), *Misa di defuntos* (Spanish), *Messe des morts* or *Messe funèbre* (French), and *Totenmesse* or *Trauersmesse* (German). Virtually all of the works cited in this guide, with the exception of the Eastern Rite, bear one of these names. In the Eastern tradition, the requiem is recognized as *Panikhida* (Russian), *Opelo* (Serbian), and *Parastasos* (Greek).

Masses for the dead have been celebrated by Christians since the earliest recorded history of the Church. This service is mentioned in several sources from the Second Century, among them the *Apology of Aristides*, the apocryphal *Acts of John*, and three works of Tertullian (*De Corona, De Castitate*, and *De Monogamia*).

The requiem's musical history parallels the majority of significant trends and styles in that of Western music. The Gregorian mass stands as the form's oldest extant. The requiem is a style that had gradually devel-

oped, matured, and declined more than 1,000 years ago. It realized a pivotal status in music history because of its melodic content and spiritual
quality, which exercised a prominent influence upon subsequent musical
styles, both sacred and profane.

Throughout the development of measured music and polyphony (800–
1400), the requiem continually utilized monophonic Gregorian melodies.
Settings of the mass ordinary and motets employed metered, polyphonic,
multivoiced textures a full century before composers ventured to do likewise with requiem music. It is not exactly clear as to why this was so.
Perhaps the requiem was not considered an eminent musical festival, or
polyphony was deemed too frivolous and distracting to be performed on
such a solemn occasion.

A notable and somewhat unusual work mentioned in this book is the
polyphonic, folk-style setting of a requiem mass from Corsica. This music
is a unique and curious blend of Eastern and Western musical traditions.
Although some of its melodies are derived from the Greek tradition, the
harmony senses to be of Western provenance. A striking aspect of its history is the fact that the musical polyphony of the Corsican requiem was
initially improvised, learned, and passed down through the generations
by means of oral tradition. This brings up the possibility that a polyphonic tradition of requiem composition, now vanished, had once filled
the historical era during which the development of notated polyphony
had taken place.

The first polyphonic requiems began to appear in the Lowlands during
the fifteenth century. What had begun as a rather modest compositional
trickle in the early years of the Renaissance with either Guillaume Dufay
or Johannes Ockeghem had eventually broadened into a stream of some
fifty works during the sixteenth century, and still a greater abundance of
settings, several hundred, in fact, throughout the Roman Catholic world
after 1615.

A scarce number of Renaissance requiems receive great recognition
today, yet the era produced a collection of veritable masterpieces that are
truly deserving of our attention. The majority of them quote, emulate, or
paraphrase the Gregorian melodies, thus serving as an important link to
a past musical tradition. Among the pieces languishing in obscurity are
works by Giovanni de Palestrina, Manuel Cardoso, Duarte Lôbo, Thomas
da Victoria, and Eustâche Du Caurroy. The tenor and emotions conjured
up by these outstanding composers reach across the enormous abyss of
time, establishing their impression upon the musical and spiritual sensibilities and passions to millions of people throughout the centuries. To
this day, they remain stellar appearances from a spiritual world that has
been long since forgotten.

Decisions made at the Council of Trent (1545–1563) regarding church music had enormous and far-reaching effects not only upon the liturgy, but upon the entire realm of Western music. At this Council, the text of the Roman Catholic requiem was standardized, and the sequence poem, *Dies irae* (c. 1308), along with its spiritual message placing emphasis on God's judgment and condemnation, was directly incorporated into the requiem liturgy. This message was further illuminated through vivid descriptions in *The Divine Comedy* by Dante Alighieri, a work roughly contemporary with the *Dies irae* sequence.

The theological foundation of the requiem mass rests in the concept that, through prayer and sacrifice, the living can assist the escape of their deceased family members from the netherworld of Purgatory. A proliferation of votive and memorial masses designed to promote this deliverance, after a nominal compensation of monies from bereaved families, generated interest in music for the requiem mass. Throughout the seventeenth century, musical settings of the requiem spread like wildfire as hundreds of new settings were composed. It would be reasonable to say that during this era, the requiem became somewhat recognized in Italy as a national musical form, much in the same sense as the chorale had been noted as a national form associated with German Lutherans.

The theological issues associated with the funeral mass, as well as the economics behind it, in particular, the sale of indulgences [monies paid for the remission of temporal damnation to Purgatory], were anathema to many Christians. It was those very same issues and grievances that eventually helped to fuel the Protestant Reformation. It is important to note that although both the Lutheran and Anglican churches maintained some form of the regular mass liturgy after their break with Rome, they had both abolished the use of the traditional Latin requiem mass. To this day, both persuasions employ a greatly abridged memorial service, and from these forms mainline Protestant denominations have created even more extensively abbreviated funeral rites.

During the turbulent years of the early seventeenth century, Church authorities and musicians both adopted a new declamatory, monodic style, espoused by the *Camerata*, a group of Florentine intellectuals and scholars. This style was a musical reaction against the vocal polyphony of the Renaissance, which was instrumental in ushering in the musical era known as *Baroque*. At the same time, church musicians became greatly enthralled by the ornamental and decorative possibilities of music. Where once the music had been composed to serve the needs of the liturgical text, the text had since become subservient to the needs and whims of the music. This era attained its full maturity in the creation of works by Bach and Handel. Ironically, neither of these composers had ever produced a requiem setting. Bach, a Lutheran, was a master craftsman of the musical forms implemented in the Lutheran rite, while the opera-oratorio-composer-turned-impresario Handel settled in an English kingdom that observed the Anglican rite. Neither man had any compelling reason, culturally or spiritually, to compose a Latin requiem.

It was during this period that an alternative requiem with its roots based in Germany came into existence. The first of such works were the *Musikalische Exequien* by composer Heinrich Schütz, and *Deutsche Sprüch von Leben und Tod* by Leonhard Lachner. Although they were actually a Protestant version of the requiem, several examples were destined to follow its lead. Hassler, Scheidt, Schein, Bach, and Praetorius, among other Protestant composers, eventually replaced the requiem with the funeral motet or cantata. The ides of the German requiem soon passed into the hands of Catholic composers who continued to cultivate its concept and form. The text of this requiem was composed in the vernacular, generally paralleling that of the Latin rite. Similar works followed from many noted composers, including Thomas Selle, Georg Vogler, Johann Fasch, Franz Schubert, Michael Haydn, Franz Gruber, Hugo Kaun, Helmut Barbe, and César Bresgen. *Ein Deutsches Requiem* by Johannes Brahms has emerged as the most famous example of this type of requiem.

In 1694, Henry Purcell performed his memorial composition at the funeral of Queen Mary, primarily using music he had composed prior to this time and drawing upon texts from the 1660 *Book of Common Prayer*. Various other composers, including Bingham, Rutter, Davies, Harington, and Howells, have also contributed significant requiem works that can be classified in this category of Anglican requiem.

This new trend was further nourished in part by the polychoral techniques developed at St. Mark's in Venice by composers Adrian Willaert and Giovanni Gabrieli, as well as the mature madrigal style of Claudio Monteverdi. Instruments had been adopted into the musical performance of the requiem liturgy. In an ironic twist, the Roman Catholic Church, which at the Council of Trent had previously attempted to exclude all secular music and profane influences from its liturgical presentation, elected to court a new, popular style that proved highly effective and appropriate for the world of opera and madrigal. In the end, all of the influences that had been once deemed undesirable had been introduced, albeit in a completely new form, into the liturgy, and not with mere subtlety, but with a resounding vengeance. By mid-century, the music of the Counter Reformation had adopted all the sound qualities and nuances of the seventeenth-century opera and instrumental style.

It is quite unfortunate that very few of the numerous requiems composed in the early baroque era are frequently performed or well-known by today's audiences. The setting composed by Francesco Cavalli remains a spectacular, hair-raising work that greatly deserves to be reintroduced into the active repertoire of concert music. Its madrigalesque, polychoral qualities are enormously attractive, and its sense of drama continues to be absolutely stunning. A host of other gifted composers, such as Giuseppe Pitoni, Christoph Strauss, Francesco Brusa, Antonio Lotti, Adam Michna, and the Royal Hapsburg Emperor Leopold I, had also bequeathed exquisite models of early baroque-style requiems to musical posterity.

Magnificent middle and late baroque requiems were contributed to the genre by Benedetto Marcello, Adolphe Hasse, Marc-Antoine Charpentier, Alessandro Scarlatti, and Jan Dismas Zelenka. Heinrich Biber's dazzling *Requiem for Fifteen Voices* includes some breathtaking virtuoso vocal and choral writing. There is not a single melancholy expression throughout this entire work. In the *Sanctus*, the choral and instrumental voices on *Hosanna* flit back and forth with tremendous speed, encompassing a potent energy that generates a fierce momentum.

Also, Italian composer Domenico Cimarosa penned a requiem in G minor that can easily be described as one of the most melodious pieces ever composed in this genre. Concise, joyous, and energetic, the work has something for everyone, be they soloists, choruses, instrumentalists, or audience members. Flawless in its construction, it embodies an extensive array of moods, tempi, and colorful orchestration.

The Viennese school of Mozart, Haydn, and Beethoven, with its elegance, grace, and balance, in turn, left its unmistakable imprint upon the music of the requiem. These composers also left behind a very important legacy: the first truly symphonic requiem (and mass) models. Perhaps the most famous and continuously performed work of the genre is the requiem setting composed by Mozart. Never mind the fact that the piece is actually a collective effort involving Mozart and two other composers, Franz Süssmayr and Joseph Eybler, both of whom had created their own settings for the requiem. Eybler had been designated as the first choice to complete what Mozart had begun, but after concentrating most of his work on the Sequence, he decided to jettison the assignment. A glance at Eybler's *Requiem in C Minor* immediately reveals a composer of a much different temperament. Subsequently, Constance Mozart engaged Süssmayr to complete the remainder of the unfinished work.

An ample number of classical composers, including Ignace Pleyel, Michael Haydn, and Luigi Cherubini, adopted the Viennese tradition, and in so doing, left some truly splendid requiems in their wake. Pleyel's elegant setting is filled with exceptional melodic grace. The sonorities similar to the music of his mentor Haydn and his friend Mozart are clearly evident. The two requiems composed by Michael Haydn, brother of the more famous Franz Joseph, are also superlative creations, most notably the unfinished B Flat Minor, his ultimate composition. Although he was not fortunate enough to live to see it to completion, the portion that exists is a truly incomparable piece of music.

With their florid vocal styles and elegant choruses, important contributions to eighteenth century symphonic requiem music were made by Neapolitan composers Niccolo Jommelli, Giovanni Paisiello, and Giovanni Mayr. Jommelli's requiem overflows with operatic drama and virtuoso writing. It is certainly no accident that his bust, adorned with his name in gold letters, forms part of the musical pantheon displayed at the right-side facade of the Paris Opera House. His requiem, rich with virtuoso coloratura writing, is greatly deserving of much more esteemed recognition than it presently receives.

Luigi Cherubini's two requiems stand as masterpieces of religious drama. Beethoven had even stated that if he himself were to compose a requiem—something he never did do—he would model his work after that of Cherubini.

As orchestral music, such as the symphony and concerto, began to ascertain their prominence during the eighteenth century, the orchestra naturally evolved into an invaluable confederate for the choir.

From the mid-century onward, orchestral accompaniments began to display a genuine independence from the vocal lines. The orchestra was no longer restricted to playing short introductions or postludes in the various movements, as in the setting by Marc-Antoine Charpentier, nor was it confined, as in the Strauss requiem, to the doubling of choral and vocal parts designed to maintain that the soloist or choir remain in tune. The orchestral parts had acquired an independent existence, giving color to the entire work while occasionally providing support to the vocal and choral lines. In this manner, the liturgical concert requiem was born. Large and sumptuous, these works were performed as part of the funeral services for a variety of notables, often royalty. With the increase in the size and instrumental make-up of the orchestra came the expanded interest from philharmonic choruses and societies toward private performance of these requiem settings.

During the romantic era, the requiem made the journey from the sanctuary to the concert hall. Requiems composed by Berlioz and Dvořak, as well as Gounod's *Mors et Vita* (an oratorio containing a complete setting of requiem text), were specifically created for performance on the stage. Although the premiere performance of Berlioz's requiem took place at the Church of Les Invalides, it was clearly a concert occasion. The later settings by Dvořak and Gounod were composed for the Birmingham Festival. In all three works, the repetition of text, as well as the re-structuring of the liturgical texts, offers further indication of this development.

Composed in 1760 during the final years of France's old regime, immediately prior to the French Revolution, Francois Joseph Gossec's requiem stands as one of the first romantic settings of the genre. A model known to Mozart, its sense of drama and colorful orchestration blazed the trail for nineteenth-century composers who had designed their requiem works more for the concert hall than for the religious sanctuary. The romantic era stood witness to the creation of many new settings of the requiem text. Two of the most cherished choral works in the repertoire, the requiems of Brahms and Verdi, masterworks that have captured a special place in the hearts of those who love music, were composed during this prolific historical period.

During the nineteenth century, dramatic musical art was seen to follow two very distinct trends. The first involved the development of composition written with a spontaneous, improvisational spirit. This aspect of romantic art is embodied in such works as symphonic program music, lieder, and the short character pieces written for piano. The second trend, demonstrating a much more conservative slant toward past musical forms and values, is discernable in those compositions that had adopted a renewed style of classicism.

This penchant toward classicism can be interpreted as a debt of homage to past styles, be they from the Renaissance, baroque, or Viennese schools. The trend presents itself early within the works of Mozart and Haydn in their use of the fugue. Romantic composers were known to adapt this form and texture as well, suggesting their respect for and obligation to tradition. Such reverence for the past can also be cited in the revival of the Gregorian chant and Renaissance polyphony. Felix Mendelssohn had attempted to revive the music of Johann Sebastian Bach, while Johannes Brahms studied the vocal forms of the Renaissance, composing various choral motets rooted in polyphonic style, and baroque chorale melodies. Brahms was interested in the fugue as well, and included four in *Ein Deutsches Requiem*. In his oratorios *Elijah* and *St. Paul*, Mendelssohn made an effort to capture the grandeur of the music from the baroque era. Franz Liszt, the inventor of the symphonic tone poem, had also employed fugue techniques in his *Fugue on BACH* (organ) and in the opening orchestral symphony of his oratorio, *The Legend of St. Elizabeth*.

Just as it had been believed at the time of the Tridentine Council, the Roman Catholic Church again expressed concern that the encroachment of the secular, operatic musical style was stripping its liturgical music of its exceptional spiritual qualities. Thus, the Caecilian Movement was organized in an attempt to redirect the course of the Church's music by pursuing its goal of encouraging the use of Gregorian chant and Palestrina-style polyphony in its compositions. For the majority of this organization's members, pieces that featured vocal soloists and large symphonic orchestras were considered *musica nongrata*. The movement was fortunate to experience a measure of success in return for its efforts. The requiem settings by Franz Liszt, Anton Bruckner, Charles Gounod, and Josef Rheinberger, as well as the twentieth-century composers Pietro Yon, Licinio Refice, Karl Höller, Lorenzo Perosi, and Vincenzo Tommasini, serve as extraordinary models of the devotional style that had been sanctioned and applauded by the Caecilianists. This type of literature provided a distinct alternative to the more spectacular symphonic settings by Hector Berlioz, Franz von Suppé, Antonin Dvořak, Joao Bomtempo, Gaetano Donizetti, and Guiseppe Verdi.

Other important requiems in the romantic style remain, including those composed by Théodore Gouvy, Felix Draeseke, Daniel De Lange, Otto Olsson, Theodor Kiel, Charles Villiers Stanford, and Georg Henschel. Today, these significant works are virtually unknown not only to the musical public, but to many members of the music profession as well. Gouvy's large-scale setting was admired by Berlioz, who had once lamented that Gouvy's talent was often passed over in favor of other less-qualified composers, whom he pejoratively referred to as "mosquitos."

Capturing the spirit and essence of late romanticism is De Lange's unaccompanied requiem, a genuine masterpiece imbued with the Renaissance polyphonic ideal. The superb settings of Stanford, Kiel, and Olsson serve as late examples of the romantic symphonic requiem and stand as masterpieces of melodic and harmonic beauty. Lastly, the *Messa per Rossini*, a collaborative effort of twelve luminaries under the auspicious guidance and leadership of Verdi, whose idea it was to create the work, deserves to be hailed as one of the towering achievements of the nineteenth century. The remarkable musical unity of this monumental composition was strictly imposed by Verdi upon the other participants.

The output of new requiem settings continued to enjoy an unabated flow during the twentieth century. The works created at this time, which closely parallel the general course of contemporary forms of musical expression, can be categorized into three principal types: liturgical requiems, secular (nonliturgical) requiems, and war requiems. Some, including those settings by Maurice Duruflé, Daniel Pinkham, Alfred Descenclos, Roger Calmel, Guy Ropartz, and Le François, are heavily influenced by French Impressionism. Others, like those by Erich Urbanner, Rafael Kubelik, Erikki Tüür, Paul Patterson, and Boris Blacher, are modeled after the German expressionist idiom. Works reaching into the world of unpitched sound are found in settings by György Ligeti, Luboš Fišer, and Renaud Gagneaux.

More traditional harmonic works have come courtesy of Andrew Lloyd-Webber, Healey Willan, Kryzstof Penderecki, Virgil Thompson, Elinor Remick Warren, and James De Mars. Most secular requiems maintain a textural continuity with the Latin requiem, utilizing secular poetry to gloss the traditional requiem texts. Notable models of this style include

Pehkonen's *Russian Requiem*, Bryar's *Cadmeon Requiem*, Victory's *Ultima Rerum*, Szokolay's *Déploration*, and Vycpálek's *Czech Requiem*. Many, such as Sandro Gorli's *Requiem for Fourteen Unaccompanied Voices*, employ original, nonliturgical poetry.

The war requiem, a new style in the genre, evolved into an important form during the century. The Great War (World War I) ignited the composition of the earliest war requiems of this era by such composers as Kastalsky, Delius, Reger, and Foulds. The best-known pieces in this style, however, are Benjamin Britten's *War Requiem*, Kabalevsky's *War Requiem*, Mauersberger's *Dresden Requiem*, and Tomasi's *Requiem pour la Paix*, all inspired by the tragic history of the World War II. A grand example of this model is the *Requiem of Reconciliation*, composed in 1995, a monumental setting executed by thirteen contemporary composers. Like an encyclopedia of twentieth-century musical style, the work commemorates the fiftieth anniversary of the end of World War II. A special subset of the war requiem is the Holocaust requiem, examples of which have been composed by Senator, Lazar, and Rosenfeld.

A chapter of this volume is devoted specifically to the German requiem, an early, pioneering model of which is the *Musikalische Exequien* composed by Heinrich Schütz. What had begun as a Protestant requiem setting was promptly adopted by Catholic composers, including Schubert, Bresgen, Kaun, Barbe, Gruber, Vogler, and Brahms, who created a stream of notable works subsequent to the Reformation.

This guide also covers the important Anglican requiem. Although there are fewer of these particular models, those that do exist stand collectively as an indispensable contribution to the literature. Composers who have dipped into the *Book of Common Prayer* include Purcell, Webbe, Bingham, Howells, Davies, and Rutter.

A chapter is devoted to the independent settings of the *Dies irae* text. The poetic imagery of this medieval hymn has exerted a powerful influence upon many generations of gifted composers. Lully, Charpentier, and De Lalande were among the composers who contributed the earliest manifestations of this type of piece in France during the reign of Louis XIV. A steady stream of pieces continues up to Stravinsky and Penderecki.

In an effort to produce a comprehensive overview of the vast world of requiem music, the history and significance of the funeral music of the Eastern Christian traditions are also detailed. In contrast to the traditions of the West, the East has engaged its music primarily for liturgical purposes. There is no history regarding concert-liturgical music in the Orthodox Rite, yet pieces have been composed in this style that can be adapted to a concert setting. Although polyphonic in style, the Russian *Panikhida* and the Serbian *Opelo*, similar to the Roman Rite, contain multiple monophonic versions of the chants. The Greek requiem (*Parastasos*) remains in monophonic style to the present day, with the occasional use of an organal voice. Based on available information, the setting by Mikos Theodorakis is possibly the sole concert version of this particular liturgy.

The majority of composers discussed in these chapters are currently recognizable only to specialists in the field and study of music. It is this goal of this guide to introduce the names of these gifted individuals and the glory of their phenomenal works to a much wider audience.

And so the response to the opening question, "Why a book on the requiem?" has hopefully been sufficient. Within the covers of this inclusive guide is a great deal of diverse and detailed information, equally useful to the professional musician, the musical scholar, and the interested amateur. The enclosed data will also prove helpful to choirmasters and conductors because most of the works mentioned are suitable for serious performance. No attempt is made to determine the best or worst pieces, although some are obviously superior to others.

A significant portion of the information used to compile this guide was acquired through the analysis of musical scores located in the libraries of Yale University in New Haven, Connecticut, and Columbia University in New York City. Additional works, including substantial pieces by Fišer, Stanford, and Hristič, were located through resources posted on the Internet. In certain cases in which the score for the work was unavailable, a general description based on careful, meticulous listening is provided.

The undertaking of such a copious project proved quite daunting to say the least, yet the preparation of the work was continuously fascinating, if at times arduous. The history of music extends far beyond the Three B's. It includes a multitude of stories involving numerous talented, highly skilled and devoted individuals, many of whom to this day remain stranded in obscurity from both the public and the music profession. Discovering the number of diverse styles of requiem settings and the many unique ways in which these composers confronted the task of creating such a work is inherently interesting. Collecting the tales of their lives and their works was akin to strolling through a graveyard of great luminaries, the difference being that these musical stars—as many had truly been in years past—have the ability to communicate from beyond through their precious music legacies. For this reason, when it came time to decide which composers would be included in this volume, I chose to adhere to a simple, straightforward concept: There's always room for one more on the bus.

1

The Gregorian Requiem Mass

The mass for the dead of the Roman Catholic Church is called the *Requiem Mass*. It is celebrated as an intercessory prayer on behalf of the deceased person and its name comes from the first words of the opening introit, *Requiem aeternam*. The requiem is celebrated in memory of all the faithful departed on All Souls' Day, the second day of November. This liturgy can also be sung on the day of burial, on successive annual anniversaries, as well as on the third, seventh, and thirtieth day following the death.

During the thirteenth and fourteenth centuries, there was an explosion of votive masses (a mass not part of the liturgical calendar), particularly the requiem. This rapid growth was caused by the belief that offering prayers for souls in Purgatory was the most effective way of assisting those departed souls to attain their eternal glory. This practice led to abuses, particularly the notorious practice of selling indulgences, for the remission of temporal punishment, by the Church. This practice was one of the major theological issues that helped to precipitate the Protestant Reformation. Ultimately, the Catholic Church began to restrict this practice and the excessive requiem celebrations of that period.

Monophonic Gregorian chant is named after Pope Gregory I (reigned 590–604). Although it is probable that he wrote few, if any, of the chant melodies, it was he who started to collect and codify the chants that were used in churches throughout the Christian world. These chants were used for the musical portions in the cycle of mass celebrations of the liturgical year and the daily divine office. The chant reached the highest point of its development between 750 and 850. After this time, the earliest attempts at polyphony began to take place and monophonic chant composition was gradually replaced by this newer, multivoiced style.

The music of the Gregorian requiem mass was written for unaccompa-

1

nied male voices, usually clergy, in monophonic style and its structure developed over the Middle Ages. Its present shape was in place by the 1300s, although the sequence hymn, *Dies irae,* was the last piece to be included into the requiem mass by the Council of Trent (1543–63). It had been used in the Italian rite during the 1300s, but was not employed in the French rite until the 1400s. It was unofficially dropped from the rite by the Second Vatican Council (1962–65), yet there are parishes (Paris) where it is still sung.

The requiem was many centuries in formation but during the lifetime of the Tridentine Council, the liturgies of the Mozarabic (Spain) and Gallican (France) rites were discarded in favor of the Roman Rite. Only the Ambrosian Rite (Milan) was spared; to this day, the funeral mass, as celebrated in Milan, varies somewhat from the Roman version.

The musical pieces of the Requiem Mass are almost the same as those of any other mass setting, except that in the mass Ordinary (the prayers said at every mass: Kyrie, Gloria, Creed, Sanctus, and Agnus Dei), the Gloria and Creed are always omitted. The concluding words of the Ordinary, *Agnus Dei, Miserere nobis,* and *Dona eis pacem* are changed to the Requiem Proper, *Dona eis requiem* and *Dona eis requiem sempiternam.* In the Proper, the Offertory, one of the medieval verses, *Hostias et preces tibi,* is retained and a fragment of the original psalm, *Requiem aeternam,* is kept.

INTROIT

The oldest text of the requiem is that of the Introit, *Requiem aeternam.* The Introit is a chant sung during the procession of priests and attendants from the sacristy to the altar. Its opening lines are based upon a passage from the Apocryphal Fourth Book of Esdras (2:34–35), a book considered canonical until the late fifth century. The verse, *Te decet hymnus in Sion,* are the words of Psalm 64 (65):1–2. Consisting of mostly a few notes, F, G, and A, the florid Gregorian melody of the Introit, sung by the *schola,* is smooth and peaceful. The contrasting melody of the psalm verses, sung by a soloist, is more of a recitation.

Requiem aeternam dona eis, Domine et lux perpetua luceat eis.	Grant them eternal rest, O Lord, and may perpetual light shine upon them.
V. Te decet hymnus, Deus, in Sion,	V. In Zion a hymn is fitting to You, O God,
et tibi reddetur votum in Jerusalem.	a vow is paid to You in Jerusalem.
V. Exaudi orationem meam, ad te omnis caro veniet.	V. O hear my prayer: all flesh shall come to Thee.
Requiem aeternam. . . .	Grant them eternal rest. . . .

KYRIE

The *Kyrie* is one of the oldest texts in the requiem mass. Its Greek text bears witness to its antiquity. Originally, it was said by the congregation as part of a litany, in dialogue with the officiating priest or cantor. The A-B-A structure of the current version of the *Kyrie* text dates from the early ninth century. There are 226 known *Kyrie* melodies, coming from manuscripts dating from the tenth to the eighteenth centuries. The melody associated with the requiem *Kyrie* is velvety-smooth in shape and confident in mood.

Kyrie eleison.	Lord have mercy.
Christe eleison.	Christ have mercy.
Kyrie eleison.	Lord have mercy.

GRADUALE

The Graduale has been in use since the ninth century and is sung after the reading of the Epistle. During the early liturgy, a psalm was probably sung between the readings of the Old and New Testament. The florid, ornate nature of the existing gradual tunes indicates that this was a passage in which the soloist demonstrated his vocal technique. The timing is ideal for ornamentation because there is no liturgical action occurring at the moment when this chant is sung. Before the Council of Trent, an alternative Graduale, *Si ambulem in medio umbrae mortis* was used; afterward, only one choice remained, *Requiem aeternam*. The verse is taken from Psalm 111 (112):6–7.

Requiem aeternam dona eis, Domine	Grant them eternal rest, O Lord
et lux perpetua luceat eis.	Let perpetual light shine upon them.
V. In memoria aeterna erit justus:	V. The just shall be in everlasting
ab auditione mala non timebit.	memory:
[alternate graduale for French usage]	He shall not fear evil tidings.
Si ambulem in medio umbrae mortis	Though I walk through the shadow of death,
non timebo in mala:	I shall fear no evil
quoniam tu mecum es, Domine;	for Thou art with me, O Lord.
virga tua et baculus tuus,	Thy rod and staff
ipsa me consolata sunt.	they comfort me. [Psalm 23:4]

TRACT

The Tract, *Absolve, Domine*, was originally sung after the second Epistle. The text of the Tract is usually a portion of a Psalm text, but in the requiem, the text is not taken from the Bible. The elaborate, melismatic passages of chant indicate that the music of the Tract is an important, early form of solo performance. *Absolve, Domine* was chosen by the Council of Trent to be used for the requiem mass. The text, *Sicut cervus*, taken from the Sarum Rite (English), was normally used for the Tract before the Council.

Absolve, Domine, animas omnium fidelium defunctorum ab omni vinculo delictorum. V. Et gratia tua illis succerente, mereantur evadere judicium ultionis. V. Et lucis aeternae beatitudine perfrui.	Lord, release the souls of all the faithful departed from every bond of sin. V. By the help of your grace enable them to escape avenging judgement. V. And to enjoy bliss in everlasting light.
[alternate tract] Sicut cervus desiderat ad fontes acquarum, ita desiderat anima mea ad te Deus. Sitivit anima mea ad Deum vivum: quando veniam at apparebo ante faciem Dei mei? Fuerunt mihi lacrime mei panes die ac nocte, dum dicitur mihi per singulos dies: Ubi erat Deus tuus? [Psalm 42:1–3]	Like as the hart pants after the water brooks, so pants my soul after Thee, O God. My soul thirsts for the living God: When shall I come and appear before God? My tears have been my meat day and night, while they continually say unto me, Where is thy God?

SEQUENCE HYMN

The last piece to be inserted into the Requiem mass by the Tridentine Council was the sequence, *Dies irae*. This medieval text is unlike anything found in the texts of the Orthodox tradition and is unique to Roman Catholicism. This picturesque, angry text was ascribed to the Franciscan monk, Thomas of Celano, but his authorship is now disputed and it is generally recognized that the poem came from an earlier time period. Given the plagues, wars, famine, and unsanitary quality of life so common in the thirteenth to fifteenth centuries, the pessimism of the text is hardly surprising. Even Dante, in the *Divine Comedy*, spelled out in great detail, the tortures and punishments that awaited the evil-doers of his own time and place.

The words of the *Dies irae* are a commentary upon the Biblical text of Zephaniah:

> The great Day of the Lord is at hand: . . .
> That Day is a day of wrath . . . of trouble and distress . . .
> of waste and desolation . . . of darkness and gloom . . .
> of clouds and thick darkness . . . a day of the trumpet and alarm . . .
> against the fenced cities . . . and high battlements. . . .
> [Zephaniah I]

This very popular poem has over 150 English translations and the Gregorian melody is possibly the best-known tune of the chant repertory. The incipit of this tune was employed numerous times by composers of the nineteenth and twentieth centuries. (For detail, see the chapter, *Dies irae*.)

Dies irae, dies illa,	Day of wrath, that day
Solvet saeclum in favilla	Will dissolve the earth into ashes
Teste David cum Sibilla.	As David and the Sibyl testify.
Quantus tremor est futurus	What dread there will be
Quando judex est venturus	When the Judge shall come
Cuncta stricte discussurus.	To judge all things strictly.
Tuba mirum spargens sonum	The trumpet shall spread a wondrous sound
Per sepulcra regionum	Through every grave, in all lands,
Coget omnes ante thronum.	It will drive mankind before the throne.
Mors stupebit et natura	Death and nature shall be astonished
Cum resurget creatura	When all creation rises again
Judicanti responsura.	To answer to the Judge.
Liber scriptus proferetur	A book, written in, will be brought forth
In quo totum continetur,	In which is contained everything that is,
Unde mundus judicetur.	Out of which the world shall be judged.
Judex ergo cum sedebit	When the Judge is seated
Quidquid latet apparebit,	Whatever is hidden will reveal itself.
Nil inultum remanebit.	Nothing will remain unavenged.
Quid sum miser tunc dicturus,	What then shall I say, wretch that I am,
Quem patronem rogaturus,	What advocate is there to speak for me,

Cum vix justus sit securus?

When even the righteous are not
  secure ?

Rex tremendae majestatis,
Qui salvandos salvas gratis,
Salve me, fons pietatis.

King of awe-ful majesty,
Who freely saves the redeemed,
Save me, O fount of goodness.

Recordare, Jesu pie
Quod sum causa tuae viae,
Ne me perdas illa die.

Remember, blessed Jesus,
That I am the cause of Thy pilgrimage,
Do not forsake me on that day.

Quaerens me sedistis lassus,
Redemisti crucem passus,
Tantus labor non sit cassus.

Seeking me, Thou sat down weary,
Thou didst redeem me, suffering on
  the Cross.
Let not such toil be in vain.

Juste judex ultionis
Donum fac remissionis
Ante diem rationis.

Just and avenging Judge,
Grant pardon
Before the day of reckoning.

Ingemisco tamquam reus,
Culpa rubet vultus meus,
Supplicanti parce, Deus.

I groan like a guilty man.
Guilt reddens my face.
Spare a suppliant, O God.

Qui Mariam absolvisti
Et latronem exaudisti,
Mihi quoque spem dedisti.

Who didst absolve Mary Magdalene
And who didst hearken to the thief,
To me also hast Thou given hope.

Preces meae non sunt dignae,
Sed tu bonus fac benigne,
Ne perenni cremer igne.

My prayers are not worthy,
But Thou in Thy mercy, grant
That I burn not in everlasting fire.

Inter oves locum praesta,
Et ad haedis me sequestra,
Statuens in parte dextra.

Place me among the sheep
And separate me from the goats,
Setting me on Thy right hand.

Confutatis maledictis

When the accursed have been
  confounded
And given over to the bitter flames,
Call me with the blessed.

Flammis acribus addictis,
Voca me cum benedictus.

Oro supplex et acclinis,
Cor contritum quasi cinis,
Gere curam mei finis.

I pray in supplication on my knees.
My heart contrite as the dust,
Safeguard my fate.

Lacrimosa dies illa
Qua resurget ex favilla
Judicandus homo reus.
Huic ergo parce, Deus.
Pie Jesu, Domine,
Dona eis requiem.

Mournful that day
When, from the dust shall rise
Guilty man to be judged.
Therefore spare him, O God.
Merciful Jesus, Lord
Grant them rest.

OFFERTORY

The Offertory, *Domine Jesu Christe*, is a chant sung as the faithful bring forward their offerings to the altar. Most Offertory texts are taken from the Psalms, but this is not the case with the requiem Offertory. It originated in the Gallican (French) Rite and was imported into the Roman liturgy sometime between the ninth and eleventh centuries. The chant is an ornamented version of the second of the eight possible Psalm-tone formulas.

Domine Jesu Christe, Rex gloriae,
libera animas omnium fidelium
defunctorum de poenis inferni,
et de profundo lacu:
libera eas de ore leonis,
ne absorbeat eas tatarus, ne
cadant in obscurum,
sed signifer sanctus Michael
repraesentet eas in lucem sanctam,
quam olim Abrahae promisisti
et semini ejus.

Lord Jesus Christ, King of glory,
deliver the souls of all the faithful
departed from the pains of hell
and from the bottomless pit.
Deliver them from the lion's mouth.
Neither let them fall into darkness
nor the black abyss swallow them up.
Let St. Michael, Thy standard-bearer,
lead them into the holy light
which once Thou didst promise
to Abraham and his seed.

V. Hostias et preces, tibi, Domine,
laudis offerimus;
tu suscipe pro animabus illis,
quarum hodie memoriam facimus:
fac eas, Domine, de morte transire
quam olim Abrahae promisisti
et semini ejus.

V. We offer unto Thee this sacrifice
prayer and praise.
Receive it for those souls
whom, today we commemorate
from death into life
which once Thou didst promise to
Abraham and his seed.

SANCTUS

The Sanctus is a portion of the Eucharistic prayer that follows the Preface. The text is taken from Isaiah 6:3, *Sanctus Sanctus, Sanctus*, which is a Greek translation of the original Hebrew, threefold *Kadosh, Kadosh, Kadosh*. Benedictus is drawn from the Gospel of Matthew 21:9, *Blessed is He who comes in the name of the Lord*. It seems to have been incorporated into the liturgy at a very early date, though its use before 400 cannot be proved. These words are also found in the Eastern liturgy. The historian, Josef Jungmann (*The Mass of the Roman Rite*, 1959) suggests that the text may have been taken from the Gallican liturgy and inserted into the Roman liturgy between the fourth and sixth centuries. Originally, the *Sanctus* was sung by the congregation, but by the ninth century it was sung by the trained choir.

The ringing of bells, used during the elevation of the Host, seems to have been introduced as far back as the thirteenth century. Composers from the Renaissance to the twentieth century, who set the *Sanctus* to music, have introduced bell-like, melodic intervals into the choral lines of the requiem *Sanctus*. The *Sanctus* is part of the mass Ordinary. The two-fold division of the text has allowed composers, especially from the Baroque era to the present day, to create two separate musical movements to express the contrasting moods (joy and reflection) of each text.

Sanctus, sanctus, sanctus	Holy, holy, holy,
Dominus Deus Sabaoth!	Lord God of Sabaoth!
Pleni sunt coeli et terra	Heaven and earth are full of
gloria tua.	Thy glory.
Osanna in excelsis.	Hosanna in the highest.
Benedictus qui venit in	Blessed is he who comes
nomine Domine.	in the name of the Lord.
Osanna in excelsis.	Hosanna in the highest.

AGNUS DEI

The *Agnus Dei* is one of the Ordinary mass sections and its text has been associated with Christian worship since the earliest days of the Church. The image of a lamb was designed to symbolize Christ's sacrifice. The *Agnus Dei* is primarily a theme of the Western church since the Middle Ages because its use was banned in 692 by the Byzantine Church. The earliest reference to the chant for this text is found in the *Liber pontificalis I.* Pope Sergius I (687–701) mentions that it is sung by both the people and clergy. The threefold repetition of the text began sometime in the tenth century and the text proved to be popular with the clergy for amplification and extension by troping the text. The Council of Trent purged the core text of the various tropes that had become attached to it.

In Germany, the *Agnus Dei* was sung at the Communion itself, but in France and Italy it was sung during the fraction (breaking) of the consecrated loaves of bread. The melody is fairly simple and straightforward; the syllabic chant hovers around its two principal notes, G and A.

Agnus Dei, qui tollis peccata	O Lamb of God, that takest away the
mundi: dona eis requiem.	sins of the world, grant them rest.
[repeated]	
Agnus Dei, qui tollis peccata	O Lamb of God, that takest away the
mundi: dona eis requiem	sins of the world, grant them
sempiternam.	eternal rest.

COMMUNION

The text of the Communion contains a recapitulation of the themes of eternal peace and light that are at the core of the Introit. Following the Communion, a brief prayer is said at the requiem mass: *Requiescant in pace. Amen.* This prayer replaces the *Ite missa est, Deo gratias*, a text used in every mass Ordinary. The chant melody for this Proper is quite beautiful and filled with spiritual fervor.

Lux aeterna luceat eis, Domine:	May eternal light shine on them, O Lord,
cum sanctis tuis in aeternum,	with thy saints forever,
quia pius es.	because thou art gracious.
V. Requiem aeternam dona eis	V. Grant the dead eternal rest, O Lord
Domine, et lux perpetua luceat	and may perpetual light shine on them,
eis, cum sanctis tuis in aeternam	with thy saints forever,
quia pius es.	because thou art merciful.

RESPONSORY: LIBERA ME

Sometime around the fourteenth century, the Responsory, *Libera me*, was included in the requiem mass. It is actually sung after the requiem service and replaces the *Subvenite, sancti Dei* ("Come to his help, all saints of God") that had been used from at least as far back as the ninth century. This text is sung over the coffin, placed on a stand and covered with a black pall that is ornamented with a gold cross. As the chant is sung, the priest sprinkles the coffin with holy water and then swings the censer over it. It is a solemn moment as the Church cares for the departed soul.

Libera me, Domine de morte aeterna	Deliver me, Lord from eternal death,
in die illa tremenda,	on that dreadful day,
quando coeli movendi sunt et terra,	when the heavens and earth shall move,
dum veneris judicare	when you come to judge
saeculum per ignem.	the world through fire.
Tremens factus sum ego, et timeo,	I am made to tremble and fear,
dum discussio venerit,	at the coming destruction,
atquae venture ira	and also at your coming wrath.
Dies illa, dies irae	That day, day of wrath,
calamitatis et miseriae	calamity and misery.
dies magna at amara valde.	great and exceedingly bitter day.
Requiem aeternam	Rest eternal
dona eis, Domine.	grant them, Lord.
Et lux perpetua luceat eis.	And may perpetual light shine on them.

IN PARADISUM

There remains a concluding text, often set by French composers: *In Paradisum*. The Gregorian melody that accompanies this text projects a mood of serenity and hope and is one of the most beautiful chants in the repertory. The text refers to the beggar Lazarus, who is mentioned in Jesus' parable of Dives and Lazarus (St. Luke 16:19–31).

In Paradisum deducant te Angeli;	May the angels lead you into Paradise;
in tuo adventu	at your coming
suscipiant te martyres,	may the martyrs receive you,
et perducant te	and conduct you
in civitatem sanctam Jerusalem.	into the holy city, Jerusalem.
Chorus Angelorum te suscipiat,	May the chorus of Angels receive you,
et cum Lazaro quondam paupere	and with Lazarus, once a pauper,
aeternam habeas requiem.	eternally may you have rest.

BASIC DATA

EDITION

The Liber Usualis
edited by the Benedictines of Solesmes
Desclée and Cie., Tournai (Belgium) New York. 1956
(The chants are written in square Gregorian notation.)

DISCOGRAPHY

Gloria Dei Cantores, GDCD 021, Gregorian Requiem, Richard Pugsley, cond.

2

Traditional Sacred Polyphonic Requiem of Corsica

The origin of the traditional Corsican polyphonic music remains shrouded in mystery. This improvised folk-music style appears to be the remnants of a much older oral tradition, with roots that probably extend back into the Middle Ages. Although polyphony is often considered to be the product of a learned educated musical training, here exists a polyphony created by a people untrained in music and dependent upon oral tradition.

The Corsican polyphonic style possesses a number of archaic traits, for example, the parallel harmonic movements of thirds, fourths, and fifths. The earliest form of this type of vocal polyphony is called *parallel organum*. It seems to have originated in France around 1,200 years ago. In this style, secondary voices double the principal melody at the fourth and fifth degrees of the scale. The word *organum* is used to describe the duplication of a melody at a different pitch. The use of melodic parallel thirds, employed in the Corsican idiom, was also found in the music of Scandinavia and the British Isles more than 1,000 years ago.

Notated examples of vocal *organum* styles have existed since 850. The original voice, usually a Gregorian chant, is called the *vox principalis*. The doubling voices are called *vox originalis*. In the Corsican style, the traditional three-voice parts are designated *secunda* (principal voice), the *bassu* (lowest voice), and *terza* (highest voice).

How did this musical style evade detection for so long and why was it not set to notation? Were there other places where polyphony developed by oral tradition? Did polyphony arise and pass among those peoples

11

who maintained commerce in the Mediterranean ports? These questions await a definitive response.

Much of the music of the Gallican (French) and Celtic (Irish) liturgies is now lost because it developed and disappeared before a musical notation had been created to preserve it. The music of the Corsican style was passed on in much the same way: oral tradition. Even the earliest musical notation, such as staffless diastematic notation, remains difficult to read. This is because it was designed as an aid to assist those singers who already knew the chants, melodies they had learned by oral transmission.

A number of Corsican requiem chants are preserved in a Kyriale that is believed to date from the eighteenth century. This Kyriale was not rediscovered until the beginning of the twentieth century and is currently located in Bastia, Corsica (Franciscan provincial monastery). Several of the Corsican chants were discovered by Soulange Corbin, a liturgical music specialist, to be of Greek and Byzantine origin. For example, the *Kyrie* of the mass is similar to the Greek *Kyrie,* a number of intonations are Greek and the Benedictus is of an Eastern origin.

The full triadic sonorities of the Corsican music are more typical of the Western musical style, but the timbre and manner of singing are very different than that used in the Roman Rite. The chordal, three-part polyphony remains constant throughout the work.

Basic Data

EDITION
None found.

DURATION
six movements, perf., c. 24"

VOICING
Choir: TBarB

OUTLINE
Requiem-Kyrie
Sequence
Offertory
Agnus Dei
Lux aeterna
Libera me

DISCOGRAPHY

1. ADES, 111622, Messa Corsa in Rusiu.
2. Harmonia Mundi, HMD 941 495, Ensemble Organum, dir. Marcel Pérès.

3

The Renaissance and the Franco-Flemish School: The Beginnings of the Polyphonic Requiem

BACKGROUND

The years between 1460 and 1470 form a significant interval in the history of musical literature. During this time, a major musical form, the polyphonic requiem mass, enjoyed its most substantial development. This development marks the beginning of the gradual replacement of the Gregorian requiem with the polyphonic model. The requiem settings discussed in this chapter were composed over a 100-year period from approximately 1461 through 1560. The earliest settings composed by Dufay and Ockeghem are followed by a forty-year gap before the more extensive ensemble of Franco-Flemish requiems began to appear. The requiems of Févin, Brumel, Prioris, de la Rue, and Richafort appear to have been written somewhere after the turn of the sixteenth century, while the suave compositions of Vaet and Manchicourt were born in the twilight of the Franco-Flemish era.

The first mention of such a requiem is found in the will of Guillaume Dufay, a Burgundian composer, dated July 8, 1474. In this document, Dufay explains that this piece had been copied by Simon Mellet in 1470 and requests that it be performed at his funeral in the cathedral at Cambrai, where he had been not only a canon, but also Master of Music.

Unfortunately for modern music scholars and enthusiasts, the score for this particular piece has never been recovered.

Although Dufay is credited with creating the first known polyphonic requiem, the first setting composed in this style that remains in existence was written by Johannes Ockeghem (circa 1461), possibly in recognition of the death of King Charles VII of France. This setting, however, if designed for this particular occasion, raises the question as to who should actually be credited with the composition of the first polyphonic requiem. Should it be Dufay or Ockeghem? It is known that Ockeghem was a younger contemporary of Dufay, yet there are no firmly established composition dates for either of their works. Speculation suggests that the two settings were composed within a short time of each other, but the question as to which man completed his piece first has yet to be answered.

The fifteenth century was a period of immense activity in the development and composition of polyphonic music. Only a century earlier, the poet-musician Guillaume de Machaut (1300–1377) created the *Messe de Notre Dame*, the first complete polyphonic setting, by one person, of the mass Ordinary. By the mid-1400s, Franco-Flemish composers (often called *Netherlanders*) stepped to the forefront of musical creativity and composition. Among these composers were Johannes Ockeghem and the Burgundians, Guillaume Dufay and Gilles Binchois. The trail was thus blazed for the succeeding consortium of Netherlanders, Johannes Prioris, Antoine de Févin, Claudin Sermisy, Jean Richafort, Pierre de La Rue, Antoine Brumel, and the later notables, Pierre de Manchicourt and Jacobus Vaet, who were the first to leave settings of the requiem. It is rather peculiar, and quite ironic, that no independent setting by Josquin dès Prés, the most renowned and influential composer of this pléiade, has been unearthed, and a collaborative requiem to which he had contributed his talents also remains lost.

In the years preceding the Netherlanders, composers and singers had been equally content to perform the requiem mass using Gregorian chant. Eventually, there had been a significant signal event that triggered an inclination toward the polyphonic style, however, the *why*, *how*, and even the precise *who* that had served as the catalyst for this fundamental development may never be discovered. One theory suggests that the weight of the tradition coaxed musical innovation to drift slowly toward the funeral ceremony, as opposed to the regular mass. It is also conceivable that in this older, more-established tradition, a simpler form of music had been both the desired and accepted standard. It is quite possible that the polyphonic style was found to be much too colorful and therefore distracting for such a solemn occasion.

The first two polyphonic requiem settings were ordained for very specific people; the first for a clergyman and the second for a king. At first glance, it would appear that the more elaborate polyphonic requiems were available to persons of a different social class until it is pointed out that Dufay and Ockeghem were not only musicians and clergymen, but also members of the privileged class who enjoyed unlimited access to the inner circles and higher echelons of Renaissance society. Requiem settings by other composers were also created to serve the wealthy upper classes, and in many cases, royalty.

It is interesting to note that the composers of this era, their lives spanning three or four generations, did in fact know each other personally. Typically, these men led peripatetic lives that revolved around singing, training, conducting, and composing for the choirs with whom they were personally associated. It is likely that within their respective generations, and over their generational gaps, they had at one time broken bread, celebrated, and sang mass together, and both coached and studied musical art amongst themselves. It is also possible they may have accompanied one another in their recreational pursuits, such as horseback riding or fishing. What of those wintry mornings when their feet and fingertips became numb from the frigid air as they sang the liturgy? Brumel, Prioris, and Vaet in particular were known to leave the Belgium and French lands behind and travel to Italy for a welcome change of scenery.

Ockeghem and Josquin were recognized as the most influential and esteemed of the Netherlanders, having their styles and techniques frequently emulated by many successive generations of Franco-Flemish composers. Testimony of the friendship and mutual admiration they felt toward each other remains evident.

THE DÉPLORATION

The lament, an old form now addressed as the *Déploration*, surfaced during the early years of the Renaissance. Similar in style to the motet, the *Déploration* is a piece in which its composer mourns the loss of a colleague. Other names are often mentioned within these compositions. The majority of Franco-Flemish composers at one time created a *Déploration*. The death of Binchois moved Ockeghem to compose such a work. Later, Ockeghem himself, considered the grand old master of the Netherlanders, was mourned in *Déplorations* written by various composers, including Josquin, Jean Molinet, Guillaume Crétin, and Johannes Lupi. Vaet expressed his grief musically upon the death of Clemens, while Jean Mouton lamented to the passing of Févin, and Pierre Certon bemoaned the loss of Sermisy. Josquin's younger contemporaries, Benedictus Appenzeller, Nicolas Gombert, and Jerome Vinders all composed *Déplorations* in his honor upon his death. Jean Richafort was considerate enough to insert two of Josquin's most appreciated melodies into his setting of the requiem mass, causing one to wonder if Richafort's music was actually sung at Josquin's funeral.

Composers of this era worked with four basic types of mass settings: the *tenor mass*, which does not employ Gregorian chant; the *Gregorian mass*, which either uses or paraphrases the Gregorian melody; the *free mass*, which applies completely new vocal parts; and the *parody mass*, which borrows entire segments from pre-existing compositions. Interestingly, although not surprising, every Franco-Flemish requiem setting is a Gregorian mass.

TEXTURE

By the early sixteenth century, Franco-Flemish four-part writing had come to replace the three-part texture that had been employed by the Burgundian school of composers, and has remained the norm up to the present day. With the exceptions of the settings composed by Ockeghem and Richafort, the polyphonic requiem of the Franco-Flemish tradition is solidly based in the four-part writing texture. Deviations from this prevailing sonority can be found in the occasional excursions into two, three, or five part writing experiments. For example, *Virga tua* (from the *Graduale*) or *Sicut servus* (from the tract) employed a florid two-part, contrapuntal writing by Prioris, Févin, Vaet, de la Rue, and Ockeghem. (This ornate melodic style was actually a carry-over from the original solo scoring of the Gregorian *versicle*.) Sporadic models of five-part writing were utilized by de la Rue and Févin in their pursuit of a deeper, more resonant harmony.

In their requiem settings, Manchicout and Richafort virtually expanded the four-part texture, employing respectively a five- or six-part harmony. Settings by Févin, Richafort, and Ockeghem also include three-part texture. As a result, in their pieces, four-part texture *becomes* the contrasting sonority.

INSTRUMENTAL PERFORMANCE

To this day, questions remain about the practice of performance. There is no absolute definitive evidence declaring whether or not the earliest choirs to sing these pieces were furnished with instrumental accompaniment. A partial answer may very well be provided by a choir book dating from ca. 1520 (MS Musica C, located in Munich, Germany, Bayerische Staatsbibliothek) that also contains La Rue's *Missa pro fidelibus defunctis*.

Included in this book is an illustration of a choir performing a mass with a musician accompanying them on the positive organ. (*Corpus Mensurabilis Musicae* 97, Vol. V, p. LI, Introduction) Thus, it appears probable that at least some of these early requiems, along with other liturgical pieces, had been accompanied by instrumental support. The CD recording of the Brumel setting (listed in the section on Brumel) employs a modest accompaniment of several Renaissance sackbuts.

A hallmark of the Franco-Flemish school is its composers' willingness to experiment with the vocal range. Dufay was one of the first to move the vocal range downward to the lowest registers of the bass, a trend that continued with later Netherlands composers. F 3 and E 3 are commonly used. The uppermost line, performed by either boy sopranos or countertenors, is seen rarely to exceed D 6, although some of these requiem settings display instances of G 6 and F 6. The prominent low tessitura of the soprano line provides the evidence suggesting that this music was performed primarily by men's choirs.

COMPOSING STYLE

Franco-Flemish composers were endowed with what appeared to be an immeasurable supply of melodic and harmonic invention, all of which was tremendously enhanced by their intrepid experimentation and imitative polyphony. Their imitative techniques (canon, point of imitation, and imitative voice pairing) did more than merely furnish an engine by which the music could be driven. They also allowed for a fluid treatment of the texture and a varied series of chord progressions. Tension, color, and drama in the harmonic and melodic fabric were enhanced by the use of suspensions.

A novel feature of the Franco-Flemish texture is the gradual appearance of homophonic chordal passages appropriated to provide a greater sense of emotion and expressive quality to the text. These quasi-declamatory passages are present throughout the requiem, but are especially prevalent in the *Sanctus* and *Agnus Dei* movements, providing a foil to the more lyric, polyphonic settings of the text. In the same manner that Gregorian chant had long been recognized as the ideal means for expressing objective spiritual sentiment, Franco-Flemish composers, as well as clergy, believed polyphony to be more appropriate for imparting that same, objective attitude.

The vocal lines and phrases composed by the Netherlanders have a tendency to be smooth, energetic, intense, passionate, and, most notably in the case of Ockeghem, unusually long. Later Renaissance composers often emulated this archetype of melodic writing.

Early requiem settings of Févin, Brumel, and especially de la Rue make use of imitative voice pairings. Canonic writing and points of imitation are customarily used techniques appearing in virtually every Franco-Flemish requiem setting. After the turn of the sixteenth century, imitation is cited in every vocal line, and as the time interval between imitative entries became gradually shorter, their harmonic texture became progressively more rich and dense. The integration of all four or five vocal parts ultimately led to an equality among and similarity within the various musical lines. The lyrical style of melodic writing of Josquin dès Prés, as well as his mastery of imitative techniques, was clearly awarded great appreciation by his students and younger contemporaries.

GREGORIAN CHANT

The Gregorian *cantus*, which had once been rigidly affixed to the tenor voice, appears in the top-most vocal line (cantus), along with the tenor. Composers began perceiving the Gregorian melody as material that had the potential to be paraphrased from both a rhythmic and melodic standpoint. No longer were they restricted to a long, sustained tenor vocal part, but they were free to create a novel approach that infused new life into the oft-used chant.

All Franco-Flemish requiem settings possess fragments of older plainchant tunes, primarily the chant incipits that were still sung before most of the principal sections of the requiem mass. These include the Introit (*Requiem aeternam* and verse, *Te decet hymnus Deus in Sion*), Graduale (*Si ambulem*), Offertory (*Domine Jesu Christe* and verse, *Hostias et preces tibi Domine offerimus*), Sanctus (*Sanctus* and *Benedictus*) Agnus Dei (*Agnus Dei*), and Communion (*Lux aeterna* and verse, *Requiem aeternam dona eis, Domine*). These opening phrases, as well as the composer's subsequent paraphrases of the original chant, were instrumental in preserving a significant and familiar link to the musical past.

STRUCTURE

The original arrangement of the mass texts and the liturgical practices of saying or chanting them during the mass were regularly followed by the structuring of new and innovative musical ideas. The Introit, for instance, had always been divided into two parts, *Requiem aeternam* and *Te decet hymnus*. Vaet is the sole composer (as recognized in this volume) who took it upon himself to create a third musical section for *Exaudi orationem*, the concluding portion of the text. The *Kyrie* was traditionally set in a tri-partite arrangement, however, Brumel added a section to his setting, while Richafort subtracted one, both for the sake of musical diversity and repetition. In his quest to create an extensive variety of contrasting textures, Ockeghem employed seven different sections for the *Kyrie*. Still, Manchicourt proved to have an even more unique touch by being the only composer to join all three sections into one continuous movement.

The Graduale, *Si ambulem* (peculiar to the French liturgy), was usually split into two musical sections, *Si ambulem* and the verse, *Virgo tua*. Vaet and Prioris applied an additional break at the text, *Fuerunt mihi*.

The Tract, *Sicut cervus*, was utilized only by Ockegham, Févin, and de la Rue, the latter two choosing to divide up the text into three sections: *Sicut cervus, Sitivit anima mea*, and *Fuerunt mihi*. Ockeghem, on the other hand, chose to include an additional section, *Ubi est Deus*.

In most cases, the Offertory was divided into two large sections, *Domine Jesu Christe* and its verse *Hostias*, but both Vaet and Ockeghem divided the music into five sections by setting the *Quam olim Abrahae* and *Tu suscipe* into their own units. The *Sanctus* has been split up in many different ways, occasionally into its two principal parts, *Sanctus* and *Benedictus* (Richafort, Prioris, and Manchicourt), and other times into three, four, and five musical sections by the subdivision of the *Pleni sunt coeli* and *Osanna* from the balance of the text.

In the vast majority of settings, the *Agnus Dei* music was broken down into three sections designated *Agnus* I, II, and III. In cases where Brumel and de la Rue chose to repeat a section, the *Agnus* then contained only two sections of original music. The Communion was, without exception, divided into two parts, *Lux aeterna* and *Requiem aeternam*, in every Franco-Flemish requiem, other than that of Ockeghem, who did not employ this particular text, choosing instead to apply a polyphonic setting.

The Netherlanders were recognized for their sense of individual style, and as such, every composer's requiem setting exhibits its own distinct personality. Ockeghem's setting demonstrates the greatest diversity in its textural fabric. Its movements chiefly employ three-part writing, similar to the tradition of the earlier Burgundian composers, yet there are several sections that utilize two- and four-part writing designed for six distinct voices. As a whole, the setting plays more like a collection of self-contained individual pieces than a complete stylistically unified work.

CODA

Brumel's setting is the first and only Franco-Flemish model to include a polyphonic setting of the sequence, *Dies irae*. De la Rue's requiem incorporates numerous examples of paired imitative writing, obviously influenced by Josquin, who was well-known for his employment of this particular contrapuntal device. Richafort's requiem also exemplifies the era's acceptance of individuality. Not only is it the only setting scored for six-part writing, but it is also the only one to quote two melodies associated with Josquin. The first, *Circumdederunt me*, can be cited in several of Josquin's own compositions, while the second, *C'est douleur non pareille*, appears in his chanson, *Faulte d'argent*.

A sense of austerity is discerned in the requiem setting by Prioris, which for much of the work employs a rather simple chordal structure. In contrast, de Févin's work sings out with elaborate and ornate melodic writing, as well as a vast range of vocal combinations and part-writing.

Of all the composers of this era, Jacobus, Vaet, and Pierre de Manchicourt create what could be described as the most "modern"-sounding versions of the requiem, which is not surprising, considering they were all contemporaries of Palestrina and Di Lasso, who both scored requiem settings for five-part choir.

Finally, the advent of printed music and publishing in Venice (Petrucci in 1498 and Scotto in 1481) and Paris (Pierre Attaingnant), resulted in the opportunity for composers to make their new music more readily available to various performing entities. Choirmasters no longer found themselves completely dependent upon the few circulating handwritten copies of any particular work. Enjoying the advantage and greater exposure created by these pre-eminent printing firms were the published works of Brumel, Févin, Prioris, Richafort, and Sermisy.

ANTOINE BRUMEL
c. 1460–c. 1515

Brumel cut a famous figure during the sixteenth century. The renowned English composer, Thomas Morley, mentions him numerous times in *A Plaine and Easie Introduction to Practicall Musicke*, while the Swiss humanist, Heinrich Glareanus (1488–1563) refers to five of Brumel's compositions in his *Dodekachordon* (1547), a book about music theory. The Italian poet, Teofilo Folengo (1496–1544) noted, in *Le Maccheronee*, that Brumel was a famous singer, and the publisher, Ottaviano Petrucci (1466–1539), included a number of Brumel's compositions in his first collection, *Harmonice Musices Odhecaton A* (1501).

In spite of the fame, very little is now known about his life. He was a pupil of Ockeghem and appears to have led a peripatetic existence as a singer-cleric in Chartres Cathedral (c. 1483) and in Geneva (1492). In 1498, he was appointed *Cantor Princeps* for the choirboys at Notre Dame (Paris) and for five years (1505–1510), occupied the position of *maestro di cappella* at the court of Alfonso d'Este in Ferrara, one of the most prestigious and important posts available to a musician during the Renaissance. When the chapel was disbanded in 1510, he retired to Rome, where he appears to have remained until his death.

Brumel composed about fifteen known mass settings, most for four voices, but one for twelve. Five of these works are parody masses; the remainder are based upon a Gregorian *cantus firmus*. He wrote another three dozen sacred works as well as a handful of instrumental and secular vocal pieces.

The *Missa pro defunctis* was first published by Andrea de Antiquis (Rome), on May 9, 1516, in *Liber quindecim missarum electorum quae per excellentissimos compositae ferunt*. It is not known for whom the *missa pro defunctis* was composed, but the presence of the *Dies irae* suggests an Italian patron, perhaps someone associated with the court at Ferrara.

The prevailing, polyphonic SATB texture is contrasted only by unison or fauxbourdon versions of the Gregorian melody, employed in the even-numbered verses of the sequence hymn, *Dies irae*. One further contrast is provided by the fifth and fifteenth verses (*Liber scriptus* & *Inter oves*), which are scored for a florid, two-part contrapuntal arrangement for soprano and alto. Brumel's contrapuntal writing is enhanced by use of imitative techniques, such as canon (prominent in the Communion) and point of imitation (found throughout).

Unlike those works of Brumel that possess full, "modern" harmonic sonorities, the requiem summons up an archaic tonal language, one more familiar to Ockeghem or the Burgundians, Binchois and Dufay. The Introit, *Kyrie*, Sequence Hymn, and the Communion verse employ the empty, final cadence of an earlier era. Only the *Sanctus*, *Agnus Dei* and the first section of the Communion possess "modern," complete harmonies. The polyphonic fabric is occasionally relieved by brief, chordal passages, such as *et tibi reddetur*, *Pie Jesu*, *Sanctus*, *Osanna*, *Benedictus*, *Agnus Dei*. This procedure suggests to the listener a mood, more austere and solemn.

The plainchant melody, usually assigned to the tenor line by Brumel, occasionally appears in the soprano. His treatment of the chant varies from a straightforward presentation of the original to elaborate paraphrase. The long, flowing melodic lines are an inheritance from Ockeghem's teaching.

The most unique feature of this requiem setting is the presence of a polyphonic setting of the *Dies irae*. It appears that Brumel, with his connections to the Papal Court, was the first composer to introduce it into the Franco-Flemish polyphonic requiem. At this time, the *Dies irae* was peculiar to the Roman, not the French, liturgy and it is the first known polyphonic arrangement of the text.

Basic Data

EDITIONS

1. Das Chorwerke #68
Antoine Brumel Requiem
ed. Albert Seay
Karl Heinrich Moseler Verlag,
Wolfenbuttel 1959

2. Corpus Mensurabilis Musicae
Antonii Brumel, Opera Omnia
Vol. IV
ed. Barton Hudson
American Institute of Musicology
1970

DURATION

Six movements, 674 mm.

VOICING

Choir: SATB range: S-B flat 5 [C6 rare], B-G3 [F3 rare]

OUTLINE

Introit: 104 mm., 2 sections [*Requiem* & *Te decet*, satb]
Kyrie: 92 mm., 4 sections [*Kyrie, Christe, Kyrie, Kyrie*, satb]
Sequence, *Dies irae*: 300 mm., 6 sections. All satb unless otherwise noted.
 [1 *Dies irae*; 3/9 *Tuba mirum* & *Recordare*; 5/15 *Liber scriptus* & *Inter oves*, sa; 7/
   13 *Quid sum* & *Qui Mariam*; 11/17 *Juste judex* & *Oro supplex*; 20 *Pie Jesu*]
Sanctus: 79 mm., 4 sections. [*Sanctus, Osanna, Benedictus, Osanna*, satb]
Agnus Dei: 51 mm., 2 sections. [*Agnus* I/II, *Agnus* III, satb]
Communion: 48 mm., 2 sections. [*Lux aeterna* & *Requiem aeternam*, satb]

DISCOGRAPHY

Sony Vivarte, Sk 46348, Huelgas Ensemble, dir. Paul van Nevel [*Dies Irae* only]

ANTOINE DE FÉVIN
c. 1470–1511/1512

Antoine de Févin was probably born in Arras, his family home, and died
in Blois, a seat of the French royal court. His family belonged to the
French nobility and father, Pierre, was Lord of Graincourt and Garinet, as
well as alderman (district leader or governor) of Arras. Antoine worked
as a priest and singer in the service of the French king, Louis XII.

He is mentioned in several musical compositions, including a *Déploration* composed by Jean Mouton. In 1515, Petrucci published a volume of
Févin's masses, *Misse Antonii de Fevin*. This volume contains three masses
by Févin and one mass each, by Pierre de La Rue and Robert de Févin
(brother of Antoine). There exist an additional ten masses by Févin, four
of which are parody masses. Fifteen motets, three settings of the *Magnifi-*

cat, three settings of the Lamentations, and seventeen secular chansons constitute the remainder of his extant works.

The composition date of the *Missa pro fidelibus defunctis* remains unknown, though it might have been written in the first decade of the 1500s when Févin was in his mid-thirties. It is likely to have been composed for nobility at the French court.

Although the predominant choral texture is SATB, Févin furnishes several contrasts in the fabric with two-part writing for the Graduale verse, *Virga tua*, the Offertory verse, *Hostias et preces tibi*, and the opening passage of the Tract, *Sicut cervus*. Three-part writing is employed in a portion of the Tract (*Sitivit*) and five-part writing is used throughout the *Sanctus* and *Agnus Dei*.

Throughout the composition the texture remains polyphonic, laced with numerous imitative passages. The *Agnus Dei* and *Te decet* (Introit) possess a contrasting, elaborate, homophonic weave. With the exception of the *Sanctus*, the concluding chords of every movement are missing the third of the triad. This conservative technique adds an archaic, somber feeling to the mood of the music.

This beautiful work is based upon the melodies of the plainsong requiem, paraphrased in the uppermost melodic line. Févin's ornate melodic lines abide as exquisite examples of free and imitative contrapuntal writing. Some passages, such as *Virga tua*, *Sicut cervus*, and *Tu suscipe*, are particularly ravishing.

Basic Data

EDITION

Les Oeuvres Complètes D'Antoine de Févin
Collected Works, Vol. XI/I
ed. Edward Clinkscale
Institute of Mediaeval Music, Ltd.
Henryville, Ottawa, Binningen c. 1980

DURATION

Eight movements, 378 mm.

VOICING

Choir: SATTB range: S-C6 [D6 rare], B-F3

OUTLINE

Introit: 41 mm., 2 sections [*Requiem* & *Te decet*, satb]
Kyrie: 22 mm., 3 sections [*Kyrie, Christe, Kyrie*, satb]
Graduale, *Si ambulem*: 31 mm., 2 sections [*Si ambulem*, satb & *Virga tua*, sa]
Tract, *Sicut servus*: 90 mm., 3 sections [*Sicut servus*, tb; *Sitivit*, sab; *Fuerunt*, satb]

Offertory: 80 mm., 3 sections [*Domine Jesu Christe, Quam olim*, satb; *Hostias*, sa]
Sanctus: 53 mm., 3 sections [*Sanctus, Pleni sunt coeli, Benedictus*, sattb]
Agnus Dei: 38 mm., 3 sections [*Agnus* I, II, III, sattb]
Communion: 20 mm., 2 sections [*Lux aeterna, & Requiem aeternam*, satb]

DISCOGRAPHY

None found.

PIERRE DE MANCHICOURT
c. 1510–October 5, 1564

De Manchicourt was born near Arras, Spain, where he began his musical career as a choirboy in the cathedral at Arras. He later served as chapel-master at the Cathedral of Tours (1539) and at Notre Dame in Tournai (1545). His most significant appointment was chapel-master to King Philip II of Spain. He was selected for this position in 1559 and remained in it until his death. During his lifetime he was quite famous and enjoyed the respect and friendship of the composers, Clemens non Papa, Claudin Sermisy, Orlando Di Lasso, and Tielman Susato, one of his many publishers. He was one of the last composers of the Franco-Flemish school and his musical style seems to have been influenced by Josquin and his contemporary, Clemens non Papa.

His setting of the *Missa pro defunctis* was probably composed in the late 1550s. It was first published in *Liber quatuor missarum* (c. 1560). The individual for whom the work was composed is unknown, but may have been someone associated with the Spanish court, to which he had just been appointed. The work is scored for five-part SATTB writing throughout, with a brief contrast of four-part SATB writing in the Graduale verse, *Virgo tua*. One of the unique aspects of the composer's writing is the brief, chromatic passages, similar to the "cross relations" used by Purcell. These colorful passages appear in every movement and function in nearly the same way that secondary dominants work in Bach's chorale settings.

The prevailing imitative polyphonic texture is rarely disturbed by chordal passages, though de Manchicourt falls back on the "empty" final cadences in the Graduale, Offertory, *Agnus Dei*, and Communion. Perhaps these archaic sonorities, at least in the "mind's-eye" of the composer, were associated with a sense of solemnity and were seen as a link to past tradition. Plainchant melodies appear clearly in the uppermost vocal line, except for the Communion, when the chant is placed in the tenor. The suave, "spun out" melodic lines, in all likelihood, are based upon the convention established by Ockeghem and Josquin and the compact polyphonic texture, with its numerous imitative passages, is derived from the models of Josquin and non Papa.

One of the endearing qualities of this *missa,* is the elegantly balanced, five-part writing, with its chromatic coloring. A second, novel quality is the integration of the three sections of the *Kyrie,* (*Kyrie, Christe, Kyrie*) into one continuous movement. Of the other Franco-Flemish composers, only Richafort made this type of structural change in the requiem, who joined without break, the *Christe* text to *Kyrie* I.

Basic Data

EDITION

Corpus Mensurablis Musicae #55
Pierre de Manchicourt, Opera Omina, Vol. 4
ed. Lavern J. Wagner
American Institute of Musicology, Hanssler Verlag. 1982

DURATION

Seven movements, 712 mm.

VOICING

Choir: SATTB range: S-D6 [E flat 6, rare], B-F3

OUTLINE

Introit: 76 mm., 2 sections [*Requiem* & *Te decet*, sattb]
Kyrie: 125 mm., 1 continuous section [*Kyrie, Christe, Kyrie,* sattb]
Graduale: 119 mm., 2 sections [*Si ambulem* sattb & *Virgo tua*, satb]
Offertory: 210 mm., 2 sections [*Domine Jesu Christe* & *Hostias*, sattb]
Sanctus: 71 mm., 2 sections [*Sanctus* & *Benedictus*, sattb]
Agnus Dei: 55 mm., 3 sections [*Agnus* I, II, III, sattb]
Communion: 56 mm., 2 sections [*Lux aeterna* & *Requiem aeternam*, sattb]

DISCOGRAPHY

None found.

JOHANNES OCKEGHEM
c. 1420–February 6, 1497

Probably born in East Flanders, Ockeghem, clergyman and master musician, was respected and beloved by his colleagues. Testimony of this respect is divulged in the *Déploration sur le mort d'Ockeghem* by Guillaume Crétin. (A *déploration* was a type of lament or homage arranged in the form of a motet.) There is further, the positive eye-witness account of

Francesco Florio, an Italian humanist who visited and met him at Tours in the 1470s.

Ockeghem may have been a pupil of the Burgundian, Gilles Binchois, for he, too, wrote a similar *Déploration* (1460) upon the death of Binchois. There remains virtually no doubt that the two men knew each other personally.

His professional life was spent in France. In the 1440s, he served Charles I, Duke of Bourbon (Moulins), and, in 1453, he entered into the service of Charles VII, King of France, as *premier chapelain*. Ockeghem continued to serve in this position throughout the reigns of Louis XI and Charles VIII. A miniature portrait still exists of this Franco-Flemish musician, directing his cappella, whilst wearing eyeglasses! Ockeghem's pupils included Pierre de La Rue and Josquin Dès Prés.

He did not leave an enormous number of works, but those extant include ten motets, twenty-one secular chansons, and sixteen mass settings. Many of his mass settings are parody masses; a form that the Council of Trent tried to abolish. Of the mass settings, two are great masterpieces; the *Missa Mi-Mi* and the *Missa Prolationum*. The former is a beautiful, moody work; the latter, a marvel of canonic complexity and ingenuity. Ockeghem's *Requiem pro defunctis* is the oldest extant polyphonic setting of the funeral text. It was probably composed for the funeral of Charles VII in July of 1461.

One puzzling aspect of the work is the dissimilarity in style and scoring of the movements. Although the prevailing texture of this work is for three voices (more in keeping with the Burgundian tradition), simple two-part and three-part writing exist side by side with more sophisticated four-part texture (Graduale, Tract, and Offertory). Although six different voice parts are called for, the scoring never exceeds four vocal lines and his constantly shifting scoring provides the work with sonic variety and interest.

He was the only Franco-Flemish composer to provide the *Kyrie* with such a wide melodic variety (seven independent sections), while at the same time, scoring the *Kyrie* for, variously, two-, three-, and four-part writing. It appears to be an *ad hoc* collection of pieces, coming from different sources and different periods of the composer's *oeuvre*. Be that as it may, this *missa* is a compositional form in its infancy. Rules about how to create a correct version of the requiem did not exist. Ockeghem miraculously and successfully prepared a composition in which the continuous unfolding of musical ideas accurately reflects the meanings of the text. It served as a model for several later generations of composers.

His requiem mass employs traditional plainsong melodies, blended with the contours of the French chanson, for melodic inspiration. Any contemporary of Ockeghem, who sang or heard this requiem, would have easily recognized the Gregorian *cantus firmus* because the melody was placed in the *superius* [soprano] line.

This work possesses all the requisite qualities of piety, contemplation, and spiritual depth. These characteristics are summoned up by the long, supple melodies and fluid harmonies so typical of Ockeghem's writing style.

Basic Data

EDITIONS

1. American Musicological Society, Studies & Documents, No. 1 Johannes Ockeghem Collected Works, Vol. 2 Columbia University Press, New York, N.Y. 1947 [C clefs used]

2. Johannes Ockeghem Requiem für sechstimmigen Chor Eulenburg Octavo Edition # 10135 c. 1977 [Edition Music, Budapest]

DURATION

five movements, 803 mm., perf. c. 30"

VOICING

Choir: SS [contratenor] ATB range: S-D 6 [E 6-rare], B-B flat 3

OUTLINE

Introit: 120 mm., 2 sections [*Requiem* & *Te decet*, sctt]
Kyrie: 155 mm., 7 sections [*Kyrie* 1 & 3, stb; *Kyrie* 2, sct; *Christe* 1 & 3, sct; *Christe* 2, stb; *Kyrie* 1, stb; *Kyrie* 2, sct; *Kyrie* 3, scttb]
Graduale, *Si ambulem*: 219 mm., 2 sections [*Si ambulem*, sctt; *Virga tua* scttb]
Tractus, *Sicut cervus*: 167 mm., 4 sections [*Sicut*, sct; *Sitivit*, tb; *Fuerunt*, sctt; *Ubi est*, scttb]
Offertory: 142 mm., 5 sections [*Domine Jesu Christe*, scttb; *Sed signifer*, stb; *Quam olim*, scttb; *Tu sucipe*, cctt; *Hostias*, st]

DISCOGRAPHY

1. Harmonia Mundi, HMC 901441, Ensemble Organum, cond. Marcel Pérès.
2. Gaudeamus 168, The Clerkes Group, dir. Edward Wickham.

JOHANNES PRIORIS
c. 1460–c. 1514

Of Johannes Prioris' life and existence, only the slightest shadow remains. Nevertheless, his work reminds us of his accomplishments as an accomplished composer and musician. He might have been born in Brabant, in the town of Vorst (his Flemish name, De Vorste), a village near Brussels.

By 1491, he was a member of the choir of St. Peter's (Rome). In 1503, the ambassador from the Ferrara Court, working at the Court of Louis XII, wrote to Duke Ercole I that he had received a mass from *"Prioris, suo* (Louis XII) *maystro de capella."* In a *Déploration*, composed by Crétin for Ockeghem, Prioris is referred to as *"notre bon père et maistre."* (Groves Dictionary, vol. 15, p. 275)

Six mass compositions are known. Three are based upon French chansons, two upon plainchant (including the requiem), and one is lost. There are about twenty other sacred pieces, including six *Magnificat* settings, and a dozen secular chansons.

The *Missa pro defunctis* was first published, posthumously, by Pierre Attaignant in 1532 (*Viginti missarum musicalium. Quintus liber tres missas continet*). Richard Wexler (Groves Dictionary, vol. 15, p. 275) suggests that it may have been composed to commemorate the death of Anne of Brittany (d. Jan. 9, 1514).

The predominant SATB scoring for the *missa* is in homophonic texture, with one brief excursion into two-part writing during the Graduale verse, *Virga tua*. This texture lends a deepened sense of sadness to an already severe text.

Prioris used simple chordal style for the *Te decet* (Introit), *Sanctus & Benedictus*, *Agnus Dei*, and *Et lux* (Communion). For the remainder of the work, he used an elaborate, nonimitative polyphonic texture. Imitative polyphony is found in the *Kyrie*. Except for the *Kyrie* and one section of the *Agnus Dei*, Prioris used the archaic, "empty" cadence on the final chords of the remaining movements.

The paraphrased chant melodies are placed in the uppermost line and appear in every movement. The overall mood of the work is somewhat austere, even haunting. One of the most emotional moments in the *missa* is the touching duet for soprano and countertenor for the Graduale verse, *"Virga tua."* This emotional piece clearly owes its genesis to the florid contrapuntal writing of Ockeghem.

Basic Data

EDITION

Corpus Mensurabilis Musicae #90
Johannes Prioris
Opera Omnia II
editors, T. Herman Keahey and Conrad Douglas
American Institute of Musicology, Hanssler Verlag, 1982

DURATION

Seven movements, 596 mm.

VOICING

Choir: SA [counter-tenor] TB range: S-C6 [D6 rare], B-G3

OUTLINE

Introit: 83 mm., 2 sections [*Requiem* & *Te decet*, satb]
Kyrie: 66 mm., 3 sections [*Kyrie, Christe, Kyrie*, satb]
Graduale: 140 mm., 3 sections [*Si ambulem*, satb; *Virga tua*, sa; *Consolata sunt*, satb]
Offertory: 219 mm., 2 sections [*Domine Jesu Christe* & *Hostias*, satb]
Sanctus: 33 mm., 2 sections [*Sanctus* & *Benedictus*, satb]
Agnus Dei: 30 mm., 3 sections [*Agnus Dei* I, II, III, satb]
Communion: 28 mm., 2 sections [*Lux aeterna* & *Requiem aeternam*, satb]
An alternate *Agnus Dei* III [satb] is provided [16 mm.].

DISCOGRAPHY

None found.

JEAN RICHAFORT
c. 1480–c. 1548

His birthplace is believed to have been in or near Hainaut. The first clear fact about this composer is that he was *maitre de chapelle* at St. Rombout's Cathedral in Mechelen, Belgium, but his tenure there was quite short (1507–1509). Two significant musical personalities of the twentieth century, Jules van Nuffel and Flor Peeters, worked together in St. Rombout's; the former as composer-conductor for the 200-voice choir; the latter as organist.

Richafort was connected with the French royal chapel during the reign of Louis XII, although it is not clear in what capacity he served. His motet, *Consolator captivorum*, mentions the king's name and offers a prayer for him. It is possible that this piece was composed for the king's funeral in 1515.

Pope Leo X mentioned Richafort's name as a singer in the French chapel. His last-known position, *maitre de chapelle* (1542–1547), was at St. Gilles in Bruges. In a work by Pierre Ronsard, titled *Livre des méslanges*, (Paris, 1560) the author states that Richafort was a pupil of Josquin. (Richafort's motet *Misereatur mei* is clearly modeled on the same, exact ostinato as is found in Josquin's *Miserere mei*).

Although the biographical evidence is slender, the compositions speak for the man. In 1556, Le Roy & Ballad (Paris) published a collection of nineteen motets by Richafort (*Joannis Richafort modulorum quatuor quinque & sex vocum, liber primus*). There are three known masses (one requiem and two parody), more than a dozen settings of the *Magnificat*, about

twenty motets, and an equal number of secular chansons. His compositions are found in some seventy anthologies, published from 1519–1583,
thereby attesting to his fame.

In 1532, the *Missa pro defunctis* was published by Pierre Attaingnant
(Paris), in a collection titled, *Sextus liber duas missas habet.* . . . Because this
composition includes two texts and melodies, liked and used by Josquin,
there exists the possibility that Richafort wrote it for Josquin's funeral service in 1521. Bruno Turner suggests the possibility that the work was performed for the funeral of King Philip II of Spain, in September 1598. (CD
notes, p. 3)

For this composition, Richafort created a canon, based upon the melody
and text of *Circumdederunt me* (the same melody used by Josquin in several of his own works) and placed it in every movement. It is located in
the middle of the six-part texture, (third and fourth melodic lines)
between the outer four voices, SA and TB. The second text, *C'est douleur
non pareille,* (found in Josquin's chanson, *Faulte d'argent*) is employed
briefly, and only in the Graduale and Offertory.

At the same time, in each movement, paraphrases of the traditional
Gregorian funeral melodies are intermingled with Josquin's canon. The
chant is placed not only in the uppermost voice, but also in the other three
outer lines.

The predominant texture of the requiem is six-part polyphony. The
number of voices was increased, evidently to accommodate the two voice
parts for the canon. Contrast is accomplished by a thinning of the usual
SATB parts, for example, the number of voice parts in the Graduale verse,
Virga tua, or the Offertory verse text, *Tu suscipe,* is reduced to passages
employing only three or four voices. At the same time, the canon is also
omitted. The harmonic elements are quite beautiful and possess a full,
"modern" sound, even on the final chords of each movement.

Richafort was one of the most skilled composers of the Franco-Flemish
school. His requiem setting is replete with contrapuntal devices, such as
canon and points of imitation. He employed *canti firmus,* ostinati, and
paraphrase in his music, yet he attempted to make the relationship
between music and text a close knit. His work served as a model for later
composers, such as Mouton, Morales, and Palestrina.

Basic Data

EDITIONS

1. Das Chorwerke
Jean Richafort Requiem
ed., Albert Seay
Pub. Karl Heinrich Moseler Verlag
Wolfenbüttel and Zurich 1976.

2. Corpus Mensurabilis Musicae #81
Johannes Richafort, Opera Omnia
ed., Harry Elzinger
American Institute of Musicology
Hanssler Verlag 1979

DURATION

Seven movements, 672 mm.

VOICING

Choir: SA [canon I, canon II—both are tenor] TB range: S-D6, B-G3

OUTLINE

Introit: 72 mm., 2 sections [*Requiem* & *Te decet*, satttb]
Kyrie: 86 mm., 2 sections [*Kyrie/Christe* & *Kyrie*, satttb]
Graduale, *Si ambulem*: 134 mm., 2 sections [*Si ambulem*, satttb; *Virga tua*, sat—
   satb—satttb]
Offertory: 186 mm., 2 sections [*Domine Jesu Christe*, satttb; *Hostias*, satb—satttb
Sanctus: 75 mm., 2 sections [*Sanctus*, satttb; *Benedictus*, satb—satttb]
Agnus Dei: 55 mm., 3 sections [*Agnus* I, II, III, satttb]
Communion: 64 mm., 2 sections [*Lux aeterna* & *Requiem aeternam*, satttb]

DISCOGRAPHY

Signum Records, SIGCD005, Chapelle du Roi, cond. Alistair Dixon.

PIERRE DE LA RUE
c. 1460–December 20, 1518

Pierre de la Rue was a member of the Franco-Flemish school of composers
that included Jacob Obrecht, Josquin dès Prés, and Johannes Ockeghem.
Information about his early years remains scant, yet the unusual number
of his compositions preserved in the archives of the Papal Chapel suggests that they were spent in Rome.

   A singer at the chapel of the Burgundian Court from 1492 until 1516,
he accompanied Philippe Le Beau on visits to Spain in 1502 and 1506.
Following the death of this ruler, he entered into the service of Margaret
of Austria. La Rue died in Courtrai, where he was a canon in Notre Dame
Church.

   La Rue composed a number of polyphonic compositions, including
thirty masses and an almost equal number of motets. Several of the mass
settings are based upon chanson melodies, including the famous
L'Homme Armé tune, while the majority are built upon Gregorian melodies.

   From Ockeghem, de la Rue received a sense of fluid melodic line; from
Josquin, canon and the contrapuntal technique of paired melodic and
rhythmic imitation. In this technique, one pair of voices imitates another.

   The *Missa pro defunctis* was composed sometime around 1500. The earliest source for this work is a choirbook dating from c. 1520. (Corpus Mens-

urabilis Musicae 97, Vol. V. Critical Notes.) The individual for whom it was written is unknown, although it has been suggested that Margaret of Austria was the recipient. (Jean-Pierre Ouvrard, CD notes)

The dominant feature of the vocal writing is the persistent, four-part ATBarB and five-part ATBarBB. This arrangement provides a basic "dark," serious color. At the same time, de la Rue employed a very wide range of contrasting choral groupings, including TB, SA, AT, ABar, SATB, BarB, and ATBarBB. The somber sonorities of the *missa* are greatly enhanced by the omission of a soprano line. It appears only in *Sicut cervus* (Tract), *Quam olim Abrahae* (Offertory), *Sanctus* (but not *Benedictus*) and the Communion. It is optional for the Offertory. For the remainder of the composition it remains silent, thereby elevating the balanced voice pairings and intensifying the powerful sense of spiritual awe.

Earlier, Ockeghem used the same technique for dark coloring in his *Missa Mi-Mi*. When the soprano line is added, the music radiates light, dispelling every shadow.

One of the most interesting aspects of the requiem is the composer's skill in handling the paired imitations that occur in every movement of the requiem. Every conceivable pairing (A/T-B/B, S/A-BarB, S/A-T/B, T/B-Abar, and A/B-BarB) is imaginatively written.

The overall musical fabric is fairly dense and compact, with occasional thinning of the voice parts. The harmony is complete and sonorous, with most final cadences possessing a complete triad. There are some exceptions, such as sections found in the Introit, Tract, Offertory, and *Sanctus*. Although most of the texture is imitative polyphony, there are scattered, intimate chordal passages that further intensify the serious mood of the music.

Fragments of the Gregorian melodies or newly composed melodies, suggestive of the Gregorian originals, are not limited to the tenor line; they are found in every vocal part and section of the *missa*.

Basic Data

EDITIONS

1. Kalmus Study Scores, # 703
The Flemish and German Schools
Edwin Kalmus, Publisher of Music
1968

2. Corpus Mensurabilis Musicae
Pierre de la Rue, Opera Omnia, Vol. V
editors, St. John-Davison, Nigel and
J. Evan Kreider and T. Herman Keahey
American Institute of Musicology,
Hanssler Verlag 1996

3. Das Chorwerk XI
Pierre de la Rue
Requiem und eine Motette
ed. Freidrich Blume 1931

DURATION

Seven movements, 400 mm., perf. c. 21'

VOICING

Choir: SA [or counter-tenor] TBarBB range: S-F6 [G6 rare]; B-E3

OUTLINE

Introitus: 34 mm., 2 sections [*Requiem* & *Te decet*, atbarb]
Kyrie: 44 mm., 3 sections [*Kyrie, Christe, Kyrie*, atbarb]
Tract-*Sicut Servus*: 58 mm., 3 sections [*Sicut servus*, sa; *Sitivit*, tbar; *Fuerunt*, satbar]
Offertory: 116 mm., 4 sections [*Domine Jesu Christe*, satbar; *Quam olim*, satbarb; *Hostias*, satbar; *Quam olim*, satbarb]
Sanctus: 80 mm., 5 sections [*Sanctus*, satbarb; *Pleni sunt coeli*, satbar; *Osanna*, satbarb; *Benedictus*, atbarb; *Osanna*, satbarb]
Agnus Dei: 34 mm., 2 sections [*Agnus* I, *Agnus* II, atbarbb]
Communion: 34 mm., 2 sections [*Lux aeterna* & *Requiem aeternam*, satbar]

DISCOGRAPHY

Harmonia Mundi, HMT 7901296, Ensemble Clément Janequin.

CLAUDIN DE SERMISY
c. 1490–October 3, 1562

Sermisy, a recognized master of the Renaissance chanson, was an important composer of sacred music. He may have come from Burgundy or Picardy. The earliest documentary reference refers to him as a cleric at Sainte Chapelle (Paris). In 1532, he was in Paris, as the *sous-maitre* of the royal chapel (for Louis XII), and he probably continued to work for successive French kings, up until the time of his death in Paris. In September 1553, he was nominated to the 11th canonry of Sainte Chapelle, a position that gave him revenue and a home.

He enjoyed a good reputation among his colleagues. Claude Chappuys, librarian and personal attendant to King Francis I, called Sermisy the "father of musicians." The composer, Pierre Certon, in his *Déploration de Sermisy,* called Sermisy *"grand maistre, expert et magnifique compositeur."* He might have been a pupil of Josquin.

Sermisy's vocal compositions include more than 100 sacred works and about 175 chansons. There exist a dozen mass settings; of those, one is a requiem. The majority of the settings are parody masses; the models often selected from his motets. Some, such as the requiem, are derived from plainchant.

The style of the polyphonic chanson was a source of inspiration for his musical fabric. Points of imitation, occasional canonic treatment of the melodies, short phrases, and general lightness in the musical texture are typical characteristics.

Sermisy's *Missa pro defunctis* was first published in *Viginti Missarum,* by Pierre Attaingnant in 1532. A constant SATB texture is maintained throughout the work, with occasional thinning of the vocal lines, particularly in the Graduale verse, *Virga tua,* where much of the texture is reduced to three-part writing. Although much of the writing bristles with imitative polyphony, the *Agnus Dei* employs a more solemn, chordal texture.

Exact or paraphrased fragments of the Gregorian melodies are found in the tenor line of every section of this setting. A distinctive feature of this *missa* is the polyphonic setting of the complete *Benedictus* text. Sermisy and Brumel were the only composers of this school to set the entire text (in a requiem setting) in this manner.

Basic Data

EDITIONS

1. Musica Liturgica, Vol. 1, Fasciculez
Claudin De Sermisy
Missa Pro Defunctis
ed. Robert Snow, March 1958
Pub. World Library of Sacred Music

2. Corpus Mensurabilis Musicae #52
Opera Omnia
Claudin de Sermisy, Vol. 5
American Institute of Musicology,
Hanssler Verlag, 1977

DURATION
Seven movements, 588 mm.

VOICING
Choir: SATB range: S-F6, bass-F3

OUTLINE
Introit: 62 mm., 2 sections [*Requiem* & *Te decet*, satb]
Kyrie: 60 mm., 3 sections [*Kyrie, Christe, Kyrie,* satb]
Graduale, *Si Ambulem*: 114 mm., 2 sections [*Si ambulem* & *Virga tua*, satb]
Offertory: 176 mm., 2 sections [*Domine Jesu Christe* & *Hostias*, satb]
Sanctus: 93 mm., 4 sections [*Sanctus, Pleni sunt coeli, Hosanna, Benedictus*, satb]
Agnus Dei: 41 mm., 3 sections [*Agnus Dei* I, II, III, satb]
Communion: 42 mm., 2 sections [*Lux aeterna* & *Requiem aeternam*, satb]

DISCOGRAPHY
None found.

JACOBUS VAET
c. 1529–1567

Vaet was born, probably in Courtrai, where he began his musical career as a choirboy at Notre Dame. By 1550, he was a member of the chapel of

Emperor Charles V. Ten years later, he entered into the service of Arch-duke Maximilian as Master of the chapel, a position he held until his death in Vienna. Among his pupils was the outstanding composer, Jacob Regnart. Among his friends were Di Lasso, Clemens non Papa, and Gombert.

There are nine extant masses, of which one is a requiem and the remainder parodies from secular or sacred pieces. During his lifetime, he was famous for his motets. There are two books of motets, *Modulationes, liber* I & II, published in Venice (1562). Other motets were published from 1553 to 1568. The remainder of his sacred pieces includes eight settings of the *Magnificat*, eight settings of the *Salve Regina* for four to eight voices, and a number of miscellaneous pieces. Only three secular chansons survive.

His style is marked by smooth vocal writing and by the use of bor-rowed material. Gabrieli's influence is seen in the use of expressive homo-phonic textures and polychoral scoring. Vaet's harmonic sense leans away from modality, closer to tonality, and with a fondness for dominant-tonic relationships.

The *Missa pro defunctis,* for five voices, was written sometime after 1550. A prevailing SATTB texture is used for five of the seven movements, while the Tract and Offertory employ a reduced scoring. The Tract, *Sicut cervus,* its verse, *Sitivit,* and concluding line, *Fuerunt,* were scored for a more inti-mate SA, TB, and SATB voicing, respectively. The Offertory was set in an SATB arrangement.

Vaet employs a paraphrased version of the plainchant melody in the tenor and soprano lines throughout the various movements. The conser-vative quality of the *missa* is produced by the use of imitative polyphony throughout the work.

Basic Data

EDITION

Denkmäler der Tonkunst in Österreich
Jacobus Vaet
The Complete Works, Vol. IV
Masses, Vol. I
ed. Milton Steinhardt
Akademische Druck und Verlagsanstalt
Graz and Vienna, 1964

DURATION

Seven movements, 523 mm.

VOICING

Choir: SA [Quintus-tenor I] TB range: S-E6; B-D3

OUTLINE

Introit: 49 mm., 3 sections [*Requiem aeternam* , *Te decet*, *Exaudi*, saqtb]

Kyrie: 59 mm., 3 sections [*Kyrie*, *Christe*, *Kyrie*, saqtb]

Tract, *Sicut cervus*: 90 mm., 3 sections [*Sicut cervus*, sa; *Sitivit*, tb; *Fuerunt*, satb]

Offertory: 144 mm., 5 sections [*Domine Jesu Christe & Quam olim*, satb; *Hostias*, Gregorian chant; *Tu suscipe & Quam olim*, satb]

Sanctus: 70 mm., 4 sections [*Sanctus, Sanctus, Pleni sunt coeli, Benedictus,* saqtb]

Agnus Dei: 50 mm., 3 sections [*Agnus Dei* I, II, III, saqtb]

Communion: 61 mm., 2 sections [*Lux aeterna & Requiem aeternam*, saqtb]

The motet, *Ne recorderis*, [20 mm., saqtb] is included at the end of this requiem.

DISCOGRAPHY

None found.

4

The High Renaissance

BACKGROUND

The mid-sixteenth century proved to be a prosperous time for the art of vocal music, thanks to many notable developments. The most significant advance to take place was the gradual yet beneficial unification of the Franco-Flemish and Italian musical traditions. The Netherlanders, with their science of counterpoint, and the Italians, with their sense of harmonic fullness, combined to create a liturgical repertory that displayed a remarkable balance of the horizontal and vertical formations of music. Joining together with this already vibrant and arousing music was the spiritual fire and mystical passion of the Iberians. This extraordinary marriage of melody and harmony set the stage for an era often referred to as the *Golden Age of Polyphony*.

The most historically significant Renaissance musical forms are the mass, the motet, and most certainly the secular madrigal. A special form of the mass, the polyphonic *missa pro defunctis*, was, to some extent, a rarity in the late fifteenth and early sixteenth centuries. It was the materialization of a handful of settings from the Netherlanders that inadvertently burst open the creative doors for many composers, and as the new musical styles traveled throughout the Catholic lands, more and more musicians jumped at the chance to become members of this adventurous fraternity. Unfortunately, despite the vast number of mass compositions written during this era, the percentage of surviving requiem settings remains sadly miniscule.

For inspiration, composers often adapted pre-existing Gregorian chant melodies or popular tunes into their new mass settings. Works that employ old plainchant melodies are designated *cantus firmus* masses.

With the exception of the requiem composed by De Monte, virtually every setting cited in this chapter is based upon the traditional Gregorian melodies.

All composers of the late Renaissance spoke contrapuntal polyphony, the *lingua franca* of that era, and by the mid-sixteenth century, great efforts were made on the parts of many creative minds to add a greater sense of density and uniformity to that musical texture. Continuous musical movement, be it in the harmonic fluidity or the melodic flow, stands as the prime attribute of the period's compositions. Regardless of whether it was written by Flemish composers, such as De Monte, Vaet, Di Lasso, Clemens non Papa, and De Kerle, or by Italians, such as Palestrina, Asola, Vecchi, and Porta, requiem music was embedded in the soil of musical tradition and innovation.

The Frenchmen, Du Caurroy, Certon, Clereau, and Maillard, the Spaniards, Victoria, Guerrero, and Vasquez, and the Portuguese, Brito, Lôbo, and Cardoso, spoke the language of melodic counterpoint and smooth chordal succession equally well.

A more modern and uniform sound was acquired through the use of perfect, full harmony. Zarlino, the Renaissance theorist, referred to this phenomenon as "complete triadic harmony." A fascinating merit of this language rests in the fact that each composer could utilize it in a manner that allowed for the establishment of a personal identity. Although the use of imitative polyphonic texture permitted most compositions to sound somewhat similar, individual personality and charisma prevented any two composers from creating works that sounded exactly alike. This individuality was displayed in various ways. For instance, certain composers, such as Palestrina and Porta, regularly applied chromaticism to their harmonic textures, but others, such as Lôbo and Victoria, used it sparingly with spectacular effect. Manchicourt, who was especially fond of "cross" relations, employed it frequently, a practice that cleverly disrupted the routine harmonic and melodic flow.

SCORING

Another avenue by which late Renaissance composers affirmed their individuality was the use of a wide, although chiefly standard, variety of vocal scoring. This diversity extended from the prevailing four-part SATB (ATTB) and five-part SATTB textures to a more resonant six-part SAATTB or SAATBB arrangement, the latter of which was most notably adapted by the Iberian composers Lôbo, Maghalães, Cardoso, and Victoria. Also of note were the colossal eight-part combinations of SSAATTBB and SATB-ATTB invoked by Vecchi and Lôbo.

Simple two- and three-part scorings, although cited in approximately a dozen of the works discussed in this chapter, tended to be less frequently employed. Although these lighter textures were made use of by Di Lasso and Porta, this sonority was found most appealing by the Spanish and Portuguese, namely Guerrero, Lôbo, Morales, Vasquez, and Victoria. Of the numerous requiems discussed in this chapter, those of Brudieu, Brito, Cardoso, Guerrero, Lôbo, Maghalães, Morales, Pujol, and Vasquez bring into play an intimate, reduced scoring for *In memoria*, the Graduale verse. Among the vocal groupings are SST, SAT, SSAT, ATT, and SATB arrangements, all of which are clear reductions of the prevailing textures found in the parent work. Anerio, Cardoso, Maghalães, Morales, Palestrina, and Porta chose to apply a reduced scoring for *Hostias et preces*, the Offertory verse, a style that was commonly adopted during the era. The *Christe* and *Benedictus* texts or verses of the Sequence, *Dies irae*, would on occasion be granted a more modest and intimate scoring, but this use of technique was not widespread enough to indicate a tradition or, for that matter, even a trend.

GREGORIAN CHANT

Composers had various ways of handling the treatment of the chant melody. Lôbo and Maghalães, in an effort to ensure that the melody would be easily recognized, put the chant melodies into long, sustained note values. Most composers placed the Gregorian melody in the uppermost line, yet some preferred to put it in the alto and tenor. Still others, most notably Di Lasso, Pujol, and Vecchi, worked out paraphrases of the melody in nearly every line. De Monte, the madrigal composer, completely eliminated the plainsong melody, yet managed to capture the essence of the Gregorian original. Similar to the composers of the Franco-Flemish school, some late Renaissance composers made use of the chant incipits as a means of introducing the polyphonic settings of the text.

COUNCIL OF TRENT

Renaissance composers witnessed two paramount milestones during their creative era: the Council of Trent (1543–1563) and the experiments with monody of the Florentine Camerata. The Council of Trent proved significant for its attempt to reform church music by restoring the primacy of Gregorian chant, as well as its efforts to purge all sacred polyphonic music of the secular influences that had gradually seeped in throughout the decades. It had been decreed by certain members of the clergy that the parody mass, which included far too many secular tunes, was an unaccepted style of music and therefore not permissible in the liturgy. Those with a more hard-line approach insisted polyphony should be banned altogether. The use of intertwining voices and texts, an identifying characteristic of the polyphonic style, was scorned by still others who insisted that it made the sacred texts completely incomprehensible. As the Council tried to initiate some standards for musical reform, it simultaneously worked to counter the Protestant Reformation and somehow fill the ensuing chasm that had widened between political and religious ideologies. Finally, on September 17, 1562, in the famous decree, *Decretum de observandis et evitandis in celebratione Missae*, Canon IX, the Council recommended that all secular influences be eliminated from any music performed as part of the mass. It also reaffirmed the primacy of Gregorian chant, but at the same time, acknowledged polyphony as a legitimate form of liturgical expression. Despite this recognition, the Council insisted upon a simpler form of polyphony, one in which the words of the sacred text were clearly recited so as to be distinctly coherent without distraction.

Composer Jacobus De Kerle was commissioned by Cardinal Otto Truchess of Augsburg, his long-time patron, to compose *Preces speciales pro Gerneralis Concilii successu* (1562), a set of polyphonic responsories for the meetings of the Council. Regularly performed at the Trent meetings, their continuous exposure served as a tool for promoting the cause of polyphony.

The Council of Trent ultimately decided to maintain four special chants. Referred to as "sequences," they included *Victimae paschali, Stabat Mater, Veni Sancti Spiritus,* and *Dies irae.* Although the Council chose to include *Dies irae* in the funeral liturgy, it was not formally incorporated into the Roman Missal until 1570 during the papacy of Pius V. This resolve to enlist changes in the liturgy encouraged many composers to create polyphonic settings of the *Dies irae* and the Responsory text, *Libera me.* Earlier requiems composed by the Netherlanders included only one arrangement of the *Dies irae* and lacked a setting of the *Libera me.* In response to the Council's decision, the *Dies irae* soon became common within polyphonic arrangements.

Cited in this chapter are seven composers, Anerio, Asola, Porta, Vecchi, Lôbo, Morales, and Esquivel, who created polyphonic arrangements of the Sequence text. Morales chose to set only the ultimate verse, *Pie Jesu,* while Esquivel concentrated on the penultimate verse, *Lacrimosa.* Three other composers, Anerio, Asola, and Porta, created complete arrangements of the text, alternating each verse between plainchant and polyphonic passages. Lôbo's version was similar, but contained only eleven sections. Vecchi was the sole as well as, by all recorded accounts, the first composer among his contemporaries to create a completely polyphonic setting.

During the late fourteenth and early fifteenth centuries, *Libera me*, the Responsory, also appeared with greater frequency in polyphonic settings of the requiem. Settings by Brito, Brudieu, Du Caurroy, Guerrero, Lôbo, Pujol, and Victoria were some of the earliest versions of this text, all notably composed after the Council of Trent had effectively concluded its business.

Also appearing in the requiem mass during and after the tenure of the Council of Trent was the Tract, *Absolve me*, associated with the Roman rite. This replaced the *Sicut cervus*, which had been previously adopted by the Netherlanders, Ockeghem, Févin, and La Rue. Vasquez appears to be the first to embrace *Absolve me* in specific adaptation for the requiem. *Agenda Defunctorum*, his monumental 1556 setting, incorporates a version of this text at the conclusion of the twenty-seven compositions that comprise a complete polyphonic setting of the funeral office and requiem. Clemens non Papa, Di Lasso, Esquivel, and Guerrero are among the others who composed versions of the Tract as part of their requiem masses. *Si ambulem*, the version of the Graduale long associated with the French rite, was adapted into various polyphonic versions by most of the earlier Franco-Flemish composers, yet the Tridentine Council selected the *Requiem aeternam*, the version used in the Roman rite, to serve as the standard throughout the Catholic lands. This newly designated text was immediately embraced by virtually every Spanish and Portuguese composer of the era. Evidence suggests, however, that this decision was met with some degree of resistance because many composers with close ties to the Franco-Flemish traditions, such as De Monte, Di Lasso, Du Caurroy, and De Kerle, as well as the Italian Vecchi, persisted in composing *Si ambulem* well into the seventeenth century.

FLORENTINE CAMERATA

Of equally significant influence upon Renaissance composers were the Florentine Camerata experimentations with monody, a form of recitative-like solo singing supported by a thorough bass accompaniment. The soon-to-follow polychoral (*cori spezzati*) compositions of Giovanni Gabrieli, combined with monody, forever altered the face of Renaissance music. The blending of Renaissance polyphony with Gabrieli's expressive and declamatory sacred melodies blazed the trail for the ensuing baroque era, while simultaneously fulfilling the Council of Trent's desire for a simplified form of polyphony. In an ironic twist, this new style was perfectly suited for the development of opera. It ultimately lured what would be noted as the ideal style of church music away from Gregorian chant and "Palestrina" style polyphony toward a devotional music with a more ornamental and personal sound, often deemed "operatic."

In the late Renaissance, transitional requiem settings of such composers as Vecchi, Di Lasso, and Anerio exuded traces of the newer baroque style. Vecchi's 1607 setting for double chorus appears to have its roots in the polychordal techniques attributed to Gabrieli. The vivacious, homophonic settings of the text present throughout the work, predominantly in the *Dies irae*, bear the imprint of the Venetian writing style. The requiems of Anerio and De Kerle (c. 1614 and 1614) feature more chordal, homophonic passages than all other Renaissance settings.

Expressive chordal composition is present in all requiem settings from the Renaissance. The *Agnus Dei* was always set in a format that was both poignant and easy to understand, while, in contrast, the *Kyrie* was almost always set in an imitative polyphony, presuming the text to be readily understood given its numerous repetitions. *Te decet*, the opening portion of the Introit verse (if not larger sections), was generally scored with a homophonic texture. Other homophonic passages are rarer and vary from one composer to the next.

Although composers continued setting the *Sanctus* in a variety of ways, dividing it into as few as two up to as many as five separate sections, there appears to have been a tendency during the mid-fourteenth century to split it into two major musical units: *Sanctus* and *Benedictus*. The composers responsible for this trend—if it can be described as such—included Palestrina, Porta, Vecchi, De Monte, Morales, and Victoria.

INSTRUMENTAL SUPPORT

What can be noted of the instrumental support for the requiem settings? Although the Sistine Chapel enforced a steadfast tradition of unaccompanied vocal music, iconographic evidence supports the likelihood that other chapels did not. Engravings, oil paintings, miniatures, and cover pages depict choral ensembles both with and without instruments. Those images without instruments include a picture by Hans Muelich (sixteenth century) of the Chapel Choir at Munich under the direction of Orlando Di Lasso. The title page of a volume of masses published by Attaignant (1532) features an image of a group of singers standing around the choirbook in the Chapel of King Francis I of France. An illumination by Fabian Puler, located in the Teplice Graduale, depicts a group of the Literary Bretheren (c. 1560) circled around the choir book.

Images featuring instruments alongside singers are equally numerous. A well-known picture of Heinrich Schütz depicts him surrounded by the choir of the Chapel of the Elector of Saxony (Dresden) with an organ, a section of trombones, and other instruments visible in the balcony. Also in existence is the famous image of Di Lasso and the chapel musicians of the Duke of Bavaria. The large group of singers is shown supported by flutes, recorders, cornets, sackbut, dulzian, and a keyboard. A woodcut located in *Spiegel der Orgelmacher und Organisten* (Arnold Schlick, 1511) displays the image of an organist behind a positive organ, a cornetist, and a group of musicians singing from a manuscript. Van Eyck's *Ascension and Coronation of the Virgin* (c. 1480) is a portrayal of a celestial choir accompanied by two ensembles of angels playing instruments, one being a "soft" consort of lute, fiddle, harp, and portative organ, the other a "hard" consort of trumpet and three shawms.

Adrian Collaert's engraving entitled *A Religious Service*, created in the late sixteenth century, after Johannes Stradanus, records the existence of a group of instrumentalists (sackbuts and cornets) sharing the choir book with the choral ensemble. The *Coronation of the Virgin Mary*, created circa 1520 and credited to Gangolf Herlinger (although his artisanship is not universally confirmed), adorns the Cisterian monastery at Osek in the Czech Republic. It depicts angelic choirs supported by three cornets, four crumhorns, and a recorder consort. The Litomerice Graduale (c. 1515) includes an illumination displaying a group of singers in the upper left-hand side of the musical score, while three groups of instrumentalists, half human and half angel, playing harp lutes, portative organ, conical trumpets, cornet, shawms, triangle, and bells appear in the right and lower borders.

Evidence of the collaboration between vocal and instrumental musicians appears in written records as well. One such chronicle associated with the performances at the Council of Trent is especially informative. The journal of concilar secretary Angelo Massarelli includes the passage, "a solemn mass was heard sung, with music of voices and instruments." (Romano Vettori, Essay for the CD recording of De Kerle's *Preces speciales*)

Di Lasso's 1578 four-part requiem setting was provided with an instrumental bass part, signifying the presence of a rudimentary form of the basso continuo. The 1614 Anerio requiem does not have a part designated for organ continuo, but several of his masses do.

Various contemporary conductors producing CD recordings of the Renaissance requiem employ instrumental support for their vocal ensembles. Cornets and trombones can be heard on a twentieth century recording of Di Lasso's 1578 four-voice requiem, while a recording of Guerrero's 1582 setting features such instruments as cornet, shawm, sackbuts, dulzian, harp, tabor, and organ. A CD recording of Morales five-part requiem (1548–51) utilizes a full consort of strings, as well as cornet, two sackbuts, serpent, bassoon, and organ. A recording of Vasquez's *Agenda Defunct-*

orum (1556), on the other hand, employs merely organ and the occasional bassoon. The Brumel requiem (1516) employs the talents of three instrumentalists playing sackbuts.

Rui Viera Nery, author of the liner notes for the CD recording of the Morales requiem, states that Renaissance Iberian and Latin American liturgical performances almost always included instrumental support (CD Notes, p. 15, see Morales).

CODA

Compositions of Palestrina and Di Lasso continue to serve as the quintessential models of High Renaissance style, having influenced nearly every contemporaneous writer in their wake. The late appearance in the Iberian Peninsula of "Palestrina" style composition in the works of Lôbo, Cardoso, and Maghalães remains a Renaissance musical curiosity. This trio composed what may be considered the most luminous "Palestrina" style requiem settings during the second and third decades of the seventeenth century, a period when most others had discarded this style in favor of the new baroque.

The emergence of music publishing during this era proved to be a monumental development in the career of the Renaissance composer. Before the advent of publishing, compositions had to be copied slowly and laboriously by hand. Printers immediately revolutionized the way music was distributed. Publishing allowed a vast quantity of musical pieces to become accessible to an ever-widening and geographically expanding audience. Musical scores were not only made readily available throughout Europe, but were even sent all the way to the New World. Continental works were ultimately performed by choirs in such far-away countries as Mexico, Guatemala, and Peru.

Some of the most notable publishers of this era included Ottaviano Petrucci and Andre Antico of Italy, LeRoy & Ballard, and Pierre Attaignant of France, Tielman Susato of the Netherlands, and Lawrence Van Craesbeeck of Portugal.

GIOVANNI FRANCESCO ANERIO
1567–June 12, 1630

Giovanni came from a distinguished musical family. His father, Maurizio, was a musician at the Castel St. Angelo and trombonist for the church of St. Louis de France. A younger brother, Bernadino, played cornet for the Confraternity of the Holy Cross, while his elder brother, Felice, succeeded

Palestrina as composer for the Papal Chapel. His first music studies were received from his elder brother.

He spent most of his life in and around Rome, holding a succession of positions; possibly as choirmaster at St. John Lateran (1600–03) and similar positions at St. Spirito, Sassia (1606) and Verona Cathedral (1608). In 1613, Giovanni was appointed music prefect at the *Collegio Romano* and in 1620, the *maestro* at St. Maria dei Monti. Anerio became a priest in 1616. Finally, he was the choirmaster of King Sigismund III of Poland from 1624 to 1628. He died in 1630 in Graz, Austria, on his return home from Poland.

Anerio wrote more than 100 motets, numerous masses for four to six, eight, and twelve voices, several litanies, antiphons, spiritual madrigals, Psalm settings, and responsories. His *Teatro armonico spitituale* (1619), written for the Oratory of Filippo Neri (an organization with which he was associated early in his career), is an important work as it was the pioneer form of the vernacular oratorio.

The sacred compositions of Anerio follow closely the polyphonic style developed by Palestrina. He was one of the first composers to use the eighth note and its subdivisions; a new development related to the influence of the then-current idiomatic instrumental writing upon vocal technique.

The *Missa pro defunctis* was first published in a collection of masses for four, five, and six voices (*Missarum Quatuor, Quinque & sex vocibus*, 1614), printed in Rome by Giovanni Robletti. Dedicated to Clementia Muti di Nari, Anerio's patroness, this anthology must have been quite popular as it was reprinted three times during the seventeenth century. Because Anerio was clearly influenced by the "Palestrina" style of polyphony, his setting of the requiem bears the impress of late sixteenth-century composition, yet a substantial portion of the work is composed in homophonic, chordal texture. The composer maintained a remarkable balance between the linear and vertical elements. This work seems to be one of the earliest requiems to employ such a substantial amount of intimate, homophonic writing.

The *Missa pro defunctis* is scored for SATB choir. A four-part texture is maintained throughout the work, with a few reductions to intimate, three-part writing for the Offertory verse, *Hostias* (ATB), and the Responsory, *Dies illa* (SAT). Occasionally, Anerio thickened the texture to SATTB, writing in *Agnus Dei* III and *Judicandus* (Sequence) or altered the prevailing SATB scoring to other four-part textures in sections of the Sequence (*Quid sum miser*, STTB and *Juste Judex*, SSAT).

Canonic writing is found throughout the work, but is especially notable in the *Kyrie*, Offertory, and Communion sections. The second *Kyrie* employs a remarkable double canon. The ever-present, fluid, polyphonic passages are relieved by expressive homophonic passages, everything in perfect balance. The Sequence, *Dies irae*, is fully set in alternating passages of Gregorian chant and short, expressive homophonic sections.

As in the case of every other Renaissance requiem, this work makes an extended use of the Gregorian melody, usually in the uppermost line, but sometimes in the tenor. Although the first edition of the *missa* lacked a *continuo* part (*basso segunte*) for the organ, it was included in a 1649 edition. (It is a curiosity that all of the masses in the 1614 edition, except the requiem, possessed a *continuo* part.) The earlier *Missa pro defunctis* of Di Lasso (1580) and the *missa* of Anerio are unique in that both appear to be the only Renaissance requiems with extant *continuo* parts.

Basic Data

EDITION

Giovanni Anerio
Missa Pro Defunctis
ed. Anthony Petti
J. and W. Chester, JWC 8841. 1966
[edition supplied with a reduction for accompaniment]

DURATION

Nine movements. 410 mm., perf. c. 38'

VOICING

Choir: SATB range: S-F6; B-A flat 3

OUTLINE

Introit: 29 mm., 2 sections [*Requiem aeternam* & *Te decet*, satb]
Kyrie: 31 mm., 3 sections [*Kyrie, Christe, Kyrie,* satb]
Sequence, *Dies irae*: 137 mm., 10 polyphonic sections
    Quantus tremor, satb; *Mors stupebit*, satb; *Judex ergo*, satb; *Rex tremendae*, sttb;
    Quarens me, satb; *Ingemisco*, ssat; *Preces meae*, satb; *Confutatis*, satb; *Lacrymosa*,
    satb; *Pie Jesu*, sattb
Offertory: 95 mm., 2 sections [*Domine Jesu Christe*, satb & *Hostias*, atb]
Sanctus: 12 mm., 2 sections [*Sanctus* & *Pleni sunt coeli*, satb]
Benedictus: 12 mm., 1 section [*Benedictus*, satb]
Agnus Dei: 37 mm., 3 sections [*Agnus Dei* I, II, satb & *Agnus Dei* III, sattb]
Communion: 43 mm., 2 sections [*Lux aeterna* & *Requiem aeternam*, satb]
Responsory, *Libera me*: 110 mm., 6 sections [*Libera me*, satb; *Tremens factus*, atb;
    Quando coeli, satb; *Dies illa*, sat; *Dum veneris*, satb; *Requiem aeternam*, satb]
Kyrie in absolution: 13 mm., 2 sections [*Kyrie* and *Kyrie*]

DISCOGRAPHY

Hyperion, CDA 66417, Choir of Westminster Cathedral, cond. James O'Donnell.

GIOVANNI MATTEO ASOLA
c. 1532–October 1, 1609

Asola studied in Verona, his birthplace, with Vincenzo Ruffo (1508–1587) and later worked, successively, as *maestro di capella* at the cathedrals in Trevisio and Vincenza. He died in Venice.

He left a large body of sacred music that includes about two dozen mass settings, polyphonic arrangements of the Psalms, Vespers, liturgical motets, several sets of *Lamentations*, and Passion music. The funeral music is comprised of a published *Officum defunctorum* (1586) and the *Officium defunctorum addito cantico Zachariae* (1593). In addition, there are four requiem masses: two for four voices (1574 and 1576), a *Missa pro defunctis* for two choirs (1580), and a *Missa defunctorum* for three voices (c. 1600). Asola composed secular and spiritual madrigals. In 1592, he and other composers published and presented to Palestrina a collection of Vesper settings.

Asola was greatly influenced by the "Palestrina" style of composition. His musical textures are sprinkled with imitative, contrapuntal lines that can be described as supple and flowing. Although he was aware of the new polychoral techniques and the colorful, chromatic vocabulary of the Venetian school, his own musical language reflected those innovations less often.

The *Missa pro defunctis*, for four voices was first published in the collection, *Il secondo libro della a quatro voci* (1586), by the Venetian printers, Jacob Vincenti and Riccardo Amadino. The requiem was later reprinted in the 1860s, along with a large number of Renaissance works, in the collection, *Musica Divina*. This nineteenth century anthology was edited by Karl Proske, a leading figure of the Caecilian Movement.

The unchanging scoring for alto, two tenors, and bass is an arrangement that provides an especially solemn color to the work. The prevailing texture of the requiem is imitative polyphony with passages of homophonic writing in the Sequence and *Agnus Dei*. The full, rich harmony of the High Renaissance is employed throughout the work.

Asola was one of the few composers who made a polyphonic setting of the *Dies irae*. His version consists of twenty alternating sections, in which odd-numbered verses employ the original Gregorian tune and even-numbered verses are set in polyphonic arrangements. This movement bears the imprint of the Venetian school and its experiments with expressive, declamatory, homophonic writing, and polychoral technique.

The chant tune is present in every movement and placed in the tenor line, but Asola's paraphrase technique so cleverly disguises the melody, that it is often difficult, if not impossible, to hear it. This seldom-heard work deserves to be performed more often.

Basic Data

EDITION

Musica Divina, Vol. 1
ed. Karl Proske
Johnson Reprint Corp., New York, London. 1973
[uses C (alto and tenor) and F clefs]

DURATION

Seven movements, 438 mm.

VOICING

Choir: ATTB range: A-G5; B-F3

OUTLINE

Introit: 50 mm., 2 sections [*Requiem aeternam* & *Te decet*, attb]
Kyrie: 38 mm., 3 sections [*Kyrie, Christe, Kyrie*, attb]
Sequence, *Dies irae*: 137 mm., 20 sections. Odd-numbered verses-chant; Even-numbered verses-polyphony. Included are the polyphonic verses: *Quantus-tremor, Mors stupebit, Judex ergo, Rex tremendae, Quaerens me, Ingemisco, Preces meae, Confutatis, Lacrymosa, Pie Jesu* & *Amen*, attb]
Offertory: 97 mm., 3 sections [*Domine Jesu Christe, Quam olim, Hostias*, attb]
Sanctus: 42 mm., 3 sections [*Sanctus, Pleni sunt coeli* & *Benedictus*, attb]
Agnus Dei: 32 mm., 3 sections [*Agnus* I, II, III, attb]
Communion: 42 mm., 2 sections [*Lux aeterna* & *Requiem aeternam*, attb]

DISCOGRAPHY

None found.

ESTEVAO DE BRITO
c. 1575–December 2, 1641

The Portuguese composer, de Brito probably studied with Felipe de Maghalães. In 1597, he was appointed to the position of *maestro de capilla* at Badajoz Cathedral and in 1613, to a similar position at the Cathedral at Malaga, where he remained until his death. His surviving works are few in number and include an *Officum Defunctorum* for four to six voices, nine settings of the Psalms, twenty-nine hymns, and twenty-five motets for four to eight voices.

The *Missa pro defunctis* is taken from the *Officum Defunctorum*. This excellent work was written, in all likelihood, after 1600 and scored for SATB choir. Polyphonic texture is employed throughout, except for the Graduale verse, *In memoria*, where the composer chose a delicate, three-part (SAT) fabric.

The composer resorted to a simple, homophonic texture for the Introit verse, *Te decet* and the third statement of the *Agnus Dei*. The Responsory, *Libera me*, is arranged in nineteen alternating sections of Gregorian chant and polyphony. An alternate Responsory, *Memento mei*, arranged in nine alternating sections of chant and polyphony, is provided in the modern edition. Imitative devices such as canon and point of imitation are commonly used.

De Brito made use of fragments of the Gregorian melody in every movement, placing them in the uppermost voices. This *missa* is imbued with the intense spiritual piety, so commonly found in many of the Iberian vocal composers of that time.

Basic Data

EDITION

Portugaliae Musica
Series A, Vol. I
Estevao de Brito
Motectorum Liber Primus, Officum Defunctorum . . .
Trans. Miguel Querol Gavalda
Lisbon, 1972

DURATION

Nine movements, 364 mm.

VOICING

Choir: SATB range: S-E flat 6; B-F 3

OUTLINE

Introit: 44 mm., 2 sections [*Requiem aeternam* & *Te decet*, satb]
Kyrie: 25 mm., 3 sections [*Kyrie, Christe, Kyrie*, satb]
Graduale: 56 mm., 2 sections [*Requiem aeternam*, satb & *In memoria*, sat]
Offertory: 61 mm., 2 sections [*Domine Jesu Christe* & *Quam olim Abrahae*, satb] The verse, *Hostias et preces* not set.
Sanctus: 41 mm., 3 sections [*Sanctus, Pleni sunt coeli* & *Benedictus*, satb]
Agnus Dei: 37 mm., 3 sections [*Agnus Dei* I, II, III, satb]

Communion: 43 mm., 2 sections [*Lux aeterna* & *Requiem aeternam,* satb] Responsory: 64 mm., 19 sections [*Libera me, Quando coeli, Dum veneris, Tremens factus, Quando coeli, Dies illa, Dum veneris, Requiem aeternam, Kyrie* I and *Kyrie* II are polyphonic. satb]
Alternate Responsory, *Memento mei*: 34 mm., 9 sections [satb]

DISCOGRAPHY
None found.

JOAN BRUDIEU
c. 1520–May 10, 1591

The earliest information available about this French-Catalonian composer dates from 1538, when he conducted the music for Christmas mass in La Seo de Urgel Cathedral. His appointment as permanent choirmaster at the Cathedral took place in the following year. In 1546, Brudieu was ordained a priest.

He became *maestro de capilla* and organist of Santa Maria del Mar in Barcelona in 1578, but in the following year returned to his former position in Urgel. In 1586, he went to Barcelona to supervise the publication of his collection of Spanish madrigals, *De los Madrigales del muy reverendo Ioan Brudieu maestro de capilla de la sancta yglesia de La Seo de Urgel a quatro bozes* (1585). In 1589, he was recalled to active duty as a priest at Urgel, where he died several years later.

Brudieu left a manuscript of the *Missa pro defunctis* at Urgel Cathedral. The work was composed in the style of the late Renaissance, yet the concluding empty cadences, employed in every movement, disclose an affinity to the earlier Franco-Flemish tradition. The presence of the Roman Graduale and the Responsory, *Libera me*, indicate that the composition was written according to the reforms ordered by the Council of Trent.

Brudieu scored the *missa* for SATB choir and maintained this arrangement throughout, except for the Graduale, where he employed a lighter SSAT scoring. Its verse, *In memoria*, employs an even more intimate, angelic SST grouping. He rarely departed from the prevailing imitative texture, doing so only at the expressive, homophonic setting of the Introit verse, *Te decet*, the *Agnus Dei*, and the Responsory. The Gregorian melodies are paraphrased in the soprano and tenor lines.

Basic Data

EDITION

Els Madrigal i la Missa de difunts d'en Brudieu
Transcription and critical and historical notes by Felip Pedrell and Higini Angles

Institut d'Estudis Catalans
Palau de la Diputacio, Barcelona
1921 [C [soprano, alto, tenor] and F clefs]

DURATION
Seven movements, 458 mm.

VOICING
Choir: SATB range: S-E6; B-F3

OUTLINE
Introit: 59 mm., 2 sections [*Requiem aeternam* & *Te decet*, satb]
Kyrie: 113 mm., 3 sections [*Kyrie, Christe, Kyrie*, satb]
Graduale: 76 mm., 2 sections [*Requiem aeternam*, ssat & *In memoria*, sst],
Offertory: 88 mm., 1 section [*Domine Jesu Christe*, satb]
Sanctus: 54 mm., 2 sections [*Sanctus* & *Benedictus*, satb]
Agnus Dei: 43 mm., 3 sections [*Agnus Dei* I, II, III, satb]
Responsory: 25 mm., 3 sections [*Libera me, Dies illa, Kyrie*, satb]

DISCOGRAPHY
None found.

MANUEL CARDOSO
bapt. December 11, 1566–November 24, 1650

Manuel Cardoso was born in Fronteira, Portugal. At nine, he was enrolled in a choir school operated by Evora Cathedral. We learn from the *Rules of the Choristers' College* that all choristers, at the close of the morning choir service, went to their lessons where they spent two hours studying the rules of plainsong and vocal polyphony. This routine lasted from September to May. At nightfall, the choristers devoted themselves to study and composition. At 8 P.M., they had their evening meal; following that, were allowed to talk or sing for an hour. On Sundays and holy days, they were required to sing for mass so that they might practice the singing they had learned in class. Their studies lasted for four years. At seventeen or eighteen years of age, the students entered either into theological studies or a different career.

Cardoso later joined the Carmelite order, taking priestly vows in the *Convento do Carmo* on July 5, 1589. This wealthy institution maintained singers, an organist, and wind and brass players. He was attached to this institution, where he worked as organist and choir director for most of his career.

Cardoso also spent some time, in the early 1620s, at *Vila Vicosa*, a ducal household, where he made the friendship of the young Duke of Barcelos, who later became King John IV. It was this king who later helped pay the costs of publishing two large collections of Cardoso's music, *Liber primus missarum*, for four to six voices (1625), and the *Livro de varios motetes* for four voices (1648). A second book of masses (1636) contains parody masses based upon motets, written by the future King John IV. These masses are scored for four to six voices. A third book of masses (1636) contains six settings (two each for four, five, and six voices) that are based upon a Marian motet written by King Philip IV of Spain. *Livro de varios motetes*, a collection of motets for four voices, was published in 1648.

He was a master of Renaissance contrapuntal style and at the dawn of the baroque era, when most composers were occupied with the newer innovations of polychoral writing and declamatory style associated with the Venetian school, it is noteworthy that he continued to write in the conservative "Palestrina" style. Like Duarte Lôbo and Felipe de Maghalães, Cardoso was one of a small group of composers whose music represented a late blossoming of High Renaissance style.

The *Missa pro defunctis* was first published in *Liber Primus Missarum* (1625), by the royal printer, Pieter van Craesbeeck. This collection includes seven masses for four, five, and six parts, two five-part motets, two antiphons, and a four-part response. Five parody masses found in this collection are based upon motets by Palestrina.

A brief glance at his requiem reveals a mastery of Renaissance contrapuntal style, imbued with intense spiritual feeling. Perhaps his priestly vows of silence nurtured the introspective sonic qualities of his music. The choice of SSAATB voicing bestows upon the music a light, angelic quality. The preponderant, six-part texture is occasionally interrupted by the thinning of voices within a section, as well as, the even-lighter, four-part settings of *Christe* (SSAT), Graduale verse, *In memoria* (SSAT), and the Offertory verse, *Hostias* (SATB). *Agnus Dei* is scored in an elaborate, homophonic setting, while much of the requiem employs imitative polyphony.

The composer placed the Gregorian melody in the top-most part while paraphrasing it within the other vocal lines. In the Offertory and Communion, his paraphrases are written as inversions of the chant melody. This work is a masterpiece of spiritual expression and luminous beauty.

Basic Data

EDITION

Portugaliae Musica, Series A
Frei Manuel Cardoso
Liber Secundus Missarum

Transcription and study by Jose Augusto Alegria
Calouste Gulbenkian Foundation, Lisbon, 1970

DURATION

Seven movements, 753 mm., perf., c. 38'

VOICING

Choir: SSAATB range: S-D6, B-F3

OUTLINE

Introit: 81 mm., 3 sections [*Requiem, Te decet & Exaudi,* ssaatb]
Kyrie: 83 mm., 4 sections [*Kyrie,* ssaatb; *Christe,* ssat; *Christe,* ssaatb; *Kyrie,* ssaatb]
Graduale: 141 mm., 2 sections [*Requiem aeternam,* ssaatb & *In memoria,* ssat]
Offertory: 235 mm., 3 sections [*Domine Jesu Christe, Quam olim,* ssaatb & *Hostias,* satb]
Sanctus: 66 mm., 3 sections [*Sanctus, Pleni sunt coeli & Benedictus,* ssaatb]
Agnus Dei: 55 mm., 3 sections [*Agnus Dei I, II, III,* ssaatb]
Communion: 92 mm., 2 sections [*Lux aeterna & Requiem aeternam,* ssaatb]

DISCOGRAPHY

Gimell, 454 921-2, The Tallis Scholars, dir. Peter Phillips.

EUSTACHE DU CAURROY
bapt. April 2, 1549–August 7, 1609

Although his name is scarcely a household word, he was a master of
French Renaissance polyphony. He was baptized in Beauvais and entered
into royal service as a singer around 1570. Du Caurroy held the position
of *vice-maitre de la chapelle royale* until 1595, when he received the title *surintendant de la musique* for Henri IV. At the same time, he was advanced to
composer for the royal chamber and by the end of the sixteenth century,
he had achieved great fame and recognition. The music theorist, Marin
Mersenne, praised Du Caurroy for his "rich counterpoint and harmoniousness of composition" (*Harmonie Universelle,* 1636).

Today, little of his music is performed, owing to the lack of published
editions. The bulk of his compositions are the liturgical motets composed
for the French royal court during the reigns of Charles IX, Henri III, and
Henri IV. His published works include: *Preces ecclesiasticae,* Paris, 1609
(forty-four motets, four Psalms, three settings of the *Te Deum* for four to
seven voices), *Méslanges de la musique,* Paris 1610 (ten Psalms, thirty-six
chansons, fifteen Noëls for four to six voices), and several other works,
including the *Missa pro defunctis.*

The *Missa pro defunctis* for five voices [SATBarB] was performed, probably for the first time, in 1606 at the funeral of Henri IV. It remained the
"official" requiem that was sung for the funerals of later French mon-
archs. The *Missa* was published, for the first time, by Pierre Ballard in
1636.

This work, like many in the Renaissance, reflects the Parisian usage.
Instead of using the Roman Graduale text, *Requiem aeternum*, Du Caurroy
set two verses of Psalm Twenty-three, *Si ambulem* and *Virga tua*. Slight
variations in the Offertory text can be explained by the Parisian usage.

Elegant, imitative polyphony was employed in nearly every movement.
Du Caurroy derived his musical style from that of Palestrina, but the
expressive homophonic arrangements of the Introit verse, *Te decet*, and the
three sections of the *Agnus Dei*, descended from the traditions of the
Franco-Flemish school.

The composer maintained SATBarB writing throughout the requiem,
except for the SATB arrangement of the *Benedictus*. Other contrasts in the
texture were generated by occasional thinning of the vocal parts.

Like other contemporaries, Du Caurroy employed, in highly disguised
paraphrase, the Gregorian funeral melodies. These melodies were usually
placed in the *quintus* (baritone) line. This work is one of the most brilliant,
spirited settings of the Renaissance requiem—one brimming over with
energy and possessing great beauty.

Basic Data

EDITION

Le Pupitre
E. Du Caurroy
Missa pro defunctis. Quinque vocum
Edition by Michel Sanvoisin
LP. 65
Heugel & Cie. 1983

DURATION

Eight movements, 402 mm., perf. c. 24'

VOICING

Choir: SATBarB range: S-D6; B-F3 [D3 rare]

OUTLINE

Introit: 18 mm., 2 sections [*Requiem aeternam* & *Te decet*, satbarb]
Kyrie: 32 mm., 3 sections [*Kyrie, Christe, Kyrie*, satbarb]
Graduale, *Si Ambulem*: 32 mm., 2 sections [*Si ambulem* & *Virga tua*, satbarb]
Offertory: 104 mm., 2 sections [*Domine Jesu Christe* & *Hostias*, satbarb]

Sanctus: 59 mm., 4 sections [*Sanctus, Pleni sunt coeli, Osanna*, satbarb; *Benedictus*, satb]

Agnus Dei: 31 mm., 3 sections [*Agnus Dei* I, II, III, satbarb]

Communion: 32 mm., 2 sections [*Lux aeterna* & *Requiem aeternam*, satbarb]

Responsory: 94 mm., 3 sections [*Libera me, Dies illa, Quando coeli*, satbarb]

DISCOGRAPHY

1. Collins Classics, 14972, The Choir of New College, Oxford, dir. Edward Higginbottom.
2. Astrée, E 8660, Doulce Mémoire, cond. Denis Raisin Dadre.

CLEMENS NON PAPA [JACOB CLEMENT]
c. 1510/15–1555/56

Clemens, a prolific Franco-Flemish composer, was well-known for his sacred music. Although many details of his life remain obscure, it is known that he was *succentor* (choir leader) at Bruges cathedral for little more than a year (1544–45). At the time, he formed a business relationship with the Antwerp publisher, Tilman Susato. He was employed briefly by the Marian Brotherhood in s'Hertogenbosch (1550).

His music compositions include texts that offer homage to Charles V or the Duke of Aerschot (a general of Charles V) indicating that Clemens probably had some connection with the royal court. He might have been employed in Leiden, too, because much of the music in the choirbooks at St. Pieterskerk are works written by him. In 1558, Jacob Vaet published a *Déploration* upon Clemens' death.

Judging by the dates of his published works, he appears to have done most of his composing within fifteen years. He wrote fifteen complete masses, more than 200 motets, two *Magnificat* cycles, eighty-eight French chansons, and 159 *Souterledekens* and *lofzangen*. The *Souterledekens* (little psalters) were polyphonic settings of the Psalms in Dutch, based upon popular tunes. *Lofzangen* were songs of praise.

The *Missa defunctorum* was first published in Louvain (1580) and scored for four-part (SATB) choir. A dense, compact texture, with occasional thinning of the voice parts, is maintained throughout the work. Expressive, homophonic texture is employed only for the Introit verse, *Te decet*, the *Agnus Dei*, and the initial bars of the Offertory.

This work is a remarkable polyphonic composition in which the Gregorian *cantus firmus*, when used, is surrounded by constant imitative texture. Virtually all lines of this texture are derived from the Gregorian melody. This contrapuntal device, later known as *Vorimitation* ("pre-imitation"), can be found in the opening movement of the requiem. Di Lasso's requiem settings, written at the same time, possess hints of this technique, too.

Basic Data

EDITION

Clemens non Papa: Opera Omnia
Corpus Musicae Mensurabilis, Vol. VIII
ed., K. P. Bernet Kempers
American Institute of Musicology, Rome 1959

DURATION

Seven movements, 326 mm.

VOICING

Choir: SATB range: S-C6; B-F3

OUTLINE

Introit: 40 mm., 2 sections [*Requiem aeternam* & *Te decet,* satb]
Kyrie: 33 mm., 3 sections [*Kyrie, Christe, Kyrie,* satb]
Tract, *Absolve Domine*: 43 mm., 2 sections [*Domine Deus* & *Et gratia,* satb]
Offertory: 102 mm., 3 sections [*Domine Jesu Christe, Quam olim, Hostias,* satb]
Sanctus: 32 mm., 3 sections [*Sanctus, Pleni sunt coeli, Benedictus,* satb]
Agnus Dei: 29 mm., 3 sections [*Agnus Dei* I, II, III, satb]
Communion: 47 mm., 3 sections [*Lux aeterna, Requiem aeternam, Cum sanctis,* satb]

DISCOGRAPHY

ERAS, 121, Cappella Palestrina, cond., Maarten Michielsen.

JUAN ESQUIVEL
c. 1563–after 1613

Esquivel spent most of his life in his birthplace, Cuidad Rodrigo, Spain. He studied with the local choirmaster, Juan Navarro. Sometime around 1608, he became the choirmaster of the Cathedral in Cuidad Rodrigo, remaining there until the end of his life.

He was the author of three music collections that included: *Missarum . . . liber primus* (1608) (four to six voices), *Motecta festorum et dominicarum* (1608) (four to six and eight voices), and *Liber secundus psalmorum, hymnorum, magnificarum* (1613) (four to six and eight voices). His music was sung widely throughout Spain and Portugal in the seventeenth century.

Esquivel wrote two settings of the requiem; one for four voices, the other for five. (The latter remains in incomplete condition because the only known surviving copy has been damaged.) The *Missa pro defunctis* for four voices was first published in *Liber secundus* (1613). The prevailing SATB texture is employed for all but two of the requiem movements, the Offertory and *Sanctus*, which utilize a contrasting, STTB, scoring. Like other composers of the Iberian Peninsula, Esquivel frequently used canonic writing and a harmony, colored with accidentals, which created a particularly intense, emotional musical idiom. The expressive, chordal texture of the Introit verse, *Te decet*, and the *Agnus Dei* provides a contrast to the prevailing imitative polyphonic garb.

Virtually every movement of the requiem employs fragments or large sections of the Gregorian tunes. These melodies are usually placed in the soprano line. The *Missa pro defunctis* is an elegant work in which the spirit of the original Gregorian lines has been preserved.

Basic Data

EDITION

Missa pro defunctis for four voices.
Transcribed and edited by Clive Walkley
Mapa Mundi Renaissance Performing Scores
Series A: Spanish Church Music, No. 87
Vanderbeek & Imrie Ltd. 1996

DURATION

Eight movements & two responses, 441 mm.

VOICING

Choir: SATB range: S-E 6 (F 6 rare); B-G 3

OUTLINE

Introit: 60 mm., 2 sections [*Requiem aeternam* & *Et tibi*, satb]
Kyrie: 39 mm., 3 sections [*Kyrie, Christe, Kyrie*, satb]
Tract: 53 mm., 1 section only [*Absolve me*, satb]
Sequence: 44 mm., 1 section only [*Lacrimosa*, satb]
Offertory: 76 mm., 1 section only [*Domine Jesu Christe*, sttb]
Sanctus: 67 mm., 3 sections [*Sanctus, Caeli et terra, Qui venit*, sttb]
Agnus Dei: 61 mm., 3 sections [*Agnus Dei* I, II, III, satb]
Communion: 32 mm., 1 section only [*Lux aeterna*, satb]
Two short responses, (*Requiescant* [ssat] & *Amen* [ssatb]: 9 mm.) are included.

DISCOGRAPHY

None found.

FRANCISCO GUERRERO
May 1528–May 8, 1599

Francisco Guerrero was one of the most important Spanish composers of the second half of the sixteenth century and a noted composer of sacred music. He studied music with his elder brother, Pedro, and with Cristobal de Morales. Guerrero was master-of-all-skills in the field of music, for he not only composed and conducted, but also played a number of instruments, including the harp, cornett, vihuela, and organ. He is known to have possessed an exceptionally fine tenor voice. At seventeen, he was recommended by Morales for the position, *maestro de capilla* at the cathedral in Jaen. In 1549, he removed to Seville, where he accepted a singing position at the cathedral and in 1551, he was offered the position of assistant choirmaster at the cathedral. During his life-long tenure there, he produced numerous outstanding sacred compositions for his choir, many of which were subsequently published. In 1574, he became the *maestro de capilla*, a position that he held until his death by plague in 1599. His compositions were well-known during his lifetime and continued to enjoy popularity throughout Europe and South America for more than two centuries after his death.

Guerrero's published works include *Sacrae Cantiones* (1555) (sacred motets for four and five voices), *Psalmorum, liber primus & missa pro defunctis* (1559) (settings of the Psalms for four voices), *Missae, Liber primus* (1556) (masses for four and five voices), *Liber secundus* (1582) (masses for four to six voices), Songs to the Blessed Virgin (1563) (four to six voices), Book of Vespers (1584) (four to six voices), The Passion according to St. Matthew (1585), *Canciones y villanescas espirituales* (1589) (sixty-one works, for three to five voices), and motets for four to eight voices (1570), as well as a number of other works. Guerrero is known to have employed instruments, such as shawm, recorder, cornett, and bassoon to support and ornament the vocal passages of his choral works, when sung at the cathedral.

The *Missa pro defunctis* was published in Paris (1566) in the *First Book of Masses*. It was probably written during the sitting of the Tridentine Council, for the text of Roman Graduale, *Requiem aeternam*, is present. Although this setting is not the first appearance of the newly chosen text, it is among the earliest. (The first setting seems to be in Morales's five-part requiem, 1544.) This work exists in two versions. The later version (1582) is a revision of the earlier 1566 work. Because it was composed after the Council meetings, its make-up reflects the liturgical reforms enacted and carried out in the spirit of the Council's recommendations.

The prevailing ATTB texture includes imitative polyphonic writing, coupled with numerous reductions and additions in the vocal scoring. In fact, one of the unusual features of Guerrero's textures is the diverse vocal groupings, which encompass ATTB, ATB, AT, ATT, TTTB, and AATBB. No other requiem in this chapter employs such a variegated approach. Guerrero, too, was a skilled contrapuntalist and frequently employed point of imitation, canon, and paired imitation in his wide-ranging textures.

The Gregorian melody is present throughout the work and placed in several different melodic lines. However, the *Kyrie* melodies used are taken from local repertory, rather than the Roman usage. These melodies are found in the later publications: Montanos, *Arte de canto llano* (1610 and 1616) and Villasagra, *Arte de canto llano* (1756).

Guerrero provided two versions of the Tract, one for local usage, *Dicit Dominus*, and one for the Roman usage, *Sicut cervus*. The former was sung at the cathedral in Seville during the Pascal season, before its removal by the Council from the liturgy. His polyphonic setting of the Responsory, *Libera Me*, appears to be one of the earliest examples, if not the first, included in the Renaissance requiem.

Basic Data

EDITION

Francisco Guerrero
Missa pro Defunctis (1566)
Transcribed and edited by Martyn Imrie
Vanderbeek & Imrie Ltd. 1998

DURATION

Ten movements, 776 mm.

VOICING

Choir: ATTB range: A-G 6; B-F 3

OUTLINE

Introit: 62 mm., 2 sections [*Requiem aeternam* & *Te decet*, attb]
Kyrie: 48 mm., 3 sections [*Kyrie, Christe* & *Kyrie*, attb]
Graduale: 91 mm., 2 sections [*Requiem aeternam*, attb & *In memoria*, att, the bass enters at *Non timebunt*]
Tract I, *Dicit Dominus*: 97 mm., 3 sections [*Dicit Dominus*, aatb, *Et omnis*, at & *In aeternam*, aatb]
Tract II, *Sicut cervus*: 116 mm., 2 sections [*Sicut cervus*, aatb & *Sitivit anima*, tttb]
Offertory, *Domine Jesu Christe*: 93 mm., 1 section [*Domine Jesu Christe*, attb, & *Hostias*, Gregorian chant].
Sanctus: 82 mm., 3 sections [*Sanctus, Pleni sunt coeli* & *Benedictus*, attb]
Agnus Dei: 66 mm., 3 sections [*Agnus Dei* I, II, & III, aatb]
Communion I: 57 mm., 1 section [*Lux aeterna*, aatb]
Communion II: 64 mm., 1 section [*Lux aeterna*, aatbarb] alternate version

DISCOGRAPHY

1. Glossa, GCD 921402, Orchestra of the Renaissance, Michael Noone, cond.
2. Signum, SIG CD 017, Chapelle du Roi, cond. Alistair Dixon.

A second version of the earlier *Missa pro defunctis* was printed in the *Second Book of Masses* (1582). Although the earlier edition contains settings of the Tracts, *Dicit Dominus* and *Sicut Cervus*, both are missing from the revised version, reflecting the liturgical reforms of the Tridentine Council. The original Introit, *Kyrie*, Graduale, Offertory, *Sanctus*, and *Agnus Dei* were carried over from the first version, although the *Benedictus* was substantially rewritten and the *Agnus Dei* was modified. In this version of the mass, Guerrero included the Responsory, *Libera Me,* and a motet, *Hei mihi*.

This *missa* is a model of excellent, polyphonic writing. The long, flowing melodic lines are composed in the spirit of the Gregorian melodies and the texture employs frequent use of points of imitation, thereby driving the pulse of the music forward.

Basic Data

EDITION

Francisco Guerrero
Missa pro Defunctis (1582)
Transcribed by Martyn Imrie
Vanderbeek & Imrie Ltd. 1998

DURATION

Eleven movements, 746 mm.

VOICING

Choir: ATTB

OUTLINE

Introit: 62 mm. [same as the 1566 version]
Kyrie: 48 mm. [same as the 1566 version]
Graduale: 91 mm. [same as the 1566 version]
Tract, *Absolve Domine*: 45 mm., 3 sections [*Absolve Domine, Et gratia* & *Et lucis*]. Only the *Absolve Domine* is polyphonic.
Offertory: 90 mm. [same as the 1566 version]
Sanctus: 84 mm. [same as the 1566 version]
Agnus Dei: 62 mm. [same as the 1566 version] *Agnus Dei* III has a slightly longer ending.
Communion I, *Lux aeterna*: 34 mm., 1 polyphonic section [*Lux aeterna*, attb]
Communion II, *Lux aeterna*: 41 mm., 2 sections [*Lux aeterna* & *Requiem aeternam*, aattb]
Responsory, *Libera me*: 144 mm., 6 sections [*Libera me, Tremens factus, Dies illa, Requiem aeternam, Kyrie* I & II] Gregorian intonations are provided in between the polyphonic passages. This newly composed movement employs a mixture of polyphonic and imitative polyphonic textures.
Motet, *Hei mihi*: 75 mm., 1 section, scored for six-part choir: aatbarbarb.

Woe is me, O Lord, for I have sinned exceedingly in my life.
What will I, wretched one, do ? Where will I seek refuge ?
Only with Thee, my God.
Have pity on me until Thou comest on the Last Day.

DISCOGRAPHY
None found.

JACOBUS DE KERLE
1531/32–July 1, 1591

De Kerle was a southern Netherlands organist and member of the Franco-Flemish fraternity whose professional career first took him to Ieper (Flanders) as *maitre de chapelle* and then to Orvieto, as cathedral organist and town carillonneur. Later, he was in Cambrai, as a chapter member (*cantore*) of the cathedral.

In Rome, he composed the *Preces speciales* for the Council of Trent. His ever-peripatetic lifestyle led him to Augsburg, as vicar-choral and cathedral organist, and then Vienna, as a chaplain of the imperial court. He finally settled in Prague for the remaining years of his life.

He traveled widely and had numerous friends in high places, both within the clergy and secular nobility. He was once excommunicated because of a dispute with one of the chapters he served, yet he must have been politically adept, for the sentence was removed through his good connections with Rome. His musical work for the Council of Trent also resulted from these connections.

The *Preces speciales*, commissioned specifically for the Council, was perhaps as influential in the cause for retaining liturgical polyphony as the famed *Pope Marcellus Mass* of Palestrina. This monument of late Renaissance musical art, the *Preces speciales*, was commissioned by De Kerle's famous patron, Cardinal Truchess. It consists of ten responsories, parts of which were sung three times weekly during the meetings of the Council of Trent. In addition, he composed more than a dozen masses for four and five voices, many settings of the *Magnificat*, and numerous motets. Most of his secular madrigals have been lost.

De Kerle's music is generally written in imitative polyphony, balanced by sections of homophonic texture, thus following a tradition developed and nurtured by a long line of Franco-Flemish composers.

His requiem setting, *Officum mortuorum*, exists in a manuscript dating from 1614. For a long time, the work was ascribed to Di Lasso and curiously, is currently included in the *Collected Works* of Orlando Di Lasso. It is scored for SATB choir. The four-part texture remains constant in every part of the requiem. The habit of setting the *Agnus Dei* in expressive homophonic texture and of retaining the Graduale text, *Si ambulem,* inform us about De Kerle's Franco-Flemish origins. Like all other composers of the era, De Kerle wrote a Gregorian *cantus-firmus* requiem. The chant melody is paraphrased in the tenor and soprano lines, but is often hidden from view in the complex, linear fabric.

Basic Data

EDITION

Academie Royale de Belgie-Bayerische Akademie der Wissenschaften
Orlando Di Lasso
Neue Reihe/Band 11 [Vol. 11]
Masses 56–63
ed. Siegfried Hermelink
Bärenreiter. Kassel, Basel, Tours, London 1971

DURATION

Seven movements, 322 mm.

VOICING

Choir: SATB range: S-C6 [D6, rare]; B-F3

OUTLINE

Introit: 41 mm., 2 sections [*Requiem aeternam* & *Te decet,* satb]
Kyrie: 35 mm., 3 sections [*Kyrie, Christe, Kyrie,* satb]
Graduale, *Si ambulem:* 56 mm., 2 sections [*Si ambulem* & *Virga tua,* satb]
Offertory: 103 mm., 2 sections [*Domine Jesu Christe* & *Hostias,* satb]
Sanctus: 33 mm., 4 sections [*Sanctus, Osanna, Benedictus, Osanna,* satb]
Agnus Dei: 31 mm., 3 sections [*Agnus* I, II, III, satb]
Communion: 23 mm., 1 section [*Requiem aeternam,* satb]

DISCOGRAPHY

None found.

ORLANDO DI LASSO [DE LASSO, LASSUS]
1532–June 14, 1594

Orlando di Lasso was one of the most prolific composers in the history of Western music. He was born in Mons, Hainaut, and died in Munich at the age of 62. During his childhood, he sang as a choirboy and there is an enduring legend that he was kidnapped three times because of his beautiful voice, but it is only a tale. In his teenage years, he was in Ferrara,

Naples, and Rome gaining valuable experience in the musical art and at the age of 21, was appointed *Maestro di Capella* at St. John Lateran. Di Lasso returned to Antwerp in 1555 and in the following year published his first book of madrigals for five and six voices.

In 1556, Di Lasso accepted an invitation to join the court of Duke Albrecht V of Bavaria in Munich where he was responsible for the education of the choirboys, the composition of music for the morning services and other special occasions (state visits, banquets, and hunting parties), and the copying of manuscripts. During his own lifetime, his fame grew as he traveled extensively throughout Europe. Two of his sons became musicians. He resided in Munich until the end of his life.

The bulk of his output is truly extraordinary: nearly sixty masses (of which two are requiems), four settings of the Passion, 101 settings of the *Magnificat*, a dozen settings of the *Nunc Dimittis*, the music for the Offices of Christmas, Easter and Pentecost, the *Seven Penitental Psalms of David*, several sets of the Lamentations, fourteen Litanies, 525 motets, 171 madrigals, 144 French chansons, ninety-two German Lieder, as well as other miscellaneous liturgical pieces. Most of this material was published in more than 100 editions issued during his lifetime.

Di Lasso possessed a flawless composing technique and his work with compositions in four different languages reveals a wide variety in style and genre. He was able to write fluent imitative polyphony (though he does not always use this technique) and yet his music has a strong orientation toward chordal harmony. For example, the modern edition of his *Missa pro defunctis* for five voices includes a *basso continuo* part for the organ. Like Palestrina, he was very conservative in the use of chromatic coloring.

The first edition of the *Missa pro defunctis,* for SATTB, appeared in 1580. The prevailing texture of this work is polyphonic, including points of imitation and canonic writing that push the energy and pulse of the music forward. The opening of the Introit, which employs this procedure, is based upon an ascending melodic motive, derived from the Gregorian original. This motive is further employed in several, simultaneous rhythmic adaptations, yet the chant melody, found in the tenor, is presented in a fairly straightforward manner. What is truly remarkable is that this type of compact writing is found throughout the work.

The dense, five-part sonority is relieved only at two passages, *Et gratia* (Tract) and the *Benedictus*. Here, Di Lasso employed a lighter, three-part (SAT) sonority. Each movement of the requiem utilizes the Gregorian melody, usually employed in the tenor, but because of the imitative paraphrasing, other vocal lines often resemble the plainchant.

It is very likely that Di Lasso performed this work with instrumental

support because the scholarly edition, found in the *Collected Works*, provides a *basso continuo* part for the organ.

Basic Data

EDITION

Orlando Di Lasso
Sämtliche Werke [Collected Works]
Vol. V
Bärenreiter. Kassel, Tours, London 1966

DURATION

Seven movements, 439 mm., perf., c. 35'

VOICING

Choir: SATTB range: S-E6; B-F3 [D3, once on *"profundo lacu"*]

OUTLINE

Introit: 51 mm., 2 sections [*Requiem aeternam* & *Te decet*, sattb]
Kyrie: 52 mm., 3 sections [*Kyrie, Christe, Kyrie*, sattb]
Tract, *Absolve Domine*: 78 mm., 3 sections [*Absolve*, sattb, *Et gratia*, sat, *Et lucis aeter-
    nae*, sattb]
Offertory: 130 mm., 2 sections [*Domine Jesu Christe* & *Hostias*, sattb]
Sanctus: 52 mm., 4 sections [*Sanctus*, sattb, *Pleni sunt coeli*, sattb, *Benedictus*, sat,
    Hosanna, sattb]
Agnus Dei: 37 mm., 3 sections [*Agnus* I, II, III, sattb]
Communion: 39 mm., 2 sections [*Lux aeterna* & *Requiem aeternam*, sattb]

DISCOGRAPHY

Deutsche Harmonia Mundi, 77066-2-RG, Ensemble Pro Cantione Antiqua, London, cond. Bruno Turner.

The *Missa pro defunctis* for four voices (SATB) was first published (1578)
in Paris by Adam Le Roy & Robert Ballard. It was part of the collection,
Missae variis concentibus ornatae, ab Orlando de Lassus . . . which included
eighteen masses in arrangements for four, five, six, and eight voices.

The dominant, four-part sonority of this requiem is suspended only
twice; once at the Graduale verse, *Virga tua*, and a second time at the *Benedictus*. Here, he used TB and SAT scoring, respectively. The greater part
of the texture is composed in imitative polyphony, much like his five-part
requiem. The Gregorian melody is set in the tenor line, yet it echoes
throughout the remaining vocal lines.

This composition is a work of great solemnity and to underscore that
quality, the range of the vocal parts lies especially low, thereby creating

an intensely sober and shadowy sonority. Of particular interest is the presence of the Tract, *Si ambulem*, used only in the French Rite. Not only did Di Lasso make a polyphonic setting of this text, he further scored the *Virga tua* for two-parts (TB), much in the spirit of the older Franco-Flemish school. For these reasons, we can assume that this requiem setting may have been destined for performance in the Lowland countries.

Basic Data

EDITION

Orlando Di Lasso
Sämtliche Werke, Neue Reihe [Collected Works, New Edition]
Vol. 4
Bärenreiter Kassel, Basel, Tours, London 1964

DURATION

Seven movements, 468 mm., perf., 36'

VOICING

Choir: SATB range: S-C6; B-G3

OUTLINE

Introit: 59 mm., 2 sections [*Requiem aeternam* & *Te decet*, satb]
Kyrie: 54 mm., 3 sections [*Kyrie, Christe, Kyrie*, satb]
Graduale, *Si ambulem*: 85 mm., 3 sections [*Si ambulem*, satb, *Virga tua*, tb, *Ipsa me*, satb]
Offertory: 106 mm., 2 sections [*Domine Jesu Christe* & *Hostias*, satb]
Sanctus: 71 mm., 5 sections [*Sanctus, Dominus Deus, Pleni sunt coeli*, satb, *Benedictus*, sat, *Hosanna*, satb]
Agnus Dei: 45 mm., 3 sections [*Agnus I, II, III*, satb]
Communion: 48 mm., 2 sections [*Lux aeterna* & *Requiem aeternam*, satb]

DISCOGRAPHY

Hyperion, CDD22012, Pro Cantione Antiqua, dir. Mark Brown.

DUARTE LÔBO [EDWARDUS LUPUS]
1565–September 24, 1646

This once-famous Portuguese composer learned his musical craft at Evora cathedral with Manuel Mendes. His great talent was recognized by the cathedral authorities and, in due time, he was appointed *maestro de capilla*. At a later date, he removed to Lisbon where he was appointed to a similar position at the *Hospital Real* and in 1594, the cathedral in Lisbon, where he remained for more than forty years. His talent was recognized and honored by the royal court.

During his lifetime he managed to publish six volumes of sacred music. Sadly, much of his music was destroyed in the Lisbon earthquake (1755). The works that survive show him to be a composer strongly rooted in Renaissance musical tradition, even in a time when composers were attracted to the newer trends in baroque composition. His musical style was influenced by the pre-eminent Spanish composer, Tómas Luis da Victoria. As contemporaries (Victoria was seventeen years older), it is even likely that the two men knew each other. We note with interest that Victoria's patroness, the Empress Maria of Austria, died in February 1603 and that Victoria's requiem, published in 1605, was performed at the funeral of the Empress. Was Lôbo acquainted with this requiem? Fond of the music of Francisco Guerrero (1528–1599), Lôbo based several of his parody masses upon the former's compositions.

From the extant music, Lôbo seems to have preferred the commonly used, four-part choral sonority, although there is some music for six- and eight-part choir, as his two requiem settings attest.

The *Liber Missarum* (Antwerp, 1621) contains settings of the mass for four to six and eight voices. A second book of mass settings, *Liber secundus missarum*, (four to six voices) was published in Antwerp (1639). In 1605, he published sixteen *Magnificat* settings. A volume of funeral music, *Officium defunctorum* (Lisbon, 1603), is lost.

The *Missa pro defunctis, octo vocum* (SSAATTBB), was published in 1621 in the *Liber Missarum*. Although the piece was originally written for two separate choirs, its texture is rather like one large choir. Antiphonal effects, created by two separate choirs, in dialogue with each other, are absent from this work. The modern edition of this work treats the music as if it were written for one large group with eight vocal lines. Its eight-part texture is often trimmed to fewer parts for variety and contrast. Although the writing is polyphonic, much of the time it sounds more like an elaborate homophonic texture. Frequently, syllables are aligned in the various voice parts, thereby creating an expressive chordal sonority.

Melodic and rhythmic imitation are employed throughout the work, but most extensively in the *Kyrie*, Graduale, and Offertory. The *Agnus Dei* is set in homophonic texture. Gregorian melodies are most often quoted in the uppermost vocal line, but are paraphrased in other lines, particularly in the Graduale and Offertory as the texture of these sections is imitative polyphony.

Basic Data

EDITION

Mapa Mundi Renaissance Performing Scores
Duarte Lôbo

Missa Pro Defunctis [Requiem Mass for Eight Voices]
Transcribed and edited by Bruno Turner
Vanderbeek & Imrie Ltd. 1985 [reprinted in 1994]

DURATION

Seven movements, 356 mm., perf. c. 25′

VOICING

Choir: SSAATTBB range: S-G6; B-G3

OUTLINE

Introit: 61 mm., 2 sections [*Requiem* & *Te decet*, ssaattbb]
Kyrie: 43 mm., 3 sections [*Kyrie, Christe, Kyrie*, ssaattbb]
Graduale: 65 mm., 2 sections [*Requiem aeternam*, ssaattbb; *In memoria*, sat]
Offertory: 59 mm., 1 section [*Domine Jesu Christe*, ssaattbb] the verse, *Hostias*, has
   been omitted.
Sanctus: 53 mm., 3 sections [*Sanctus; Pleni sunt coeli; Benedictus*, ssaattbb]
Agnus Dei: 38 mm., 3 sections [*Agnus Dei* I, II, III, ssaattbb]
Communion: 37 mm., 2 sections [*Lux aeterna* & *Requiem aeternam*, ssaattbb]

DISCOGRAPHY

Hyperion, CDA 66218, Masterpieces of Portuguese Polyphony, The William Byrd
Choir, cond., Gavin Turner.

The *Requiem for Six Voices* was first published in *Liber secundus missarum*
(1639) and is arranged for six-part choir (SAATTB). The six-part, contrapuntal texture is peppered with rhythmic and melodic imitation and is
frequently thinned to provide contrast with the prevailing, full texture.
This practice appears in the shortened Sequence poem, *Dies irae*, the Graduale verse, *In memoria*, the Offertory verse, *Hostias*, and the final Responsory, *Memento mei*.

   The Gregorian melodies are perceptible in the uppermost melodic
lines. Lôbo was one of the few Iberian composers of the era to set the
Sequence in a polyphonic arrangement. This requiem setting includes an
incomplete, polyphonic version (six verses) of *Dies irae*. The overall
impression is one of utmost melodic and harmonic beauty. Its spiritual
sentiment and religious fervor are commensurate with the better-known
setting of Victoria.

Basic Data

EDITION

No modern edition is yet available. Mr. Bruno Turner made a transcription for
   the CD performance listed in the Discography. Because a modern edition was
   unavailable, measure lengths are replaced by the CD performance times.

DURATION

Nine movements, perf. c. 37'

VOICING

Choir: SAATTB

OUTLINE

Introit: 7' 12", 2 sections [*Requiem aeternam* & *Te decet*]
Kyrie: 5' 11", 4 sections [*Kyrie* I, *Kyrie* II, *Christe* & *Kyrie*]
Graduale: 4' 18", 2 sections [*Requiem aeternam* & *In memoria*]
Sequence, *Dies irae*: 5' 15", 11 sections—polyphony and chant set in alternating
     sections: odd-numbered verses are the polyphonic *Dies irae, Tuba mirum, Liber
     scriptus, Rex tremandae, Preces meae,* and *Huic ergo;* the even numbered verses
     are the Gregorian *Quando judex, Mors stupebit, Quid sum miser, Qui Mariam,* and
     Lacrymosa.
Offertory: 6' 13", 2 sections [*Domine Jesu Christe* & *Hostias*]
Sanctus: 2' 37", 3 sections [*Sanctus, Pleni sunt coeli, Benedictus*]
Agnus Dei: 2' 33", 3 sections [*Agnus Dei* I, II, III]
Communion: 3' 09", 2 sections [*Lux aeterna* & *Requiem aeternam*]
Responsory, *Memento mei*: 3' 55," 1 section

DISCOGRAPHY

Gimell, CDGIM 028, The Tallis Scholars, dir. Peter Phillips.

FELIPE DE MAGHALÃES
c. 1571–December 12, 1652

Like Duarte Lôbo, this composer studied with Manuel Mendes in the
cloister school at Evora cathedral. In 1602, he joined the choir of the royal
chapel in Lisbon and in 1623 became *mestre* of the choir. He remained in
this position until 1641.

When composers in Catholic Europe were eager to write music in the
emergent baroque style, Duarte Lôbo, Manuel Cardoso, and Felipe Maghalães constituted a small but significant group who continued to write
music in the conservative "Palestrina" style. As it turned out, their works
represent a late blossoming of the Renaissance in Portugal.

Their music is infused with spiritual fire and energy. The musical texture is smooth and highly refined, yet at the same time, the sonorities are
absolutely gorgeous and expressive, enhanced by a judicious use of chromaticism. One cannot help but wonder if this trio, observing vows of
silence, were able to see, hear, and imagine more clearly than others of
their time.

Maghalães' published works include *Cantus ecclesiasticus* . . . (Lisbon, 1614) for three to five voices, the *Missarum liber cum antiphonis dominicali-bus in principio, et motetto pro defunctis* (Lisbon, 1636), for four to six voices, and *Cantica beatissimae virginis* (Lisbon, 1636).

The *Missa pro defunctis* for six voices was first published in the *Missarum* of 1636. This collection of masses and antiphons was issued by Lourenço Craesbeeck, printer to King Philip IV. The work is scored for six-part (SAATBB) choir. This full, ample texture is interrupted only twice as the composer chooses a lighter, four-part fabric (SATB) for the more intimate passages: the Graduale verse, *In memoria*, and the Offertory verse, *Hostias*. Every movement employs imitative polyphony, except the *Agnus Dei*, which is scored in an elaborate, homophonic texture. Maghalães employs the Gregorian melody in the soprano voice throughout the requiem.

Basic Data

EDITION

Portugaliae Musica
Maghalhães. Missarum Liber
transcribed by Luis Pereira Leal
Foundation Calouste Gulbenkian, Lisbon 1975

DURATION

Eight movements, 588 mm.

VOICING

Choir: SAATBB range: S-D6; B-D3

OUTLINE

Introit: 74 mm., 2 sections [*Requiem aeternam* & *Te decet*, saatbb]
Kyrie: 81 mm., 3 sections [*Kyrie, Christe, Kyrie*, saatbb]
Graduale: 104 mm., 2 sections [*Requiem aeternum*, saatbb & *In memoria*, satb]
Offertory: 170 mm., 2 sections [*Domine Jesu Christe*, saatbb & *Hostias*, satb]
Sanctus: 56 mm., 2 sections [*Sanctus* & *Benedictus*, saatbb]
Agnus Dei: 56 mm., 3 sections [*Agnus* I, II, III, saatbb]
Communion: 47 mm., 2 sections [*Lux aeterna* & *Requiem aeternam*, saatbb]
A motet, *Commissa mea*: 61 mm., ssaatb, is included in the modern edition.

DISCOGRAPHY

None found.

PHILIPPE DE MONTE
1521–July 4, 1603

De Monte was born in Mechelen, Belgium, and probably received his earliest musical training at the cathedral of St. Rombout. He moved to Italy and by 1542, was working for the Pinelli family of Naples. Later on, he went to England where he was responsible for the choir in the private chapel of Philip II of Spain, husband of Mary Tudor. By 1568, a year after the death of Jacobus Vaet, court *Kapellmeister* to Emperor Maximilian II, De Monte was offered Vaet's position and once he accepted, remained in it until his death. In this position, he served the emperor variously in Vienna and Prague. He had been the Hapsburg emperor's second choice for the position; Palestrina, the first. Before he died, he expressed a wish to be buried in St. Jakub's Church, Prague.

De Monte composed thirty-eight masses and about 260 other liturgical pieces, including motets and *Magnificat* settings. The most imposing part of his *oeuvre*, however, is the more than 1,100 madrigals (secular and spiritual) and fifty chansons. During the span of his career, he published thirty-four volumes of secular madrigals and five volumes of sacred madrigals.

He was a master of parody technique, drawing upon the music of Palestrina, Di Lasso, Josquin, and de Rore, as well as his own compositions, for melodic inspiration. He seemed to prefer light, contrapuntal textures, more typical of the madrigal and his melodic lines tend to be smooth with occasional angular movement.

It is not known precisely when De Monte wrote the *Missa pro defunctis*, but it was probably after 1550. The manuscript of this work is located in Codex 15948, of the National Library in Vienna. The five-part vocal arrangement, (standard for the madrigal) of the requiem is for soprano, alto, tenor I, tenor II, and bass. Except for the expressive, chordal fabric of the *Agnus Dei*, the prevailing texture of the requiem is imitative polyphony.

Although Gregorian intonations are included at the beginning of each movement, De Monte seems not to have quoted the plainsong in his composition; rather, the melodic material seems to have been gleaned from the spirit of the chant melodies and the madrigal. The absence of the Gregorian melodies is one of the more unusual aspects of this setting. Because he had composed so many madrigals, most of which did not depend upon a pre-existent melody, it would have been no problem to dispense with the chant.

Several interesting features of the requiem are the use of *Si ambulem*, the Graduale of the French Rite, and an unchanging, five-part texture throughout the requiem. It is a very moving work, filled with spiritual awe and possessing a beautiful, vibrant sound.

Basic Data

EDITION

Phillipi Da Monte
Opera Omnia, #13

editors, Charles van den Borren & Julius van Nuffel
L. Schwann, Düsseldorf. 1930

DURATION

Eight movements, 376 mm., perf. c. 18'

VOICING

Choir: SATTB range: S-D6; B-F3

OUTLINE

Introit: 56 mm., 2 sections [*Requiem aeternam* & *Te decet*, sattb]
Kyrie: 41 mm., 3 sections [*Kyrie, Christe, Kyrie*, sattb]
Graduale, *Si Ambulem*: 56 mm., 2 sections [*Si ambulem* & *Virga tua*, sattb]
Offertory: 99 mm., 2 sections [*Domine Jesu Christe* & *Tu suscipe*, sattb]
Sanctus: 30 mm., 2 sections [*Sanctus* & *Pleni sunt coeli*, sattb]
Benedictus: 20 mm., 1 section [*Benedictus*, sattb]
Agnus Dei: 31 mm., 3 sections [*Agnus I, II, III*, sattb]
Communion: 37 mm., two sections [*Lux aeterna* & *Requiem aeternam*, sattb]

DISCOGRAPHY

Panton, LC 1430, Kühn Chamber Soloists, cond. Pavel Kühn.

CRISTÓBAL DE MORALES
c. 1500–c. September 7, 1553

Morales, a key figure in Spanish sacred music of the early sixteenth century, was born in Seville. He evidently maintained a great deal of pride in his Spanish heritage, for the sixteen masses that were published in Rome (1544) bore his name, *Christophorus Morales Hyspalensis*, not only in the book title but also at the beginning of each mass. In 1526, he was appointed *maestro de capilla* at the cathedral in Avila and by 1535, he was a singer in the Papal Choir. For a decade, he remained a member of this prestigious organization, where he appears to have been a baritone. Morales left Rome in 1545 and may have returned to Seville.

There are about two dozen mass settings, 100 motets, eighteen settings of the *Magnificat*, four arrangements of the *Lamentations*, and a number of secular pieces. His fluent, smooth writing style influenced his younger contemporaries, Palestrina and Francisco Guerrero, his most famous pupil. His fame extended far and wide, for his music was performed not only throughout Europe, but also in Guatemala and Mexico.

The *Missa pro defunctis*, along with several other works for the Office of the Dead, was composed sometime between 1548 and 1551, while he was employed by the Duke of Arcos (Marchena). The work was dedicated to Juan de Giron, Fourth Duke of Urena, and scored for SATB choir.

Four-part texture is maintained throughout the work. Contrast is provided with occasional thinning of the voices. Variety in the contrapuntal texture is provided by occasional expressive homophonic passages such as the Introit verse, (*Te decet*), *Kyrie* II, *Sanctus*, and *Agnus Dei*. Paraphrases of the Gregorian melodies are found in every movement.

Basic Data

EDITION

Musica Hispana. Serie B: Polifonia, 3
Christophori de Morales, Pro Defunctis Missa á 4
Transcription, Alicia Muniz Hernandez
Prologue, Miguel Querol Gavalda
Instituto Espagnol de Musicologia
Consejo Superior de Investigaciones Cientificas, Barcelona. 1975

DURATION

Six movements, 416 mm.

VOICING

Choir: SATB range: S-E6; B-F3

OUTLINE

Introit: 59 mm., 2 sections [*Requiem* & *Te decet*, satb]
Kyrie: 40 mm., 3 sections [*Kyrie, Christe, Kyrie*, satb]
Graduale: 71 mm., 2 sections [*Requiem aeternam* & *In memoria*, satb]
Offertory: 90 mm., 1 section [*Domine Jesu Christe*, satb]
Sanctus: 84 mm., 3 sections [*Sanctus; Pleni sunt coeli; Benedictus*, satb]
Agnus Dei: 72 mm., 3 sections [*Agnus Dei* I, II, III, satb]

DISCOGRAPHY

None found.

In addition to the *Requiem* for four voices, there exist two other works, associated with the Liturgy for the Dead, composed by Morales. The first is a set of pieces for the *Officum defunctorum*, which includes:

1. Invitatory motet: a setting of Psalm 94 along with a polyphonic setting of the chant verse, *Regem cui omnia vivunt*; a verse that recurs throughout the Psalm;
2. Motet, *Circumdederunt me gemitus mortis*, for Matins;
3. Polyphonic settings of the readings for First Nocturne: *Parce mihi*

Domine (Job 7:16–21), *Taedet animam* (Job 10:1–7), and *Manus tuae* (Job 10:8–12);
4. Second Nocturne: a setting of the third responsory, *Ne recorderis peccata mea, Domine.*

Most of this stunning music was found in the music archives of the cathedral in Puebla, Mexico. Its probable first performance was in Mexico City (November 1559), during the funeral services held for the death of Emperor Charles V.

The second work, the *Missa pro defunctis* for five voices, was first published in 1544 (*Missarum liber secundus*). The requiem and mass settings found in this volume were composed for the Papal choir. The composer, Francisco Guerrero, wrote that he had studied with Morales in 1545. One wonders if the inspiration for his first requiem (1566) came from the earlier model by Morales.

The five-part scoring of the 1544 requiem is for soprano, alto I, alto II, tenor, and bass. The five-part texture is occasionally relieved by four part writing (*Hostias*) and three-part texture (*In memoria*). The predominant weave of imitative polyphony (canon, points of imitation), is broken up by contrasts of expressive, homophonic writing. This haunting, serious work uses large segments of the plainsong melody, usually in the soprano, for its melodic inspiration. The chant appears to be paraphrased in all five vocal parts of the Communion.

Of particular interest is the presence of a polyphonic *Pie Jesu*, the final verse of the sequence, *Dies irae*. Apparently the remainder of the poem was sung in chant. Morales is one of the few Renaissance composers to make a polyphonic setting of this text.

Basic Data

EDITION
Cristóbal de Morales
Opera Omnia, Vol. 3
Missarum Liber Secundus, Rome 1544
Transcription and Essay by Higinio Angles
Consejo Superior de Investigaciones Cientificas
Delegation de Roma. 1954

DURATION
Nine movements, 668 mm., perf., c. 43'

VOICING
Choir: SAATB range: S-D6; B-F3

OUTLINE
Introit: 85 mm., 2 sections [*Requiem* & *Te decet*, saatb]
Kyrie: 65 mm., three sections [*Kyrie, Christe, Kyrie,* saatb]

Graduale: 126 mm., 3 sections [*Requiem*, saatb; *In memoria*, aII,tb; *Non timebit*, saatb]

Sequence: 33 mm., 1 section [Pie Jesu, saatb]

Offertory: 194 mm., 3 sections [*Domine Jesu Christe*, saatb; *Hostias*, satb; *Quam olim*, ssatb]

Sanctus: 47 mm., 3 sections [*Sanctus; Sanctus; Pleni sunt coeli*, saatb]

Benedictus: 24 mm., 1 section [*Benedictus*, saatb]

Agnus Dei: 47 mm., 3 sections [*Agnus* I, II, III, saatb]

Communion: 47 mm., 2 sections [*Lux aeterna & Requiem aeternam*, saatb]

DISCOGRAPHY

1. Astree, E 8765, La Capella Reial de Catalunya and Hesperion XX, dir. Jordi Savall. (A performance, lightly supported by period instruments.)
2. Archive, 457 597-2, Gabrieli Consort, cond. Paul McCreesh.

GIOVANNI DA PALESTRINA
1524/25–February 2, 1594

Palestrina was one of the most prolific composers of the late Renaissance. His first important professional position was the appointment as choirmaster of the *Cappella Giulia*, where he remained from 1551 to 1555. In the latter year, he succeeded Orlando Di Lasso as music director of St. John Lateran and simultaneously became a member of the Pontifical Choir. From 1561 to 1567, Palestrina was choirmaster at Santa Maria Maggiore. At the end of this period, he entered into the service of Cardinal Ippolito d'Este.

Among his works are ninety-four masses for four, five, six, and eight voices; 244 motets for four-, five-, six-, seven-, eight-, and twelve-voice parts; twenty-nine settings of the Songs of Solomon; a dozen *Cantiones sacrae*; thirty-five *Magnificats*; eight sets of *Lamentations*; seventy-one offertories; four settings of the Psalms for twelve voices; seven litanies; fifty-nine sacred madrigals for three, four, and five voices; forty-one hymns for four voices; and 107 secular madrigals. His first published book of masses dates from 1554, the first book of motets, 1563, and a second and third book of masses from 1560 and 1570. Between 1581 and 1594, he published no less than sixteen collections of original music.

Palestrina's *Missa pro defunctis* is not one of his better-known pieces, yet it is a sparkling gem. It is his only requiem and it came from the period of time when he directed the *Cappella Guilia* (1551–1555). The first edition is dated 1554, a time of relative well-being and happiness for the composer. The birth of two sons (1549 and 1551), his appointment to the *Cappella* and the publication of his first book of masses (1554) seem to indicate that his career was going well. Even the music and mood of this requiem seems to possess a sunny disposition. Given the very large number of masses that Palestrina composed, it is a little unusual that he did not write several requiems. His sponsor, Pope Julius III, died only three months after appointing Palestrina to the *Cappella* and between 1572–1580, he lost both sons, two brothers, and his wife.

Palestrina set only the *Kyrie*, Offertory, *Sanctus*, *Benedictus*, and *Agnus Dei* in a polyphonic arrangement for five voices (SAATTB). The prevailing texture is imitative polyphony. The *Kyrie* contains two separate canons: one functioning in the soprano and alto, the other in the second tenor and bass. The canon in the upper two voices is derived from the Gregorian melody; the canon in the two lower voices forms an accompaniment. Meanwhile, the first tenor line contains a rather straightforward version of the Gregorian *cantus*. It is strict contrapuntal writing of the most complex kind, yet the sound is serene and the writing, transparent and light.

The contrapuntal fireworks of the *Kyrie* are found throughout the work. A prevailing, five-part imitative polyphonic texture is broken only once, at the Offertory verse, *Hostias*, as the composer employs a light, ethereal SATT scoring. Like all other Renaissance requiems, the Gregorian melodies were utilized everywhere in the work and in the various vocal lines, especially of the *Sanctus* and *Benedictus*. This rarely performed requiem deserves to be better known.

Basic Data

EDITIONS

1. Giovanni da Palestrina
Missa Pro Defunctis for Five Voices
ed. Dr. Hermann Bauerle
Breitkopf & Härtel, Leipzig
B. 2035

2. Pierluigi da Palestrina
Werke. Vol. 10
ed. Franz Haberl
Breitkopf & Härtel, Leipzig
Reprint by Gregg International Printers, Ltd.
1968

DURATION

Five movements, 344 mm.

VOICING

Choir: SATTB range: S-E6; B-G3

OUTLINE

Kyrie: 49 mm., 3 sections [*Kyrie, Christe, Kyrie,* sattb]
Offertory: 120 mm., 3 sections [*Domine Jesu Christe,* sattb; *Hostias,* satt; *Quam olim,* sattb]
Sanctus: 50 mm., 1 section [*Sanctus,* sattb]

Benedictus: 33 mm., 1 section [*Benedictus*, sattb]
Agnus Dei: 92 mm., 3 sections [*Agnus Dei* I, II, III, sattb]

DISCOGRAPHY

1. De Roo & Partners, WVH 042, Cappella Palestrina, cond. Maarten Michielsen.
2. Das Alte Werk, 94561, Chanticleer.

CONSTANZO PORTA
1528/9–May 19, 1601

Porta was one of the many exceptionally skilled composers of the late
Renaissance. Born in Cremona, he probably received his musical training
in the Convent of Porta St. Luca, located in Cremona. He received later
training with Adrian Willaert, the choirmaster of St. Mark's and among
his classmates were the composer Claudio Merulo and the theorist Gio-
seffe Zarlino. His first professional position was that of *maestro di cappella*
of Osimo Cathedral. Following this position, he held similar positions in
Padua and Ravenna. In 1587, he was elected to membership in the *Congregazione Romana dei Musici di St. Cecilia;* an elite group of musicians that
included Palestrina and Di Lasso. In the twilight of his career (1595), he
returned to the *Cappella Antoniana* in Padua.

He was a lifelong member of the Minorite Friars, for whom he wrote
much of his sacred music. Most of his extant pieces are motets that were
published at regular intervals throughout his career. Seven books of
motets survive. He wrote fifteen masses, twelve of which were published
in 1578. He wrote more than 100 madrigals.

Porta, an adherent to the "Palestrina" style, was a gifted writer of polyphonic textures, including those that used double and triple invertible
counterpoint. Paired imitation and points of imitation are common features in his music. Yet, he had close connections with the Venetian school
and experimented with polychoral writing. His Vesper Psalms and *Magnificat* settings are models of polychoral splendor and brilliance.

He applied the techniques of madrigal writing to composition of sacred
music, especially when the texts called for descriptive treatment. In particular, he was one of the few Renaissance composers who set the *Dies
irae* to polyphony, not only in the requiem for four voices, but also in a
five-voice setting. Porta seemed to realize the opportunities for exploring
the dramatic possibilities of this picturesque text.

The two requiems were first published in a collection of masses, *Missarum Liber Primus* (1578). The twelve masses in this anthology were composed to celebrate an approaching Jubilee Year (1575), for the Basilica in
Ravenna.

The imitative, polyphonic textures of both works remain remarkably consistent throughout. Although there is little deviation from the four- or five-part scoring of the respective works, both settings include three short passages of contrasting texture. The four-voice requiem employs two-part writing (SA) for *Liber scriptus* (Sequence) and three-part writing (SAT) for *Qui Mariam* (Sequence) and the Offertory verse, *Hostias*. The requiem for five voices departs from five-part writing to three-part texture (TTB) only at *Lacrimosa* (Sequence), the Offertory verse, *Hostias,* and the *Benedictus.* Occasional passages of expressive chordal writing provide a contrast to the prevailing polyphony.

Both requiems are based upon the Gregorian chant melody and usually found in the tenor line. Of particular interest is the presence in both settings of the *Dies irae,* arranged in alternating passages of Gregorian chant and polyphony; the usual way in which the earliest composers handled the enormous amount of text.

Basic Data

EDITION

P. Constantii Porta
Opera Omnia, Vol. IX
Missarum Liber Primus, pars secunda 1578
Transcription by Syri Cisilino
Biblioteca Antoniana. Padova, Italy
1969

DURATION

Eight movements, 498 mm.

VOICING

Choir: SATB range: S-C6; B-F4

OUTLINE

Introit: 50 mm., 2 sections [*Requiem aeternam* & *Te decet,* satb]
Kyrie: 34 mm., 3 sections [*Kyrie, Christe, Kyrie,* satb]
Sequence, *Dies irae*: 188 mm., 12 sections [*Dies irae* & *Tuba mirum,* satb; *Liber scriptus,* sa; *Quid sum miser* & *Recordare* & *Juste judex,* satb; *Qui Mariam,* sat; *Inter oves* & *Oro supplex* & *Judicandus,* satb; *Pie Jesu,* plainchant & *Dona eis,* satb]
Offertory: 107 mm., 3 sections [*Domine Jesu Christe,* satb; *Hostias,* sat; *Quam olim,* satb]
Sanctus: 35 mm., 3 sections [*Sanctus, Pleni sunt coeli, Hosanna,* satb]
Benedictus: 7 mm., 2 sections [*Benedictus* & *Hosanna,* satb]
Agnus Dei: 27 mm., 2 section [*Agnus I* & *II, Agnus III,* satb]
Communion: 42 mm., 2 sections [*Lux aeterna* & *Requiem aeternam,* satb]

DISCOGRAPHY
None found.

Basic Data

EDITION
P. Constantii Porta
Opera Omnia, Vol X
Biblioteca Antoniana, Basilica del Santo Padova
Italy. 1971

DURATION
Eight movements, 651 mm.

VOICING
Choir: SATTB range: S-E6; B-F3

OUTLINE
Introit: 89 mm., two sections [*Requiem aeternam* & *Te decet*, sattb]
Kyrie: 72 mm., 3 sections [*Kyrie, Christe, Kyrie*, sattb]
Sequence, *Dies irae*: 197 mm., 12 sections [*Dies irae*, Gregorian chant; *Quantus tremor, Mors stupebit, Judex ergo, Rex tremendae, Quaerens me, Ingemisco, Praeces me*, sattb; *Confutatis*, ttb; *Lacrymosa, Pie Jesu, Amen*, sattb]
Offertory: 129 mm., 3 sections [*Domine Jesu Christe*, sattb; *Hostias*, ttb; *Quam olim*, sattb]
Sanctus: 45 mm., 3 sections [*Sanctus, Sanctus, Sanctus*, sattb]
Benedictus: 27 mm., 2 sections [*Benedictus*, ttb; *Hosanna*, sattb]
Agnus Dei: 39 mm., 2 sections [*Agnus* I & II, *Agnus* III, sattb].
Communion: 51 mm., 2 sections [*Lux aeterna* & *Requiem aeternam*, sattb]

DISCOGRAPHY
None found.

JUAN PUJOL
c. 1573–May 1626

Pujol, a Spanish composer about whom little is known, wrote a rather substantial amount of sacred music. In November 1593, he was appointed *maestro de canto* at Tarragona Cathedral and in 1596, to the organist's position at El Pilar, Saragossa. He became a priest in 1600 and in 1612, choirmaster at Barcelona Cathedral, remaining in that position until his death.

He composed thirteen masses for four and eight voices, eight settings of the *Magnificat*, six settings of the *Nunc Dimittis*, seventy-four Psalm settings, nineteen villancicos, four settings of the *Lamentations*, nine Passions, and numerous other works, including secular pieces.

The *Missa pro defunctis* was probably composed in the early years of the seventeenth century, possibly after 1612. The presence of the Responsory, *Libera Me*, and the Roman Graduale, *Requiem aeternam*, attest to its post-Council origins. Scored for SATB choir, the work was clearly modeled after the style of Palestrina. A smooth, imitative polyphonic texture is found throughout the work and the prevailing SATB scoring is maintained, except for a brief change to a darker, AATB sonority during the Graduale verse, *In memoria*. As was the usual custom, the *Agnus Dei* was written in expressive, homophonic texture.

The composer paraphrased the appropriate plainchant melodies in the soprano line, although fragments of the chant can be found in every line when the imitative process is employed.

Basic Data

EDITION

Johanis Pujol 1573–1626
Opera Omnia, Vol. 1 edition & Study by Higini Angles
Publicationes del Departamento de Musica de la Biblioteca de Catalune . . . Barcelone.
Biblioteca de Cataluna 1926 [C (soprano, alto, tenor) & F clefs]

DURATION

Eight movements, 453 mm.

VOICING

Choir: SATB range: S-D6; B-F♯3

OUTLINE

Introit: 68 mm., 2 sections [*Requiem aeternam* & *Te decet*, satb]
Kyrie: 47 mm., 3 sections [*Kyrie, Christe, Kyrie*, satb]
Graduale: 90 mm., 2 sections [*Requiem aeternam*, satb & *In memoria*, aatb]
Offertory: 135 mm., 2 sections [*Domine Jesu Christe* & *Hostias*, satb]
Sanctus: 45 mm., 2 sections [*Sanctus* & *Benedictus*, satb]
Agnus Dei: 13 mm., 3 sections [*Agnus Dei* I, II, III, satb]
Communion: 55 mm., 2 sections [*Lux aeterna* & *Requiem aeternam*, satb]
Responsory: 55 mm., 4 sections [*Libera me, In die illa, Quando coeli* & *Requiescant*, satb]

DISCOGRAPHY

None found.

JUAN VASQUEZ
c. 1510–c. 1575

Juan Vasquez was born in Badajoz, Spain, and died in Seville. In 1530, he was admitted as a chorister at Badajoz Cathedral and within three years he became the singing instructor for the choirboys and prebendaries (adult members of the Cathedral who received a stipend for officiating at stated times within that church). Within five years, he served as *succentor* (assistant director). In 1541, he moved to Madrid at the request of the musical director for the Archbishop of Toledo. He later returned to Badajoz.

Vasquez was famous for his settings of the villancico, a kind of madrigal with a strong dance rhythm and scored for three to five voices. Twenty-six of them were published in *Villancicos i canconies* (Osuna, 1551). The last published collection of his secular music, *Recopilacion de (6) sonetos y villancicos*, appeared in 1560 (Seville).

The *Agenda Defunctorum* is his only sacred work. In 1551, he was employed by Antonio de Zuniga, a Sevillian nobleman. The most momentous result of this appointment was that Vasquez came into contact with the great Spanish composers, Juan Bermudo, Cristóbal Morales, and Francisco Guerrero. This contact was a crucial determinant in the creation of his *Agenda Defunctorum*, one of the great monuments of Renaissance musical art. Although each member of the trio wrote at least one setting of the requiem, it was Morales who may have established the model for the Iberian requiem mass with his *Officium Defunctorum* (Office of the Dead). It is more than likely Vasquez was familiar with this work and fashioned his own setting after it.

The *Agenda* is a major work that has a complete set of pieces for the Office of the Dead. It was published in Seville (1556), when Vasquez was in his forties. The volume is dedicated to *"Johanni Bravo, viro nobilissimo ac domine suo."* Of the twenty-seven pieces that constitute this opus, only six are not based upon the Gregorian melodies. Following is an outline of the work:

Matins

Title	Voices	Theme	Style
1. *Regem cui*	satb	Gregorian	homophonic
1st Nocturne			
2. *Dirige, Domine*	satb	Gregorian	imitative polyphony
3. *Convertere, Domine*	satb	Gregorian	imitative polyphony
4. *Nequando rapiat*	satb	Gregorian	imitative polyphony
5. *Parce mihi*	ssat	original	homophonic
6. *Taedet animam*	satb	original	homophonic
7. *Manus tuae*	satb	original	homophonic
2nd Nocturne			
8. *In loco pascuae*	satb	Gregorian	polyphony
9. *Delicta*	satb	Gregorian	polyphony
10. *Credo videre*	satb	Gregorian	polyphony
11. *Responde mihi*	satb	original	polyphony

3rd Nocturne

12. *Complaceat tibi*	satb	Gregorian	imitative polyphony
13. *Sana Domine*	satb	Gregorian	polyphony
14. *Sitivit anima mea*	satb	Gregorian	polyphony
15. *Spiritus meus*	satb	original	imitative polyphony
16. *Libera me*	satb	Gregorian	polyphony

Lauds

17. *Canticum Zachariae*	satb	Gregorian	homophonic
18. *Requiescant in pace*	satb	Gregorian	homophonic

Mass

19. Introit	satb	Gregorian	polyphony
20. Kyrie	satb	Gregorian	polyphony
21. Graduale	atb	Gregorian	polyphony
22. Tract, *Sicut servus*	satb	Gregorian	imitative polyphony
23. Offertory	satb	Gregorian	imitative polyphony
24. Sanctus	satb	Gregorian	imitative polyphony
25. Motet, *Sana me*	ssat	Gregorian	imitative polyphony
26. Agnus Dei	satb	Gregorian	polyphony
27. Motet, *Absolve*	satb	Gregorian	imitative polyphony

Because Vasquez included all of the plainsong melodies used in the polyphonic requiem mass and office, the *Agenda Defunctorum* functions as a catalogue that indicates how the Gregorian melodies, both in original form and in paraphrase, were employed by Renaissance composers in the polyphonic mass setting.

The music of the *Agenda* is very elegant and expressive and within it are two kinds of pieces; those that have texts that are usually sung during the service and those that are read. The latter are the readings from the Book of Job, which are a part of the service for First Nocturne and the invitatory of the Matins. The former are those pieces that are normally sung during the requiem service.

Kinship to the Franco-Flemish tradition can be clearly seen and heard in the music of the *Agenda*. This relationship is found in the continued use of the Gregorian melodies for the melodic framework and the incomplete triadic harmonies, especially those of the final chord.

The prevailing texture of the work is imitative polyphony, with only six works set in expressive homophonic writing. A notable exception to the routine use of expressive homophony for the *Agnus Dei* is found in the *Agenda*. The primary, four-part (SATB) writing is relieved only once by the three-part (ATB) texture of the Graduale verse, *In memoria*, the motet, *Sana me* (SSAT), and by the occasional thinning of the voice parts in other movements. The Gregorian melodies are placed, variously, in the soprano or tenor line, although it is found in all lines of the Offertory.

Basic Data

EDITION

Juan Vasquez
Agenda Defunctorum, Sevilla, 1556.
Transcription, stylistic and technical studies by Samuel Rubio.
Real Musical Editores, Madrid c. 1975

DURATION [Mass only]

Nine movements, 665 mm.

VOICING

Choir: SATB range: S-D6 [F6 in the motets]; B-F3

OUTLINE

Introit: 81 mm., 2 sections *[Requiem* & *Te decet*, satb]
Kyrie: 45 mm., 3 sections [*Kyrie, Christe, Kyrie*, satb]
Graduale: 57 mm., 2 sections [*Requiem*-plainchant & *In memoria*, atb]
Tract: 81 mm., 1 section [*Sicut servus*, satb]
Offertory: 115 mm., 1 section [*Domine Jesu Christe*, satb]
Sanctus: 102 mm., 4 sections [*Sanctus, Hosanna, Benedictus, Hosanna*, satb]
Motet, *Sana Me*: 79 mm., 1 section [*Sana me Domine*, ssat]
Agnus Dei: 61 mm., 2 sections [*Agnus Dei* I & II, satb]
Motet, *Absolve Domine*: 44 mm., 1 section [*Absolve*, satb]

Motet translations
SANA ME DOMINE
Wash me Lord and I shall be washed.
Make me safe and I shall be safe,
because You are my praise and strength.
Have mercy Lord, because I am infirm.
Cleanse my soul because I have sinned against Thee.

ABSOLVE, DOMINE
Absolve, O Lord, their souls from all chains of punishment;
so that resuscitated,
they will breathe among Your holy ones
in the glory of the resurrection.

DISCOGRAPHY

Almaviva, DS 0122, Capilla Peñaflorida, dir., Josep Cabre.

ORAZIO VECCHI
bapt. December 6, 1550–February 19, 1605

Vecchi, born in Modena, held a number of positions, including *maestro di cappella* at the cathedral in Modena (at two different times), and *maestro di corte* at the distinguished Este court. He worked occasionally with Gabrieli for such special events as the marriage of the Grand Duke Francesco (1579). On this occasion, they composed music for the nuptial ceremony. In 1591, Vecchi, Gabrieli, and Ludovic Balbi were chosen to help with the revisions and corrections of the newly published Roman Graduale. Throughout his career, he moved within a close circle of Venetian composers, thereby guaranteeing, for himself, a first-hand knowledge of the developments that were giving birth to the baroque style.

Orazio Vecchi was a prominent composer of secular music. He wrote numerous madrigals, six books of canzonettas (published in the 1580s), and the madrigal comedy, *L'Amfiparnasso, comedia harmonica* (1597). The work, *Il convito musicale*, contains sixty-five secular compositions of various forms and styles. In addition to his contributions to the madrigal and other secular forms, Vecchi produced a respectable quantity of church music. There are motets for four to eight voices (1590), the *Lamentations* (1587), *Sacrarum cantionum liber secundus* (1597), *Missarum liber primus* (1607) (published posthumously), and a *Magnificat* for five voices.

The *Missa pro defunctis* for eight voices was included in the *Missarum liber primus* (1607). His familiarity with polychoral music is amply evident in the handling of the two choirs, worked variously together and antiphonally. This music clearly stands on the threshold between two musical worlds: the Renaissance and the baroque. The *Missa* is scored for double chorus (SATB and ATTB). Vecchi's fluent contrapuntal technique and mastery of dramatic homophonic texture is evident at every moment. The seams of his musical fabric are seemingly without flaw, as the smooth, fluid transitions flow from one style to another.

Passages of four-part writing alternate and contrast with eight-part texture and are found in most of the movements. However, the Sequence, *Dies irae*, is exclusively scored for four-part writing, as the two choirs take turns in singing each of the nineteen verses. The prevailing, homophonic texture of the Sequence was derived from the experiments of the Venetian school. The imitative, contrapuntal texture of the *Kyrie* had its genesis in the "Palestrina" style. Like most of the Renaissance settings of the requiem, this one is based upon the Gregorian melodies. Vecchi usually places the chant in the tenor or soprano line.

Several novel features include the Graduale, *Si ambulem*, of the French Rite and the absence of a polyphonic setting of the Offertory verse, *Hostias*. Even more notable is the presence of a complete polyphonic setting of the *Dies irae*. It is, possibly, the first such example. This spectacular work is rarely performed today.

Basic Data

EDITION

Musica Divina, Vol. 8
ed. Karl Proske

Johnson Reprint Corp.
New York, London 1973 [C (soprano, alto, tenor) & F clefs]

DURATION
Nine movements, 514 mm.

VOICING
Choir: choir I, SATB choir II, ATTB range: S-D6; B-F3

OUTLINE
Introit: 43 mm., 2 sections [*Requiem aeternam* & *Te decet*, satb/attb]
Kyrie: 44 mm., 3 sections [*Kyrie, Christe, Kyrie*, satb/attb]
Graduale, *Si ambulem*: 32 mm., 1 section [*Si ambulem*, satb/attb]
Sequence, *Dies irae*: 273 mm., 20 sections [*Dies irae*, choir I; *Quantus tremor*, choir
   II; *Tuba mirum*, choir I; *Mors stupebit*, choir II; *Liber scriptus*, choir I; *Judex ergo*,
   choir II; *Quid sum miser*, choir I; *Rex tremendae*, choir II; *Recordare*, choir I; *Quae-
   rens me*, choir II; *Juste judex*, choir I; *Ingemisco*, choir II; *Qui Mariam*, choir I; *Preces
   me*, choir II; *Inter oves*, choir I; *Confutatis*, choir II; *Oro supplex*, choir I; *Lacrymosa*,
   choir II; *Judicandus*, choir I; *Pie Jesu*, choir I & II]
Offertory: 54 mm., 1 section [*Domine Jesu Christe*, satb/attb]
Sanctus: 18 mm., 1 section [*Sanctus*, satb/attb]
Benedictus: 7 mm., 1 section [*Osanna*, satb/attb]
Agnus Dei: 19 mm., 2 sections [*Agnus Dei* I, II, satb/attb]
Communion: 24 mm., 2 sections [*Lux aeterna* & *Requiem aeternam*, satb/attb]

DISCOGRAPHY
None found.

TOMÁS LUIS DE VICTORIA
1548–August 20, 1611

Victoria was born in Avila and died in Madrid. For a long time, he was
considered the greatest composer of the Spanish Renaissance, yet, in reality, he was but one of many outstanding Iberian composers during that
era. He learned the fundamentals of music while serving as a choirboy at
Avila cathedral and after his voice changed, he was sent in 1565 to study
at the Jesuit *Collegio Germanico* in Rome. He was enrolled as a singer. The
next years were spent working in several different positions, including
one at the Germanic College. It is probable that Victoria studied with Palestrina, a personal friend, during these years in Rome. A symbol of that
friendship was his participation in Palestrina's funeral cortège. He was
also close to his fellow countryman, Francisco Guerrero.
   After the death of his wife, he entered the priesthood and was installed

as a canon of the cathedral in Avila (1577). A year later, he was appointed chaplain at the church of St. Girolamo, where he lived for five years with one of the most important spiritual leaders of his time, St. Philip Neri. From 1581 to the end of his life, he worked in Madrid as chaplain to the Dowager Empress Maria, wife of Maximillian II. Here, he held the position of *maestro* for the convent choir at the Monastery de las Descalzas until 1604. After that time, he held the position of organist at the convent.

During a lifetime of sixty-three years, he published a great number of compositions, though nothing on the scale of Palestrina or Di Lasso. These publications include *The First Book of Masses* (Venice, 1576); thirty-three motets for four to six and eight voices (Venice, 1572); *The Second Book of Masses* for four to six voices (1583); fifty-three motets for four to six and eight and twelve voices (1583); thirty-two masses, *Magnificats*, motets, and Psalms for three, four, eight, nine, and twelve voices (Madrid, 1600); Requiem Responsories (1592); and an *Officium defunctorum* for six voices (Madrid, 1605). Many of these collections contained music from previously issued editions. In total, he composed about twenty-two masses of which two are requiems, eighteen *Magnificats*, twenty-five responsories, thirteen antiphons, fifty-two motets, thirty-eight hymns, and three sequence settings. His compositions for Holy Week (*Officum Hebdomae Sanctae*) include nine sets of *Lamentations*, eighteen responsories, two settings of the Passion, and several other pieces.

His music comes from a time in which older modal harmony was being gradually replaced by tonal harmony. Chromatic alterations, found in his melodic lines, make the older modes sound more like major and minor keys. He was fond of imitative procedures such as paired imitation (a process in which two vocal lines imitate two other vocal lines). A common arrangement is for tenor-bass and soprano-alto. This grouping is found in the well-known Christmas motet, *O magnum mysterium* as well as the Introit of the *Missa pro defunctis* for four voices (1583).

Finally, it should be noted that many musicians have considered Victoria to be the greatest practitioner of religious mysticism in music. However, familiarity with the later compositions of Duarte Lôbo, Manuel Cardoso, and Felipe de Maghalães permits us to modify this view somewhat, when we realize that he was but one member of an important group of successful composers bent on a similar path.

The *Missa pro defunctis* for six voices was composed for the funeral of the Dowager Empress, Maria of Austria, who died on February 26, 1603. The first published edition reads: *Officium defunctorum, sex vocibus. In obitu et obsequiis Sacrae Imperatricis.* In addition to the mass proper, he composed a setting of the Matins lesson, *Taedet animam meam* ("My soul is weary of my life . . .") and a motet, *Versa est in luctum cithara mea* ("My harp is turned to mourning"). For the fifth responsory at absolution after mass is included the *Libera me* ("Deliver me, O Lord").

The prevailing six-part, polyphonic texture (SSATTB) is broken only three times in the course of the work; the passages for *Christe* (SSAT), *Dum veneris* (SAB), and *Quando coeli* (SSAT). The latter two texts are found in the Responsory. Victoria continued the practice of setting the *Agnus Dei* in expressive, homophonic style, although the texture might be better designated as elaborate homophony. Fragments of the Gregorian melodies are placed in the soprano line of every movement. This work, with its smooth, velvety polyphonic texture, is one of the better-known masterpieces of the golden era of polyphony.

Basic Data

EDITION

1. Tomas Luis de Victoria
Missa pro defunctis cum sex vocibus
for mixed chorus, a cappella
Arista Edition. 1981 AE 100

2. Thomae Ludovici Victoria
Opera Omnia. Tomus VI
ed. Philippo Pedrell
Missarum Liber Tertius
Leipzig, Breitkopf & Härtel. 1909

3. Tomas Luis de Victoria
Missa pro Defunctis (1583)
Requiem Responsories (1592)
Officium Defunctorum (1605)
Trans. and ed., Michael Noone
Boethius Press, Aberystwth, Wales 1990

DURATION

Ten movements, 231 mm., perf., c. 43'

VOICING

Choir: SSATTB range: S-G6; B-F3

OUTLINE

Introit: 29 mm., 2 sections [*Requiem aeternam* & *Te decet*, ssattb]
Kyrie: 22 mm., 3 sections [*Kyrie*, ssattb; *Christe*, ssat; *Kyrie*, ssattb]
Graduale: 22 mm., 2 sections [*Requiem* & *In memoria*, ssattb]
Offertory: 39 mm., 2 overlapping sections [*Domine Jesu Christe*, ssattb; *Quam olim*, ssattb]
Sanctus: 29 mm., 3 sections [*Sanctus*, ssattb; *Pleni sunt coeli*, ssattb; *Benedictus*, ssattb]
Agnus Dei I & II: 8 mm., 1 section [*Agnus Dei*, ssattb]
Agnus III; 10 mm., 1 section [*Agnus Dei*, ssattb]
Communion: 28 mm., 2 sections [*Lux aeterna*, ssattb; *Requiem aeternam*, ssattb]

Responsory, Libera Me: 38 mm., 5 sections [*Libera me*, ssattb; *De morte*, ssattb; *Dum veneris*, sab; *Quando caeli*, ssat; *Requiem aeternam*, ssattb]
Alternate Kyrie: 6 mm., 3 sections [*Kyrie, Christe*-Gregorian, *Kyrie*, ssattb]

DISCOGRAPHY
1. Gimell, CDGIM 012, The Tallis Scholars, dir. Peter Phillips.
2. DGG, Archiv 447 095-2, Gabrieli Consort, dir. Paul McCreesh.

Victoria's *Missa pro defunctis* for four voices was first published in the collection, *Missarum libri duo* (1583), an edition dedicated to Philip II of Spain. It was later reprinted (1592) in the anthology, *Missae, una cum antiphonis Asperges*. The edition used for this study is based upon the 1592 print.

The established four-part, imitative texture (SATB) is employed throughout this requiem, except for the passage at *Christe eleison*, where the texture is reduced to three voices (SAT). However, in tune with the usual Renaissance practice, *Agnus Dei* is set in expressive homophonic texture.

Victoria generally placed the Gregorian tune in the uppermost line, but in the *Kyrie* and Graduale, it appears paraphrased in several of the vocal parts. The opening movement begins with paired imitation (soprano-alto and tenor-bass); one of Victoria's favorite contrapuntal devices. From the very first notes of this piece, it is clear that he had fully absorbed the lessons of "Palestrina" style.

In addition to the usual requiem movements, Victoria provided music for the fifth responsory at Absolution after mass (*Libera me, Domine*), the responsory for the 1st lesson, and 7th lesson at Matins (*Credo quod Redemptor* and *Peccantem me quotidie*), respectively.

Basic Data
EDITION
Tomas Luis de Victoria
Masses, Vol. 11
Requiem Mass for Four Voices with settings for the Office of the Dead
Transcribed and edited by Jon Dixon
JOED Music JOED V49 1993
[In addition to the arrangement for SATB, JOED has an alternate version for ATBarB; JOED V50]

DURATION
Eight movements, 469 mm.

VOICING
Choir: SATB [ATBarB] range: S-E6; B-G3

OUTLINE
Introit: 58 mm., 2 sections [*Requiem* & *Te decet*, satb]
Kyrie: 47 mm., 3 sections [*Kyrie*, satb; *Christe*, sat; *Kyrie*, satb]

Graduale: 78 mm., 2 sections [*Requiem aeternam*, satb; *In memoria*, satb]

Offertory: 133 mm., 4 sections [*Domine Jesu Christe*, satb; *Quam olim*, satb; *Hostias*, Gregorian chant; *Quam olim*, satb]

Sanctus: 36 mm., 2 sections [*Sanctus & Pleni sunt coeli*, satb]

Benedictus: [set separately] 21 mm., 1 section [*Benedictus*, satb]

Agnus Dei: 56 mm., 3 sections [*Agnus Dei* I, II, III, satb]

Communion: 40 mm., 2 sections [*Lux aeterna & Requiem aeternam*, satb]

DISCOGRAPHY

None found.

5

The Baroque Requiem

INTRODUCTION

The seventeenth century was witness to several monumental developments in the world of music, which simultaneously included the rise and
burgeoning art of the opera and the birth of a vast instrumental literature.
Composers throughout this era freely intertwined vocal and instrumental
idioms, and, as a result, inspired a revolution in the sound, style, and face
of music. The restrained and somewhat aloof idiom of the Renaissance
liturgical music eventually gave way to a style of church music that
proved to be more personal, passionate, and emotionally intimate.

Originating in Italy as part of the Counter-Reformation, the spirit and
influence of the baroque movement traveled quickly throughout Europe,
and was especially embraced in the predominantly Catholic lands, such
as southern Germany, France, Poland, Moravia, Bohemia (Czech Republic), Slovakia, and later, the Iberian Peninsula.

The primary patrons for seventeenth century composers tended to be
the royal courts and the Church, however, a small but growing middle
class, eager to indulge in the upper crust "good life," consequently began
lending its support to the musical arts. The two styles of music—opera
and pure instrumental—were ideally suited to meet the entertainment
needs of these groups, with their desire for pleasure ultimately spilling
over into the genre of sacred music.

A significant number of composers mentioned in this chapter were
commissioned by both the Church and the court. Cavalli and Hasse, two
uniquely gifted artists, were responsible for composing several pieces of
magnificent church music, as well as a series of successful, highly celebrated operas. Likewise, the late-Renaissance composers Da Monte and

Di Lasso had written many acclaimed masses and motets, but had turned out an even greater number of secular madrigals. Monteverdi, recognized as one of the most noteworthy composers of the early baroque era, held the authorship of the colossal *Marian Vespers*, as well as the operas *Orfeo* and *Il Ritorno d'Ulisse*. An enormous quantity of secular madrigals is credited to his efforts.

In 1621, in a collaborative effort with Giovanni Battista Grillo and Francesco Usper (Sponga), Monteverdi composed a requiem for the funeral of Duke Cosimo II of Toscana. Grillo created the music for the *Kyrie* and Offertory, Usper wrote the Tract and Graduale, and Monteverdi contributed the Introit, *Sanctus, Agnus Dei, Libera Me*, along with other responsories. Sadly, this collective endeavor by these three uniquely talented composers has completely vanished, a tremendous loss to musical literature.

This era marks the first time in the history of Western music that two distinct musical styles surfaced and flourished side-by-side, not merely prospering, but mutually sustaining each other as continual sources of artistic inspiration and nourishment. In the early seventeenth century, liturgical music accompanied primarily the liturgical action, but with the passing of the decades, it began to assume a more decorative function. This ground-swell evolution in attitude eventually became all-important, successfully stimulating a spirit and style distinctly baroque. At the close of the seventeenth century and continuing throughout the eighteenth, this decorative purpose eventually helped to emancipate music from its former subordinate role. Liberated from the restrictions of liturgical requirements and traditions, it managed to progress and develop its own independent existence.

Distinct musical styles eventually emerged. Differences were easily cited between *stile antico*, the older Renaissance style, and *stile moderno*, the newer style of baroque. The former is represented by the even-flowing and restrained vocal polyphony of church music, an *a cappella* style with imitative techniques, and the use of *cantus-firmus*, while the latter is represented by the opera, *bel-canto* style of solo singing, declamatory choral style, and extended instrumental or keyboard support for the choral forces. The so-called *concertante* requiem, which had surfaced as early as 1636 with such composers as Strauss, stands as an expression of *stile moderno* art, although it is also comprised of various older, conservative elements, such as imitative polyphony. Evidence suggests this form to have been developed and favored by the Germans.

STILE ANTICO

Despite the evolution of musical forms during this time, the *stile antico* continued to be employed by many seventeenth-century composers. The requiems of Casciolini, Stadlmayr, and Pitoni demonstrate a conscious implementation of the Palestrina model. There are several possible explanations as to why they had chosen to do this. Some theories suggest they felt an obligation to maintain the *a cappella* tradition of the Sistine Chapel, or that their works were composed for performance in churches with small choirs or whose funds were too limited to produce expensive, concerted music. Another possible theory proposes that these particular pieces were designed to portray practical, everyday settings aimed toward audiences who might not have been famous, wealthy, or well-schooled in the musical arts.

POLYCHORAL ART

Many of the changes in musical composition quietly came to fore with the polychoral (*cori spezzati*) style developed by Giovanni Gabrieli at St. Mark's in Venice and Heinrich Schütz in Dresden. Their implementation of multiple vocal choirs or instruments—performing in contrast to or in union with each other—allowed for a dramatic presentation of sacred text. This, coincidentally, succeeded in fulfilling the Council of Trent's desire that the sacred liturgical text be made accessible and intelligible to the lay listener. The use of opposing polychoral forces led to a system of expressive and contrasting sound levels called "terraced dynamics," which were later applied to instrumental works as well. Naturally, the presence of multiple choirs had an inbred system for producing changes in timbre and dynamics. An early expression of this technique can be found in the *concertante* style of writing, which employs contrasts of choral and soloist passages. The *concertante* requiems and masses developed and performed in the seventeenth century were actually fledgling forms of the mature instrumental *concerto grosso* with its *soli* and *tutti* sections.

CHORAL TEXTURE

The requiem settings composed during the first half of the seventeenth century appear to have adopted a choral writing exemplar related to the simplified polyphonic style of De Kerle and Viadana, as well as the expressive polychoral experiments identified with the Venetian school. Of the requiems cited in this chapter, only the setting designed by Etienne Moulinié (1636), a Frenchman, bears a strong affinity to the "Palestrina" style, yet even in this work, the Offertory is composed in declamatory, chordal style. The French composers Poitevin (c. 1680–1690) and Chein (1690), who are credited with the composition of two separate settings dating from the latter half of the seventeenth century, embraced a style that strictly adhered to the traditions of the Franco-Flemish school. The tendency to reinforce a highly emotional musical style is underscored by an extended use of expressive homophonic textures, which had been formerly reserved for the *Agnus Dei* and Introit verse, *Te decet* of the Renaissance requiem.

Of the requiems acknowledged in this chapter composed prior to 1650, only three (Viadana, Stadlmayr, and Cererols) employ four-part texture. Three others (Viadana, Lienas, and Moulinié) utilize five part, while one (Bernardi) uses six part, one (Cererols) seven part, and another (Strauss) ten part. Styles fluctuated by the middle of the century. After 1650, seven (Cererols, Charpentier, Michna, Pitoni, Stadlmayr, and Viadana) use four-part texture; six (Biber, Kerll, Leopold I, Lienas, Moulinié, and Viadana) use five-part writing; three (Bernardi, Biber, and Gilles) employ six-part texture, and six (Cavalli, Cererols, Charpentier, Galan, Pitoni, and Strauss) use seven- to eight-part writing. Throughout the eighteenth century, however, an extraordinary development had occurred—a shift toward four-part writing. Of the twenty requiems (listed in the book), half (Zelenka [twice], Casciolini, Cimarosa, Hasse, Lotti, Pergolesi, Salas, Werner, and Zach) employ four-part texture, three (Brusa, Runcer, and Cordans) use three-part texture, two (Campra and Fux) use five-part writing, and three (Herrera [twice], Lopez, and Marcello) incorporate six or more vocal parts.

This conversion to four-part writing is a direct response to the development of an independent orchestral accompaniment. Once the orchestra appropriated a more central role in liturgical music, composers set out on a mission to invigorate and consolidate the choral forces in an effort to maintain equilibrium between the instrumental and vocal sonorities. Concurrently, polyphonic texture gave way to a greater use of chordal, homophonic settings of the text.

GREGORIAN CHANT

More evidence of the requiem's evolution can be cited in the gradual waning and eventual extinction of the *cantus firmus* requiem and the requiem that was melodically inspired by plainsong. During the early baroque era, the Gregorian paraphrase was initially supplanted by original melodies designed to capture the spirit of plainchant. Ultimately, it found itself intertwined with melodies more consonant with those of "expressive" secular music.

In the first half of the century, most requiem settings required the Gregorian intonations for the Introit, Graduale, Offertory, *Sanctus*, *Agnus Dei*, and Communion because of the fact that the polyphonic portions of the mass did not include that specific part of the text. In the later half of the century, however, most composers had come to include these brief phrases within their polyphonic arrangements.

Two of the more innovative intonation settings can be found in the requiems composed by Cavalli and Galan. Cavalli chose to harmonize several of them for the choir, while Galan provided all Gregorian incipits sung by a unison choir accompanied by two oboes and *basso continuo*.

DECORATION: REQUIEM LENGTH

The trend toward a more ornate, decorative music surfaced in a variety of ways. One of the more obvious factors was the evolution in the expanded length of the new requiem settings. During the Renaissance, the performance of the requiem, for the purpose of fulfilling its liturgical duty, was regulated to a length of approximately thirty to thirty-five minutes. Unencumbered by the restrictions of the religious ceremony, Biber, Cordans, Kerll, Strauss, Cererols, Gilles, and Zelenka extended their texts by an additional ten minutes. Marcello and Hasse, in turn, created settings with performance times stretching from fifty minutes to one hour, far exceeding liturgical limitations and demands.

DECORATION: TEXT REPETITION

In the final years of the seventeenth century, musical considerations were viewed as more pivotal to a requiem's success than the previously required mass text. Repetition of liturgical text, gratuitous and redundant for any theological or philosophical purpose, became a common aspect within every movement of the requiem mass. The requiem settings of Biber, Gilles, and Charpentier display prime examples of this technique. Text repetition was put to greater use in the fancier, more elaborate eighteenth century settings composed by Fux, Lopez, Pergolesi, Cimarosa, Marcello, Hasse, Zelenka, and Campra in order to satisfy the demands of musical structure and balance.

TEXT STRUCTURE

Evolution in the art of the requiem had taken place with the small yet significant innovations that had been enveloped within the traditional structure of the texts. The first such alteration, put into place by Cererols, involved the restructuring of the tri-partite sectioning of the texts for the *Kyrie* and *Agnus Dei*. His decision to continuously unfold the texts without sectional breaks is likely to have served as a model for later composers.

In the first half of the eighteenth century, composers began experimenting with the concept of linking one requiem movement with another. Lotti, Biber, Zelenka, and Kerll combined the *Christe* and the second *Kyrie* passages into one section or movement. Zelenka and Pitoni, on the other hand, connected the first *Kyrie* to the Introit, while Herrea and Zach unified the Introit and *Kyrie* into one large movement. Lopez and Werner also engaged in this practice by connecting the *Agnus Dei* with the Communion texts.

When *Dies irae*, the Sequence hymn, had served as part of the requiem mass, composers had either set only small portions of the text to polyphony while employing plainsong for the remainder, or unfolded the text by alternately setting the individual verses with either Gregorian chant or polyphony. Viadana and Casciolini were the only composers (recognized in this volume) who chose the latter course of action.

Most composers set the Sequence in a series of short sections (not yet referred to as "movements") that included various vocal combinations, such as solos, duets, trios, and choral pieces. This compositional technique was modeled from the *concertante* masses and requiems of the early baroque. Settings of the Sequence *Dies irae* verses by Kerll, Strauss, Michna, Pitoni, Biber, and Galan continuously unfold in a series of one-movement pieces.

Because of the poem's extended length, some composers chose to break down the various verses into more manageable units. Brusa, Strauss, Charpentier, Zach, and Hasse divided the Sequence verses into as few as three and as many as seven movements. Cimarosa arranged them into ten movements, while Marcello went as far as to create eleven. Zelenka omitted two verses and divided the remaining ones into seven movements, presenting several verses simultaneously through the use of duets, trios, and overlapping texts.

DECORATION: INSTRUMENTAL MUSIC

Nowhere are the decorative, ornamental tendencies of music more apparent than in the presence of the purely instrumental melodies in the sacred liturgy. The 1636 Strauss requiem setting is possibly the first model provided with an opening *sinfonia*. Leopold I and Adam Michna, among other subsequent composers, began embellishing their settings with a greater number of introductory instrumental pieces. The creation and evolution of the opening *sinfonia* stands as a significant and remarkable development in the history of the requiem, even if it is merely acknowledged in writing a technique that might have been informally applied during earlier times. Composers from Strauss, Charpentier, and onward began inserting introductions (*sinfonias*) and interludes (*ritornelli*) into various movements of the requiem.

INSTRUMENTATION

The origins of colorful orchestration are solidly rooted in the Viennese requiem *instrumentarium*, an outgrowth of a much wider interest in instrumental composition and performance. Through their arrangements, composers of this era attempted to synthesize the passion and emotional fortitude of opera into the instrumental medium.

A speculative presentation of the early five-part Viadana requiem (see Viadana, Discography) was performed in *concertante* fashion, despite the fact that the composer had not specifically indicated which instruments were to be used. Other requiem settings of this period could be handled much the same way, the most notable exception being the conservative Mouliné work, which appears to be designed solely for *a cappella* performance.

One of the most colorful requiem orchestrations is attributed to Adam Michna, whose *Dies irae* includes a series of remarkably fluid, ever-changing sonorities that succeed in illuminating the text in a most telling fashion.

In the earliest *concertante* requiems, the orchestra's purpose was to double the choral lines, thus limiting its role in the overall piece. Although Charpentier employed a pair of flutes and Biber had written expressive parts for trumpets, the main body of strings did little more than reinforce the choral lines. It was not until the eighteenth century that the fully independent orchestral requiem accompaniment was heard.

BASSO CONTINUO

The *basso continuo* or *basso segunte* [organ part] was a mainstay as a means of providing instrumental support for nearly all baroque composers. The earliest settings, such as those of Cavalli and Cererols, employed the *basso segunte*, a simple doubling of the bass line. Scored for choir, vocal soli, strings, trombones, and organ, the Strauss requiem appears to be one of the first for which the *concertante* parts are specifically cited. In this piece, the primary onus of the instruments is to double the vocal lines and provide color to the musical texture. There are independent instrumental passages, however, that presage the totally independent symphonic accompaniments of the Mannheim or Viennese traditions. By the time of Charpentier, Gilles, Fux, and Hasse, a more intricately developed system of the *basso continuo* had evolved, and the organ, violone, viola de gamba, bassoon, or therobo emerged as the most popular options for use as a *basso continuo* instrument.

ORCHESTRAL ACCOMPANIMENTS

During that latter part of the seventeenth century, the requiem's instrumental accompaniments began to assert their independence from the choral lines. By the mid-eighteenth century, they had become completely liberated from the vocal matrix. Many turn-of-the-century requiems featured pieces scored solely for orchestra as well as instrumental introduction and *ritornelli*. Biber, Kerll, Michna, Charpentier, and Gilles were some of the pioneers in the field of orchestration and the orchestral accompaniment of choral and vocal works. The subsequent eighteenth-century requiem settings composed by Hasse, Zach, Pergolesi, and Cimarosa include fully independent accompaniments scored for chamber ensembles of strings, woodwinds, and brass.

Requiem settings of Herrera, Werner, Fux, Marcello, and Pergolesi feature *obbligati* for various instruments with solo voice. They later became commonplace in the works of Cimarosa, Hasse, and Zelenka. It appears that the earliest *obbligati* were scored for strings, however, there are some notable exceptions that featured trombone and trumpet. During the era of high baroque, the oboe, flute, and violin often served to provide a counter-melody for the vocal soloist. Pieces featuring trumpet and French horn were reserved for special occasions, customarily events related to the state.

The purpose of the *obbligati* was to bring a distinct mood or emotional tone to the music and illuminate the liturgical texts. The Viennese style of Mozart and Haydn incorporated sections of instrumental players, as opposed to instrumental soloists.

INSTRUMENTS: INFLUENCE ON
THE VOCAL LINE

Throughout the Renaissance, instrumental and vocal idioms were perceived as being interchangeable. During the era of baroque, however, individual instruments were systematically explored with the aspiration of discovering their own idiomatic potential. The result was an interesting phenomenon: instruments, most notably the violin and keyboard, developed a recognized influence upon the vocal line. Sixteenth notes and dotted rhythms, common in pieces scored for those instruments, were not typically found in vocal music, yet for the purpose of matching the unique quality of a particular instrument, composers adapted these rhythms to the vocal line with increasing frequency. An example of this can be found as early as Cavalli, who displays the most elaborate melodic rhythms in the *Inter oves* and *Rex tremendae* (Sequence) of his requiem. The French had also become noted for employing keyboard trills and ornamentation for vocal and choral music.

NEW PIECES: SEQUENCE AND RESPONSORY

Because it was commonly sung in plainchant, few Renaissance composers set the sequence *Dies irae* in polyphonic style. Such was not the case for baroque composers. After the Tridentine Council opted to incorporate the *Dies irae* into the liturgy, virtually every baroque composer set the text in polyphony. Cererols, however, was the only one to create a completely polyphonic setting. Most of that era's composers set the text verses in alternating sections of chant and polyphony. Only the French (D'Helfer, Poitevin, and Moulinié), along with the Austrian emperor Leopold I (Hapsburg), chose to dispose of the text completely.

A great many baroque composers explored the dramatic potential of the sequence poem in intimate detail. The French composers in particular, including Lully, DeLalande, and Charpentier, created dramatic settings of the *Dies irae* by embracing a newly developed musical form called the *grand motet* that features a succession of solos and choral pieces. The era's composers regarded such compositions as sacred concertos.

Only a handful of seventeenth-century composers, including Cavalli, Cererols, Moulinié, Pitoni, and Casciolini, set the Responsory *Libera me* in polyphonic style. It appears that this piece was more commonly sung at the burial service than at the *cantafalque* (resting place for the coffin) within the church. Also, the fact that the *Libera me* belongs to the Burial Rite as opposed to the Requiem mass may account for the relatively few settings composed.

VOCAL STYLE AND THE NEAPOLITANS

By mid-century, vocal arias had moved away from the syllabic, declamatory style, as found in the Monteverdi madrigal, toward a more lyrical

and melodic, if not *bel-canto*, style. The *bel-canto* style of singing is concerned with the perfection of the lightness, agility, and flexibility of the
voice in the course of delivery of the melodic phrase. Requiem settings of
the late seventeenth century were more likely to feature vocal solos, duets,
and the occasional trio. Settings composed by Kerll, Michna, Leopold I,
Gilles, and Charpentier are among the earliest to make use of such pieces
with the purpose of favoring the individual voice, and more importantly,
emphasizing the expressive qualities of the text. The rapid development
and favorable audience response to the Neapolitan opera resulted in the
greater use of vocal solos, duets, and trios in the liturgical music of the
eighteenth century. The Neapolitan School and its musical language, with
its formal structures and *bel-canto* singing style, had a tremendous impact
upon the music composed for the requiem setting.

Early pioneers of this style include Francesco Durante (1684–1755) (five
requiems: gm, cm, am, FM, GM for SSB or SATB choir, and strings), Francisco Feo (1691–1761) (one requiem: SSAATTBB choir, strings, and woodwinds), Francesco Provenzale (1627–1704) (one requiem: SATB choir and
strings), and Domenico Sarri (1679–1744) (one requiem: SSATB choir and
strings). Their style can be cited in the choral passages of the requiems
composed by Pergolesi and Hasse.

The two-part, binary structure, which was also favored by Scarlatti
among other Neapolitans, was employed in the Introit (*Te decet*), Sequence
(*Tuba mirum*), Offertory (*Non peccavi*), and the *Benedictus* of the requiem
that is attributed to Pergolesi.

The Neapolitan influence continued to be felt for many subsequent
years, culminating in the later requiems of Salas, Jommelli, Paisiello, and
Mayr. In the latter three works, singers were obligated to improvise additional ornamentation and virtuoso vocal cadenzas in the final phrases of
their arias.

Finally, it should be noted that the Neapolitans played a vital role in
the development of an independent orchestral accompaniment that was
actually on par with the dramatic choral forces. French composers also
expected their soloists and choirs to adorn their music through improvisation with the appropriate trills and embellishments derived from
instrumental style.

By the mid-sixteenth century, the stage had become set for the emergence of the more elaborate symphonic requiem.

STEFFANO BERNARDI
c. 1585–1636

Bernardi served as a chaplain at Verona Cathedral (1603) and in 1610 as
maestro di cappella of the Church of the Madonna dei Monti (Rome). In

the following year, he returned to Verona to assume a similar post at the cathedral. In 1622, he entered into the service of Archduke Carl Joseph, Bishop of Breslau and Bressansone. Ultimately, Bernardi moved to Salzburg, where he remained until his death.

He wrote and published a significant amount of church music that includes masses with *basso continuo*, motets and settings of the Psalms. Seven books of madrigals were published from 1611 to 1623. He composed a *Te Deum* for twelve choirs, now lost, for the consecration of Salzburg Cathedral.

The *Missa pro defunctis sex vocum* was written during the first third of the seventeenth century and scored for SSATTB choir. Much of the work was composed in the "Palestrina" polyphonic style. At the same time, sections such as the second *Kyrie* or the *Tuba mirum* and *Inter oves* of the *Dies irae* employ the techniques of the Venetian school and its method of dramatic text declamation. It remains a clear example of the turn-of-the-century *stile misto* (mixed style).

With two soprano and two tenor vocal lines (in addition to the frequent thinning of voice parts), the overall texture and sound remains light and airy. During the course of the work, Bernardi reduced the full, six-part texture to achieve greater contrast in the musical fabric; three times during the Sequence (*Liber scriptus*, SAT; *Qui Mariam*, SATB; and *Oro supplex*, SSA) and once again at the Benedictus (SAT).

Bernardi set the Sequence hymn in the most commonly used method of the early baroque; alternate verses of chant and polyphonic style. All of the usual movements are provided with the Gregorian intonations. Paraphrased segments of the chant melody, in the soprano or tenor line, can be found in most movements, including the Sequence.

Basic Data

EDITION
Denkmäler der Tonkunst in Öesterreich
Vol. XXXVI. 1
Kirchenwerke
ed. Karl August Rosenthal
Universal Edition, Vienna, 1929. [C clefs (soprano, alto, tenor) & F clef]

DURATION
Eight movements, 467 mm.

VOICING
Choir: SSATTB range: S-E6; B-F3

OUTLINE
Introit: 37 mm. [*Requiem aeternam*; *Te decet*, ssattb]
Kyrie: 59 mm. [*Kyrie*; *Christe*; *Kyrie*, ssattb]

Sequence: 182 mm. (even # verses sung in chant)
  Dies irae, ssattb; *Tuba mirum*, ssattb; *Liber scriptus*, sat; *Quid sum miser*, ssattb;
  Recordare, sat; *Juste judex*, ssattb; *Qui Mariam*, attb; *Inter oves*, ssattb; *Oro supplex*,
  ssa; *Judicandus*, ssattb; *Pie Jesu*, ssattb
Offertory: 91 mm. [*Domine Jesu Christe*; *Quam olim*; *Hostias*, ssattb]
Sanctus: 46 mm. [*Sanctus*, ssattb; *Benedictus*, sat]
Agnus Dei: 20 mm. [*Agnus Dei* I, II, III, ssattb]
Communion: 32 mm. [*Lux aeterna*; *Requiem aeternam*, ssattb]
Responsory: 33 mm. [*Libera me*; *Tremens factus*; *Requiem aeternam*, ssattb]

DISCOGRAPHY
None found.

HEINRICH BIBER
August 12, 1644–May 3, 1704

Biber was the finest violinist of the seventeenth century. His fame originated in his stunning violin sonatas, some of which are played in a nor-
mal fashion and others that require *scordatura* tuning. He also happened
to be a first-rate composer. In the mid-1660s, he entered into the service
of Prince-Bishop Karl, Count Liechtenstein-Kastelkorn of Olomouc. By
1670, he was employed as a violinist in the Kapelle of the Salzburg court,
an orchestra that was one of the best in the princely courts of Europe. Its
excellent reputation was achieved through the efforts of Georg Muffat
and Heinrich Biber. Later in the decade, he began to train the Salzburg
Cathedral choirboys in the singing of florid, contrapuntal writing. In
1679, he was made vice-*Kapellmeister* and by 1684, dean of the chorister's
school and *Kapellmeister* of the court orchestra.

Much of the composer's music was printed during his lifetime. The sixteen *Mystery (Rosary) Sonatas* were published in 1676 and the *Mensa sonora*
(a set of six violin partitas) in 1680. *Harmonia artificiosa-ariosa* was published posthumously in 1712. Biber wrote three operas and the famous
Sonata St. Polycarpi, scored for eight trumpets and timpani.

Biber excelled in the composition of church music, writing a thirty-two-
part setting of the *Vespers* for soli, choir, strings, trumpets, trombones,
timpani, and four *basso continuo* instruments. He penned two particularly
spectacular works, the *Missa Bruxellensis* (1700) for twenty-three parts and
the *Missa Salisburgensis* (1682?) for an astonishing fifty-three parts. These
works, along with those of his contemporary, Orazio Benevoli (1605–
1672), are models of "colossal" baroque style. Several other *concertante*
requiems and masses (including one *a cappella* setting), a *Laetatus sum*, a
second setting of the Vespers and an Offertory, constitute the bulk of his
efforts.

Biber's two requiem settings reveal his gift for inventing beautiful melody, as well as his mastery of contrapuntal writing. A century after the invention of monody (a style of vocal-solo writing in which the melody is supported by a simple, chordal accompaniment), Biber wrote florid, coloratura melodies for the solo and choral parts; a melodic style derived from the idiomatic playing style of the violin. A century later, Bach employed the same style of writing in the *Cum Sancto spiritu* and *Et resurrexit* of the *B Minor Mass*.

The *Requiem* for five voices was probably written in the last decade of the seventeenth century and is in the key of F minor, a key linked to sorrow and lamentation. The work is scored for *concertante* SSATB choir and soloists, two violins, three violas, three trombones, and *basso continuo* organ, cello, and bass violin. As was the usual custom, the strings and trombones double the upper and lower voice parts, respectively. There exist several solo instrumental introductions and a semi-independent first-violin part, while the bulk of the orchestral writing doubles or ornaments the vocal lines. The first performance was probably given in Salzburg Cathedral, a location noted for its sumptuous, magnificent sacred music.

The texture is a mixture of homophonic and polyphonic writing, with an abundance of imitative passages. The prevailing five-part texture is frequently broken up by *concertante* writing, as well as the presence of duets and solos, particularly in the Sequence. Fugal writing is found in many passages, including the *Kyrie, Quam olim Abraham, Hosanna in excels is, Benedictus,* and *Agnus Dei.*

Biber, like many other middle and late baroque composers of the requiem, ceased paraphrasing and quoting the traditional Gregorian tunes by inventing his own melodies. The shape and contour of his choral and vocal lines was strongly influenced by the idiomatic string writing so familiar to him. The parallel thirds of the opening choral lines of the Introit and the florid, coloratura passages of the bass solo, *Domine Jesu,* and soprano solo, *Hostias et preces tibi,* give ample testimony of this influence.

Vivid word painting is present. "Fanfare" motifs on the word, *repraesentet,* depict the Archangel Michael. Sharp dissonances on the words *de poenis* and a "wailing" eighth-note figuration of parallel thirds and sixths in the Introit illustrate the poetic vocabulary of baroque "affections."

Finally, Biber helped to reshape the various sections of the requiem (particularly the *Kyrie* and *Agnus Dei*) into through-composed single movements. Subsections of the mass movements, as in the case of the Sequence, were built into multisectional, single movements. A novel feature of the work is the union of the *Agnus Dei* and Communion texts into one movement. Altogether, this work is a very moving testament to Biber's musical imagination and spiritual sentiment.

Basic Data

EDITIONS

1. Heinrich Biber
Denkmäler der Tonkunst in Öesterreich
Vol. XXX (59)
Drei Requiem (Kerll-Strauss-Biber)
Ed. Guido Adler
(C [soprano & tenor] and F clefs)

2. Requiem for five-part chorus of mixed
   voices [F minor]
   Ed. Robert DeCormier
   Lawson Gould Music Publishers
   (#51923) 1976

DURATION

Seven movements, 583 mm., perf., c. 25'

VOICING

Choir: SSATB range: S-F6 [G6 rare]; B-F3 [E3 & C3, occasional]
Instruments: vn. I/II, vla. I/II/III, tbn. I/II/III, *basso continuo* [org. or vc.]

OUTLINE

Introit: 61 mm.
  Requiem aeternam, ssatb-tutti; *Te decet*, B solo/SSAT-soli; *Requiem aeternam*, ssatb-tutti]. Repetition of the *Requiem aeternam* differs from opening section.
Kyrie: 39 mm.
  Kyrie, Christe, Kyrie, SSATB soli & tutti.
Sequence, *Dies irae*; 175 mm.
  Dies irae, ssatb-tutti; *Quantus tremor*, SS soli; *Tuba mirum*, TB soli; *Mors stupebit*, A solo; *Liber scriptus*, ssatb-tutti; *Judex ergo*, B solo; *Quid sum miser*, SSA soli; *Rex tremendae*, ssatb-tutti; *Recordare*, T solo; *Quarens me*, S solo; *Juste judex*, A solo; *Ingemisco*, S solo; *Qui Mariam*, ssatb-tutti; *Preces meae*, ssatb-tutti; *Inter oves*, SST soli; *Confutatis*, B solo; *Oro supplex*, SSAB soli; *Lacrimosa*, ssatb-tutti; *Huic ergo*, T solo; *Dona eis*, ssatb-tutti.
Offertory: 116 mm.
  Domine Jesu Christe, B solo/ssatb-tutti; *Libera eis*, SSATB duets & soli/ ssatb-tutti; *Quam olim Abrahae*, ssatb-tutti; *Hostias*, SB soli/TA duet; *Quam olim Abrahae*, ssatb-tutti.
Sanctus: 73 mm.
  Sanctus, ssatb-tutti; *Osanna*, SSATB soli & tutti.
Benedictus: 16 mm.
  Benedictus, SAB soli. *Osanna* is repeated.
Agnus Dei: 103 mm.
  Agnus Dei, SSTB soli/SA soli/ssatb-tutti; *Lux aeterna*, SSATB soli; *Cum sanctis tuis*, ssatb-tutti; *Requiem aeternam*, ssatb-tutti; *Cum sanctis tuis*, ssatb-tutti.

DISCOGRAPHY

1. L'Oiseau Lyre, 436 460-2, New London Concert, dir. Philip Pickett.
2. Deutsche Harmonia Mundi, 05472-77277-2, Choir and Orchestra of the Netherlands Bach Society, dir. Gustav Leonhardt.

The festive *Requiem à 15 in Concerto* of Biber was probably composed in
1687 for the funeral of Archbishop Maximillian von Khuenberg. The ceremonies that surrounded this funeral lasted for six days and this requiem
was most likely performed at the concluding mass. The music was scored
for a six-part choir (SSATBB) and a vocal cappella of six soloists; one for
each section. The choir is accompanied by a string section of four *viole di
brazzio*, two *trombe basse*, three trombones, and two *piffari*, (oboe) *ad libitum*. The organ, violone, and bassoon executed the *basso continuo*. Because
trumpets were often reserved for state occasions, their presence indicates
that the funeral was one of exceptional importance. Trombones play or
double the lower vocal parts, *colla parte*, while the trumpets play an independent role.

The texture of the work is polyphonic throughout, with numerous passages of fugal writing. The term *fugue* designates an imitative style or procedure in composition and fugal style evolved in the second half of the
seventeenth century, during Biber's lifetime. His setting of *Quam olim
Abrahae* employs an emergent fugue style. Many other passages contain
imitative episodes that could be called *fuga* or *fughetta*.

Double canon (the use of two melodies simultaneously) can be found
on the words, *Et lux perpetua* (Introit), *Kyrie eleison* (*Kyrie*), *Quam olim Abrahae* (Offertory), *Osanna in excelsis* (*Sanctus*), and *Cum Sanctis tuis* (Communion). Paired imitation can be found on the words *Et lux perpetua* (Introit).
Imitative canonic writing can be found virtually everywhere.

Chordal, homophonic spots are rare and were employed for short sections, such as *Requiem aeternam* (Introit), *Dies irae, Lacrimosa, Huic ergo, Oro
supplex* (Sequence), *Hostias* (Offertory), *Pleni sunt coeli* (*Sanctus*), and
Requiem aeternam (Communion). These passages are so infrequent, that
they create a very striking and impressive effect when used. Terraced
dynamics, a hallmark of baroque style, are present in every movement of
the *Requiem*. Biber was almost certainly familiar with the Strauss
Requiem, a work in which the *concertante* orchestration and voicing
employed continuous change. None of the movements in Biber's fifteen-
part requiem maintains an unchanging sound palette. (see Outline)

Although this work employs substantial instrumental support, Biber
rarely uses the orchestra in a solo capacity. Only the *Sanctus* and Communion have orchestral introductions of seven and four measures, respectively. There also exist rare, brief instrumental interludes in the Introit,
Sanctus, and Communion. Another interesting stylistic innovation is the

presence of a vocal and choral writing that has assumed the features of idiomatic string writing. This difficult-to-sing and florid writing style, coupled with fast tempi, point to the presence of well-trained singers. Expressive word painting, a hallmark of baroque music, can be found on such works as *In excelsis* and *Gloria*. The absence of Gregorian intonations (no longer needed), and the traditional Gregorian *cantus-firmus*, give ample testimony to the growing attraction for an ornamental, decorative music for the liturgy.

A significant, structural innovation is present in Biber's *Requiem à 15 in concerto*. The linking of individual sections, such as the *Kyrie* and *Agnus Dei* (in which Biber intermingled the texts), blurred the older division of the texts. These pieces were molded into one-movement compositions in which the harmonic motion, used between the principal sections (tonic to dominant or vice versa), gave a sense of tonal correctness and completeness. In this way, the movements of the requiem become more like movements of an instrumental symphony or a keyboard dance suite. In this work, musical principles superseded text primacy.

The musical splendor that this requiem generates originated in the division of the instrumental and vocal forces, which were placed in the four galleries at the crossing of Salzburg Cathedral. In Biber's time, each gallery possessed an organ. The original performance must have been hair-raising. The key of A major, not particularly a key used for mourning, is the predominant key of this requiem.

Basic Data

EDITION

Beitrage zur Musikforschung, Band 5. Herausgegeben von Reinhold Hammerstein und Wilhelm Seidel
Werner Jaksch
H.I.F. Biber, Requiem à 15
Untersuchungen zur höfischen, liturgischen und musikalischen Topik einer barocken Totenmesse.
Musizverlag Emil Katzbichler. Munich-Salzburg. 1977

DURATION

Eight movements, 712 mm., perf. c. 45′

VOICING AND ORCHESTRATION

Choir: soprano I/II, alto, tenor, bass I/II. range: S-A6; B-D3
Soloists: soprano I/II, alto, tenor, bass I/II
Orchestra: 4 viole di brazzio, 2 trombe basse, 3 tbn, 2 piffari *ad libitum* [ob., bsn. db. & org. (*basso continuo*)]

OUTLINE

Introit: 80 mm.

Requiem aeternam, ssatbb-tutti, *à* 15; *Te decet*, SSATBB soli *à* 6/*à* 15; *Requiem aeternam* is repeated. ABA structure.

Kyrie: 49 mm.

Kyrie, SSATB soli & tutti, *à* 15; *Christe*, SAB soli, *à* 5; *Christe-Kyrie*, ssatbb-tutti, *à* 15. ABA structure.

Sequence: 244 mm.

Dies irae, ssatbb-tutti; *Quantus tremor*, ATB soli; *Tuba mirum*, TB soli; *Mors stupebit*, B II solo; *Liber scriptus*, S I solo; *Judex ergo*, S II solo; *Quid sum miser*, T solo; *Rex tremendae*, ssatbb-tutti; *Recordare*, A solo; *Quaerens me*, SS soli; *Juste Judex*, B I solo; *Ingemisco*, B II solo; *Qui Mariam*, SST soli, ending with *mihi quoque* ssatbb-tutti; *Preces meae*, A solo; *Inter oves*, T solo; *Confutatis*, BB soli; *Oro supplex*, ssatbb-tutti; *Lacrymosa*, ssatbb-tutti; *Huic ergo*, SS soli; *Amen*, ssatbb-tutti.

Offertory: 128 mm.

Domine Jesu Christe, BB soli; *Libera animas*, ssatbb-tutti; *Libera eas*, SS & BB soli/ssattb-tutti; *Sed signifer*, AT soli; *Quam olim Abrahae*, ssatbb-tutti; *Hostias*, SSAT soli/BB soli; *Quam olim Abrahae*, ssatbb-tutti.

Sanctus: 39 mm.

Sanctus, ssatbb-tutti, *à* 15; *Osanna*, SSATBB soli, *à* 6/*à* 15.

Benedictus: 35 mm.

Benedictus, SSATB soli, *à* 5; *Osanna* repeat, ssatbb-tutti, *à* 15.

Agnus Dei: 44 mm.

Agnus Dei, SSATB soli & ssatbb-tutti, *à* 8/*à* 15.

Communion: 68 mm.

Lux aeterna, BB soli, *à* 6; *Cum Sanctis*, ssatbb-tutti, *à* 7/*à* 15.

DISCOGRAPHY

Deutsche Harmonia Mundi, 05472 77344 2, Choir and Orchestra of the Netherlands Bach Society, cond. Gustav Leonhardt.

FRANCESCO CAVALLI
February 14, 1602–January 17, 1676

Francesco Cavalli was one of the leading composers of the mid-1600s. His father, Italian composer-organist-singer, G. B. Caletti, was his earliest music teacher. Francesco took his name from his protector, Federico Cavalli, Venetian governor of Crema. In 1616, Cavalli entered into the *cappella* of St. Mark's (Venice) at the age of fourteen. He maintained a sixty-year relationship with the cathedral and for the first twenty-seven years, was guided by Claudio Monteverdi.

In 1620, he took on an additional position as organist at Saints Giovanni and Paolo, a position that he kept for ten years. An advantageous marriage to a well-to-do widow, Maria Sozomeno (1630), gave him sufficient financial support to allow him to develop a second career in opera. In 1639, he was appointed to the position of second organist at St. Mark's and in 1665 to the position of principal organist. He was finally appointed to the position of *maestro di cappella* of St. Mark's in 1668, where he remained until his death.

Cavalli maintained a double career in music during his mature years; first as a church musician and second as a successful opera composer for various Venetian opera houses. He spent a two-year period in Paris as an opera composer while he simultaneously maintained his position in Venice. Such was his fame. He wrote about thirty operas over a thirty-year period (1639–1669) and penned a significant amount of church music that included two *concertante* masses, an oratorio, three sets of Vespers, five *Magnificat* settings, and more than two dozen other liturgical pieces.

The *Missa pro defunctis per octo vocibus* was composed in 1675, shortly before his death. This *stile antico* requiem was scored for double choir (SATB-SATB) and employed a *concertante* treatment of the voices in both choirs. The predominant, eight-part texture is skillfully molded into ever-changing passages of intimate, two-, three-, or four-part writing that contrasts with colossal blocks of eight-part sound. Both choirs have their own *soli* and *tutti* scorings.

He illuminated the requiem text through various vocal combinations; some with dark sonorities; yet others with dazzling brilliance. A predominantly imitative texture, in "Palestrina" style contrasts with the expressive, declamatory homophonic passages of *Dies irae, Confutatis, Dona eis, Pie Jesu* (Sequence), *Domine Jesu Christe* (Offertory), *Benedictus* (*Sanctus*), and other short phrases. There are no truly sad moments in this music, yet an awesome majesty and a quiet solemnity are present. Powerful rhythm and pulsating energy exists throughout.

One of the novel features of this requiem is the almost complete absence of the Gregorian intonations and chant paraphrase. The Introit and its verse, *Te decet,* and the *Agnus Dei* are the only movements to employ the intonation, but they do so in harmonized or unison versions for the basses of both choirs. Cavalli preserved the original divisions and structure of each movement, as did his Renaissance predecessors.

Parts of the *Dies irae* are reminiscent of the *concertante* style found in Monteverdi's "Madrigals of War & Love" (*Madrigali Guerrieri*, Book VIII). Word painting on such liturgical phrases as *cum resurget, tuba mirum,* and *Dies irae* parallels the hammers (*martelli*) and water (*aqua*) of the madrigal texts in Book VIII.

Sensing that his life was drawing to a close, Cavalli wrote this *Missa* for his own funeral and left precise instructions for the organization of his own funeral rites. It was probably not performed at the time of his death, but was at later commemorations. We learn this from his will, in which he states that he wishes his funeral to be held in the Church of San Lorenzo, with a concerted mass for the dead. He further specified that the performance should include singers and instrumental musicians, who should number at least twelve concerted parts. The instruments consisted of two violins, four violas, two cornets, two theorboes, trombones, bassoon, bass viol, and three organs. The requiem mass was to be performed "by whomever may undertake the task of composing this mass. . . ." (T. Weil, Francesco, *Cavalli e la sua musica scenica*, Venice 1914). In the second paragraph, he states,

> I also desire that two . . . further exequies be instituted
> for me *in perpetuo*, the first to be held in the Ducal Church
> of St Mark, and the second in . . . Church of San Lorenzo . . .
> It is my wish that during these rites a Mass for the dead shall
> be sung, composed by myself for this purpose. All the Canons
> of this Church of St Mark and all the chapel singers shall take
> part in these rites . . . and since this mass, which I wish to be
> sung, necessarily requires a low instrument for the basso continuo,
> it is my wish that . . . Signor Paulo Mansina with his bass viol be
> called upon to play this part.

From this will, it can be deduced that Cavalli had a *basso continuo* or *basso segunte* in mind. The bass viol part (contained in the new edition) was composed by R. G. Kiesewetter (1773–1850), a collector of *musicalia*.

This work is a true masterpiece: every piece is a gem, and each movement forms a long string of pearls. The music possesses enormous spiritual depth and insight. The writer and musicologist, August Ambros, maintained that its spiritual qualities were on the same level as Mozart's requiem.

Basic Data

EDITION

Francesco Cavalli
Missa pro Defunctis for Eight Voices, with the Responsory, "Libera me" for Five
    Voices. 1675
Critical edition by Francesco Bussi,
Edizioni Suvini Zerboni. Milan. 1978

DURATION

Seven movements, 704 mm., perf., 30'

VOICING

Two choirs: Choir I [SATB]. Choir II [SATB] range: S-F6: B-F3
Instruments: the modern edition includes a violone "*grosso*" part.

OUTLINE [*tutti* indicates both choirs]

Introit: 86 mm., 4 sections [*Requiem aeternum; Te decet; tutti; Exaudi;* ATB soli & tutti; *Requiem; tutti*]

Kyrie: 50 mm., 2 sections [*Kyrie; tutti, Christe;* SATB soli of both choirs] The *Kyrie* is repeated.

Sequence, *Dies irae*: 321 mm., 22 sections.

   Dies irae, tutti-Quantus tremor, ATB soli-*Tuba mirum,* SST soli-*Mors stupebit, tutti-Liber scriptus,* TB soli-*Judex ergo,* ATB soli-*Quid sum miser,* SAB soli-*Rex tremendae, tutti-Recordare,* SAT soli-*Quaerens me,* ATB soli-*Juste judex,* SST soli-*Ingemisco,* ATB soli-*Qui Mariam,* SATB soli-*Preces meae, tutti-Inter oves,* SATB soli-*Confutatis,* sat *tutti-Voca me,* SAT soli-*Oro supplex,* satb *tutti-Lacrymosa,* satb *tutti-Pie Jesu,* satb *tutti-Dona eis, tutti-Amen,* satb *tutti.*

Offertory: 116 mm., 4 sections [*Domine Jesu Christe, Quam olim* & *Hostias, Quam olim, tutti*]

Sanctus: 66 mm., 4 sections [*Sanctus; Sanctus, tutti; Benedictus, tutti* soli, *Hosanna, tutti*]

Agnus Dei: 65 mm., 3 sections [*Agnus Dei* I, II, III], *tutti* but considerable thinning of voice parts.

The modern edition includes:

Responsory, *Libera me*: 138 mm., [sattb]

DISCOGRAPHY

Pierre Varany, PV793052, Akademia Ensemble Vocal Régional de Champagne Ardenne, cond. Françoise Lasserre.

JOAN CEREROLS
September 9, 1618–August 28, 1676

Although Cererols spent most of his career at the Monastery of Montserrat, first as a choirboy and novice, and later as a monk, relatively little is known about him. In addition to composing, he apparently played organ and several string instruments. There still exists a small number of his liturgical works and Spanish villancicos. Among the sacred pieces are four masses, eleven psalm settings, a setting of the *Magnificat* and the *Nunc dimittis,* as well as several hymns and antiphons. Many of these works were scored for eight voices and were presumably performed at the monastery.

   The *Missa pro defunctis* is one of two mass settings scored for four voices (SATB) in which the composer maintained a balance of elaborate four-part, homophonic texture and imitative polyphony throughout the work. The four-part fabric is contrasted with occasional points of imitation and thinning of voices. The *Kyrie,* Graduale, *Sanctus,* and Communion employ imitative polyphony while the remainder of the work is homophonic.

Most notable is a complete, chordal setting of the *Dies irae* text in an arrangement similar to fauxbourdon style.

Cererols based this *missa* upon the Gregorian melody, which is paraphrased throughout the composition and usually in the tenor line. Gregorian intonations are present for all of the usual movements except the Graduale verse, *Hostias et preces meae*, for which he composed a polyphonic setting. As is the case for a majority of early baroque settings, a *basso seguente* for the organ was furnished.

One of the striking, modern features of this work is the structuring of the *Kyrie* into one continuous movement. Cererols was among the earliest composers to break down the traditional, tri-partite division of this three-sentence text. He achieved the same result with the unification of the usual, three-part division of the *Agnus Dei* into one movement. Here, only the uppermost vocal lines sing *Agnus Dei* (traditionally sung three times . . . and he maintained the tradition), while the lower lines manage the remainder of the text.

Another important aspect of the work is the division of the *Sanctus* and *Benedictus* into two separate parts. This separation is indicative of a growing trend that permitted later composers, such as Mozart, to arrange both text sections into separate movements, each with its own choral or vocal soloist ensemble, as well as contrasting orchestrations.

Basic Data

EDITION

Mestres de L'Escolania de Montserrat
Vol. II
Joan Cererols. Missa
ed., D. Pujol
Imprenta del Monestir de Montserrat. 1931 [Clefs, C (soprano, alto, tenor) & F]

DURATION

Ten movements, 944 mm.

VOICING

Choir: SATB range: S-E flat 6; B-D3
Instrument: org. [*basso seguente*]

OUTLINE

Introit: 75 mm. 2 sections [*Requiem aeternam*; *Te decet*, satb]
Kyrie: 48 mm., 1 section [*Kyrie, Christe, Kyrie*, satb]
Graduale: 34 mm., 1 section [*Requiem aeternam*, satb] The verse, *In memoria*, plainchant.
Sequence: 335 mm., 19 sections [satb]

Offertory: 205 mm., 3 sections [*Domine Jesu Christe*; *Quam olim*; *Hostias*, satb]
Sanctus: 65 mm., 1 section [*Sanctus*, satb]
Benedictus: 46 mm., 1 section [*Benedictus*, satb]
Agnus Dei: 46 mm., 1 section [*Agnus Dei* I, II, III, satb]
Communion: 83 mm., 2 sections [*Lux aeterna*; *Requiem aeternam*, satb]
Responsory: 82 mm., 5 sections [*Libera me*; *In die illa*; *Dies illa*; *Kyrie*; *Kyrie*, satb]

DISCOGRAPHY

None found.

The *Missa pro defunctis* for seven voices is arranged for two separate
choirs, Choir I-SAT and Choir II-SATB, which often function as a unified
ensemble, but at other times, as a dramatic double choir in antiphonal-
dialogue fashion. Daniele Becker suggests that an outbreak of plague in
Barcelona (1650–51), might have motivated Cererols to write this work.
(CD notes for the Astrée recording. See Discography)

The prevailing seven-part texture of the composition is imitative style,
with expressive, homophonic passages reserved for the Sequence, *Agnus
Dei*, and Communion texts. Contrasts in the texture are achieved by thinning the vocal lines or reducing the vocal parts to a more personal and
intimate three-line fabric (SAT) in the Graduale verse, *In memoria*, and the
Responsory, *Dies illa*. A dance-like, triple meter, employed only in the
Sequence, is highly expressive and animated. This departure from the
pervasive, austere duple rhythm is quite striking.

Cererols' polyphonic *missa* does not appear to be a *cantus-firmus* work,
although Gregorian intonations are used for the Introit (and verse), Offertory (but not the verse), and the opening of *Agnus Dei*. Plainchant is
employed for the even-numbered verses of the *Dies irae* as well as the *Benedictus*. The traditional structure of the *Kyrie* and the *Agnus Dei* was
altered when the composer condensed the tri-partite division of each
movement into two separate, through-composed compositions.

Cererols provided a *basso continuo* for organ and the vocal parts might
have been augmented by doubling instruments.

Basic Data

EDITION

Mestres de L'Escolania de Montserrat
Vol. II
Joan Cererols. Missa
Imprenta del Monastir de Montserrat. 1931 [C (soprano, alto, tenor) & F clefs]

DURATION

Ten movements, 401 mm., perf., c. 37'

VOICING

Choir I, SAT; Choir II, SATB range: S-F6; B-D3
Instruments: *basso continuo*

OUTLINE

Introit: 58 mm., 2 sections [*Requiem aeternam*; *Te decet*, sat/satb]
Kyrie: 19 mm., 1 section [*Kyrie, Christe, Kyrie*, sat/satb]
Graduale: 36 mm., 2 sections [*Requiem aeternam*, sat/satb; *In memoria*, sat]
Sequence, *Dies irae*; 150 mm., 11 sections. [Odd-numbered verses: sat/satb] *Dies irae-Tuba Mirum-Liber scriptus-Quid sum miser-Recordare-Juste judex-Qui Mariam-Inter oves-Oro supplex-Lacrimosa-Pie Jesu* [Even-numbered verses: plainchant]
Offertory: 58 mm., 3 sections [*Domine Jesu Christe; Quam olim; Hostias*, sat/satb]
Sanctus: 30 mm., 1 section [*Sanctus*, sat/satb] *Benedictus*: plainchant.
Motet, *Hei mihi*: 3 sections [*Hei mihi*, sat/satb; *Anima mea*, sat; *Miserere*, sat/satb]
Agnus Dei: 21 mm., 1 section [*Agnus Dei* I, II, III, sat/satb]
Communion: 29 mm., 3 sections [*Lux aeterna; Requiem aeternam; Cum sanctis*, tutti]
Responsory: 63 mm., 5 sections [*Libera me; Quando coeli*, sat/satb; *Dies illa*, sat; *Kyrie; Kyrie*, sat/satb]

DISCOGRAPHY

1. Accent, ACC 94106, D Currende, cond. Erik Van Nevel.
2. Astrée, E8704, La Capella Reial, dir. Jordi Savall.

MARC ANTOINE CHARPENTIER
1645/50–February 24, 1704

This prolific composer, along with Johann Kerll, studied with Giacomo Carissimi for several years in Rome. He later worked for the Grand-Dauphin (eldest son of the king) and, for that service, was granted a pension in 1683. Charpentier also collaborated with Moliére, after the latter had a falling-out with Lully, but never managed to receive a significant position with the royal establishment. During the 1680s, he was employed as composer and *maitre de musique* for the Jesuit church, St. Louis. A large portion of his sacred music was written for this church and the singers from the *Opera*, who attended mass there. Finally, in 1698, he was named *maitre* for Ste. Chapelle, the important royal church. Some of his best music was penned for this institution.

Little of Charpentier's output was published in his lifetime. Fortunately, the bulk of his manuscripts were purchased by the King's Library in 1727, thereby preserving it for posterity. Among his works are eleven masses, four sequences, thirty-seven antiphons, nineteen hymns, ten settings of the *Magnificat*, nine settings of the *Litany of Loretto*, fifty-four lessons and responsories for Tenebrae, four settings of the *Te Deum*, eighty-four Psalm settings, and 207 motets of various types. Of the eleven masses, three are requiems: *Messe pour les trépasses* (eight parts), *Messe des morts* for four voices, and the *Messe des morts et simphonie* for four voices.

The *Prose des morts* (*Dies irae*) is composed in the form of a grand motet. These exquisitely beautiful works appear to have been written in the final decade of the composer's life. The specific events for which the funeral music was written remain unknown.

The *Messe des morts à quatre voix et simphonie* (H 10), written between 1697–1698, is a *concertante* work employing a four-part (SATB) choir and solo (SATB) quartet. Unlike its predecessor, the Gilles requiem, the four-part choral texture is primarily imitative polyphony. Occasional homophonic passages (such as *Judex ergo Quaerens me, Confutatis* [Sequence] and *Pleni sunt coeli* and *Hosanna* [*Sanctus*]) relieve this imitative fabric. Contrast is further provided by the numerous vocal solos. Although a chamber orchestra is used to double and color the choral lines, there are several independent orchestral pieces: the opening sinfonias of the *Kyrie* and Sequence (*Kyrie, Christe, Dies irae, Tuba mirum,* and *Oro supplex*). The orchestra employs the usual strings, two oboes, and flutes, as well as *continuo* instruments.

Charpentier did not set the Introit, Offertory, and Communion in any of his requiems, although he included settings of the *Pie Jesu* (sung during the elevation of the Host) in all three works.

Basic Data

EDITIONS

1. Messes à 4 voix et orchestre	2. Messe des morts à 4 voix et orchestre
Messes, Vol. 2 Edition de Catherine	Editions Costallat C-3610
Cessae Editions du Centre de Musique	60, Chausée d'Antin, Paris. 1979
Baroque de Versailles.	
1997 [full score]	

DURATION

Twelve movements, 660 mm., perf., c. 20'

VOICING AND ORCHESTRATION

Choir: SATB [dessus, haute-contre, taille, basse] range: S-A6; B-F3
Instruments: vn., vla., vc., db.. 2 fl., 2 ob., bsn., *Basso Continuo*

OUTLINE

Kyrie: 180 mm. [gm] 3 movements.
   Orchestral symphony; Kyrie: satb choir & soli; Christe: symphony; *Christe*; ATB trio; Kyrie is repeated.
Sequence, *Dies irae*: 326 mm. 5 movements [complete text]
   Dies irae: orchestral prelude; *Dies irae*, ATB trio [cm] Tuba mirum: *Tuba mirum &
   Judex ergo*, satb choir [CM] Quid sum miser: *Quid sum miser*, SSB trio [CM]
   Quaerens me: *Quarens me*, satb choir [CM]; *Ingemisco*, AT duet [CM] & *Qui
   Mariam*, A solo & satb choir [cm] Oro supplex: orchestral prelude; S solo [cm];
   Lacrymosa, ATB trio [cm] & *Pie Jesu*, satb choir [cm]
Sanctus: 38 mm.
   Sanctus & Pleni sunt coeli, satb choir] [gm]
Elevation, *Pie Jesu*: 32 mm.
   Pie Jesu, SA duet [gm]
Benedictus: 25 mm.
   Benedictus, ATB trio & satb choir [gm]
Agnus Dei: 59 mm.
   Agnus Dei I, satb choir; *Agnus Dei* II, ATB trio; *Agnus Dei* III, satb choir [gm]

DISCOGRAPHY

Erato, Musique Sacrée, Vol. 10, Westvlaams Vocaal Ensemble, Musica Polyphonica, Con. Louis Devos.

The *Messe des morts à quatre voix* (H 7) was composed in the early 1690s and scored for *concertante* SATB choir and soli. Unlike the *Messe des morts* (H 10), this requiem has no independent sinfonias, instrumental introductions or *ritornelli*. String instruments and *basso continuo* are used solely to support the choral and vocal lines.

The prevailing four-part texture is a mixture of chordal writing and imitative polyphony. Charpentier's poignant, expressive harmony generates an overwhelming sense of serenity and tranquility throughout the work. Musical and emotional contrast is provided by the numerous passages for one or more soloists, just as in the *concerto grosso*.

The composer followed some novel procedures in the structuring of the mass movements. For example, he divided the *Kyrie* text into three virtually separate movements (much like Bach's *B Minor Mass*) and consolidated the *Sanctus* text into one movement.

Occasional trills, performed by the choir and soloists, ornament their elegant melodic lines. These trills, derived from the string instruments, make visible the impact of instrumental writing upon the choral and vocal solo technique.

Basic Data

EDITION

None found.

DURATION

Five movements, perf., c. 25'

VOICING AND ORCHESTRATION

Choir: SATB
Soloists: SSATB
Instruments: [*basso continuo*] therobo, viola da gambe, org.

OUTLINE

Kyrie: 6' 30" 3 movements.
  Kyrie I: satb choir/TB soli.
  Christe: satb choir/ATB trio.
  Kyrie II: satb choir/AT soli.
Sanctus: 2' 19"
  Sanctus, satb choir; *Sanctus*, SAT soli; *Sanctus*, satb choir; *Dominus* & *Pleni sunt coeli*, satb choir/SATB soli, *Gloria* & *Hosanna*, satb choir/AT soli.
Elevation, Pie Jesu: 2'
  Pie Jesu: SI/SII duet.
Benedictus: 2' 08"
  Benedictus, ATB soli; *Hosanna*, satb choir; *Hosanna*, ATB soli, *Hosanna*, satb choir.
Agnus Dei: 3' 06"
  Agnus Dei, satb choir; *Dona eis*, AB duet, *Dona eis*, satb choir; *Agnus Dei*, AB soli; *Agnus Dei*, satb choir; *Dona eis*, AT soli; *Dona eis*, satb choir.
Motet, *De profundis*: satb choir/SATB soli

DISCOGRAPHY

1. Calig, CAL 50874, Hanover Boys Choir, cond. H. Henning.
2. Erato, Musique Sacrée, Vol. 10, Westvlaams Vocaal Ensemble and Musica Polyphonica, dir. Louis Devos.

The *Messe pour les trépasses* was composed in the late 1690s, if not the early years of the eighteenth century. It is the grandest of his requiem settings, employing double SATB choir, SATB soli, four-part string orchestra, two flutes, and organ. (A grand motet, *Miseremini mei* [H 311], found next to the *Messe* in the composer's *Méslanges*, replaced the Graduale and Offertory.)

An independent grand motet, *Dies irae* (see: *Dies Irae* Chapter) also found in the *Méslanges* might have been performed along with the *Messe pour les trépasses*. The prevailing texture of the work is imitative polyphony, with occasional homophonic passages, such as those at the end of the *Kyrie*, on the phrase, *Hosanna in excelsis*, and in the *Agnus Dei*. The interplay and sweep of the choral mass is designed to overwhelm the senses and emotions with the grandeur and power of the text. As in all *concertante* masses, contrast is achieved by use of the *tutti* and *soli* ensembles. The strings double the choral lines while the flutes lend a pastoral, even plaintive, quality to the music.

Basic Data

EDITION

Marc Antoine Charpentier
Oeuvres Complètes
Méslanges Autographes, Vol. 1
Fac-simile du manuscript, Paris Bibliothèque Nationale, Res Vm1 259
Minhoff France Editeur, Paris. 1990 [C (soprano, alto, tenor) & F clefs]

DURATION

Seven movements, 348 mm., perf., c. 40'

VOICING & ORCHESTRATION

Choir: double SATB choirs range: S-F6; B-F3

OUTLINE

Kyrie: 74 mm. 2 movements [am] *andante*
  Forty-measure *symphonie*; *Kyrie*, satb choirs/SATB soli.
Christe: 55 mm., 2 sections, 2 movements [am] *andante*
  Fifteen-measure *symphonie*; *Christe*, SAB soli; Opening *symphonie* and Kyrie I are repeated.
Sanctus: 73 mm. [am] *andante*
  symphonie; *Sanctus*, SATB soli/satb choirs; *Dominus Deus* & *Hosanna*, SS soli/satb choirs.
Elevation, *Pie Jesu*: 44 mm. [am]
  Pie Jesu: SATB soli/satb choirs
Benedictus: 17 mm. [am]
  Benedictus, SA soli; *Hosanna* is repeated.
Agnus Dei: 85 mm. [am] 4 sections, 2 movements [am]
  Symphonie; *Agnus Dei* I, SATB soli/satb choirs; *Agnus Dei* II, satb choirs; *Agnus Dei* III is nearly identical to *Agnus Dei* I.

DISCOGRAPHY

Erato, 4509.97238-2, Choeur Symphonique et Orchestre de la Fondation Gulbenkian de Lisbonne, dir. Michel Corboz.

CRISTÓBAL GALAN
c. 1630–September 24, 1684

The Spanish composer Galan began his musical career in the choir at the Morella and Teurel cathedrals. He also worked in Corsica and Sardinia before he was thirty years old. He was appointed *maestro de capilla* at Segovia Cathedral in 1664. He later became music director at the wealthy, royal institution, *Real Convento de Senoras Descalzas* in Madrid. Because of his fame as a composer of polyphonic music, he was appointed *maestro* of the royal chapel in 1680 (King Carlos II), the most important post in Spain.

He wrote more than 100 secular villancicos (Spanish poetry, consisting of several stanzas and refrain), two masses (one for nine voices and the *Misa de difuntos*), numerous Latin liturgical pieces, and three settings of the *Stabat Mater*.

The *Misa de difuntos* is a spectacular work, composed after 1680 and arranged for twelve voices in three choirs. The scoring was set out in the following plan: Choir I (Soprano 1, two oboes, and *basso continuo* instruments), Choir II (SSAT), and Choir III (SATB). *Basso continuo* instruments include harp and organ. Because of the *cori spezzati* (divided choirs) technique and the *instrumentarium*, Galan's *Misa* can be considered to be a model of *stile moderno*.

Yet, conservative traces of the older Renaissance requiem style remain. Most noticeable is the continued presence of the Gregorian chant. The chant melody, including the intonations, is always sung by the soprano of Choir I, either in large, recognizable chunks of melody or in suggestive paraphrase. The chant is, on every occasion, surrounded and supported by an instrumental accompaniment of two oboes and *basso continuo* instruments. At other times, the melody appears in the tenor voice. Constant imitative polyphony also suggests Renaissance technique. On the other hand, the presence of sixteenth notes, occasional thirty-second notes, dotted rhythms, and instrumental-like writing in the vocal lines reveal the composer's modernistic tendencies.

The three choirs perform antiphonally, coming together at various points to create tremendous sonorous effects and a majestic, expressive presentation of the text. Other passages use a thinner texture to create a more intimate musical expression. With the exception of the *Kyrie* (written in imitative polyphony), the remainder of the *misa* employs a mixture of polyphonic and homophonic fabric.

Like many composers of the second half of the seventeenth century (Cavalli, Michna, and Kerll), Galan composed one-movement versions of the *Kyrie*, *Agnus Dei*, and the Sequence. Yet Galan went a step further and composed one-movement settings of the Offertory and its verse as well as the *Sanctus*, without the *Benedictus*. He set the Introit and Communion and their verses into four separate movements.

Basic Data

EDITION

Collected Works, Vol. XII/I
Obras Completas de Cristobal Galan
Part 1, Misa de Difuntos
ed., John H. Baron
Institute of Medieval Music, Ltd.
Henryville, Ottawa, Binningen. 1982

DURATION

Eight movements, 256 mm.

VOICING

Choirs: Choir I [Soprano I, 2 oboes, *basso continuo*], Choir II [SSAT], Choir III
   [SATB] range: S-G6; B-D3
Instruments: 2 ob., *arpa* [harp], org.

OUTLINE

Introit: 25 mm., 2 sections: *Requiem aeternam* & *Te decet,* choirs I/II/III
Kyrie: 22 mm., 1 movement: *Kyrie* & *Christe,* choirs I/II/III
Tract: 9 mm., 1 section: *Absolve Dominus,* choirs I/II/III
Sequence: 83 mm., 1 movement: choirs I/II/III
Offertory: 42 mm., 1 movement: *Domine Jesu Christe,* choirs I/II/III
Sanctus: 22 mm., 1 movement: *Sanctus,* choirs I/II/III
Agnus Dei: 20 mm., 1 movement: *Agnus Dei,* choirs I/II/III
Communion: 23 mm., 2 sections: *Lux aeterna* & *Requiem aeternam,* choirs I/II/III
Motet, *Deficit gaudium*: choir I, sst/choirs II/III, satb

DISCOGRAPHY

None found.

JEAN GILLES
January 8, 1668–February 5, 1705

At the age of eleven, Gilles, enrolled in the choir school of St. Sauveur Cathedral (Aix-en-Provence). In 1687, he left the choir school, but continued to work there as assistant choirmaster, organist, and, ultimately, *maitre de musique* (1693). Four years later, he was appointed to a similar position at Toulouse Cathedral, where he remained until his death.

Among his exclusively sacred compositions there exist fourteen *grands* motets (four to five voices), ten *petits* motets (one to two voices), a mass for five voices, and a requiem.

Gilles' *Messe des morts* was one of the better-known requiem settings of the eighteenth century. It was composed about 1696. He received a commission from two families who were members of the Toulouse Parliament. Upon learning the cost of the requiem, they refused payment. Gilles apparently put the work away, along with his will, and a note requesting that the *Messe* be performed at his own funeral. It was performed on that occasion (conducted by André Campra), and almost a century later, for the funeral services of Jean-Philippe Rameau (1764) and Louis XV (1774). Its popular appeal stemmed from its use of folk-like melodies and dance rhythms of Gilles' Provencal heritage. After the eighteenth century, the work fell into oblivion until a revival performance by the Jean Pailliard Ensemble, in the 1950s.

The scoring of the requiem is for SSATTB (*dessus, haute-contre, taille-haut, taille-basse,* and *basse*) and chamber orchestra. In this *concertante* setting, the six-part choir is paired with a four-part (SATB) soloist ensemble. Gilles greatly expanded the role of the orchestra in the requiem. Every movement, except the *Kyrie*, was given an instrumental prelude, a self-contained piece of music, called *symphonie*. This composer went a step further than his predecessors; he added instrumental interludes and postludes, called *ritornelli*, in five of the seven mass movements. The chamber orchestra began to assume a more independent role. Although the orchestra could and did support the singers, the idiomatic violin obbligati and pastoral flute melodies contrasted with the choral and vocal fabric as the instruments illuminated the text and brought it to life. One final observation is in order; Gilles not only gave the traditional requiem movements a sense of being "little" symphonies, he also transformed the verse sections, such as *Te decet, Benedictus, Sed signifer, Hostias,* and *In memoria,* into movements. This structuring of the requiem has remained a standard procedure, in one form or another, up to the present.

The prevailing choral fabric of the Messe is an expressive homophonic texture, with the exception of the *Domine Jesu Christe* (Offertory), *Benedictus,* and concluding *Requiem aeternam,* which employ imitative polyphony. It may be considered a triumph of harmony over counterpoint. The only fugue in the requiem is the concluding chorus, *Et lux perpetua.* Contrast in the texture is created by the presentation of the text by choir and soloists *concertante* style. Numerous instrumental *ritornelli* divide the text sections. The orchestra also uses *concertante* techniques, so the overall texture of the work is constantly shifting from a *grand* to a *petit* sound.

His engaging music possesses numerous pictorial elements. The steady rhythm of the Introit clearly suggests a funeral cortège. When this rhythm is combined with the sustained notes on the word, *aeternam,* a mood of peace and repose is created. Perpetual light is suggested by the melodic notes of an ascending F major triad, followed by a series of quick eighth notes on the text, *Et lux perpetua.* Darkness is hinted at by the use of a descending melodic line in the bass. The overall tone of this requiem setting is solemn and sad. In the fifty-minute timespan of the work, there are only four short sections that use an *allegro* tempo, designated "gay," to relieve the pervasive solemnity.

Basic Data

EDITION

Recent Researches in the Music of the Baroque Era. Vol. XLVII
Messe des Morts. Jean Gilles
ed., John Hajdu
A-R Editions. 315 West Gorham St., Madison Wisconsin 53703. 1984

DURATION

Twelve movements, 1120 mm., perf., c. 47'

VOICING & ORCHESTRATION

Choir: SSATTB range: S-G6; b-F3 S♯soloists: SATB [dessus, haute contre, taille, basse]

Orchestra: dessus de violon [vn. I], haute-contre de violon [vn. II], taille de violon [vla.], basse de violon [vc.], viola da gambe, 2 fl., org. In keeping with eighteenth-century performances of the music, a baroque *tambour* [drum] should be used.

OUTLINE

Introit: 310 mm., [FM] 2 movements.
   Requiem: *symphonie; Requiem,* T solo (lentement); *Et lux,* SB duet/sattb choir (*gay*); *ritornello; Et lux,* B solo/sattb choir.
   Te decet: *Te decet,* S solo; *ritornello; Et tibi,* B solo; *ritornello; Et tibi,* SB duet; *ritornello; Exaudi,* sattb choir; *ritornello.*
Kyrie: 51 mm., [FM]
   Kyrie, T I solo; *ritornello; Christe,* ST duet; *Kyrie,* sattb choir.
Graduale: 166 mm., [gm]
   symphonie; Requiem, B solo with *ritonelli; In memoria,* sattb choir/B solo (*gay*).
Offertory: 281 mm., [gm] 3 movements
   Domine Jesu Christe: *symphonie; Domine Jesu,* bass solo; *Domine Jesu,* SATB soli/ B solo. Sed signifer: *symphonie* (*gay*); *Sed signifer,* SA duet; *ritornello; Sed signifer,* sattb choir; *Sed signifer,* SSA trio/B solo; *Quam olim,* sattb choir. Hostias: *symphonie; Hostias,* T solo; *Fac eas,* B solo/sattb choir.
Sanctus: 103 mm., [GM] 2 movements.

Sanctus: *symphonie*; *Sanctus*, B solo/BT duet; *Osanna*, B solo/ssattb choir; *Osanna*, sattb choir/SSA trio.

Benedictus: *symphonie*; *Benedictus*, ATB trio. *Osanna* repeated.

Agnus Dei: 90 mm., [GM]

symphonie; *Agnus Dei*, B solo (two times); *Agnus Dei*, sattb choir; *ritornello*; *Qui tollis*, sattb choir.

Communion: 119 mm., [GM] 2 movements.

Lux aeterna: symphonie; *Lux aeterna*, B solo; *ritornello*; *Requiem*, B solo; *Requiem*, sattb choir (fugue).

Et lux perpetua: (*vivement*) *Et lux*, B solo; *Et lux*, sattb choir; *Et lux*, SA duet/sattb choir.

DISCOGRAPHY

Erato, 2292-45989-2, The Boston Camerata, dir. Joel Cohen.

LEOPOLD I (HAPSBURG)
June 9, 1640–May 5, 1705

Leopold I was the second son of Emperor Ferdinand III, the Holy Roman Emperor. He received an excellent humanistic education and was trained in music by Antonio Bertali and the brothers, Markus and Wolfgang Ebner. Later, he hired such famous musicians as Johann Fux, Johann Kerll, and Johann Schmeltzer as his court musicians.

He wrote a considerable amount of music, including stage works, oratorios, and sacred vocal music. Some of those works include a four-part mass, a *Stabat Mater*, an arrangement of the *Magnificat*, a setting of the *Dies irae* for four voices, one requiem, five Marian antiphons, and numerous other works.

The *Missa pro defunctis* shows his formidable composition skills and is dated 1673, the same time as the death of his first wife. It is scored for five-voice (SSATB) choir, soloists, and instruments. Although this *concertante* work was written in the Venetian tradition, its immediate Viennese predecessors were the settings by Kerll (1669), Michna (1654), and Strauss (1636). Interplay between the strings, brass, and *basso continuo* instruments, as well as the kaleidoscopic combinations of choir and soloists, highlights the remarkable variety of timbre in the composer's instrumental-vocal palette. Brasses and strings are treated as choirs, which may perform separately for a more expressive, emotional effect, play *en masse* for the more powerful, climatic passages.

The prevailing texture of the music is imitative style, with numerous, contrasting homophonic passages. Leopold I wrote three instrumental pieces, which function as preludes for the Introit, *Sanctus*, and Communion. "Echo" effects on *Osanna* are used at the end of the *Sanctus*.

Gregorian intonations are not needed for this setting, in fact, the Gregorian funeral melodies are absent from this work. Melodic inspiration for the *missa* came from the composer's own reservoir of musical ideas.

The music possesses a great deal of drama and passion, generated by his control and balance of the expressive and contrapuntal idioms. The music is never dull or uninteresting; consequently, the listener is rewarded with new color or an attractive turn of musical phrase.

Basic Data

EDITION

None found.

DURATION

Six movements

VOICING AND ORCHESTRATION

Choir: SSATBAR
Soloists: SSATBAR
Instruments: 3 vla., vc., violone. 2 zink [tpt.], 2 posaune, dulzian [bsn], org.

OUTLINE

Introit: 3 sections: *Requiem aeternam*, ssatbar choir; *Et lux perpetua*, SSATBar soli; *Requiem aeternam*, ssatbar choir]; instrumental *sinfonia*.

Kyrie: 3 sections: *Kyrie*, ssatbar soli/choir; *Christe*, ssatbar choir; *Kyrie*, ssatbar soli/choir.

Sanctus: 3 sections: *Sanctus*, ssatbar choir/soli; *Pleni sunt coeli*, S solo/AT duet/ ssatbar choir; *Osanna*, TB duet/ssatbar choir]; instrumental *sinfonia*.

Benedictus: 1 section: *Benedictus*, ssatbar soli. *Hosanna* is repeated.

Agnus Dei: 3 sections: *Agnus Dei* I, S solo; *Dona eis*, TA soli; *Agnus Dei* II, T solo; *Dona eis*, SBar duet; *Agnus Dei* III, ssatbar choir, *Dona eis*, ssatbar choir/soli.

Communion: 2 sections: *Lux aeterna*, ssatbar choir/SA soli; *Requiem aeternam*, ssatbar choir/soli; instrumental *sinfonia*.

DISCOGRAPHY

Preiser, 90067, Choir of the Basilika Maria Treu, Convivium Musicum Vidobonense, dir. Gerhard Kramer.

CHARLES D'HELFER
d. after 1664

This French composer was associated with the cathedral at Soissons, where he served as priest and *maitre de musique* in 1648. In 1653, he was

appointed chaplain at one of the twelve chapels in the cathedral and in
1664 became a canon of the cathedral. D'Helfer seems to have written only
sacred music. There remain only four *a cappella* masses. Several other
known masses and Vespers music have been lost.

The *Missa pro defunctis* for SATB voices (unaccompanied) was first published in Paris by Robert Ballard (1656). There exist several later manuscript versions of the *Missa*, one of which was used in 1774 for the funeral
service for Louis XV. Its conservative, *stile antico* tendencies are found in
the *a cappella* setting, the need for the Gregorian intonations and subsequent chant paraphrases found in the soprano and tenor. Furthermore,
the structure of the various mass sections faithfully follows earlier Renaissance models.

The prevailing texture, a four-part, imitative polyphony, is occasionally
interrupted by voice thinning or homophonic texture employed in the
Introit verse, *Te decet*, and the motet, *Pie Jesu* (inserted between *Sanctus*
and *Osanna*).

The modern edition contains two versions of the Graduale: one for the
Parisian and the other for the Roman usage. The presence of two Graduales indicates that the demands for liturgical uniformity set forth by the
Council of Trent (1545–1563) were not always realized. Although the original score of the music does not contain any instrumental accompaniment, it is possible that instruments could have been used for doubling
the vocal parts.

Basic Data

EDITION

Missa pro Defunctis
Charles d'Helfer
Transcription and adaptation by Jean Charles Leon
Editions Aug. Zurfluh, A. Z. 1343. 1991

DURATION

Nine movements, 600 mm., perf. c. 26'

VOICING

Choir: SATB range: S-A6; B-F3

OUTLINE

Introit: 88 mm., 2 sections [*Requiem aeternam* & *Te decet*, satb]
Kyrie: 53 mm., 3 sections [*Kyrie, Christe, Kyrie*, satb]
Graduale, *Si ambulem*: 59 mm., 2 sections [*Si ambulem* & *Virga tua*, satb]
Graduale, *Requiem aeternam*: 75 mm., 2 sections [*Requiem aeternam* & *Virga tua*,
   satb]

Offertory: 142 mm., 2 sections [*Domine Jesu Christe* & *Hostias*, satb]
Sanctus: 42 mm., 2 sections [*Sanctus* & *Osanna*, satb]
Motet, *Pie Jesu*: 26 mm. 2 sections [*Miserere* & *Dona eis*, satb].
Benedictus: 34 mm., 2 sections [*Benedictus* & *Osanna*, satb]
Agnus Dei: 36 mm., 2 sections [*Agnus Dei* I, II, satb]
Communion: 45 mm., 2 sections [*Lux aeterna* & *Requiem aeternam*, satb]

DISCOGRAPHY

Astrée, E 8521, A Sei Voci, dir. Bernard Fabre Garrus. [The performance includes instrumental pieces and a reconstruction of the obsequies for two of the Dukes of Lorraine: Charles III (1608) and Henry II (1624).]

JOHANN CASPAR KERLL
April 9, 1627–February 13, 1693

Johann Kerll, began his musical studies with his father, an organist in Adorf. In his youth, he served as organist at the Viennese Imperial Court. He later worked with Giovanni Valentin and was sent to Rome to study with Carissimi and Frescobaldi. By 1656, he had been appointed vice *Kapellmeister* in Munich. His career took him through a succession of other positions, including organist of St. Stephen's Cathedral (Vienna, 1674) and, once again, organist for the Viennese Imperial Court (1677).

Kerll composed eleven known operas (none survive) and a small quantity of keyboard and instrumental music. He wrote eighteen masses, one of which is a requiem for five accompanied voices. This *concertante* requiem mass, composed in 1669, was modeled after the setting of Christoph Strauss. Its musical language is a blend of "Palestrina" style contrapuntal writing, and baroque *concertante* techniques for choir and soloists. Its numerous vocal solos are supported and embellished by a more vigorous and independent orchestral accompaniment than that of the earlier Strauss model.

The prevailing five-part choral texture is written in imitative-polyphonic style, with occasional homophonic passages in the Sequence (*Dies irae, Ingemisco, Oro supplex, Huic ergo*), the Offertory (*Sed signifer*), the Agnus Dei (*Dona eis*), and the Communion (*Cum sanctis*). The *Quam olim Abrahae* and *Osanna* texts are early examples of choral fugues. Canonic writing can be found in *Qui Mariam, Inter oves*, and many other places.

Kerll usually employed instruments in the following fashion: strings doubled the SATTB choral passages, but were reduced to a simple *basso continuo* for the *concertante*, SATTB soli passages. However, accompaniments for solo arias were far more colorful and independent from the vocal line. In the aria, *Quantus tremor*, the bass soloist is accompanied by four-part strings, playing *tremulando*. In the tenor solo, *Tuba mirum*, the strings play a martial, trumpet-like figuration. Dramatic, dotted rhythms accompany the alto solo, *Mors stupebit.*

The choral fabric is set in *stile antico* while the solos are composed in *stile moderno.* Purely instrumental passages are rarely found. A six-measure interlude between the *Domine Jesu Christe* and *Sed signifer* passages of the Offertory is the only example found in this work.

The structuring of the *Kyrie* and *Agnus Dei* into clear, one-movement pieces is a reflection of the composer's emphasis upon music, rather than liturgical text. Yet, Kerll was able to successfully illuminate, through his music, the meaning of the text. The remainder of the movements, even with their separate sections, suggests a similar trend. The work does not need any of the usual Gregorian intonations, although the Offertory verse, *Hostias,* is missing from this polyphonic setting.

Basic Data

EDITION

Denkmäler der Tonkunst in Österreich. Vol. XXX/I, Band 59
ed., Guido Adler
Graz, Austria. 1960 [C (soprano, alto, tenor) & F clefs]

DURATION

Seven movements, 537 mm., perf., c. 38′

VOICING AND ORCHESTRATION

Choir: SATTB range: S-E6; B-E3
Soloists: SATTB
Orchestra: vla. I/II/III, db. or bsn., & org.

OUTLINE

Introit: 52 mm. [FM] 2 sections:
  Requiem aeternam & *Te decet,* sattb soli/choir; *Requiem aeternam* is repeated. ABA form.
Kyrie: 31 mm. [FM] *adagio.* 2 sections:
  Kyrie, Christe-Kyrie, sattb soli/choir. ABA form.
Sequence, *Dies irae:* 228 mm., 17 sections:
  Dies irae, [em] satb choir; *Quantus tremor,* [CM] B solo; *Tuba mirum,* [em] T solo; *Mors stupebit,* [DM] A solo; *Liber scriptus,* [em] satb choir; *Judex ergo,* [em] satb choir; *Quid sum miser,* [em] S solo; *Recordare,* [GM] T solo; *Quaerens me,* [GM] T solo; *Juste judex,* [em] satb choir; *Ingemisco,* [em] satb choir; *Qui Mariam,* [bm] ATB soli; *Inter oves,* [em] SA soli; *Confutatis,* [em] S solo; *Oro supplex,* [em] satb choir; *Lacrymosa,* [GM] S solo; *Huic ergo,* [em] satb choir.
Offertory: 89 mm. [gm] 3 sections:
  Domine Jesu Christe; Sed signifer, SATTB soli/choir; *Quam olim,* sattb choir. Fugue.

Sanctus: 72 mm. [FM] 3 sections:
  Sanctus, sattb choir; *Osanna*, SATTB soli/choir (Fugue); *Benedictus*, SAT soli trio
  Osanna is repeated.
Agnus Dei: 32 mm. [FM] 1 section:
  Agnus Dei, SATTB soli/choir
Communion: 33 mm. [FM] 2 sections:
  Lux aeterna, ATB trio; *Requiem aeternam*, SAT soli/sattb choir.

DISCOGRAPHY

Scene, MDG 614 0739-2, Hassler Consort, cond. Franz Raml.

DON JUAN DE LIENAS
fl. 1620–1650

The ancestry of Juan de Lienas is quite obscure. There exists the possibility that he may have come to Mexico from Spain, but the use of the title
"Don" might indicate that he was a *hidalgo* (member of the Spanish lesser
nobility). It could also suggest that he was an Indian prince (*cacique*) who
had taken the name of his sponsor at the time of his baptism. He was a
married man and is thought to have been active in Mexico City sometime
between 1620 and 1650.

All of his music is found in a manuscript found at the Convento del
Carmen, near Mexico City, and the Newberry Choirbooks (located in Chicago). The Newberry Choirbooks were for use in the Encarnacion Convent, a wealthy convent situated in Mexico City. His known music
includes a mass for five voices, two *Magnificats*, two sets of *Lamentations*,
a handful of motets, and one requiem for five voices.

The current edition of his requiem includes only the Graduale, *Requiem
aeternam* and its verse *In memoria*. The verse is arranged in two sections,
In memoria and *Ab auditione*. The Graduale and the concluding line of the
verse, *Ab auditione* are scored for SSATB, while the verse opening, *In
memoria*, is set for a reduced SSAT arrangement. The prevailing texture is
imitative polyphony. Although the Gregorian intonation is provided, the
polyphony following it seems to be freely composed.

Basic Data

EDITION

Tesoro de la Música Polifonica en Mexico
Vol. I
El Codice del Convento del Carmen
Transcription and notes by Jesus Bal y Gay
Mexico 1952

DURATION

Two movements, 84 mm.

VOICING

Choir: SSATB range: S-G6; B-C4

OUTLINE

Graduale: 84 mm., 3 sections: *Requiem aeternam*, ssatb, *In memoria*, ssat; *Ab auditione*, ssatb.

DISCOGRAPHY

None found.

ADAM VÁCLAV MICHNA
c. 1600–November 2, 1676

Adam Michna was the outstanding seventeenth-century composer in the Czech musical landscape. He probably received his earliest musical education from his father, the town organist and leader of the castle trumpeters in Jindrichhuv Hradec. He later studied at the town's local Jesuit Gymnasium. Sometime around 1633, Michna was appointed to the position of organist in his hometown. He possessed a licensed wine vault, which brought him revenue, and owned a considerable amount of land.

Except for a collection of lute pieces, most of his music seems to have been lost. The remaining works are liturgical compositions. A setting of the *Magnificat*, two hymnals (*Czech Marian Music* and *Music for the Liturgical Year*), the *Missa Sancti Wenceslai*, and an important collection, *Sacra et litaniae* (Prague, 1654), still exist. The collection is significant because it contains six masses, a requiem, two litany settings, and a *Te Deum* (all works scored for four to eight voices and instruments). The *Cantiones pro defunctis* (1647, 1661) include nine pieces in Czech.

Michna's style is a mixture of the *stile antico* and *stile moderno*. A Palestrina style of polyphonic choral writing stands, side by side, with the newer, expressive techniques of the baroque idiom. Most of the solo vocal melodies of the requiem have ornate, elaborate figurations, similar to the mature madrigals of Monteverdi or the *Geistliche Concerte* by Schütz.

The *Missa pro defunctis*, except for the opening *Sinfonia* and *Lacrymosa* (Sequence), remains in manuscript. Composed in 1654, this work is scored for six to ten parts, and includes a *concertante* SATB choir and SATB soli, violins I and II, three trombones, and *basso continuo* for organ and theorbo. The strings double the upper vocal parts while the trombones duplicate the bass and tenor lines. The addition or subtraction of either group from the scoring adds expressive color to the vocal solos.

Four requiem movements (Introit, Tract, Sequence, and *Sanctus*) possess instrumental introductions, more than any other early baroque requiem listed in this study. This trend will come to full flower in the last decade of the century. The choral fabric employs a mixture of homophonic and imitative polyphonic textures, with the latter playing a predominant role.

Although most of the melodic material for the requiem was freely invented, Gregorian intonations for the Introit and verse, *Te decet*, the Offertory and verse, *Hostias*, and the opening of the *Agnus Dei* were still needed. The intonations preserved an important link to an older liturgical tradition as it was gradually transformed by the baroque composer.

Michna employed some "word painting" in the passages, *Quantus tremor* (vocal shakes) and *Tuba mirum* (trombone solo) of the Sequence. One novel feature of the *missa* is the slight rearrangement, in the order of the fifteenth through seventeenth verses of the *Dies irae* sequence and the insertion of a rarely used verse, *Ne me perdas . . . .*

Basic Data

EDITION

The *Sinfonia* and *Lacrymosa* in:
Dějiny České Hudby v Příkladech [History of Czech Music in Examples]
Jaroslav Pohanka
Státní nakladatelství krásné literatury, hudby a umení, Prague. 1958
[State Publishing House for *Belles Lettres*, Music and Art]
A performing edition for the CD, listed below, was prepared by Robert Hugo.

DURATION

Nine movements, perf. c. 28′

VOICING AND ORCHESTRATION

Choir: SATB range: S-F6; B-G3
Soloists: SATB [alto or counter-tenor]
Instruments: vn. I/II, 3 tbn., and *basso continuo* [org. & therobo]

OUTLINE

Introit: 4′
    Requiem aeternam, Te decet, satb choir/soli. *Requiem aeternam* is repeated.
    Instrumental *sinfonia.*
Kyrie: 1′50″
    Kyrie, Christe, Kyrie, satb choir/soli.
Tract: 2′16″

Chapter 5

Absolve Domine, satb choir/soli. Instrumental *sinfonia.*
Sequence: 6'26", 4 "movements" [*Dies irae, Quid sum miser, Qui Mariam, Lacrymosa*]
Instrumental sinfonia.
Dies irae, satb choir; *Quantus tremor,* STB soli; *Tuba mirum,* A solo; *Mors stupebit,* T
solo; *Liber scriptus,* B solo; *Judex ergo,* satb choir. *Quid sum miser,* ST soli; *Rex
tremendae,* AB soli; *Recordare,* ST soli; *Quaerens me,* AB soli; *Juste Judex,* SATB soli;
Ingemisco, satb choir. *Qui Mariam,* SA soli; *Preces meae,* TA soli; *Oro supplex,* A
solo; *Ne me perdas,* ST soli; *Inter oves,* ATB soli; *Confutatis,* satb choir. *Lacrimosa,*
S solo; *Judicandus homo,* B solo; *Pie Jesu,* satb choir.
Offertory: 5'
Domine Jesu Christe & Hostias, satb choir/soli.
Sanctus: 2'12"
Sanctus, satb choir/soli. Instrumental *sinfonia.*
Agnus Dei: 1'52"
Agnus Dei I, II, III, SATB soli.
Communion: 2'18"
Lux aeterna & Requiem, satb choir/soli.
Post Communion: 2'
Requiem aeternam, satb choir/soli.

DISCOGRAPHY

Matous, OSA BIEM Capella Regia Musicalis, dir. Robert Hugo.

ETIENNE MOULINIÉ
c. 1600–after 1669

In his youth, Moulinié was a singer at Narbonne Cathedral. In 1628, he
entered into the service of Gaston of Orleans, the younger brother of the
French king, as music director. He remained in this position until Gaston's death in 1660. During the same period (1634–1649), he also worked
for Gaston's daughter. Moulinié composed the bulk of his musical compositions for this family. For Gaston, he wrote *ballets de cour* (a type of
ballet that included pantomime, choruses, and dances) and for his daughter, Mlle. de Montpensier, *airs* (solo songs with lute accompaniment).

   In 1661, he was appointed Director of Music to the estates of Lan-
guedoc, where he remained until his death. Among Moulinié's surviving
works are ten volumes of *airs,* the *Méslanges* (an anthology of sacred
pieces, including motets, cantiques, and litanies), and a *Missa pro defunctis*
for five voices.

   The *Missa pro defunctis* was first published in 1636 by Peter Ballard
(Paris). It might have been performed at the funeral service for the composer's brother, Antoine (1658) and for the death anniversary service of

his employer, Gaston d'Orleans (March 21, 1661). Scored for SATBarB choir, this work is a masterpiece of Renaissance-style, vocal writing, employing both florid melodic lines and imitative contrapuntal techniques. Imitative, contrapuntal texture is found in each movement, except for one line of the Offertory verse, *Tu suscipe*, which is set in a fiery, declamatory passage. The *Benedictus* is scored for a reduced, contrasting SAT texture.

Gregorian intonations are present in the Introit, the opening of the two Graduale settings (Parisian and Roman), Offertory, *Sanctus,* and Responsory. The plainsong *Kyrie* is paraphrased in the appropriate movement and the *Dies irae* melody is employed in the Responsory. The spirit of the plainchant melodies permeates the entire *Missa*.

Basic Data

EDITION

Missa Pro Defunctis
Transcription de D. Launay
Heugel & Cie., Editeurs, Paris 1952 H. 31630

DURATION

Seven movements, 425 mm.

VOICING

Choir: SATBarB range: S-G 6; B-E 3

OUTLINE

Introit: 67 mm., 2 sections: *Requiem aeternam, Te decet,* satbarb.
Kyrie: 90 mm., 3 sections: *Kyrie, Christe, Kyrie,* satbarb.
Graduale: 59 mm., 2 sections: *Requiem aeternam,* satbarb, *In memoria,* sat.
Graduale: 28 mm., 2 sections: *Si ambulem, Virga tua,* satbarb.
Offertory: 78 mm., 3 sections: *Domine Jesu Christe, Quam olim, Hostias,* satbarb.
Sanctus: 36 mm., 3 sections: *Sanctus, Hosanna,* satbarb, *Benedictus,* sat.
Responsory: 67 mm., 3 sections: *Libera me, Dies illa, Dum veneris,* satbarb.

DISCOGRAPHY

Ensemble Vocal Sagittarius and La Fenice, cond. Michel Laplénie.

GIUSEPPE OTTAVIO PITONI
March 18, 1657–February 1, 1743

Pitoni was noted for an exceptionally large output of church music. His parents enrolled him in a music school in his fifth year and his early career was marked by a succession of positions; chorister at St. Giovanni dei Fiorentini, Rome (1665), *maestro di cappella* at Monterotondo, near Rome (1673), and *maestro* at Rieti Cathedral (1676). In the following year, he was appointed to a similar post at the Collegiate Church of St. Marco, in the Palazzo Venezia, Rome. He remained in this post until his death. At the same time, he held several other important positions; *maestro di cappella* at St. John Lateran (1708–19) and at the *Cappella Giulia* at St. Peter's (1719).

His compositions include 270 mass settings and mass sections (four, six, and eight voices), 205 introits, at least 230 graduales, numerous alleluia settings, fifteen sequences (two, four, six, eight, and ten voices), 210 offertories, sixteen communions, thirty-seven litanies, about 780 psalms, 220 canticles, twenty-five sets of the *Lamentations*, about 640 antiphons, 250 hymns, more than 235 motets, and numerous settings of the *Magnificat* and the Passion.

Although many of these pieces are simple monodic or four-part settings, there are works that include as many as sixteen voice parts. At the time of his death, he was working on a complete setting of the mass, arranged for twelve choirs. His musical language is a mixture of the contrapuntal Palestrina style and the *concertante* techniques of the Venetians. Many of the late works are primarily chordal in texture. He wrote four books on music theory and current musical practices.

The *Missa pro defunctis* for four voices (SATB) was first published on January 22, 1688, in Rome. This conservative piece, composed in *stile antico,* is an excellent model of unaccompanied writing. These conservative traits include the *a cappella* setting of the text, the constant use of imitative polyphony (paired imitation, canon, and points of imitation), and paraphrase of the Gregorian melodies.

The absence of the Gregorian intonations and melodic passages that include wide leaps or arpeggiated contours, as well as dramatic dotted-patterns and sixteenth-note figures, suggest the influence of the *stile moderno.* Although many requiems of the period (Strauss, Galan, Michna, and Kerll) were already using a fuller instrumental support and an increased role for the solo voice, Pitoni seems to have consciously chosen a path toward what he might have considered to be a restoration of "true" liturgical style.

The prevailing four-part (SATB) texture of the music is frequently reduced to a more intimate, three-part (SST or ATB) fabric. The soprano line is often divided between soprano I and II in the reduced scorings. (see Outline) The reduced passages can be sung by the choir or by soli in *concertante* style. No Gregorian intonations are needed for this work, but chant paraphrases are usually found in the soprano or tenor lines and, occasionally, the other vocal lines.

Basic Data

EDITIONS

1. Giuseppe Ottavio Pitoni. Requiem with Libera for mixed voicesed., Eugen Leipold, Willy Muller. Süddeutscher Musikverlag. Heidelberg. 1983 [This edition does not include the *Dies irae*.

2. Musica Divina, Vol. I ed. Karl Proske Johnson Reprint Corp. London. 1973 [C (soprano, alto, tenor) & F clefs] [This edition includes the *Dies irae*.]

DURATION

Nine movements, 1048 mm.

VOICING

Choir: S[S]ATB range: S-F6; B-E3

OUTLINE

Introit: 61 mm., 2 sections [*Requiem aeternam*, satb; *Te decet*, sst] *Requiem aeternam* is repeated.
Kyrie: 40 mm., 3 sections [*Kyrie*, satb; *Christe*, atb; *Kyrie*, satb]
Tract: 84 mm., 1 section [*Absolve*, satb]
Sequence: 325 mm., 16 sections
  Dies irae, satb; *Quantus tremor*, sst; *Tuba mirum*, atb; *Mors stupebit*, satb; *Liber scriptus*, sst; *Judex ergo*, atb; *Quid sum*, satb; *Rex tremendae*, sst; *Recordare*, atb; *Quaerens me*, satb; *Ingemisco*, sst; *Qui Mariam*, satb; *Inter oves*, atb; *Confutatis*, satb; *Oro supplex*, satb; *Lacrymosa*, satb.
Offertory: 176 mm., 4 sections [*Domine Jesu Christe*, satb; *Sed signifer*, atb; *Quam olim*, satb; *Hostias*, sst] *Quam olim Abrahae* is repeated.
Sanctus: 32 mm., 1 section [*Sanctus*, satb]
Benedictus: 37 mm., 2 sections [*Benedictus*, atb; *Hosanna*, satb]
Agnus Dei: 56 mm., 1 section [*Agnus Dei*, satb]
Communion: 50 mm., 2 sections [*Lux aeterna*, satb; *Requiem aeternam*, satb]
Responsory: 187 mm., 7 sections [*Libera me*, satb; *Tremens factus*, sst; *Quando caeli*, satb; *Dies illa*, atb; *Dum veneris*, satb; *Requiem aeternam*, sst; *Kyrie*, satb]

DISCOGRAPHY

None found.

The *Missa pro defunctis* for eight voices (SATB-SATB) was composed during the period from February 1734 to October 1735. An additional, separate Introit and *Kyrie* (included in the 1959 edition) was composed earlier in 1721. This dramatic, polychoral setting for double choir employs a chordal, homophonic texture throughout. Dynamic and texture contrasts are achieved by the union or separation of the two choirs.

Pitoni maintained the traditional, smaller divisions of individual movements, such as the Graduale, Offertory, and *Sanctus-Benedictus*, yet he linked the Introit and *Kyrie* texts to form one continuous movement. The three sections of the *Agnus Dei* and the two of the Communion are fused into single, through-composed movements. The multi-sectional Responsory, *Libera me*, is consolidated into one movement, too. Particularly noteworthy is the novel setting of the Introit and *Kyrie* in which both sections are joined together to form one continuous movement. A *basso seguente* is provided in the 1959 edition.

Basic Data

EDITION
Documenta Maiora. Liturgiae Polychorlis
Sanctae Ecclesiae Romanae. No. 5
G. O. Pitoni
Missa Pro Defunctis per 8 voci
ed., Lorenzo Feininger
Societas Universalis Sanctis Ceciliae. Tridenti, 1959
[C (soprano, alto, tenor) & F clefs]

DURATION
Eight movements, 386 mm.

VOICING
Choir: Choir I [SATB] Choir II [SATB] range: S-F#6; B-F3 [C3 rare]
Instruments: organ [*basso seguente*]

OUTLINE
Introit-Kyrie: 82 mm., 1 movement, [choirs I/II]
Graduale: 39 mm., 5 sections [*Requiem aeternam*, choirs I/II; *In memoria*, choir I; *Absolve*, choirs I/II; *Et gratia tua*, choir II; *Et lucis eterne*, choirs I/II].
Offertory: 121 mm., 4 sections [*Domine Jesu Christe*; *Quam Olim*; *Hostias, Quam olim*, choirs I/II]
Sanctus & Benedictus: 64 mm., 2 sections [choirs I/II]
Agnus Dei: 43 mm., 1 movement [choirs I/II]
Communion: 37 mm., 1 movement [choirs I/II]
Responsory: 123 mm., 1 movement [choirs I/II]
Additional: Introit-Kyrie: 104 mm., 3 sections [*Requiem aeternam*, choirs I/II; *Te decet*, sst; *Kyrie*, choirs I/II]

DISCOGRAPHY
None found.

JOHANN STADLMAYR
c. 1575–July 12, 1648

This German composer was probably born in Freising, Bavaria. In 1603, he was in the service of the Archbishop of Salzburg and in the following year was married and made vice-*Kapellmeister* there. Shortly afterward, he became *Kapellmeister*. He kept this post until 1607, when he was appointed to a similar position at the court in Innsbruck. He remained at Innsbruck for the remainder of his life, in the service of the Hapsburg Archdukes, Maximillian II and Leopold V.

Stadlmayr was quite famous and considered one of the best composers of his time. Praetorius mentioned him in his encyclopedia, *Syntagma musicum*, Vol. III (1618), and Johann Gottfried Walther referred to him in his *Musikalishes Lexicon* (1732). A selection of his compositions appeared in Italian and Dutch anthologies. He was, almost exclusively, a composer of church music. His works show the typical traits of the era: a contrapuntal "Palestrina" style, blended with the new, expressive baroque idiom.

Stadlmayr was a prolific composer, writing about thirty masses, numerous settings of the *Magnificat*, and about 250 motets, psalms, hymns, introits, or vesper settings. These works are arranged for four, five, six, seven, eight, nine, and twelve voices and most use some form of instrumental accompaniment, ranging from a simple *basso continuo*, to those scored for full strings and brass.

The one requiem that he composed is scored for SATB choir and *basso continuo*. First published in 1641 (Innsbruck), it bears the title, *Missae breves a IV cum una pro defunctis et alia. V voc: concertatae*. This anthology of masses is dedicated to the widow of Leopold I, Claudia von Medici. The *missa* is rather conservative in style, recalling the older polyphonic style of Palestrina. The occasional expressive homophonic passages, particularly of the *Agnus Dei* and the Introit verse, *Te decet*, reveal his debt to the Franco-Flemish school, but the presence of a *basso continuo* informs us of his awareness of the newer baroque spirit.

Except for occasional voice thinning, the four-part fabric is maintained throughout most of the work. The prevailing, homophonic texture of the Sequence, *Dies irae*, includes unison, two-, three-, and four-part writing, with which the Gregorian melody is harmonized. Plainsong intonations are provided for the appropriate movements and virtually every movement of this work contains a paraphrase of the proper Gregorian funeral melody.

Basic Data

EDITION

Missa Pro Defunctis
Johann Stadlmayr
ed. Wolfgang Furlinger
Musikverlag Alfred Coppenrath, Altötting. 1981

DURATION

Nine movements, 381 mm.

VOICING

Choir: SATB range: S-D6; B-F3
Instruments: organ [*basso continuo*]

OUTLINE

Introit: 19 mm., 2 sections: *Requiem aeternam* & *Te decet*, satb.
Kyrie: 35 mm., 3 sections: *Kyrie*; *Christe*; *Kyrie*, satb.
Graduale: 21 mm., 1 section: *Requiem aeternam*, satb.
Tract: 31 mm., 1 section: *Absolve, Domine*, satb.
Sequence, *Dies irae*: 116 mm., 18 sections:
   Dies irae, satb; *Quantus tremor*, unison alto; *Tuba mirum*, unison tenor; *Mors stu-pebit*, unison soprano; *Liber scriptus*, unison bass; *Judex ergo*, satb; *Quid sum miser*, sat; *Rex tremendae*, unison bass; *Recordare*, satb; *Quaerens me*, at; *Juste judex*, satb; *Ingemisco*, atb; *Qui Mariam*, satb; *Preces meae*, sa; *Inter oves*, satb; *Confutatis*, sat; *Oro supplex*, tb; *Lacrimosa*, satb.
Offertory: 79 mm., 2 sections: *Domine Jesu Christe* & *Hostias*, satb.
Sanctus: 34 mm., 2 sections: *Sanctus* & *Benedictus*, satb.
Agnus Dei: 23 mm., 3 sections: *Agnus* I, II, III, satb.
Communion: 23 mm., 2 sections: *Lux aeterna* & *Requiem aeternam*, satb.

DISCOGRAPHY

None found.

CHRISTOPH STRAUSS
c. 1575/80–June 1631

Christoph Strauss came from a musical family that had served the royal Hapsburg family for many years. One of his earliest appointments was as organist of the court church of St. Michael (1601). In 1617, he was appointed director of the music for the court, a position held only for a short time. Finally, he was appointed organist to St. Stephen's Cathedral (Vienna) in 1626, a position occupied until his death.

   He published two volumes of sacred music, the first (1613) consisted of thirty-six motets for five to ten voices and instruments, and the second (1636), sixteen masses for eight to twenty voices with *basso continuo* and instruments. Two requiems are included among the mass settings. His musical style is a combination of the older Renaissance vocal tradition and the newer Venetian technique with its use of divided choirs (*cori spezzati*) of voices and instruments; a blending of traditional polyphony and the dramatic presentation of declamatory, expressive homophony.

The *G Major Requiem*, first published in 1636, is one of four masses designated *"concertata."* This composition, probably written during his tenure at St. Stephen's, is of singular importance because it likely served as a model for later composers, such as Heinrich Biber, Leopold I, Adam Michna, and even Johann Kerll (himself a student of Carissimi). It is *concertante* music in the fullest sense of the word. The gradual shift away from a purely liturgical music, toward a decorative, soul-stirring church music is clearly expressed and felt in this composition.

This composition of this music represents a defining moment for the *stile nuovo*. Earlier baroque requiem settings employed *bassi continuo* and *bassi segunte*; some composers doubled the vocal lines with organ and string or wind instruments (without indicating which, where, or when), but Strauss clearly spelled-out his scheme for instruments and voices. In the *G Major Requiem*, both voices and instruments are employed in *tutti-soli* fashion and even though the instruments are frequently used to double the vocal lines, there are those occasional passages or lines that are independent from the vocal fabric. The contrasts between *soli* and *tutti* passages are powerful and vivid. Strauss made his music palette more colorful and appetizing in comparison with older settings.

The musical forces for the requiem are divided into two groups; Choir I (four-part, SSTT, vocal, or instrumental) and Choir II (six-part, TBarBarBarBB, vocal or instrumental). Choir II is scored for six parts, and only for *tutti* vocal or instrumental passages. However, Choir I is scored for four parts, and employs both *tutti* and *soli* instrumental or vocal passages. During the *tutti* passages, instrumental doubling takes place. Strauss indicates the use or disuse of the instruments with the words, *Son*, (*sonant*) or *Ta* (*tacent*). This approach allows for a wide range of timbre and dynamic control. Strauss seems to have preferred to use instruments in family groups (trombones or viols) for the *Requiem*. Present throughout is an organ *basso continuo*.

The *Requiem* begins with an instrumental *symphonia ad imitationem campanae*, in which the composer depicted the tolling of the funeral bells of St. Stephen's. The prevailing, ten-part texture of the double, choral-instrumental ensemble is a mixture of imitative polyphonic and expressive homophonic writing. This massive texture is further enhanced or reduced by vocal-part thinning, canonic writing, vocal solos, duets, quartets, massed choral passages, and changes in orchestration.

The setting of the *Dies irae* is somewhat novel; verses seven to seventeen are omitted, while the remainder are grouped into three large, continuous sections (Verses 1–3, 4–6, and 18–19). The omitted verses might have been sung in plainchant. Although the Gregorian intonations are needed for the Introit, Offertory, *Sanctus*, *Agnus Dei*, and Communion, the polyphonic music does not appear to be based upon the Gregorian melodies.

Several ornamental passages, such as the "bell" effects of the opening sinfonia, word painting on *Et lux* (Communion) and *Et semini* (Offertory), as well as the string tremolo on the text, *Quantus tremor* (Sequence), add a dramatic, decorative touch to the music.

Basic Data

EDITION

Denkmäler der Tonkunst in Öesterreich
Vol. XXX (59)
Drei Requiem (Kerll-Strauss-Biber)
Editor, Guido Adler [C (soprano, tenor)] & F clefs]

DURATION

Eight movements, 673 mm.

VOICING AND INSTRUMENTATION

Choir I, SSTT or vn. I & II, vla. I & II
Choir II, TBarBarBarBB or vn. I/II/III/IV/V, violone [or vla., vc. I/II/III/IV and db.], org. [*basso continuo*]. Range: S-F6; B-F3 [occasional E3, D3, C3, G2]

OUTLINE

Sinfonia: "Bell" symphony: 29 mm., seven-part strings and organ *b.c.*
Introit: 84 mm.
    Requiem aeternam; Te decet, ten-part choir/strings
Kyrie: 80 mm.
    Kyrie; Christe; Kyrie, ten-part
Sequence: 119 mm.
    Dies irae; Mors stupebit; Lacrimosa, ten-part
Offertory: 121 mm.
    Dominie Jesu Christe, ten-part. Verse, *Hostias* sung in plainchant
Sanctus: 104 mm.
    Sanctus; Benedictus, ten-part
Agnus Dei: 69 mm.
    Agnus Dei I; *Agnus Dei* II; *Agnus Dei* III, ten-part
Communion: 67 mm.
    Lux aeterna; Requiem aeternam, ten-part

DISCOGRAPHY

None found.

LODOVICO DA VIADANA
c. 1560–May 2, 1627

This composer, born in Viadana, near Parma, was a member of the Grossi family. He took the name *Viadana* when he entered the order of the Minor

Observants, sometime around 1588. He might have been a pupil of Constanzo Porta. Viadana was *maestro di cappella* at Mantua cathedral from 1594 to about 1597. By 1602, he held the same position at the convent of St. Luca in Cremona. Similar cathedral positions followed at Concordia and Fano. He finally settled into the Convent of St. Andrea, Gualteri.

Viadana's compositions are, for the most part, written in the sacred *a cappella* vocal style, but from Opus 12, onward, he began to add a *basso per l'organo* to his compositions. This bass line was not a true *basso continuo*, but rather an early type of thoroughbass that duplicated, usually on the organ, the lowest part of the composition. His *Cento Concerti ecclesiastici*, Op. 12 (1602) is chronologically the first publication to provide a *basso continuo* with sacred music.

Stylistically, his music stands between the polyphonic writing of Palestrina and the emerging *concertante* style of the early baroque. His *Salmi* (Psalms) for four choirs (Op. 27) includes one choir of five solo voices and three choirs of voices and instruments. Three organs and a chitarrone realize the harmony; strings, cornetts, bassoons, and trombones double the vocal lines.

Some of his published works include *Missarum liber primus* for four voices (1596), *Concerti ecclesiastici, libro secondo* (1607), *Lamentationes*, Op. 22 (1609), *Il terzo libro de concerti ecclesiastici*, Op. 24, *Salmi per cantare e concertare* for four choirs, Op. 27 (1612), and the *Responsoria ad lamentationes, libro primo*, Op. 23. There exist two volumes of canzonettas (1590 and 1594) and other secular pieces as well. Viadana composed three requiems; *Missa defunctorum* for three voices and *basso continuo* (1598), *Officium defunctorum* for four voices, Op. 11 (1600), and *Officium ac Missa defunctorum* for five voices, Op. 15 (1604). Opus 11, *Officium Defunctorum*, (Venice, 1600) was published by Jacob Vincenti.

This work is scored for SATB (TTBarB) choir. A dense, four-part texture is maintained throughout the work, broken only by occasional rests in the vocal lines. The writing appears to have been influenced by the Franco-Flemish tradition because the Introit verse, *Te decet*, and the *Agnus Dei* were written in expressive homophonic style. The *Benedictus* and parts of the Tract are homophonic, too, and the remainder of the work is a blend of imitative and nonimitative polyphony.

Although the melodic design of this requiem is based upon the Gregorian chant, the composer's use of melodic snippets effectively hides the original from view. This use of fragments embodied a general trend in which the Gregorian tune was replaced with original material.

The only modern edition of this work (1966) does not include the setting of the Sequence, *Dies irae*, found in the first-edition. This work includes not only the music for the requiem mass, but also music for the complete Office for the Dead, as follows:

- Vespers: *Dilexi, quoniam* (Psalm 114), *Ad Dominum cum tribularer* (Psalm 120), *De profundis* (Psalm 129), *Confitebor tibi Domine* (Psalm 137).
- Matins: *Regem cui omnia* & *Venite exultemus* (Invitatory), *Verba mea auribus* (Psalm 5), *Domine, ne in fu rore* (Psalm 6), *Domine Deus meus* (Psalm 7).
- The three Responsories: *Credo quod Redemptor-Qui Lazarum-Domine quando.*
- Lauds: *Ego sum resurrectio* (Antiphon), *Benedictus Dominus* (Canticle of Zachary), the Litany, *De profundis* (Psalm 129), *Miserere mei* (Psalm 50). Finally, the edition of 1600 also contains the songs for Second and Third Nocturne, with the responsories.

Basic Data

EDITION

Musica Divina, Heft 19
Ludovico Grossi da Viadana
Missa pro defunctis
Vier gleiche oder gemischte Stimmen, a cappella
ed. August Scharnagl
Verlag Friedrich Pustet, Regensburg. 1966

DURATION

Eight movements, 292 mm.

VOICING

Choir: SATB [TTBarB] range: S-G6; B-F3

OUTLINE

Introit: 26 mm., 2 sections: *Requiem aeternam* & *Te decet*, satb.
Kyrie: 33 mm., 3 sections: *Kyrie, Christe, Kyrie*, satb.
Graduale: 27 mm., 2 sections: *Requiem aeternam* & *In memoria*, satb.
Tract: 35 mm., 4 sections: *Absolve Domine, Et gratia tua, Et lucis*, satb.
Offertory: 86 mm., 3 sections: *Domine Jesu Christe, Quam olim, Hostias*, satb.
Sanctus: 23 mm., 2 sections: *Sanctus* & *Benedictus*, satb.
Agnus Dei: 31 mm., 3 sections: *Agnus Dei I, II, III*, satb.
Communion: 30 mm., 2 sections: *Lux aeterna* & *Requiem aeternam*, satb.

DISCOGRAPHY

None found.

The *Officium ac Missa defunctorum a cinque voci* (SATTB), Opus 15 was published in 1604 by Jacob Vincenti. In addition to the music of the requiem mass, Viadana included other pieces for the Office. Among them are: Matins: Invitatory, *Regem cui* (antiphon), and *Venite exsultemus Domino* (Psalm 94) First Nocturne: *Verba mea* (Psalm 5), *Domine, ne in furore* (Psalm 6), *Domine Deus meus* (Psalm 7) and the three responsories, *Credo quod Redemptor, Qui Lazarum,* and *Domine quando veneris.*

The *Officium* contains three other responsories: *Subvenite* (Burial service), *Ne ricorderis* (Second Nocturne), and *Libera me Domine* (Third Nocturne).

The requiem mass for five voices, SATTB, is an extremely moving and beautiful work. It possesses both conservative and forward-looking elements; conservative in its use of a supple vocal polyphony; modern with its application of the *concertante* style. Its Gregorian intonations provide a link with the musical and liturgical past, yet the chant paraphrases melodic passages in which the chant tune is scarcely recognizable, pointing toward a future in which the time-honored, *cantus-firmus* technique will be abandoned.

Basic Data

EDITION

A modern transcription, made by Rodobaldo Tibaldi for the CD performance, is listed in the discography. Because no edition was available to the writer, performing times, rather than number of measures, are used in the Outline.

DURATION

Seven movements, perf. c. 28'

VOICING

Choir: SATTB
Instruments: 2 cornets, 3 sackbuts, double bass gamba and org. All instruments double the vocal lines.

OUTLINE

Introit: 3'36", 4 sections: *Requiem aeternam, Te decet, Et tibi, Exaudi.*
Kyrie: 2'28", 3 sections: *Kyrie, Christe, Kyrie.*
Sequence: 10' 40", 21 sections alternating polyphony (odd-numbered verses) and Gregorian chant (even-numbered verses) (H = homophony, P = polyphony, IP = imitative polyphony) *Dies irae,* H; *Tuba mirum,* H; *Liber scriptus,* IP; *Quid sum miser,* P; *Recordare,* IP; *Juste judex,* H; *Qui Mariam,* IP; *Inter oves,* P; *Oro supplex,* P; *Judicandus,* IP; *Dona eis requiem,* P.
Offertory: 5', three sections: *Domine Jesu Christe, Hostias, Quam olim Abrahae*
Sanctus: 1'51", 2 sections: *Sanctus & Benedictus.*
Agnus Dei: 1'54", 3 sections: *Agnus I, II, III.*
Communion: 2' 15", 2 sections: *Lux aeterna & Requiem aeternam.*

DISCOGRAPHY

Stradivarius, DULCIMER STR 33430, Vox Hesperia, cond. Romano Vettori.

FRANCESCO BRUSA
c. 1700–after 1768

Very little is known about this Venetian composer, but he was appointed organist at St. Mark's in December 1726. By this time, he had already composed a number of operas. He was the manager of his own opera company in 1756. Finally, he is known to have been choirmaster of the *Ospedale degli Incurabli* in Venice, from 1766 to 1768. During this period, he composed a *Messa pro defunctis* for three voices (SSA) and instruments. He has also composed a small quantity of other sacred pieces, as well as a number of operas from the earlier part of his career.

The *Messa pro defunctis* (1767), a *concertante* work, is a superior piece, full of life, energy, and vitality. It is scored for SSA choir, strings, and organ (*continuo*). The prevailing choral texture is a mixture of imitative polyphony and expressive declamatory writing. A number of canonic passages are similar to the one found in the initial *Requiem aeternam*. Brusa was also fond of using suspensions, "walking" basses, and the interplay of the major and minor modes.

The chamber orchestra plays a semi-independent role in this requiem setting. Although it supports the three-part choir, there are also a number of instrumental introductions and bridges throughout the work, as well as very modest obbligati for the solo and choral passages. Many of its numerous eighth-note rhythmic patterns serve as an engine for driving the work along at a fast pace. Dramatic dotted rhythms accompany the *Dies irae*. Although several quiet moments are in the work, not a sad passage is to be found.

Basic Data

EDITION

Peter Simtich prepared a modern edition for the listed recording. [see Discography]

DURATION

Nine movements, perf., 20′

VOICING AND ORCHESTRATION

Choir: SSA

Instruments: vn. I/II, vc. Org. [*basso continuo*]

OUTLINE

Introit: 3 sections, 1 movement. ABA form
Requiem aeternam, [*allegretto*] ssa choir; *Te decet*, ssa choir; *Requiem aeternam* is repeated.
Kyrie: 3 movements
Kyrie, [*allegro*] ssa choir
Christe, [*andante*] ssa choir
Kyrie, [*allegro*] ssa choir
Sequence, *Dies irae*: 3 movements. Verses 1-3; Verses 4 & 5; Verses 6-18.
Dies irae: [*Dies irae* [*largo*] ssa choir; *Quantus tremor* [*allegretto*] ssa choir; *Tuba mirum* [*alle gretto*] ssa choir]
Mors stupebit: [*Mors stupebit* [*adagio*] SA duet; *Liber scriptus* [*adagio*] A solo]
Judex ergo: [*Judex ergo* [*allegro*] ssa choir; *Quid sum miser* [*andante*] S solo; *Rex tremendae* [*allegro*] ssa choir; *Recordare* [*andante*] S solo; *Quaerens me* [*allegro*] SA solo; *Juste Judex* [*allegro*] ssa choir; *Ingemisco* [*allegro*] ssa choir; *Qui Mariam* [*andante*] SA duet; *Preces meae* [*andante*] A solo; *Inter oves* [*allegro*] ssa choir; *Confutatis* [*allegro*] ssa choir; *Oro supplex* [*allegro*] SA duet; *Lacrymosa & Pie Jesu* [*allegro*] ssa choir]
Sanctus: 3 sections, 1 movement
[*Sanctus*, [*allegretto*] ssa choir; *Benedictus*, SA duet; *Hosanna*, ssa choir]
Motet, *Adoramus Te* [*adagio*] ssa choir

Adoramus te Christe et benedicimus tibi;	We adore Thee, O Christ and bless Thee:
quia per sanctam crucem tuam redemisti mundum.	for that by Thy holy Cross didst Thou redeem the world.

Agnus Dei: 3 sections, 1 movement
[*Agnus Dei* I [*adagio*] SS duet; *Agnus Dei* II & III, ssa choir]

DISCOGRAPHY

The Chorus America Program, #9909, with the Ospedale Chorus of the San Francisco Girl's Chorus, dir. Sharon Paul.

ANDRÉ CAMPRA
December 4, 1660–June 29, 1744

By the beginning of the eighteenth century, André Campra was a stellar figure in the universe of French sacred music. He began his career as a choirboy at St. Sauveur and undertook his theological studies in 1678 at the age of thirty-four. By 1681, he was made a chaplain and appointed *maitre de musique* at St. Trophime, Arles. In 1694, he became *maitre de musique* at Notre Dame Cathedral in Paris, leaving this position six years later. In 1696, he received a canonicate at St. Jean-le-Rond.

However, this man had another side to his musical personality. He loved the world of the theatre and composed more than twenty-seven operas, numerous secular cantatas, ballets, and intermezzi. This interest in the secular world caused friction with his ecclesiastical superiors on more than one occasion, but finally, in 1718, Louis XV granted Campra a heady sum of 500 livres "in recognition of his talents . . . and as an incentive to continue such composition" (Groves Encyclopedia, Vol. 3, p. 663). Gradually, he built up support from the royal family and from about 1723, a period of dual alliance to the royal chapel and the stage began. Campra continued to train the boy sopranos for the royal chapel until he was seventy-five years old.

One of Campra's important contributions to music was the creation of the *opera-ballet*. He was further responsible for bringing Italian influences into the French musical style. His contribution to the field of sacred music was significant, too. He composed several masses, but the *petit motet* and the *grand motet* were the more favored forms of the French royal court. These compositions were, in their mature forms, a succession of airs and ensembles; they included instrumental overtures and *ritornelli*. Campra wrote a great many of these pieces and although many have been published, a great number yet remain in manuscript.

Campra's only requiem, the *Messe des Morts*, was composed sometime around 1722 and scored for five-part choir SATBarB, SSATB soloists, and chamber orchestra. Its structure resembles that of a *grand motet*.

For the most part, the choral texture is a highly expressive, homophonic fabric. The only exceptions are the well-spaced passages of imitative polyphony in the opening *Requiem aeternam* (Introit) and *Libera eas* (Offertory), as well as two choral fugues, *Et lux perpetua* (Graduale) and concluding *Cum sanctis tuis* (Communion).

The syllabic *air*, (solo) with its accompaniment of delicate orchestral color and expressive vocal ornamentation, is a prominent feature of the Campra *Requiem*. There are nearly a dozen solos as well as several duets and trios. The union of the *da capo* structure and *ritornello* form, present in these *airs*, represents a combination of French and Italian musical styles.

The orchestra occupies a prominent role in this work. Every movement of the requiem has a substantial, sometimes lengthy, opening prelude and the *Sed signifer* (Offertory) and *Requiem aeternam* (Communion) passages also possess instrumental introductions. Numerous *ritornelli* (interludes) are in most movements and independent accompaniments for the vocal solos. *Ritornelli* helped to shape expansive musical canvases by giving added length and by highlighting the prevailing mood of a particular movement. For example, the three concluding instrumental *ritornelli* of the *Kyrie* create an unexpected emotional intensity in the choral sections. The orchestra was also used to double the choral lines.

Solo passages, vocal choruses, and orchestral accompaniment bristle with elaborate trills and ornamentation. Although most of the melodic invention sprang from the composer's reservoir of musical ideas, there remains a brief link to the liturgical past; the incipit of Gregorian Introit melody is imbedded in the first notes of the bass line.

The overall mood of the work is one of great seriousness and solemnity. During the course of this fifty-two-minute piece, only four sections have a lively tempo and festive mood (*Et lux perpetua, Osanna, Sed signifer,* & *Cum sanctis tuis*).

Basic Data

EDITIONS

1. Requiem de Campra
Reconstruction by H. A. Durand
Editions Costallat, 60 Rue de la Chausée
    d'Antin, Paris.
1958

2. Requiem
Messe des Morts
ed. Elisabeth van Stratten
Editions Costallat, Paris. 1983

DURATION

Seven movements, 1048 mm., perf., c. 42'

VOICING AND ORCHESTRATION

Choir: SATBarB range: S-A6; T-B flat 6; B-F3
Soloists: SSTTBarB orchestra: vn. I/II, vla., vc. *basso continuo*, [chitarrone and org.]

OUTLINE

Introit: 116 mm.
    orchestral intro. [FM]; *Requiem aeternam,* satbarb choir; *Te decet,* TTB-soli trio. *Requiem aeternam* repeated. ABA form
Kyrie: 104 mm.
    orchestral intro. [fm]; *Kyrie,* S [or T] solo; *Christe,* B solo; *Kyrie,* satbarb-choir
Graduale: 131 mm.
    orchestral intro. [dm]; *Requiem aeternam,* B solo/satbarb-choir; *Et lux perpetua,* satbarb choir (Fugue); *Et lux perpetua,* T solo/satbarb choir; *In memoria,* (orchestral intro.) Bar solo/satbarb choir.
Offertory: 251 mm.
    orchestral intro. [gm]; *Domine Jesu Christe,* TTB trio/satbarb choir; *Sed signifer,* (orchestral intro.) T II solo; *Quam olim Abrahae,* T II solo/satbarb choir; *Hostias,* B solo. *Quam olim Abrahae* is repeated.
Sanctus: 86 mm.
    [orchestral intro. [cm]; *Sanctus,* SS duet/satbarb choir; *Pleni sunt coeli,* B solo; *Osanna,* SSB trio/satbarb choir
Agnus Dei: 72 mm.

orchestral intro. [AM]; *Agnus Dei,* S [or T] solo; *Agnus Dei,* dialogue for ST soli/
satbarb choir
Communion: 288 mm.
  orchestral intro. [AM]; *Lux aeterna,* B solo; *Requiem aeternam,* (orchestral intro.)
  satbarb choir; *Et lux perpetua,* SS duet/satbarb choir; *Cum sanctis tuis,* satbarb
  choir. (Fugue).

DISCOGRAPHY

1. Erato, 2292-45993-2, Monteverdi Choir, English Baroque soloists, cond. John
   Eliot Gardner.
2. Veritas, 7243 5 61528, La Grande Ecurie et La Chambre du Roy; Les Pages de la
   Chapelle, cond., Jean-Claude Magloire.

CLAUDIO CASCIOLINI
December 9, 1697–February 18, 1760

Casciolini's career was centered in one church, St. Lorenzo (Damaso) for
the length of his days. Here, he worked, first as a cantor until 1726, and,
subsequently, as *maestro di cappella* until the end of his life. He held a
membership in the prestigious *Congregazione & Accademia di St. Cecilia* in
Rome and composed numerous works for this organization. Although his
life span fell within the baroque era, his musical language was firmly
rooted in Renaissance style.

This master of *a cappella* style counterpoint composed a number of
sacred compositions, including motets, a *Stabat Mater,* three masses
(three, four, and fourteen voices), and two requiems (three and four
voices). The *Missa pro defunctis* for four voices (SATB *a cappella*) was written for the Academy of St. Cecilia. It is a model of Palestrina-style writing
and possesses enormous melodic charm.

Homophonic passages and voice thinning frequently interrupt the prevailing four-part, imitative texture. All of the traditional Gregorian intonations are needed because Casciolini, following Roman tradition, set in
polyphonic style, only the texts which came after the incipit. These polyphonic passages do not appear to be based upon the Gregorian melodies,
but they do evoke the spirit of the older chant style. One of the curious
features of the work is Casciolini's liberal use of archaic empty cadences.

Basic Data

EDITION

Missa Pro Defunctis für vierstimmigen gemischten Chor a cappella
ed., Dr. Ernst Tittel
Musikverlag Alfred Coppenrath, Altötting 1955

DURATION

Ten movements, 439 mm.

VOICING

Choir: SATB-a cappella range: S-G6; B-F3

OUTLINE

Introit: 23 mm., 2 sections [FM] *Requiem, Te decet*, satb. *Requiem aeternam* is repeated.
Kyrie: 27 mm., 3 sections [FM] *Kyrie, Christe, Kyrie*, satb.
Graduale: 12 mm., 2 sections [FM] *Requiem aeternam, In memoria*, satb.
Tract: 10 mm., 3 sections [FM] *Absolve, Et gratia, Et lucis*, satb.
Sequence, *Dies irae*: 123 mm., [dm] 20 alternating sections: polyphonic verses only listed. Odd-numbered verses are sung in chant. *Quantus tremor*, satb; *Mors stupebit*, satb; *Judex ergo*, satb; *Rex tremendae*, satb; *Quaerens me*, satb; *Ingemisco*, satb; *Preces meae*, satb; *Confutatis*, satb; *Lacrimosa*, satb; *Pie Jesu*, satb.
Offertory: 81 mm., 4 sections [am] *Domine Jesu Christe, Libera eas, Quam olim Abrahae*, satb; *Hostias*, atb. *Quam olim Abrahae* is repeated.
Sanctus: 20 mm., 3 sections [am] *Sanctus, Sanctus, Pleni sunt coeli*, satb.
Benedictus: 12 mm., 1 section [GM] *Benedictus*, satb.
Agnus Dei: 33 mm., 3 sections [GM] *Agnus Dei* I, II, III, satb.
Communion: 17 mm., 2 sections [GM] *Lux aeterna, Requiem aeternam*, satb.
Responsory: 81 mm., 8 sections [dm-FM] *Libera me; Tremens factus; Quando coeli; Dies illa; Dum veneris; Requiem aeternam; Kyrie* (*Christe*-plainsong); *Kyrie*, satb.

DISCOGRAPHY

None found.

LOUIS CHEIN
c. 1636–June 17, 1694

Chein began his musical career as a choirboy at Ste. Chapelle in 1645. He continued to work at the chapel for the remainder of his life. Chein was also appointed chaplain for the cathedral in Quimper. He published three masses and one requiem. All, except for the *Missa pro defunctis*, are currently lost.

The *Requiem* is scored for SATB choir, unaccompanied, and was first published in 1690 by Christophe Ballard of Paris. The work is fashioned after the models of the Franco-Flemish school. Its prevailing imitative, four-part texture is broken only in the *Agnus Dei* and *Pie Jesu*. These two movements employ expressive, homophonic writing. Fragments of the Gregorian melodies can be found in the tenor line of the Introit, *Kyrie*, and Graduale, while Gregorian intonations are provided for all of the usual movements. One novel feature is the inclusion of *Pie Jesu* into the Sanctus movement.

Basic Data

EDITION

Louis Chein
Missa pro defunctis
Cahiers de musique 40
Editions du Centre de Musique Baroque de Versailles 1997.

DURATION

Nine movements, 580 mm.

VOICING

Choir: SATB range: S-E6; B-F3

OUTLINE

Introit: 47 mm., 3 sections: *Requiem aeternam* and *Te decet*, satb; *Requiem aeternam* repeated.
Kyrie: 46 mm., 3 sections, *Kyrie, Christe, Kyrie*, satb.
Graduale, *Si ambulem*: 67 mm., 2 sections: *Si ambulem, Virga tua*, satb. [Parisian usage]
Graduale, *Requiem aeternam*: 53 mm., 2 sections: *Requiem aeternam, In memoria*, satb. [Roman usage]
Offertory: 129 mm., 2 sections: *Domine Jesu Christe, Hostias*, satb.
Sanctus: 85 mm., 5 sections: *Sanctus, Pleni sunt coeli, Osanna, Pie Jesu, Benedictus*, satb. *Osanna* repeated.
Agnus Dei: 42 mm., *Agnus Dei* I, II, III, satb.
Communion: 51 mm., 2 sections: *Lux aeterna, Requiem aeternam*, satb.
Responsory, *Ne recorderis*: 60 mm., 2 sections: *Ne recorderis, Dirige Domine*, satb.

DISCOGRAPHY

None found.

DOMENICO CIMAROSA
December 17, 1749–January 11, 1801

Cimarosa was a talented singer as well as an able harpsichordist, organist, and violinist, but was known as the leading composer of *opera buffa* in the late 1700s. He worked in St. Petersburg (1787–91) as *maestro di cappella* at the court of Catherine II. In 1791, he was appointed *Kapellmeister* to Emperor Leopold II in Vienna and in the following year, his most famous work, the opera *Il matrimonio segreto,* was performed. He returned to Italy in 1793.

During his career, he wrote sixty-five operas, most of which were *opera buffa*. He also wrote some instrumental music and a substantial amount of church music. Included in the latter category are twenty masses (two requiems, G minor and F major), mass movements, motets, a Magnificat, and *Te Deum*. Most of the church music employs instrumental accompaniment.

The *Requiem in G Minor* was quickly composed in 1787 for the Duchess of Serra Capriola, the wife of Cimarosa's patron. It was written just after he arrived in St. Petersburg, on December 2, 1787. Scored for SATB choir and soloists, strings, two French horns, and *basso continuo*, this hour-long work possesses a great variety in musical material and texture, as well as a huge range of emotional feelings. The only mood not present is grief. Feelings of serenity, joy, introspection, majesty, and hope permeate the work.

The most commonly used choral texture is a mixture of polyphony and chordal homophonic writing. Cimarosa included three *stile antico*, choral fugues (*Christe, Amen* [Sequence], and *Cum sanctis tuis* [Communion]). Canonic writing was employed in the *Confutatis* section of the Sequence hymn. A constant alternation of the choral textures maintains a delicate balance between the chordal and linear fabric.

The composer grouped the requiem texts into eighteen complete movements and subdivided most of the Sequence verses into a pairing of contrasting slow-fast movements. The *Requiem in G Minor* possesses all of the characteristics of the Neapolitan school of instrumental writing. Elaborate, ornate, and independent obbligato lines for the first and second violins contrast with the slower-moving choral passages in virtually every movement. Short orchestral introductions were composed for a number of movements, including the Introit, *Judex ergo, Recordare, Preces meae, Inter oves, Lacrimosa,* Offertory, and *Agnus Dei*. The only passages played *colla parte* with the choir are the fugue movements.

Cimarosa replaced the older *concertante* requiem form with a more modern structure that included separate choral movements and *bel canto* arias.

A special melody (designated "motto" by this writer) was used by Cimarosa as type of *Leitmotiv*. This motif, always played by the violins, was employed throughout the work. It suggests the funeral cortège and appears in the Introit, Sequence (*Dies irae, Judex ergo, Recordare, Ingemisco, Inter oves,* and *Lacrimosa*), Offertory, and Communion.

French horns are sparingly employed and are always used to underscore the meaning of the text (*Tuba Mirum, Lacrymosa,* Offertory, *Agnus Dei,* and Communion).

Basic Data

EDITION

Domenico Cimarosa
Requiem pro Defunctis für Soli, Chor und Orchester
ed., Etienne Krähenbühl
Edition: Eulenburg Zurich GmbH #10087. 1976

DURATION

Eighteen movements, 1227 mm., perf., c. 59'

VOICING AND ORCHESTRATION

Choir: SATB range: S-A6; B-G3
Soloists: SATB
Instruments: vn. I/II, vla. [colla parte with the vc.], vc. 2 Fh., Org. [basso continuo]

OUTLINE

Introit: 46 mm., ABA form
   Requiem aeternam [gm] largo. satb choir. "motto;" Te decet [gm] andante. satb
   choir; Requiem aeternam is repeated.
Kyrie: 61 mm., ABA form.
   Kyrie [gm] largo. satb choir; Christe [gm] allegro. satb choir. Fugue; Kyrie [gm]
   largo. satb choir.
Graduale: 41 mm.
   In memoria [gm] andante. satb choir.
Sequence: 707 mm., 10 paired movements.
   Dies irae, 8 mm. [cm] largo. satb choir. "motto" & Quantus tremor, 8 mm. [cm]
   allegro. satb choir.
   Tuba mirum, 15mm. [E flat M], largo. S solo/vn. I/II obbligato & Mors stupebit,
   40 mm. [B flat M-fm] allegro. satb choir. ABA form.
   Judex ergo, 16 mm. [A flat M-fm] piu lento. A solo. "motto" & Rex tremendae, 37
   mm. [fm-cm] allegro marcato.
   Recordare, 18 mm. [fm] largo. SA solos. "motto" & Juste judex, 136 mm. [fm]
   allegro. SA duet. Canon.
   Ingemisco, 5 mm. [cm] largo. S solo/satb choir. "motto" & Supplicanti parce, 30
   mm. [E flat M] allegro molto. satb choir.
   Qui Mariam, 7 mm. [fm-GM] largo sempre piano. S solo/satb choir/vn. obbligato & Mihi quoque, 44 mm. [cm] allegro molto. satb choir.
   Preces meae, 100 mm. [E flat M] andante. T solo/vn. obbligato.
   Inter oves, 10 mm. [gm] largo. S solo. "motto" & Confutatis, 30 mm. [B flat M]
   allegro presto. B solo/vn. obbligato & Oro supplex, 11 mm. [E flat M] largo. A solo.
   Oro supplex-Inter oves-Confutatis, 115 mm. SAB trio. [E flat M-cm-cm-gm]
   largo-allegro-largo-allegro. The allegro sections are written as canons. Vn. obbli-
   gato.
   Lacrimosa, 29 mm. [cm] largo molto. satb choir/soloists (concertante). "motto" &
   Amen, 60 mm. [cm] allegro. satb choir. Fugue.

Offertory: 123 mm.

Domine Jesu Christe, 77 mm. [cm] *allegro.* satb soli/choir. "motto;" *Hostias*, [cm] *allegro.* satb soli/choir; *Quam olim*, [cm] *allegro.* satb choir.

Sanctus: 51 mm.

Sanctus, [gm] *allegro non tanto.* satb choir; *Osanna*, [gm] *allegro.* satb choir. (only piece to use 6/8 meter)

Benedictus: 14 mm.

Benedictus, [gm] *largo.* S solo/satb choir. *Osanna* is repeated.

Agnus Dei: 117 mm.

Agnus Dei, [cm] *andante con moto.* satb soli/choir; *Lux aeterna*, [gm] *largo pesante.* SATB soli/choir; *Cum sanctis*, [gm-B flat M] *allegro.* satb choir.

Communion: 64 mm.

Requiem aeternam, [gm] *largo.* satb soli/choir. "motto;" *Cum sanctis*, [gm] *allegro.* satb choir. Fugue.

DISCOGRAPHY

Phillips, 442 657-2, Choeur du Festival de Montreux, Orchestre de Chambre de Lausanne, dir. Vittorio Negri.

BARTOLOMEO CORDANS
February 12, 1698–May 14, 1757

Many details of Cordans' early life remain obscure, but he is known to have become a member of a Franciscan Order at the age of sixteen. However, in 1724, he left the organization in order to become a secular priest. In 1735, he was accepted for the position of music director of the cathedral in Udine.

The majority of his 400 surviving sacred compositions were written for the choir at Udine. Among these pieces are masses (five requiems), mass movements, motets, psalm settings, hymns, and antiphons. He was also involved with composing operas for various opera houses in Venice, but that music has been lost.

The *Messa da Requiem a tre voci virili* was composed in 1738 and scored for three-part male choir (TTB) and organ. This utilitarian composition was probably written for use at the Cathedral in Udine.

Cordans' musical language is a mixture of expressive homophonic writing and imitative polyphony. The work contains no less than seven three-part fugues, a half-dozen canons, and numerous imitative passages. The piling up of melodic lines, one after another, and the liberal use of suspensions give a great deal of energy and tension to the musical drive.

The *concertante* nature of this work comes about from the use of solo, choral unison, and TTB *tutti* passages. Although this work is not particularly dramatic, numerous tempi changes and dynamic variety were employed by the composer to enhance that facet of the music. Although the composer left a simple figured-bass part for the organist, the editor of the modern edition, Daniele Zanettovich, has written a complete realization of that figured bass. This reconstruction, written in the spirit of a free improvisation, is as Frescobaldi might have played it. Cohesion and continuity are provided to the fragmentary structure of the choral passages.

A novel feature is the brief, harmonized quasi-chant intonation for the Introit and Communion.

Basic Data

EDITION

Messa da requiem a tre voci virili e organo
Revised edition, ed. Danielle Zanettovich
Pizzicato Edizioni musicali, via M. Ortigana 10, 33100 Udine, Italy
P. 319 E (1998) [Source of the original manuscript: State Archives, Udine]

DURATION

Eight movements, 946 mm., perf., c. 42′

VOICING AND ORCHESTRATION

Choir: TTB range: T-F6; B-G3
Soloists: TTB
Instrument: org.

OUTLINE

Introit: 94 mm. [gm]
  Requiem aeternam, ttb choir (Fugue); *Te decet*, tt choir; *Et tibi reddetur*, ttb choir (Fugue). *Requiem aeternam* is repeated.
Kyrie: 121 mm. [gm]
  Kyrie, ttb choir (Fugue); *Christe* ttb choir (Fugue); *Kyrie*, ttb choir (Fugue).
Sequence: 388 mm.
  Dies irae, ttb choir; *Quantus tremor*, ttb choir (canonic); *Tuba mirum*, TT soli; *Mors stupebit*, ttb choir (canonic); *Liber scriptus*, T 2 solo; *Judex ergo*, ttb choir; *Quid sum miser*, TT soli (canon); *Rex tremendae*, ttb choir (canon); *Recordare*, T 1-unison choir; *Juste judex*, ttb choir (Fugue); *Ingemisco*, BT duet (canon); *Qui Mariam*, ttb choir; *Preces meae* & *Inter oves*, B solo; *Confutatis*, ttb choir; *Oro supplex*, TT soli (canon); *Lacrymosa*, ttb choir; *Judicandus*, bass-unison choir; *Pie Jesu* & *Amen*, ttb choir (Fugue).
Offertory: 91 mm. [B flat M]
  Domine Jesu Christe & *Quam olim Abrahae*, ttb choir; *Hostias* (Fugue) & *Quam olim Abrahae*, ttb choir.
Sanctus-Benedictus: 47 mm.
  Sanctus, ttb choir; *Benedictus*, ttb choir (canon).

Agnus Dei: 24 mm. [gm]
  Agnus Dei I & II, ttb choir (canonic).
Communion: 43 mm. [gm]
  Lux aeterna, ttb choir; *Requiem aeternam*, ttb choir (canon).
Responsory: 138 mm. [gm]
  Libera me; Tremens factus; Quando coeli; Requiem; Libera me, ttb choir.

DISCOGRAPHY

RS 951-0026, Coro Polifonico di Ruda, cond. Andrea Faidutti.

JOHANN ERNST EBERLIN
bapt. March 27, 1702–June 19, 1762

Born in Bavaria, Eberlin began his professional career in Salzburg (1721).
He was appointed fourth organist of the Salzburg Cathedral in 1726. By
1749, Eberlin had become the *Kapellmeister* of both the Cathedral and
Royal Court. He knew the Mozart family well and was held in high
esteem by them. The young Wolfgang Mozart studied the contrapuntal
writing of Eberlin.

The only collection of Eberlin's music that was published during his
lifetime is the nine toccatas and fugues for organ (1747). In the nineteenth
century, two collections of organ music, one of sixty-five preludes and
postludes and another of 115 verses and cadences, were published about
1830. His sacred music includes almost seventy masses, of which nine are
requiems, 160 offertories, thirty-seven litanies, three settings of the *Te
Deum*, and many other liturgical pieces.

The *Requiem in B flat Major* is one of his short requiem settings and was
composed around 1750. This *concertante* setting is scored for SATB choir,
SATB soli, strings, and organ (*continuo*). The addition of trombone, trumpet, timpani, and cello, made by Eberlin's younger contemporaries, P.
Georg Pasterwiz and Friedrich Kramel, was done so that performance-
practice would conform to Viennese tradition.

Its musical style includes elements of the Viennese and Neapolitan traditions. The orchestration with its *concertante* treatment of choir and soloists,
as well as the doubling trombones, confirms the former, and the binary
form and the virtuoso, *bel canto* style of the soprano solo (*Benedictus*), the
latter. The prevailing choral texture is a mixture of polyphonic and chordal
writing. The violin obbligati duets that accompany the choir and vocal soloists also represents a blend of Viennese and Neapolitan styles.

One of the novel structural features of this shortened setting is the linking of the Introit and *Kyrie* as well as the *Agnus Dei* and Communion
movements. Another unique hallmark of this piece is the presence of a

recurring melody, designated as "floating," eighth-note theme. It appears in the Introit, *Kyrie*, Sequence, and *Agnus Dei* and is employed by a variety of instruments and voices. Although the choral parts of this utilitarian setting are not difficult to manage, skilled soloists are needed.

Basic Data

EDITION

Johann Eberlin
Requiem in B für Soli und gemischte Chor, zwei Violinen und Basso continuo.
Erstdrucke [first edition] edited by Wolfgang Fürlinger
Musikverlag Alfred Coppenrath, Altötting. 1979

DURATION

Six movements, 379 mm.

VOICING AND ORCHESTRATION

Choir: SATB range: S-G6; B-E flat 3
Soloists: SATB
Instruments: vn. I/II, db. 2 tpt., 2 tbn., timp., org. [*continuo*] [2 tbn. doubling the alto & tenor; 2 clarini with mutes]

OUTLINE

Introit-Kyrie: 43 mm. ABA form.
    Requiem aeternam [B flat M] *adagio.* satb choir/soli, "floating" theme; *Te decet*, SATB soli; *Requiem aeternam - Kyrie*, satb choir. "floating" theme.
Sequence, *Dies irae*: 176 mm. [Verses 1-4, 7-9, 12, 17-19] The "floating" theme appears throughout.
    Dies irae, andante [B flat M] satb choir/soli; *Quantus tremor*, S solo; *Tuba mirum*, A solo; *Mors stupebit*, satb choir; *Quid sum miser*, T solo; *Rex tremendae*, satb choir; *Recordare*, B solo; *In-gemisco*, SA duet; *Oro supplex*, TB duet; *Lacrymosa*, satb choir/soli; *Huic ergo*, satb choir/soli.
Offertory: 74 mm.
    Domine Jesu Christe [B flat M] *andante.* satb choir/soli; *Libera eas* [E flat M] *allegro.* SATB soli/choir; *Hostias* [gm-B flat M] *andante.* SATB soli/choir.
Sanctus: 14 mm.
    Sanctus [B flat M] *andante.* satb choir/SA duet.
Benedictus: 26 mm.
    Benedictus [B flat M] *andante.* SA duet/satb choir.
Agnus Dei-Communion, 46 mm.
    Agnus Dei [B flat M] *adagio.* SATB soli/choir; *Cum sanctis tuis*, Fughetta. "floating" theme.

DISCOGRAPHY
None found.

JOHANN JOSEPH FUX
1660–February 13, 1741

The biographical details of Johann Joseph Fux's life remain sketchy. Born in humble circumstances, he attended the Jesuit Universities in Graz and in Ingolstadt and was an organist in St. Moritz up until 1688. The emperor, Leopold I, by chance heard mass settings by Fux and liked them. From that time on, Fux enjoyed royal favor. He became organist of the Schottenkirche (Vienna) in 1696, and, in 1698, the emperor appointed Fux to the position of court composer. In addition to his duties at Court, Fux took on the position of vice-*Kapellmeister* at St. Stephen's Cathedral (Vienna) in 1705. Finally, in 1715, he was appointed to the important position of Court *Kapellmeister*, a post he held until his death. Among his pupils were Gottlieb Muffat and Jan Dismas Zelenka.

Fux was primarily a composer of church music who wrote more than 600 liturgical pieces. Included are eighty masses, three requiems, numerous motets, antiphons, Vespers and Psalms, and a *Te Deum* for double choir. In addition, there are fourteen sacred oratorios. His secular compositions include twenty operas, fifty church sonatas, about eighty partitas, and many other keyboard compositions. Several treatises on music theory, including the *Gradus ad Parnassum* [study of counterpoint] (1725) and the *Singfundament* (published posthumously in 1832) round out his *oeuvre*.

The *Emperor's Requiem* was composed for the funeral of the widow of Emperor Leopold I, whose funeral took place on March 5, 1720, in Vienna. It was repeatedly performed at royal funeral services up until 1743. The *Requiem* is scored for five-part *concertante* (SSATB) soli and choir, four-part *concertante* strings, two trombones (to double the lower vocal lines), two cornetti (for solo work and doubling the higher choral lines), and an organ *continuo*.

Many traits of the *Requiem* (1636) by Christoph Strauss (at an earlier time, organist of St. Stephen's Cathedral and musical director Viennese Court), are found in the instrumentation and *concertante* writing of the *Emperor's Requiem*.

The choral writing also reveals its Germanic orientation by its heavy use of imitative polyphonic texture, which includes canonic and fugal writing. *Kyrie* II, *Quaerens me, Preces meae, Pie Jesu, Quam olim Abrahae*, and *Cum sanctis* are models of fugal style and writing. Canonic writing is employed in the duets for two sopranos, *Quid sum miser* and *Ingemisco* (Sequence).

Expressive homophonic writing is rarely used, but is found in the Sequence (*Dies irae* and *Inter oves*), Offertory (*Hostias*, opening phrase), *Sanctus* (*Pleni sunt coeli*), and several passages in the *Agnus Dei*.

Although the French were already writing imposing instrumental symphonies for their requiem masses, Austrian composers lagged somewhat behind in their efforts. The Viennese orchestra was still used principally for doubling the *tutti* choral passages, though it is generally reduced to a *basso continuo* during the *soli* passages of the *concertante* fabric. Although the orchestral forces cannot yet be called symphonic, the scoring used by Fux displays perceptible movement toward a more independent role for the chamber orchestra. Modest instrumental preludes, placed at the head of the Introit and *Kyrie* movements, as well as the far more adventurous preludes and accompaniments for the vocal-solo passages, *Ingemisco* and *Inter oves*, and the trombone obbligato for *Tuba mirum*, too, bring to light this trend. The orchestral instruments play in *concertante* style, matching the solo voices with a more intimate scoring.

Basic Data

EDITION

Joseph Johann Fux
Requiem K 51-K 53
Vorgelegt von Klaus Winkler
Continuo von Klaus Winkler
Akademische Druck und Verlagsanstalt
Graz, Austria 1992

DURATION

Eight movements, 808 mm., perf., c. 39'

VOICING AND ORCHESTRATION

Choir: SSATB range: S-G6; B-F3 [E3 rare]
Orchestra: vn. I/II, vla., vc., violone. 2 cornetti, 2 tbn. Bsn. and org. [*continuo*]

OUTLINE

Introit: 117 mm. [fm]
 Requiem aeternam; et lux perpetua, SSATB soli/choir; *Te decet,* SSATB soli, *Exaudi,* ssatb choir; *Requiem aeternam,* SSATB soli/choir. Brief instrumental prelude.
Kyrie: 47 mm. [cm]
 Kyrie, ssatb tutti; *Christe,* SSATB soli & *Kyrie,* ssatb tutti. Brief instrumental prelude.
Sequence: 324 mm.
 Dies irae, ssatb choir; *Quantus tremor,* SSB soli; *Tuba mirum,* A solo; *Mors stupebit,*

ssatb choir; *Liber scriptus*, ATB soli; *Quid sum miser*, SS duet; *Rex tremendae*, ssatb choir; *Recordare*, SIIAT soli; *Quarens me*, ssatb choir; *Juste Judex*, SSATB soli; *Ingemisco*, SS duet; *Qui Mariam*, SIIA duet; *Preces meae*, ssatb choir; *Inter oves*, SSA soli; *Confutatis*, ssatb choir; *Oro supplex*, ATB soli; *Pie Jesu*, ssatb choir (Double fugue).

Offertory: 137 mm. [FM]
   Domine Jesu Christe, concertante SSATB soli/choir; *Sed signifer*, SS duet/ ATB trio; *Quam olim Abrahae*, ssatb choir (Fugue); *Hostias*, ATB trio; *Quam olim Abrahae*, ssatb choir (Fugue).

Sanctus: 30 mm. [cm]
   Sanctus; Pleni sunt coeli; Osanna, ssatb choir.

Benedictus: 66 mm. [E flat M-cm]
   Benedictus, ssatb choir; *Osanna*, SS duet/ATB soli trio.

Agnus Dei: 24 mm. [cm]
   Agnus Dei I, SS duet; *Agnus Dei* II, ATB trio; *Agnus Dei* III, ssatb choir.

Communion: 63 mm. [E flat M]
   Lux aeterna, SSATB soli; *Cum sanctis*, ssatb choir (Fugue); *Quia pius es*, ssatb choir; *Requiem aeternam*, SAT trio; *Cum sanctis & Quia pius es*, ssatb choir (Fugue).

DISCOGRAPHY

Arte Nova Classics, 74321 27777 2, Clemenic Consort, cond. René Clemenic.

JOHANN ADOLPHE HASSE
March 25, 1699–December 16, 1783

In 1718, Hasse joined the Hamburg Opera Company as a tenor, but his true interest lay in opera composition. In the early 1720s, he went to Italy, where he studied with Alessandro Scarlatti. His earliest theatrical compositions date from the mid 1720s. He was employed as *Kapellmeister* at the Dresden court in 1730 and married the famous soprano, Faustina Bordoni in 1731. His life was spent in Dresden, with frequent return trips to Italy, where he did much composing, too. Hasse maintained a warm relationship with the opera librettist, Pietro Metastasio, setting many of the latter's texts to music. After the death of his patron, Hasse was dismissed because the new prince lacked the funds to continue support for the lavish entertainments his father had enjoyed. After going to Vienna, where he composed yet more opera, he ultimately returned to Venice.

Though he is nearly forgotten today, Hasse was one of the truly prolific composers of the baroque, writing more than 100 operas, eleven oratorios, ninety-one cantatas for voice and *basso continuo*, and cantatas with one or two obbligato instruments or with orchestra. His liturgical music includes nineteen masses, three requiems, many separate mass movements, ten offertories, a dozen hymns, forty-one solo motets, and eighteen anti-phons. Among the instrumental works are twenty-one concerti, trio sona-tas, and keyboard sonatas.

Hasse wrote three settings of the requiem mass, two in E flat major and one in C major. The splendid *Requiem in C Major* was composed in 1763 in memory of his Dresden benefactor, Prince Augustus III, who died on October 5, 1763. Its first performance took place on November 22, 1763, and the work was so popular that it continued to be performed on the anniversary date of every year. This tradition lasted into the nineteenth century. The *Requiem* is scored for SATB choir, SSAATB soloists, and orchestra and bears the hallmarks of both the Viennese and Neapolitan styles. A colorful instrumental palette was used to support and color the *bel-canto* style, solo singing. An organist is expected to realize the figured bass *continuo*.

Most of the choral writing, with a few exceptions, is homophonic. This kind of texture allowed the text to stand out, in relief, against the more complex orchestral writing that Hasse, as well as the Neapolitans, were fond of using. The only significant polyphonic passage is the *stile antico* fugue of the *Christe*. The treatment of the orchestral forces, from the 1740s onward, represents a turning point in the evolution toward a true sym-phonic accompaniment for the requiem text. Hasse scored for the orches-tra in three basic ways: a full, rich sound for the most festive and majestic passages; second, the strings and woodwinds for most of the accompa-nied solos; and third, strings and *basso continuo* for the most intimate, per-sonal solos.

Hasse's *Requiem in C Major* is one of the earlier requiem settings to employ an independent symphonic accompaniment. Early baroque orchestral forces tended to double or support the choral lines and fabric. Hasse goes a step beyond this; he used the orchestra, as a free entity, to color or heighten the meanings implied in the sung texts. A notable exam-ple of this technique can be seen in the writing for *Inter oves*.

> With thy sheep a place provide me
> From the goats afar divide me.

The pastoral nature of the text is evoked by dividing the orchestra into two antiphonal groupings. Flutes and strings are pitted against the oboes and bassoons, similar to Bach's orchestration of the *Pastorale Symphony* in Part Two of the *Christmas Oratorio*.

For Hasse, instrumental obbligati for the choral sections and vocal solos were usually performed by an instrumental section and not just a soloist, as was done in the earlier eighteenth century. Obbligato passages, for oboes and flutes, are always doubled by violins. In the *Tuba mirum*, Hasse employed trumpets to play fanfare-like passages to depict the apocalypse of the Last Judgement.

Four separate layers of sound are used in the *Lacrymosa*, one of which doubles the choral parts. The four layers are used to create a massive tonal effect. The bassoon and continuo line are, for the most part, independent of the choral line. Violins execute a descending arpeggio figure and the brass and timpani punctuate the rhythm. Only the violas and oboes double the choral lines. Nearly every movement in the requiem has an orchestral introduction and coda.

The vocal soloists need an excellent singing technique, breath control, and light voices for the execution of the numerous *bel canto* arias. Most of these solos have lengthy and difficult, ornate lines, as well as a flashy concluding cadenza that must be improvised.

Some of the work's highlights are the dance-like soprano solo, *Exaudi orationem*, the dazzling *bel canto* solo for tenor, *Mors stupebit*, the plaintive alto solo, *Recordare*, and the warm trio for soprano and two altos, *Hostias*.

Basic Data

EDITION

David James Wilson
The Masses of Johann Adolphe Hasse
University Microfilms, A Xerox company
Ann Arbor, Michigan. 1974

DURATION

Nineteen movements, 1017 mm., perf., c. 50'

VOICING AND ORCHESTRATION

Choir: SATB range: S-A6; B-F3
Soloists: SSAATB
Orchestra: vn. I/II, vla., vc., db. 2 ob., 2 fl., 2 bsn., tpt., timp. org. [or clavecin]

OUTLINE

Introit: 121 mm., three movements
    Requiem aeternam: 31 mm., [CM] *Non troppo lento, ma maestoso.* satb choir/full orchestra. Te decet: 13 mm., [FM] *andante.* unison tb choir/*bc.* Plainsong harmonized. Exaudi orationem: 78 mm., [FM] *moderato,* A solo/strings/ww. Binary form.
Kyrie: 128 mm.
    Kyrie: 40 mm., [CM] *andante.* satb choir/str./ww; *Christe*: 76 mm. [cm] *allegro.* satb choir/str./ww. (*Stile antico* fugue. The fugue subject [G-A flat-F #-G] is a direct quotation from the second *Kyrie* in Bach's *B Minor Mass*.); *Kyrie*: 12 mm., [cm] *adagio.* satb choir/str./ww. Coda. AB[A truncated] form.

Sequence: 743 mm., seven movements (verses 12-14 omitted, *Ingemisco, Qui Mariam & Preces meae*)

Dies Irae: 69 mm. [cm] *andante. Dies irae*, satb choir/str./ww.; *Quantus tremor*, A solo/str./ww.; *Tuba mirum*, [CM] *allegro*. satb choir/full orchestra. 3 vv.

Mors stupebit: 74 mm. [E flat M] *andante. Mors stupebit*, T solo/str.; *Liber scriptus*, AT duet/str./ww.; *Judex ergo*, B solo/str./ww.; *Quid sum miser*, T solo/str.; *Rex tremendae*, satb choir/str./ww. 5 vv.

Recordare: 64 mm. [fm] *un poco lento*. A solo/str./ww. ABA form.

Quaerens me: 127 mm. [B flat M] *andante*. T solo/str./ww. Binary form.

Juste judex: 9 mm. [E flat M] *largo*. satb choir/str./ww. An accompanied choral recitative.

Inter oves: 80 mm. [FM] *andante. Inter oves; Confutatis & Oro supplex* [GM] *adagio*. A solo/str./ww. 3 vv. AB[A truncated] form.

Lacrymosa: 71 mm. [cm] *andante. Lacrymosa*, satb/choir/full orchestra; *Huic ergo*, SA duet/str.; *Dona eis*, satb choir/full orchestra. 3 sections.

Offertory: 107 mm., two movements, ABA form

Domine Jesus Christe: 41 mm. [B flat M] *andante*. 2 sections, *Domine Jesu & Sed signifer*, satb choir/ str./ww.

Hostias: 66 mm., [cm] *andantino*. 3 sections. *Hostias*, SSA soli/str.; *Quam olim Abrahae* [E flat M] & *Domine Jesu Christe* (*da capo*) [B flat M] satb choir/str./ww.

Sanctus: 40 mm.

Sanctus [FM] *andante; Pleni sunt coeli, andante*. satb choir/str./ww.; *Osanna*, SA soli/satb choir/ str./ww.

Benedictus: 74 mm.

Benedictus [CM] *Un poco lento*. A solo/str.. *Osanna* is repeated.

Agnus Dei: 39 mm.

Agnus Dei [cm] *andante*. AA duet/str.

Communion: 13 mm.

Lux aeterna [FM] *andante*. unison TB choir, Gregorian intonation of the *Te decet; Requiem aeter-nam*: The first movement, *Requiem aeternam*, is repeated.

DISCOGRAPHY

Opus 111, OPS 30-80, Il Fondament, dir. Paul Dombrecht.

JUAN DE HERRERA
c. 1670–February/March 1738

De Herrera was born in Bogota, Colombia (New Grenada), where he apparently received his education and spent his career. He was a chaplain and music teacher at Santa Ines Convent. From 1703 until the end of his life, he was the choirmaster of Bogota's Santa Fe Cathedral.

Of the existing three-dozen compositions, most are polychoral. There are two complete masses for eight voices, a partial *Officum Defunctorum*, a *Laudate Dominum* for three choirs and *continuo*, three requiem settings (for five, eight, and nine voices), and, lastly, a dozen villancicos for two–five and seven voices. The *Misa de Difuntos* for five voices was probably composed for the Santa Fe Cathedral in the early years of the eighteenth century. For its period, it remains a conservative, *stile antico* model of requiem writing. Its scoring for four vocal parts (SSAT) and one instrumental part (*basso segunte*) gives the work a light and airy quality.

The prevailing texture is elaborate homophony, with occasional passages of simplified, imitative polyphony, such as those found in the Introit and *Kyrie*. There are curious one-measure breaks in the choral writing, causing one to speculate whether these breaks were used by the composer to explore the resonant acoustics of the cathedral or whether they were filled with the interludes of an accompanying organ.

Gregorian intonations are needed for the Introit, Graduale, Offertory, *Sanctus, Benedictus*, and *Agnus Dei,* and the subsequent polyphonic paraphrases appear to be taken from the few opening notes of those chant portions that follow the intonations.

Although the musical style is strongly influenced by Renaissance style, traces of the early baroque are found, too. The one-movement structure of the *Kyrie*, with overlapping and abbreviated texts is a peculiar, *stile moderno* trait that is found in all three of his requiem settings.

Basic Data

EDITION

Tres Misas de Difuntos para coro, solistas y continuo
Transcripción y Edición: Margarita Restrepo
Consejo Nacional de la Cultura & Instituto Colombiano de Cultura
Catedral de Santa Fe de Bogotá
Caracas, Venezuela. 1996
[Misa de Difuntos a cinco voces]

DURATION

Six movements, 437 mm., perf. c. 11'

VOICING AND ORCHESTRATION

Choir: SAT range: S-D 6; T-F 4
Instruments: portative organ [*basso continuo*]

OUTLINE

Introit: 89 mm., 2 sections: *Requiem aeternam* & *Te decet*, ssat.
Kyrie: 26 mm., 1 section: *Kyrie*, ssat.

Graduale: 72 mm., 2 sections: *Requiem aeternam* & *In memoria*, ssat.
Offertory: 145 mm., 1 section: *Domine Jesu Christe*, ssat. *Hostias* sung in plainsong.
Sanctus: 73 mm., 3 sections: *Sanctus, Pleni sunt coeli,* & *Benedictus*, ssat.
Agnus Dei: 32 mm., 1 section: *Agnus Dei*, ssat. Agnus II & III sung in plainsong.

DISCOGRAPHY
Les Chemins du Baroque-Nouvel Grenade, K 617077-2, Camerata Renacentista de
Caracas, dir. Isabel Palacios.

The *Misa de Difuntos a Ocho Voces* [Requiem for eight voices], a *concertante*
work, was composed in the polychoral Venetian style. Choir I (SSA) and
Choir II (SAT) unfold the texts in an ongoing dialogue and a *basso continuo*
(organ and bassoon) is used to support the vocal ensembles.

The prevailing texture of the *Misa* is two homophonic blocks of choral
text employed in polyphonic fashion. Contrast in the texture is created by
the addition or withdrawal of one or the other choirs and by the use of
the soloists.

The structure of the requiem possesses several novel features. The
Introit and *Kyrie* are linked together in one continuous movement;
polyphony is employed only for the Graduale verse, *In memoria;* and the
Sequence is set into one continuous movement of multiple sections. Herrera did not set the *Agnus Dei* or Communion in polyphonic arrangements.

Basic Data

EDITION
[see above]

DURATION
Five movements, 253 mm.

VOICING AND ORCHESTRATION
Choir: choir I, SSA; choir II, SAT range: S-F6; T-F4
Instruments: bsn., org.

OUTLINE
Introit-Kyrie: 55 mm., 1 movement: *Requiem aeternam, Kyrie*, choirs I/II/AT duet/
S I solo.
Graduale: 20 mm., 1 movement: *In memoria*, choirs I/II. *Requiem aeternam.* Sung in
plainchant.
Sequence, *Dies irae*: 53 mm., 18 sections, one movement:
    Dies irae, choir I; *Quantus tremor*, choir II; *Tuba mirum*, choir I, S solo; *Mors stu-
pebit*, choirs II/I; *Liber scriptus*, choirs I/II; *Judex ergo*, SA duet/S choir I/choir

II; *Quid sum miser,* choir I; *Rex tremendae,* choir II; *Recordare,* choir I/S solo; *Quae-rens me,* choirs I/II; *Juste Judex,* choirs I/II; *Ingemisco,* SA duet/S (choir I)/choir II; *Qui Mariam,* choir I; *Preces meae,* choir II; *Inter oves,* choir I/S solo; *Confutatis,* choirs II/I; *Oro supplex,* choirs I/II; *Judicandus,* SA duet/S (choir I)/choir II.
Offertory: 68 mm., 2 sections, 1 movement: *Domine Jesu Christe* & *Sed signifer,* choirs I/II/SA duet. The verse, *Hostias,* sung in plainchant.
Sanctus: 57 mm., 2 sections, 1 movement: *Sanctus* & *Benedictus,* choirs I/II.

DISCOGRAPHY
None found.

The *Misa de Difuntos a nueve voces* (Requiem mass for nine voices) is scored for three choirs of female voices (choir I, SSA; choir II, AA; choir III, SS) and *basso continuo.* The absence of male voices bestows a light, angelic quality to the choral sound. The designation, nine voices, comes from the seven-part choral tutti and the occasional two-part soli (SA) passages. A *basso continuo* is employed to underpin the choral mass.

The prevailing texture of this *concertante* requiem is seven-part, elaborate homophonic writing, with frequent voice thinning. Duet passages, supported by the *continuo,* contrast with the choral writing and allow for a more intimate presentation of the liturgical text. Two of the novel features of this work are the one-movement Introit and *Kyrie* and absence of a bass vocal part.

Basic Data
EDITION
[see above]

DURATION
Four movements, 244 mm.

VOICING AND ORCHESTRATION
Choir: choir I, SSA; choir II, AA; choir III, SS range: S-B6
Instruments: org. or bsn. [*basso continuo*]

OUTLINE
Introit-Kyrie: 76 mm., 1 movement: choirs I/II/III/SA soli.
Offertory: 95 mm., 3 sections, 1 movement: *Domine Jesu Christe,* choirs I/II/III; *Sed signifer,* SA duet; *Quam olim Abrahae,* choirs I/II/III. The verse, *Hostias,* sung in plainsong.
Sanctus: 21 mm., 1 movement: choirs I/II/III. *Benedictus* sung in plainsong.
Agnus Dei: 52 mm., 1 movement: choirs I/II/III/SS or SA duets.

DISCOGRAPHY
None found.

MIGUEL LOPEZ
February 1, 1669–1723

The Spanish organist and composer Miguel Lopez entered the Escolania
of Montserrat about 1678. In 1686, he became a full member of the Benedictine Order. He served St. Martin's Monastery in Madrid (1689–1696) as
organist and he was twice appointed choirmaster at Montserrat (1696–
1705 and 1715–1718). He was also the organist for the Monastery of St.
Benito, Valladolid (1705–1715).

His compositions are found in one folio entitled, *Miscellanea musicae.*
Contained within this manuscript are five masses, thirty-two vesper and
compline psalms, three sets of *Lamentations*, nineteen motets, sixty-two
villancicos, cantatas, and many organ pieces. Among the masses is a
Missa Defunctorum à 12, for three choirs, composed in 1716. The scoring
of the mass is as follows: Choir I, violin I/II, violone and unison-alto
choir; Choir II, SSAT voices; and Choir III, SATB voices. A *basso continuo*
supports the instrumental-vocal ensembles. This somewhat unusual polychoral scoring was modeled after the almost-identical, earlier requiem of
Cristóbal Galan (c. 1630–1684). A succession of polychoral requiems from
the monastery at Montserrat (Cererols, Galan, and Lopez) highlights the
important musical tradition of this institution.

Choir I contains the Gregorian melody, sometimes in the original
melodic form, other times in fragments or paraphrase, in the unison-alto
line. This line functions as *cantus firmus*, while Choirs II and III comment,
in dialogue fashion, on the liturgical text. Choir I is always supported by
an elaborate instrumental accompaniment. This structure is reminiscent
of the opening chorus in Bach's *St. Matthew Passion*.

A *"concertante"* sound is achieved by the variety of choral combinations; sometimes in antiphonal dialogue, or a massed *tutti* and at yet other
times in duet or solo scoring. The musical texture ranges from predominantly chordal homophony to polyphonic points of imitation. The Gregorian melodies of the Roman tradition are present in every movement,
except the *Agnus Dei*.

The *Kyrie*, Tract, Sequence, and *Sanctus* were composed in single,
through-composed movements while the remaining movements retain
their traditional sectional structures. In some instances, the essence of the
original structure is preserved in the dialogue between Choir I and Choirs
I and II. The threefold partitioning of the *Kyrie* text is preserved as Choir
I introduces each line of the text before Choir II and II comment upon it.

(This procedure is also employed in the Introit.) Other movements use cadences to indicate the major divisions of the text. Lopez linked the *Agnus Dei* and Communion while omitting the opening line of the latter movement, *Requiem aeternam*, into a single movement. A single Gregorian intonation is needed only for the Introit because Lopez did not set the incipit in polyphonic style.

Basic Data

EDITION

Mestres de L'Escolania de Montserrat
Vol. VIII
Miguel Lopez, Obres Completes, II
Missa Defunctorum for 12
Transcription and notes by Ireneu Segarra
Monastir de Montserrat. 1958

DURATION

Eight movements, 669 mm.

VOICING AND ORCHESTRATION

Choir: choir I: unison alto, violin I/II, violone. Choir II: SSAT, choir III: SATB
range: S-G6; B-D3 [C3 rare]
Instruments: vn. I/II, violon [vc.], org. [*basso continuo*]

OUTLINE

Introit: 82 mm.
  Requiem aeternam, choirs I/II/III (*Requiem aeternam* is repeated in altered form.)
Kyrie: 32 mm.
  Kyrie, choirs I/II/III.
Tract: 27 mm.
  Absolve me, choirs I/II/III.
Sequence: 219 mm.
  Dies irae, dialogue between choir I and choirs II & III.
Offertory: 116 mm.
  Domine Jesu Christe; Hostias, choirs I/II/III.
Sanctus: 42 mm.
  Sanctus, choirs I/II/III.
Motet, *O, Mors:* 103 mm. Same vocal and instrumental forces as other movements.
Agnus Dei-Communion: 54 mm.
  Agnus Dei; Lux aeterna, choirs I/II/III.
Responsory: 97 mm.
  Libera me, Tremens factus, Dies illa, choir I; *Requiem aeternam, Kyrie* I, *Kyrie* II (Gregorian intonations sung before *Tremens factus* & *Kyrie* II), choirs I, II, III.

DISCOGRAPHY
None found.

ANTONIO LOTTI
c. 1667–January 5, 1740

Lotti spent most of his professional life in Venice, except for a brief interlude in Dresden, where he worked for the Saxon Elector, Friedrich
August II. He studied with Legrenzi, a composer admired by Johann
Sebastian Bach. In 1687, he began his career as a singer at St. Mark's Basilica. He was later appointed second organist (1692) and in 1704, to the
position of first organist; a position he held until his appointment as *primo
maestro di cappella* in 1733.

His second career, that of an opera composer, began in the early 1690s,
where he started to produce stage works for local Venetian theaters. He
penned a string of twenty-nine operas over the duration of his career.

He was a noted teacher and among his more famous pupils were
Domenico Alberti (of *Alberti-bass* fame), Baldassare Galuppi, and Benedetto Marcello.

In his musical production are twenty-nine operas, seven oratorios,
ninety solo cantatas, and a small amount of instrumental music. The
sacred music includes motets, numerous masses, two requiems for four
voices, and one requiem for five voices. Most of this repertory was written
for St. Mark's.

The *F Major Requiem*, discussed here, is scored for SATB voices and
written in *stile antico*. The date of the work cannot be precisely determined, but it is possible that it came from the time when he was choirmaster for St. Mark's. Its likely post-1726 date suggests that the work
included, at the very least, a *basso segunte*. Its Roman origins are evident
in the continued use of intonations (Introit and *Agnus Dei)*, the *a cappella*
scoring, and in the enormous volume of imitative polyphony, modeled
after Palestrina. This *missa* employs a number of imitative techniques.
Paired imitation is used in the Introit, *Kyrie* I, *Christe*, *Kyrie* II, *Sanctus*, and
Benedictus. There are two choral fugues, one on *Dona eis pacem* (Sequence)
and the second, on *Agnus Dei* I. Imitation throughout all the vocal parts
and points of imitation are commonly used devices.

The four-part, imitative texture is broken by chordal writing in nearly
half of the expressive passages of the Sequence (*Liber scriptus, Judex ergo,
Quid sum miser, Quaerens me, Preces me, Oro supplex, Judicandus*, and *Pie
Jesu*). Chordal passages are also used at the beginning phrases of the
Offertory (*Domine Jesu Christe, Quam olim Abrahae*, and *Hostias*) and *Agnus
Dei* II.

Basic Data

EDITION

Denkmäler Deutscher Tonkunst
I. Folge, Band 60
Antonio Lotti, Messen
ed. Arnold Schering
Verlag Breitkopf & Härtel, Wiesbaden 1959
[C (soprano, alto, tenor) & F clefs]

DURATION

Seven movements, 590 mm., perf., c. 27'

VOICING AND ORCHESTRATION

Choir: SATB range: S-F6; B-F3
Instruments: violone [*basso segunte*]

OUTLINE

Introit: 56 mm. *Requiem aeternam* & *Te decet*, satb.
Kyrie; 50 mm. *Kyrie, Christe, Kyrie*, satb.
Sequence, *Dies irae*: 301 mm. [satb] [H = homophonic; IP = imitative polyphony]
    Dies irae, H; *Quantus tremor*, H/IP; *Tuba mirum*, IP; *Mors stupebit*, H; *Liber scriptus*, IP/H; *Judex ergo*, H; *Quid sum miser*, H; *Rex tremendae*, IP; *Recordare*, IP; *Quaerens me*, H/IP; *Juste judex*, H; *Ingemisco*, IP; *Qui Mariam*, IP; *Preces meae*, H/IP; *Inter oves*, IP; *Confutatis*, IP; *Oro supplex*, H; *Lacrymosa*, IP; *Pie Jesu*, H/IP (*Amen*)
Offertory: 91 mm. *Domine Jesu Christe* & *Hostias*, satb.
Sanctus: 24 mm. *Sanctus*, satb.
Benedictus: 22 mm. Benedictus, satb.
Agnus Dei: 36 mm. *Agnus Dei* I (II), *Agnus Dei* III, satb.

DISCOGRAPHY

Arion, ARN 68154, Ensemble Metamorphoses de Paris, dir. Maurice Bourbon.

BENEDETTO MARCELLO
July 24/August 1, 1686–July 24/25, 1739

Benedetto Marcello, one of the better early eighteenth-century composers, learned violin from his father and singing and counterpoint from Francesco Gasparini (1668–1727). During an active political career, Marcello continued to issue a number of new musical works that included five oratorios, eight stage works, 348 secular cantatas, ten masses, and a collection of twenty-five psalm settings, *Estro poetico-armonico*. His first publication was a set of twelve concerti, issued in 1708. He also composed instrumental and keyboard music.

Among his *concertante* mass settings is a *Requiem in G Minor* scored for double SATB chorus, SATB soloists, and instruments. This little-known masterpiece is a remarkable work that employs a great deal of fugal writing, inspired by a composer with phenomenal contrapuntal skills and a sparkling musical imagination. The musicologist, Marco Bizzarini, suggests that the requiem might have been written between 1728 and 1733 (p. 9, CD Notes, 1999).

The larger portion of the choral fabric was spun in imitative contrapuntal fashion. In addition to the "usual" *stile antico* polyphonic writing, Marcello employed a number of fugues and passages of canonic writing for setting the text. Eloquent, chordal passages, such as those of *Kyrie* and *Rex tremendae*, as well as the "sighing" portions of *Qui Mariam*, make a significant contrast to the prevailing intense, horizontal texture.

Although the orchestra often doubles the choral lines, there are independent obbligati for violin, viola, and cello that pepper the vocal solos. The movements *Kyrie, Christe, Dies irae, Tuba mirum, Liber scriptus, Recordare*, and *Oro supplex* possess orchestral introductions and orchestral ritornelli.

Typical baroque *affections* include the "shaking" rhythms of the strings on *Quantus tremor*, the "sighing" figures on the choral lines at *Qui Mariam*, and the martial dotted rhythms of *Tuba mirum*. Almost no traces of the Gregorian melodies can be found in the requiem settings of this era, yet Marcello suggested the plainsong melodies in unison, chant-like passages found at the beginning of the Introit and Communion movements and in the Offertory verse, *Hostias*.

Following a Venetian tradition, Marcello replaced the traditional *Sanctus* and *Agnus Dei* movements of this requiem with an organ sonata and a motet, *Dulcis Jesu Mater cara*.

Basic Data

EDITION
Critical edition prepared by Alessandro Borin

DURATION
Seventeen movements, perf., (with sonata and motet) c. 60'

VOICING AND ORCHESTRATION
Choir: double SATB choir
Soloists: SATB
Orchestra: vn. I/II, vla., vc., db. 2 ob., bsn. Fh. *basso continuo* instruments: harpsichord, org., therobo.

OUTLINE

Introit: 4'29"
> *Requiem aeternam,* satb choirs (fugal); *Et lux perpetua,* satb choirs; *Te decet,* unison soprano choirs. *Requiem aeternam* is repeated. ABA form.

Kyrie I-II: 7'08"
> *Kyrie* I, orchestral intro., satb choirs/SATB soli; *Kyrie* II, orchestral intro., SATB soli; *Kyrie* III, satb choirs/SATB soli. ABA form.

Christe: 2'50"
> *Christe,* orchestral intro., SATB soli (canonic)

Kyrie III: 5'38"
> *Kyrie,* satb choirs. Double Fugue.

Sequence: 21'14," 11 movements.
> Dies irae: 1'25" orchestral intro.; *Dies irae,* satb choirs/SATB soli; orchestral postlude. Fugal writing.
> Quantus tremor: 0'39" *Quantus tremor,* satb choirs/vn. obbligato.
> Tuba Mirum: 1'12" orchestral intro.; *Tuba mirum,* satb choirs; orchestral postlude.
> Mors stupebit: 1'52" *Mors stupebit,* satb choirs. Canonic writing.
> Liber scriptus: 2'46" orchestral intro.; *Liber scriptus,* SA duet; *ritornello; Judex ergo,* TB duet; *ritornello; Quid sum miser,* SA duet; orchestral postlude. vn. I/II obbligato.
> Rex tremendae: 1'00" *Rex tremendae,* satb choirs.
> Recordare: 3'16" orchestral intro.; *Recordare,* A solo; *ritornello; Quaerens me,* S solo; *ritornello; Juste judex* & *Ingemisco,* T solo/A solo; *ritornello]* vn. and vla. obbligato.
> Qui Mariam: 2'12" *Qui Mariam,* satb choirs; *Preces meae,* A solo/vn. obbligato; *ritornello; Inter oves,* satb choirs; orchestral postlude.
> Confutatis: 0'55" *Confutatis,* satb choirs (Fugue).
> Oro supplex: 1'38" orchestral intro.; *Oro supplex,* S solo; *ritornello; Cor contritum;* orchestral postlude. Violin I/II obbligato.
> Lacrymosa & Pie Jesu: 3'40" *Lacrymosa* & *Pie Jesu,* satb choirs. Prelude and fugue structure.

Offertory: 5'42"
> *Domine Jesu Christe,* satb choirs; *Libera animas-Sed signifer-Quam olim Abrahae* (fugal) & *Hostias,* satb choirs/unison altos; *Tu suscipe-Fac eas-Quam olim Abrahae,* satb choirs (fugal).
> Sanctus: replaced by an organ sonata, according to Venetian usage.
> Motet, *Dulcis Jesu Mater:* replaced the *Agnus Dei.*
> Communion, *Lux aeterna:* 0'35" *Lux aeterna,* plainchant; *Requiem aeternam* & *Et lux aeterna,* satb choirs. Fugal.

DISCOGRAPHY

Chandos, CHAN 0637, Athestis Chorus, Academia de li Musici, cond. Filippo Maria Bressan.

GIOVANNI BATTISTA PERGOLESI
January 4, 1710–March 16, 1736

This prolific Italian composer lived an even shorter life than did Mozart, yet he produced an enormous amount of music. He was trained at the *Conservatorio dei poveri di Gesu Christo* in Naples. His teachers included Gaetano Greco and Francesco Durante, leading figures of the Neapolitan school. This group of composers pioneered the development of comic opera and oratorio.

In 1732, he was appointed *maestro di cappella* for Prince Stigliano of Naples. Although Pergolesi became famous for his operatic works, he composed a limited amount of sacred music. The Naples earthquakes of November-December (1732) led to commissioning of his most famous sacred pieces. Three psalms, a large motet and the *Mass in D major*, for two choirs and two orchestras were written at this time. Two years later, he received a similar appointment, as chapel-master, in the service of the Duke of Maddaloni. In the meantime, he was busy fulfilling commissions for new operas, among them, *La serva padrona*, his most famous work. By his twenty-sixth birthday, he had written eleven operas, several oratorios, numerous vocal arias, some instrumental music, and a quantity of church music that included four masses (one for ten parts), Psalm settings, and many motets, most of which had an instrumental accompaniment. His last composition was the *Stabat Mater*.

There exists a question about the authorship of the *Requiem in B flat Major* (listed in *Grove's* as C Major), however, it was included in this book because of its historical interest and its musical qualities, which appear to mirror Pergolesi's musical style. The manuscript of the *Requiem in B flat major* is located in the Bibliothèque Nationale, Paris. Perhaps it was commissioned in memory of those lost in the Naples earthquakes. It is scored for SATB choir, SATB soli, and orchestra.

Much of the text is presented in an animated, declamatory style, typical of the Neapolitans. Although the prevailing choral texture is homophonic, Pergolesi was also capable of writing in the polyphonic *stile antico*, as the *Kyrie* fugue attests. Contrasts within the total work are created by the alternation of the vocal solo and the choral passages; a technique that stemmed from the earlier *concertante* structure.

The *bel-canto* melodies of this requiem setting are more ornate than those of the Viennese and Venetian style. The composer's method of melodic organization includes the frequent use of binary form found in the opening section of the Introit, *Requiem aeternam*, the bass solo, *Tuba mirum*, and the tenor solos, *Non peccavi* and *Libera me*.

The string orchestra generally functions independently of the choral

passages (except for the *Kyrie*) and there are numerous orchestral introductions (*Te decet, Tuba mirum,* Offertory, *Non peccavi,* and *Benedictus*). It is
also used to intensify the drama of the text, especially the dotted rhythms
that accompany *Quantus tremor* and the fanfare-like motive on the text,
Tuba mirum. Of special interest is the unusual Offertory text, Job 17:1–3
and 11–15, taken from the seventh lesson at Matins.

Basic Data

EDITION

Opera Omnia di Giovanni Battista Pergolesi
ed., F. Caffarelli
Vol. 27
Rome. 1942

DURATION

Six movements, 634 mm.

VOICING AND ORCHESTRATION

Choir: SATB range: S-G6; B-F3
Soloists: SATB
Instruments: vn. I/II, vla., vc., 2 Fh., org.

OUTLINE

Introit: 131 mm.
   Requiem aeternam, [B flat M] satb choir (Binary form); *Te decet,* [E flat M] SA duet.
   Binary form, modified.
Kyrie: 125 mm.
   Kyrie [B flat M] satb choir. *Stile antico* Fugue.
Sequence, *Dies irae*: 157 mm.
   Dies irae: 12 mm. [B flat M] satb choir;
   Quantus tremor: 22 mm. [fm] SA duet/satb choir; *Tuba mirum*: 86 mm. [B flat
   M—FM] TB soli/duet. Binary form; *Mors stupebit*: 31 mm. [gm] satb choir; *Huic
   ergo* & *Pie Jesu*: 56 mm., [B flat M] satb choir.
Offertory: 160 mm.
   Spiritus meus, 23 mm. [B flat M] satb choir; *Non peccavi,* 73 mm. [fm] T solo.
   Binary form; *Libera me,* 31 mm. [dm] satb choir; *Si sostenuto,* 33 mm. [B flat M]
   TB duet/satb choir.
Sanctus: 18 mm.
   Sanctus [FM] satb choir.
Benedictus: 43 mm.
   Benedictus [E flat M] SA duet [soli or choir not indicated] Binary form.

DISCOGRAPHY

None found.

GUILLAUME POITEVIN
October 2, 1646–January 26, 1706

Poitevin was trained at St. Troiphime, Arles, and in 1667 appointed *maitre de musique* at the cathedral, St. Sauveur, Aix-en-Provence. He trained two famous composers, Jean Gilles and André Campra, both of whom wrote superior requiem settings. The *Messe des Morts*, scored for SATB choir and *basso continuo*, employs a mixture of imitative polyphony and expressive homophonic style. Its conservative qualities reflect the tradition of the Franco-Flemish school and are evident in the placement of homophonic texture in *Agnus Dei* and *Pie Jesu*, as well as the use of Gregorian intonations.

The prevailing, four-part writing is relieved by voice thinning in all three movements and two-part writing employed in *Sed signifer* and *Hostias*. The smooth, contrapuntal passages reveal a masterly control of the imitative Palestrina style.

Basic Data

EDITION

Messe des Morts à IV parties
attribuée à Guillaume Poitevin
ed. H. A. Durand
Procure du Clerge, Musique Sacrée (PC 636 MS) 1962.

DURATION

Three movements, 166 mm.

VOICING AND ORCHESTRATION

Choir: SATB range: S-G6; B-F3
Instruments: org. [*b.c.*]

OUTLINE

Introit: 38 mm., 3 sections: *Requiem aeternam, Te decet*; satb choir; *Requiem aeternam* repeated.
Offertory: 96 mm., 5 sections: *Domine Jesu Christe*, satb; *Sed signifer*, tb; *Quam olim Abrahae*, satb; *Hostias*, tb; *Quam olim Abrahae*, satb.
Communion: 32 mm., 2 sections: *Lux aeterna; Requiem aeternam*, satb.

GEORG REUTTER
June 14, 1708–March 11, 1772

Georg Reutter received his first musical training from his father, the *Kapellmeister* and organist of St. Stephen's Cathedral (Vienna). He studied composition with Antonio Caldara. Around 1736, he assumed the same position once held by his father. Reutter is the choirmaster that hired and released the child chorister, Franz Joseph Haydn. In fact, he lived in the Reutter household for ten years.

Reutter became first *Kapellmeister* of the Court Chapel in 1769. He enjoyed fame as an outstanding composer, yet his poor management of the royal chapel caused the musical activities to enter a period of serious decline. He was further criticized for not taking his Cathedral duties seriously enough.

He produced more than three dozen operas, a small amount of instrumental music, and a number of sacred works, including eighty-one masses, six requiems, 126 motets, seventeen graduals, one hundred-fifty psalm settings, and numerous other liturgical pieces.

The *Requiem in C Minor* for SATB choir, SATB sol, and orchestra was composed in 1753. Its style follows the traditional Viennese *concertante* model created earlier by Christoph Strauss. The *concertante* principle is applied to the instruments, specifically their addition to and withdrawal from the choral passages. Strings provide support and rhythmic drive for the choral passages and first and second violins furnish obbligati for the vocal soloists. Cornetti and trombones double the choral lines, but in colorful, dramatic passages, such as those in the *Dies irae*, provide fanfares or obbligati for the choir and soloists. Particularly noteworthy is the virtuoso trombone solo that accompanies the alto solo, *Tuba mirum* and the trumpet fanfare passages of the *Sanctus*.

The predominant choral texture is a mixture of imitative polyphonic and expressive homophonic writing. There are four fugal passages (*Kyrie, Huic ergo, Quam olim Abrahae,* and *Cum sanctis*). Vocal solos are similar to those of the typical Viennese requiem. An exceptionally dramatic passage for the strings and voices occurs in the Introit where Reutter employed rapidly alternating, *piano-forte* dynamics, in typical Mannheim fashion.

Basic Data

EDITION
Denkmäler der Tonkunst in Österreich. Band 88
Georg Reutter. Kirchenwerke

ed. P. Norbert Hofer
Öesterreicher Bundeverlag, Wien. 1952

DURATION

Eight movements, 628 mm.

VOICING AND ORCHESTRATION

Choir: SATB range: S-G6; B-F3
Soloists: SATB
Instruments: vn. I/II, vla., db., 2 cornetti, 2 tbn., bsn. & org. [*continuo*]

OUTLINE

Introit: 47 mm.
  Requiem aeternam [cm] *adagio* satb choir; *Te decet* [fm] *andante*. satb choir. *Requiem aeternam* is repeated.
Kyrie: 32 mm.
  Kyrie [cm] satb choir. Fugue.
Sequence: 12 sections, 1 movement
  Dies irae [cm] satb choir; *Tuba mirum-Mors stupebit* [fm] A solo/TB duet; *Judex ergo* [cm] satb choir; *Quid sum miser* [cm] S solo; *Rex tremendae* [A flat M] satb choir; *Recordare* [fm] ST duet; *Quaerens me* [fm] B solo; *Juste judex & Ingemisco* [gm] satb choir & A solo; *Qui Mariam & Confutatis* [gm] STB soli, satb choir; *Oro supplex* [gm] STB soli; *Lacrymosa* [gm] satb choir; *Huic ergo* [cm] satb choir. Fugue.
Offertory: 71 mm.
  Domine Jesu Christe, [fm] *adagio*. satb choir; *Sed signifer,* T solo; *Quam olim Abrahae, andante*. satb choir (fughetta); *Hostias,* A solo. *Quam olim Abrahae* is repeated.
Sanctus: 18 mm.
  Sanctus, [cm] *adagio*. satb choir.
Benedictus: 68 mm.
  Benedictus [E flat M] *andante*. B solo; *Hosanna* [cm] satb choir.
Agnus Dei-Communion: 58 mm., [cm] 3 sections. *Adagio*
  Agnus Dei [cm] *adagio*. ATB soli/satb choir; *Lux aeterna,* SA duet; *Cum sanctis,* satb choir (fughetta); *Requiem aeternam,* SA soli/satb choir.

DISCOGRAPHY

None found.

GIOVANNI BATTISTA RUNCHER
March 9, 1714–February 21, 1791

Runcher appears to have studied in Venice and, from 1750 on, held the post of cathedral choirmaster in Trieste until his death. Little of his life is known and only a handful of works remain. Among the surviving pieces are three masses for men's choir and organ, a *Magnificat*, and a motet, *Dixit Dominus*. The latter two pieces are scored for choir and orchestra.

The *Messa da Requiem*, scored for TTB choir and organ, is similar to the Cordans requiem setting (1738), although it employs little imitative texture as does the latter work. It is a conventional liturgical setting, designed for general usage. The date of its composition is sometime around 1770. The predominant, three-part texture is written in homophonic style, with occasional passing tones.

Basic Data

EDITION

Giovanni Battista Runcher
Messa da requiem a tre voci en organo in Fa maggiore
trans. Roberto Gianotti
Partitura e Parti
Stamperia Musicale E. Cipriani, Rovereto. 1995

DURATION

Twenty-four movements that are sections, 554 mm.

VOICING AND ORCHESTRATION

Choir: TTB range: T-G6; B-G3
Instruments: org.

OUTLINE

Introit: 47mm., 2 sections: *Requiem aeternam* [FM], *Te decet* [dm-FM].
Kyrie: 64 mm., 1 section: *Chirie*.
Sequence: 171 mm. (10 sections-even-numbered verses only, except for *Pie Jesu*). *Quantus tremor-Mors stupebit-Judex ergo-Rex tremendae-Quaerens me-Ingemisco-Preces meae-Confutatis-Lacrimosa-Pie Jesu*] (gm throughout) Odd-numbered verses sung in chant.
Offertory: 89 mm., 3 sections: *Domine Jesu Christe* [dm], *Quam olim Abrahae* [FM], *Hostias* [dm]. *Quam olim Abrahae* repeated.
Sanctus: 83 mm., 3 sections: *Sanctus* [FM], *Pleni sunt coeli* [B flat M], *Benedictus* [gm].
Agnus Dei: 47 mm., 3 sections: *Agnus Dei* I [FM], II [B flat M], III [FM].
Communion: 53 mm., 2 sections: *Lux aeterna* [CM], *Requiem aeternam* [FM].

DISCOGRAPHY

None found.

ESTEBAN SALAS Y CASTRO
December 25, 1725–July 14, 1803

This Cuban composer was *maestro de capilla* of Santiago de Cuba Cathedral from 1764 to 1803. He established a music school at the cathedral for singers and instrumentalists. Other activities included working with the earliest chamber music ensemble in Cuba, conducting works by European composers, such as Haydn, Paisiello, Righini, and Pleyel. Late in life, he was ordained a priest (1790).

His compositions include five masses, three requiems, a *Devotions for the Virgin Mary*, three Passions, a *Stabat Mater*, and various other church pieces. There also exists a work for voices and orchestra, *Las siete ultimas palabras* (The Seven Last Words) and thirty villancicos for one to six voices; some with instruments. His musical style is derived from the Neapolitan models of Scarlatti and Durante.

Composed after 1762, the *Requiem* is a charming chamber work scored for SATB choir, strings, two flutes, and *basso continuo*. The presence of two flutes throughout the work, adds a gentle, pastoral quality. The choral fabric is written in a simple polyphonic texture with some imitative passages.

The instrumental writing often doubles the choral lines, though the first and second violins, as well as the two flutes, are scored with some independence from the vocal lines. The orchestration remains constant for all movements. This liturgical setting includes the Gregorian intonations, *Te Decet* (Introit), *Requiem aeternam* (Graduale), *Domine Jesu Christe* (Offertory), and *Requiem aeternam* (Communion). It is a gentle work that radiates peace and hope. *In memoria* is particularly lovely.

Basic Data

EDITION
None available.

DURATION
Eight movements, perf., c. 16′

VOICING AND ORCHESTRATION
Choir: SATB
Instruments: vn. I/II, fl. I/II, *basso continuo* [org., harp and vc.]

OUTLINE
Introit: 3′04,″ 2 sections [E flat M] [*Requiem*, satb choir] *Requiem*, repeated. ABA form.
Kyrie: 1′02,″ 1 section [E flat M] [*Kyrie*, satb choir]
Graduale: 2′39,″ 2 sections [fm] [*Domine Jesu Christe*, satb choir; *In memoria*, satb choir, *a cappella*]
Offertory: 2′53,″ 1 section [fm] [*Libera animas*, satb choir]
Sanctus: 1′35″ 1 section [fm] [*Sanctus*, satb choir]
Benedictus: 0′42,″ 1 section [fm] [*Benedictus*, satb choir]

Agnus Dei: 1'26," 1 section [fm] [*Agnus Dei*, satb choir]
Communion: 2'26," 2 sections [A flat M] [*Lux aeterna & Cum sanctis*, satb choir]

DISCOGRAPHY
Jade, 35808-2, Exaudi Choir of Cuba, dir. Maria Felicia Perez.

GREGOR JOSEPH WERNER
January 28, 1693–March 3, 1766

This Austrian composer was, for a short time, organist at the famous Melk Abbey (1715–1716). In 1728, he left Vienna for Eisenstadt, where he had been appointed *Kapellmeister* to the Esterhazy Court. Here, he was responsible for the writing of sacred music for the court. Slightly more than thirty years later, in 1761, Franz Joseph Haydn was placed on the Esterhazy staff as the chief composer, however, Werner remained on at Esterhazy as *Oberhofkapellmeister*, responsible still for the composition of sacred music. He clearly resented Haydn, referring to him as a "little songmaker." Even so, when the genial Haydn had reached old age, he wrote a set of introductions and fugues for string quartet on themes taken from Werner's oratorios.

Werner's compositions include eighteen oratorios, about sixty-five masses (including three requiems), three settings of the *Te Deum*, about seventy-five Marian antiphons, litanies, vespers, and various Christmas arias, pastorales, and cantilenas. There exists a small amount of instrumental music.

The date of his *Requiem in G Minor*, scored for SATB choir, SATB soli, strings, and organ, seems to be unknown, but the general *concertante* style, the use of instruments, and the imitative polyphonic texture suggest a strong affinity with the Viennese tradition of Strauss, Kerll, and Fux. He was a master of contrapuntal writing and virtually every movement of this requiem employs imitative texture. Only a few brief passages (*Et lux perpetua* and *Agnus Dei* III) utilize expressive homophonic writing. There are five vocal fugues; (*Kyrie*; *Ad te* (antiphon), *Hosanna* (*Benedictus*), and *Cum sanctis tuis* (Communion). There is paired imitation on *Confundantur* (antiphon) and canon *Pleni sunt coeli* (*Sanctus*).

The chamber orchestra is used primarily to double the vocal lines, however an independent part can be found in the accompaniment of the tenor solo, *Te decet*, the bass solo, *Quid est homo*, the duet, *Neque irrideant me*, the choral passage, *Agnus Dei* II, and bass solo, *Lux aeterna*. This usage of the orchestra conforms with the Viennese tradition of the early- to mid-eighteenth century.

Several novel features, all related to the requiem structure, include a one-movement Introit, an integrated, one-movement *Kyrie* (with a reduction of *Kyrie* II), the Lesson for First Nocturne, *Parce mihi*, the Antiphon, *Ad te levavi*, a linked, one-movement *Agnus Dei* and Communion, and a separate movement for the Communion verse, *Requiem aeternam*.

Basic Data

EDITION

Gregor Joseph Werner
Requiem G moll für Solo-Quartett, gemischten Chor, Streicher und Orgel
ed., Imre Sulyok
Verlag Doblinger, D. 13 084 Vienna & Munich
[Editio Musica, Budapest] 1969

DURATION

Eight movements, 305 mm.

VOICING AND ORCHESTRATION

Choir: SATB range: S-G6; B-G3
Soloists: SATB
Instruments: vn. I/II, vc., org. [*continuo*]

OUTLINE

Introit: 20 mm., 2 sections: [gm] *Requiem aeternam*, satb choir/soli; *Te decet*, TB soli
Kyrie: 21 mm., 1 movement: [gm] *Kyrie*, satb choir. Fugue.
Lesson, 1st Nocturne [Job 7, 16-21]: 25 mm., 4 sections: [gm] *Parce mihi*, satb choir; *Quis est homo*, B solo; *Quare me*, SATB soli; *Ecce nunc*, satb choir.
Antiphon: 60 mm., 3 sections: [dm] *Ad Te levavi*, satb choir (Fugue); *Neque irrideant*; SA duet; *Confundantur omnes*, satb choir.
Sanctus: 40 mm., 3 sections, 1 movement: [dm-FM] *Sanctus*, satb choir; *Pleni sunt coeli*; SB duet (Canon); *Hosanna*, satb choir.
Benedictus: 50 mm., 2 sections: [dm] *Benedictus*, SATB soli; *Hosanna*, satb choir. Fugue.
Agnus Dei-Communion: 50 mm., 2 sections: [gm] *Agnus Dei* I, SATB soli; *Agnus Dei* II, T solo; *Agnus Dei* III, satb choir; *Lux aeterna*, B solo & *Cum Sanctis*, satb choir. Fugue.
Communion, Requiem aeternam: 39 mm., 2 sections: [gm] *Requiem aeternam*, SATB soli/satb choir [same material as in opening movement]; *Cum sanctis*, satb choir. Fugue.

DISCOGRAPHY

Preiser Records, 90067, Chor der Basilika Marie Treu, Convivium Musicum Vindobonense, dir. Gerhard Kramer.

JAN ZACH
November 13, 1699–May 24, 1773

Zach began his musical career as a violinist at the Prague churches of St. Gallus and St. Martin. He later became the organist at St. Martin. He was a pupil of organ and composition with the great Czech organist, Bohuslav Černohorsky and seems to have learned counterpoint from Fux's *Gradus ad Parnassum*. In 1745, he was appointed *Kapellmeister* to the Elector's court in Mainz. He remained in this position for only five years, when he was suspended from his duties and ultimately dismissed. For the remainder of his career, he appears to have led a peripatetic existence.

He composed both sacred and secular music. Among the sacred works are twenty-nine masses, three requiems, and other miscellaneous liturgical pieces. The instrumental music includes sonatas, sinfonias, partitas, and works for the harpsichord and organ. The C minor *Requiem* is a dramatic and dynamic piece that is divided into sixteen separate movements. It was scored for SATB choir, SATB soli, and orchestra. The exact date of composition seems to be unknown.

Its musical language and style comes from two musical worlds; the Viennese tradition of Strauss (four *stile antico* fugues [*Kyrie, Dona eis, Quam olim Abrahae*, and *Cum sanctis tuis*] and one canon, *Agnus Dei*) and the *bel canto* solo of the Neapolitan school. The melodies, which Zach invented for the *Requiem*, were derived from Czech folksong and dance models. With the exception of the choral fugues, the primary choral texture is homophonic.

Although the orchestra doubles the choral lines, it often functions independently of the choir, providing rhythmic impetus and graceful, elegant contrapuntal melodies. It also provides introductions and conclusions for various movements. Trumpets and French horns are discretely employed to provide a nearly full ensemble sound. The instrumental obbligati, played by sections of instruments, rather than soloists, indicate that the *Requiem* probably dates from the mid-century.

Basic Data

EDITION
None found.

DURATION
Sixteen movements, perf., c. 31'

VOICING AND ORCHESTRATION
Choir: SATB
Soloists: SATB
Orchestra: vn. I/II, vla., db., 2 Fh., 2 tpt., org.

OUTLINE

Introit-Kyrie: 6'47" 3 movements
  Requiem aeternam, satb choir; *Te decet,* S solo; *Kyrie,* satb choir. Fugue.
Sequence: 7'05" 4 movements
  Dies irae: *Dies irae,* satb choir; *Quantus tremor,* S solo; *Tuba mirum,* B solo/trum-
  pet obbligato. (vs. 1, 2 & 3) Recordare: *Recordare,* AT duet. (vs. 9) Lacrimosa:
  Lacrimosa, satb choir. (vs. 18) Dona eis: *Dona eis,* satb choir. Fugue. (vs. 19, con-
  clusion)
Offertory: 8'20" 3 movements
  Domine Jesu Christe, satb choir/SATB soli; *Sed signifer,* S solo/string obbligato;
  Quam olim Abrahae, satb choir. Fugue.
Sanctus: 4'06" 3 movements
  Sanctus, satb choir; *Benedictus,* SA duet/violin obbligato; *Hosanna:* ATB trio/
  satb choir.
Agnus Dei: 1'52" 1 movement, SATB quartet/solo violin. Canon.
Communion: 3'00" 2 movements
  Lux aeterna, satb choir; *Cum sanctis tuis,* satb choir. Prelude and Fugue.

DISCOGRAPHY

Arte Nova, Musikland Rheinland-Pfalz, Vol. I, 74321 54241 2, Mainz Domchor and
Domorchester, cond. Mathias Breitschaft.

JAN DISMAS ZELENKA
October 16, 1676–December 22, 1745

Zelenka, an important contemporary of Bach and Handel, was born in
Bohemia. His father was an organist in the town of Lounovice. Jan is
believed to have studied at the Jesuit *Clementinium* (Prague). He later
studied with Johann Fux in Vienna and Antonio Lotti in Venice. In 1720,
he returned to Dresden, where he remained for the rest of his life. In Dresden, he gradually took over the duties of the *Kapellmeister,* Johann Heinichen. However, when Heinichen died in 1733, the position was not
given to Zelenka, but Johann Adolph Hasse, instead. Zelenka had to settle
with a lesser title, *Kirchen-compositeur.* This fact is believed to have caused
the very talented Zelenka to become withdrawn, spending his last years
in solitude and disappointment.

Like Johann Sebastian Bach, Zelenka was considered to be an "old-
fashioned" composer. Zelenka's music had two salient features, contrapuntal mastery and harmonic daring and inventiveness. The harmonic
progressions and fugue subjects found in the two requiems discussed
here give ample proof of both those qualities.

In the instrumental field, he composed five magnificent *Capriccios* for orchestra, a *Sinfonia à 8*, a *Concerto à 8*, an *Overture à 7*, and the *Hipocondrie à 7*; all works are the musical equivalents of Bach's *Brandenburg Concerti* or the *Six Concerti, Opus 3* of Handel. There are *Six Trio Sonatas* for violin, oboe, bassoon, and *basso continuo*. He wrote several oratorios of which, one, *Gesu al Calvario*, is still occasionally performed. There are about a dozen masses from his pen, of which three are requiem masses, (D minor, C minor, D major), two settings of the *Magnificat*, numerous responsories, three cantatas, and about a half-dozen concerted motets.

The *Requiem in D minor* was probably written in 1721 and was commissioned by Maria Josepha, a daughter of the emperor, Joseph I, on the tenth death anniversary of her father (1711). It is scored for SATB choir, SATB soli, and orchestra. It is a representative work of the South German school of composition. The prevailing choral texture is a mixture of imitative polyphony and expressive, homophonic writing. There are no less than six fugues, *Requiem aeternam*, *Kyrie* II, *Huic ergo*, *Quam olim Abrahae*, *Sanctus*, and *Benedictus*. The remarkable *Benedictus* combines, within its fugal procedure, a canon between the soprano and alto voices. Many of the vocal chromatic fugue subjects are characteristic of the South German organ school.

The restructuring and overlapping of the requiem texts, such as in the various verses of the Sequence hymn, *Dies irae*, is quite unusual. Yet, the linking of *Kyrie* I to the Introit movement is not that unusual in the musical settings of the requiem during this period. The need for Gregorian intonations (*Te decet* [Introit], *Domine Jesu Christe* & *Hostias* [Offertory], and *Lux aeterna* [Communion]) in this late-date work is somewhat noteworthy when compared with other requiem settings of the period. Several other unique features of the *D Minor Requiem* are the wide variety of tempi, scoring, and texture of the numerous short sections of text. Zelenka's repetition of the Introit (*Requiem aeternam*) music during the concluding Communion is one of the early examples of the unifying and rounding-out of musical ideas found at opposite poles of the work. This tradition was nurtured and employed by many later composers.

Basic Data

EDITION

Music Antiqua Bohemica. Series II, 14
Jan Dismas Zelenka
Requiem—D Moll, ZWV 48
Partitura [full score]
ed. Vratislav Belsky
Editio Supraphon H 7701, Prague. 1997

DURATION

Nine movements, 849 mm., perf., c. 42'

VOICING AND ORCHESTRATION

Choir: SATB range: S-A6; B-F3
Soloists: SATB
Orchestra: vn. I/II, vla. I/II, vc., db., 3 tbn. [2 double the vla. lines], 2 ob., chalu-
meau, bsn., org.

OUTLINE

Introit: 84 mm., 2 movements
    Requiem aeternam: 53 mm. [dm] *Requiem aeternam* & *Et lux*, satb choir/soli/full
    orch. Fugue. Te Decet: 29 mm. [FM] *Te decet*, SAT soli/ob.; *Exaudi* & *Ad Te*, SATB
    soli/full orch.; *Kyrie I*, satb choir/soli/full orch.
Christe: 114 mm., [dm] *Christe*, SB duet/str. (canon); [dm] *Kyrie*, satb choir/str./
ww. Fugue.
Sequence: 369 mm., [vv.10 & 13, *Juste Judex* & *Preces meae* omitted]
    Dies irae: 32 mm., [dm] satb choir/full orchestra.
    Quantus tremor-Quid sum miser-Rex tremendae: 67 mm., [dm] SB duet/vn. I/
    II/chalumeau obbligato.
    Tuba mirum: 63 mm., [CM] *Tuba mirum*, B solo; [dm] *Recordare*, A solo; [am]
    Tuba mirum & *Quaerens me*, SB duet; [am] *Mors stupebit* & *Juste Judex*, SB duet.
    All sections-vn. I/II & chalumeau obbligato.
    Liber scriptus: 116 mm., [am] *Liber scriptus*, SB duet,; *Qui Mariam*, TB duet. Both
    sections use str., ob. & chalumeau obbligato.
    Judex ergo: 35 mm., [am] *Judex ergo* & *Confutatis*, TB duet/bsn. I/II obbligato;
    Oro supplex, T solo/vn. I/II obbligato.
    Lacrimosa: 10 mm., [am] *Lacrimosa*, satb choir/full orch. (tbn. tacent)
    Huic ergo: 53 mm., [dm] *Huic ergo*, satb choir/full orch. (tbn. tacent). Fugue.
Offertory: 103 mm., 2 movements
    Domine Jesu Christe: 22 mm., [dm] *Libera me*, satb choir/full orch.; *Libera eas*,
    [FM] SA duet/vn. I/II obbligato; *Ne cadant*, TB duet/*b.c.*; [gm] *Quam olim Abra-*
    hae, satb choir/full orch. Fugue. Hostias: 13 mm., [FM] *Tu suscipe*, satb choir, *a*
    cappella/b.c. Quam olim Abrahae is repeated.
Sanctus: 55 mm.
    Sanctus [am] satb choir/str./ww. (fugue); *Dominus Deus*, satb choir *a cappella/*
    b.c.; *Deus Sabbaoth*, SAT soli *a cappella/b.c.*; *Pleni sunt coeli*, satb choir/full orch.;
    Osanna, SATB soli *a capella/b.c.*
Benedictus: 97 mm.
    Benedictus, [am] satb choir/str./ww. Fugue and canon.
Agnus Dei: 22 mm.
    Agnus Dei I, II, III [dm] satb choir/soli/str./ww.
Communion: 4 mm.
    Cum sanctis, [FM-dm] satb choir/str./ww. Repeat opening *Requiem aeternam*.

DISCOGRAPHY

Supraphon, SU 0052-2-231, Ensemble Baroque 1994 & the Czech Chamber Choir, dir. Roman Valek.

The *Requiem in C Minor* is a serious, restrained work, full of musical beauty. This masterpiece is scored for SATB choir and soloists, strings, three trombones and *basso continuo*. Trombones double the lower vocal lines and are used in every movement. The general style of the work, with its contrapuntal fabric and orchestration, is that of southern Germany.

The date of the composition is unknown, but likely comes from his last years of resignation and withdrawal. Perhaps this accounts for the even, sober quality of the music. Zelenka called his last masses *"Missae ultimate"* and one wonders if, in view of their great length (up to ninety minutes), there was any intention of having them performed, a similar question often asked of Bach's *Mass in B Minor*.

The predominant choral texture is imitative polyphony, including several fugues (*Kyrie* I, *Osanna* & *Huic ergo*), canons (*Et lux* and *Te decet*, violins, *Christe* SA duet, and *Pleni sunt coeli* ST duet) and other forms of imitative writing. The orchestra regularly doubles the choral parts, but there are a large number of independent orchestral *ritornelli*, as well as introductions and concluding passages.

Many of its pieces, especially the duets and solos, appear to be on the exalted spiritual level of a Johann Sebastian Bach. The duet for alto and tenor, *Te decet*, the soprano solo, *Tuba mirum*, or alto solo, *Liber scriptus*, are stunning pieces of virtuoso writing. Zelenka's *C Minor Requiem* was performed for the first time on Good Friday of 1984 in the Cathedral at Berne, Switzerland.

Basic Data

EDITION

None available.
Source: Muzeum ceské hudby, Prague, sign. XLVI C 115a and XLVI C 115b

DURATION

Six movements, perf., c. 47'

VOICING AND ORCHESTRATION

Choir: SATB
Soloists: SATB
Orchestra: vn. I/ II, vla., vc., db., 2 ob., bsn., 3 tbn., org. or harpsichord

OUTLINE

Introit: perf., 8'
 Requiem aeternam, satb choir/str./tbn.; *Et lux*: ST duet/vn. I/II. Canon and *ritornelli* employed; *Te decet*: AT duet/vn. I/II. (canon and *Ritornelli*). *Requiem aeternam* is repeated. ABA form.
Kyrie: perf., 9'30"
 Kyrie: satb choir/str./tbn. (Fugue); *Christe*, SA duet (canon)/vn. I/II obbligato. *Ritornelli*. *Kyrie* is repeated. ABA form.

Sequence: perf., c. 17' [abbreviated text in 7 sections]
  Dies irae: satb choir/orch.; *Quantus tremor*, SA duet; *Tuba mirum*, S solo; *Mors stupebit*, B solo; *Liber scriptus*, A solo/vn. obbligato; *Lacrymosa*, satb choir/orch.; *Huic ergo*, satb choir/orch. Fugue.
Sanctus: perf., 5'
  Sanctus, satb choir/orch.; *Pleni sunt coeli*, ST duet (canon); *Osanna*, satb choir/orch.; *Benedictus*, SAB trio; *Osanna*, satb choir/orch.
Agnus Dei: perf., 5'46'
  Agnus Dei I, satb choir/orch.; *Agnus Dei* II, T solo/SAT trio/satb choir/tbn./*b. c.*; *Agnus Dei* III, satb choir/orch.
Communion: perf., 2'54"
  Lux aeterna, B solo/vn. I/II obbligato; *Cum sanctis*, satb choir/str./tbn.

DISCOGRAPHY

1. Claves, CD 50-8501, Berne Chamber Chorus & Orchestra, cond. Jörg Dähler.
2. Bonton Music, 71 0368-2, Prague Madrigal Singers & Musica Aeterna, dir. Pavel Baxa.

6

The Symphonic Requiem

INTRODUCTION

During the mid-eighteenth century, a number of important musical styles—the baroque, the Neapolitan, the rococo, and the Viennese Classical—established an interesting artistic coexistence. Even as the baroque, with works by such renowned composers as Händel, J. S. Bach, Zelenka, and Scarlatti, approached its zenith in the 1750s, the rococo, a "simplified" version of the baroque style, had already appeared some thirty years prior. Johann Christian Bach, Georg Reutter, and Johann Ernst Eberlin were recognized for creating rococo requiem settings. All of these works were composed in the 1750s, yet they each possessed some of the noticeable stylistic characteristics later identified with the baroque.

Having originated in the late seventeenth century, the Neapolitan school bequeathed a vast array of masterful requiem settings, including early works by Feo, Durante, and Scarlatti, as well as the slightly later Pergolesi. Symphonic settings by Jommelli and Paisiello were first heard in the latter half of the eighteenth century. *G Minor Requiem*, the extraordinary setting composed by Mayr in 1815, stands as a landmark work in the Neapolitan requiem tradition.

The second half of the eighteenth century witnessed the steady ascendancy of the Viennese style, which reached its full maturity shortly before that century's end. During these years, Michael Haydn, Dittersdorf, Gassmann, Mozart, Pleyel, Salieri, and Eybler produced a series of elegant symphonic requiems. Inclusion of Ferdinand Schubert, Tomášek, and Cherubini in this pantheon of Viennese composers thus extends the lifespan of the classical style well into the second decade of the nineteenth century.

STURM UND DRANG

After the 1760s, a powerful movement and an early style of literary romanticism called *Sturm und Drang* (storm and stress) was embraced by composers working in the Viennese musical style. Its influence became apparent when the art form that had originally been presented as a refined, patrician music gradually drifted away from a tradition of structured, intellectual reflection toward a state of tremendously expressive emotion. Such influence was well articulated with the requiem settings of Eybler, Ferdinand Schubert, Gossec, Tomášek, and Cherubini. The fiery, picturesque settings of the *Dies irae* present in the Eybler requiem, as well as two works by Cherubini, serve as quintessential manifestos of this influence.

Mozart's settings of the *Dies irae* feature elements of *Sturm und Drang*, but they tend to be much more muted and controlled than those of Eybler and Cherubini. Cherubini's requiems in particular demonstrate more volatility and explosiveness than those of his contemporaries, yet the presence of the classical sense of restraint, balance, and decorum remains clearly evident.

CLASSIC FORMS

The second half of the eighteenth century saw the growth and evolution of two distinct artistic forms: the Viennese tradition of classicism and the Neapolitan opera's melodic *bel-canto* style. The more consequential forms of this era include the orchestral symphony, string quartet, piano sonata, solo concerto, opera and chamber music, and symphonic mass and requiem. These larger musical forms served as the foundation molds into which composers of the day poured their creative instincts and innovative ideas. Imbedded within these large structures were smaller musical forms, such as the sonata, minuet and trio, and rondo. These forms were platforms for the expression of rational thought with an orderly presentation and judicious unfolding of the melody. They were perceived as models of Enlightenment reasoning and a means by which to create what most considered a "pure" form of music.

This penchant for structure, elegance, and tradition is clearly apparent in the classic style. Composers did strive to portray feelings, sensations, and emotions, but communicated such things through their choice of mode (major-minor), melodic contour, contrasting dynamics, orchestral color, and tempo, elements that are found in the classical requiem setting as well.

As the eighteenth century came to a close, the emotional, programmatic elements began infiltrating the period's classical church music, especially the settings of the *Dies irae* text.

MANNHEIM SCHOOL

Forerunners of the classical style, the Mannheim composers bequeathed to the musical canon such orchestral effects as string tremolos, broken chords played out in quick notes, abrupt and unforeseen fortes and pianissimos, and the chamber-size orchestra that preceded the larger classic symphony.

The delicate melodies of a "simplified" baroque idiom are present in the requiem settings of Eberlin, J. C. Bach, Werner, and Reutter, with the most commonly employed obbligato instruments being the first and second violins. Many of their more decorative and flowery melodies are constructed upon repeated or arpeggiated figurations. Taking the style one step further was Schmittbaur, who included fragments of folk songs and virtuoso hunting-call *obbligati* scored for the French horn.

The Viennese tradition of the symphonic requiem built upon the pioneering work of the composers of the Mannheim school by expanding the orchestra so that the strings no longer carried the burden of all the important roles, sharing such duties with sections of woodwinds, brass, and percussion.

NEAPOLITAN STYLE

Scarlatti, Cimarosa, Paisiello, Pergolesi, Jommelli, Mayr, and Hasse stand as the most celebrated representatives of the Neapolitan requiem style. Their works feature the virtuoso *bel-canto* arias with trills, ornamentation, and improvised vocal cadenzas that stand as the true hallmarks of this tradition. Pasquale Cafaro (1715?–1787) and Fedel Fenroli (1730–1818) are lesser-known but genuinely significant Neapolitan composers who contributed requiem settings scored for SATB choir and strings. A requiem by Francisco Fago (1677–1745) is scored for SSATB soli and choir, strings, and brass. Mayr and Hasse, German disciples of the Neapolitan style, created requiems that possess an even greater colorfulness in their orchestration than those of their Italian counterparts. The Neapolitan influence is also evident in the requiem created by the Polish composer Wojciech Dankowski (c. 1760–c. 1836), which exhibits its notable melodic and orchestral characteristics.

Throughout the eighteenth century, the range of choral and vocal solo parts followed a steadily upward trend. High, A, B, and C are cited in

many of the soprano and tenor lines of the Neapolitan requiems, and high
E, F, and G occur frequently in the alto and bass range. Tenor solos in
Mayr's *G Minor Requiem, Preces meae* include four high B flats (B flat 6),
while his *Quid sum miser* calls for six A flats (A flat 6). This technical progression was eventually embraced and absorbed by the Viennese composers as well.

UNIQUE SETTINGS

Several requiems composed during the second half of the eighteenth century follow their own distinct artistic paths, differing from the styles
established by the Neapolitans and the Viennese. One such setting, a single requiem movement, was composed by Righini and scored for SATB *a
cappella* choir.

The gargantuan Gossec setting entitled *Messe des Morts* (1760) stands as
the most elaborate work of its era. Its enormous proportions and militant
orchestration were a foreshadowing of the grandiose musical style
adapted for public occasions during the French Revolution. The large
brass section employed by Gossec in the *Messe* was presented to the audience from a perch on an elevated platform. Berlioz created a similar effect
by including four brass bands in his own setting some seventy-seven
years later.

Smaller settings by Brusa (1767), Runcer (c. 1770), Cordans (1738), and
Mayr, appeared in the late 1700s, composed in a plain, nonsymphonic
style. Scored for choir and organ, and designed for general use and presentation, they are more akin to the routine liturgical models of the late
eighteenth century.

STRUCTURE

To provide musical interest, the *solo* versus the *ripieno* structure of the
baroque concerto gross, as cited in Vivaldi's *The Seasons*, Bach's *Branden-
berg Concerto*, and Händel's *Six Concerti, Opus 3*, employed a system of
"terraced" dynamics and instrumental variation. The classical era's
expression of these techniques came in the form of the *concertante* mass/
requiem. In the years following 1750, however, the vocal solo and chorus
replaced the concept of the baroque solo versus *ripieno* sections with a
smoother, even, and more natural flow of the orchestral coloring between
the movements and the dynamic contrasts.

Formal key relationships, utilized for the purpose of creating interest
and contrast, can be found in the music composed in both the baroque
and classic styles. The ABA form impressed upon so many requiem

Introits was derived from the tri-partite structure of the liturgical text. A tonic to dominant to tonic (I-V-I) key relationship is employed by most ABA forms, while several other possible key relationships between movements also follow a customarily prescribed pattern.

It should be noted that while developing the *da capo* aria, the Neapolitan composers retained their binary forms, especially when creating arias for their requiem settings.

In the late eighteenth century, the Introit and *Kyrie* texts, along with the *Agnus Dei* and Communion, were often linked together. Dittersdorf, Mozart, Salieri, Eybler, Eberlin, Mozart, Cherubini, Reicha, and Garcia-Nuñes combined both sets, while Schmittbauer and J. C. Bach joined only the Introit and *Kyrie*. Because Bach never completed his requiem setting, his possible means for presenting the *Agnus Dei* will remain forevermore left to conjecture. Biber (1690s) and Lopez (1716) were among the earliest composers who chose to connect the *Agnus Dei* and the Communion, a linkage Reutter later made in his requiem as well.

The polyphonic textures and melodic independence of the musical lines found in the baroque are altered and refined in the classic style. The era's prevailing imitative polyphonic texture was replaced by a homophonic texture in which the top musical line, in most cases the melody, became supported by the harmony of the lower lines. Baroque's linear contrapuntal conception is replaced by a chordal, vertical approach. This style is dominant in the majority of requiem settings composed after 1750. The employment of a fugue or canonic-style piece was often presented as a conscious recall of the older *stile antico*. Certain post-1750 texts, interestingly enough, were often arranged as fugues. *Quam olim Abrahae* was used by Reutter (1753), Jommelli (1756), Haydn (1771), Mozart (1791), Eybler (1803), Salieri (1816), Reicha (1803–09), Cherubini (1816 and 1834), and Tomášek (1820). This same text had been previously employed by Biber (1687), Marcello (after 1716), and Fux (1720). *Cum sanctis tuis*, a second text was frequently used in the second half of the eighteenth century. *Hosanna* and *Kyrie* were among the other popular, although less-often utilized, texts deemed proper for fugal treatment.

VOICING

Throughout the seventeenth and early eighteenth centuries, a wide variety of choral settings—SATB, TTB, SSA, SATTB, SATB-SATB—were in existence. Scores for the works that emerged during the progression of the eighteenth century, however, suggest that most composers favored the SATB format, possibly a result of an expanded orchestral role. There are only three post-1750 requiems (listed in this study), the settings of J. C.

Bach, Eybler, and Paisiello, that depart from the four-part format, opting instead for the double choir (SATB-SATB).

CODA

Music composed during the classical era was designed to serve as entertainment for an elite, sophisticated, well-to-do, aristocratic society. The formal elegance and beauty of classical music structure reflected this social position, even in the melodies composed for the requiem. The classical liturgical requiems evolved into concert works with the average performance time ranging from forty-five to sixty minutes. Performance of Gossec's colossal setting is an undertaking that runs nearly an hour and a half.

Composers during the era of the Enlightenment enjoyed the patronage of both the Church and the court, and their symphonic requiems illustrate this support. Late eighteenth- and early nineteenth-century settings by such composers as Paisiello, Righini, Bach, Cherubini, Cimarosa, Eybler, Jommelli, Mozart, and Nuñes-Garcia were written specifically for members of the royal court and the noble class. Other composers, however, sought to target expanded and divergent audiences. Salieri, Cherubini, Gossec, and Nuñes-Garcia specifically wrote for other composers and musicians. Haydn, Schmittbaur, and Mayr, on the other hand, focused their concentration on serving the clergy, while Mayr and Tomášek created settings deemed appropriate for "ordinary" people.

The composer's role in society began to change in the later years of the eighteenth century as the patronage system of the clergy and aristocracy gradually faded and artists discovered a new source of support from the newly emerging merchant class. Unfortunately, the merchants, though of sound wealth, did not support musicians and composers to the same degree as they had done in previous years. As the decades passed into the nineteenth century, composers began to resemble today's modern independent agents, contracting their services for whatever commission they were offered.

Public concerts and performances designed for the emerging upper and middle classes became more popular, similar to displays and programs put on at public museums and zoos. The early part of the nineteenth century witnessed the establishment of new music schools and conservatories. The dissolution of the aristocratic support led to the phasing out of the traditional system of music guilds that had existed for the purpose of training musicians and protecting their livelihood. Publication of music and journalism about the musical arts, which had first appeared during the mid-1700s, proliferated and flourished along with the new middle class that expressed such great interest in music, its history, and its performance.

JOHANN CHRISTIAN BACH
September 5, 1735–January 1, 1782

Johann Christian, the youngest son of Johann Sebastian Bach, received his musical training from his older brother, Carl Philip Emmanuel. In 1754, he traveled to Bologna to study with Padre Giovanni Battista Martini. After his conversion to Catholicism, he was appointed in 1760 to the organist's position at Milan Cathedral. Two years later, he left for England, where he began to make a reputation as an opera composer. By 1772, he had returned to Germany where he continued to produce stage works and instrumental music.

During his life, Johann Christian composed twelve operas and virtually every kind of instrumental music including symphonies, concertos, chamber music, keyboard works, and sacred music. His setting of the *Requiem* was composed in or about 1757 and was probably written for a family member of Count Agostino Litta, Bach's patron. The *Requiem* was never completed for there exists only the Introit, *Kyrie,* and sections of the *Dies irae.* An additional five pieces, all of which are for the Office of the Dead, include (an Invitatory, *Regem cui omnia sunt,* (Psalm 94 [95]), from Matins; three readings from First Nocturn, *Parce mihi Domine* (Job 7:16–21), *Taedet animam meam* (Job 10:1–7), *Manus tuae* (Job 10:8–12), and a setting of *Miserere* (Psalm 50 [51]). With the exception of the Introit (SSAATTB), the remainder of the work is scored for double SATB choir, SATB soli and small chamber orchestra of strings, oboes, organ, and French horns.

The prevailing choral texture is imitative polyphonic, with no less than three double fugues (*Kyrie* and *Amen*), a three-voiced fugue (*Rex tremendae*), and fugal writing in *Juste Judex*. Rare homophonic passages can be found in the short declamatory sections *Mors stupebit, Judex ergo, Huic ergo,* and *Pie Jesu.* Much of the choral writing is composed with dramatic antiphonal effects devised between the two ensembles. This choral dialogue, a legacy of the Venetian polychoral tradition, is accompanied by an independent orchestral accompaniment that drives the work forward. It is worth noting that Bach's setting for double chorus is one of few such models from the second half of the eighteenth century. The settings of Eybler (1803) and Paisiello (1789) also belong to this group.

Virtuoso Neapolitan *bel canto* solos and violin obbligati provide a foil to the contrapuntal choral idiom of the Germanic north. First and second violins play especially striking obbligati for the bass solo, *Quantus tremor,* the alto solos, *Quid sum miser* and *Oro supplex,* as well as the solo quartet, *Confutatis.*

The larger structure of the *Dies irae* is quite similar to the French grand motet or a German cantata. It is a suite of contrasting choral and solo pieces, unified by text, yet individualized by the moods and imagery of the text. The linking of the *Christe* and *Kyrie* II into one large section is accomplished in this work. Mozart, the Haydn brothers, and Beethoven learned from the work of Christian Bach. This excellent music is rarely played today. It deserves a much better fate.

Basic Data

EDITIONS

1. The Collected Works of Johann Christian Bach ed., Ernest Warburton A Garland Series in 48 volumes, Vol. 21 Music for the Office of the Dead & Mass for the Dead. Garland Publishers, Inc. New York, London. 1986	2. Accademia Musicale Vol. 20 Joh. Chr. Bach Dies Irae. Partitura [Full Score] First Edition. Ed. James Bastian Universal Edition. 1972

DURATION

Sixteen movements, 1052 mm.

VOICING AND ORCHESTRATION

Choir: choir I, SATB; choir II, SATB range: S-G6; B-G3 [F3 rare]
Soloists: SATB
Orchestra: STR: vn I/II, vla., vc., db. OTHER: 2 ob., 2 Fh., org.

OUTLINE

Introit: 32 mm., 2 movements. ABA form.
    Requiem aeternam: 18 mm. [FM] ssaattb choir.
    Te decet: 14 mm. [FM] ssaattb choir. *Requiem aeternam* is repeated.
Kyrie: 67 mm.
    Kyrie [FM] Double fugue; *Christe & Kyrie,* satb choirs I/II. Double fugue.
Sequence: 951 mm., 12 movements.
    Dies irae: 96 mm. [cm] *allegro moderato.* orch. intro.; *Dies irae (adagio),* satb choirs
      I/II *Quantus tremor:* 56 mm. [gm] *largo.* B solo/violin obbligato.
    Tuba mirum: 124 mm. [E flat M] orch. intro; *allegro maestoso.* S solo.
    Mors stupebit: 73 mm. [cm] *allegro.* orch. intro.; *Mors stupebit,* satb choirs I/II
      (Canon); *Liber scriptus,* S solo; *Judex ergo,* satb choirs I/II.
    Quid sum miser: 92 mm. [fm] *allegro con espressione.* A solo. Binary form.
    Rex tremendae, Recordare & Quaerens me: 72 mm. [E flat M] *allegretto.* SAB soli.
      Fugue.

Juste judex: 40 mm. [cm] *tempo moderato*. satb choirs I/II

Ingemisco: 56 mm. [cm] *andante*. T solo/violin I/II obbligato. Binary form.

Qui Mariam & Inter oves: 86 mm. [GM] *allegretto*. TA duet. Canon.

Confutatis: 87 mm. [gm] *non tanto allegro*. SATB soli. Binary form.

Oro Supplex: 87 mm. [CM] *allegro svelto*. A solo. Binary form.

Lacrimosa: 82 mm. [cm] *Lacrimosa, grave*; *Qua resurget, andante*; *Judicandus, grave*; *Huic ergo, andante*; *Pie Jesu, grave*; *Dona eis requiem, allegro,* satb choirs I/II. Double fugue.

DISCOGRAPHY

None found.

LUIGI CHERUBINI
September 14, 1760–March 15, 1842

From the early 1780s, Cherubini began to compose opera, the medium that most interested him. He studied with Giuseppi Sarti (1729–1802). In 1795, he was appointed an inspector [composer] of the Paris Conservatoire. He lost this position because of difficulties with Napoleon, but was reappointed as a professor of composition in 1816. He became director of the conservatoire in 1821.

The most famous of his theoretical works, *Cours de Contrepoint et de la Fugue*, resulted from his classroom teaching at this institution. By the age of sixteen, he had composed three masses, a setting of the *Magnificat*, two settings of *Dixit Dominus*, and an oratorio. His life's work includes thirty-nine operas (French and Italian), fifteen masses, thirty cantatas and ceremonial works, numerous vocal solos, and nearly 100 sacred pieces.

Beethoven regarded Cherubini as his greatest musical contemporary and Mozart, Haydn, Schumann, Brahms, and Mendelssohn held him in high esteem. Cherubini introduced Mozart's Requiem to French audiences.

The two requiem settings are among his best works. The earlier *Requiem in C Minor* was composed in 1816; a commission by Louis XVIII, who wanted to commemorate the deaths of Louis XVI and his wife, Marie Antoinette. It was first performed on January 21, 1816, in the Crypt of St. Denis. It is likely that this work was the first such work composed after the French Revolution. The last colossal requiem of French provenance had been composed by Gossec in 1760.

Cherubini scored the work for SATB choir and orchestra. A unique aspect of the orchestration is the absence of vocal soloists. Unison choral lines replace vocal soloists. It is also one of the principal methods used by the composer to create contrast in the choral fabric. The general harmonic language of the work is that of the Viennese classical tradition, but there are other qualities, such as the wide range of emotions, ranging from the seething anger of the *Dies irae* to the martial rhythm of the Offertory. A "sighing" instrumental motive played during the *Recordare* through *Inter oves* section adds a plaintive obbligato to the unison choral lines. A particularly violent orchestral accompaniment is found at the text, *de ore leonis* (in the lion's mouth). The absence of violins in the Introit, Graduale, *Sanctus*, and *Pie Jesu* creates a dark, somber timbre. In the concluding, ethereal passage (*Requiem aeternam*) the choir sings a sustained "C" while the orchestra revels in a variety of shifting harmonies. Of course, the expanded emotional character of this work is always controlled and balanced.

A large portion of the choral writing is homophonic, chordal texture. There is only one fugue (*Quam olim Abrahae*) and several passages of canonic writing (*Dies irae* and *Confutatis*).

The usage of a separate *Pie Jesu*, is a peculiarity of the French liturgy. Cherubini appears to be the second composer to include a symphonic version of the Elevation text. Gossec also included it in his requiem setting of 1760.

The *Requiem in C Minor* is a great work because the music, at every turn, works to illuminate the spiritual content of the text. This piece held a special place in Beethoven's mind. He once said that if he were to write a requiem, he would choose the *C Minor* of Cherubini as a model. Ironically, he never composed one, but this was the work performed at his own funeral!

Basic Data

EDITIONS

1. Cherubini	2. Luigi Cherubini
Requiem Mass in C Minor	Requiem in c
Four-Part Chorus of Mixed Voices	ed. Wolfgang Hochstein
ed. Eduardo Marzo	[full score]
G. Schirmer (ed. 537) c. 1902	Carus Verlag (40.086/01) 1995

DURATION

Seven movements, 937 mm., perf., c. 48'

VOICING AND ORCHESTRATION

Choir: SATB range: S-A flat 6; B-F3
Orchestra: vn. I/II, vla., vc., db., 2 ob., 2 cl., 2 bsn., 2 Fh., 2 tpt., 3 tbn. timp., tam-tam.

OUTLINE

Introit & *Kyrie*: 43 mm.
  Requiem aeternam [cm] *largo sostenuto*; *Te decet* [E flat M]; *Kyrie* [cm] satb choir. ABA form.

Graduale: 28 mm.

Requiem aeternam [gm] *andantino largo*, satb choir.

Sequence: 321 mm.

Dies irae [cm] *allegro maestoso*, Canonic (vv. 1–8) satb choir; *Recordare* [A flat M] *dolce assai*, (vv. 9–14), unison stb choir, "sighing" motive; *Inter oves* [gm-cm] satb choir, (vv. 15–19) Canonic.

Offertory: 243 mm.

Domine Jesu Christe [E flat M] *andante; Quam olim Abrahae, allegro,* Fugue; *Hostias, larghetto; Quam olim Abrahae* is repeated. satb choir.

Sanctus: 37 mm.

Sanctus [A flat M] *andante*, satb choir.

Pie Jesu: 78 mm.

Pie Jesu, [fm] *larghetto*, soprano & tenor choral unisons & satb choir.

Agnus Dei & Communion: 87 mm.

Agnus Dei [cm] *sostenuto*, satb choir; *Requiem aeternam*, satb choir.

DISCOGRAPHY

1. EMI, CDC 7496782, Ambrosian Singers and Philharmonia Orchestra London, cond. Riccardo Muti.
2. Multiple listings in Schwann Catalogue.

The *Requiem in D Minor* was composed between 1834 and 1836. It is one of the few big concert requiems scored for male voices (TTB) and orchestra. The composer chose this scoring because when he tried to have his *C minor Requiem* performed for his famous pupil, François Boïeldieu (1775–1834), the Archbishop of Paris raised objections to the presence of female voices.

It was given its premiere by the Concert Society of Paris on March 25, 1838. When Cherubini died in 1842, he was given a state funeral and this piece was performed on that occasion.

Contrasts in the choral texture are made by dividing the TTB into TT or TTTBB groupings. Although much of the texture is homophonic, there are passages of imitative polyphony in the Introit, Graduale, *Dies irae, Quam olim Abrahae* (Fugue), and *Pie Jesu*. For yet more variety, there are *a cappella* passages (*Pie Jesu*, the Graduale, *Voca me*, and *Dona eis*).

The full orchestra appears only in selected passages of the *Dies irae* and the Sanctus movement. Despite the limited possibilities for the choral scoring, this requiem is rich in orchestral color and emotional fire.

Basic Data

EDITIONS

1. Cherubini	2. Cherubini
Requiem [piano-vocal score]	Requiem für Mannerstimmen, D Moll
Edwin Kalmus,	Partitur [full score]
Publishers of Music, New York, NY	Edition Peters (#2005)

DURATION

Seven movements, 972 mm., perf., c. 47'

VOICING AND ORCHESTRATION

Choir: TTB [frequently divisi, TTTBB]
Orchestra: vn. I/II, vla., vc., db., pic., 2 ob., 2 cl., 2 fl., 2 bsn., 2 tpt., 3 tbn., bass
tbn., timp.

OUTLINE

Introit & *Kyrie*: 177 mm.
  Requiem aeternam [dm] *un poco lento*, ttb choir; *Te decet*, [FM]; *Requiem aeternam*
  [dm]; *Kyrie* [B flat M] Fugal writing. ABA form.
Graduale: 46 mm.
  Requiem aeternam [am] *lento*, ttb choir. Canonic writing.
Sequence: 302 mm. [complete text]
  Dies irae [dm] *vivo*; *Rex tremendae* [AM] *maestoso*; *Confutatis* [EM] *presto*; *Voca mea*
  [EM] *lento*; *Oro supplex* [am-dm] *andantino*; *Lacrymosa* [dm] *grave*, ttb choir.
Offertory: 196 mm.
  Domine Jesu Christe [FM] *andante*, ttb choir; *Sed signifer* [CM] tt choir; *Quam olim*
  Abrahae [FM] *allegro*, ttb choir, Fugal; *Hostias* [DM] *larghetto*, ttb choir; *Quam olim*
  Abrahae [FM] *allegro vivo*, ttb choir. Fugue.
Sanctus: 40 mm.
  Sanctus [B flat M] *maestoso*, ttb choir.
Pie Jesu: 67 mm.
  Pie Jesu [gm] *adagio*, ttb choir *a cappella* & instrumental interludes.
Agnus Dei & Communion: 144 mm.
  Agnus Dei & *Requiem aeternam* [dm] *lento*, ttb choir.

DISCOGRAPHY

Melodia, 74321 40723 2, Estonian State Academic Male Choir and Estonian Radio
Symphony Orchestra, cond. Neeme Järvi.

CARL DITTERS VON DITTERSDORF
November 2, 1739–October 24, 1799

Dittersdorf was an important figure in the Viennese school and a prolific
composer of symphonies and *Singspiel*, a form of music drama. He was
also an accomplished violinist. His first position was in the private
orchestra of Prince Hildburghausen (Vienna). At the time, he was twelve
years old. Dittersdorf remained a member of this ensemble for ten years
as he gained experience and an education. Later, he played in the court
orchestra that was conducted by Christoph Willibald Gluck.

  In 1765, Dittersdorf became *Kapellmeister* to the bishop of Grosswardein

(Hungary), a position that Michael Haydn had earlier occupied and finally, in 1769, was appointed to a similar position at the episcopal palace of Johannisberg. He remained there for twenty-six years. He was a good friend of Wolfgang Mozart, Johann Vanhal, and Joseph Haydn and played string quartets with them when visiting Vienna.

Dittersdorf, the composer, penned about 120 symphonies and more than forty solo concerti. The *Singspiel* occupied a prominent place in his output, turning out thirty-nine of them. His sacred compositions include a dozen masses, several oratorios and litanies, one requiem, a Vespers setting, and many offertories, antiphons, and hymns.

The *Requiem in C minor* was written before 1787 and scored for SATB choir, SATB soli, string orchestra, trumpets, trombones, timpani, and organ. In typical Viennese fashion, trumpets double the upper voices, the trombones, lower. The predominant choral texture is homophonic, with points of imitation employed in the opening passage of the *Kyrie*. The core of the orchestral writing rests with the string section. It supports the choir and provides obbligati for the soloists and choir. A descending chromatic scalar passage, played by the violins, is especially noteworthy. This recurring pattern suggests fear and dread and is played throughout the *Dies irae*. A foreboding string tremolo accompanies the text, *Quantus tremor*. Brass and timpani are relegated to a rather modest, coloristic role.

The musical language and style of the *Requiem in C Minor* descends from the long line of Viennese requiem tradition initiated by Christoph Strauss more than a century earlier.

Basic Data

EDITIONS

1. Karl Ditters von Dittersdorf
Requiem in C Minor for Mixed Choir, Solo Quartet, Chamber Orchestra and
   Organ.
Practical First Edition. Harmonization of Basso Continuo, and Piano Reduction
   by Rudolf Walter
Edition Gravis, Bad Schwalbach. [Vocal Score EG 199] 1990

2. Karl Ditters von Dittersdorf
Requiem C moll für gemischten Chor, Solo Quartet, Orchester und Orgel
Praktische Erstausgabe und Generalbass-Aussetzung von Rudolf Walter
[Full Score] Edition Gravis. Bad Schwalbach EG 199

DURATION
Seven movements, 416 mm., perf., 28′

VOICING AND ORCHESTRATION
Choir: SATB range: S-G6; B-F3
Soloists: SATB
Orchestra: vn. I/II, vla., vc., db., 2 tpt. (clarino), 3 tbn., timp., Org.

OUTLINE

Introit: 49 mm.

Requiem aeternam [cm] *andante*. satb choir/TB duet; *Te decet* [E flat M] S solo; *Requiem aeternam* is repeated. ABA form.

Kyrie: 32 mm.

Kyrie, [gm] *allegro*. satb choir; *Christe* & *Kyrie* [E flat M-gm] SA duet/ satb choir. ABA form.

Sequence: 138 mm.

Dies irae [cm] satb choir; *Quantus tremor*, satb choir; *Tuba mirum*, satb choir; *Mors stupebit*, B solo; *Liber scriptus*, S solo; *Judex ergo*, T solo; *Quid sum miser*, A solo; *Rex tremendae*, B solo; *Recordare*, S solo; *Juste judex*, A solo; *Ingemisco*, T solo; *Qui Mariam*, B solo; *Preces meae*, S solo; *Inter oves*, A solo/satb choir; *Oro supplex*, SA duet; *Lacrimosa* & *Huic ergo*, satb choir.

Offertory: 57 mm.

Orch. intro; [E flat M]; *Domine Jesu Christe, andante*. T solo; *Quam olim Abrahae*, satb choir; *Hostias*, T solo; *Quam olim Abrahae*, satb choir.

Sanctus: 39 mm.

Sanctus [cm] *adagio*. satb choir; *Pleni sunt coeli*, SA duet; *Hosanna*, satb choir.

Benedictus: 59 mm.

Benedictus [E flat M] *andante*. A solo; *Hosanna* repeated, satb choir.

Agnus Dei-Communion: 42 mm.

Agnus Dei I [fm] *largo*. S solo; *Agnus Dei* II [A flat M] T solo; *Agnus Dei* III [cm] satb choir. Introit *Requiem aeternam* repeated.

DISCOGRAPHY

Ars Musici, AM1158-2, Consortium Musicum München and the Regensburger Domspätzen, cond. Georg Ratzinger.

JOSEPH LEOPOLD EYBLER
February 8, 1765–July 24, 1846

Joseph Eybler grew up in eighteenth-century Vienna. A friend of Haydn and Mozart, he knew Salieri and Schubert, as well as Albrechtsberger, who had been his teacher. He maintained a life-long friendship with Mozart, whom he assisted and cared for during the latter's final illness. After Mozart died, his widow, Constanza, commissioned Eybler to complete the requiem. After completing the orchestration for large parts of the *Dies irae*, he relinquished the commission.

Eybler held the position of choirmaster in the Carmelite Church (Vienna) and later, the Schottenkloster, where he worked for thirty years. When Salieri retired in 1824 as *Hofkapellmeister*, Eybler was chosen to succeed him. In 1833, he suffered a stroke while conducting Mozart's *Requiem* and spent his final years with his family. He was ennobled in 1835.

Eybler's compositions are not as numerous as other composers of his generation. He wrote some instrumental music, several vocal works, and a number of liturgical compositions, including three-dozen masses, thirty-nine graduales, thirty-three offertories, and other liturgical pieces.

The *Requiem in C minor* was commissioned by Empress Maria Theresia, wife of Emperor Franz II. It was performed at a memorial service for Emperor Leopold II, in 1803. Eybler scored the music for SATB soli, double SATB choir, and symphonic orchestra. Although the music superficially resembles that of Haydn and Mozart, the large, independent orchestra and advanced chromatic language reveal an impulse toward the romantic idiom.

This symphonic mass is full of dramatic surprises. Hallmarks are abrupt changes in the dynamic levels (Communion), a legacy of the Mannheim tradition and unexpected harmonic turns and melodic chromaticism (*Agnus Dei*), an inheritance from the literary *Sturm und Drang* movement.

The *Dies irae*, scored for double choir, strings, brass, and timpani paints a spectacular depiction of the Last Judgment. Seething string obbligati in the *Dies irae*, *Confutatis*, and *Quam olim Abrahae* passages drive the music relentlessly forward. Yet Eybler frequently turned to the older *concertante* style when composing for the soloists and choir. Such passages are found in the *Domine Jesu Christe* (Offertory), the *Benedictus*, and *Requiem aeternam* (Communion). Two hair-raising choral fugues *Quam olim Abrahae* and *Cum sanctis tuis* are a carry-over of past tradition. The fugue was the classical version of the baroque *stile antico*; a homage to the liturgical past. The use of double-choir dialogues (*Dies irae*, *Confutatis*, and *Libera me*) suggest an equally remote past; the polychoral style of the Venetians, Gabrielli, and Cavalli.

The virtuoso clarinet obbligato (one of the earliest in the requiem literature) of the soprano solo, *Recordare* was indicative of the expanded use of a "military" instrument. The clarinet had been accepted into the Viennese symphonic orchestra during the latter part of the century. Mozart's *Clarinet Quintet*, K581 and *Clarinet Concerto*, K622 (1789 and 1791, respectively) predate this obbligato by only a few years. Eybler infused the Viennese classical style with a sense of drama, foreshadowing the advent of nineteenth-century musical romanticism.

Basic Data

EDITION

Joseph Eybler
Requiem für Soli, Chor und Orchester
ed. Martin Derungs
Edition Kunzelmann GmbH # 9M 932
Lottstetten/Waldhut. 1980

DURATION

Twelve movements, 1075 mm., perf., c. 58'

VOICING AND ORCHESTRATION

Choir: Choir I, SATB; Choir II, SATB range: S-B flat 6; B-E flat 3
Soloists: SATB
Orchestra: vn. I/II, vla., vc., db., 2 ob., 2 cl., 2 bsn., 4 tpt., alto, tenor, bass tbn.,
  timp.

OUTLINE

Introit-*Kyrie*: 166 mm.
  Requiem aeternam [cm] *adagio.* satb choir; *Te decet* [E flat M] *andante.* satb choir;
  Requiem aeternam & *Kyrie* [cm] *adagio.* satb soli; satb choir only in *Kyrie.* ABA
  form.
Sequence: 280 mm., 5 movements.
  Dies irae: 69 mm. [cm] *Dies irae* & *Quantus tremor, andante.* satb choirs I/II; *Tuba
  mirum,* B solo; *Mors stupebit, adagio.* satb choirs I/II. *Liber scriptus:* 46 mm. [gm]
  Liber scriptus, andante. A solo; *Judex ergo* [B flat M] B solo; *Quid sum miser* [cm]
  A solo; *Rex tremendae* [A flat M] satb choir, *divisi. Recordare:* 124 mm. [fm-D flat
  M] *Recordare, andante cantibile.* A solo; *Quaerens me,* A solo/satb choir; *Juste
  judex* & *Qui Mariam* [D flat M] T solo; *Preces meae* [A flat M] B solo; *Inter oves* [E
  flat M] satb choir. *Confutatis:* 24 mm. [gm] *andante.* satb choirs I/II; *Voca me* [E
  flat M] *adagio.* satb choirs I/II. *Lacrimosa:* 17 mm. [cm] *largo.* T solo; *Huic ergo,*
  satb choir.
Offertory: 179 mm., 2 movements.
  Domine Jesu Christe: 105 mm. [gm] *andante.* SATB soli/satb choir; *Sed signifer,* S
  solo/sat choir; *Quam olim Abrahae,* satb choir. Fugue. *Hostias:* 74 mm. [E flat M]
  andante. TB duet/SATB soli/satb choir; *Quam olim Abrahae* fugue repeated.
Sanctus: 41 mm.
  Sanctus [cm] *andante.* satb choir; *Osanna,* satb choir. Fughetta.
Benedictus: 137 mm. [E flat M] *andantino.* SATB soli/satb choir. *Osanna* is repeated.
Agnus Dei: 176 mm.
  Agnus Dei [cm] *adagio.* ATB soli/satb choir; *Lux aeterna,* S solo/satb choir; *Cum
  sanctis tuis,* [cm] *allegro.* satb choir. Fugue. Communion: 10 mm. *Requiem aeter-
  nam* [A flat M] *adagio.* satb choir; *Cum sanctis tuis* repeated. Fugue.
Responsory: 88 mm. [gm] satb choirs I/II.

DISCOGRAPHY

CPO 999 234-2, Alsfelder Vokalensemble and Steintor Barock Bremen, dir. Wolfgang Helbich.

FLORIAN LEOPOLD GASSMANN
May 3, 1729–January 20, 1774

Gassmann was born in Bohemia and was probably educated by the Jesu-
its in Chomutov. In 1757, he was working in Venice. He is believed to have

studied with Padre Martini and is known to have been familiar with Fux's *Gradus ad Parnassum*. He was appointed composer, in 1764 or 1765, to the Viennese royal court, succeeding Christoph Willibald Gluck. Shortly afterward, in 1772, he was also appointed *Kapellmeister* for the court, in the footsteps of Georg Reutter.

Gassmann composed about twenty operas, thirty-three symphonies, ten wind quartets, eight string quartets, nine quartets for flute, oboe, and strings, twenty-six fugues for string quartet, and many other pieces. The liturgical compositions include five masses, one incomplete requiem, ten graduales, seven offertories, eight motets for choir and orchestra, vespers, and a *Stabat Mater*.

It is not known when the three-movement Requiem (Introit, *Kyrie*, and Sequence) was composed, but the musicologist, Mark Suderman, suggests that the probable date of composition was between 1772 and 1774 (p. 26, "Comparisons between the requiems . . ." Suderman). He also suggests that Mozart might have been influenced by this work when composing his own setting of the requiem. (There exist similarities between the key choice and melodic shapes.)

The *C Minor Requiem* is scored for SATB choir, strings, two oboes, two trombones, bassoon, and organ (*continuo*). Both the violin I/II and viola play in *concertante* fashion. The orchestral accompaniment is often independent of the choral mass, but from time to time, doubles it. The orchestral writing bears many similarities to that found in Jommelli's requiem setting. The choral textures include imitative polyphony (*Kyrie, stile antico* fugue) and homophonic writing (*Exaudi orationem*).

This work was performed at least once, annually, at the Imperial Chapel (Vienna) from 1788 to 1843 (Sudermann). One of the unique features of this piece is the absence of the *Christe* text in the *Kyrie* movement.

Basic Data

EDITIONS

1. Denkmäler der Tonkunst in Österreich [XLV 83]
Florian Leopold Gassmann
Kirchenwerke
ed. Franz Kosch
Universal Edition, Wien 1938. [Introit & *Kyrie* only]

2. Florian Gassmann's Requiem: A critical edition and conductor's analysis.
Mark Suderman
DMA Essay (University of Iowa)
[Introit, *Kyrie* & Sequence]

DURATION
Two movements, 282 mm.

VOICING AND ORCHESTRATION
Choir: SATB range: S-G6; B-F4
Orchestra: vn. I/II, vla., db., 2 ob., bsn., 2 tbn., org. [*basso continuo*]

OUTLINE

Introit: 153 mm., 3 movements
  Requiem aeternam: 63 mm. [cm] *adagio*, satb choir.
  Te decet: 82 mm. [A flat M] *andante*, satb choir.
  Requiem aeternam: 8 mm. [fm] *grave*, satb choir.
Kyrie: 129 mm.
  Kyrie [fm] *alla breve*, satb choir. (no *Christe*)

DISCOGRAPHY

None found.

FRANCOIS-JOSEPH GOSSEC
January 17, 1734–February 16, 1829

Gossec was born in Hainaut Province, Belgium. He sang in several different chapel choirs and around 1751 he became a member of an orchestra
conducted by Jean Phillipe Rameau in Paris. During that time, he also
became acquainted with Johann Stamitz. This connection permitted him
to become familiar with the music of the Mannheim school. In 1762, he
became director of a private theater and, in 1769, he founded the *Concert
des Amateurs*, an organization supported by public support. He eventually
left to work with an older organization, the *Concert Spirituel*. During the
French Revolution, he turned his musical energies to composing a style of
patriotic, state music that involved massive musical forces. These works
foreshadow the colossal works of Berlioz, such as his *Requiem*.

Gossec's musical compositions consist of twenty-three stage works,
more than forty symphonies, forty chamber works and thirty-three revo-
lutionary vocal pieces. The output of sacred music includes a dozen compositions, the oratorio *La Nativité*, and the massive *Grande Messe des Morts*.

His *Requiem* was first performed in May 1760 at the Jacobean monastery
of the rue St. Jacques. It appears that Gossec dedicated the composition at
a later date to the administrators of the *Concert des Amateurs de Paris*. It is
scored for SATB choir, SATB soli, and orchestra. Its massive proportions,
(2,518 measures in length, large orchestra, and seventy-five-minute performance time) are models for the gargantuan, out-of-door, massed performances held in Paris during the French Revolution.

The work is arranged into twenty-five movements but is missing the
Kyrie. There are several novel features in this work: The powerful brass
orchestration of the *Tuba mirum* and *Mors stupebit* calls for four clarinets,
eight bassoons, four trumpets, three trombones, and four French horns,
all placed on a raised platform (an idea later used by Berlioz and Verdi);
operatic recitative style (*Quid sum miser*) and *Vado et non revertar*; and

striking dynamic contrasts (*Agnus Dei*). A vocabulary of pictorial orchestral effects includes a depiction, by the brass choir, of the Last Judgment (*Tuba mirum*), string pizzicato (*Quantus tremor* & *Recordare*), string tremolo (*Confutatis*), and "sighing" motives in the first violins (*Vado et non revertar*).

Gossec composed orchestral introductions for many of the movements, especially those of the Sequence (*Tuba mirum, Mors stupebit, Recordare, Inter oves, Confutatis,* and *Lacrymosa*). The *Exaudi* passage of the Introit and Offertory also possess introductions.

The *Grande Messe* seems to have taken on the features of a Handelian oratorio, complete with an orchestral overture, lengthy arias, recitative-like sections and choruses. One tenor aria in Neapolitan style, *Spera in Deo*, is composed in binary form. It includes vocal trills and ornaments and its range extends upward to B flat 6 (eight times) before reaching the high C7.

The choral writing is predominantly homophonic texture but there are passages of imitative polyphony, including the two *stilo antico* fugues, *Et lux perpetua* and *Amen*. The Offertory, is that of the then-current French usage, *Vado et non revertar*.

Vado et non revertar	I go and shall not return
Aeternitatem pavide conspicio	With fear I view eternity.
sors immutabilis tamen contingit me.	Immutable fate confronts me.
Jam apertum video monumentem,	I already see the open tomb,
vocem tenebrosam audio	I hear the somber voices
ad judicium evocantem me.	calling me to judgement.
Quid sum dicturus	What shall I answer?
Heu me miserum.	Alas, woe is me. I shall suffer
Iram Domini portabo quia peccavi.	the wrath of the Lord, for I have sinned.
Quare tristis anima mea?	Why are you sorrowful, my soul,
et quare conturbas me?	and why do you disquiet me?
Spera in Deo, quoniam adhuc confitebor illi,	Hope in God, for I will trust in Him as before.
salutare vultus mei, et Deus meus.	Savior of my soul and my God.
Cedant hostes in adventu eius,	Foes shall yield at His coming
contremiscant et fugiant in infernum.	and flee in trembling to Hell.
Confundantur erubescant;	They shall be confounded and humbled
iter impedire non audeant.	and shall not dare to oppose Him.

Basic Data

EDITION

Francois Joseph Gossec
Grande Messe des Morts

Partition Choeur et Piano
Editions à Coeur Joie, "Les Passerelles"
24 Avenue Joannes Masset, 69009 Lyon, France. 1989

DURATION

Twenty-five movements, 2518 mm., perf., c. 1' 30"

VOICING AND ORCHESTRATION

Choir: SATB range: S-A flat 6; B-F 3
Soloists: SATB
Orchestra: vn. I/II, vla., vc., db., 2 fl., 2 ob., 4 cl., 8 bsn., 4 tpt., 3 tbn., 4 Fh., timp.,
    org.

OUTLINE

Overture: 69 mm.
Introit: 561 mm., 5 movements.
    Requiem aeternam: 35 mm. [cm] *grave*. satb choir.
    Te decet: 161 mm. [E flat M] *allegro moderato*. SA duet/satb choir. Canon.
    Exaudi: 93 mm. [fm] *largo*. S solo.
    Requiem aeternam: 13 mm. [CM] *grave*. satb choir.
    Et lux perpetua: 259 mm. [cm] *moderato*. satb choir. Fugue. No *Kyrie*.
Sequence: 1127 mm., 11 movements. (vv. 5-6 omitted)
    Dies irae, 87 mm. [gm] *grave; maestoso*. SATB soli. (vv. 1–2)
    Tuba mirum: 153 mm., [E flat M] *grave*. Bar solo. (v. 3)
    Mors stupebit: 159 mm. [CM] *allegro*. satb choir. (v. 4)
    Quid sum miser: 27 mm. [FM] *lento*. *Recit*, A solo. (vv. 7–8)
    Recordare: 95 mm. [fm] *largo*. SAB trio. (vv. 9–14)
    Inter oves: 175 mm. [FM] *allegretto*. S solo [C7 required] (v. 15)
    Confutatis: 131 mm. [gm] *allegro molto*. satb choir. (v. 16)
    Oro supplex: 16 mm. [E flat M-cm] *grave*. satb choir. (v. 17)
    Lacrymosa: 77 mm. [fm] *lento*. SS duet. (v. 18, 2 lines)
    Judicandus: 17 mm. [B flat M] *grave*. satb choir. (v. 18, line 3 & v. 19, line 1)
    Pie Jesu & Amen: 190 mm. [gm] *andante*. satb choir. *Amen* (fugue). (v. 19, line
        2–3)
Offertory: 341 mm., 3 movements.
    Vado et non revertar: 67 mm. [cm] *lento*. *Recit*, T solo.
    Spera in Deo: 102 mm. [E flat M] *largo*. T solo. Binary form. [C7]
    Cedant hostes: 172 mm. [cm] *allegro*. satb choir & AB duet.
Sanctus: 15 mm.
    Sanctus [fm] *maestoso*. satb choir.
Pie Jesu: 60 mm.
    Pie Jesu [FM] *largo*. TB duet & satb choir.
Agnus Dei: 33 mm.
    Agnus Dei [cm] *moderato*. satb choir.
Communion: 312 mm., 2 movements.

Lux aeterna: 175 mm. [CM] *allegretto*. SAB trio.
Requiem aeternam: 137 mm. [cm] satb choir, *grave*; *Et lux perpetua*, *allegro*. Fugue.

DISCOGRAPHY

Capriccio, 10 616, Kölner Rundfunkchor and Cappella Coloniensis, cond. Herbert Schernus.

JOHANN MICHAEL HAYDN
bapt. September 14, 1737–August 10, 1806

Following in the steps of his older brother, Michael Haydn began his musical career as a chorister at St. Stephen's Cathedral in Vienna. At the age of twenty, he was appointed *Kapellmeister* to the bishop of Grosswardein in Hungary, currently Oradea, Romania. In 1763, he began a life-long tenure as court musician and concert-master with the court of Archbishop Schrattenbach in Salzburg. Among his more famous pupils were Carl Maria von Weber and Anton Diabelli.

He wrote a significant amount of instrumental music including twelve concertos, forty symphonies, thirty divertimentos, twelve string quartets, as well as dances, marches, partitas, cassations, and serenades. He composed twenty dramatic works and numerous vocal solos. However, Haydn also left a significant amount of sacred music that included thirty-two masses (three requiems), six settings of the *Te Deum*, twelve litanies, four vespers, six responsories, and about 340 smaller works, such as motets, Latin works, and German masses.

The autograph score of the *Requiem* (dated December 31, 1771) was written in a period of two weeks after the death of his patron, Archbishop Schrattenbach. Scored for SATB choir, SATB soli, string orchestra, brass, timpani, and organ, it was first performed at Salzburg Cathedral.

The choral textures are evenly balanced between homophonic and imitative polyphonic writing. There are three fugues, *Kyrie*, *Quam olim Abrahae*, and *Cum sanctis tuis*, of which two are used twice. Other imitative passages include *Requiem aeternam* and the *Amen* of the Sequence.

Vocal solos are models of melodic beauty and restraint. Missing are the fiery and florid Neapolitan arias with their virtuoso cadenzas. Long movements, such as the Sequence, *Agnus Dei*, and the Offertory, tend to be through-composed, instead of divided into smaller movements. SATB soli are frequently used with the satb choir in *concertante* fashion. Strings form the nucleus of the orchestration for the *Requiem in C minor*, providing support for the choir and obbligati for the vocal solos and choir. Trumpets and trombones play only a modest, coloristic role.

Haydn sought to preserve a balance between the liturgical text and the music. The liturgical requirements of the service seem to be met, for the Caecilian Movement, a group of nineteenth-century musicians that attempted to reform church music by removing operatic influences and other improper elements from it, approved of Haydn's church music. Although this group generally frowned upon symphonic liturgical music, they felt that Haydn's approach was appropriate for church usage.

Basic Data

EDITIONS

1. Johann Michael Haydn
Missa pro defuncti Archepiscopo
  Sigismundo
Musicum Edition Vol. 8
Universal Edition #25 C008. 1970

2. Academia Musicale
A University of Missouri Collegium
Universal Edition & University of
Missouri Press
Johann Michael Haydn
Missa pro defunctis
Universal Edition 1969.

DURATION

Eight movements, 950 mm., perf., c. 42′

VOICING AND ORCHESTRATION

Choir: SATB range: S-A flat 6; B-E flat 3
Soloists: SATB
Orchestra: vn. I/II, vc., db., bsn., 2 clarini, 2 tpt., 3 tbn., timp., org.

OUTLINE

Introit-*Kyrie*: 70 mm.
> *Requiem aeternam* [cm] *adagio.* satb choir; *Te decet* [E flat M] satb choir/SATB soli; *Requiem aeternam* [cm] SATB soli; *Kyrie,* [cm] SATB soli/satb choir. Fugue. ABA form (modified). Fugue.

Sequence: 291 mm.
> *Dies irae, Quandus tremor* & *Tuba mirum* [cm] *andante maestoso.* satb choir; *Mors stupebit* & *Liber scriptus,* S solo; *Judex ergo* & *Quid sum miser,* A solo; *Rex tremendae, Recordare* & *Quaerens me,* satb choir; *Juste judex* & *Qui Mariam,* T solo; *Preces meae* & *Inter oves,* B solo; *Confutatis,* satb choir; *Oro supplex,* SATB soli; *Lacrimosa,* satb choir/SATB soli.

Offertory: 177 mm., 2 movements
> *Domine Jesu Christe*: 103 mm. [gm] *andante moderato.* satb choir/SATB soli; *Fac eas,* S solo; *Quam olim Abrahae,* satb choir. Fugue. *Hostias*: 73 mm. [gm] *andante.* A solo; *Fac eas,* TB duet; *Quam olim Abrahae* (*vivace e piu allegretto*) satb choir. Fugue.

Sanctus: 46 mm.
> *Sanctus* [cm] *andante.* satb choir; *Osanna,* ATB soli/satb choir.

Benedictus: 97 mm.

   Benedictus & *Osanna* [E flat M-cm] *allegretto*, ATB soli/satb choir.

Agnus Dei-Communion: 269 mm., 2 movements.

   Agnus Dei: 148 mm. [cm] *adagio con moto*. S solo/satb choir; *Agnus Dei*, B solo/satb choir; *Agnus Dei*, T solo/satb choir; *Lux aeterna*, S solo/satb choir; *Cum sanctis tuis*, satb choir. Fugue.

Requiem aeternam: 121 mm. [E flat M] *adagio*. SATB soli in duet pairs/satb choir; *Cum sanctis tuis*, satb choir. Fugue.

DISCOGRAPHY

René Gailly, CD87-125, Vivente Voce and Capella Vivente, dir. Philippe Benoit.

The *Requiem in B Flat Major*, of which only a fragment remains, was composed at the very end of the composer's life. He had been able to complete an exceptionally fine Introit and *Kyrie* as well as the first three verses of the *Dies irae* before he died in 1806. The work was commissioned by the Empress, Maria Theresa, the very same person for whom Haydn had written solo soprano passages in other works. Haydn scored the work for SATB choir, SAB soli, two oboes, two bassoons, two French horns, two trumpets, three trombones, strings, timpani, and organ.

The dramatic setting of the Introit, *Requiem aeternam*, is scored for SATB choir and soprano soloist. The text and music are arranged into an ABA form with an attached *Kyrie*, (fugue) which develops directly out of the first movement. Although two different fugues are used for the *Kyrie* and *Christe* texts, both are employed in the second Kyrie. The *Dies irae* is scored for satb choir and a raging orchestral accompaniment. *Tuba mirum* is scored for soprano and alto soloists with a trombone obbligato. The *Liber scriptus* text, set for bass solo, was only partially completed.

Because the musical imagery of the extant music is so good, one can only wonder what might have happened had Haydn lived to complete his vision.

DISCOGRAPHY

Hanssler Classic, CD 98.144, Gächinger Kantorei Stuttgart, Bach Collegium Stuttgart, Stuttgart Chamber Orchestra, cond., Helmuth Rilling.

NICCOLO JOMMELLI
September 10, 1714–August 25, 1774

Jommelli was an important composer of opera and sacred music, who began his musical training in the cathedral choir at Aversa, Italy. He was later befriended by Johann Adolphe Hasse, a man whose music greatly influenced him. Jommelli maintained a lifelong friendship with one of his teachers, Padre Martini. During the 1740s, he received numerous commission to write operas and oratorios for every important Italian city. In 1749, he received an important commission from Vienna. His Neapolitan-style music had a significant influence upon the music of the early Viennese symphonists, Dittersdorf and Wagenseil.

For several years, he was musical director for the *Ospedale degli Incurabili* in Venice. From 1754 to the late 1760s, he worked as *Ober-Kapellmeister*, in Stuttgart, for Duke Karl Eugen of Württemberg. He finally moved to Naples after the death of his wife in 1769, where he continued to compose opera and some church music, despite a stroke and ill health. He penned some 160 operas, sixteen oratorios, passions, and sacred cantatas, more than a dozen masses (including two requiems, both in E flat; 1756 and 1764), and numerous other liturgical pieces. Much of his sacred music was written for the *Accademia di St. Cecilia* in Rome.

The *Missa pro defunctis in E Flat* was composed in 1756 for the death of the Duchess of Württemberg, the mother of Duke Karl Eugen. This magnificent composition, scored for SATB choir, soloists, string orchestra, and organ, has all of the stylistic hallmarks for which Jommelli was noted; a remarkable variety of violin obbligati, an important role for the second violin, a *concertato* style for soloists and choir and an ever-changing homophonic and imitative polyphonic choral texture.

In virtually every one of the fourteen movements, first and second violins play an astonishing variety of melodic counterpoints for the soloists and choir. Each of these string duets enhances, ornaments, or underlines the meaning of the liturgical text. The choral texture is a balanced mixture of imitative polyphony and chordal writing. There are no less than ten fugues (or fugal passages), as well as canons and other imitative devices. All vocal solos employ ornate, florid, *bel canto* passages that require an excellent technique.

The orchestra rarely doubles the choral lines. Instead, it is used to provide an inexhaustible supply of melodic and rhythmic counterpoints to the choral and vocal ensembles. Only the opening of the majestic, *stile antico* fugue, written at the end of the requiem, is accompanied without instrumental ornamentation.

Basic Data

EDITION

Niccolo Jommelli
Requiem for Solo Voices, Chorus, String Orchestra and Organ
ed. Hermann Müller
Second edition [Full score]
Edition Kunzelmann (#10225) Adliswil, Zurich. 1986

DURATION
Thirteen movements, 984 mm.

VOICING AND ORCHESTRATION
Choir: SATB range: S-A6; B-G3
Soloists: SATB
Orchestra: vn. I/II, vla., vc., db., org. [*continuo*]

OUTLINE
Introit: 32 mm.
  Requiem aeternam [E flat M] *larghetto*, satb choir; *Et lux* [B flat M] SA soli; *Luceat eis*, satb choir. *Te decet* not set. ABA form.
Kyrie: 129 mm.
  Kyrie [E flat M] SATB soli. Fugato; *Christe* [cm] *un poco adagio*. satb choir/SATB soli; *Kyrie* [E flat M] satb choir. Fugue.
Sequence: 392 mm., 4 movements. All verses included.
  Dies irae: 72 mm., [E flat M] *moderato*. *Dies irae*, satb choir/SATB soli; *Quantus tremor*, T solo; *Tuba mirum*, B solo; *Mors stupebit*, A solo; *Liber scriptus*, S solo; *Judex ergo*, satb choir/SA duet; *Quid sum miser*, A solo; *Rex tremendae*, satb choir. *Salva me*: 212 mm., [B flat M] *andantino*. *Salva me/Recordare*, SAT trio; *Quaerens me*, B solo; *Juste Judex*, T solo; *Ingemisco*, A solo; *Qui Mariam*, S solo; *Preces meae*, BT duet; *Inter oves*, SA duet; *Confutatis*, satb choir/SAT trio. *Oro supplex & Lacrymosa*: 39 mm., [cm] *larghetto*. *Oro supplex*, satb choir/SATB soli; *Lacrymosa*, satb choir/SATB soli. *Pie Jesu*: 70 mm., [E flat M] satb choir. Fugue.
Offertory: 258 mm., 2 movements.
  Domine Jesu Christe: 136 mm., [E flat M] *tempo giusto*. *Domine Jesu Christe*, satb choir; *Libera eas*, (*andante assai*) satb choir; *Quam olim*, SATB soli. Fugue. *Hostias*, 122 mm., [cm] *andantino*. *Hostias*, SATB soli/satb choir; *Quam olim*, satb choir. Fugal.
Sanctus: 103 mm.
  Sanctus [E flat M] *larghetto*. satb choir/SA duet; *Hosanna*, satb choir. Fugue.
Benedictus: 34 mm.,
  Benedictus [cm] *largo*. S solo/string trio (*fughetta* obbligato); *Hosanna* is repeated.
Agnus Dei: 113 mm., 2 movements.
  Agnus Dei: 23 mm., [E flat M] *moderato*. satb choir/SATB soli. *Dona eis*: 90 mm., *andante*. satb choir/SATB soli. Fugal.
Communion: 111 mm.
  Lux aeterna [E flat M] satb choir. Fugue; *Requiem aeternam*, satb choir/SATB soli.

DISCOGRAPHY
Bongiovanni, GB 2215-2, Orchestra Sinfonica Moldava, Coro dell'Accademia Nazionale, dir. Silvano Frontalini.

JOHANNES SIMON MAYR
June 14, 1763–December 2, 1845

Mayr was a highly gifted keyboard performer. At the age of eleven, he attended the Jesuit School in Ingolstadt, and later, in 1781, the university where he learned how to play most of the string and woodwind instruments. In 1789, he began his formal musical studies with Carlo Lenzi, the choirmaster of St. Maria Maggiore (Bergamo). Ten years later, he made his debut at La Scala with his opera, *La Lodoiska*. During the following years, he established himself as a serious, first-rate opera composer. In 1802, Mayr succeeded Lenzi as choirmaster at St. Maria Maggiore and, in 1805, he was appointed director of the cathedral choir school. His most famous pupil was Gaetano Donizetti.

Mayr was a prolific composer, leaving an output of sixty-eight operas, ten oratorios, forty-six cantatas, eighteen masses, six requiems, 213 mass movements, twenty requiem movements, 111 pieces for the Office of the Dead, 159 works for Vespers, twenty-nine works for Holy Week, and numerous other liturgical pieces. He further composed a significant amount of instrumental music, including two symphonies, and a handful of solo keyboard works and chamber music. His musical style is a mixture of the melodic fireworks and harmonic language of the Neapolitan School coupled with a colorful Germanic orchestration.

The *Requiem Mass in D minor* belongs to a group of three requiems (#1, F major; #2, D minor; #3, F Major) for three mixed voices (S [or A] TB). These pieces are scored for organ and violone accompaniment and are designed for practical use in parishes with small or nonprofessional choirs. The vocal range and demands of the melodic line are fairly simple and easy, yet the music is quite satisfying.

The *Requiem in D minor* employs an elaborate homophonic texture throughout, with some polyphonic writing in *Christe*, the *Amen* section of the *Dies irae* movement and the *Benedictus*.

Basic Data

EDITION

Messa da Requiem in Re minore
Ed. D. Giuseppe Pedemonti
Edizioni Carrara. Bergamo. 1963

DURATION

Nine movements, 538 mm.

VOICING AND ORCHESTRATION

Choir: S (or A) TB range: S-G6; B-F3
Instruments: org., violone

OUTLINE

Introit: 46 mm., *Requiem aeternam* & *Te decet*, stb choir.
Kyrie: 41 mm., *Kyrie, Christe* & *Kyrie*, stb choir.

Sequence: 175 mm., 19 sections [odd-numbered verses-STB; even-numbered verses-Gregorian chant]
Offertory: 76 mm. *Domine Jesu* & *Hostias,* stb choir.
Sanctus: 18 mm. *Sanctus,* stb choir.
Benedictus: 25 mm. [GM] *Benedictus,* stb choir.
Agnus Dei: 32 mm. *Agnus Dei* I, II, III, stb choir.
Communion: 35 mm. *Lux aeterna* & *Et lux perpetua,* stb choir.
Responsory: 90 mm. [gm] [*Libera me,* satb choir].

DISCOGRAPHY

None found.

The *Gran Messa da Requiem in Sol minor,* Mayr's most extensive piece of this genre, was composed around 1815 and received its premiere on August 25, 1815, in the Basilica of St. Maria Maggiore. This monumental setting (one of the longest in the eighteenth and nineteenth centuries) is scored for SATB choir, SATB soli, and large symphonic orchestra. The only other contemporary work that can match its length is the setting by Gossec, which exceeds the *Gran Messa* by 355 measures for a total length of 2,518 measures. However, the *Gran Messa* is the most massive Neapolitan requiem setting.

The musical style of this requiem is an apotheosis of Neapolitan operatic, *bel canto* style, traditional eighteenth-century diatonic harmonic language, and colorful Germanic orchestration. The choral texture is a balanced mixture of imitative polyphony and dramatic, chordal homophony. There are a half-dozen fugues and fugal passages (*Kyrie, Cuncta stricte, Amen, Benedictus, Requiem aeternam,* and *Et lux*).

Although a number of choral passages were composed in *concertante* style (Introit, Offertory, and *Agnus Dei*), almost every movement contains similar passages for virtually every string and woodwind instrument. Obbligato and solo passages pepper the instrumental fabric. The orchestration of the *Gran Messa* suggests that Mayr relied abundantly upon this older technique, more than any other composer of requiem settings up to that time.

Mayr wrote instrumental introductions for the Introit, *Agnus Dei,* and Responsory, as well as solo pieces of the Sequence hymn, *Dies irae.* Included are *Dies irae, Tuba mirum, Liber scriptus, Rex tremendae, Ingemisco, Qui Mariam, Preces meae, Confutatis, Oro supplex,* and *Lacrymosa.* Because most are vocal solos, it is probable that their instrumental introductions represent a stylistic carryover from the solo works found in the then-current opera style.

A novel characteristic with Mayr is the predisposition for the contrasting sonorities of woodwind and string ensembles. They are found throughout the work. The binary form, popular with the Neapolitan School, was used by this composer for the solo movements, *Tuba mirum*, *Ingemisco*, and *Qui Mariam*.

The *bel canto* style of Mayr employed wide melodic leaps, a spacious vocal range, numerous trills, grace notes, patterns, short note values (sixteenth and thirty-second notes) and taxing vocal cadenzas that were placed at the end of every solo movement. While perusing the score, it can be seen that he treated the voice just like any other instrument of the orchestra. Even the bassoon and string bass did not escape Mayr's notice. Their *bel canto* passages show that they were expected to perform up to the same rigorous standard he set for the solo vocalists or the violins.

It has occasionally been said that Verdi's *Manzoni Requiem* was his greatest opera; the same might also be said of Mayr's *Gran Messa da Requiem*. This rarely performed work is one of the important milestones in the history of the requiem.

Basic Data

EDITION

Mayr, Giovanni Simeone
Messa da requiem [full score]
Pub. Calegraphia Cogliate e Co, Milano. [1855]

DURATION

Sixteen movements, 2153 mm., perf., c. 90'

VOICING AND ORCHESTRATION

Choir: SATB range: S-G6; B-F3
Soloists: SATTB
Orchestra: vn. I/II, vla., vc., db., 2 fl., 2 cl., 2 ob., 2 bsn., 2 Fh., 2 tpt., 2 tbn., timp.
    Additional instruments for *Libera me*: 2 basset horns, 4 Fh. Org.

OUTLINE

Introit: 218 mm.
    orch. intro; *Requiem aeternam* [gm] satb choir; orch. interlude; *Te decet* [E flat M]
    SATB soli/satb choir; *Requiem aeternam* [gm] ST soli/satb choir. ABA form.
Kyrie: 288 mm.
    Kyrie, [gm] SATB soli/choir; *Christe*, B flat M] AB duet/cello obbligato; *Kyrie*,
    [gm] SATB soli/satb choir, fugue. ABA form.
Sequence: 1220 mm., 8 movements
    Dies irae: 213 mm. [cm-CM] orch. intro.; *Dies irae & Quantus tremor*, satb choir.
    Fugal passage on *Cuncta stricte*. ABABAB form. (vv. 1–2). *Tuba mirum*: 147 mm.
    Tuba mirum & Mors stupebit [FM] B solo/trombone obbligato. Binary form. (vv.
    3–4). *Liber scriptus*, 170 mm. [GM & em] orch. intro.; *Liber scriptus & Judex ergo*;
    T solo/flute obbligato; orch. interlude; *Quid sum miser & Judex ergo*. two-part

form. (vv. 5–7). *Rex tremendae*: 125 mm. [E flat M] ST soli/satb choir; orch. intro.; *Rex tremendae; Recordare; Quarens meae & Juste judex*, ABCA form. (vv. 8–11). Ingemisco: 93 mm. [fm] orch. intro.; *Ingemisco*, S solo/violin obbligato. Binary form. (v. 12). *Qui Mariam*: 135 mm. [am] orch. intro.; *Qui Mariam*, T solo/TB duet/B solo. Binary form. (v. 13). *Preces meae*: 170 mm. [B flat M] *Preces meae & Inter oves*, T solo; orch. intro.; *Confutatis*, T solo/satb choir/clarinet obbligato. (vv.14–16). *Lacrymosa*: 167 mm. [cm] [orch. intro.; *Lacrymosa*, satb choir; *Huic ergo*, SATB soli; *Amen*, satb choir. Fugue.(vv. 17–19).
Offertory: 116 mm.
   Domine Jesu Christe; Sed signifer & Hostias, [B flat M] *concertante* SATB soli/choir.
Sanctus: 35 mm.
   Sanctus; Pleni sunt coeli & Hosanna [B flat M] satb choir.
Benedictus: 29 mm.
   Benedictus, [FM-B flat M] SATB soli (Fugue) & *Hosanna*, satb choir.
Agnus Dei: 38 mm.
   Agnus Dei I, II, III, [FM] SATB soli & *Dona eis*, satb choir.
Communion: 62 mm.
   Lux aeterna [FM] SAB soli; *Requiem aeternam*, satb choir (Fugue); *Et lux*, SATB soli/satb choir (fugal).
Responsory: 147 mm. [cm]
   [orch. intro; *Libera me*, ST soli/satb choir; *Tremens factus*, S solo; *Quando coeli*, satb choir; *Dies illa*, SATB soli (fugal); *Dum veneris*, satb choir & *Requiem aeternam*, ST soli/satb choir (*Libera* & *Requiem* are same music.)

DISCOGRAPHY

Agora, AG 131-2, Civico Coro Fiharmonico di Milano, Orchestra Stabile di Bergamo, cond. Pierangelo Pelucchi.

WOLFGANG AMADEUS MOZART
January 27, 1756–December 5, 1791

Mozart wrote nineteen masses, including the *Requiem* (K. 626), several Litanies, Vespers, and Vesper Psalms. Twenty-five other short pieces round out the output of sacred choral works by this master. Of course, he wrote wonderful music in virtually every other medium.

K. 626 is probably the most famous requiem ever written and is possibly the most-often performed work of the genre. There are numerous editions and myriad articles, not to mention the recent monograph by Christoph Wolff, *Mozart's Requiem*, devoted to this work. The musicologists Mark Suderman and Jeffrey Poland have suggested that Mozart might have been influenced by the earlier requiem settings of Gassmann and Michael Haydn as he composed his own setting. Others have proposed that Mozart's setting subsequently influenced the requiem of Eybler. Mozart's father wrote a requiem setting. Was the son influenced by it? These points remain quite interesting, yet speculative. Irving Kolodin, in his book, *The Continuity of Music*, dealt with the topic of how composers make use of their predecessors' works, both at the conscious and subconscious levels. He suggests that fundamental ideas present in all music and the musical insights expressed by one composer could be used by another as the basis for the development of a new work or style.

Mozart composed his *Requiem in D Minor*, in the twilight of his young life, June or July to December of 1791. Unfortunately, he did not live to see its completion. Michael Haydn and Charles Gounod suffered the same fate, although the latter was putting the finishing touches on the work when he died and Haydn got only as far as the first few measures of *Liber scriptus*. Mozart scored the *Requiem* for SATB choir, SATB soli, and orchestra. It was commissioned by Count Franz von Walsegg-Stuppach, who had hoped to perform it on the first anniversary of his wife's death.

Mozart was able to complete the Introit and *Kyrie* and sketch out the Sequence, up to the first eight measures of the *Lacrymosa*. He further notated the choral parts and figured bass for the Offertory; Süssmayr completed its orchestration in addition to the *Lacrimosa*. The material for the Communion was taken from the Introit and *Kyrie*, music already composed by Mozart. His pupil, Süssmayr, composed much of the *Sanctus* and *Agnus Dei*. Incidentally, Süssmayr is believed to have composed, upon Mozart's request, the recitatives for the opera *La Clemenza di Tito*. He also wrote two requiems himself. He was anything but an *amanuensis* or musical "hack," rather he was a composer whom Mozart held with respect and esteem.

The orchestration of the Sequence was also worked on and completed up to the *Lacrimosa* by another of Mozart's close friends, Joseph Eybler. He had been Constanze Mozart's first choice to complete Mozart's unfinished requiem, but he declined to finish the task. This *Requiem* is considered a masterpiece; a remarkable fact when we consider that the work was written by three different individuals.

The choral textures employ both imitative contrapuntal and expressive chordal writing. There are three fugues (one a double fugue, used two times), *Kyrie, Osanna,* and *Quam olim Abrahae*. The double fugue of the *Kyrie* is a powerful piece, derived from the musical style of Bach. Like other requiem settings of the period, the orchestra doubled the choral passages in the *stile antico* fugal writing, but which provided colorful melodic counterpoint and rhythmic drive in other choral passages and the solos. Five of the movements were furnished with brief, but telling, orchestral introductions (Introit, *Rex tremendae, Recordare, Lacrymosa,* and *Benedictus*).

Some of the pictorial elements in the orchestral accompaniment include the dramatic dotted-rhythms of the stately *Rex tremendae*, the churning melodic motives of the *Confutatis*, the "weeping" melody of the *Lacry-mosa*, and the tranquil harmonies of the *Recordare*.

The structural changes to the mass sections (the union of the Introit and *Kyrie*, as well as the *Agnus Dei* and Communion), typical of the late eighteenth-century requiem, are also present in the Mozart work. Also, like the slightly earlier Dittersdorf setting, the music of the opening Introit material was brought back at the conclusion of the work. This technique "rounded off" the melodic structure of the piece.

Despite the fact that the finished work was the result of several individuals, this work possesses an uncommon depth of spiritual feeling. Carl Czerny (1791–1857), friend of Beethoven and teacher of Liszt, was an excellent composer. Although known today as a composer of velocity exercises for piano, Czerny wrote a substantial amount of music for two pianos. Among these pieces are arrangements of Haydn's *Creation* and Handel's *Messiah*. He is further supposed to have made an arrangement for two pianos (long out of print) of the Mozart *Requiem*, although the writer has not been able to confirm this.

Basic Data

EDITIONS

1. W. A. Mozart
Requiem
C. F. Peters Corporation, # 8337
New York-London-Frankfurt

2. Wolfgang A. Mozart
Neue Ausgabe, Sämtliche Werke
Series I, Geistliche Gesangswerke
Abteilung 2: Requiem
vorgelegt von Leopold Nowak
Bärenreiter. Kassel, Basel, Paris 1965

3. Mozart
Requiem, K. 626
[full score]
Ed. & revised by Friedrich Blume
Edition Eulenburg #954
Ernst Eulenburg, Ltd. London

DURATION

Twelve movements, 881 mm., perf., 48'

VOICING AND ORCHESTRATION

Choir: SATB range: S-B flat 6; B-F3
Soloists: SATB
Orchestra: vn. I/II, vla., vc., db., 2 bassett horns [cl.], 2 bsn., 2 tpt., 3 tbn., timp., org.

OUTLINE

Introit-*Kyrie*: 101 mm. [Prelude & Fugue]
    orch. intro.; *Requiem aeternam* [dm] *adagio.* satb choir; *Te decet* [B flat M] S solo/

satb choir; *Requiem aeternam* [dm] satb choir; *Kyrie*: 52 mm., *allegro*, satb choir. Double fugue.

Sequence: 352 mm., 6 movements

Dies irae: 68 mm. [dm] *allegro assai*. satb choir. (vv. 1–2).

Tuba mirum: 62 mm. [B flat M] *andante*. *Tuba mirum*, B solo; *Mors stupebit & Liber scriptus*, T solo; *Judex ergo*, A solo; *Quid sum miser*; S solo. (vv. 3–7).

Rex tremendae: 22 mm. [gm–B flat M] *grave*. satb choir. (v. 8).

Recordare: 130 mm. [B flat M-FM] *andante*. satb soli. (vv. 9–15).

Confutatis: 40 mm. [am–FM] *andante*. satb choir. (vv. 16–17).

Lacrymosa: 30 mm. [dm] *larghetto*. satb choir. (vv. 18–19).

Offertory: 191 mm., 2 movements.

Domine Jesu Christe: 78 mm. [gm] *andante*. satb choir; *Sed signifer*, SATB soli; *Quam olim Abrahae*, satb choir. Fugue. *Hostias*: 54 mm. [E flat M] *larghetto*. satb choir. *Quam olim* is repeated.

Sanctus: 28 mm., 2 movements.

Sanctus: 11 mm. [DM] *adagio*. satb choir.

Osanna: 28 mm. [DM] *allegro*. satb choir. Fugue.

Benedictus: 76 mm.

Benedictus: [B flat M] *andante*. SATB soli; *Osanna, allegro*. satb choir.

Agnus Dei-Communion: 133 mm.

Agnus Dei [dm] *larghetto*. satb choir; *Lux aeterna*, [B flat M] *adagio*. S solo/satb choir; *Requiem aeternam* [dm] satb choir [material from first movement]; *Cum sanctis tuis* [dm] *allegro*. satb choir. (Same as the *Kyrie* fugue.)

DISCOGRAPHY

1. Philips, 432 087-2, Academy & Chorus of St. Martin in the Fields, cond., Sir Neville Mariner.
2. Multiple listings in the Schwann Catalogue.

JOSE MAURICIO NUÑES-GARCIA
September 20/22, 1784–April 18, 1830

Nuñes-Garcia spent his entire life in Rio de Janeiro. Fluent in six languages, he was noted for his intellectual and musical abilities. He helped to found the Brotherhood of St. Cecilia, an important musical organization, and, in 1791, entered the Brotherhood *Sao Pedro dos Clergios*. He was ordained a priest in the following year. A formidable improviser at the keyboard, he was appointed *mestre de capela* of the cathedral in Rio de Janeiro in 1798, and remained there for twenty-eight years. In 1808, he secured a similar position at the royal chapel. It was for these positions that he wrote the bulk of his 237 known works.

Among his sacred compositions are nineteen masses, funeral music, music for Holy Week, motets, and liturgical pieces of all kinds. Much of this music includes instrumental accompaniment. Garcia's musical library was apparently rather extensive and there is little doubt that he was unacquainted with the latest musical trends in Europe. He gave the Brazilian premieres of Haydn's *Creation* and Mozart's *Requiem.*

The *Requiem in D minor* was composed in 1816 at the request of the exiled Portuguese King Joao VI for his mother, Maria I. The composer's mother, too, died in the same year and it is possible that he considered the work an honor to his mother's memory. It is one of four requiem masses that Nuñes-Garcia wrote. There are two *Oficio de defuntos* for SATB choir and instruments (1799 and 1816) and an *Oficio funèbre* for two SATB choirs and two organs.

The *Requiem in D Minor* is scored for SATB choir, SATB soli, and orchestra. Traces of the choral *concertante* style are found in the Graduale, Sequence, and *Sanctus.* The predominant choral texture is homophonic, with imitative polyphony used only in the *Kyrie.* The pairing of the Introit and *Kyrie,* as well as the *Agnus Dei* and Offertory (a Viennese tradition), is suggested by the use of a concluding dominant chord in the initial movement of each pair. This pairing technique was also employed by Anton Reicha (Nuñes-Garcia's European contemporary).

The musical language and elegance of this work are similar to that of Haydn and Mozart. The theme of the *Kyrie* fughetta bears a strong resemblance to that of Mozart's *Kyrie* subject and Nuñes-Garcia's chromatic harmonies suggest those typical of early romanticism.

Basic Data

EDITION

Jose Mauricio Nuñes-Garcia
Requiem Mass for Four-Part Chorus of Mixed Voices
and Alto, Tenor and Bass Solos with Piano Accompaniment
ed. Dominique-René de Lerma
Associated Music Publishers, Inc. (#47667) 1977

DURATION

Eight movements, 742 mm., perf., c. 35'

VOICING AND ORCHESTRATION

Choir: SATB range: S-A6; B-F3
Soloists: SATB
Orchestra: vn. I/II, vla., vc., 2 ob.[opt.], 2 Fl., 2 cl., 2 bsn. [opt.], 2 Fh., tpt., timp., *ad libitum.*

OUTLINE

Introit: 46 mm.
 Requiem aeternam, [dm] *larghetto; Te decet* [FM]; *Requiem aeternam* [dm] satb choir. ABA form, segue to *Kyrie.*

Kyrie: 38 mm.
  Kyrie-Christe, [dm] *allegro*; *Kyrie*, satb choir. Fughetta.
Gradual: 50 mm. *Requiem aeternam*, [gm] *larghetto*. satb choir; *In memoria*, A solo;
  Ab auditione, satb choir; *Et gratia*, B solo; *Et lucis*, satb choir.
Sequence: 341 mm.
  Dies irae: 114 mm. [dm] satb choir (vv. 1–3); *Mors stupebit*, SATB soli/satb choir
    (v. 4); *Liber scriptus*, A solo (vv. 5–6)
  Quid sum miser: 85 mm. [B flat M] T solo/satb choir (vv. 7–11)
  Ingemisco: 73 mm. [B flat M] *adagio*. T solo (vv. 12–14) ABA form.
  Inter oves: 69 mm. [dm] *allegro*. satb choir (vv. 15–19)
Offertory: 120 mm. *Domine Jesu Christe*, [E flat M] *andantino*. B solo/satb choir;
  Quam Olim Abrahae & *Hostias*, B solo; *Fac eas*, satb choir.
Sanctus: 24 mm.
  Sanctus, [CM] *allegro*. SATB soli/satb choir.
Benedictus: 20 mm.
  Benedictus, [FM] *andante*. S solo/satb choir.
Agnus Dei: 39 mm. ABA form. [segue to Communion]
  Agnus Dei, [dm] *allegretto*. satb choir.
Communion: 64 mm.
  Lux aeterna, [dm] *L'istesso tempo*. satb choir.

DISCOGRAPHY

Columbia Masterworks, M33431, Morgan State College Choir, Helsinki Philharmonic Orchestra, cond. Paul Freeman [Black Composers Series].

GIOVANNI PAISIELLO
May 9, 1740–June 5, 1816

Paisiello, the famous and successful opera composer, flourished in the late eighteenth century. His first major position was *maestro di cappella* at the court of Catherine II in St. Petersburg, where, from 1776 to 1784, he produced the earliest of his eighty operas. He eventually returned to Naples and was given the title, by Ferdinand IV, *compositiore della musica de drammi*.

Napoleon was a great admirer of Paisiello's music, so much so that he brought Paisiello to Paris in 1802 as music director of his chapel. By 1804, Paisiello returned to Naples. His political problems began when Joseph Buonaparte, brother of Napoleon, removed Ferdinand IV from his position and installed Paisiello as director of sacred and secular music at his own court. When Ferdinand returned to Naples in 1815 to assume his former position as king, Paisiello lost all of his positions, save one, *maestro della real cappella*, thereby losing the bulk of his income. Nevertheless, he continued to compose opera and church music during his final year.

The bulk of his compositions include eighty operas, ten cantatas, seventeen masses, a requiem, about three-dozen liturgical pieces, and some instrumental music.

The *Requiem in C Minor* was composed in 1789 as a memorial for the two sons of Ferdinand IV, both of whom had perished during an outbreak of smallpox in Naples. The orchestral overture (sinfonia) attached to the requiem was composed later (1797) for a different occasion; the death of one of Napoleon's generals, Lazare Hoche. It is one of the few, late eighteenth-century symphonic requiems scored for double SATB choir, soloists, and orchestra. Like its earlier Neapolitan "ancestor," the Cimarosa *Requiem* (1787), the Paisiello setting utilizes a recurrent "motto" theme in the orchestral accompaniment (*Requiem aeternam* [Introit], *Quantus tremor* & *Pie Jesu* [Sequence], *Hosanna* [*Sanctus*], *Requiem aeternam* [Communion], *Dies illa*, & *Kyrie* [Responsory]).

The orchestral accompaniment functions independently from the choir and the instrumental introductions for the Introit, *Kyrie,* and various dramatic or emotional sections of the Sequence (*Tuba mirum, Rex tremendae, Confutatis, Oro supplex, Lacrymosa, Huic ergo,* and *Pie Jesu*) highlight the mood of the particular text. The binary form, frequently used by Neapolitan composers, is employed in several solos (*Absolve me* [SA duet], *Confutatis* [A solo], *Oro supplex* [T solo], and *Domine Jesu Christe* [SATB soli]). This requiem is a showcase for *bel canto* singing. The soprano arias, *Confutatis* and *Lacrymosa*, are models of this style and require additional ornamentation, far beyond the printed notes.

Basic Data

EDITION

Giovanni Paisiello
Messa da Requiem per soli, doppio (double) coro e orchestra
Transcribed by Giuseppe Piccioli
[full score]
Edizioni Curci-Milan, Galleria del Corso, 4 (E. 7084 C) 1960

DURATION

Twelve movements, 1615 mm., perf., c. 57'

VOICING AND ORCHESTRATION

Choir: Choir I SATB & Choir II SATB range: S-B flat 6; B-G3
Soloists: SATB
Orchestra: vn. I/II, vla., vc., db., 2 ob., 2 cl., 2 bsn., 2 Fh., 2 tpt., org. [pianoforte for *Agnus Dei* only].

OUTLINE

Sinfonia: 111 mm.
Introit: 131 mm.

Requiem aeternam [cm] *largo e maestoso.* choirs I/II; *Te decet*, [fm] *andante* S solo.
(Theme & two variations); *Requiem aeternam* is repeated. ["motto"] ABCA form.
Kyrie: 76 mm. (3 "verses")
    Kyrie, Christe, Kyrie [FM] *andantino,* SA duet/choirs I/II. ABA form.
Graduale: 70 mm.
    Requiem aeternam, [gm] *moderato,* B solo; *In memoria,* [B flat M] *allegro,* choirs I/
II.
Tract: 51 mm.
    Absolve Domine, [gm] *maestoso con devozione,* SA duet/choirs I/II. Binary form.
Sequence: 659 mm. (The first six sections are paired verses.)
    Dies irae [cm] *moderatamente mosso,* B solo & *Quantus tremor* [cm] choirs I/II
basses. ("motto"); *Tuba mirum* [E flat M] B solo & *Mors stupebit,* [E flat M] choir
I/II basses; *Liber scriptus* [cm] B solo & *Judex ergo* [cm] choirs I/II basses; *Quid
sum miser* [E flat M] *largo,* choirs I/II; *Rex tremendae* & *Recordare* [gm] *moderato,*
S solo; *Quarens me* [CM] *andantino affetuoso,* SA duet & *Ingemisco* [CM] *piu mosso
e con energia,* A solo & *Preces meae* [GM] soprano solo. *Inter oves* [CM] *dolce e con
affeto,* SA duet; *Confutatis* [FM] *allegro,* A solo (Binary form); *Oro supplex* [B flat
M] *andante molto sostenuto,* T solo (Binary form); *Lacrymosa* [E flat M] *andante
molto sostenuto,* S solo; *Pie Jesu* [CM] *largo e maestoso,* choirs I/II ("motto")
Offertory: 113 mm.
    Domine Jesu Christe [gm] *andante,* SATB soli; *Hostias,* SATB soli. Binary form.
Sanctus: 80 mm.
    Sanctus [dm] choirs I/II *a capella; Pleni sunt coeli, allegro molto,* choirs I/II & *Bene-
dictus* [B flat M] *moderatamente con solennita,* SATB soli/choirs I/II. ("motto")
Agnus Dei: 63 mm.
    Agnus Dei I [gm] *andante,* SA duet, choirs I/II; *Agnus Dei* II, ST duet, choirs I/
II; *Agnus Dei* III, AB soli, choirs I/II; (*Agnus Dei-*soli, *Dona eis* choirs I/II.
Communion: 68 mm.
    Lux aeterna [cm] *largo,* SA duet; *Cum sanctis* [cm] *andante,* choirs I/II; *Requiem
aeternam* [cm] *largo maestoso,* choirs I/II ("motto").
Responsory: 244 mm.
    Libera me [cm] choirs I/II, *sostenuto e solenne; In die illa,* choirs I/II, *allegro molto
ed energico; Tremens factus,* B solo, *andante; Quando coeli,* choirs I/II, *allegro molto;
Dies illa,* B solo, choirs I/II, *allegro* ("motto"); *Requiem,* choirs I/II, *largo maestoso,*
("motto")" *Libera me,* choirs I/II, *sostenuto e solenne; In die illa,* choirs I/II, *allegro
molto ed energico; Kyrie,* choirs I/II, *andante molto* ("motto").

DISCOGRAPHY

Italia Fonit Cetra, CDC 92, Cambridge University Choir, Orchestra del Festival di
Martina Franca, dir. Alberto Zedda.

IGNACE PLEYEL
June 18, 1757–November 14, 1831

Pleyel was born in Rupperthal, Austria. His teachers were Jan Vanhal and
Franz Joseph Haydn. He became Haydn's pupil in 1772 and lived on the

Esterhaza estate for five years. While there, he wrote the overture (and possibly the first two movements) for Haydn's puppet opera, *Das abgebrannte Haus*. Pleyel was invited to London in 1791–92 to conduct the Professional Concerts series. Haydn was there at the same time, conducting a rival concert series, yet there appears to have been no friction or competition between them and both were well-received by the London public.

Sometime around 1784, Pleyel was appointed second *Kapellmeister* at Strasbourg Cathedral. He succeeded to the top position five years later. During his years at the cathedral, much of his church music was composed. In 1795, he started a music-publishing business. Shortly afterward, in 1807, he founded a piano factory, which soon began to prosper. His pianos were so well-received that he gave up composition altogether. Pleyel was a popular composer and during his lifetime Pleyel societies sprung up in the centers of the musical world, as well as less-traveled locations, such as Nantucket.

He wrote forty-one orchestral symphonies, seventy quartets, five books of string quintets (seventeen pieces), six symphonies *concertantes*, forty-eight trios, six quartets for flutes and strings, and much more. Little is known about his church music and much is assumed to have been lost. Several masses and motets are believed to have perished in a fire. There remains a requiem and a *Tantum Ergo* for soprano, counter-tenor, tenor, bass, and orchestra.

The elegant *Requiem in E flat Major* was written sometime between 1781 and 1791 and scored for SATB choir, SATB soli, and orchestra. It was clearly modeled after the Haydn masses. Its harmonic language, melodic shapes, and orchestration follow the Viennese classical style, though a few unique features, such as the muted brass (also found in the requiem by Eberlin, c. 1750), are employed in the *Dies irae*. The use of the mute appears not to have been the custom in this period.

In nearly every movement, the first violins play *bel canto* obbligati derived from arpeggiated chords or repeated note motifs. They create a rich counterpoint to the choral music while a sustained, "organistic" use of the woodwinds and horns reinforces the harmonic background. The texture of the choral sections is usually chordal, but these sections often begin with imitative polyphony, adding a touch of elegance to the simpler homophonic style.

Of special interest are the soprano and alto duet, *Benedictus* and the tenor solo, *Qui Mariam,* as well as the *Kyrie* fugue. From the beginning to the end, this fine piece has that "magical," elegant Viennese sound. A published edition is needed.

Basic Data

EDITION

None currently available.
The manuscript is located in the Bibliothèque Nationale, Paris.

8

Cat. #MS 2376
Requiem di me Ignazio Pleyel
[178 pp.] [clefs: C (soprano, alto, tenor) & F]

DURATION

Fifteen movements, 1018 mm, perf., c. 43'

VOICING AND ORCHESTRATION

Choir: SATB range: S-A flat 6; B-F3
Soloists: SATB
Orchestra: vn. I/II, vla., vc., db., 2 ob., 2 bsn., 2 Fh.

OUTLINE

Introit: 137 mm., 2 movements
  Requiem aeternam: 42 mm. [E flat M] *largo non troppo*. satb choir.
  Te decet: 95 mm. [e flat m] *andante*. SAT soli/satb choir.
Kyrie: 143 mm.
  Kyrie [E flat M] *alla cappella*. satb choir. Fugue; *Kyrie*, coda.
Sequence: 305 mm., 4 movements
  Dies irae: 103 mm. [cm] *allegro spiritoso*. satb choir/SATB soli.
  Judex ergo: 62 mm. [A flat M] *maestoso*. satb choir/SATB soli.
  Qui Mariam: 78 mm. [E flat M] *andante*. T solo.
  Lacrymosa: 62 mm. [cm] *moderato*. satb choir/SATB soli. ABA form.
Offertory: 167 mm., 3 movements
  Domine Jesu Christe: 33 mm. [E flat M] *andante*. satb choir.
  Hostias: 128 mm. [gm] *andante*. SATB soli (duet and quartet)
  Quam olim Abrahae: 6 mm. [E flat M] *andante*. satb choir.
Sanctus: 66 mm.
  Sanctus [E flat M] *adagio*. satb choir; *Pleni sunt coeli* [E flat M] *allegro*. satb choir.
Benedictus: 112 mm., 2 movements
  Benedictus: 92 mm. [gm] *andante*. SA duet.
  Osanna: 20 mm. [E flat M] *allegro*. satb choir.
Agnus Dei: 37 mm.
  Agnus Dei [gm] *andante*. SATB soli/satb choir.
Communion: 51 mm.
  Lux aeterna [E flat M] satb choir.

DISCOGRAPHY

Erol, 2CD-90001, L'Ensemble Vocal Jean Pierre Loré, L'Ensemble Vocal Pythagore, L'Orchestre Francais d'Oratorio, dir. Jean Pierre Loré.

ANTON REICHA
February 26, 1770–May 28, 1836

Born in Prague, Reicha learned violin and piano from an uncle. By 1787, he was in Bonn, studying and conducting. During the Bonn years, he supported himself by teaching piano, harmony, and composition. In 1799, he moved to Paris, but soon left for Vienna, where he made friendships with Haydn and Beethoven. He studied with Salieri and Albrechtsberger. In this environment, his musical style took on the Viennese sound. In 1818, he was appointed professor of counterpoint and fugue at the Paris Conservatoire. Among his more famous pupils were Franz Liszt, Hector Berlioz, and César Franck.

His ability with counterpoint, fugue, and musical variation were exceptional. The *Thirty-Six Fugues for Piano, Op. 36*, (1803) use original themes as well as those of Mozart, Scarlatti, Bach, Haydn, Frescobaldi, and Händel. *Opus 36* is a nineteenth-century version of Bach's *Wohltemperite Klavier*: a treatise on the fugue for piano. The twenty-four compositions of the *Practische Beispiel* (1803) reveal his thinking about modulation, musical form, and bitonality. At the same time, they are concert pieces. Even his singular requiem shows the composer how to put various musical elements together in order to create a good work.

Reicha wrote music of all genres; theatrical works, choral music, solo voice with orchestra, orchestral music (including symphonies and concertos), piano solo, and chamber music. Among the large choral works are a *Te Deum* for SATB choir and orchestra and the *Missa pro defunctis* for SATB choir, SATB soloists, and orchestra. It was written sometime between 1803 and 1809 when he lived in Vienna. The stringed instruments and choir form the main body of sound for this setting. Woodwinds and brass color the orchestral sound and highlight the poetry of the text. Trumpets are used only in the climatic moments of the *Tuba mirum* and *Confutatis*.

The choral texture is a mixture of homophonic and imitative polyphonic writing. There are four fugues or fugal sections in the *Requiem in C Minor* including the *Kyrie*, *Quam olim Abrahae*, *Hosanna*, and final *Requiem aeternam*. Two important Viennese features are present in *Opus 36*; the three trombones used for doubling the lower vocal lines and the linked Introit-*Kyrie* and *Agnus Dei*-Communion movements.

Basic Data

EDITION

Anton Reicha's "Missa Pro Defunctis"
Performing edition & commentary
Amy Goodman
Stanford University, Doctoral Dissertation
UMI Dissertation Services, Ann Arbor, Michigan. 1989

DURATION

Thirteen movements, 1415 mm., perf., c. 55'

VOICING AND ORCHESTRATION

Choir: SATB range: S-A flat 6; B-G3
Soloists: SATB

Orchestra: vn. I/II, vla., vc., db., 2 fl., 2 ob., 2 cl., 2 bsn., 2 Fh., 3 tpt., 3 tbn., timp., org.

OUTLINE

Introit-*Kyrie*: 150 mm.
  Requiem aeternam [cm] *lento*. satb choir; *Kyrie* [cm] *allegro*. satb choir. Fugue.
Sequence: 617 mm., 7 movements.
  Dies irae: 57 mm. [gm] *allegro*. satb choir. (vv. 1–2)
  Tuba mirum: 32 mm. [CM] *andante poco adagio*. T solo/trumpet obbligato. (vv. 3–4)
  Liber scriptus: 139 mm. [am] *andantino*. SATB soli; *Quid sum miser* [AM] SATB soli (vv. 5–7)
  Rex tremendae: 98 mm. [dm] *allegro assai*. satb choir (v. 8)
  Recordare: 75 mm. [E flat M] *Recordare*, SATB soli; *Quaerens me*, SATB soli/satb choir; *Juste judex*, SATB soli; *Ingemisco*, satb choir; *Qui Mariam*, SATB soli; *Preces meae* & *Inter oves*, SATB soli/satb choir (vv. 9–15)
  Confutatis: 115 mm. *Confutatis* [cm] *allegro*. satb choir; *Oro supplex* [cm] *lento*. satb choir. (vv. 16–17)
  Lacrimosa: 101 mm. [gm] *allegro non troppo*. satb choir. (vv. 18–19)
Offertory: 301 mm., 2 movements.
  Domine Jesu Christe: 246 mm. *Domine Jesu Christe* [B flat M] *maestoso*. satb choir/SATB soli; *Quam olim Abrahae* [B flat M] satb choir. Fugue. *Hostias*: 55 mm. *Hostias* [gm] *andante*. satb choir. *Quam olim Abrahae* is repeated.
Sanctus: 60 mm.
  Sanctus [dm] *lento*. satb choir; *Osanna*, *allegro*. satb choir. Fugue.
Benedictus: 62 mm.
  Benedictus [DM] *andantino*. S solo/flute/violin/oboe obbligati/satb choir; *Osanna*. Fugue repeated.
Agnus Dei-Communion: 21 mm.
  Agnus Dei [E flat M] *lento*. SATB soli/satb choir; *Lux aeterna* [CM] *lento*. satb choir. Fugue; *Cum sanctis* [cm] *allegro moderato*. satb choir. Fugue.

DISCOGRAPHY

Supraphon, 11 0332-2, Soloists and Choir of the Czech Philharmonic, Dvorak Chamber Orchestra, dir. Lubomir Matl.

VINCENZO RIGHINI
February 11, 1756–September 19, 1812

This Italian composer composed his first opera in 1776 for the Bustelli opera troupe of Prague. He was a tenor with the same company. In 1787, he was appointed *Kapellmeister* at the Electoral court in Mainz, for which he wrote a number of stage works. At the same time, he was a highly respected voice teacher who wrote a singing method, *Exercises pour se per-*

fectionner dans l'art du chant. By 1793, he was appointed to a similar position in Berlin and simultaneously, the directorship of the Italian Opera in Berlin.

He composed sixteen operas, a number of cantatas, and several sacred pieces. Included are a *Te Deum*, the oratorio, *Der Tod Jesu*, several masses, and a brief, incomplete *Missa pro defunctis*. Righini's *Requiem* fragment was written while he worked in Berlin as director of the Italian Opera. It was composed upon the death of Queen Louise, in March 1810. Its scoring is quite different from other contemporary requiem settings because it was arranged for *concertante* SATB *a cappella* choir. The only texture used is an expressive homophony. Its length is 123 measures and consists of a complete setting of the Communion text.

Basic Data

EDITION

Vincenzo Righini
Requiem a cappella für gemischten Chor
Breitkopf & Härtel, Wiesbaden
Chor-Bibliothek (Nr. 5118) 1978

DURATION

One movement. 123 mm.

VOICING

Choir: SATB range: S-A6; B-E3
Soloists: SATB

OUTLINE

Communion, 123 mm. ABA form.
   Requiem aeternam [cm] *grave*. satb choir/SATB soli; *Cum sanctis tuis* [A flat M] *larghetto*. satb choir/soli; *Requiem aeternam* is repeated.

DISCOGRAPHY

None found.

ANTONIO SALIERI
August 18, 1750–May 7, 1825

Salieri was born in Verona, Italy, but spent most of his professional life with the Royal Court in Vienna. Beethoven, Schubert, and Liszt were among his pupils. He maintained a close relationship with Haydn and

Gluck, the latter helping him with his career as opera composer and conductor. He became court conductor in Vienna in 1788, retiring from that position in 1818.

He wrote forty operas, four oratorios, a setting of the Passion, a handful of oratorios, five masses, one requiem, and a quantity of other church music. Among the orchestral pieces are several concertos for organ, a concerto for two pianos, and one for flute and oboe.

The *Requiem in C minor* was finished at the end of 1804. Although the preface to the first published edition (1978) designates the work as a *Grand Requiem*, Salieri gave it the following title: Antonio Salieri: *Piccolo requiem composto da me, e per me, Antonio Salieri, piccolossima creatura, Viena, Agosto 1804* (A little requiem composed by me and for me, Antonio Salieri, the smallest creature . . .). Its first performance took place on June 22, 1825, at Salieri's funeral service. Salieri scored the work for SATB choir, SATB soli, and orchestra.

The choral and solo parts are predominantly homophonic and are set in the baroque *concertante* fashion of solo & *ripieno* (only partially indicated in the current score). The music and orchestration reveals his talent for musical drama and instrumental coloring, much of which stemmed from his activity as a composer of opera. The bulk of the orchestration is for strings, but when the composer wanted to suggest solemnity, he used the trombones; for brilliance and majesty, the timpani and trumpets. For elegiac feelings or moods related to lamentation, he used the English horn. The harmonic chromaticism clearly foreshadows the drama of nineteenth-century romanticism.

Like the Cherubini's *Requiem in C Minor* (1816), there are no solo arias in this setting of the requiem. The passages, *Quam olim Abrahae* and *Osanna in excelsis* are the only examples of *stile antico* imitative polyphony. Much of the work follows the general stylistic traits of the Viennese classical idiom.

Basic Data

EDITION

Antonio Salieri
Requiem für vier Solostimmen, Chor und Orchester
Edited for the first time by Johannes Wojciechowski
Henry Litolff's Verlag/C. F. Peters
Frankfurt. New York. London #8311 1978

DURATION

Seven movements, 932 mm., perf., 43'

VOICING AND ORCHSTRATION

Choir: SATB range: S-A flat 6; B-E3
Soloists: SATB
Orchestra: vn. I/II, vla., vc., db., 2 ob., Eh., 2 bsn., 2 tpt., 3 tbn., timp.

OUTLINE

Introit-*Kyrie*: 141 mm.

> orch. intro.; *Requiem aeternam* [cm] *larghetto*; *Te decet* [E flat M] *allegretto*; *Requiem aeternam-Kyrie* [cm] *larghetto*. SATB soli/satb choir. ABA form.

Sequence: 353 mm.

> *Dies irae* [cm] *andante maestoso*. satb choir (vv. 1–2); *Tuba mirum* [AM-dm] *allegro molto*. satb choir/SATB soli (vv. 3–7); *Rex tremendae* [FM] *adagio*. satb choir (v. 8); *Recordare* [B flat M] *andante con moto*. SATB soli/satb choir (vv. 9–17); *Lacrimosa* [GM] *andante maestoso*. satb choir (v. 18); *Huic ergo* [E flat M]-cm] *andante*. satb choir/SATB soli (v. 19)

Offertory: 123 mm.

> *Domine Jesu Christe* [CM] *andante maestoso ma con moto*. (*Quam olim Abrahae*, fughetta); *Hostias* [FM] *larghetto*. *Quam olim Abrahae* is repeated. satb choir/ SATB soli.

Sanctus: 59 mm.

> *Sanctus* [CM] *largo e maestoso*. satb choir; *Osanna* [CM] *allegretto non molto*. Fugue.

Benedictus: 66 mm.

> *Benedictus* [AM] *andante con moto*. SATB soli/satb choir; *Osanna* [CM] *allegretto non molto*. Shortened fugue.

Agnus Dei-Communion: 149 mm.

> *Agnus Dei* [cm] *larghetto*. satb choir/SATB soli; *Dona ei* (*s*) [CM] *poco allegro*. satb choir; *Requiem aeternam* [cm] *larghetto*. satb choir/SATB soli; *Cum sanctis* [A flat M-cm] *poco allegro*. satb choir.

Responsory: 41 mm.

> Several short sections, including two Gregorian intonations. [cm] *andante*. satb choir.

DISCOGRAPHY

Milan Vlcek Music Productions, SY 0008-2 131 Concertino Notturno Praha and The Italian Chamber Choir, dir. Andreas Kroper.

JOSEPH ALOIS SCHMITTBAUR
November 8, 1718–October 24, 1809

Schmittbaur was raised in the home of the German organ builder J. P. Seuffert, from whom he also received his education in music. He stated that he had been a student of the Neapolitan, Jommelli. Schmittbaur worked initially as concertmaster (1753) and subsequently as *Kapellmeister* (1765) in the Rastatt court until it was dissolved in 1771. He later held several other similar positions.

His musical output includes several stage works, some instrumental music, and a small amount of church music. Included in the last category are five masses, one requiem, and a *Passion according to St. Matthew*. The *Requiem in E flat major* was written in memory of Clemens Faulstich, a priest-choirmaster at Ebrach Cloister. The music is scored for SATB soli, SATB choir, and orchestra. The editor of the current edition of this music, Hans Peter Eisenmann, believes that Schmittbaur might have assembled a number of earlier-written pieces and joined them together to form a new work.

The composer included most of the expected movements, except the *Kyrie*, the *Te decet* (Introit), and the Communion. Of course, these sections could have been sung in Gregorian chant, but at a time when composers were composing all of the usual mass pieces, Schmittbauer's omissions seem a little unusual.

This requiem has several distinctive features, peculiarities that set this composition apart from other contemporary requiem models. For example, the Offertory and *Benedictus* include quotations of folk songs (as Charpentier made in the *Messe de Noel*) and hunting horn signals (like Haydn used in the oratorio, *Die Jahreszeiten*). This personal touch is very charming, for it gives us a glimpse into the life of the deceased, provided that the music was not previously written for someone else!

Although the string section of the orchestra provides the main support for the choral and solo forces, the virtuoso solo horn and clarino parts add enormously to the orchestral ensemble. Normally brass players were restricted in church music to simpler melodies and harmony notes.

The bulk of the choral writing is simple SATB chordal harmony, but there are two *stile antico* fugues (*Huic ergo* and *Lux aeterna*). The composer evidently liked the fugue subject for he set both texts to the same fugue subject. The virtuoso arias *Quantus tremor* and *Benedictus*, scored for coloratura soprano and complete with runs, trills, and ornaments (and the latter with a "high" C), are a legacy from the Neapolitan, Jommelli. Elaborate instrumental obbligati for the Offertory, the *Quam olim Abrahae*, and portions of the Sequence are also derived from the *bel canto* style.

The music, be it borrowed from earlier compositions or newly composed, is quite charming and elegant.

Basic Data

EDITION

Joseph Alois Schmittbaur
Requiem in Es [E flat] für Clemens Faulstich
für Sopran, Alt, Tenor und Bass, vierstimmigen Chor, zwei Oboen, zwei Hörner in Es, zwei Trompeten in Es, Pauken, Streichorchester und Basso continuo
[Practical edition based upon the manuscripts in the Pfarrbibliothek in Ebrach and the Bibliothek of Kloster Ottobeuren]
ed., Hans Peter Eisenmann
Edition Walhall (#EW 12) 1997

DURATION

Nine movements, 852 mm.

VOICING AND ORCHESTRATION

Choir: SATB range: S-G6; B-F3
Soloists: SATB
Orchestra: vn. I/II, vla., vc., db., 2 ob., bsn., 2 E flat Fh., 2 E flat tpt., timp., org. [*basso continuo*].

OUTLINE

Introit: 68 mm., *Te decet* omitted.
   Orch. intro.; *Requiem aeternam*, [E flat M] *adagio molto*. satb choir.
Sequence: 269 mm., 3 movements. (vv. 1–3, 19).
   Dies irae: 23 mm., [E flat M] satb choir; *Quantus tremor*, S solo *Tuba mirum*: 123 mm., [E flat M] *adagio molto*. orch. intro., AT duet; orch. interlude, *Mors stupebit*, B solo; *Tuba mirum*, AT duet; orch. postlude. ABA form. *Huic ergo*: 123 mm., [E flat M] *moderato*. satb choir. Fugue.
Offertory: 210 mm., 2 movements.
   Domine Jesu Christe: 109 mm., [gm] *adagio*. satb choir; *Libera eas* [B flat M] soprano solo; *Quam olim Abrahae*, satb choir. ABC structure. *Hostias*: 101 mm., [E flat M] *adagio*. TB duet/satb choir; *Quam olim Abrahae*, satb choir.
Sanctus: 48 mm.
   Sanctus, [E flat M] *adagio*. satb choir; *Pleni sunt coeli, poco vivace*. satb choir.
Benedictus: 93 mm.
   Benedictus, [cm] *andante*. S solo.
Agnus Dei-Communion (*Lux aeterna*): 164 mm.
   Agnus Dei, [cm] *adagio molto*. satb choir; *Lux aeterna*, [E flat M] *allegro*. satb choir. Fugue.

DISCOGRAPHY

None found.

FERDINAND SCHUBERT
October 18, 1794–February 26, 1859

Ferdinand, the older brother of Franz Schubert, was a composer, but, unlike Franz, his music remains virtually unknown. Most of his pieces are of a sacred nature. There are two requiems, a German requiem, and another 100 miscellaneous works. He further scored some fifty of his brother's works. He was a professor of organ at the Viennese Kirchen-musikschule.

The *Requiem in G Minor* was composed in 1828 and is considered by his biographer, Dr. Otto Biba, to be his best work. It was dedicated to the memory of his brother (*"Dem Andenken des verblichenen Tonsetzers Franz Schubert geweiht von seinem Brüder"*) and performed at the funeral of Franz Schubert. Scored for STB soli, SATB choir, and orchestra, its musical style and harmonic language is in the late classical Viennese-early romantic tradition. The predominant choral texture is homophonic except for the one fugal passage on *Quam olim Abrahae*. The vocal solos employ a simple, syllabic setting of the text, with none of the ornamentation and *bel canto* style of the Neapolitan school.

The basic orchestral string color is expanded by frequent use of the French horns and trumpets for obbligati and rhythmic drive. Trombones were used to double the alto and tenor choral lines. (Schubert allowed for the possibility of replacing the trombones with waldhorns.)

Schubert employed the two sets of linked movements, Introit-*Kyrie* and *Agnus Dei*-Communion, following a century-old Viennese tradition.

Basic Data

EDITION

Ed. Musica Sacra des 19 Jahrhunderts
Band III
Requiem in G Minor, Op. 9
S T B Soli, Mixed Choir and Orchestra
ed. Otto Biba [full score]
Musikverlag Alfred Coppenrath, Altötting. 1978

DURATION

Seven movements, 434 mm.

VOICING AND ORCHESTRATION

Choir: SATB range: S-B flat 6; B-F3
Soloists: STB
Orchestra: vn. I/II, vc., db., 2 Fh., 2 tpt., 2 tbn. [double the alto & tenor choral parts], timp.

OUTLINE

Introit-*Kyrie*: 46 mm.
  Requiem aeternam [gm] *largo*. satb choir; *Kyrie* [gm]
Sequence: 107 mm. [incomplete setting]
  Dies irae [gm] *vivace*. satb choir; *Quantus tremor* [B flat M] B solo/satb choir/ trombone obbligato; *Tuba mirum* [B flat M] *larghetto*. B solo/trumpet solo; *Mors stupebit*, SATB soli; *Huic ergo* & *Pie Jesu* [gm] *adagio*. satb choir.
Offertory: 146 mm., 2 movements.
  Domine Jesu Christe: 68 mm. [dm] *andante*. satb choir; *Quam olim Abrahae* [gm] satb choir. Fugue. *Hostias*: 78 mm. [E flat M] *larghetto*. S solo/French horn duet-obbligato; *Quam olim Abrahae*, satb choir. Fugue.
Sanctus: 27 mm.
  Sanctus [B flat M] *andante*. satb choir.

Benedictus: 44 mm.
  Benedictus [B flat M] *cantabile*. satb choir. AAA form.
Agnus Dei: 64 mm.
  Agnus Dei [gm] *largo*. STB soli/satb choir; *Lux aeterna* [gm] *largo*. satb choir; *Cum sanctis* [gm] *allegro moderato*. satb choir.

DISCOGRAPHY

Esoldun, MOS 1003, Petit Chanteurs de Notre Dame, Ensemble Vocal Jean Pierre Loré, French Oratorio Orchestra, cond. J. P. Loré.

VÁCLAV JAN TOMÁŠEK
April 17, 1774–April 3, 1850

Tomášek, a gifted child, received his formal musical training in organ and theory from Donat Schuberth, a teacher at the Jihlava Gymnasium. On his own, he studied theoretical works by Fux and Marpug. During his years of law study at Prague University, he earned his living by giving music lessons. From 1806, he worked for sixteen years as a private tutor and composer for a local nobleman. By 1825, he started his own music school, attracting many young composers and among his more famous pupils was the piano virtuoso, Alexander Dreyschock. Tomášek became an important figure in the musical life of Prague.

His musical style is based upon the classic-romantic forms and harmonies used by Cherubini, Eybler, and other turn-of-the-century figures. He composed and published a great deal of piano music and vocal songs. There exist several operas and a small amount of church music that includes a *Missa Solemnis* in C Major (for the coronation of Ferdinand V of Bohemia, 1836), two requiems, and a setting of the *Te Deum*.

The *Requiem Mass in C Minor*, op. 72 was composed in 1820, not for an individual, but rather for the people who perished in the village of Strán (Bohemia) during a massive flood. Tomášek traveled to see this disaster and was greatly moved by what he experienced. Consequently, he was prompted to compose a requiem in their memory. Tomášek privately printed the work, but it was later published by Marco Berra of Prague. Although the late date of the work would appear to exclude it from the Viennese classical tradition, its harmonic style and vocabulary identify its eighteenth-century orientation.

The *Requiem Mass* is scored for double SATB choir, SATB soli, and orchestra. It is one of the rare period settings for two choirs. Solo voices and choir interact in old-fashioned *concertante* fashion throughout most of the work. Like most symphonic requiem settings, the orchestra operates independently of the choir. Pictorial writing is occasional employed. A "sighing" motive played by the violins is present throughout the Introit and reappears in the final bars of the last movement. Agitated triplet passages (reminders of our mortality) are sounded by the full orchestra and recur throughout the Sequence at *Dies irae, Rex tremendae, Lacrymosa,* and *Dona eis.*

There is a curious, structural parallel to some of Handel's choruses. The pieces *And the Glory, Hallelujah,* and *His yoke is easy (Messiah)* conclude with a dramatic pause preceding the final choral statement. Tomášek liked this effect, too, and he used it in the *Requiem,* but with a difference; the dramatic pause is always preceded by a secondary dominant (diminished VII7) instead of the V7 chord. It is used frequently enough to be designated a stylistic hallmark.

Basic Data

EDITION

Hymni, in sacro pro defunctis Cantari soliti pleno concentu Musico redditi a Wenceslawo Joane Tomaschek.
Opus 70. Bohemo. [1820?]

DURATION

Ten movements, 963 mm., perf., c. 45′

VOICING AND ORCHESTRATION

Choir: SATB range: S-A6 ; B-G3
Soloists: SATB
Orchestra: vn. I/II, vla., vc., db., 2 fl., 2 ob., 2 cl., 2 bsn., 2 Fh., 2 tpt., 3 tbn., timp., org.

OUTLINE

Introit-*Kyrie*: 118 mm.
   Requiem aeternam [cm] *andante.* satb choir/satb soli; *Kyrie.* ABA form.
Sequence: 346 mm., 3 movements. [vv. 10–13 & 15 omitted]
   Dies irae: 144 mm. [cm] *allegro. Dies irae & Quantus tremor,* satb choir; *Tuba mirum,* T solo; *Mors stupebit,* satb choir; *Liber scriptus,* T solo; *Judex ergo,* A solo; *Quid sum miser,* S solo/SATB soli; *Rex tremendae,* satb choir. Recordare: 83 mm. [A flat M-GM] *andante. Recordare,* T solo; *Preces meae,* SATB soli; *Confutatis,* SB solo; *Oro supplex,* T solo/satb choir. Lacrimosa: 119 mm. [cm] *allegro. Lacrimosa,* satb choir; *Pie Jesu,* satb choir/SATB soli. Fugue.
Offertory: 193 mm., 3 movements.
   Domine Jesu Christe: 87 mm. [E flat M] *andantino. Domine Jesu Christe,* SATB soli/satb choir; *Sed signifer,* BS soli; *Quam olim Abrahae,* B solo/satb choir. Hostias: 36 mm. [cm] *adagio. Hostias,* SATB soli; *Quam olim Abrahae* [E flat M] *allegro.* satb choir. Fugal writing.

Sanctus: 23 mm. [CM] *adagio. Sanctus*, satb choir/SATB soli; *Pleni sunt coeli &*
Osanna, allegro. S solo/satb choir. Fugue.
Benedictus: 183 mm. [FM] *adagio con moto. Benedictus*, A solo/SATB soli/satb choir;
Osanna repeated. Fugue.
Agnus Dei-Communion: 100 mm.
Agnus Dei [cm] *andante maestoso.* BST soli; *Lux aeterna*, SB soli/satb choir.

DISCOGRAPHY

Multisonic, 31 0395-2, Kühn Mixed Choir and the Prague Philharmonic, cond.
Bohumil Kulínský.

GEORG JOSEPH VOGLER
June 15, 1749–May 6, 1814

The organist-theorist-composer Abbé Joseph Vogler left seven requiem
settings, including a German requiem (see chapter 10). He also
bequeathed to posterity nine settings of the mass ordinary.

The *Requiem in E Flat Major* was composed in 1809 and first published,
posthumously, in 1822. Vogler scored the work for SATB soli, SATB choir,
and orchestra. His plan was to have it performed at the funeral of Franz
Joseph Haydn, but it was never realized. The choral texture is a mixture
of polyphonic writing and chordal homophony. There are two fugues,
Pleni sunt coeli and *Lux aeterna.* Imitative writing is employed in *Huic ergo*
and *Osanna.* The harmonic language is typical of the late Viennese-early
romantic style.

Except for two bass solos, *Tuba mirum* and *Dum veneris*, the SATB soli
are used as a classical version of the *concertante* second choir. The florid
melodic lines of the *Tuba mirum* solo reflect the influence of the Neapolitan school.

Although the orchestra frequently doubles the choral lines, it also plays
an independent role, providing dramatic, rhythmic accompaniments for
the *Dies irae, Mors stupebit, Juste judex*, and *Confutatis*, an ostinato bass for
the Introit and a pastoral background for *Inter oves.* Most of the movements have been provided with an orchestral introduction.

The Protestant hymn, *Herzlich tut mich verlangen*, is quoted in the *Te*
decet section of the Introit and the Gregorian *Agnus* melody is employed
in *Agnus Dei* II.

Basic Data
EDITION

G. J. Vogleri Abbatis Requiem
Seu missa pro defunctis accomadata clavicembalo a C. H. Rink.

Moguntiae ex Magno-ducal Hassiaca musices officina B. Schott filiorum.
No. 1648 [piano-vocal score, Munich] 1822.

DURATION

Eight movements, 1473 mm. [There are 27 separate pieces in the 1822 edition.]

VOICING AND ORCHESTRA

Choir: SATB range: S-A6; B-E flat 3
Soloists: SATB
Orchestra: vn. I/II, vla., vc., db., 2 fl., 2 bsn., Fh., tpt., tbn.

OUTLINE

Introit: 320 mm.
   Requiem aeternam, 82 mm. [E flat M-B flat M] *adagio.* satb choir; *Te decet,* 113 mm.
   [gm-DM] *andantino.* satb choir; *Te decet,* 61 mm. [GM] *con piu moto.* satb choir;
   Kyrie, 64 mm. [cm-E flat M] *adagio.* satb choir.
Sequence: 428 mm.
   Dies irae, 87 mm. [gm-GM] *vivace.* satb choir; *Quantus tremor,* 24 mm. [E flat M]
   satb choir; *Tuba mirum,* 73 mm. [E flat M] *piu andante.* B solo/SATB/soli/satb
   choir; *Mors stupebit,* 103 mm. [gm] *allegro molto.* satb choir. (verses 4–9); *Ingemisco,* 14 mm. [gm] *andantino.* SATB soli; *Deus, Qui Mariam,* 42 mm. [gm-DM]
   andantino. satb choir. (verses 11–15); *Voca me,* 29 mm. [GM-DM] SAT soli/satb
   choir (verses 15–16); *Lacrymosa,* 20 mm. [gm] *andantino.* SATB soli (verse 17);
   Huic ergo, 36 mm. [GM] SATB soli/satb choir. (verses 18–19).
Offertory: 131 mm.
   Domine Jesu Christe, 60 mm. [E flat M] *andante.* satb choir; *Quam olim Abrahae,* 71
   mm. [E flat M] *andante con allegretto.* satb choir.
Sanctus: 112 mm.
   Sanctus, 162 mm. [E flat M] *larghetto.* satb choir; *Pleni sunt coeli,* 63 mm. [E flat
   M] *allegro.* satb choir. Fugue; *Osanna,* 50 mm. [E flat M] *allegro.* satb choir.
Benedictus: 53 mm.
   Benedictus [E flat M] *cantabile.* SATB soli; *Osanna* is repeated.
Agnus Dei: 124 mm.
   Agnus Dei I [GM] satb choir; *Agnus Dei* II [mixolydian G] satb choir.
Communion: 48 mm.
   Lux aeterna [GM] satb choir. Fugue.
Responsory: 207 mm.
   Libera me [gm] *andante.* SATB soli/satb choir; *Dum veneris* [E flat M] B solo/satb
   choir; *Dies illa* [GM] satb choir; *Quando coeli* [E flat M] satb choir; *Requiem aeter-
   nam* [E flat M] satb choir.

DISCOGRAPHY

Arte Nova, 74321 71663 2, Chor den Staatlichen Musikhochschule, Mannheim,
Kurpfälzisches Kammerorchester, cond. Gerald Kegelmann.

PETER VON WINTER
August 28, 1754–October 17, 1825

Von Winter, the opera composer, studied with several Mannheim musicians, including Georg Vogler, founder of the Mannheim School. His eclectic musical style was also influenced by Mozart, Salieri, and Georg Benda. In 1798, he was appointed Court *Kapellmeister* in Munich and toward the end of his career, he began to write church music.

His output includes nearly forty operas, three symphonies, and chamber and vocal music. He composed twenty-seven settings of the mass, including two requiems (both in C minor), a setting of the *Stabat mater*, offertories, psalms, and motets. The *Requiem* was composed for the funeral services of Joseph II (Munich), held sometime around March 19, 1790, and scored for SATB soli, SATB choir, and orchestra.

The prevailing four-part choral texture is written in homophonic style and is contrasted with occasional fugal writing in *Kyrie, Osanna,* and *Lux aeterna.* Canonic passages are employed at *Lacrimosa* and *Amen* (Sequence).

As is common with other eighteenth-century composers, Winter employed a *concertante* treatment of the SATB soli and SATB choir (*Dies irae, Rex tremendae,* Offertory, and *Agnus Dei*). The only movement scored for solo voice is *Quid sum miser* (tenor). The elaborate solo writing exhibits some of the melodic ornateness of the Neapolitan style and includes two short recitative-like passages.

The orchestral accompaniment provides a strong rhythmic impulse for the choral matrix, but rarely rises above doubling or elaboration of the choral parts. One of the interesting features of this work is the presence of both Latin and German texts, indicating that the work was probably performed in the vernacular language when done locally.

Basic Data

EDITION
P. de Winter
Messe de Requiem à quatre voix
Arrangé pour le Piano-forte
Leipsic chez Breitkopf et Hartel [1827]
(German and Latin)
[Yale University Music Library, Rare M213 W786 R 42 +]

DURATION
Seven movements, 1013 mm.

VOICING AND ORCHESTRATION
Choir: SATB range: S-A flat 6; B-F3
Soloists: SATB
Orchestra: strings, woodwinds, probable brass, timpani, piano-forte.

OUTLINE

Requiem (Introit-Kyrie): 156 mm.

Requiem aeternam [cm] *larghetto; Te decet* [E flat M]; *Requiem aeternam; Kyrie* [cm] *alla breve*, satb choir. ABA form with four-part fugue on *Kyrie*.

Dies Irae: 85 mm.

Dies irae [cm] *allegretto*, satb choir/SA soli (vv. 1–4) *Quid sum miser*: 39 mm. *Quid sum miser*, [fm] *adagio*, T solo AA form. (v. 7) *Rex tremendae*: 271 mm. *Rex tremendae* [am] *molto grave*, satb choir/SATB soli; *Lacrimosa* [cm] *allegro*, satb choir (fugal). (vv. 8–16, 18–19)

Offertorium: 118 mm.

Domine Jesu Christe [A flat M] *larghetto*, satb choir/SATB soli.

Sanctus: 134 mm.

Sanctus [CM] *maestoso; Osanna, alla breve*, satb choir. Fugue.

Agnus Dei-(Communion): 210 mm.

Agnus Dei [cm] *adagio*, satb choir/SATB soli; *Lux aeterna, allegro.* satb choir (fugue); *Requiem aeternam* [cm] *adagio.* satb choir.

DISCOGRAPHY

None found.

MATEUSZ ZWIERZCHOWSKI
c. 1713–April 14, 1768

The Polish composer, Zwierzchowski, was organist-composer at the cathedral in Gniezno for more than thirty years. His father, who was an organist-violinist for the cathedral chapel, was his teacher. After the death of his father in 1735, he was appointed organist at the cathedral. Some time after, he was appointed conductor of the cathedral chapel, the *Capella Musices*. He remained in this post until his death. Very little is currently known about the composer and, unfortunately, only four of his compositions appear to have survived: a requiem, two pastorales, and a fragment of the Vesper service.

The *Requiem in E Flat Major* was composed in 1760 in memory of a colleague, Wojciech Wieczorkiewicz, a canon-cantor at Gniezno Cathedral. The composer scored the work for SATB choir, SATB soli, and orchestra. The *bel canto* solos *Tuba mirum* (bass), *Liber scriptus* (soprano), *Libera eas* (tenor), *Benedictus* (bass), and duet *Judex ergo* (soprano/alto) possess the same florid and elaborate figurations (including dotted rhythms, sixteenth and thirty-second notes) characteristic of the Neapolitan school. The independent orchestral accompaniment provides melodic obbligati (violins/trumpets) and rhythmic drive for the choral parts and many movements have an instrumental introduction.

The predominant homophonic, chordal texture is broken only by two fugues (*Kyrie* and *Hosanna*) and one fugal passage, *Cum sanctis tuis*. Zwierzchowski employed the solo quartet as a second choir, in *concertante* fashion, in the Introit (*Te decet*), Offertory, and Communion. Of particular interest is the *Tuba mirum* (a polonaise) with its melodic charm and folkloric spirit.

Basic Data

EDITIONS

1. Zrodla do Historie Muzyki Polskei, Vol. XIV
Mateusz Zwierzchowski
Requiem [Partytura]
ed., F. Dabrowski & Jan Jargon
Polskie Wydania Muzyczne, Krakow
1968

2. Florilegium Musicae Antiquae, II
M. Zwierzchowski
Polonez "Tuba Mirum" na bas,
2 trabki, wiolonczele i organo.
Polskie Wydawnictwo Muzyczne,
Krakow. 1962 [only the *Tuba mirum*]

DURATION

Eighteen movements, 902 mm., perf., c. 35'

VOICING AND ORCHESTRATION

Choir: SATB range: S-A flat 6; B-G3
Soloists: SATB
Instruments: vn. I/II, clarino I/II, vc., org. [*basso continuo*].

OUTLINE

Introit: 138 mm., 2 movements [incomplete text].
  Requiem aeternam: 26 mm. [E flat M] *maestoso*. satb choir *Te decet:*, 112 mm. [cm] *adagio*. S solo/satb choir; inst. Interlude; B solo/SA & TB duets/satb choir.
Kyrie: 140 mm. (no *Christe*)
  Kyrie [E flat M] *allegro*. satb choir. Fugue.
Sequence: 239 mm., 6 movements.
  Dies irae: 38 mm. [E flat M] *maestoso*. orch. intro.; satb choir; (vv. 1–2) *Tuba mirum*: 98 mm. [E flat M] *andante*. orch. intro.; *Tuba mirum*, B solo (vv. 3–4). Polonaise. *Liber scriptus*: 51 mm. [cm] *andante*. orch. intro.; SA duet. (vv. 5–6). *Juste judex*: 21 mm. [E flat M] *maestoso*. orch. intro.; *Juste judex*, satb choir (vv. 11–12). *Oro supplex*: 10 mm. [cm] *adagio*. satb choir, *a cappella*. (v. 17). *Huic ergo*: 30 mm. [E flat M] *allegro*. satb choir. (v. 19).
Offertory: 158 mm., 4 movements.
  Domine Jesu Christe: 27 mm. [E flat M] *andante*. satb choir. *Libera eas*: 33 mm. [gm] *andante*. orch. intro.; TB soli. *Quam olim Abrahae*: 48 mm. [E flat M] *allegro*. satb choir. *Hostias*: 50. mm. [gm] *adagio*. SA duet. *Quam olim Abrahae* repeated.
Sanctus: 132 mm., 2 movements.
  Sanctus: 34 mm. [E flat M] *adagio*. satb choir. *Hosanna*: 98 mm. [E flat M] *allegro*. satb choir. Fugue.

Benedictus: 58 mm.

    Benedictus [gm] *andante*, B solo; *Hosanna* repeated.

Agnus Dei: 15 mm.

    Agnus Dei [E flat M] *adagio*. T solo/SB duet/satb choir; *Cum sanctis*, satb choir.

Communion: 22 mm. [similar to opening movement]

    Lux aeterna [cm-E flat M] *adagio*. *Requiem aeternam* repeated.

DISCOGRAPHY

Muza-Polskie Nagrannia, XL 0275 (LP), Arion Choir, Bydgoszcz Philharmonia, cond. Zbigniew Chwedczuk.

7

Romanticism

INTRODUCTION

During the nineteenth century, the traditional liturgical requiem had evolved into a new independent musical form—the concert requiem. The concert requiem was designed for performance in the concert hall and on the operatic stage. An obvious indication of this transformation is the extension of the works' performance time. Although the eighteenth-century requiem's liturgical function regulated it to a performance time of forty to fifty minutes, the larger-scale models of Gossec, Paisiello, Mayr, Eybler, and Cimarosa served to foreshadow the style of what would eventually become the romantic standard. Although a number of settings, including Gounod's three settings (*C Major*, *Messe Funèbre*, *Messe Brève*), Rheinberger's Op. 84 and Op. 194, and the settings of De Lange, Liszt, Fauré, and Bruckner conform to the standards for liturgical usage, the works created by many other composers demonstrated their eagerness to take advantage of the newly established freedom from traditional time restrictions. Bomtempo (1818), Bottesini (1880), Donizetti (1835), Gouvy (1874), Henschel (1901), and Draeseke (1876–80) created requiems that required approximately one hour to perform, while settings by Berlioz (1837), Stanford (1897), Verdi (1874), Gounod (*Mors et Vita*, 1885), Sgambati (c. 1895), and Von Suppé (1855) have performance times that surpass even that. Furthermore, the collaborative *Messa per Rossini* (1869), as well as the setting by Dvořak, require almost two full hours to perform in their entirety.

ROMANTIC IDEALS

Romantic composers found inspiration due in part to their interest in numerous subjects, such as nature, romantic love, the Middle Ages, larger-than-life drama, and a sense of nationalism. All of these elements can be cited in either overt or covert manifestations in the requiem literature of the romantic century. These interests influenced and allowed for the development of program music. It is but a small step from the textless concert overture to the instrumental overtures present in the requiems of Donizetti, Gounod, and Paisiello, or the programmatic requiem introductions by Berlioz, Draeseke, Henschel, and Saint-Saëns.

Engaging and highly charged sentiments are often cited in the orchestral accompaniments for Italian grand opera solos. Such a wide range of passionate and dramatic emotions lends itself nicely to the programmatic illumination of the solo text. An identical writing style was adopted for their sacred counterparts—the vocal solos, duets, trios, and quartets of the Romantic-era requiem. Examples of this are abundant, including the bass solo, *Hostias* (Suppé); the soprano-tenor duet, *Benedictus* (Gounod's C Major Requiem); the soprano solo, *Libera me* (Verdi); and the tenor-bass duet, *Judex ergo*; bass solo, *Oro supplex*; and tenor solo, *Ingemisco* (Donizetti).

Contained within the *Messa per Rossini* are a great many virtuoso arias: *Agnus Dei* (alto), *Ingemisco* (tenor), *Quid sum miser* (soprano/alto duet), *Recordare* (satb quartet), and *Lux aeterna* (tenor/baritone/bass trio). *Recordare*, a setting by Gouvy for solo SATB quartet and choir, is one of the most poignant examples of romantic literature. Operatic recitative is included in the settings of both Verdi and Saint Saëns (*Liber scriptus* and *Libera me*).

The requiem text, especially that of the *Dies irae*, proved to be fertile soil in which composers could sow their imaginations. The poetry of the Sequence hymn, verses 1–3 (*Dies irae-Quantus Tremor-Tuba mirum*) and verses 8–9 (*Rex tremendae-Confutatis*) were ripe material for dramatic settings. Accompanying orchestrations demonstrate similarities to those of opera settings depicting violent acts of nature and malevolent human behavior.

Some composers, including Fauré and Rheinberger, chose to preclude the violent aspects of the *Dies irae* simply by eliminating the Sequence from their settings. They instead emphasized the tranquil, serene guise of the requiem text. The variations of tone and attitude of the overall setting can be distinctly recognized based on the particular aspects the composer chose to accentuate. For instance, the Verdi and Fauré settings were composed only fourteen years apart, yet they represent two uniquely different musical worlds—one of external fire and fury, the other of internal peace and serenity. Despite these different approaches, each work manages to inspire and move the spirit in its own distinctive manner.

Nationalism, a key component in many romantic works, is more difficult to detect in the Romantic requiem. Nevertheless, its presence can be resolutely affirmed. The setting by Berlioz is a fine example. Its colossal musical forces, most notably the four brass bands and twenty-four muffled drums (used during the cortege) are an obvious vestige of a musical tradition that had been finely honed during the height of the French Revolution. Verdi also drew upon this tradition in the *Manzoni Requiem* with his decision to commemorate Manzoni, the renowned Italian poet and writer, and Rossini, the celebrated Italian musician, through music as his way of affirming his national pride.

In the Dvořak *Requiem*, the opening phrase of *Recordare* resonates with a melody that, if not previously composed as an actual folk song, encompasses all the qualities of folk music. Nearly every romantic composer applied the technique of incorporating folk melodies or well-known patriotic tunes into their settings. Such music was instrumental in attracting the attention of the emerging middle class and garnered many composers an expanded audience.

Artists' fascination with the Middle Ages is discernible in the literary works of the romantic era, such as Tennyson's *Idylls of the King*, Hugo's *Hunchback of Notre Dame*, and Shakespeare's *Romeo and Juliet*, as well as in musical works that witnessed a revival in the use of Gregorian chant. The Caecilian Movement (Germany) was steadfast in its effort to restore medieval chant and Renaissance polyphony to liturgical use. In 1890, the Plainsong and Medieval Music Society of England began issuing its publications, successfully stimulating a new awareness and interest in musical styles of the past.

The opening phrase of the Gregorian *Dies irae* melody was made famous by its use in a variety of romantic works, such as Liszt's *Totentanz*, Berlioz' *Symphonie Fantastique*, and *Variations on a Theme of Paganini*, by Rachmaninoff. Saint Saëns (1878), Alfred Bruneau (1896), and Sgambati (c. 1895) also quoted it when creating their requiem settings.

ROLE OF THE COMPOSER

Romantic era composers were quite different from their classical predecessors from both a professional and creative perspective. Although most classical composers had some connections to the older system of patronage, the romantics were comparable to modern independent agents, creating their works upon commission. The majority of classical composers wrote in a fashion that was both elegant and restrained, fostering unifor-

mity in the musical style of the eighteenth century. Less interested in stylistic unity, the romantics cherished their individuality, rejecting
restrictions or traditions that might impose limitations on their artistic
expression. Composers of this era thoroughly enjoyed placing their personal imprint upon their works. Paganini, Liszt, and Chopin created sin-
gularly individualized pieces designed to showcase their spectacular
virtuosity. So personal and complex were some of these creations that
Liszt was actually forced to rewrite a number of his works just so other
musicians would be able to play them. Virtuosity permeated all musical
forms.

The shift toward vocal virtuosity, initially exhibited by Beethoven in
Missa Solemnis and *Ninth Symphony*, continued to develop in the romantic
requiem setting, evident in the complex choral lines and frequent high
notes included in the vocal and choral arrangements. In most romantic
settings, precise choral tuning, especially in chromatic passages, is more
difficult to maintain than in earlier works. The settings of Draeseke, Henschel, and De Lange provide an array of intonations and challenges for
the singer. Less apparent in the eighteenth-century requiem, the pitches A
6 up to C 7 ("high" C) are more commonly found in the romantic settings.
Because of its unusually high pitches, extensive range of dynamics, and
fiercely dramatic intensity, performance of Verdi's *Libera me* requires the
talents of a virtuoso soprano soloist. The Bottesini requiem, *Quantus
tremor, Judex ergo, Confutatis*, includes instrumental bass lines with a vast
range and intricate passages that call for the flair of a highly skilled musician. For the romantics, the dexterity of performance, technical prowess,
and personal charisma are reflected in the music.

Despite their need for individual artistic liberties, a connection was
maintained between romantic composers and musical tradition through
the revival of the baroque *concertante* style. Although the *concertante*
proved inspirational to the romantics, they still felt the need to emboss
the traditional style with their own unique, contemporary stamp. This, in
turn, led them to design arrangements that had the choir and solo quartet
(or soloist) function as contrasting groups. In addition, a number of composers chose to embellish their requiem settings with the addition of a
fugue or canon. The text *Quam olim Abrahae* was most frequently used in
this fashion (Dvořak, Gounod, Lachner, Rheinberger, Stanford, and Von
Suppé). The *Kyrie* text, also a popularly adapted piece, became part of the
settings composed by Donizetti, Lachner, Lange, Von Suppé, and Buzzola
[*Messa per Rossini*]. Other texts set as fugues include *Hosanna* (Gouvy, Berlioz, and Plantania), *Judex ergo* (Bomtempo and Lachner), *Dies irae* (Gounod and Lange), *Cum sanctis tuis* (Von Suppé), *Amen* (Donizetti and
Coccia), and *Libera me* (Verdi).

LANGUAGE AND STYLE

During the eighteenth century, classic diatonic harmony evolved into chromatic harmony, resulting in an ever-increasing number of tonal relationships between one chord and the next. The earlier requiem settings of Cherubini, Bomtempo, Tomášek, Schubert, and Eybler include passages that show traces of this developing chromaticism. This style was continued by the romantics, Bottesini and Bruckner, but by the second half of the century, the ultra-chromaticism of Wagner's *Tristan* made its presence known in most requiem settings, especially those of Dvořak, Liszt, Stanford, Draeseke, Henschel, and Gounod. In the late romantic period, it was common to hear keys with five or more sharps/flats, leading to the widespread application of enharmonic modulation, as frequently found in settings by Draeseke, Henschel, Dvořak, and Gounod.

The basic four-part SATB scoring so prominent in the eighteenth century gave way to the romantic four-part (*divisi*) fabric, with variations including SSAATTBB, SSAATB, SATTBB, and SAATTB.

In the classic tradition, composers made general indications regarding dynamic and tempo because these particular elements related directly to the music's structure. In the romantic era, composers left very precise, often quite fussy, directions for tempo and dynamic changes, of which they were meticulously insistent. The Introit of Draeseke's requiem, for example, notes ten tempo changes, while the Sequence designates a total of fifteen. Henschel's setting of the *Dies irae* specifies nineteen tempo changes. Any given romantic movement is likely to exhibit profuse subtle, and in some cases dramatic, changes in tempo, key, and dynamics. The *Dies irae* of the Liszt *Requiem* serves as a fine model of this trend, incorporating more than a dozen changes of key signature. Regardless of these extraordinary complexities, the romantic composer did everything necessary to ensure that the music flowed and unfolded in a natural progression.

Credit for the development of such intricacies can be partially awarded to the arrival of the Industrial Revolution, whose impact led to the production of state-of-the-art musical instruments that provided romantic composers with more power and versatility than their predecessors had ever known.

Berlioz' treatise on orchestration deals not only with technical matters, but also with the emotional temperament of the high, medium, and low ranges of various instruments. In his *Requiem*, he put his theories into practice, none more overt than the brass fanfare present in the opening of the *Tuba mirum* passage. Berlioz had learned this technique from Gossec, and Verdi, in turn, had learned from Berlioz, with all three composers making special efforts for this text.

Berlioz was fascinated with the exploration of the emotional and psychological effects of orchestration. His orchestration treatise concerns itself as much with the emotional reaction to the use of differing timbre and the various ranges of the instrument's sound as it does with the nature of the instrument itself. He employed a melodic device called *idée fixe* to create thematic unity.

Heavily influenced by Schopenhauer, Wagner developed a great interest in the psychological impact of his musical concepts. He expounded the *Leitmotiv*, a kind of musical "theme" that held different levels of psychological interpretation, based on the way in which it was orchestrated. Dvořak, Gounod, and Stanford also employed a form of Wagnerian *Leitmotiv* in their requiem settings. Verdi liked to incorporate prayer scenes into his operas (*Aida*, *Othello*), and also employed a contemplative type of prayer scene (in a recitative style) into the *Libera me* of his *Manzoni Requiem*.

The classic forms continued to be cherished by composers like Dvořak, Cherubini, Verdi, and Rheinberger, yet their creators gave them a sense of the romantic individualism by filling them with the new spirit of drama and emotion. Berlioz and Liszt, among others, chose to abandon the classic forms in favor of structures and forms that allowed for greater improvisation.

The merging of the Introit and *Kyrie* movements into one continuous movement, a practice initiated by the Viennese classicists, was sustained by virtually all romantic composers. Some composers, such as Gouvy, Liszt, Berlioz, and Bruckner, used the *Kyrie* as little more than a coda for the Introit. The romantics also adopted the Viennese tradition of coupling the *Agnus Dei* with the Communion. Differences in the two schools become more apparent in their presentation of the Sequence text, *Dies irae*. While the Viennese preferred to divide this text into smaller, more manageable chunks by writing separate movements, numerous romantic composers, including Bruckner, Draeseke, Henschel, Lange, Stanford, and Verdi, chose to set all nineteen verses into one continuous movement. At the other extreme, however, is Donzetti, who composed the Sequence in nine movements and the *Messa per Rossini* in only seven.

The romantics, for the most part, did not set the Responsory, *Libera me*, to music, although several composers, including Donizetti, Bottesini, Liszt, Von Suppé, Verdi, and Fauré, did create musical accompaniment for that particular text. The Frenchmen Gounod and Fauré set scores for the *Pie Jesu*.

The nineteenth century saw a rise in popularity of choral societies as institutions, and many choral works, including requiem settings, were created specifically for these singing societies. Dvořak's *Requiem* and Gounod's *Mors et Vita* were commissioned by England's Birmingham Festival.

Schumann and Lachner worked directly with choral groups and composed pieces specifically for their voices. Bottesini's *Requiem in C Minor* was given its premiere in an opera house. The French government provided its sponsorship for the premiere of the massive Berlioz *Requiem*, which despite being performed in a church, had a connection to the liturgy that, at best, could be described as tenuous. Composed under the direction of Verdi, the monumental *Messa per Rossini* could not be performed in the church because of a papal ban that denied female singers the opportunity to participate in the liturgy. The plan for a subsequent opera house premiere also dissolved before it could reach fruition. More than a century had passed since its composition before this masterpiece would receive its maiden performance.

During the eighteenth century, little resistance was evident toward the development of the symphonic requiem, with its elaborate ornamentation, or the adoption of Neapolitan operatic and classic instrument styles.

CAECILIAN MOVEMENT

The response to the symphonic-operatic requiem culminated in the formation of the Caecilian Movement, a reform that embraced Gregorian chant and the Palestrina polyphonic style, but rejected sacred music that made use of large orchestras and vocal soloists. Although Johann Fux, whose setting integrated only modest orchestral accompaniment, found his requiem considered acceptable, Donizetti, Von Suppé, Verdi, and Paisiello, whose settings adopted an "operatic" style, were informed that their works, along with the grand *Messa per Rossini*, had been branded *musica non grata*.

The Caecilian Movement was begun by Franz Xavier Witt (1834–1888) specifically for the German churches and church musicians, but this reform rapidly spread to all Catholic countries. Dr. Karl Proske, a canon and choirmaster of the Ratisbon Cathedral, was also an important figure in this musical movement. His ten-volume anthology, *Musica Divina* (1853–1878), included many choices, but neglected Renaissance choral works. In 1868, the establishment of the Schola Gregoriana at the Lateran by Pope Pius IX further encouraged the restoration of chant and polyphonic music.

Those who followed the Caecilian Movement held steadfast to the belief that all contemporary religious music should adhere to the spirit and tradition of the "ages of faith." These ideals are generally respected in the requiem settings of Bruckner, Liszt, DeLange, Gounod, and Rheinberger. Numerous Caecilian requiem settings were born of such composers as Joseph Auer, Ludwig Bonvin, Eduard Brunner, Michael

Dachs, Vincenzo Goller, Peter Griesbacher, Karl Hegmann, Michael Hir-blinger, Oswald Joos, Thaddaeus König, Karl Kraft, Johann Meurer, Ignaz Mitterer, Joseph Renner, Sr., Joseph Renner, Jr., Bruno Stein, Josef Stein, Georg Zoller, among others. Their works were published by the Coppenrath firm, based in Altötting, Germany.

CODA

A few words remain to be said concerning several of the composers mentioned in this study. A majority of the artists whose careers are expounded upon in this chapter are well known and have secured their niche in musical history. However, a number of other outstanding composers whose contributions are terribly underrated, and, in way too many instances, are completely unknown. The requiem settings of Théodore Gouvy (1819–98), Charles Villiers Stanford (1852–1924), Friedrich Kiel (1821–83), and Daniel De Lange(1841–1918) are truly extraordinary works of art. The first three are scored for choir, soloists, and orchestra, while the De Lange setting is an unaccompanied requiem for two SATB choirs and two sets of SATB soloists. This composition ranks in quality with such other renowned unaccompanied pieces as Vaughan-Williams' *Mass in G Minor*, Schoenberg's motet, *Friede auf Erde*, and Poulenc's *Figure Humaine*.

Modern-day performance of these particular requiems is hindered by the lack of current editions. The Théodore Gouvy Society, based in Hombourg-Haut, France, is in possession of some detailed information regarding many rare compositions, and a full score of the Stanford *Requiem* can be found in the collections of Cornell University and the Library of Congress. Microfilm versions of both Kiel requiems are available at the New York Public Library. At the time of this writing, the De Lange requiem was about to receive its first published edition.

HECTOR BERLIOZ
December 11, 1803–March 8, 1869

Hector Berlioz was an uncommonly gifted musical visionary. His music, especially the *Requiem* (1837) and *Te Deum* (1850), was influenced by the musical tradition and style that arose during the French Revolution. This type of national music often called for gigantic musical forces for the out-of-door musical performance. These concerts were designed by the government to create support of the populace for the Revolution as well as to display its national fervor and dignity. Hints of this grandiose style were already evident in the *Messe des Morts* of Gossec (1760).

When Berlioz wrote his *Requiem*, he was concerned with how to fill the cathedral with majestic, powerful sonorities. At the same time, he wanted the *Requiem* to glorify France and reaffirm its national honor. He scored the work for tenor solo, SSTTBB choir, orchestra, four brass bands, and an enormous amount of percussion. Commissioned by the French government in 1837, it was scheduled for a ceremony honoring those who lost their lives in the July Revolution of 1830. This date passed, however, without a performance. It was not until December 5, 1837, that it was finally performed at the Cathedral of St. Louis des Invalides for the entombment of General Charles de Damremont. The premiere went well and received an enthusiastic response from the press.

Viewed as a whole, the *Requiem* is a titanic canvas of the Last Judgment. Its hybrid form employs elements of the requiem mass and grand opera. His setting of the *Requiem* is the first completely romantic-era model. His contemporary, Cherubini, wrote two requiems. These pieces contain a substantial amount of romantic fervor, but they are old-fashioned when compared to the Berlioz setting. Berlioz bypassed the classic ideals of balance and restraint and achieved a hair-raising grandeur through the use of three brass choirs in the *Tuba mirum*, *Rex tremendae*, and *Lacrymosa*. At the same time, he provided a contrast to the colossal quality of these movements by writing three quiet movements, *Quid sum miser*, *Quaerens me*, and *Domine Jesu Christe* to follow each massive movement.

The choral writing of the *Requiem* is highly varied. There are solo choral passages for tenors, basses, and sopranos (*Quid sum miser*); four-part chordal writing (*Hostias*); fugal texture (*Hosanna*); choral unisons (*Domine Jesu Christe*); and mixed polyphonic-homophonic texture (*Rex tremendae*). Berlioz used the SI, SII, TI, TII, BI, BII choir in yet another version of a romantic "*concertante*" style. Throughout most of the work, the soprano, tenor, or bass lines are added or omitted to create "solo" or "full" choral sections. The texts of the requiem are repeated for emphasis and the order of the words occasionally changed to suit the dramatic intentions of Berlioz. The only vocal solo is for tenor and SSA choir in the *Sanctus*.

The work is scored for a very large orchestral ensemble. The *Messe des Morts* possesses all of the dramatic qualities of earlier classic and early-romantic requiem settings, but on a greatly expanded level. One of the novel features employed by the timpani is the use of sponge coverings for the mallets in order to subdue the dynamic volume of the powerful drum rolls executed during the *Tuba mirum*. The *Sanctus* and final *Requiem aeternam* possess an angelic and ethereal character, imparted by the strings and four-part flute scoring.

The chromatic elements of the harmonic vocabulary are more daring and colorful than any previous composer. Berlioz was, in some ways, fortunate to have no ability to play the piano or any other instrument. This situation allowed him to write a music based upon aural imagination and free from any limitations based upon technical proficiency.

Basic Data

EDITIONS

1. New Edition of the Complete Works   2. Hector Berlioz
Hector Berlioz   Requiem for Tenor Solo,
Grande messe des morts.   SSTTBB Chorus & Orchestra
ed., Jurgen Kindermann   [Choral score]
Bärenreiter. Kassel. Basel. London.   Kalmus (K 06092)
New York. Prague 1978

DURATION

Ten movements, 1517 mm., perf., c. 82'

VOICING AND ORCHESTRATION

Choir: SI/II, TI/II, BI/II range: S-B flat 6; B-D3
80 sopranos, 60 tenors, 70 basses [specified by the composer]
Soloists: T
Orchestra: 50 vn., 20 vla., 20 vc., 18 db.,. 4 fl., 2 ob., 2 Eh., 4 cl., 8 bsn., 12 Fh., timp.
    (8 pairs), 10 players, 4 tamtams, cymbals (10 pairs).
Orchestra I: 4 cornets á pistons, 4 tbn., 2 tubas.
Orchestra II: 4 tpt., 4 tbn.
Orchestra III: 4 tpt., 4 tbn.
Orchestra IV: 4 tpt., 4 tbn., 4 ophicledes [tuba].

OUTLINE

Introit & *Kyrie*: 209 mm.
    Requiem aeternam, [gm] *andante un poco lento*; *Te decet*, [B flat M-gm]; *Kyrie* [gm]
    SSTTBB choir.
Sequence: 703 mm., 5 movements.
    Dies irae: 251 mm. [am] *moderato*. ssttbb choir/four brass choirs/orchestra. (vv.
    1–6). *Quid sum miser*: 49 mm. [g # m] *andante un poco lento*. T I unison & BT
    II, (vv. 7–9). *Rex tremendae*: 111 mm. [EM] *andante maestoso*. ssttbb choir/four
    brass choirs/orchestra. (vv. 8, 9, 16). *Quaerens me*: 84 mm. [AM] *andante soste-*
    nuto. ssttbb unaccompanied choir. (vv. 10–15). *Lacrymosa*: 208 mm. [am]
    andante non troppo lento. ssttbb choir/four brass choirs/orchestra. (vv. 18–19).
    Orchestral ostinato figure.
Offertory: 201 mm., 2 movements.
    Domine Jesu Christe: 154 mm. [dm] *moderato*. unison stb choir. *Hostias*: 47 mm.
    [gm-B flat M] *andante non troppo lento*. Unaccompanied ttbb choir, punctuated
    by short orchestral interludes.

Sanctus: 203 mm.

Sanctus [D flat M] *andante un poco sostenuto e maestoso.* T solo/ssa choir; *Hosanna,* stb choir, Fughetta; *Sanctus*, T solo/ssa choir; *Hosanna*, stb choir. Fughetta.

Agnus Dei-Communion: 201 mm. [abbreviated *Agnus Dei* text]

Agnus Dei I [CM signature-multiple keys] *andante un poco lento.* ttbb choir; *Requiem aeternam,* ttbb choir; *Te decet,* tb choir/ ssttbb choir; *Quia pius est* [GM] *un poco piu lento.* ssttb choir.

DISCOGRAPHY

1. Sony, 01-062659-10, Temple University Choir, Philadelphia Orchestra, cond., Eugene Ormandy.
2. Multiple listings in the Schwann Catalogue.

JOÃO BOMTEMPO
December 28, 1775–August 18, 1842

João Bomtempo was the son of Franz Xavier Bomtempo, an oboist at the royal chapel of Dom Jose I. Because of the political turmoil caused by the Napoleonic invasions of Portugal, he spent a number of years in France and England. A member of the Brotherhood of St. Cecilia, he occupied himself with the creation of a Portuguese "national" school of music. Toward that end, he established The Philharmonic Society (1833) and founded the Lisbon Conservatory (1835).

Bomtempo composed a number of piano concerti, piano music, quintets for piano and strings, as well as a number of sacred choral and vocal pieces. Op. 23, *Messe de requiem consacrée à Camoes,* was completed, in Paris, by 1818. Its first performance took place in London during the summer of 1819. The name *Camoes* refers to the great national poet of Portugal, Luis Vaz de Camoes (c. 1524–1580). The prevailing choral texture is homophonic with occasional passages of imitative polyphony. There are three fugues, *Judex ergo, Quam olim Abrahae,* and *Hosanna* and imitative or fugal writing on *Requiem aeternam* and *Juste Judex.*

The orchestra tends to support the work of the choir, and rarely functions as an individual entity, but it does energize the motion and mood of the text by intense, seething eighth, sixteenth, and thirty-second-note rhythmic patterns and motion, including passages in *Confutatis, Inter oves, Rex tremendae, Recordare,* and *Te decet.* Other notable coloristic effects are an orchestral "vamp" in *Juste Judex,* the brass fanfare at the opening of *Tuba mirum,* and the light, angelic coloring of *Sed signifer.*

The vocal soloists sing briefly, making occasional contributions to the greater sonorous totality. There exists none of the virtuosity associated with the Neapolitan opera tradition of vocal pyrotechnics; only expressive, lyrical melody.

The diatonic musical language employed is typical of the late-classic, early romantic era and possesses a solid measure of chromatic writing. An interesting touch is the repetition of musical material from the Introit, at the conclusion of the *Requiem*, thereby formally rounding out the greater melodic structure.

This requiem is a large-scale work, full of drama, passion, and fury. Moments of great, lyrical writing stand side-by-side with moments of turbulence and violence. It is one of the superior early romantic requiems.

Basic Data

EDITION

Bomtempo
Requiem. Opus 23
Vocal score.
ed., Christopher Bochmann
Musicoteca (Mus 012 red) 1994

DURATION

Eight movements, 1728 mm., perf., 60'

VOICING AND ORCHESTRATION

Choir: SATB range: S-A6; B-F3
Soloists: SATB
Orchestra: vn. I/II, vla., vc., db., 2 ob., 2 cl., 2 fl., 2 bsn., 2 Fh., 2 tpt., 2 tbn., timp.

OUTLINE

Introit-*Kyrie*: 188 mm., 1 movement.
  Requiem aeternam: 71 mm. [cm-GM] *larghetto*. *Requiem aeternam*, satb choir; *Te decet/et tibi*, SAT soli/satb choir; *Requiem aeternam*, satb choir. ABA form. Seque to Kyrie:
Kyrie: 117 mm. [GM-cm] *concertante* SATB soli/satb choir.
Sequence, *Dies irae*: 745 mm. [CM] 3 movements.
  Dies irae: 424 mm. [CM-GM] *allegro con fuoco*. satb choir (vv. 1–2); *Tuba mirum* [E flat M-B flat M] SATB soli/satb choir (vv. 3–5); *Judex ergo* [cm-gm] *allegro moderato*. satb choir. Fugue. (v. 6); *Quid Sum miser* [gm] *larghetto*, satb choir (vv. 7–10); *Juste judex* [CM] *allegro*, satb choir. fughetta. (v. 11). Ingemisco: 167 mm. [em] *andante commodo*. SA soli/satb choir. (vv. 12–14); *Confutatis* [FM] *allegro spiritoso*. satb choir (vv. 15–16); Lacrymosa: 154 mm. [CM/am] *moderato espressivo assai*. satb choir; *Pie Jesu*, SATB soli; *Dona eis requiem* [CM] *allegro vivace*. satb choir. (vv. 17–19).
Offertory: 319 mm.
  Domine: [G flat M] *larghetto*. satb choir; *Sed signifer* [cm] *allegro*. satb choir; *Hostias* [e flat m] *larghetto*. S solo/satb choir; *Quam olim Abrahae* [B flat M] *allegro moderato*. satb choir. Fugue.

Sanctus: 83 mm.
    Sanctus [CM] *allegro maestoso assai.* satb choir; *Hosanna* [am] *allegro.* satb choir.
    Fugal.
Benedictus: 92 mm.
    Benedictus [FM] *larghetto.* SATB soli; *Hosanna* [FM] *allegro.* satb choir.
Agnus Dei-Communion: 301 mm.
    Agnus Dei & *Requiem aeternam* [cm] *andante sostenuto.* satb choir; *Cum Sanctis*
    [CM] *allegro moderato.* satb choir; *Requiem aeternam* (taken from Introit), [cm]
    larghetto. satb choir.

DISCOGRAPHY

1. Berlin Classics, 0092452 BC, Rundfunkchor & Sinfonie-Orchester Berlin, cond. Heinz Rögner.
2. Aria Music, 592302, Orchestre et choeur de la Fondation Gulbenkian, dir. Michel Corboz.

GIOVANNI BOTTESINI
December 22, 1821–July 7, 1889

Bottesini was a famous double-bass virtuoso who received his musical training at the Milan Conservatory from Luigi Rossi. He was nicknamed the "Paganini" of the double bass. His peripatetic musical career as conductor and performer took him around the world. He was a life-long friend of Verdi and conducted the first performance of the latter's opera, *Aida*, in Cairo for the opening of the Suez Canal. Among his compositions are a dozen operas, many works for the double bass, including several concerti, a handful of orchestral works, and several sacred pieces: the oratorio *The Garden of Olivet* (1887) and the *Requiem* (1880).

The *Requiem in C minor*, is one of the fine romantic requiems for soloists, choir, and orchestra. Unfortunately, the work is not well-known. It was premiered during the Lent-Carneval season of 1879–80 at the Royal Theatre of Turin. Bottesini scored the *Requiem* for SATB soli, SATB choir, and orchestra. Its exterior form, typical of Italian grand opera (less recitative and dialogue), allows the vocal soloists to play a major role. The bass solo, *Ingemisco*, was composed specifically for the gifted Edouard de Reszke (brother of the tenor, Jean de Reszke), who sang its premiere.

This work is a dramatic, sometimes lyrical, setting of the liturgical text. Paired movements (*Dies irae-Quid sum miser, Quaerens me-Ingemisco, Confutatis-Lacrymosa, Sanctus-Benedictus,* and *Agnus Dei-Communion*) provide moments of vivid emotional contrast. The choral texture is a mixture of expressive chordal harmony and imitative polyphonic writing style. There are two complete fugues, *Confutatis* and *Cum sanctis tuis*, as well as numerous imitative passages in the Introit-*Kyrie*, *Quaerens me*, and *Benedictus*.

The vocal solos possess a lyrical character, are generally syllabic and free of the florid ornamentation associated with the Neapolitan style. The solo quartet occasionally functions as a second choir (*Introit-Kyrie, Lacrymosa,* and *Et lux perpetua*) in a romantic version of the older baroque *concertante* style.

Although Bottesini used the musical language of romanticism, the harmonic style of the *Requiem* is quite restrained and similar to the Classic era. The traditional arrangement of keys and modulations, spiced with a modest amount of chromatic alteration, was employed by the composer.

Basic Data

EDITION

Messa da Requiem per soli, coro e orchestra
Revisione di Franco Gallini
[piano-vocal score]
Edizioni Suvini Zerboni, Milan 1978

DURATION

Fourteen movements, 1403 mm., perf., c. 55′

VOICING AND ORCHESTRATION

Choir: SATB range: S-A6; B-F3
Soloists: SI/IIATB
Orchestra: vn. I/II, vla., vc., db., pic., 2 fl., 2 ob., 2 cl., 2 bsn., 4 Fh., 4 tpt., 3 tbn., bass tuba., timp., bass drum, cymbals., org.

OUTLINE

Introit-*Kyrie*: 120 mm.
    Requiem aeternam, [cm] *adagio*. Fugal; *Te decet*, [E flat M] Fugal; *Requiem aeternam* [cm] Fugal.; *Kyrie* [CM]; *Requiem aeternam*, [cm] SATB soli/satb choir.
Sequence: 659 mm., 6 movements.
    Dies irae: 226 mm. [gm] *allegro*. satb choir. orchestral postlude. (vv.1–6). *Quid sum miser*: 80 mm. [A flat M] *andante sostenuto*. T solo. (vv. 7–9). *Quaerens me*: 54 mm. [EM] *maestoso*. satb choir. (vv. 10–11). Fugal. *Ingemisco*: 125 mm.[am] *andantino*. B solo. (vv. 12–15). *Confutatis*: 61 mm. [fm] *moderato*. satb choir. (vv. 16–17). Fugue. *Lacrymosa*: 113 mm. [E flat M] *adagio*. SATB soli/satb choir. (vv. 18–19).
Offertory: 79 mm.
    Domine Jesu Christe [gm-GM] *andante*. S I solo.
Sanctus: 48 mm.
    Sanctus [BM] *allegro*. satb choir.

Benedictus: 73 mm.
> *Benedictus* [A flat M] *andantino con moto.* SATB soli.

Agnus Dei: 68 mm.
> *Agnus Dei* [E flat M] *andante.* SA duet.

Finale [Communion]: 193 mm.
> *Requiem aeternam* [CM] *grave; Cum sanctis tuis, allegro.* satb choir. Form: prelude/ fugue.

Responsory: 163 mm.
> *Libera me* [fm-CM] *andante.* ssaatb choir; *Tremens factus* [cm] S II solo; *Dies illa* [gm] *allegro.* satb choir; *Requiem aeternam* [gm] *adagio.* SATB soli; *Et lux* [cm] *allegro.* SATB soli/choir.

DISCOGRAPHY

None found.

ANTON BRUCKNER
September 4, 1824–October 11, 1896

During his early years, Bruckner held several important organist positions, including St. Florian's monastery and the cathedral at Linz, Austria. Eventually, he embarked upon a long period of study at the Vienna Conservatory with Simon Sechter. During these years, Bruckner became acquainted with Wagner, and was eventually taken into the circle of Wagner's close friends. After Sechter died, Bruckner was offered the former's position at the Conservatory. He settled in Vienna permanently and composed his most important works. Among his pupils were the conductors, Arthur Nikisch, Karl Muck, and the composer-conductor, Gustav Mahler.

Bruckner is famous for his nine symphonies, but he also wrote numerous choral works. There are thirteen masses and seven large compositions for choir and orchestra (five Psalm settings, a *Magnificat*, and a *Te Deum*). Also, forty-five smaller liturgical works exist.

The *Requiem in D Minor* was written in 1849, before his studies in Vienna. It commemorates the death of his friend and mentor, Franz Seiler, the Notary and Clerk of St. Florian Monastery. There are two other requiems, one for male voices (1845), which is lost, and a *Requiem in D minor* (1875), of which only a fragment was composed. The 1849 setting is a straightforward work, scored for SATB soli, SATB choir, and orchestra.

Although the bulk of the choral writing is homophonic chordal style, there are a number of polyphonic passages, such as *Qui Mariam* (canon), *Oro supplex* (fugal), *Quam olim Abrahae* (double fugue), and paired rhythmic imitation (*Sanctus*). The harmonic vocabulary used by Bruckner is that of the late romantic style. Although the harmony is restless, the highly charged chromaticism of Wagner's *Tristan* is absent.

The music possesses a serious and austere quality that is derived not only from the use of older, conservative musical forms, such as fugue and canon, but also from an orchestral role that, for the most part, doubles the choral fabric. The *concertante* use of solo voices and choral passages also comes from an older tradition and is always melodic and appealing.

The *Requiem in D Minor* adheres to the principles of good church music espoused by the Caecilian Movement. There is no evident trace of operatic style, with its flamboyant vocal solos and colorful orchestrations, as is found in the Verdi, Dvořak, Von Suppé, Stanford, and Donizetti requiem settings.

Basic Data

EDITIONS

1. Anton Bruckner
Requiem in D Minor for Soli, Chorus
and Orchestra.
Kalmus (K 06085) [Vocal Score]
Belwin Mills Publishing Corp.

2. Anton Bruckner
Requiem D Moll für Soli, Chor
und Orchester 1849
Klavierauszug, Ludwig Berberich
Verlag Doblinger (46 007) 1974.

3. Öesterreichische Nationalbibliothek in
   Wien
Anton Bruckner
Sämtliche Werke [Collected Works]
Band 14
Requiem D Moll [Full Score]
ed. Dr. Leopold Nowak
Musikwissenschaftlicher Verlag der
   Internationalen Bruckner-Gesellschaft
Vienna 1966.

DURATION

Ten movements, 698 mm., perf., c. 37'

VOICING AND ORCHESTRATION

Choir: SATB range: S-B flat 6; B-F3
Soloists: SATB
Orchestra: vn. I/II, vla., vc., db., 3 tbn, Fh., org.

OUTLINE

Introit-*Kyrie*: 59 mm., ABA form.
   Requiem aeternam [dm] *andante*; *Te decet* [FM]; *Requiem aeternam* [gm-dm] *Kyrie*
   [dm], satb choir.

Sequence: 261 mm. All verses included.

Dies irae [DM] *allegro.* satb choir. *Mors stupebit,* A solo; *Liber scriptus,* T solo; *Quid sum miser,* S solo; *Rex tremendae,* satb choir; *Juste judex,* B solo; *Qui Mariam,* SA duet. Canon; *Inter oves,* satb choir; *Oro supplex,* satb choir, Canon.

Offertory: 214 mm., 3 movements.

Domine Jesu Christe: 67 mm. [FM-DM] *andante.* BS soli/satb choir. *Hostias*: 15 mm. [B flat M] *adagio.* ttbb choir. *Quam olim Abrahae*: 132 mm. [fm] *con spirito.* satb choir. Double fugue.

Sanctus: 17 mm.

Sanctus [dm] *andante.* ssatb choir. Canonic pairing of ss/a and t/b.

Benedictus: 62 mm.

Benedictus [B flat M] *andante.* SATB soli/satb choir.

Agnus Dei-Communion: 85 mm.

Agnus Dei I [dm] *adagio.* A solo/satb choir; *Agnus Dei* II, T solo/satb choir; *Agnus Dei* III, B solo/satb choir; *Lux aeterna,* satb choir.

Communion: 52 mm., 2 movements.

Requiem aeternam: 20 mm. [FM] *grave.* satb choir. *Cum sanctis tuis*: 32 mm. [dm] *alla breve.* satb choir.

DISCOGRAPHY

Hyperion, CDA 66245, Corydon Singers and the English Chamber Orchestra, cond. Matthew Best.

DANIEL DE LANGE
June 11, 1841–January 31, 1918

Daniel De Lange descended from a Dutch family of organists. He studied cello at the Brussels Conservatory and later lived in Paris, where he worked as an organist and choirmaster at Montrouge (a Protestant church). From 1895 to 1913, he was director of the Amsterdam Conservatory. His final appointment was to the directorship of the Isis Conservatory in Point Loma, California. During his working years, he conducted a number of very good choirs and was involved in promoting the polyphonic music of the Renaissance.

He wrote only a handful of musical works that includes two symphonies, an opera, a cello concerto, a mass, and one requiem. The *Requiem* was composed in 1868 and scored for two SATB choirs and two SATB soli quartets, unaccompanied. Although this atypical requiem still remains largely unknown, it is one of the great settings of the romantic era.

Its conservative stylistic characteristics are derived from the imitative polyphonic idiom of the Renaissance and *concertante* choral style, developed in the early baroque. Late romantic harmony and chromaticism contribute to the modern character of the *Requiem,* yet even this harmonic vocabulary is influenced by the unisons, fifths, octaves, and "empty" cadences of pre-Renaissance harmony. Ludwig Spohr's elegant, melodious *E Flat Mass*, for two, five-part, unaccompanied choirs and soloists (1821) might have served as a model for De Lange. The *concertante* use of soloists and choir, as well as the specific vocal scoring, in both works are also quite similar.

This intimate chamber-work encompasses a broad range of moods and emotions, not the least of which is a keen sense of deep spirituality. The *Requiem* is designed for concert performance, but would not be inappropriate for liturgical usage.

Basic Data

EDITION

Performance edition by Rene Rakier (1992).
To be published by Donemus.

DURATION

Six movements, perf., c. 32′

VOICING

Choir: choir I, SATB. Choir II, SATB
Soloists: solo quartet I, SATB. solo quartet II, SATB

OUTLINE

Introit-*Kyrie*: 8′57″
   Requiem aeternam: satb choirs I/II; *Te decet*: SATB soli/satb choirs; *Requiem aeternam*: satb choir I/II; *Kyrie*: satb choirs I/II. Fugue.
Sequence: 9′47″
   Dies irae: satb choirs I/II (fugal and imitative style) (vv. 1–8, lines 1–2). *Rex tremendae*: SATB soli I/II (v. 8, line 3–v. 16). *Oro supplex*: satb choirs I/II/SATB soli I/II. *concertante* style. (vv. 17–19).
Offertory: 4′39″
   Domine Jesu Christe: SATB soli I/II/ satb choirs I/II. *concertante* style; *Libera me*: satb choirs I/II. Fugal; *Sed signifer*: SATB soli I/II; *Quam olim Abrahae*: satb choirs I/II; *Hostias*: SATB soli I/II; *Domine Jesu Christe*: (first line only), SATB soli I/II/satb choirs I/II; *Quam olim Abrahae*: satb choirs I/II.
Sanctus-Benedictus: 5′14″
   Sanctus: satb choirs I/II/SATB soli I/II; *Pleni sunt coeli*: satb choirs I/II. Fugue; *Sanctus*: satb choirs I/II/SATB soli I/II; *Benedictus*: ST solo duet; *Sanctus*: satb choir.
Agnus Dei: 3′03″
   Agnus Dei I/II: unison choir/SATB soli; *Agnus Dei* III: choirs I/II. Musical material from Introit.

DISCOGRAPHY

NM Classics, 92039, Netherlands Chamber Choir, dir. Uwe Gronostay.

GAETANO DONIZETTI
November 29, 1797–May 8, 1848

Donizetti received his earliest musical training with the choirmaster of Bergamo Cathedral, Johannes Mayr. By 1817, he worked with an opera company in Bergamo. During this period, he wrote quite a number of compositions, including sacred pieces, but it was not until 1822 when he went to Naples to work for the Teatro Nuove that he began to compose his first major operas. By 1830, his opera *Anna Bolena* brought him fame and recognition. Over the course of his career, he composed more than seventy operas. Today, he is remembered for *Lucia di Lammermoor* and *Don Pasquale*.

He wrote a considerable amount of church music, which included many smaller solo pieces, mass movements, Psalms, motets, a magnificent setting of the *Miserere*, and four requiems. A requiem (1837) written in memory of the composer, Niccolo Zingarelli and another setting (1837), for his friend, Abate Fazzini, are lost. A third requiem, composed for the blessing of Alfonso della Valle di Casanova's tomb, is scored for three voices and orchestra.

Donizetti's *Messa di Requiem*, in memory of Vincenzo Bellini, was composed in Paris (1835). This incomplete setting lacks a *Sanctus*, *Benedictus*, and *Agnus Dei*. He scored the *Messa* for SATB soli, SATB choir, and orchestra. The first-known performance took place in Bergamo (1870). This work is a combination of French grand opera and Neapolitan opera and is a showcase for the tenor and bass soloists. The soprano is given little solo work and the alto virtually confined to the quartet ensembles. The duet *Judex ergo* for tenor and bass and the tenor solo *Ingemisco* are masterfully composed and are among the best pieces of the *Messa*.

The choral texture is a mixture of chordal writing and imitative polyphonic style. The two fugues, *Lacrymosa* and *Amen* (double fugue) and fugal writing on *Kyrie* II and *Rex tremendae* are romantic remnants of the baroque *stile antico*. Traces of the earlier *concertante* style are found in the Introit, *Confutatis* (Sequence), and Responsory. In these passages Donizetti employs the SATB soli as a second choir. The harmonic vocabulary of this work is characteristic of the early romantic period, includes a modest amount of chromaticism, and frequent usage of that hallmark of the era, the *Neapolitan* sixth.

Basic Data

EDITION

Gaetano Donizetti
Messa di Requiem for Soprano, Contralto, Tenor, 2 Bass Soloists
Four-part mixed Chorus and Orchestra.
Latin & English texts
Piano-Vocal score, Edited by Vilmos Lesko
Casa Ricordi, Milano. #131956. 1997

DURATION

Sixteen movements, 1539 mm., perf., 64′

VOICING AND ORCHESTRATION

Choir: SATB range: S-A6; B-G3
Soloists: SATBI/BII
Orchestra: vn. I/II, vla. vc., db., 2 fl., 2 ob., 2 cl., 2 bsn., 4 Fh., 2 tpt., 3 tbn., timp.,
   org.

OUTLINE

Orchestral introduction: 41 mm.
Introit: 143 mm.
   Requiem aeternam [dm] *maestoso*. satb choir; *Te decet* [FM] *andante*. SATB soli/satb
   choir; *Requiem aeternam* [FM-dm] *maestoso*. SATB soli. *Kyrie* [dm] *maestoso*.
   satb choir. (prelude/concluding fughetta).
Graduale: 97 mm., 2 movements.
   Requiem aeternam: 35 mm. [dm] *maestoso*. satb choir. (Same musical material as
   Introit). *In memoria aeterna*: 62 mm. [FM] *andante*. satb choir.
Sequence: 910 mm., 9 movements.
   Dies irae: 126 mm. [cm] *allegro*. B solo/satb choir. *Tuba mirum*: 77 mm. [A flat M]
   andante. TBB soli trio. *Judex ergo*: 116 mm. [fm] *larghetto*. T solo/TB duet. *Rex
   tremendae*: 92 mm. [CM] *maestoso*. SB soli/satb choir. *Ingemisco*: 110 mm., [am]
   larghetto. T solo. Binary form. *Praeces meae*: 57 mm. [E flat M] *larghetto*. ATB
   soli trio. *Confutatis*: 112 mm. [cm] *allegro*. SATB soli/satb choir. *Oro supplex*:
   66 mm. [FM] *larghetto*. B solo. Binary form. *Lacrymosa*: 154 mm. [cm] *maestoso*.
   satb choir. Double fugue on *Amen*.
Offertory: 97 mm.
   Domine Jesu Christe [EM] *larghetto*. B solo/ttb choir.
Communion: 37 mm.
   Lux aeterna [AM] *allegro*. satb choir.
Responsory: 182 mm.
   Libera me [em] *larghetto mosso*. satb choir; *Tremens factus* [GM] B solo; *Quando
   coeli* [em] satb choir/SATB soli; *Dies irae* and *Dum veneris* [CM] *larghetto*.
   SATB soli; *Requiem aeter nam* [CM] *larghetto*. satb choir (repeat of earlier mate-
   rial); *Libera me* [em] *larghetto mosso*. satb choir (repeat of opening *Libera*); *Kyrie*
   [EM] *larghetto*, SATB soli/satb choir.

DISCOGRAPHY

1. Orfeo, C 172 881 A, Bamberg Choir and Orchestra, cond. Miguel Angel Gomez-Martinez.
2. Koch Discover International, DICD 920519, Virtuosi di Praga, Prague Chamber Choir, dir. Alexander Rahbari.

FELIX DRAESEKE
October 7, 1835–February 26, 1913

During the early years of his career, Draeseke was greatly influenced by the "modernist" tendencies of Wagner's music dramas and Liszt's program music. Eventually, he moved to Switzerland and there began to develop an interest in older classical forms. In 1884, he was appointed to a professorship at the Dresden Conservatory.

He composed a half-dozen operas, five symphonies, symphonic overtures, string quartets, and other chamber music. His most grandiose undertaking was *Christus* (1895–1899), a cycle of three oratorios and orchestral prelude. Other choral works include the *Requiem in E Minor* for five-part, unaccompanied voices, a *Grand Mass* in A minor, three Psalms settings for choir and orchestra, and the *Requiem in B Minor*.

The *Requiem in B Minor* was composed over a period of years. The *Lacrymosa*, written as an independent work in 1865, eventually became the reason for completing a full requiem setting. The remaining movements were composed during 1876–1880. The *Requiem* was first published in 1887. Scored for SATB soloists, SATB (*divisi*) choir, and orchestra, this work is one of the major requiem settings of the late romantic era.

In 1883, the General Union of German Musicians held a Wagner Memorial Service (May 3, 1883) at St. Thomas Church in Leipzig. At this memorial service, held only three months after Wagner's death, was performed Draeseke's *B Minor Requiem*. The work seems to have enjoyed a brief popularity afterward, but has since fallen into complete neglect.

Its harmonic style is late romantic and influenced by the chromatic harmonies of *Tristan*, yet the composer's interest in older forms is evident in his use of no less than four fugues (*Kyrie, Quam olim Abrahae, Osanna,* and *Cum sanctis*), several canons (*Recordare,* ST duet, and *Dona eis,* ST vocal lines), a chaconne (Introit), and polyphonic writing. The SATB soli are generally used as a second choir to the SATB (*divisi*) choir, following the older *concertante* practice. The prevailing choral texture is a balance between expressive chordal style and imitative polyphony.

Romantic traits are expressed in the fussy dynamics, shifting tempi, and frequent modulation, and chromaticism. The condensation of the nineteen verses of the Sequence into one continuous movement, as well as the reduction of the Introit-*Kyrie* and the *Agnus Dei*-Communion into single movements, is a romantic trait, but had its origins in earlier classical style.

The orchestra plays an independent role throughout the work, and especially notable are the coloristic and rhythmic accompaniments of the Introit, *Lacrymosa*, Offertory, and *Sanctus*.

Basic Data

EDITION

Felix Draeseke
Requiem h-moll für vier Solostimmen, Chor und Orchester, Op. 22
Veröffentlichungen der Internationalen Draeseke-Gesellschaft
Band II
Herausgegeben von Udo-R. Follert
Coburg. 1988. [photocopy of the original Kistner Edition]

DURATION

Five movements, 1138 mm.

VOICING AND ORCHESTRATION

Choir: SATB (*divisi*) range: S-A6 B-F3
Soloists: SATB
Orchestra: vn. I/II, vla., vc., db., ob., fl., cl., bsn., Fh., tpt., tbn., timp.

OUTLINE

Introit-*Kyrie*: 173 mm.
> *Requiem aeternam* [bm] *andante grave.* SATB soli; *Et lux*, satb choir; *Te decet* [GM] SATB soli; *Requiem aeternam* [bm-F♯M], satb choir; *Kyrie* [DM-bm] satb choir. Double fugue.

Sequence: 503 mm. 1 movement, several sections.
> *Dies irae* [dm] *presto agitato.* satb choir. (vv. 1–2); *Tuba mirum* [B flat M] *piu largo ritenuto.* satb choir/SATB soli. (vv. 3–8); *Recordare* [dm] *andantino con moto.* satb choir/SATB soli. (vv. 9–17) Rondo form; *Lacrymosa* [dm] *larghetto.* satb choir/SATB soli. Canon. (vv. 18–19).

Offertory: 287 mm.
> *Domine Jesu Christe* [DM] *allegro moderato.* satb choir; *Sed signifer, un poco animato.* satb choir; *Quam olim Abrahae*, satb choir. Fugue; *Hostias* [CM] *andantino.* satb choir/SATB soli; *Quam olim Abrahae* [bm-BM] satb choir.

Sanctus: 105 + 82 mm.
> *Sanctus*, 105 mm. [EM] *allegro.* satb choir; *Osanna*, satb choir. Fugue.

Benedictus: 82 mm. [GM] *andantino.* SATB soli/satb choir. *Osanna* is repeated.

Agnus Dei-Communion: 148 mm.
> *Agnus Dei* [bm] *andantino grave.* satb choir/SATB soli; *Et lux*, satb choir; *Cum sanctis tuis* [bm] *molto tranquillo.* satb choir. Fugue.

DISCOGRAPHY

(Schwann) Polyphonia, POL 63007 [LP], Leichlinger Kantorei, Collegium Köln, cond. Udo R. Follert.

The restless *Requiem in E Minor* for unaccompanied SATBB choir was composed in 1909, several years before the composer's death. It remained unpublished for eighty-eight years and received its first performance only in 1930 on Reformation Day (October 30). This intimate, yet moody and expressive, work is saturated with polyphonic writing, reminiscent of Renaissance imitative style. Draeseke composed the *Osanna* and *Quam olim Abrahae* texts as fugues. Its constant five-part texture is occasionally relieved by a reduction in the number of voice parts.

The late romantic harmonic language of the work is suffused with lyric melodic writing. This excellent work deserves much wider recognition.

Basic Data

EDITION

Felix Draeseke
Requiem für fünf Gesangsstimmen (SATBB) a capella
WoO 35 (1909)
ed. Udo-R. Follert
Strube Verlag GmbH Edition 1128, München-Berlin
1997

DURATION

Six movements, 997 mm.

VOICING

Choir: SATBB range: S-B flat 6; B-E3

OUTLINE

Introit-Kyrie: 141 mm. [ABA with Kyrie].
  Requiem aeternam, [langsam und getragen]; Te decet hymnus; Requiem aeternam; Kyrie]
Sequence: 373 mm. [seven sections].
  [Dies irae-Tuba mirum-Rex tremendae-Recordare-Confutatis-Oro supplex-Lacrimosa]
Offertory: 207 mm. [four sections].
  [Domine Jesu Christe-Quam olim Abrahae (fugue)*-Hostias-Quam olim Abrahae.* (fugue)].
Sanctus: 101 mm. [two sections].
  [Sanctus-Osanna (fugue)].
Benedictus: 58 mm. [*Osanna* omitted].
Agnus Dei: 117 mm. [two sections].
  [Agnus Dei-Et lux perpetua].

DISCOGRAPHY
None found.

ANTONIN DVOŘAK
September 8, 1841–May 1, 1904

Antonin Dvořak received instruction in viola, piano, organ, and figured bass from his first teacher, Anton Liehmann. He later attended the Prague Organ School, first as a student, then as a professor in 1890, when the Conservatory merged with the Organ School. He finally became its director in 1901. Dvořak wrote more than 115 works of music, including nine symphonies, ten operas, seven solo works with orchestra, five symphonic poems, orchestral overtures and dances, chamber music, vocal songs and duets, piano music, and choral music.

Among the sacred pieces are a *Stabat Mater*, Op. 58 (1876–77); the oratorio, *St. Ludmilla*, Op. 71 (1885–86); *Psalm 149*, Op. 79 (1879 & 1887); *Mass in D Major*, Op. 86 (1887 & 1892); a *Te Deum*, Op. 103 (1892); and the *Requiem*, Op. 89 (1890).

The *Requiem*, Op. 89 is one of his ambitious sacred choral pieces and is scored for SATB soli, SATB choir, and orchestra. It is not conceived as a liturgical work; rather, as a grand oratorio. It was composed for the Birmingham Music Festival of 1890. Originally, the committee that commissioned Dvořak was looking for a work based upon the text "The Dream of Gerontius," but he never warmed to the subject. He chose in its place, the requiem text. It took eight months to complete this impressive work. He conducted its premiere on October 9, 1891, in Birmingham.

Dvořak was strongly influenced by the structures of the Viennese classical style. It is seen in his choice of musical forms; sonata, concerto, symphony, mass, and quartet. At the same time, the chromatic harmonic style of Wagner's *Tristan* exerted a powerful influence. Consequently, there exists a great deal of harmonic fuzziness and chromaticism in Opus 89, including the frequent use of natural, yet unexpected enharmonic modulation.

The solo quartet and choir are employed in a romantic "version" of the baroque *concertante* style. The basic SATB choir is frequently altered to SSAATTBB, SATTBB, TTBB, or SSAA *divisi* arrangements. A large chorus is necessary to meet the taxing musical demands of singing for a performance time of one hour and a half. Much of the choral texture is chordal with occasional imitative style, including the fugue on *Quam olim Abrahae* and the canon, *Fac eas* (*Hostias*).

The *Requiem* also possesses a four-note chromatic theme, similar to the Wagnerian *Leitmotiv*. This four-note theme appears in nearly every movement of the work. The timing and pacing of the *Requiem* is also similar to that of the music dramas of Wagner. In each movement, much time is allowed for the unraveling of the composer's musical ideas as well as the meaning of the text. It is a wonderful work, complete with powerful drama as well as warm lyricism.

Basic Data

EDITIONS

1. Antonin Dvořak	2. Antonin Dvořak
Requiem Mass, Opus 89 for Soli, Chorus	Requiem, Op. 89
and Orchestra. [Choral Score]	Partitura [full score]
Kalmus K 06163	Artia, Prague
Belwin Mills. 15800 N.W. 48th Ave.,	1961
Miami, FL 33014	

DURATION

Thirteen movements, TWO PARTS, 1937 mm., perf., 1' 30"

VOICING AND ORCHESTRATION

Choir: SATB [all parts *divisi*] range: S-B flat 6; B-E3
Soloists: SATB
Orchestra: vn I/II, vla., vc., db., pic., 2 fl., 2 ob., Eh., 2 cl., bcl., 2 bsn., cbn., 4 Fh., 3 tr., 4 tbn., tuba, timp.

OUTLINE

PART ONE

Introit-*Kyrie*: 245 mm., 2 movements.
   Requiem aeternam-Kyrie: 150 mm. [b flat m] *poco lento*. SATB soli/satb choir.
      Requiem aeternam: 95 mm. [b flat m-GM] *andante*. S solo/ssaa choir; *In Memoria*, ttbb choir.
Sequence: 807 mm., 6 movements.
   Dies irae: 90 mm. [b flat m] *allegro impetuoso (alla marcia)*. satb choir, tb *divisi*.
   Tuba mirum: 200 mm. [e flat m] *Tuba mirum*, A solo/ttbb choir; *Mors Stupebit*, B solo/satb choir; *Liber scriptus*, T solo/bass choir; *Dies irae*, satb choir (same music as *Dies irae* movement); *Tuba coget*, ttbb choir.

   Quid sum miser: 99 mm. [e flat m-EM] *lento*; *Quid sum miser*, S solo/unison choir sections; *Rex tremendae*, SATB soli/satb choir. *Recordare*: 151 mm. [DM] *andante*. SATB soli quartet. *Confutatis maledictus*: 118 mm. [gm-BM] *moderato maestoso*. satb choir. *Lacrymosa*: 149 mm. [CM-b flat m] *L'istesso tempo*. SATB soli/satb choir.

PART TWO

Offertory: 497 mm., 2 movements.
   Domine Jesu Christe: 347 mm. [FM] *andante con moto*. SATB soli/satb choir; *Quam*

olim Abrahae, satb choir. Fugue. *Hostias*: 150 mm.[fm] *andante*. SATB soli/choir
   basses. Canon; *Quam olim Abrahae* is repeated.
Sanctus: 137 mm.
   Sanctus, 91 mm. [B flat M] *andante maestoso*. SATB soli/satb; *Benedictus*, 46 mm.
   [BM] *tempo primo*. SAT soli/satb choir.
Pie Jesu: 106 mm.
   Pie Jesu [gm-GM] *poco adagio*. SAT soli trio/ttbb choir.
Agnus Dei-Communion: 145 mm.
   Agnus Dei, [b flat m] *lento*. SATB soli/satb choir; *Lux aeterna*, satb choir/SATB
   soli.

DISCOGRAPHY

1. Deutsche Grammophon, 437 377-2, Chorus of the Czech Philharmonic and the
   Czech Philharmonic Orchestra, cond. Karel Ancerl.
2. Multiple listings in the Schwann Catalogue.

GABRIEL FAURÉ
May 12, 1845–November 4, 1924

The composer of perhaps the most beloved setting of the requiem, Gabriel
Fauré, studied at the Ecole Niedermeyer in Paris. During his professional
career, he held a number of organist positions in Paris, first at St. Sulpice
(1870) and later, St. Honore. He became choirmaster of the Church of La
Madeleine (1877) and in 1896, first organist. In 1896, he was appointed
professor of composition at the Paris Conservatoire, remaining there until
1920.

Fauré left an outstanding legacy of graceful, elegant music. Many
regard him as the master of French song, of which he wrote eighty original works. He left many compositions for piano as well as chamber music.
Among the sacred pieces are a number of shorter liturgical works, *Messe
Basse* (1881), *Cantique de Jean Racine* (1865), and the *Requiem*.

The *Requiem*, Op. 48, a small-scale work, was written in 1888 while
Fauré was at La Madeleine. The Offertory was added in 1889 and the *Libera me* in 1892. Op. 48 was scored for SATB choir (*divisi* t/b), soprano and
baritone soloists, and small orchestra. In 1893, Fauré revised the orchestration to get a bigger sound, adding bassoons, French horns, and trumpets. A violin part for the *In paradisum* was added at this time, too. In
1900, an even yet larger orchestration was prepared (probably by Roger
Ducasse) with Fauré's permission.

It was long believed that the composer wrote the work in memory of
his parents, but he, himself, said that it was written just for the pleasure
of doing it. Typical of most French requiem settings is the absence of the

Sequence, *Dies irae*. In fact, the only passage in which *Dies irae* text appears is in the *Libera me*.

The bulk of the choral writing is chordal style, with imitative polyphonic passages in the Offertory (*O Domine Jesu Christe*). The setting of *In Paradisum* is among the more ethereal passages in choral literature and the soprano solo, *Pie Jesu*, possesses one of the most engaging arrangements found in any requiem setting. Fauré's piece is a warm and tender work, designed to give consolation and hope in time of sorrow. Its melodies and tender, romantic harmonies are particularly beautiful and draw forth the full meaning of the text.

Basic Data

EDITIONS

1. Requiem
Gabriel Fauré
English Text edited by Mack Evans
Piano/Vocal reduction by Roger Ducasse
Vocal Score
H. T. Fitzsimmons Company, Inc.
   Chicago

2. Gabriel Fauré
Requiem, Op. 48
Partitions d'Orchestre de Poche
Hamelle et Cie, Editeurs. Paris

DURATION

Six movements, 576 mm. perf., c. 35′

VOICING AND ORCHESTRATION

Choir: SATB [TB *divisi*] range: S-F # 6; B-F flat 3
Soloists: SBar
Orchestra: vla. vc., db., vn. solo, harp, timp., org. [A later version adds: 2 f., 2 cl., 2 bsn., 4 Fh., 2 tpt., 3 tbn.]

OUTLINE

Introit-*Kyrie*: 91 mm.
   Requiem aeternam [dm] *molto largo.* sattbb choir; *Requiem aeternam*, tenor choral unison; *Te decet*, soprano choral unison/sattbb choir; *Kyrie*, satb choir.
Offertory: 94 mm., ABA form.
   O Domine Jesu Christe [DM] *adagio molto.* atb choir (canon); *Hostias* [DM] *andante moderato.* Bar. solo; *O Domine Jesu Christe* [bm-BM] *adagio molto.* satb choir. Canon.
Sanctus: 62 mm.
   Sanctus [E flat M] *andante moderato.* s & tb choir (canon); *Hosanna*, sattbb choir.
Pie Jesu: 38 mm.
   Pie Jesu [B flat M] *adagio.* S solo.
Agnus Dei-Communion: 94 mm.
   Agnus Dei [FM] *andante.* choral tenor unison/satb choir; *Lux aeterna* [A flat M]

sattbb choir; *Requiem aeternam* [dm] *molto largo.* (music from Introit is repeated).
Responsory: 136 mm., ABA form.
　　Libera me [dm] *molto moderato.* Bar. solo; *Tremens factus-Dies illa,* satb choir; *Libera me* [dm] sattbb choir/Bar. solo.
In Paradisum: 61 mm.
　　In Paradisum [DM] *andante moderato.* unison choral sopranos/attbb choir.

DISCOGRAPHY

1. Telarc, CD 80135, Atlanta Symphony Orchestra and Chorus, cond. Robert Shaw.
2. Multiple listings in the Schwann Catalogue.

CHARLES GOUNOD
June 17, 1818–October 18, 1893

Gounod received his musical education at the Paris Conservatory and won the Grand Prix de Rome for composition in 1839. After study in Rome, he returned to Paris, where he was appointed organist and choirmaster at the Eglise de Missions Etrangères. During this time, he prepared for the priesthood, but in the end, abandoned the idea. He became a composer of opera. The work by which he is best remembered, *Faust*, was written in 1859.

He wrote most of his church music during the latter years of his life. From 1870 to the year of his death, he wrote a dozen settings of the mass and numerous liturgical pieces. During his career, he composed a total of seventeen masses, three of which are requiems: *Messe brève pour les Morts* (1872–73); *Messe funèbre* (1883), and the *C Major Requiem* (1893). The *Requiem in C major*, his last work, was published posthumously in 1895. Gounod died while editing this piece at the piano. Dedicated to the memory of his grandson, Maurice Gounod, there exist four versions of the work; the first, for SATB choir, SATB soli, and piano; the second, for SATB soli and organ; the third, two equal voices and organ (harmonium); and the fourth, SATB soli, SATB choir, and orchestra.

The work is one of the simpler, practical-usage requiem settings of the romantic era; a piece closer to the ideals of the Caecilian Movement than his grand, Victorian oratorio, *Mors et Vita.* The four-part, choral texture is principally homophonic. Tenors and basses are frequently scored *divisi.* *Pie Jesu* is the only movement with a consistent imitative texture and the ST duets, *Recordare* and *Benedictus,* are written in canonic style. Solo vocalists are not used as a second *concertante* choir, as is the case with a number of requiem settings. Gounod's solo melodies are characterized by a sense of piety and tenderness, if not melancholia. Perhaps this is so because he was writing for his grandson.

Several unique features of this setting are the C pedalpoint of the Introit, accompanied by shifting, kaleidoscopic harmonies and the concluding instrumental postlude; a tranquil, last "farewell" to his grandson.

Basic Data

EDITION

Requiem
Ch. Gounod
Transcrit par Henri Busser
[Piano-Vocal Score] A. C. 9791
Choudens, Editeur. Paris 1895
[There exist four versions by the same publisher: Choir, Soloists & Piano;
Four Solo Voices & Organ; Two Equal Voices & Organ [harmonium]; or Grand Organ.
Arrangements available for all versions, either symphonic orchestra or string quartet, harp, & pipe organ.]

DURATION

Six movements, 598 mm., perf., c. 36'

VOICING AND ORCHESTRATION

Choir: SATB [TB, *divisi*] range: S-A6; B-G3
Soloists: SATB
Orchestra: vn. I/II, vla., vc., db., 2 fl., 2 ob., 2 cl., 2 bsn., 2 tpt., tbn., Fh., timp., harp, org.

OUTLINE

Introit-*Kyrie*: 89 mm.
> *Requiem aeternam* [CM] *molto moderato.* sa/tb choir; *Te decet* [A flat M] satb choir; *Requiem aeternam* & *Kyrie* [CM] satb choir.

Sequence: 274 mm., 4 "movements."
> *Dies irae*: 73 mm. [cm-E flat M] *allegretto moderato,* satb choir. (vv. 1–4). *Liber scriptus*: 36 mm. [A flat M] *adagio. Liber scriptus* & *Judex ergo*, satb choir; *Quid sum miser* [cm] TB duet. V7 ostinato. (vv. 5–7). *Rex tremendae*: 44 mm. [CM] *andante maestoso.* satb choir; *Recordare*, [CM] S solo/satb choir. *Quaerens me*: 118 mm. [am-CM] *andante. Quaerens me*, SATB soli; *Juste judex-Pie Jesu*, satb choir.

Sanctus: 31 mm.
> *Sanctus* [FM] *molto moderato e maestoso.* satb choir/org.

Benedictus: 60 mm.
> *Benedictus* [B flat M] *andante quasi adagio.* ST duet. Canon; *Benedictus*, SA choir; *Hosanna*, satb choir. [An alternate version of the *Benedictus*, ST duet is included in the organ-vocal score.]

Pie Jesu: 54 mm.

    Pie Jesu [am-AM] *andante.* SATB soli/satb choir.

Agnus Dei-Communion: 90 mm.

    Agnus Dei [FM] *andante con moto.* satb choir; *Lux aeterna,* satb choir; 22 mm. orchestral postlude.

DISCOGRAPHY

1. Forlane, 16759, Matrise des Hauts-de-Seine and Orchestre Bernard Thomas, cond. Françis Bardot.
2. Claves, CD 50-9326, Choeur de Chambre Romand, Quartet Sine Nomine, dir. André Charlet.

Messe brève pour les Morts was composed between 1872–1873 and scored for double SATB choirs, SATB soloists (the latter group scored as a third choir), and organ. It was designed as a practical, liturgical setting. Typical of the French rite, the *Dies irae* is omitted, while *Pie Jesu* is included.

    With the exception of the Introit, (in which the choral parts are fully written out), the remainder of the work is written as if the four-part writing was for one SATB choir. However, both choirs are expected to perform these remaining movements. In the remaining movements the *concertante* alternation of choir I and choir II (or soloists) is indicated by a + sign in the score. Except for the opening passages of the *Agnus Dei*, the prevailing choral texture is homophonic chordal style. The late-romantic harmonic vocabulary varies in intensity from movement to movement. The Introit is written in simple, diatonic style that is slightly chromatic, yet the Offertory employs highly chromatic musical language.

    The Latin text of the 1873 edition is provided with an English translation, indicating usage in British services. An optional piano/organ accompaniment is provided, though ideally, the work should be sung *a cappella.* Gounod was clearly influenced by the ideals of the conservative, liturgy-oriented Caecilian Movement while he wrote this setting.

Basic Data

EDITION

Messe Brève pour les Morts (Requiem)
Henry Lemoine, Editeur, Paris. 1873

DURATION

Five movements, 292 mm.

VOICING AND ORCHESTRATION

Choir I, SATB; choir II, SATB range: S-A6; B-F3
Soloists: SATB [used as a quartet]
Instruments: optional org. or piano

OUTLINE

Introit-*Kyrie*: 84 mm.

    Requiem aeternam [FM] *andante*; *Te decet* [Fm-B flat M]; *Kyrie* [B flat M-CM] choirs I/II.

Offertory: 81 mm.

    Domine Jesu Christe [fm-FM] *andante*; *Hostias*, sattbb choirs I/II.

Sanctus: 41 mm.

    Sanctus [CM] *moderato maestoso*. sattb choirs I/II (bass *divisi*). The *Benedictus* is omitted.

Pie Jesu: 46 mm.

    Pie Jesu [FM] *adagio*. SATTBB soli/ sattbb choirs.

Agnus Dei: 34 mm.

    Agnus Dei I/II [fm] [*andante*]; *Agnus Dei* III [FM] satb choirs I/II

DISCOGRAPHY

None found.

The *Messe Funèbre a quatre voix* is a straightforward liturgical work, composed in 1883. Its tonality is F major and is scored for four-part mixed choir [SI, SII TB] and organ. The Introit, Offertory, and Sequence are not included in this setting. Except for the polyphonic style *Hosanna in excelsis*, the remainder of the music is composed in an intimate, homophonic, chordal style.

The diatonic harmony is colored with some chromatic elements. Although this fine work is designed for practical usage and adheres to the ideals of the Caecilian Movement, it has probably not been performed recently. The role of the organ is very modest, designed to keep the choir in tune.

Basic Data

EDITION

Messe Funèbre à quatre voix, avec accompaniment d'orgue.
Le Beau, editeur. Paris 1883.

DURATION

Four movements, 147 mm.

ORCHESTRATION AND VOICING

Choir: S I/II TB range: S-G6; B-F3
Instrument: org.

OUTLINE

Kyrie: 34 mm.

    Kyrie [FM] *grave*. satb choir; *Christe* [E flat M-dm] satb choir; *Kyrie* [FM].

Sanctus: 37 mm.
  Sanctus [cm] *moderato*. satb choir; *Hosanna in excelsis*. satb choir. *Benedictus* not
     included.
Pie Jesu: 34 mm.
  Pie Jesu [GM] *largo*. satb choir.
Agnus Dei: 48 mm.
  Agnus Dei [am-FM] *adagio*. satb choir.

DISCOGRAPHY
None found.

The grand Victorian oratorio, *Mors et Vita*, one of the more unusual works
of the genre, was written in the early 1880s. Within this large work is contained a complete setting of the requiem text set in oratorio-opera style.
Gounod scored the work for SATB choir, SATB soli, and large symphony
orchestra.

  Mors et Vita is the second part of a planned sacred triology, *La Rédemption*. Dedicated to Pope Leo XIII, it was composed for the Birmingham
Festival of 1885. After a brief vogue in England, it soon fell into oblivion,
along with *La Rédemption*. Dvořak, who composed his *Requiem* for the
same festival organization in 1890, complained to the publisher, Novello,
with whom he was in negotiation, about the squandering of 100,000
francs on Gounod's *Mors et Vita*.

  The work, despite its musical shortcomings, (thematic similarity among
the various movements, sameness of tempo, lack of explosive choral or
vocal movements, and bland writing), has some historical significance in
the study of requiem settings. It appears to be the only complete setting
of the requiem mass within the larger dimensions of an oratorio. *Mors et
Vita* is divided into three principal sections: Death, Judgment, and Life.
This description will be concerned with only the first, Death, which Gounod further divided into two sub-sections: *Prologus* and *Requiem*.

  Gounod employed several Wagnerian-style *Leitmotivs*, based on the tritone, throughout the work. The first of these themes is a descending four-
note motive, designed to depict the terror inspired by Divine Justice. A
second theme, the melodic leap of the tritone (both ascending and
descending) portrays Divine Justice and Human Suffering. The interval of
the augmented-fifth is employed to depict the Awakening of the Dead.
Last, a motive built on an ascending, step-wise line and followed by a
descending major-sixth leap represents the Happiness of the Blessed.

  The dominant choral texture is homophonic chordal writing, with the
exception of the fugue, *Quam olim Abrahae*, and a short fugato passage at
the beginning of the *Dies irae*. The pastoral aria for tenor, *Inter oves*, and
the motet, *Felix culpa*, scored for soprano solo and choir are two of the best
pieces in the work. Both can be excerpted and performed separately.

Basic Data

EDITION

Mors et Vita, A Sacred Trilogy
The Vocal Score, with pianoforte accompaniment, arranged from the orchestral
   score by O. B. Brown of Boston, Mass. U.S.A.
Novello and Company, Ltd., London. 1885

DURATION

Part I, fifteen movements, 1557 mm., perf., c. 95'
Part II, seven movements & Part III, eight movements. perf., c. 156'

VOICING AND ORCHESTRATION

Choir: two SATB choirs. range: S-B flat 6; B-E flat 3
Soloists: SATB
Orchestra: vn. I/II, vla., vc., db., 2 ob., Eh., 2 fl., 2 cl., bcl., 2 bsn., cbn., tpt., Fh.,
   tbn, tuba , timp., tam-tam, bass drum. 4 harps. org.

OUTLINE

PART I
Prologus: 87 mm.
   Horrendum est incidere [cm-CM] *andante maestoso*. satb choir; *Ego sum Resurrectio
   et Vita*. Bar solo/satb choir.

> It is a fearful thing to fall into the hands of the ever-living God.
> I am the Resurrection and the Life. Whosoever believes
> in Me, although he die, yet shall he live, and I will
> raise him up on the last day.

Introit-*Kyrie*: 158 mm.
   Requiem aeternam [cm] *adagio-andante*. satb choir; *Te decet* [A flat M] SATB soli;
   Requiem aeternam [cm] SATB soli; *Kyrie* [CM] satb choir.
Motet, *A custodia matutina*: 65 mm.
A custodia matutina [GM] *moderato maestoso*. satb choirs I/II, unaccompanied.

> A custodia matutina usque ad noctem, speret Israel in Domino;
> quia apud Dominum misericordia; et copiosa apud Eum redemptio.
> Et ipse redimet Israel ex omnibus iniquitatibus ejus.
> From the morning watch till the evening, trust thou, Israel, upon
> the Lord; for with Him is mercy found, and loving kindness, and
> with the Lord is also redemption, and He Himself will save
> Israel from all his sins and his iniquities freely.

Sequence: 150 mm. 7 movements.
   Dies irae: 150 mm. [cm-DM] *andante maestoso*. *Dies irae*, satb choir. Fugato;
   Quantus tremor [cm-B flat]; *Mors stupebit-Judex ergo* [CM-DM]. (vv. 1–6)

Quid sum miser: 87 mm. [DM-E flat M] *Quid sum miser-Rex tremendae molto moderato.* SATB soli/satb choir. *Leitmotiv; Recordare,* SATB soli/satb choir. (vv. 7–9)

Motet, *Felix culpa*: 85 mm.,
   Felix culpa [A flat M] *andantino.* S solo/satb choir.

> Felix culpa, quae talem meruit habere Redemptorem.
> Happy are we, with such a Saviour fulfilling our redemption.

Sequence: *Quaerens me*: 99 mm. [gm-cm] *andante non troppo.* SA soli; *Juste Judex,* satb choir. (vv. 10–11). An augmented-fifth *Leitmotiv* employed in the orchestral accompaniment. *Ingemisco*: 136 mm. [A flat M-FM] *molto moderato.* SATB soli/satb choir. Canonic writing. (vv. 12–14).
Inter oves: 43 mm. [B flat M] *molto moderato.* T solo. (v. 15).
Confutatis: 122 mm. [CM-GM] *andante.* satb choir; *Oro supplex,* T solo/SATB soli. (vv. 16–17).
Lacrymosa: 73 mm. [cm] *andante.* satb choir/SATB quartet. (vv. 18–19).
Offertory: 166 mm.
   Domine Jesu Christe [dm] *andante.* satb choir I/II; *Sed signifer* [DM] *molto Moderato.* S solo; *Quam olim Abrahae* [DM] satb choir, Fugue; *Hostias* [f#m] satb choir; *Quam olim Abrahae* [DM] *allegro.* satb choir.
Sanctus: 57 mm.
   Sanctus [GM] *molto moderato.* T solo/satb choir. *Benedictus* not included.
Elevation: 84 mm.
   Pie Jesu [GM-EM] *andante.* SATB soli quartet. A tritone *Leitmotiv* employed in the orchestral accompaniment. Descending, "sighing" figure in violins.
Agnus Dei-Communion: 100 mm.
   Agnus Dei [A flat M] *andante non troppo.* S solo/satb choir; *Lux aeterna* [D flat M] *andante.* ssattbb choir.
Orchestral epilogue: 45 mm. [CM].

PART II, *Judicium* [Last Judgement]. The Prelude, *Somnus Mortuorum,* and movement three, *Resurrection Mortuorum,* include frequent references to the Gregorian *Dies irae* melody.

PART III, *Vita,* is based upon the Vision of St. John.

DISCOGRAPHY

EMI Classics, CDS 7 54459 2, Orféon Donostiarra and L'Orchestre du Capitole de Toulouse, dir. Michel Plasson.

THÉODORE GOUVY
July 3/5, 1819–April 21, 1898

Although he began his professional training as a lawyer, he later began musical studies by his twentieth year. Initially, he studied piano and theory but later, composition in Germany and Italy. Although a number of his compositions were performed in Paris, they were better received in Germany. This might be accounted for by the fact that he was born and raised in Alsace-Lorraine, a German province during the composer's lifetime. Berlioz had great respect and praise for Gouvy as a composer; nevertheless, after the latter's death, his music fell into complete neglect; claimed by neither France nor Germany.

Gouvy wrote nearly 100 works of all genres, yet few, if any, remain in the active repertory of the twentieth-century musician. Among the compositions are an opera, many songs, seven symphonies, chamber music, and a large quantity of piano pieces for four-hands. There are some choral pieces including four Greek tragic oratorios, a *Stabat Mater*, a *Missa Brève*, and the *Requiem*, Op. 70 (1874).

The *Requiem* is scored for SATB solo, SATB choir, and orchestra. His writing is masterful and dramatic. Most of the choral writing is a mixture of four-part imitative polyphony and expressive chordal style. The use of fugue (*Hosanna*) and imitative polyphony (*Qui Mariam, Inter oves, Lacrymosa, Libera nos, Hostias,* and *Quam olim Abrahae*), as well as the *concertante* structuring of the SATB choir and SATB quartet are traditional techniques that contrast with his late romantic chromatic harmony and rich orchestral coloring. His tightly knit arrangements of soli and choir are a hallmark of his style.

Although most of the vocal solos are short in duration, the tenor solo, *Benedictus*, occupies an entire movement. The orchestra also provides an important rhythmic impetus to the choral and vocal forces. Gouvy was a composer whose musical ideas contained substantial content and value. The *Recordare*, for solo voices and choir, is particularly elegant, yet poignant.

Basic Data

EDITION

Requiem für vier Solostimmen, gemischten Chor und Orchester, Op. 70
[Orgel, ad libitum]
(Klavierauszug)
Breitkopf und Härtel, Leipzig (#15542) 1874

DURATION

Seven movements, 1155 mm., perf., c. 59'

VOICING AND ORCHESTRATION

Choir: SATB range: S-B flat 6; B-E flat 3
Soloists: SATB

Orchestra: vn. I/II, vla., vc., db., 2 fl., 2 ob., Eh., 2 cl., 2 bsn., 4 Fh., 2 tpt., 3 tbn., tuba, timp. harp.

OUTLINE

Introit-Kyrie: 93 mm.
   Requiem aeternam [e flat m] *grave.* satb choir (*Et lux*, ssaa choir); *Te decet* [E flat M] *poco piu mosso.* satb choir; *Requiem aeternam*, satb choir, (*Dona eis*, ttbb choir); *Kyrie*, SATB soli. ABA form.
Sequence: 572 mm., 4 movements.
   Dies irae: 289 mm. [f#m] *allegro molto.* satb choir (vv. 1–2); *Tuba Mirum* [DM] satb choir. canon; *Mors stupebit* [fm] *allegro.* satb choir (vv. 4–5). *Judex ergo*: 63 mm. [b flat m] *larghetto.* B solo; *Quid sum miser*, T solo/SA duet; *Rex tremendae* [D flat M-G flat M] T solo/satb choir. *Recordare*: 84 mm. [D flat M] *lento non troppo.* A solo; *Quaerens me*, T solo; *Juste judex*, S solo; *Ingemisco*, B solo; *Tu Mariam* SATB soli; *Preces meae*, SATB soli quartet; *Inter oves*, satb choir. *Confutatis*: 135 mm. [dm] *andante con moto.* satb choir/SATB soli; *Oro supplex* [B flat M] satb choir; *Oro supplex*, satb choir/SATB soli; *Lacrymosa*, satb choir/SATB soli; *Huic ergo*, ttbb choir/satb choir; *Parce eis-Pie Jesu*, STB soli/satb choir.
Offertory: 188 mm.
   Domine Jesu Christe [E flat M] *larghetto maestoso.* satb choir; *Hostias*, SATB soli/satb choir (fugal); *Domine Jesu*, satb choir. ABA form.
Sanctus: 171 mm.
   Sanctus: 45 mm. [GM] *andante con moto.* S solo/satb choir; *Hosanna*: 87 mm. [DM] *allegro.* satb choir (fugue); *Benedictus*: 39 mm. [GM] *andante.* T solo.
Agnus Dei: 131 mm.
   Agnus Dei I [e flat m] *adagio.* A solo; *Agnus Dei* II, SATB soli quartet; *Dona eis requiem, grave.* satb choir/SATB soli.

DISCOGRAPHY

K 617, Schola Cantorum & Philharmonie de Lorraine, cond. Jacques Houtmann.

SIR GEORGE HENSCHEL
February 18, 1850–October 10, 1934

The multi-talented Henschel was a baritone, pianist, conductor, and composer of German birth. He studied at the Leipzig Conservatory from 1867 to 1870. His teachers were Ignace Moscheles (piano), Benjamin Papperitz (organ), Hermann Goetze (singing), and Karl Reinecke and Ernest Richter (theory composition). He eventually settled in England, but for a short time lived in the United States. He was one of the first conductors of the Boston Symphony Orchestra (1881–1884) and he later established the London Symphony Orchestra, which he conducted for eleven years.

   Henschel left a significant legacy of musical composition. There are numerous vocal songs, a handful of orchestral pieces, three operas, and a number of sacred choral works. These latter pieces include a *Stabat Mater*, Op. 53 (soli, choir, and orchestra); *Te Deum*, Op. 52 (soli, choir, orchestra, and organ); an English mass for eight voices, *Psalm CXXX*, Op. 31 (soli, choir, and orchestra); and the *Missa Pro Defunctis*, Op. 59.

The *Requiem*, Op. 59 was composed in 1901, in memory of his wife who had died in the same year. It is scored for SATB soli, SATB (*divisi*) choir, and orchestra. Although much of the choral fabric is homophonic, there are exceptional passages of polyphonic style, including the fugues on *Hostias, Libera animas*, and *Quam olim Abrahae* and the canonic writing of *Dies irae, Quid sum miser, Qui Mariam*, and *Lacrymosa*. Henschel employed the older *concertante* choral style for much of the work. The SATB soli often function as a second choir and there is the noteworthy passage for twelve voices in the Offertory verse, *Hostias*. The SATB choir is generally scored *divisi* for large, massive sections.

The most important solo vocal pieces are the luminous *Lux aeterna* (tenor) and the canonic duet, *Qui Mariam* (soprano-alto). One of the notable dramatic-structural features is the statement and later repetition of the *Dies irae* text. This device is found in other late-romantic requiem settings, including Dvořak, Stanford, and Verdi.

Henschel's advanced chromatic harmony style stems from the widespread influence of Richard Wagner, as well as the composer's training at Leipzig Conservatory.

Basic Data

EDITION

Requiem (Missa pro Defunctis) für Chor, Solostimmen und Orchester, Op. 59
Georg Henschel
Klavier-Auszug mit Text
Breitkopf und Härtel, Leipzig, Brussel, London, New York. 1928

DURATION

Five movements, 1102 mm.

VOICING AND ORCHESTRATION

Choir: SATB (*divisi*) range: S-B flat 6; B-F3 [D3]
Soloists: SATB
Orchestra: vn. I/II, vla., vc., db., fl., ob., cl., bsn., Fh., tpt., tbn., tuba, timp.

OUTLINE

Introit-*Kyrie*: 109 mm.
   Requiem aeternam [B flat M] *adagio molto*. T solo/saa choir; *Te decet*, ssaattbb choir; *Requiem aeternam*, satb choir; *Kyrie-Requiem*, SATB soli/saatbb choir.

Sequence: 494 mm. 2 "movements."

> *Dies irae* [B flat M-BM] *allegro non troppo, ma con fuoco*. saatbb choir; *Quantus tremor*, saattbb choir; *Tuba mirumm*, saatbb choir; *Dies irae*, saatbb choir; *Liber scriptus*, satb choir; *Judex ergo*, satb choir; *Quid sum miser*, AB soli/SATB soli (canon); *Rex tremendae*, saattbb choir/S solo/ SATB soli. *Recordare* [gm] *larghetto*. SATB soli/satb choir/T solo; *Ingemisco*, satb choir; *Qui Mariam* [B flat M] *andante sostenuto*. SA soli duet (canon); *Inter oves*, SAT soli trio; *Confutatis*, B solo; *Oro supplex*, satb choir; *Dies irae, allegro non troppo*. saatbb choir; *Lacrymosa* [B flat M] *largo*. B solo/T solo/SATB soli/satb choir (canonic writing); *Huic ergo* [GM] *un poco piu mosso ed affrettando*. SATB soli/ssaattbb choir.

Offertory: 271 mm.

> *Domine Jesu Christe* [DM] *maestoso*. saattbb choir; *Libera animas*, satb choir. Fugue; *Sed signifer* [DM] *adagio*. SATB soli; *Quam olim Abrahae* [DM-BM] *allegro moderato*. satb choir. Fugue; *Hostias* [BM] *andante affetuoso*. Twelve solo voices-alternating ssaa/ttbb; *Hostias*, ssaattbb choir; *Tu suscipe* [GM] *largo*. satb choir; *Fac eas* [GM] *allegro sostenuto*. SATB soli; *Fac eas-Quam olim Abrahae* [DM] *allegro moderato*. satb (*divisi*) choir. Fugue.

Sanctus: 135 mm., 2 "movements."

> Sanctus [FM] *largo*. SATB soli; *Pleni sunt coeli*, SATB soli/satb choir; *Hosanna, allegro molto*. ssaattbb choir. Benedictus [FM] *adagio*. SATB soli; *Hosanna*, satb choir/SATB soli; *Hosanna, allegro*. ssaattbb choir.

Agnus Dei-Communion: 93 mm.

> *Agnus Dei* I [G flat M] *adagio molto*. AB soli/satb choir; *Agnus Dei* II, AB soli/ satb choir; *Agnus Dei* III, SATB soli/satb choir; *Lux aeterna*, [B flat M] *andante molto sostenuto*. T solo; *Requiem aeternam-Lux aeterna*, satb choir/SATB soli.

DISCOGRAPHY

None found.

FRIEDRICH KIEL
October 7, 1821–September 13, 1883

Born in Germany, Kiel's musical talents manifested themselves in his early years. Among his earliest teachers were Gaspar Kummer (composition) and the concertmaster of the local prince, Karl of Sayn-Wittgenstein-Berlberg, taught Kiel the violin. At a later time, Kiel studied counterpoint, composition, and piano with Wilhelm Dehn. He was ultimately appointed professor at the Stern Conservatory and in 1869, at the newly established Staatliche Hochschule für Musik (Berlin), where he taught composition. His pupils included Hugo Kaun (1863–1932), Ignace Paderewski; Charles Villiers Stanford (1852–1924), and the daughter of Robert and Clara Schumann.

Among his compositions are piano sonatas, *Fünfzehn Kanonen im Kammerstyl*, Op.1, *Concert overture* for grand orchestra, Op. 6, *Piano Concerto*,

Op. 30; an oratorio, *Der Stern von Bethlehem*, Op 83, *Missa Solemnis*, Op. 40, and two requiems, Op. 20 and Op. 80. The *Requiem in F minor*, Op. 20 was first published in 1862 and scored for SATB soli, SATB choir, and orchestra.

The predominant choral texture employed is imitative polyphony. Such passages include the three fugues, *Quam olim Abrahae, Hostias, Osanna*, as well the canonic settings of *Recordare, Confutatis, Pleni sunt coeli*, and *Ingemisco*. An important exception to the prevailing four-part writing is found in the *Kyrie*, where the composer splits the choral forces into two SATB choirs. The diatonic harmonic language used is colored by occasional chromaticism.

Although the orchestra generally supports the choir, it often operates in an independent fashion. There are a number of short passages for instrumental soloists, but these sections are short and integrated into the overall tonal fabric. Orchestral poetic imagery is present in the "rising flames" motive of the *Confutatis*, a "weeping" string motive in the *Lacrymosa*, sixteenth-note tremolo figures at *Quantus tremor*, and the trombone passages of the *Tuba mirum*. There are no virtuoso vocal solos, rather, soloists are employed in a romantic "version" of the baroque *concertante* style.

Basic Data

EDITION

Friedrich Kiel
Requiem (f minor)
Partitur [full score]
C. F. Peters, Leipzig. 1862
[New York Public Library, microfilm #815930A]

DURATION

Twelve movements, 1046 mm. perf., c. 55'

VOICING AND ORCHESTRATION

Choir: SATB range: S-C flat 7; B-F3
Soloists: SATB
Orchestra: vn. I/II, vla., vc. I/II, db., 2 fl., 2 ob., 2 cl., 2 bsn., 2 waldhorns, 2 tpt., 3 tbn., timp.

OUTLINE

Introit: 51 mm. [fm-CM]
  Requiem aeternam, largo. satb choir; *Te decet*, SATB soli/choir; *Requiem aeternam*, satb choir.
Kyrie: 71 mm. [FM]
  Kyrie, Christe, Kyrie, andante. ssaattbb choir.

Sequence: 487 mm., 4 movements.

    Dies irae: 201 mm. *allegro*. satb choir. (vv. 1–8). *Recordare*: 134 mm. [B flat M]
andante. *Recordare*, SA soli; *Quaerens me*, TB soli; *Juste judex*, satb choir; *Ingemisco*, SATB soli; *Qui Mariam*, SATB soli; *Preces meae*, satb choir; *Inter oves*, SATB
soli/choir. (vv. 9–15). *Confutatis*: 89 mm. [cm-CM] *moderato*. S. solo/satb
choir & soli. (vv. 16–17). *Lacrymosa*: 63 mm. [fm-FM] *grave*. satb choir. (vv.
18–19).

Offertory: 178 mm., 3 movements.

    Domine Jesu Christe: 31 mm. [E flat-B flat M] *maestoso*. STB soli/satb choir. *Quam
olim Abrahae*: 89 mm. [E flat M] *allegro*. satb choir. Fugue. *Hostias*: 58 mm. [B
flat-E flat M] *allegretto*. satb choir. Double Fugue. *Quam olim Abrahae* is
repeated.

Sanctus: 98 mm. [CM]

    Sanctus, adagio. satb choir; *Osanna, allegro*. satb choir. Fugue.

Benedictus: 89 mm. [A flat M]

    Benedictus, andante. SATB soli/choir; *Osanna, allegro*. satb choir. Fugue.

Agnus Dei-Communion: 72 mm. [fm-FM]

    Agnus Dei I, II, III, *moderato*. satb choir; *Lux aeterna, allegro*. satb choir.

DISCOGRAPHY

None found. * [Opus 40, *Missa Solemnis* recorded as Capriccio 10 587.]

The *Requiem in A flat Major*, Op. 80 was first published in 1881 and was
scored for SATB soli, SATB choir, and orchestra. The prevailing choral
texture is a mixture of homophonic writing and imitative polyphonic
style. There are no less than five fugues, *Kyrie, Quam olim Abrahae, Hostias,
Osanna*, and *Dona eis* (*Agnus Dei*), and among the imitative polyphonic
passages are *Et lux* (Introit), *Dies irae, Recordare*, Lacrymosa, and *Sanctus*.

    The harmonic language is diatonic, with several excursions into an
extreme chromaticism that employs theoretical keys, such as A # major,
D # major, and D flat minor. The orchestra is used to support the choir,
yet it often functions independently. Occasional instrumental solos
include the basset horn (Introit) and trumpet (*Hostias*). Instrumental "pic-
torialism" is employed in the *Rex tremendae* and *Flammis acribus* by the
use of dramatic, thirty-second note figurations.

    Both Opus 20 and Opus 80 are superior compositions that have been
neglected far too long.

Basic Data

EDITION

Requiem [Partitur]
Bote & Bock, Berlin. 1881
[New York Public Library, microfilm # 12270]

DURATION

Thirteen movements, 1306 mm., perf., c. 60′

VOICING AND ORCHESTRATION

Choir: SATB range: S-C flat 7 ; B-F3
Soloists: SATB
Orchestra: vn. I/II, vla., vc., db., 2 fl., 2 ob., 2 cl., 2 bsn., cbsn., basset horn, 4 Fh.,
2 tpt., 3 tbn., timp., org.

OUTLINE

Introit: 82 mm. [A flat M]
  Requiem aeternam, molto sostenuto. satb choir; *Te decet*, SATB soli/choir; *Requiem aeternam*, satb choir. ABA form.
Kyrie: 56 mm. [fm-FM]
  Kyrie, con moto. satb choir. Double Fugue.
Graduale: 47 mm. [FM]
  Requiem aeternam, andante. SATB soli; *In memoria, un pochettino piu animato.* SATB soli. Fugal.
Sequence: 594 mm., 5 movements.
  Dies irae: 210 mm. [g flat m-em] *allegro.* satb choir. (vv. 1–6). *Quid sum miser*: 27 mm. [A flat M] *andante.* satb choir. (vv. 7–8). *Recordare*: 91 mm. [BM-A♯M] *andante. Recordare, Quaerens me, Juste Judex, Ingemisco*, SATB soli; *Qui Mariam*, A solo; *Preces meae & Inter oves*, SATB soli. (vv. 9–15). *Confutatis*: 218 mm. [e Flat m-D♯M] *allegro maestoso.* SATB soli/choir. (vv. 16–17). *Lacrymosa*: 48 mm. [g♯m-A flat M] *larghetto.* satb choir. (vv. 18–19).
Offertory: 171 mm., 2 movements.
  Domine Jesu Christe: 58 mm. [E flat M] *andante.* satb choir; *Sed signifer*, SATB soli/choir; *Quam olim Abrahae*, satb choir. Fugue. *Hostias*: 113 mm. [B flat M-E flat M] *andante.* SATB soli/ choir; *Quam olim Abrahae*, satb choir. Fugue.
Sanctus: 89 mm. [D flat M]
  Sanctus, sostenuto. satb choir; *Osanna, allegro.* satb choir. Fugue.
Benedictus: 99 mm. [A flat M-D flat M]
  Benedictus, larghetto. S solo/satb choir; *Osanna, allegro.* satb choir. Fugue.
Agnus Dei-Communion: 168 mm. [fm-A flat M]
  Agnus Dei I, II, III, *poco largo.* satb choir; *Lux aeterna*; satb choir; *Dona eis requiem*, satb choir. Fugue; *Lux aeterna*, satb choir.

DISCOGRAPHY

None found.

FRANZ LACHNER
April 2, 1803–January 20, 1890

Lachner spent most of his professional life in Munich, but held his first professional position at the Lutheran Church in Vienna. He was a pupil of the Abbé Stadler and knew both Schubert and Beethoven. By 1829, he was appointed the chief conductor of the Kartnertor Theater. In 1836, he returned to Munich, where he was appointed the conductor of the Munich court opera. He made his living as a teacher and conductor. His most famous pupil was Joseph Rheinberger. He composed a small amount of chamber music, six theatrical works, eight symphonies, seven orchestral suites, an oratorio, eight masses, and one requiem.

A revised edition of the *Requiem in F minor*, Opus 146 appeared in 1872. Scored for SATB soli, SATB (*divisi*) choir, and orchestra, it was apparently successful because it received a number of performances. It was reprinted in 1990. This work employs a number of older techniques, including fugue and canon. There are no less than three double choral fugues (*Kyrie* and *Quam olim Abrahae* [two versions]) and fugal passages (*Judex ergo*, *Confutatis, Benedictus, Cum sanctis*). *Concertante* style was employed only in the *Pleni sunt coeli, Benedictus*, and *Communion*. The Sequence passages *Dies irae* and *Quid sum miser*, employ an ostinato bass figure.

There are major solos for the tenor (*Quid sum miser* and *Agnus Dei*) and alto (*Recordare*). Lachner's harmonic language is strongly influenced by the chromatic style of Wagner, coupled with forms and structures used by Beethoven and Schubert. One of the unique rhythmic passages of the *Requiem* occurs in the *Kyrie* when the composer employs simultaneous contrasting duple and triple rhythms in the melodic lines of the fugue.

Basic Data

EDITION

Franz Lachner
Requiem, Opus 146 [Piano-Vocal Edition]
Ries & Erler, Berlin (#R. 11 400 E)
1990 [clefs: C (soprano, alto, tenor) & F]
[Requiem text in Latin & German]

DURATION

Eleven movements. 1387 mm.

VOICING AND ORCHESTRATION

Choir: SATB range: S-A6; B-F3
Soloists: SATB
Orchestra: vn. I/II, vla., vc., db., fl., ob., cl., bsn., Fh., tpt., tbn., timp., org.

OUTLINE

Introit-*Kyrie*: 251 mm.
   Requiem aeternam, 80 mm. [fm] *andante*. satb choir; *Kyrie*, 171 mm. [fm] *allegro non troppo*. satb choir. Double fugue.

Sequence: 453 mm., 4 movements. (complete text)

> *Dies irae*: 169 mm. *Dies irae-Quantus tremor* [fm] *allegro.* satb choir. *Tuba mirum* [D flat M-fm] satb choir; *Judex ergo* [fm] satb choir (fugato); *Quid sum miser* [fm] T solo; *Rex tremendae* [fm] satb choir. The movement is built upon an ostinato motive and its inversion. *Recordare*: 156 mm. [D flat M] *andante.* A solo; *Ingemisco,* [c#m]; *Preces meae,* [D flat M]. ABA form. *Confutatis*: 54 mm. [b flat m-CM] *allegro molto moderato e maestoso.* satb choir. Fughetta. *Lacrymosa*: 74 mm. [fm] *andante con moto.* satb choir.

Offertory: 378 mm., 3 movements.

> *Domine Jesu Christe*: 121 mm. [A flat M] *allegro moderato e maestoso.* satb choir; *Quam olim Abrahae,* satb choir. Double fugue. *Hostias*: 125 mm. [EM-D #M] *andante con moto.* SATB solo quartet. *Quam olim Abrahae*: 132 mm. [A flat M] *allegro non troppo.* satb choir. Double fugue.

Sanctus: 87 mm.

> *Sanctus* [FM] *andante.* satb choir (*divisi*-ssaattbb); *Pleni sunt coeli,* SA soli/satb choir. Canonic writing.

Benedictus: 77 mm.

> *Benedictus* [fm] *andante con moto.* SATB soli. Canon; *Hosanna,* satb choir.

Agnus Dei-Communion: 141 mm.

> *Agnus Dei* I [fm] *andante.* T solo; *Agnus Dei* II, A solo; *Agnus Dei* III, satb choir; *Lux aeterna* [fm] satb choir; *Lux aeterna* [FM] *andante.* SATTB soli/sattb choir.

DISCOGRAPHY

None found.

FRANZ LISZT
October 22, 1811–July 31, 1886

Liszt was one of the greatest pianists that ever occupied the concert stage. Inspired by the fabulous violin artistry of Paganini, he set out to conquer every aspect of piano performance. Because he lived a long life, his compositions cover a wide spectrum of musical style, from early romanticism to a nearly atonal language in the late piano pieces. He made his living from concerts, teaching, and commissions for his music. He wrote an absolutely enormous amount of music that included symphonic poems, original solo piano music, two concerti for piano and orchestra, and the *Totentanz* (a set of variations for piano and orchestra based on the Gregorian *Dies irae* melody). He made transcriptions of opera arias, German Lieder, violin pieces, and other instrumental works; anything that was popular with the concert-going public.

Liszt composed a significant block of choral repertory. These works include two oratorios, *Christus* (1862–67) and *The Legend of St. Elisabeth* (1857–62), *Mass* for male voices (1848), *Graner* Mass (1835), *Missa Choralis* (1886), *Hungarian Coronation Mass* (1867), *Die heilige Cecilia*, three Psalm

settings, a *Requiem*, and various other short works. This music is well written. When reading through his oratorios, *Christus* or *The Legend of St. Elisabeth,* one is struck by the unexpected use of fugue and imitative
polyphony. This aspect of his work is not so well known today, perhaps
because of the flamboyant, attractive style of his better-known program
music.

The requiem settings of Liszt and Cherubini for male-voices are the two
best-known pieces of this genre from the romantic era. Although the former possesses the accompaniment of small instrumental ensemble and
the latter, the support of a full symphonic orchestra, their overall style
and mood are quite different. Liszt's *Requiem* was composed during 1867–
68. *Libera me* was not completed until 1871.

The choral writing of the *Requiem* is mainly chordal. The only exception
is a brief, imitative setting of *Pleni sunt coeli.* The choral passages were
composed in four-part TTBB scoring, while Liszt employed the choir and
TTBB solo quartet in alternating passages in *concertante* fashion throughout the piece. In several sections, the TTBB choir and TTBB quartet are
used as a double choir (*Benedictus, Hosanna,* and *Lux aeterna*).

The overall tone of the work is serious and austere and the choral
sonority is somewhat reminiscent of the unaccompanied, polyphonic
music of the nineteenth-century Russian Orthodox Church. Liszt made
the general style of the music conform to the ideals of piety and spirituality espoused by the Caecilian Movement. Yet, harmonies more in tune
with Renaissance writing stand side-by-side with Wagnerian chromatic
harmony.

Much of the choral work is sung without accompaniment, yet the organ
provides practical support and, occasionally, contrast. It also assists the
choir to stay in tune with the chromatic harmonies. Liszt supplemented
the organ with a small ensemble of brass and timpani for the more dramatic sections in the text. These sections include the *Tuba mirum, Lacrymosa,* and *Hosanna in excelsis.* All key designations in the Outline are
general because the tonality is in constant change. In 1883, Liszt made an
abridged version of the work for organ solo, giving it the title, *Requiem für
die Orgel.*

Basic Data

EDITIONS

1. Franz Liszt
Requiem for Men's Voices & Organ
Miniature Score
Kalmus, K 09383

2. Franz Liszts Musikalische Werke
herausgegeben von der Franz Liszt
   Stiftung
Band III
Messen und Requiem
Breitkopf unf Härtel, Leipzig

3. Musicotheca Classica MC 3
Liszt Ferenc
Requiem
Male Choir, organ, 2 Trumpets, 2
    Trombones, Timpani
ed. Darvas, Gabor
Editio Musica Budapest Z 7887

DURATION

Six movements, 1222 mm., perf., c. 51'

VOICING AND ORCHESTRATION

Choir: bass I/II, tenor I/II [bass I occasional *divisi*]
Soloists: bass I/II, tenor I/II
Instruments: 2 tp., 2 tbn., timp., org.

OUTLINE

Introit-*Kyrie*: 184 mm.
    Requiem aeternam [A flat M] *adagio*. TTBB soli; *Te decet* [A flat M] ttbb choir/
    TTBB soli; *Requiem aeternam* [A flat M] ttbb choir; *Kyrie* [A flat M] TTBB soli/
    ttbb choir.
Sequence: 504 mm.
    Dies irae-Quantus tremor [cm] *alla breve*; *Tuba mirum* [E flat M] ttbb choir/brass/
    timpani. *Mors stupebit*, b II choir; *Liber scriptus*, ttbb choir/organ; *Judex ergo*,
    ttbb choir/brass. *Quid sum miser* [cm] *lento*. B I solo; *Rex tremendae*, ttbb choir/
    TTBB solo quartet; *Recordare*, [E flat M] ttbb solo quartet; *Quaerens me* [B flat
    M] B II solo/TTBB quartet. *Juste Judex* [cm] ttbb choir. *Ingemisco-Qui Mariam-
    Preces meae-Inter oves* [Multiple keys] TTBB solo quartet. *Confutatis* [cm] ttbb
    choir; *Oro supplex* B I solo/ttbb choir. *Lacrymosa* [CM] *piu lento*. *Lugubre*. uni-
    son ttbb choir. *Huic ergo* ttbb choir; *Pie Jesu*, ttbb choir.
Offertory: 204 mm.
    Domine Jesu Christe [am/AM] *andante con moto*. B I solo/ttbb choir/TTBB solo
    quartet; *Hostias* [chromatic CM] *misterioso, quieto, ma non troppo lento*. TTBB
    solo Quartet/unison ttbb choir.
Sanctus: 104 mm.
    Sanctus [FM-BM] *lento maestoso assai*. ttbb choir/brass/timpani. *Benedictus* [FM]
    un poco piu lento. B I solo/TTBB solo quartet/ttbb choir/brass/timpani.
Agnus Dei: 121 mm.
    Agnus Dei [dm] *lento*. B I solo/TTBB solo quartet; *Lux aeterna*, TTBB solo quar-
    tet/ttbb choir. Responsory: 105 mm. *Libera me* [CM] *lento*. ttbb choir/T I, B I
    soli; *Requiem aeternam, un poco piu lento*. ttbb choir.

DISCOGRAPHY

Hungaroton, HCD 11267, Hungarian Army Male Chorus, cond. János Ferencsik.

OTTO OLSSON
December 19, 1879–January 1, 1964

Olsson studied at the Royal Conservatory of Stockholm from 1894 to 1901. In 1908, he became the organist for the Gustavus Vasa Church. He also began a career of teaching at the Royal Conservatory in the same year and was appointed to a full professorship in 1919.

Olsson is best known as a composer of organ music. There exists some chamber music and a *Symphony on Gregorian Themes*. Among the sacred works are the *6 Gregoriansk melodier*, Op. 60 (1910) and *6 Latinska hymner*, Op. 40 (1919). The *Te Deum*, Op. 25 for SATB choir, orchestra, harp, and organ, and the *Credo Symphonicum*, Op 50 were composed in 1906 and 1925, respectively.

The *Requiem in G Minor*, Op. 13 is scored for SSATTB choir, SATB soli, and orchestra and was composed from 1901–03, following his graduation from the Royal Conservatory, but the work was discovered only in 1971.

The predominant choral texture is homophonic, with some imitative polyphony. There are two fugues, *Osanna in excelsis* (two versions), a canonic duet for soprano and alto, *Hostias* and imitative passages on *Et lux*, *Kyrie*, *Benedictus*, and *Pleni sunt coeli*. The SATB soli are used in *concertante* fashion.

The major vocal solo is the soprano alto duet, *Hostias* and the SA duet passages in the *Agnus Dei*. The vocal solo passages do not require virtuoso singers. Olsson employed a simple, late romantic style harmony that borders on diatonic style. His music is furnished with lyric melodies that are elegant and ravishingly beautiful.

Basic Data

EDITION

Otto Olsson
Requiem, Op. 13
[Piano-Vocal score]
AB Nordiska Musikförlaget, (#NHS 6626)
Edition Wilhelm Hanson, Stockholm 1984

DURATION

Eleven movements, 1199 mm., perf., c. 54'

VOICING AND ORCHESTRATION

Choir: SATB range: S-B flat 6; B-E3
Soloists: S I/II, A, T I/II, B
Orchestra: vn. I/II, vla., vc., db., 2 ob., 2 cl., 2 fl., 2 bsn., tpt., tbn., timp., harp, org.

OUTLINE

Introit: 83 mm.
 Requiem aeternam [gm] *adagio.* ssattb choir; *Lux aeterna* [B flat M] ssattb choir; *Requiem aeternam* [gm] ssattb choir. ABA form.
Kyrie: 60 mm., ABA form.
 Kyrie [gm] *adagio*; *Christe* [GM] *molto tranquillo*; *Kyrie* [gm] ssattb choir.
Sequence: 395 mm., 4 movements.
 Dies irae: 129 mm. [cm] *andante con moto ed agitato.* ssattb choir; *Tuba mirum* [cm] *adagio.* ssattb choir; *Liber scriptus-Quid sum miser.* [cm] *allegro. Rex tremendae*: 70 mm. [E flat M] *andante maestoso.* ssattb choir/B solo. *Recordare*: 62 mm. [B flat M] *andante.* ssattb choir. *Confutatis*: 134 mm. [dm] *allegretto.* ssattb choir.
Offertory: 190 mm., 2 movements.
 Domine Jesu Christe: 116 mm. [gm] *andante. Domine Jesu Christe*, ttb choir, *Libera animas*, ssa choral dialogue. *Hostias*: 74 mm. [gm] *L'istesso tempo.* SA duet. Canon. ABA form.
Sanctus: 295 mm., (2 movements)
 Sanctus: 191 mm. [CM] *andante.* ssattb choir/SATB solo quartet; *Pleni sunt coeli.* ssattb choir; *Osanna in excelsis* [CM] *allegro moderato.* ssattb choir. (Fugue). *Benedictus*: 104 mm. [CM] *andante tranquillo.* SATB solo quartet/ssattb choir; *Osanna, allegro moderato.* ssattb choir. Fugue.
Agnus Dei-Communion: 176 mm.
 Agnus Dei [gm] *adagio sostenuto.* ssattb choir/SA soli; *Lux aeterna* [GM] *Requiem aeternam* [gm] ssattb choir.

DISCOGRAPHY

Caprice, CAP 21368, Stockholm Philharmonic Choir and Orchestra, cond. Anders Ohrwall.

GIACOMO PUCCINI
December 22, 1858–November 29, 1924

Puccini received his musical training at the Milan Conservatory, where he studied composition with Antonio Bazzini and Amilcare Ponchielli. With the latter's help, Puccini began to make a career in the world of opera. His first opera, *Le Villi*, was well received by the public and caught the attention of the publisher, Ricordi. Ricordi commissioned a new opera from Puccini, and at the same time, gave him an invaluable connection to an important publishing house. Eight of his ten operas have remained in the active repertory.

The *Requiem* is not a student work and dates from sometime before 1905. It is an incomplete requiem setting that includes the first line of the Introit and a concluding *Requiescat in pace*. The STB choir is accompanied by organ and viola obbligato.

Basic Data

EDITION

Giacomo Puccini
Requiem per coro a tre voci miste, viola e organo.
Ricordi (#132301)

DURATION

One movement, 64 mm.

VOICING AND ORCHESTRATION

Choir: STB range: S-F6; B-G4
Instruments: org., vla.

OUTLINE

Introit: 64 mm.
  Requiem aeternam [dm] *largo sostenuto*. stb choir/organ/viola solo. Homophonic
  writing with some points of imitation. ABA form.

DISCOGRAPHY

ASV 914, Gonville and Caius Choir, Cambridge, cond. Goeffrey Webber.

JOSEPH RHEINBERGER
March 17, 1839–December 25, 1901

Rheinberger was a gifted musician who became an organist at the age of
seven, in Vaduz, the capital of Liechtenstein. He later went to Munich,
where he studied theory, piano, and organ. One of his teachers was Franz
Lachner. Rheinberger eventually made his living by teaching, playing the
organ, and conducting. In 1867, he was appointed professor of composition at the Munich Conservatory; in 1877, he was appointed *Hofkapellmeister*. Among his pupils were the composer, Engelbert Humperdinck, the
conductor Wilhelm Furtwängler, and the Americans, Horatio Parker and
George Whitfield Chadwick.

His composing style was influenced greatly by Viennese classicism. He
wrote symphonic music, a number of chamber compositions, twenty
sonatas for the organ, and several stage works. His sacred music includes
thirteen masses, two settings of the *Stabat Mater*, four requiems, and a
Christmas cantata, *The Star of Bethlehem* (*Der Stern von Bethlehem*). His
liturgical music reveals the influence of the Caecilian Movement and an
interest in the older fugal and canonic forms.

Rheinberger composed and completed his first requiem in 1867 while he was a teacher of composition at the Conservatory and conductor of the Oratorio Society. He conducted the Mozart and Cherubini Requiems in the Society's programs (the former in 1865 and the latter in 1867). These two works are believed to have served as models for him in the creation of his own work, the *C Minor Requiem*. In 1869, he reworked and reorchestrated this work. By 1870, he performed it with the Oratorio Society. Two years later, the *Requiem* was published by B. Schott Sons in Mainz. It bore the dedication *"Dem Gedachtnis der im Deutschen Kriege 1870–1871 gefallenen Helden"* (In memory of those heroes who perished in the German War of 1870–1871), thus qualifying it as one of the earliest versions of the "War" requiem. Rheinberger scored it for SATB soli, SATB choir, and large orchestra.

The SATB soli are employed only as a second *concertante* choir. The prevailing texture is a mixture of imitative polyphonic style and chordal writing. Polyphonic passages include double canon, *Quam olim Abrahae*, double fugue, *Lux aeterna* & *Cum sanctis*, and fugato, *Pleni sunt coeli*, *Agnus Dei*, and *Osanna*.

An independent orchestral accompaniment is particularly colorful in the dramatic portions of the Sequence, *Quantus tremor*, *Tuba mirum*, *Confutatis*, and *Lacrymosa*. Three horns occupy a prominent role in the Offertory and the strings provide a strong, rhythmic drive to the *Cum sanctis* fugue.

Basic Data

EDITIONS

1. Josef Gabriel Rheinberger
Requiem, Op. 60 für Soli, Chor
und grosses Orchester
Reprint of the first edition. Mainz 1872.
Foreword by Harald Wanger
Carus Verlag (50.060-03) 1989

2. Josef Gabriel Rheinberger
Sämtliche Werke
Herausgegeben vom Josef
Rheinberger-Archiv, Vaduz
Abteilung I Geistliche Vokalmusik
1. Messen und Totenmessen, Band 4
Requiem, Op. 60 [full score]
Carus Verlag (50.204) 1992

DURATION
Thirteen movements, 1014 mm.

VOICING AND ORCHESTRATION
Choir: SI/II ATB range: S-B flat 6; B-E3
Soloists: SATB
Orchestra: vn. I/II, vla., vc., db., 2 fl., 2 ob., 2 cl., 2 bsn., 3 Fh., 3 tpt., tuba, timp.

OUTLINE
Introit-*Kyrie*: 89 mm.
  Requiem aeternam [b flat m] *andante molto.* satb choir.

Sequence: 358 mm., 4 movements.

    Dies irae: 105 mm. [fm] *grave*. satb choir (divisi) (vv. 1–8). *Recordare*: 83 mm. [FM] *l'istesso tempo*. SATB soli (vv. 9–10); *Juste judex*, satb choir. (vv. 11–12). *Qui Mariam*: 61 mm. [AM] *andantino*. ssatbb choir. (vv. 13–15). *Confutatis*: 109 mm. [am] *con moto, ma non allegro*. satb choir/SATB soli. (vv. 16–19).

Offertory: 193 mm., 3 movements.

    Domine Jesu Christe: 75 mm. [FM] *moderato*. satb choir. *Quam olim Abrahae*: 49 mm. [fm] *con moto*. satb choir. Double canon. *Hostias*: 69 mm. [D flat M] *adagio molto*. SATB soli; *Quam olim Abrahae* repeated.

Sanctus: 33 mm.

    Sanctus [D flat M] *grave maestoso*. satb choir; *Pleni sunt coeli* & *Osanna*, satb choir. Fugal.

Benedictus: 98 mm.

    Benedictus [B flat M] *andantino*. satb choir/SATB soli; *Osanna*, satb choir/SATB soli. Fugal.

Agnus Dei: 65 mm.

    Agnus Dei [G flat M] *andante quasi adagio*. ssattb choir.

Communion: 113 mm., 2 movements.

    Lux aeterna: 86 mm. [B flat M] *grave*. satb choir. Prelude-Fugue structure. *Requiem aeternam*: 27 mm. [B flat M] *adagio molto*. ssatbb choir.

DISCOGRAPHY

None found.

The *Requiem In E Flat Major*, Op. 84, was composed in 1867 (June 28–July 2). Scored for unaccompanied double SATB choirs, it is a model of the neo-Renaissance polyphonic style so popular with the Caecilian Movement. The work also bears striking similarities to the larger, unaccompanied Psalm settings of Mendelssohn.

    The choral texture is a mixture of imitative polyphonic style (*Kyrie, Quam olim Abrahae, Pleni sunt coeli, Osanna,* and *Agnus Dei*) with sections of chordal, homophonic writing (Introit, Graduale, Offertory, and Communion). Notable is the double canon in *Quam olim Abrahae*. Although the musical language is rooted in traditional classic harmony, it bears the imprint of late romantic chromaticism.

Basic Data

EDITION

Joseph Gabriel Rheinberger
Requiem in Es [E flat], Op. 84
Carus Verlag, Stuttgart (CV 50.084) 1986.

DURATION

Eight movements, 309 mm.

VOICING

Choir: SATB, unaccompanied. range: S-A flat 6; B-E flat 3

OUTLINE

Introit-*Kyrie*: 77 mm., 2 movements.
> *Requiem aeternam*: 30 mm. [E flat M-GM] *tempo ben moderato*. satb choir. *Kyrie*: 47
> mm. [E flat M] satb choir.

Graduale: 30 mm.
> *Absolve me* [gm] *non troppo lento*. satb choir.

Offertory: 47 mm.
> *Domine Jesu Christe* [GM] *tempo moderato*. *Quam olim Abrahae*, Double Canon.

Sanctus: 43 mm.
> *Sanctus* [E flat M] *grave*. satb choir.

Benedictus: 29 mm.
> *Benedictus* [A flat M] *moderato e espressivo*. satb choir.

Agnus Dei: 59 mm.
> *Agnus Dei* [cm] *grave*. satb choir.

Communion: 24 mm.
> *Lux aeterna* [cm-E flat m] *tempo ben moderato*. satb choir.

DISCOGRAPHY

None found.

The *Requiem in D Minor*, Op. 194 the ultimate setting of his four requiem masses, was written in 1900, a year before Rheinberger died. Scored for SATB choir and organ, this work was designed for liturgical usage, yet, like Opus 84, it can be easily included in a concert program.

The prevailing choral texture is homophonic style. Imitative polyphony is found in the Introit and *Osanna*. The only time the SATB soli are used is for a *concertante* style passage in the *Benedictus*. The work possesses a gentle, lyric quality that is brought to a musical climax in the *Sanctus*. The entire work is given a sense of completion with the musical ideas of the opening movement reappearing in the final moments of the *Agnus Dei*.

Basic Data

EDITION

Joseph Gabriel Rheinberger
Requiem in D minor, Op. 194 für vierstimmigen gemischten Chor mit Orgelbegleitung.

[Reprint of the First Edition]
Carus-Verlag (50. 194/01) 1991

DURATION

Seven movements, 289 mm., perf. time, c. 16'

VOICING AND ORCHESTRATION

Choir: SATB range: S-G6; B-F3
Soloists: SATB [*Benedictus* only]
Instruments: Org.

OUTLINE

Introit-*Kyrie*: 55 mm., ABA form.
    Requiem aeternam [dm] *andante grave*. satb choir; *Te decet* [FM] satb choir; *Kyrie*
       [same music as *Requiem aeternam*] satb choir.
Graduale: 43 mm.
    Absolve Domine [GM] *lento moderato*. satb choir.
Offertory: 62 mm., 2 movements.
    Domine Jesu Christe: 33 mm. [dm] *lento maestoso*. satb choir/sa unison or tb uni-
       son. *Hostias*: 29 mm. [B flat M] *adagio*. satb choir.
Sanctus: 30 mm.
    Sanctus: [DM] *adagio*. satb choir.
Benedictus: 38 mm.
    Benedictus [B flat M] *andante amabile*. SATB soli/satb choir.
Agnus Dei-Communion: 61 mm.
    Agnus Dei [dm] *andante*. satb choir; *Requiem aeternam*. satb choir. [same material
       as Introit]

DISCOGRAPHY

ASV Ltd., CD DCA 989, The Choir of Gonville & Caius College, Cambridge, cond.
Geoffrey Webber.

CAMILLE SAINT-SAËNS
October 9, 1835–December 16, 1921

Like Mozart, Saint-Saëns was a child prodigy, gifted as a pianist and able
to write music from his earliest years. At the age of ten, he gave his first
public concert at the Salle Pleyel. In 1848, he attended organ classes at the
Conservatoire, studying with François Benoist. In 1853, he was appointed
organist of the Eglise Sainte-Merry, where he remained until 1857, when
he was offered the same position at one of Paris' largest churches, La
Madeleine. This position was occupied, twenty years later, by Gabriel
Fauré. During the last third of the century, he achieved recognition and
fame as a composer of opera and as a champion of program music.

He was a prolific composer, writing numerous compositions for every medium, yet only a handful of works are really well-known today and include *Carnival of the Animals,* the opera, *Samson and Dalila,* and the *Third Symphony* in C minor.

The *Requiem,* Op. 54, written in 1878, is one of his lesser-known pieces. He scored it for SATB soli, SATB choir, and orchestra, yet the work is quite unlike the one Verdi had written just four years earlier. Absent from this attractive work is the drama and fury found in Verdi music. Opus 54 is quieter and lyrical, closer to the mood of the Fauré *Requiem,* even though the orchestration is much grander and more sumptuous than the latter work.

The orchestration is very colorful and varied. The "noisy" instruments, trumpets and timpani, are eliminated from the instrumental ensemble. A solo SATB quartet and SATB choir are employed in *concertante* style. A common, operatic vocal style, recitative, is a rarity in the requiem settings of the nineteenth century, yet it was employed by Saint-Saëns. There are recitatives for bass and tenor. No other requiem setting, except the Verdi, uses this singing style. Perhaps Saint-Saëns took the idea from the Verdi setting. The composer also used a "sighing" thematic motive, similar to the *Leitmotiv,* throughout the work.

The choral and quartet texture is homophonic and employs virtually no imitative polyphony. A large choir is necessary for an adequate performance.

Basic Data

EDITION

Camille Saint-Saëns
Requiem, Opus 54
Choral Score [piano-vocal]
Kalmus K 09875
[same edition published by Durand, Editions Musicales]

DURATION

Eight movements, 609 mm., perf., c. 40'

VOICING AND ORCHESTRATION

Choir: SATB range: S-A flat 6; B-F3 [C3, rare]
Soloists: SATB
Orchestra: vn. I/II, vla., vc., db., 4 fl., 2 ob., 2 Eh., 2 bsn., 2 Fh., 2 harps, 1 "offstage" tbn., org.

OUTLINE

Introit-*Kyrie:* 71 mm.
　Requiem aeternam [E flat M-CM] *andante sostenuto.* SATB soli/satb choir; *Te decet* [A flat M] SATB soli & *Kyrie* [cm] satb choir. First violin-"sighing" motive.

Sequence: 320 mm., 3 movements.

> *Dies irae*: 118 mm. [cm] *allegro*. SATB soli/satb choir. Gregorian melody in soprano; *Tuba mirum* [cm] satb choir; *Mors stupebit* [E flat M] SATB soli; *Liber scriptus*, tenor recitative; *Judex ergo*, bass recitative; *Quid sum miser* [cm] T solo/satb choir/SATB soli. "sighing" motive. *Rex tremendae*: 151 mm. [fm-A flat M] *allegro moderato*. *Rex tremendae*, satb choir;
>
> *Recordare*, T solo; *Rex tremendae*, sattb choir. (ABA form); *Quaerens me*, T solo (same melody as *Recordare*); *Juste judex*, satb choir; *Ingemisco*, T solo; *Qui Mariam*, satb choir; *Preces meae*, T solo (same melody as *Ingemisco*); *Inter oves-Confutatis*, ssattbb choir. *Oro supplex*: 51 mm. [fm] *adagio*. orchestral introduction, SAT soli; *Lacrymosa*, ssaattbb choir; *Huic ergo-Pie Jesu* [fm] SATB soli/satb choir.

Offertory: 24 mm. (Saint-Saens set only the *Hostias* verse.)

> *Hostias* [E flat M] *andantino*. sattb choir/organ/strings/harps.

Sanctus: 36 mm.

> *Sanctus* [A flat M] *allegro maestoso*. satb choir.

Benedictus: 38 mm.

> *Benedictus* [D flat M] *moderato*. satb choir/SATB soli.

Agnus Dei-Communion: 120 mm.

> *Agnus Dei* [E flat M-cm] *andante sostenuto*. SATB quartet/sattbb choir. "sighing" motive (violin I); *Lux aeterna*, sattbb choir.

DISCOGRAPHY

Premier Recordings, PRCD 1025, The Fairfield County Chorale and Horace Mann Glee Club, Amor Artis Orchestra, cond. Johannes Somary.

ROBERT SCHUMANN
June 8, 1810–June 29, 1856

Schumann was one of the great romantic composers who wrote for all of the important musical forms: Lieder, chamber music, symphonic works and, especially, solo piano. However, during the last ten years of his life, he struggled with physical and mental problems that would eventually destroy him. The two sacred compositions that he was to write, the *Mass for Chorus and Orchestra*, Op.147 and the *Requiem for Chorus and Orchestra*, Op.148, were both composed in 1852 at the very end of his career. The *Requiem* is scored for SATB soli, SATB choir, and orchestra.

The bulk of the four-part choral writing is homophonic, with occasional passages of imitative polyphony. The soloists are employed in *concertante* fashion with the choir. The harmonic style employs the typical chromatic writing of the mid-romantic period.

At the time he composed the *Requiem*, he was the municipal music director in Düsseldorf. He was responsible for weekly rehearsal of the *Gesang-Musik Verein*, the local singing society. Even though he came to see the *Requiem* as his own funeral piece, he probably had this organization in mind for a concert performance when he initially penned the work. It is regrettable that at this time his powers of composition were seriously affected by his health and mental problems. Almost since its creation, the work has been the subject of much negative criticism regarding the quality of composition and this criticism has never completely abated.

As far as it is known, Schumann never heard a public performance of the *Requiem*. The earliest known performance of the *Requiem* was in the Cathedral Church at Königsberg (November 1864). After Schumann's death in 1856, Clara Schumann sent the manuscript to Brahms, asking him to assess whether the work should be published or not. Brahms felt that it should and so it was first published in 1864. It is ironic that Brahms, who so ruthlessly destroyed his own music when he felt that it did not come up to expectations, responded positively.

After publication, the work received a number of performances, but by 1870 there were few. Although the performing groups seemed to like the work, the press reviews were generally negative. One reviewer called it "insignificant music," another said it had been "hastily and carelessly" composed. Kurt Pahlen, in his book, *The Oratorio*, (Amadeus Press, 1985) wrote, "Schumann was no longer capable of sustained concentration, so passages of great nobility are placed next to banalities. The most terrible thing is that Schumann was unaware of it."

The work certainly does not match up to some of his great chamber music pieces, his piano works, or the *Requiem für Mignon*. There are nice moments in the *Requiem*, especially the serious music of the Introit, as well as passages in the *Quid sum miser* and *Recordare*.

Basic Data

EDITIONS

1. Robert Schumann
Requiem, Opus 148 for Chorus &
  Orchestra
Choral Score
Kalmus K 06785

2. Robert Schumann
Requiem für Chor und Orchester,
Op. 148 [Partitur]
Edwin Kalmus & Co., Music

3. Robert Schumann
New Edition of the Complete Works
Series IV, Religious Works, Vol. 3
Requiem op. 148 [full score]
ed. Bernhard R. Appel
Schott.
Mainz. London. Madrid. New York, etc.
  1993

DURATION

Nine movements, 743 mm., perf., c. 39'

VOICING AND ORCHESTRATION

Choir: SATB range: S-G6; B-G3
Soloists: SATB
Orchestra: vn. I/II, vla., vc., db., 2 fl., 2 ob., 2 cl., 2 bsn., 2 Fh., 2 tpt., 3 tbn., timp.

OUTLINE

Introit: 169 mm., 2 movements.
  Requiem aeternam: 29 mm. [D flat M] *langsam*. satb choir. ABA form. *Te decet-*
  Kyrie: 140 mm. [AM] *feierlich*. satb choir/SATB soli. Fugal.
Sequence: 301 mm., 3 movements.
  Dies irae: 65 mm. [f# m] *ziemlich bewegt*. satb choir. (vv. 1–4). *Liber scriptus*: 146
  mm. [DM] *In gemessenem Tempo, doch nicht zu langsam. Liber scriptus-Judex ergo*,
  satb choir/SATB soli; *Quid sum miser*, SATB soli; *Rex tremendae*, satb choir;
  Recordare-Quaerens me, S solo; *Ingemisco*, SATB soli (canon); *Juste judex*, satb
  choir. *Qui Mariam*: 90 mm. [GM] *in massigem Tempo. Qui Mariam-Preces meae-*
  Inter oves, A solo (ABA form); *Confutatis*, satb choir; *Oro supplex*, A solo; *Lacri-*
  mosa-Huic ergo, satb choir.
Offertory: 103 mm., 2 movements.
  Domine Jesu Christe: 64 mm. [bm-BM] *feierlich*. satb choir. *Hostias*: 26 mm. [g #
  m] *dasselbe Tempo*. SA soli/satb choir.
Sanctus: 77 mm.
  Sanctus [A flat M] *dasselbe Tempo*. satb choir; *Pleni sunt coeli*, satb choir. Fugue.
Benedictus-Agnus Dei-Communion: 106 mm.
  Benedictus [b flat m] *langsam*. SATB soli; *Agnus Dei*, satb choir (canon, sa-tb
  choir); *Cum sanctis tuis* [D flat M] satb choir. Canonic.

DISCOGRAPHY

Hungaroton, HCD 11809, Budapest Chorus & Hungarian State Orchestra, cond.
  Miklós Forrai.

GIOVANNI SGAMBATI
May 28, 1841–December 14, 1914

Sgambati began as a pupil of Zingarelli and graduated from the Accademia di St. Cecilia in Rome. In 1862, he became a pupil of Liszt. He
remained a life-long friend of Liszt and championed his music.

   At a time when most Italian composers were occupied with opera,
Sgambati was involved in revitalizing the Italian instrumental tradition.
Through a series of concerts in the Sala di Dante (Rome), Sgambati, the

conductor, introduced the symphonies of Beethoven to the Roman public. His musical style was greatly influenced by the classical and romantic German musical forms. He favored the sonata form and its method of melodic organization. His music appears to have pointed the way for Ottorino Resphigi's (1879–1936) orchestral works.

He composed two quintets for strings and piano, two orchestral symphonies, numerous pieces for voice and piano, a concerto for piano, and solo piano works. The only choral music he composed was the *Requiem* for baritone soloist, SATB choir, and orchestra (c. 1895). Possibly, the composer had it in mind for a memorial service for King Vittorio Emmanuele II. The motet, *Versa est in luctum cithara mea* (Job 30, 31 and Job 7, 16) was added to the *Requiem* in 1901, after the death of King Umberto I.

This requiem setting is one of the few of the era that employs motives from the Gregorian melodies. The chant is used to give a sense of melodic unity throughout the work. Manfred Frank (CD notes, p. 17) suggests that the chant melodies are meant to represent eternity. The Gregorian *Dies irae* melody is also quoted briefly by trumpet and harp.

The prevailing choral texture is homophonic, but there are also a number of polyphonic passages, including two fugues, *Teste David* and *Confutatis,* as well as the canonic setting of *Tremens factus sum* (Sequence). A unique application of the *concertante* principle is employed by Sgambati in his use of a small, contrasting choir, drawn from the larger choral ensemble. This secondary ensemble is assigned fragments of the Gregorian chant or newly composed tunes that resemble chant melody. The small choir is employed in a wide variety of scorings; SA (*Te decet, Oro supplex, Agnus Dei*), SSAA (*Pie Jesu, Sanctus, Tremens*), B (*Mors stupebit, Liber scriptus*), SATB (*Quam olim Abrahae*), SATT (*Recordare*), and SSAAT (*Benedictus*).

Several novel features of the scoring include a major obbligato role for a first violin solo in *Inter oves* (Sequence), Offertory, *Sanctus,* and *Agnus Dei* and the use of the harp throughout the work. The composer scored the motet, *Versa est in luctum,* and the Offertory verse, *Hostias,* for baritone solo and orchestra. There are also shorter passages in the Responsory (*Dona eis requiem, Libera me, Requiem aeternam*) for the soloist.

Basic Data

EDITION

Messa da Requiem a coro misto, baritono e orchestra.
G. Sgambati
Partitura d' Orchestra
Schott & Co. Mainz. c. 1908

DURATION

Seven movements, 1641 mm., perf., c. 80'

VOICING AND ORCHESTRATION

Choir: SATB (divisi) range: S-A6; B-F3 [E flat 3, rare]
Soloists: Bar.
Orchestra: vn. I/II, vla., vc., db., 2 fl., 2 ob., Eh., 2 cl., bcl., 2 bsn., 4 Fh., 3 tpt., 3
   tbn., tuba, timp., tam-tam, cymbals, harp, org.

OUTLINE

Introit-*Kyrie*: 163 mm.
   Requiem aeternam [fm] *andante.* satb choir; *Te decet* [FM] *con moto.* small choir/
   satb choir; *Requiem aeternam* [fm] *andante.* satb choir; *Kyrie* [FM] *piu lento.* satb
   choir.
Sequence: 592 mm.
   Dies irae-Quantus tremor [cm-E flat M] *molto mosso.* satb choir; *Tuba mirum* [A flat
   M] *meno mosso.* satb choir; *Mors stupebit* [A flat M] *andante mosso.* small choir
   (b); *Liber scriptus,* small choir (b); *Judex ergo-Quid sum miser-Rex tremendae,* satb
   choir; *Recordare* [A flat M] small choir (satt); *Quaerens me-Juste judex,* tb choir;
   Ingemisco [GM] *andante espressivo.* satb choir; *Qui Mariam, un poco sostenuto.*
   sat choir; *Preces meae,* satb choir; *Inter oves,* satb choir (*divisi*); *Confutatis* [cm]
   vivace. satb choir (fugue); *Voca me, andante sostenuto.* satb choir; *Oro supplex*
   [cm] *andante solonelle.* small choir (sa)/satb choir; *Lacrymosa-Huic ergo* [cm]
   adagio. satb choir; *Pie Jesu* [CM] *andante.* satb choir/small choir, ssaa.
Offertory: 285 mm., 2 movements.
   Domine Jesu Christe: 156 mm. [E flat M] *andante maestoso e solonne.* tb choir;
   Libera eas, alla breve. ttbb choir; *Sed signifer,* ssaa choir/Bar. solo; *Quam olim
   Abrahae, andante.* small choir (satb)/satb choir. *Hostias:* 129 mm. [fm] *andante.*
   Bar. solo; *Fac eas. tranquillo, agitato molto; Quam olim Abrahae* [A flat M]
   andante. satb choir, unaccompanied.
Sanctus: 112 mm.
   Sanctus [FM] *piu tranquillo.* small choir (ssaat); *Hosanna,* ssaat choir; *Benedictus,
   lento.* small choir (saat); *Hosanna,* saat choir.
Agnus Dei-Communion: 128 mm.
   Agnus Dei I [GM] *andante con moto.* orchestral introduction/violin solo/small
   choir (sa); *Agnus Dei* II, *piu mosso.* satb choir/ small choir (sa); *Lux aeterna*
   [GM] *un poco mosso.* satb choir; *Requiem aeternam* ssat choir/violin solo; *Cum
   sanctis, tranquillo.* small choir (sa)/satb choir/ violin solo.
Responsory: 246 mm.
   Libera me [A flat M] *andante.* satb choir; *Tremens factus-Dies illa,* small choir
   (satb)/satb choir; *Requiem aeternam* [fm] *andante sostenuto.* satb choir/Bar.
   solo; *Libera me* [fm] satb choir; *Libera me* [fm] *andante.* satb choir; *Kyrie* [fm]
   piu lento. satb choir.

DISCOGRAPHY

Carus, 83.121, Philharmonischer Chor Heilbronn, Staatorchesters Stuttgart, dir. Ulrich Walddörfer.

CHARLES VILLIERS STANFORD
September 30, 1852–March 29, 1924

Stanford showed tremendous musical talent from his earliest years. In 1870, he attended Queen's College, Cambridge, and in 1873 was appointed organist of Trinity College. Later, he went on to study in Germany with Friedrich Kiel, himself the composer of two requiems. He was appointed professor of composition (1883) at the Royal College of Music. He was conductor of the London Bach Choir from 1885 to 1902 and professor of music at Cambridge (1887), all by the age of thirty-five. Among his pupils were Ralph Vaughan-Williams, Gustav Holst, John Ireland, Herbert Howells, and Benjamin Britten.

He wrote more than thirty cantatas and oratorios, seventeen stage works, orchestral music, chamber music, and music for piano, organ, and voice. His church music includes four settings of the *Magnificat & Nunc Dimittis*, six settings of the *Morning, Communion* and *Evening Services*, three masses, *Stabat Mater*, numerous motets, and one *Requiem*.

The *Requiem*, unfortunately, is not well-known, yet is a magnificent work. Scored for SATB solo, SATB choir, orchestra, and organ, it is the worthy equal of any romantic setting. It was written in memory of a close personal friend, Baron Frederick Leighton (1830–1896), an English painter and sculptor. The four-part *divisi* choral writing is elegant and always supported by an orchestral accompaniment that possesses an expansive melodic sweep and harmonic grandeur.

Although there are many chordal, homophonic sections, many choral passages are written in polyphonic style. They include the *Kyrie* and *Quam olim Abrahae* fugues and the imitative writing of *Lux aeterna, Sanctus*, and *Benedictus*. The older, choral *concertante* style is preserved throughout the work, in passages for full choir and solo quartet (*Kyrie* II, *Recordare, Pie Jesu, Domine Jesu Christe*, and *Lux aeterna*). The harmonic language is chromatic and contains passages that employ bi-tonality. A notable example is found in the Offertory, where the choral passages in C major contrast with those of the solo quartet in E major.

The presence of Wagner is suggested by the use of a *Leitmotiv*, representing human mortality. This theme appears throughout the work. (Stanford used this same device in his setting of the *Stabat Mater*.) The sensual music of the *Sanctus* was inspired by and reminiscent of Wagner's *Ride of the Valkyries*. Here, the Heavenly Choir is depicted through overlap-

ping repetitions of melody, accompanied by the full orchestra (two harps
and six-part violin writing) and a type of "galloping" rhythm. There are
beautiful, church-like, vocal solos and exquisite solo quartet writing. A
large choir is necessary for performance.

Basic Data

EDITION

Stanford
Requiem for Solo Voices & Chorus, Op. 63
Boosey & Co. H. 1752. C. [Full Score] 1897
[clefs: G & F (C for tenor soloist & tenor choral part)]

DURATION

Seven movements, 1588 mm., perf., 1' 22"

VOICING AND ORCHESTRATION

Choir: SATB (*divisi*) range: S-A6; B-E3
Soloists: SATB
Orchestra: vn. I/II, vla., vc., db., 2 fl., 2 ob., 2 cl., Eh., 2 bsn., cbn., 4 Fh., 3 tpt., 3
   tbn., tuba, timp., bass drum, harp, org.

OUTLINE

Introit: 177 mm.
   Requiem aeternam [AM] *adagio (alla breve).* ssaattbb (divisi) choir (celli-*Leitmotiv*);
      Te decet, S solo/SATB/satb choir.
Kyrie: 121 mm. ABA form.
   Kyrie [am] *allegro tranquillo ed espressivo.* satb choir, Fugal; *Christe.* SATB soli.
      fugal; *Kyrie,* SATB soli/satb (divisi) choir. Fugal.
Gradual: 83 mm. ABA form.
   Requiem aeternam [AM] *larghetto.* SATB soli/S solo; *In memoria,* S solo/violin
      solo. (violin I-*Leitmotiv*).
Sequence: 623 mm.
   *Dies irae-Quantus tremor-Tuba mirum-Mors stupebit-Dies irae-Tuba mirum-Liber
      scriptus,* 150 mm. [em] *allegro moderato ma energico.* ssaattbb choir; *Judex ergo,*
      77 mm. [CM] *con moto maestoso.* satb choir/A solo; *Rex tremendae,* 47 mm.
      [EM] *poco piu mosso.* S solo, sattbb choir/SATB soli; *Recordare,* 68 mm. [EM]
      andante tranquillo. SATB soli/satb choir. *Quaerens me-Juste judex-Qui Mariam-
      Preces me:* 84 mm. [fm-dm] *Quaerens me,* B solo/satb choir; *Juste Judex-Qui
      Mariam-Preces meae,* T solo; *Inter oves,* T solo/SATB soli. (fugal). *Confutatis-
      Oro supplex,* 49 mm. [FM-gm] *andante maestoso.* satb choir/SATB soli. *Lacri-
      mosa-Huic ergo,* 102 mm. [em] *adagio non troppo.* A solo/SATB soli/saatbb
      choir. *Pie Jesu,* 47 mm. [EM] *un poco piu mosso ma tranquillo.* SATB soli/sattbb
      choir.
Offertory: 196 mm. 2 movements.
   Domine Jesu Christe: 94 mm. [CM] *allegro.* SATB quartet/satb choir; *Libera animas,*

B solo/SATB soli/satb choir; *Quam olim Abrahae*, satb choir. *allegro vivace.* (Fugue, 69 mm.). *Hostias*: 34 mm. [A flat M] *lento tranquillo ma con moto.* SATB soli; *Quam olim Abrahae* is repeated.

Sanctus: 224 mm. 2 movements.

Sanctus: 109 mm. [AM] *allegro non troppo.* ssaatb choir/full orchestra/violins *divisi a 6*; *Pleni sunt coeli*, ssaatb choir; *Hosanna in excelsis*, ssaatb choir. ABA form. *Benedictus*: 115 mm. [FM] *andante tranquillo.* SATB soli; *Hosanna in excelsis*, ssaatb choir. (violin I, *Leitmotiv*)

Agnus Dei-Communion: 164 mm.

Agnus Dei [am] *tempo di marche funebre.* satb choir (violin I, *Leitmotiv*); *Lux aeterna* [FM] T solo/satb choir; *Lux aeterna*, A solo/satb choir; *Lux aeterna*, SATB solo quartet/saatbb choir; orchestral interlude; *Lux aeterna* [am-AM] saatbb choir. (violin I, *Leitmotiv*).

DISCOGRAPHY

Marco Polo, 8.223580-1, RTE Philharmonic Choir and the National Symphony of Ireland, cond. Adrian Leaper.

FRANZ VON SUPPÉ
April 18, 1819–May 21, 1895

Von Suppé was born in Split, Croatia, and at a very young age began singing in the cathedral at Zara (Zadar). The director of music at the cathedral, Giovanni Ferrari, gave him lessons in music theory and composition. He received flute lessons from the local military band director. In 1835, he moved to Vienna for study at the Konservatorium der Akademie der Tonkunst. In Vienna, he met Franz Pokorny, a local theatre director, who gave him his first conducting position. He remained in Vienna for many years, holding a number of different conducting positions there. During this tenure, Von Suppé enjoyed the assistance Pokorny provided and when the latter died in 1850, Von Suppé composed the *Requiem in D Minor* (1855).

Von Suppé, famous as the creator of German operettas, composed more than 200 stage works, including thirty-one operettas and 180 farces. Today, his most famous work remains the *Poet and Peasant Overture.* Among the few sacred works he wrote are the *Missa dalmatica* (1835) for three voices and organ; a large-scale Psalm setting (*Herr, strafe mich nicht*) for soli, chorus, and orchestra (late 1830s); a *Missa solemnis* in C Minor (1839); and the *Requiem in D minor.*

The *D minor Requiem* was scored for SATB soli, SATB choir, and orchestra and first performed in November 1855 at the Piarist Church (Vienna). It was well-received by the public, but critics called the Italianate-style work too operatic and cheerful for the subject matter. The last-known performance of the work took place in Vienna in 1900 and it was not until the 1990s that it reappeared.

The more conservative elements of the work are reflected in the three fugues (*Kyrie* [double fugue], *Quam olim Abrahae,* and *Cum Sanctis tuis*), and the *concertante* use of the SATB soli and SATB choir (*Rex tremendae, Preces meae, Oro supplex*).

The romantic orchestral effects represent the "modern" side of the work and include a roiling orchestral accompaniment of the *Dies irae* (continuous rolls for the timpani, one of which is twenty-six measures long), the three trombones for the dramatic choral recitative, *Domine Jesu Christe,* a very "moody" oboe solo for *Rex tremendae,* the trombone introduction and postlude for *Tuba mirum* and the string tremolos used to create a celestial aura for the *Sanctus.*

Several of the major vocal solos are in the Italian grand opera tradition. They include *Tuba mirum* (bass), *Hostias* (bass), and *Lacrimosa* (alto and choir). With the exception of the choral fugues, the primary choral texture is homophonic style.

Several unusual, if not unique, features of the work are the 15/8 meter of *Mors stupebit,* unexpected harmonic turns and the quotation of a passage from the *Lacrimosa* of the Mozart Requiem (quoted during *Tuba mirum*). Von Suppé conceived of the work as a liturgical expression and not a concert-hall piece. This remarkable requiem possesses a tremendous variety of moods, highlighted by colorful orchestration.

Basic Data

EDITIONS

1. Franz von Suppé
Missa pro defunctis (Requiem)
per Soli, Coro ed Orchestra.
First Edition edited by Gabriele Timm &
Rainer Böhm
[Full Score] Carus Verlag (40. 085/01)
  1994

2. Musica Sacra
Franz von Suppé
Requiem
Organ-Vocal score
Edition József Ács (EJA #33)
Durenerstr. 33 a
52249 Eschweiler, Germany

DURATION

Thirteen movements, 1310 mm., perf., c. 83'

VOICING AND ORCHESTRATION

Choir: SATB range: S-B flat 6; B-F♯ 3
Soloists: SATB
Orchestra: vn. I/II, vla., vc., db., 2 fl., 2 ob., 2 cl., 2 bsn., 4 Fh., 2 tpt., 3 tbn., timp., tam-tam.

OUTLINE

Introit: 166 mm.

Requiem aeternam [dm] *andante grave.* saatbb choir; *Te decet-Requiem aeternam* [FM-dm] SATB soli/satb choir; *Kyrie* (112 mm.) [dm] *allegro moderato.* satb choir. Double fugue; *Kyrie II, allegro marcato.*

Sequence: 484 mm., 5 movements.

Dies irae: 113 mm. [dm] *allegro assai.* satb choir. (vv. 1–2). *Tuba mirum*: 77 mm. [am] *andante grave. Tuba mirum,* B solo; *Mors stupebit,* ssa choir; *Liber scrip tus,* sattb choir; *Judex ergo,* B solo; *Quid sum miser,* satb choir/B solo. (vv. 3–7). *Rex tremendae*: 59 mm. [AM] *maestoso pesante.* SATB soli/satb choir. *Recordare*: 83 mm. [dm] *andante. Recordare,* T solo/satbb choir; *Quaerens me,* A solo/satbb choir; *Juste judex-Ingemisco-Qui Mariam-Preces meae,* SATB soli/satbb choir; *Inter oves,* SATB soli/sa choir. (vv. 9–15). *Confutatis*: 81 mm. [B flat M] *grave.* ssaattbb choir; *Oro supplex,* SATB soli/ssa choir. (vv. 16–17).

Lacrimosa: 71 mm. [dm] *andantino, quasi moderato.* oboe/A solo/satb choir. (vv. 18–19).

Offertory: 195 mm., 2 movements.

Domine Jesu Christe: 90 mm. [gm] *andante lugubre.* satb choir/three trombones. Choral recitative; *Quam olim Abrahae* [GM] *moderato.* satb choir. Fugue. *Hostias*: 55 mm. [cm] *larghetto.* B solo; *Quam olim Abrahae* repeated.

Sanctus: 74 mm.

Sanctus [DM] *adagio.* sattbb choir; *Osanna* [DM] *allegro giubiloso.* sattb choir.

Benedictus: 123 mm.

Benedictus [DM] *andante con moto.* SATB solo quartet, unaccompanied; *Osanna* is repeated.

Agnus Dei-Communion: 203 mm.

Agnus Dei, 91 mm. [dm] *andante grave.* satb choir; *Lux aeterna,* SATB soli quartet; *Cum sanctis tuis,* 112 mm. [dm] *allegro moderato.* satb choir. Fugue.

Responsory: 65 mm.

Libera me [dm] *andante grave.* satb choir, unaccompanied/orchestral punctuation; *Dies illa* (music from *Dies irae* movement); *Libera me,* satb choir.

DISCOGRAPHY

1. Novalis, 150 112-2, Zurich Concert Choir and Orchestra, cond. Edmond de Stoutz.
2. KSCH 312482, Cracow Philharmonic Chorus and Orchestra, dir. Roland Bader.

GIUSEPPE VERDI
October 10, 1813–January 27, 1901

Often called Verdi's "greatest opera," the *Manzoni Requiem* is one of the great musical canvases of the romantic era. Its composer received his earliest musical training from the organist of the cathedral at Busseto, Francesco Provesi. Because of his young age, Verdi was not permitted to study at the Milan Conservatory. Consequently, he took private lessons and this training must have been competent, for his first opera, *Oberto*, was produced at La Scala in 1839. During the next half century, he continued to turn out a series of masterpieces. Of the twenty-seven operas stemming from that period of Verdi's career, a majority of them remain in the active repertory.

In addition to the stage works is a string quartet and a handful of sacred pieces; the *Requiem*, an *Ave Maria*, a *Pater Noster*, and the *Four Sacred Pieces* (*Quattro Pezzi Sacri*). Verdi also attempted to create a *Messa da Requiem* to commemorate the death of Rossini. He involved a number of distinguished Italian composers in the creation of this work, with Mercadante heading a select list of thirteen composers. Even though the music was composed, arrangements for its premiere became bogged down and ultimately collapsed. The *Messa per Rossini* did not receive its premiere until 1988 with Helmut Rilling and the Stuttgart Bachakademie.

In 1873, a reason arose for Verdi to revisit the *Messa per Rossini*; the death of the poet-patriot, Alessandro Manzoni. After Manzoni's death, Verdi began to complete the *Requiem* he had begun as a collaborative effort in 1868. At that earlier time, Verdi had completed the *Libera me*. This piece was ultimately reworked and included in the *Manzoni Requiem*. By April 16, 1874, the full *Manzoni Requiem* was completed and on the first anniversary of Manzoni's death, received its premiere in the Church of San Marco, Milan. Verdi conducted for this occasion.

The *Manzoni Requiem* is scored for SATB soli, SATB choir, and large orchestra. Its style is derived from Italian grand opera, with its dramatic virtuoso solos (*Ingemisco* and *Libera*), duets (*Recordare*, *Lacrymosa*, and *Agnus Dei*), and ensemble quartet (*Domine Jesu Christe*). Classical elements, such as fugue (*Sanctus* and *Libera me*), canon (*Quaerens me*), and older *concertante* choral style (*Libera me*, *Sanctus*, *Salva me*, *Kyrie*, & *Huic ergo*), play an equally important role in the work. The predominant choral texture is a mixture of imitative polyphonic style and chordal writing. Romantic era "*stile antico*" is expressed in the prelude and fugue structure of the *Sanctus*, the four-part fugue on *Libera me*, and the fughetta at *Quam olim Abrahae*.

The independent orchestra provides very colorful and dramatic accompaniment for such passages as the *Dies irae*, in which volcanic anger is depicted by the powerful brass and timpani orchestration (an orchestration modeled upon the earlier Gossec and Berlioz requiem settings). A string tremolo is used to create an ethereal atmosphere for *Lux aeterna*.

Basic Data

EDITIONS

1. Verdi
Requiem to the memory of Alessandro
   Manzoni for Four Solo Voices &
   Chorus.
G. Schirmer (#10447) [Piano-Vocal Score]
G. Schirmer, Inc. NY. 1985

2. The Works of Guiseppi Verdi
Series III: Sacred Music
Vol. I Requiem [full score]
General editor, Philip Gosset
University of Chicago Press,
Chicago, London
Ricordi, Milano 1990

DURATION

Seven movements, 1792 mm., perf., c. 68'

VOICING AND ORCHESTRATION

Choir: SATB range: S-B6; B-E3
Soloists: SATB
Orchestra: vn. I/II, vla., vc., db., pic., 3 fl., 2 ob., 2 cl., 4 bsn., 4 Fh., 4 tpt., 3 tbn.,
   bass tuba, 3 timp., one large drum. *off-stage*, 4 tpt.

OUTLINE

Introit-*Kyrie*: 140 mm.
   Requiem aeternam [am] *andante*. satb choir; *Et lux perpetua* [AM] satb choir; *Kyrie*,
      satb choir/SATB soli (sopranos, *divisi*)
Sequence: 698 mm.
   Dies irae: 73 mm. [gm] *allegro agitato*. ssaattb choir. *Quantus tremor*: 18 mm. [B
      flat] satb choir. *Tuba mirum*: 50 mm. [a flat m] *allegro sostenuto*. satb choir.
      (ssattbb *divisi*). *Mors stupebit*: 22 mm. [dm] *molto meno mosso*. B solo. *Liber
      scriptus-Judex ergo*-67 mm. [dm] *allegro molto sostenuto*. A solo/satb choir. *Dies
      irae*: 41 mm. [gm] *allegro agitato*. satb choir. *Quid sum miser*: 52 mm. [gm] *ada-
      gio*. A solo/SAT soli trio. *Rex tremendae*: 55 mm. [cm] *adagio maestoso*. satb
      choir/SATB soli. *Recordare-Quaerens me*: 62 mm. [FM] *lo stesso tempo*. SA duet.
      Canon. *Ingemisco-Inter oves-Qui Mariam-Inter oves*: 56 mm. [CM, chromatic] T
      solo. *Confutatis-Oro supplex*:, 70 mm. [BM] *andante*. B solo. *Dies irae*: 51 mm.
      [gm] *allegro agitato*. satb chorus. *Lacrymosa-Huic ergo*: 42 mm. [b flat m] *largo*.
      AB duet/satb choir/SATB soli. *Pie Jesu*: 36 mm. [b flat m] satb choir/SATB
      soli.
Offertory: 217 mm.
   Domine Jesu Christe [A flat M] *andante mosso*. SATB soli; *Quam olim Abrahae, alle-
      gro mosso*. SATB soli. Fughetta; *Hostias* [CM] *adagio*. SATB soli; *Quam olim
      Abrahae* is repeated.
Sanctus: 139 mm.
   Sanctus [FM] *allegro*. double satb choir. Prelude and fugue structure.

Agnus Dei: 74 mm.
  Agnus Dei I, II, III [CM] *andante*. SA soli duet/satb choir.
Communion: 104 mm.
  Lux aeterna [B flat M] *molto moderato*. SAB trio.
Responsory: 420 mm.
  Libera me: 43 mm.[E flat M-cm] *moderato*. S solo/satb choir; *Dies irae*: 87 mm.
    [gm] *allegro agititato*. satb choir. Same material of the Sequence, *Dies irae*;
    Requiem aeternam: 39 mm. [b flat m] *andante*. S solo/satb choir, unaccompa-
    nied; *Libera me*: 251 mm. [cm-CM] *allegro risoluto*. S solo/satb choir. Fugue.

DISCOGRAPHY

1. Telarc, 80152, Atlanta Symphony Chorus and Orchestra, cond. Robert Shaw.
2. Multiple listings in the Schwann Catalogue.

THE MASS FOR ROSSINI
Messa per Rossini

Within four days of Rossini's death (Nov. 13, 1868), Verdi had written a letter to his publisher, Ricordi, suggesting that a group of Italy's leading composers prepare a setting of the requiem mass that would commemorate the life and work of Gioachino Rossini. The idea was received well and a committee was formed for the execution of the project. Thirteen composers were selected to compose sections of the Requiem and by September 1869, the music had been written. Yet the work was not to receive its premiere until 1988, almost 120 years later.

It seems that the political solutions of the "where and who" to perform the piece were impossible to solve. Verdi wanted the work performed at San Petronio (Bologna), but an existing Papal ban did not permit female singers to perform in church. Furthermore, the committee did not secure a capable chorus, orchestra, or soloists for the project. They assumed that the musical forces of the Teatro Comunale in Bologna would be made available, but the director of the theater refused to cooperate. The mayor of Bologna became involved, suggesting that the performance be postponed. At the beginning of November 1869, the committee met for purpose of abandoning the project. Ultimately, Verdi placed the blame on the organizing committee for their inability to settle a variety of issues that led to the ultimate demise of this remarkable project.

The *Messa per Rossini* is a unique work in the history of the requiem because it is one of the few collaborative settings of the requiem text. The only other monumental work of this type is the *Requiem of Reconciliation*, written by fourteen composers as a memorial to those who perished in World War II. It was completed in 1995.

The musical guidelines set down by Verdi and the committee allowed the composers to achieve and maintain a high degree of stylistic, tonal, and dramatic unity. Indeed, the harmonic language, key choice, and dynamics are so well integrated that the various individual movements do not sound like a mere "collection" of pieces, but rather an organic whole. Each composer was allowed about seven minutes for the length of their composition, and the committee looked after the choice of key, the tempo, the vocal and instrumental forces available, and the general form of the pieces. The work is an encyclopedia of late nineteenth-century, Italian grand opera and church music styles.

The *Messa per Rossini* is scored for SATBarB soloists, SATB choir (*divisi*), and large symphonic orchestra. Evidence of *stile antico* church music is found in the four choral fugues, *Kyrie*, *Amen* (Sequence), *Osanna*, and *Libera me* as well as Platania's *concertante* setting of the *Sanctus*. Virtuoso vocal-solo writing includes the duet (SA), *Quid sum miser;* a tenor solo, *Ingemisco;* a baritone solo, *Confutatis;* an alto solo, *Agnus Dei;* a soprano solo, *Libera me;* and the TBarB trio, *Luceat eis.* Every major solo is accompanied by choral support.

The independent orchestra provides a wide variety of accompaniments, ranging from the massive orchestration of the *Sanctus* and *Tuba Mirum* to a more intimate scoring of the *Agnus Dei* and *Recordare.*

Basic Data

EDITION

G. Ricordi [rental only]
1988.

DURATION

Thirteen movements, 2302 mm., perf., c. 1' 50"

VOICING AND ORCHESTRATION

Choir: SATB (*divisi*, 4–6 parts) range: S-B6 ; B-E3
Soloists: SATBarB
Orchestra: vn. I/II, vla., vc., db, (includes *divisi* & solo), pic., 2 fl., 2 ob., Eh., 2 cl., bcl., 4 bsn., 4 Fh., 4 tpt., 3 tbn., ophicleide, 4 timp., bass drum, cymbals, tam-tam, org.

OUTLINE

Introit-Kyrie: 129 mm. Composer: Antonio Buzzolla (3.2.1815–20.3.1871)

Buzzolla was a pupil of Donizetti and the *Maestro di capella* at St. Mark's in Venice. He wrote a handful of operas and composed sacred music for the cathedral.

Requiem aeternam: 82 mm. [gm] *andante sostenuto*. satb choir (polyphonic texture); *Kyrie*: 47 mm. [gm] satb choir. Fugue.
Sequence: 1284 mm., 7 movements.

Dies irae: 184 mm. Composer: Antonio Bazzini (11.3.1818–10.2.1897)

This virtuoso violinist was an instrumental composer who taught composition at the Conservatory in Milan and, in 1882, became its director. His pupils include Puccini and Catalani. Bazzini wrote string quartets and quintets, overtures, symphonic poems, and one opera. *Dies irae* [cm] *allegro maestoso ma non lento*. satb choir. (vv. 1–2).

Tuba mirum: 126 mm. Composer: Carlo Pedrotti (12.11.1817–16.11.1893)

Pedrotti was a conductor and composer of opera. He wrote sixteen operas and some church music. In 1868, he was appointed director of Turin Conservatory and, in 1883, director of the *Liceo Rossini* at Pesaro. Ten years later, in a fit of depression, he drowned himself. *Tuba mirum* [E flat M] *andante maestoso*. bar solo/satb choir. (vv. 3–6).

Quid sum miser: 124 mm. Composer: Antonio Cagnoni (8.2.1828–30.4.1896)

Cagnoni composed a significant quantity of church music. In 1886, he was appointed *Maestro di capella* at *Santa Maria Maggiore* in Bergamo. *Quid sum miser* [A flat M] *larghetto*. SA soli duet. (vv. 7–8). Companion piece to *Tuba mirum*.

Recordare: 161 mm. Composer: Federico Ricci (22.11.1828–10.12.1877)

Ricci was a well-known opera composer who worked from 1853 to 1869 as inspector of the vocal classes at the Imperial Theater in St. Petersburg, Russia. He composed nineteen operas, two cantatas, mass settings, and a voluminous amount of solo songs. *Recordare* [FM] *andantino*. SATB solo quartet. Themes are treated in rondo-like fashion. (vv. 9–11).

Ingemisco: 216 mm. Composer: Alessandro Nini (11.1.1805–27.12.1880).

Nini was director of the Singing School in St. Petersburg, a position he held from 1830 to 1837. In 1843, he was appointed *Maestro de cappella* at Novara Cathedral. From 1847 to the end of his career, he held a similar position at St. Maria Maggiore and the *Istituto Musicale* in Bergamo. He wrote seven operas and much church music, including one requiem. He was a close friend of Rossini. *Ingemisco* [am] *poco largo*. T solo/satb choir. Rondo-like structure. (vv. 12–14).

Confutatis: 176 mm. Composer: Raimondo Boucheron (15.3.1800–28.2.1876)

In 1829, Boucheron was appointed *Maestro di cappella* at Vigevano Cathedral and later, in 1847, at the Milan Cathedral. He remained in this position until his death. He composed only two operas, a treatise on harmony (1856), and a large quantity of church music. *Confutatis* [DM] *allegro moderato*. B solo/satb choir; *Oro supplex*, *andante sostenuto*. B solo/satb choir. (vv. 15–16).

Lacrimosa: 297 mm. Composer: Carlo Coccia (14.4.1782–13.4.1873)

During his career, Coccia wrote about forty operas and a great deal of church music. From 1823 to 1828, he was professor of composition at the Royal Academy of Music in London. *Lacrimosa* [GM] *andante*. TTBB choir, unaccompanied; *Amen* [cm] *allegro vivo*. satb choir. Fugue. (vv. 17–19).

Offertory: 213 mm. Composer: Gaetano Gaspari (14.3.1807–31.3.1881)

Maestro di cappella (1857–1866) at St. Petronio in Bologna, Gaspari was primarily a composer of church music. *Domine Jesu Christe* [CM] *moderato*. S solo/satb choir; *Quam olim Abrahae, allegro*. SAT soli/satb choir; *Hostias, andantino*. SATB quartet; *Quam olim Abrahae*, SA soli/satb choir.

Sanctus: 166 mm. Composer: Pietro Platania (5.4.1828–26.4.1907)

Platania was a conductor and composer from Milan who spent much of his career as the director of the Palermo Conservatory (1863–87) and director of the Naples Conservatory (1888–1902). He composed a half-dozen operas, some church music, including a requiem, and wrote a textbook on canon and fugue. *Sanctus* [D flat M] *maestoso*. satb choir; *Pleni sunt coeli,* [A flat M] S solo/satb choir; *Hosanna* [A flat M] satb choir (*concertante*) Fugue; *Benedictus* [D flat M] S solo/satb choir (*concertante*); *Pleni sunt coeli* and *Osanna* are repeated.

Agnus Dei: 78 mm. Composer: Lauro Rossi (19.2.1812–5.5.1885)

Rossi was a composer and conductor. He wrote twenty-nine operas, an oratorio, masses, cantatas, and a textbook on harmony. He was appointed to the directorship of Milan Conservatory (1850) and a similar position at the Naples Conservatory (1870). *Agnus Dei* [AM] *andante*. A solo. It is a companion piece to the *Sanctus*.

Communion: 155 mm. Composer: Teodulo Mabellini (2.4.1817–10.3.1897)

Mabellini was an opera composer and conductor. He was a professor of composition at the conservatory in Florence (1859–1887). He was also appointed *Maestro di cappella* to the court in Florence (1847) and a conductor at the Pergola Theater (Florence, 1848). *Lux aeterna* [A flat M] *moderato*. TBarB solo trio.

Responsory: 391 mm. Composer: Giuseppe Verdi.

This movement is the original version of the *Libera Me* that Verdi later used in the *Manzoni Requiem*. A comparison of both settings will reveal a number of minor, but significant, changes from the original setting. *Libera me* S solo/satb choir.

DISCOGRAPHY

Hanssler Classic, #98.949, Gachinger Kantorei Stuttgart, Prague Philharmonic Choir, Stuttgart Radio-Symphony Orchestra, dir. Helmuth Rilling.

8

The Twentieth Century

INTRODUCTION

The sensual, naturalistic romanticism of the nineteenth century gave way to a tense, dissonant, modernistic twentieth-century musical style in what could be described as one of the most violent and aggressive upheavals in artistic thought in the history of Western music. The most prominent result of this turmoil turned out to be a musical scheme reminiscent of a giant fresco—a mosaic of many contrasting styles that ultimately came to be labeled "isms." They include impressionism, expressionism, socialist realism, neo-classicism, serialism, minimalism, and modernism. Adding to the eclectic mixture are such genres as jazz, new age, and experimental music. A closer examination of the vast course of musical history and artistic tradition has revealed no comparable proliferation of these and many other individual styles.

The twentieth-century requiem demonstrates the influence of these many diverse genres, and has been composed in almost every style, ranging from the impressionist canvas to the aleatoric and nonpitched works of the late 1900s. Contemporary settings can be divided into three major groups: the liturgical requiem, the secular requiem, and the war requiem.

THE LITURGICAL REQUIEM

Impressionism stands as one of the twentieth century's earliest musical movements. Resembling the double-headed Roman god Janus, impressionism developed as a streamlined, more stoic version of romanticism, serving as a stepping stone from the nineteenth to the twentieth century.

The French, reacting to the hyperactive twinge of the romantic move-ment, sculpted this new genre with nebulous, evanescent harmonies, floating rhythms, fragmentary melodies, and dreamy moods. Pentatonic and whole-tone scales, as well as the older church modes, led to a fresh, new sound, and the large romantic orchestra with a pared-down arrange-ment allowed for an innovative lightness in the music's sonorities and tex-ture.

The language of impressionism was employed in the requiem settings of Henri Le François (1942–52), Alfred Desenclos (1963), and Maurice Duruflé (1947), whose requiem remains one of the most popular settings in the repertory. This language combined with a more concise rhythm and discordant harmony can be identified in the settings composed by Roger Calmel (1993), Guy Ropartz (1937–38), Jean Rivier (1953), and Dan-iel Pinkham (1962 and 1992), as well as in the ultramodern setting by Renaud Gagneux (1982).

Expressionism, an anguished and highly emotional style of music, first came to life in Germany. An outgrowth of the most overripe romanticism, this particular style often delved into the shadowy recesses of the human soul and the many nuances of the social landscape. Expressionism also differed from impressionism in its utilization of the chromatic scale as part of a highly organized and rational system that scrutinized and exper-imented with its melodic and harmonic potential. Ultimately, this style came to be known as "serialism," invoking a system in which all twelve tones of the scale were granted complete equality, a musical democracy, per se, that allowed for no single tone to take precedence over another. This accounted for a sonorous unity among the various composers who chose to adhere to this style.

Expressionism eventually paved the way for a genre of music within which was feasible a total liberation from dissonance. Throughout recorded history, Western music's harmony and melody had made use of a regulated form of consonance (relaxation) and dissonance (tension) through functional harmony, which was determined by the greater or lesser importance of the notes available within the scale. Expressionism efficiently eradicated this conventionally accepted hierarchy of notes. Some historians have identified expressionism as an agonized rendering of romanticism, while others have explained it as a breakdown and col-lapse of the traditional harmonic system.

Most often, it is recognized as atonal music. In this newer system, the wavering relay between the sensations of tension and relaxation are achieved by the wielding of a greater or lesser amount of dissonance in intermittently varying dynamic levels within the overall tonal fabric. Once the liberation of dissonance had been adequately secured, compos-ers took advantage of the new opportunities to further push the musical boundaries until they ultimately transcended themselves into the area of nonpitched sound.

Expressionism's influence can be cited in a significant number of twentieth-century concert requiem settings. Works by Erich Urbanner (1982–83), Volker David Kirchnner (1988), Rafael Kubelik (1961), Helmut Barbe (1965), Arvo Pärt (1989), Igor Stravinsky (1966), Paul Patterson (1974), Boris Blacher (1958), Andrew Imbrie (1984), Robert Wittinger (1984–86), and Sandro Gorli (1989) all expound a dependency upon expressionist techniques. Nonpitched sound is clearly employed by such composers as Geörgy Ligeti (1963–65), Erikki-Sven Tüür (1994), and Renaud Gagneux (1982).

The more traditional-harmonic, "modernist" settings of Frank Martin (1971–71), Virgil Thomson (1960), Krzysztof Penderecki (1980–1993), Joonas Kokkonen (1979), Franco Mannino (1987), Alfred Schnittke (1974–75), Elinor Remick Warren (1966), Sándor Szokolay (1964), Frank Lewin (1969), Elis Pekhonen (1986), Heinrich Sutermeister (1952), and Benjamin Britten (1961) encompass large amounts of dissonance that would have been deemed unthinkable had it not been for the prior experiments undertaken by the followers of the expressionist school. The *Requiem of Reconciliation*, a collaborative effort on the part of thirteen composers, stands as an encyclopedia of atonal musical styles, while the *Requiem*, a dramatic, aleatoric composition by Luboš Fišer (1968) surpasses even the most experimental atonal works by extending further into the universe of sound and microtonality. The Fišer piece is almost entirely characterized by nonpitched sound, yet the violent, surrealistic setting stands as one of the great contemporary requiem masterpieces.

In direct contrast to the expressionist works and the many experimental liberties their composers embraced are the neo-classic settings for choir and organ, created by their composers who chose to meticulously adhere to the spirit and ideals set forth by the Caecilian Movement. The evocation of spiritual devotion and piety are a *sine qua non* for these particular settings, with traditional harmony, rhythm, and melody establishing themselves as key features in the genre. Complete chant intonations or fragments of the Gregorian funeral melodies are prevalent within the matrix of the requiem settings by Jehan Alain (1938), Karl Koch (1955–58), Pietro Yon (1917), Ernst Tittel (1949), Lorenzo Perosi (1950), Karl Höller (1932), Licinio Refice (early twentieth century), and Vincenzo Tommasini (1944). These works, serving as exceptional models of this style of writing, continued to be regularly performed until the emergence of the Second Vatican Council (1962–65), at which time the use of Latin in the liturgy plummeted into an abyss of benign neglect.

Other neo-classic styles and traditions can be cited in the fugal and canonic composition techniques of Heinrich Sutermeister, Karl Höller, and

Frank Martin. The settings of Jehan Alain and Healey Willan (1912–18) meanwhile employed a modal harmonic style, the latter inspired by the Anglican Revival.

A revival of the polyphonic Renaissance approach was cultivated in the unaccompanied concert requiem settings by Ildebrando Pizzetti (1922), Randall Thompson (1957), Georges Migot (1953), and Humphrey Clucas (1988). Noteworthy also are the grand, large-scale, neo-romantic style requiems of 1960 composed by Marc Eychenne (b. 1933) and Roman Maciejewski (b. 1910). Popular music composers have made the foray into the genre as well, creating serious settings of the Latin requiem. Andrew Lloyd-Webber's requiem setting encompasses elements of the Broadway musical production coupled with contemporary Anglican church-music style, most discernable in the *Hosanna* fugue. Renowned Polish film composer Zbiegniew Preisner created *Requiem for my Friend*, a new wave-style piece that includes the Latin text along with several other Biblical texts. The orchestration in this work is, for the most part, "minimalist" with a sense of personal intimacy. In 1933, Swedish composer Nils Lindberg (b. 1933) developed a jazz setting of the Latin requiem scored for two soprano soloists, one tenor soloist, instrumental soloists, SATB choir, and a big jazz band. This composition is unique for its Gregorian melodies and old church modes interwoven with the jazz-style funeral music made famous in New Orleans.

THE SECULAR REQUIEM

Throughout the twentieth century, the gap between liturgical and nonliturgical requiems had grown noticeably wider, culminating in a vast diversity of requiem settings and text. The beginning of this trend can be traced back to the romantic era with the debut of Goethe's *Requiem für Mignon*. Musical settings of this text were created by Robert Schumann (c. 1849), Anton Rubenstein (1872), Hans Gál (1923), and Theodore Streicher (1913). The Friedrich Hebbel poem, *Seele, vergiss sie nicht,* was employed by Max Reger (1915) and Peter Cornelius (1872).

Of the requiems cited in this volume, only a small number of the war requiems (Levitin, Kabalevsky, Delius, Foulds), the *Requiem* by Randall Thompson, *Stones, Time and Elements: A Humanist Requiem* by Edgar Grana, and the *Requiem for Fourteen Unaccompanied Voices* by Sandro Gorli are devoid of any use of liturgical text. Virtually all other nonliturgical settings acknowledged here employ at least some portion of the Latin canon in conjunction with other poetry and prose. For his *Ultima Rerum* (Final Things), Gerard Victory adopted texts from a great variety of sources, which included poetry by Alfred Tennyson, Giacomo Leopardi,

William Blake, Walt Whitman, and James Flecker, the Norse *Edda,* a Navaho Indian chant, and passages from the Koran, to provide commentary for the requiem text. In contrast, Geörgy Ligeti and Luboš Fišer chose to limit their lyrical resources to portions of the Latin text.

Gavin Bryars applied the poetry of the *Creation Hymn,* written by Cadmeon, the oldest-known English poet, and fused it with the texts for the Introit, *Kyrie, Agnus Dei,* and in *Paradisum.* For his Czech Requiem, Ladislav Vycpálek combined the riches of the sequence hymn, *Dies Irae,* several passages from the Psalms, the story of the raising of Lazarus, the book of Ecclesiastes (taken from the Kralicka Bible), and a medieval Czech hymn entitled *Jesus Christ, thou generous knight.* For their settings, Zbiegniew Preisner and Paul Patterson compiled Biblical passages previously excluded from the requiem canon alongside the usual prayers. Thomas Beveridge wedded the Hebrew prayers to those of the Latin requiem, while Elis Pehkonen adorned the text of *Russian Requiem* with poetic passages from Pasternak's *Winter Poems* and several violent political passages from the writings of Lenin. James DeMars' *American Requiem* embraced a collection of multicultural "American" themes from the likes of Walt Whitman, Martin Luther King, and several Native American philosophers, as well as the Yizkor (Memorial) prayers of the Jewish liturgy. In a combination of contemporary language and traditional style, Frank Lewis' *Mass for the Dead* is a straightforward English translation of the Latin liturgical text.

THE WAR REQUIEM

The war requiem is truly a product of the twentieth century, during which time the concept of war had played an eminent role in the annals of civilization. History records two world wars, the Armenian genocide, the Korean War, the Vietnam War, the Russian genocides during the Stalin regime, the slaughter of uncounted millions during the Great Leap Forward and Cultural Revolution in China, the genocide in Rwanda, the Catholic versus Protestant violence of Northern Ireland, the war between Iraq and Iran, and the "ethnic cleansing" of the former states of Yugoslavia, all of which constitute an era of contemporary strife akin to the "Dark Ages." The emergence of the war requiem was a direct consequence of this brutal time in history.

Romantic composer Joseph Rheinberger's *C Minor Requiem,* dedicated to those who perished in the German War of 1870–71, appears to be one of the earliest models of this genre. The Great War (World War I) inspired the settings of Reger (1913–16), Delius (1913–1916), Hristič (*Opelo,* 1915), Walford Davies (*Anglican Requiem,* 1915), Kastalsky (*Fraternal Commemora-*

tion, 1916), and John Foulds (*World Requiem*, 1923). Of these particular settings, only those by Kastalsky, Foulds, and Delius are not liturgical, although Kastalsky eventually composed a second version that was suitable as an orthodox *Panikhida*.

Requiem settings inspired by the tragic history and events of World War II include compositions by Britten (*War Requiem*, 1961), Kabalevsky (*War Requiem*, 1962), Levitin (*Реквием памяти павших героев*, 1946), *Requiem in memory of fallen heros*), Mauersberger (*Dresden Requiem*, 1946–48), Hindemith (*Requiem, When lilacs last in the dooryard bloomed*, 1948), Zeisl (*Requiem Ebraico*, 1944–45), Tomasi (*Requiem pour la paix*, 1945), and the collaborative *Requiem of Reconciliation*, 1995). Other war requiems include Dimiter Petkov's *Sailor's requiem* (1968) and Andrey Paschenko's *Requiem in memory of the Heroic Warrior* (1942). Of all the World War II settings, only that of Tomasi is a liturgical requiem, containing a passage for trumpet and timpani in the *Agnus Dei* movement that evokes the sonorities of the military burial service.

The *Requiem of Reconciliation* and Britten's *War Requiem* both make use of the liturgical text, to which are added the composers' own unique contributions. The *Requiem of Reconciliation* employs several additional texts in the opening and closing movements, while the Britten work glosses the Latin text in every movement and adopts the World War I poetry of Wilfrid Owen. The antiwar stance expressed in Owen's poetry stands in stark contrast to the themes prevalent in the work of his contemporaries, many of whom had turned out pieces praising the glory and virtue of war. (see *Songs and Poems of the Great War*, ed. Donald Tulloch. The David Press, Worcester, Massachusetts, 1915)

The requiem settings of Levitin and Kabalevsky utilize humanistic texts, and similar to the settings of Paschenko and Petkov, are in many places heavily shaded with the language of Soviet realism. The Russian works are dedicated to the memory of those who perished in the Great Homeland War (World War II) with texts that provide a brief glimpse into an historical event that looms large in Soviet–Russian memory. Mauersberger's setting employs Biblical texts as well as a number of Evangelical German church hymns to lament the destruction of the city of Dresden, the "Venice of Northern Europe," and the war-related deaths of its citizens.

The loss of life during the American Civil War and the assassination of President Abraham Lincoln proved inspiration for the requiem setting composed by Hindemith, who utilized the poetry of Walt Whitman. Hindemith drew a parallel between the subject of Whitman's poetry and World War II and the death of Franklin Roosevelt.

A number of special compositions were created in tribute to the victims of the Holocaust, including the oratorio, *Dies Irae* (1966) by Kryzsztof

Penderecki; for the victims of Auschwitz, the *Holocaust Requiem* (1986) of Ronald Senator (based upon poems and diaries of children who had died in Theresienstadt), the *Gypsy Requiem* (*Requiem Zigeuner*) (1990) of Gerhard Rosenfeld, a *Requiem for the fate of the Jews* (1993–95) by Simon Lazar, *Kleines Requiem*, Burkhard Soll's *Korczak und seiner Kinder* (1991), the *Requiem für eine Verfolgte-in Memoriam Anne Frank* (1961) of Heine Lau, and *Requiem Ebraico* (1944–45) by Eric Zeisl. The Zeisl setting is based exclusively on the Biblical text of Psalm 92, but the others employed texts derived and compiled from many divergent sources.

INSTRUMENTAL WORKS

One other category of instrumental and orchestral requiem music emerged in the twentieth century that, although not examined within the covers of this volume, deserves recognition. Perhaps the best-known work of this type is that of Benjamin Britten, *Sinfonia da Requiem* (1940). Other works include, *Requiem Father Kolbe*, 1990s (Wociech Kilar), *Requiem for Strings*, 1960 (Toro Takemitsu), *Requiem for Three Cellos* (David Popper), *Requiem for Orchestra* (Wesley LaViolette), *Requiem, Nine Sacred Concertos*, 1990 (Hans Werner Henze, *Requiem for the Party Girl* (R. Murray Schaffer), *Symphony #4*, Op. 34, "*Requiem*," 1943 (Howard Hanson), *Requiem for Oboe and Strings*, 1951 (Robert Bloom), *Requiem for Flute*, 1956 (Kazuo Fukushima), *Requiem for Piano* (Marga Richter), *Requiem for String Orchestra*, Op. 1442, 1974 (Dimitry Shostakovitch), *Kleines Requiem für eine Polka* for piano and 13 instruments, Op. 66, 1993 (Henryk Gorecki), and *Symphonie Liturgique*, 1946 (Arthur Honegger).

JEHAN ALAIN
February 3, 1911–June 20, 1940

Jehan Alain, a highly talented French composer, studied organ with Marcel Dupré and composition with Paul Dukas and Roger Ducasse. His brief life along with his musical promise ended during the first year of the Second World War. He left a highly original body of work, most of which was composed in the last few years before his death.

These works include a number of organ works, *Litanies* (1937), *Trois Danses* (1937–38), *Deuxième Fantasie* (1936), and *Variations sur un Theme de Clément Jannequin* (1937). Among the choral pieces are several motets, an *Ave Maria* for organ and soprano; a *Messe brève* for soprano, alto, flute, organ, and string quartet (1938); and a three-movement *Requiem* written in 1938.

The *Requiem* uses Gregorian requiem themes, placed in the tenor or bass line, in each of its movements. Composed in imitative polyphonic style, it is a short, attractive work employing modal harmonies. Canonic writing can be found between the bass/soprano and the alto/tenor in the *Agnus Dei*.

Basic Data

EDITION

Messe de Requiem für gemischten Chor und Orgel
edited by Marie-Claire Alain
Orgelpartitur (organ-vocal)
Doblinger (44 121) 1991

DURATION

Three movements, 82 mm.

VOICING AND ORCHESTRATION

Choir: SATB range: S-F6; B-G3
Instruments: org.

OUTLINE

Kyrie: 19 mm. [FM] *sans lenteur*. satb choir. Chant melody in ATB lines.
Sanctus: 25 mm. [em] *molto sostenuto*. satb choir. Chant melody in B.; *Benedictus* [am] satb choir.
Agnus Dei: 38 mm. [GM] *assez lent*. satb choir.

DISCOGRAPHY

1. Arion ARN68321 Radio France.

LUCIEN-MARIE AUBE
July 1, 1889–June 3, 1953

As of 1999, the name of the French composer, Aube, does not appear in any standard biographical reference. Judging from the works listed in the card catalogue of the Bibliothèque Nationale in Paris, he appears to have been primarily a composer of French *mélodies*. Although he wrote many such pieces, he wrote a number of larger-scale compositions for other mediums: a one-act ballet, *Le mendiant de Marrakech* (The Beggar of Marrakesh) (1926), an orchestral work, *Petite Suite "1830,"* (1952), *Poème Symphonique* for orchestra, *Sur les marches d'un trône*, a dramatic interlude for orchestra (1926), *Sous les voûtes d'un temple*, a dramatic prelude for orchestra (1926), Prelude Number Two for orchestra (1930), and *Danse Russe* for orchestra (1930). There exists the *Sonate provençale* (1952) for piano. The cantata, *La Crèche merveilleuse, conte provençal du 18e siècle en 3 tableaux* (The Miraculous Creche, an eighteenth-century Provençal tale in three scenes) 1924, is scored for soli, choir, and orchestra.

Since a large portion of his music is scored for voice and piano and because this data is not readily available, it is listed here. These pieces include: *Marionettes* (words of Paul Max) 1932, *Amoroso* (Paul Max) 1932, *Flirt* (Paul Max) 1932, *Sérénata* (Paul Max) 1932, *Bathilde* (André Joubert) 1949, *C'est un vent d'amour* (Guy Sella), 1943, *Sept chansons badines* (André Canal) 1943, *Les chats* (Baudelaire) 1943, *L'examen de minuit* (Baudelaire), *Francais, reveille-toi, Chant de la France nouvel* (René Celier) 1940, *Les Galeriens* (Constant Hubert) 1950, *Je voudrais* (André Joubert) 1949, *Marie Madeleine* (Albert Willemetz) 1949, *Ne cherchez pas mon âme* (André Joubert) 1949, *Sur ton bâteau* (Jane Dumont) 1945, *Tu sais si bien les dire* (Jane Dumont) 1945, *La volière* (Ch. Pothier) 1949 and *Vos yeux* (André Joubert) 1949. Larger works include, *Le mort de Chopin* (Stephane Servant) for dramatic soprano, and the song album, *La vie et la mort d'une rose,* (Louis Poterat)—ten *mélodies* for voice and piano, 1950.

Aube composed two sets of liturgical pieces, *Six Motets* for four-part choir and organ (1943) (includes *O quam suavis, Sub tuum praesidum, Princeps glorisissimi, Tu es Petrus, In paradisum and Libera me*), and *Fumée d'encens,* eleven motets for one voice and organ (1943) (includes *Ave verum, Cor dulce, O esca viatorum, Ave Maria, Ave Regina coelorum, Maria mater gratiae, Virgo Dei genetrix, Ego sum, Pie Jesu, and Qui Lazaram*).

Judging on the basis of the people to whom Aube dedicated his pieces, he must have had a wide circle of friends, including soloists at the Opéra Comique, The National Opera, and a number of clergy at various Parisian churches. The *Pie Jesu* was dedicated to the memory of his daughter, Lucette-Thérèse, and *In Paradisum* was dedicated to the memory of his mother.

Last is the *Requiem* composed to commemorate the death of Reynaldo Hahn, a composer of *mélodies*. Reynaldo Hahn was a popular Venezuelan-born composer-conductor who worked as the conductor for the National Opera Theatre in Paris from 1945–46. The *Requiem*, scored for SATB choir, SATB soli, strings, harp, and organ was premiered on January 28, 1948, in l'Eglise de la Madeleine (Paris). The soloists, chorus, and orchestra of the National Opera Theatre, as well as the Maitrise (choir) of the Church of the Madeleine were conducted by Aube on this occasion.

Its musical style is simple and direct, much like that of the *mélodies* that Hahn composed. It is a completely tonal work, tinged with modal and impressionistic harmonies. The tranquil mood of the piece is much like the *Requiem* of Fauré, gentle and quiet. Aube chose not to set the *Dies irae*.

The basic choral fabric is a four-part homophonic texture, with occasional *divisi* in the male voices. A unique feature of the choral fabric are the textless, hummed passages (*Kyrie*-SA, *Lux aeterna*, SSAA). The arpeggiated figures of string and harp accompaniment provide a warmth and intimacy to the music.

Basic Data

EDITION

Requiem de Lucien-Marie Aube
[full score]
Enoch & Cie. Paris [E & C 9359] 1958

DURATION

Nine movements, 437 mm.

VOICING AND ORCHESTRATION

Choir: SATB [TB *divisi*] range: S-A6; B-B flat 3
Soloists: SATB
Orchestra: vn. I/II, vla., vc., db., harp, org.

OUTLINE

Introit: 52 mm.
   Requiem aeternam [CM] *modéré (sans lenteur)* satb choir/A solo; *Te decet*, A solo; *Requiem aeternam*. ABA form.
Kyrie: 57 mm. A-B-A form
   Kyrie [CM] *très modéré*. sattbb choir, unaccompanied; *Christe*, SAT soli; *Kyrie*, SATB solo quartet.
Offertory: 79 mm.
   Domine Jesu Christe [CM], *modéré, très recueilli*, B solo; *Quam olim Abrahae*, ssat choir; *Hostias*, B solo/satb choir.
Sanctus: 30 mm.
   Sanctus [DM] *large*. satb choir; *Pleni sunt coeli*, T solo; *Hosanna*, satb choir.
Pie Jesu: 52 mm.
   Pie Jesu [CM-cm] *lent, très soutenu*. T solo/satb choir, unaccompanied.
Agnus Dei: 57 mm.
   Agnus Dei I [G flat M-E flat M] *modéré*. satb choir; *Agnus Dei* II [E flat M] A solo; *Agnus Dei* III [E flat M] satb choir.
Communion: 32 mm.
   Lux aeterna [E flat M] *très modéré*. satb choir/S solo.
Responsory: 78 mm.
   Libera me [CM] *modéré*. satb choir, unaccompanied; *Tremens factus* [cm] *presque vif*. B solo; *Dies illa* [CM-cm] satb choir; *Dum veneris*, B solo; *Requiem aeternam*, sstt choir, unaccompanied; *Libera me*, satb choir.
An alternate *Kyrie* (9 mm.) and a motet, *Ego sum* (42 mm.) is included.

DISCOGRAPHY
None found.

ROGER CALMEL
May 31, 1921–July 3, 1998

The contemporary Parisian composer, Roger Calmel received his musical education at the Paris Conservatoire where he studied with Olivier Messiaen, Jean Rivier, and Darius Milhaud. In 1956, he earned the Grand Prix de la Ville de Paris; in 1959, the Premiere Prix de la Confederation national de France. In 1963, he was appointed to the position of professor to the *Maitrise* of Radio-Télévision Française and to the directorship of the Conservatoire Darius Milhaud in 1974.

Among his compositions for the stage are a musical comedy, a ballet, and an opera. His large body of work for the orchestra includes two piano concertos (1959, 1971), a *Concertino for Alto Sax and Chamber Orchestra* (1954), *Concertino for Sax Quartet and String Orchestra* (1957), *Concerto for Cello* (1963), *Concerto for Oboe and String Orchestra* (1968), *Symphony for Strings and Percussion* (1961), and an *Organ Concerto* (1968). His a small amount of chamber music and an important group of choral works include an oratorio, *La Passion* (1958); *Psaume 54* (1962); *Stabat Mater* (1971); *Triptyque liturgique* for soprano and string orchestra (1975); an oratorio, *Marie au Calvaire* (1976); and two requiems for choir, soloists, and orchestra (1979, 1993).

The *Requiem* of 1979, scored for baritone solo, SATB choir, and orchestra is dedicated to Marcel Corneloup, the leader of a choral renaissance in France, known as *Mouvement à Coeur Joie*. This movement has been active in the advancement of choral singing and the promotion of new choral works. The requiem is an impressive tonal work that employs a triadic as well as nontriadic harmonic vocabulary. At the same time, the musical language also has strong roots in impressionist harmony. The musical lines that form the harmony appear to be conceived in a linear, polyphonic fashion; although the work is scored in C, there are numerous chromatic twists in the melodic lines. The four-part choral texture is frequently reduced to unison and two-part writing. Most of the melodic phrasing is asymmetrical in shape.

Calmel employed several older musical devices; a canon for the SA duet, *Mors stupebit*, choral ostinati for the tenors and basses on the texts, *Dies irae, dies illa*, and *Lux aeterna*, numerous ostinati in the bass instruments, points of imitation in the *Kyrie*, and a repeated, quarter-note, *"e"* pedalpoint (suggesting a funeral cortège) in the Introit. The music for the *Pie Jesu* (soprano solo and trumpet) is particularly engaging and spiritual.

Unlike the better-known French requiem settings by Fauré, Duruflé, and Ropartz, the *Requiem* of Calmel includes a violent setting of the *Dies irae*.

Basic Data

EDITION

Roger Calmel
Requiem pour baryton solo, choeur mixte et orchestre.
Editions A COEUR JOIE. Les Passerelles 24, avenue Joannes Masset
69009 Lyon, France. 1983
[There also exists a choral/piano version]

DURATION

Eight movements, 740 mm.

VOICING AND ORCHESTRATION

Choir: SATB range: S-B flat 6; B-E3
Soloists: Baritone
Orchestra: vn. I/II, vla. I/II, vc. I/II, db., tpt., timp., org.

OUTLINE

Introit-*Kyrie*: 93 mm.
> *Requiem aeternam, recueilli.* satb choir; *Kyrie, plus allant.* satb choir. Ostinato fig-ure [long-short-long-short-long-long] on "e," 5/4 meter. *Divisi* strings and SATB choir unfold their musical material over the ostinato.

Sequence: 319 mm.
> *Dies irae-Quantus tremor, rude et violent.* satb choir; *Dies irae,* satb choir; *Tuba mirum, large et très lent.* tb choir; *Mors stupebit, andante.* sa choir; *Liber scriptus, très soutenu.* Bar. or A solo/tb choir (ostinato on *"Dies irae"*); *Judex ergo,* S solo/Bar. or A solo/tb choir (ostinato on *"Dies irae"*); *Rex tremendae, rude et violent.* satb choir; *Lacrymosa,* satb choir; *Dies irae, rude et violent.* satb choir.

Offertoire: 65 mm.
> *Domine Jesu Christe, andante, très sostenuto.* unison men or Bar. solo; *Libera eas de ore leonis, allegro marcato.* satb unison choir; *Signifer Sancta Michael, andante.* sa unison choir. Orchestral ostinato bass.

Sanctus: 66 mm.
> *Sanctus, large.* satb choir; *Benedictus, piu moderato.* satb choir (canon between men's and women's voices); *Hosanna, moderato.* satb choir.

Pie Jesu: 26 mm. *lent et recueilli* [slow and meditative]
> *Pie Jesu, lent et recueilli.* S solo/trumpet solo.

Agnus Dei-Communion: 77 mm.
> *Agnus Dei I, II, III, modere.* satb choir; *Lux aeterna, andante.* satb choir (tb choir ostinato *"Lux aeterna"*); *Requiem aeternam,* satb choir (spoken/sung).

Responsory: 67 mm.
> *Libera me* [very slow] Bar. solo/satb choir. Concluding pedalpoint on C 3-4. Final C major chord.

In Paradisum: 27 mm.
  In paradisum, très recueilli satb choir.

DISCOGRAPHY
None found.

The *Requiem à la mémoire de Marie Antoinette* was composed for the bicentenary commemoration of the death of Marie Antoinette, guillotined on October 16, 1793. Its tonal language and musical style are the same as the 1979 *Requiem*. A number of pieces from the 1979 requiem setting were reworked by the composer for this setting. The rhythmic ostinato found in the earlier Introit setting reappears in 3/4 meter, instead of the 5/4 meter of the 1993 work. The *Benedictus* employs the same melody of the earlier work, as well its canonic treatment. The *Mors stupebit* sections of both requiem settings are the same (both melodically and textually) and, last, there are identical rhythmic ostinati on the words *Dies irae* in both requiem settings.

Basic Data
EDITIONS

1. Roger Calmel
Requiem pour choeurs à 4 voix mixtes.
Edition M. Combre #C 5495 1993
24 Blvd Poissonnière 75009 Paris
[vocal score]

2. Requiem à la mémoire de la Reine
Marie Antoinette
[full score]
Editions M. Combre. 1993
[rental only]

DURATION
Seven movements, 603 mm., perf., c. 36′

VOICING AND ORCHESTRATION
Choir: SATB [occasional S II/Bar] range: S-G # 6; B-E3
Soloists: SBar
Orchestra: vn. I/II, vla., vc., db., fl., ob., cl., bsn., 2 Fh., 2 tpt., PERC: timp., suspended cymbals, chimes, gong, side drum, bass drum.

OUTLINE
Introit-*Kyrie*: 102 mm.
  Requiem aeternam, grave; *Et lux*; *Requiem aeternam*; *Kyrie*; *Requiem aeternam*. satb choir. Rhythmic ostinato suggests funeral cortège.
Sequence: 207 mm.
  Dies irae, allegro furioso. satb choir (Gregorian *Dies irae* melody quoted.); *Quantus tremor*, satb choir; *Dies irae*, satb choir; *Tuba mirum, andante*. Bar. solo; *Mors stupebit*, sa choir (canon); *Liber scriptus*, S solo/ssatbarb choir (strings accompany

Dies irae ostinato); *Rex tremendae,* unison satb choir (Gregorian melody); *Record-are,* satb choir; *Lacrymosa,* satb choir (canonic writing); *Dies irae,* satb choir (speaking passage). The Gregorian melody appears in the trumpet, bassoon, and string bass at various times.

Offertoire: 59 mm.

Domine Jesu Christe, andante. S solo/satb choir; *Libera me, allegro.* Bar. solo/satb choir; *Signifer Sanctus Michael. andante.* S solo/satb choir.

Sanctus-Benedictus: 81 mm.

Sanctus, vigoreux. satb choir; *Benedictus, piu moderato.* S solo/Bar solo; *Hosanna, vigoureux.* satb choir.

Agnus Dei-Communion: 58 mm.

Agnus Dei I, II, III, *dolce.* satb choir; *Lux aeterna-Requiem aeternam.* satb choir.

Responsory: 47 mm.

Libera me, somber. Bar. solo; *Tremens factus,* satb choir; *Quando coeli,* Bar. solo; *Dies irae,* satb choir (Gregorian melody); *Requiem aeternam, piu animato.* satb choir.

In Paradisum: 49 mm.

In Paradisum, recueilli et calme. satb choir. (canonic writing) Choir concludes with *Requiem aeternam.*

DISCOGRAPHY

Histoires de la Musique, 161093, Societé des Chanteurs de Saint-Eustache et orchestre, dir. Bernard Thomas.

HUMPHREY CLUCAS
November 16, 1941

Choral scholar Humphrey Clucas studied at King's College, Cambridge. He later worked as a lay vicar at Westminster Abbey. Although he is self-taught as a composer, his education and long association with important English choirs (including the Vasari Singers) provided a complete familiarity with the choral and vocal idioms. His musical language is tonal (often bi-tonal), yet he has been able to explore tonality in new ways to create an expressive and intensely spiritual body of choral music.

Among his compositions are settings of the Anglican Responses (four morning canticles; six sets of evening canticles); a *Magnificat-Nunc Dimittis*; two dozen English anthems; nine Latin anthems; a *Stabat Mater* for chamber choir, soprano, and string quartet (1992); a *Miserere, Te Deum, Evening Hymns* (1994); as well as three mass settings, including a *Requiem.* Other concert choral works and a dozen organ pieces also exist.

The *Requiem,* scored for unaccompanied soprano and mezzo-soprano soloists, and SSAATTBB choir, was composed in 1988 and premiered in Canterbury Cathedral in the same year. Clucas dedicated the work to the Vasari Singers and their conductor, Jeremy Backhouse.

Within the work Clucas explores various sonorous contrasts through numerous combinations of the choral ensemble, ranging from unison to eight-part chordal writing. The prevailing texture of the work is homophonic, with two very brief imitative passages at *Et tibi* and *Pleni sunt coeli*. Because of the amorphous tonal-modal harmonies of this work and the lack of leading tones, the key indications (see outline) are only approximate designations. The triadic harmonies of seventh chords (used extensively) and their inversions, as well as the parallel harmonies of *Pie Jesu*, suggest the impressionist style. The composer frequently employs enharmonic modulation.

Pedalpoints, such as the "f" found throughout the Introit and concluding *Kyrie* and the "e flat-g" of the alto at *Domine Jesu Christe* and *Hostias* give a sense of "key" to these otherwise chromatic passages. Ostinato-like phrases are employed in the notable 7/4 rhythm of *Pie Jesu* and the three-note repetition of the word *Requiem* in the Communion. Sustained, chordal passages that serve as support for the soloists are found throughout the eight movements. The setting of *In Paradisum* emulates the musical and spiritual tradition of Fauré, Duruflé, and Desenclos. In a broader sense, the overall style of this *Requiem* is modeled after the renaissance choral tradition.

Basic Data

EDITION

Requiem for Soprano & Mezzo-Soprano soli and Unaccompanied Choir
Oecumuse [publisher] 52a Broad St., Ely, Cambridgeshire CB7 4AH
1989

DURATION

Eight movements, 394 mm., perf., c. 19'

VOICING

Choir: SSAATTBB range: S-A flat 6; B-D flat 3
Soloists: soprano, mezzo-soprano

OUTLINE

Introit-*Kyrie*: 55 mm.
　Requiem aeternam [f] *calm, still*. saatbb choir/SS soli; *Et tibi*, sattbb choir; *Orationem meam*, satb-ssaattbb choir; *Kyrie*, S MS soli/atb choir; *Christe*, sattbb choir; *Kyrie*, SS soli/ssatbb choir. ABA form. For much of the movement the choir provides a quiet "f" pedalpoint for the soprano I/II duet.
Offertory: 72 mm.
　Domine Jesu Christe [E flat] *allegretto moderato*. satb-saatbb choir; *Libera eas*, satbb choir/MS solo; *Hostias*, MS solo/ssaatb choir. ABA form.

Sanctus: 46 mm.

Sanctus [f] *allegro, but broadly.* S MS soli/satb [divisi]; *Pleni sunt coeli*, S MS soli/ ssaattbb choir; *Benedictus*, S MS soli (*Benedictus*)/satb choir (*Hosanna*).

Pie Jesu: 28 mm.

Pie Jesu [A flat] *gently flowing, not too slowly.* S solo/ssa choir; coda (*sempiternam*), ssatb choir/S solo. Solo is accompanied by a 7/4 rhythmic choral ostinato.

Agnus Dei: 43 mm.

Agnus Dei I [f] *very moderate speed.* MS solo; *Agnus Dei* II/III, satb choir; *Dona eis requiem*, SS soli/saattbb choir.

Communion: 34 mm.

Lux aeterna, [e flat] *very moderate speed.* MS solo/ssattb choir; *Requiem aeternam*, S MS soli/satb choir. An accompanied duet.

Responsory: 84 mm.

Libera me [c] *fast, with suppressed excitement.* satb choir; *Tremens factus*, saa choir; *Dies illa*, ssatbb choir; *Requiem aeternam, calm, still.* S MS soli/satb choir; *Libera me, fast tempo.* satb choir/S MS soli; concluding *Luceat*, ssaattbb choir.

In Paradisum: 32 mm.

In Paradisum [d flat] *slow, sempre dolce.* ssaattbb choir/S MS soli.

DISCOGRAPHY

United, 88020, Vasari Singers, dir. Jeremy Backhouse.

ALFRED DESENCLOS
February 7, 1912–March 3, 1971

Alfred Desenclos entered the Paris Conservatoire in 1932, later winning prizes in harmony, fugue, and composition. In 1942, he won the prestigious Grand Prix de Rome. He was appointed choirmaster at Notre Dame de Lorette and his earliest compositions were composed for this choir. The compositions of Desenclos include a violin concerto, an orchestral symphony, an orchestral suite, *Vitrail*, saxophone quartet, a piano quintet, and a number of chamber works. Among the choral works are *Pater Noster* (1944), *Nos autem* and *Salve Regina* (1958), *Ave Maria, O salutaris*, and the *Requiem* (1963).

The *Requiem* was initially scored for SATB soli, SATB choir, and orchestra. A later version for SATB soli, SATB choir, and organ was prepared by the composer. This work follows in the tradition of Fauré and Duruflé. Its musical style is a balanced mixture of supple, melismatic, Gregorian-like melodies and impressionistic harmonies fused with an intense spirituality. Desenclos avoided leading tones, thereby creating a strong modal sense. Parallel harmonies and fluid rhythm, typical of impressionist style, are frequently employed. The prevailing four-part choral texture is chordal, with occasional imitative passages (*Te decet, Kyrie, Benedictus, Pie Jesu*, and the final *Requiem aeternam*).

Soloists function as a second choir in a modern version of the older *concertante* style. This liturgical requiem, one that preserves the essence of the Gregorian heritage, is one of the more ravishing and sensual settings of the twentieth century.

Basic Data

EDITION

Alfred Desenclos
Messe de Requiem pour soli, choeurs et orchestre
[reduction pour Chant et Orgue]
Durand. Editions Musicales [1967]

VOICING AND ORCHESTRATION

Choir: SATB [*divisi*] range: S-A6; B-E3
Soloists: SATB
Instruments: org. [or orch.]

DURATION

Seven movements, 542 mm.

OUTLINE

Introit-*Kyrie*: 122 mm.
    Requiem aeternam [bm-f#m] *molto moderato.* satb choir; *Te decet*, satb choir [fugato]; *Requiem aeternam*, satb choir; *Kyrie, non troppo lento.* satb choir [imitation]. ABA & *Kyrie*.
Offertory: 116 mm.
    Domine Jesu Christe [dm-F♯ M] *moderato*; *Libera eas*; *Quam olim Abrahae*, satb choir; *Hostias*, SATB soli;/satb choir; *Quam olim Abrahae*, satb choir.
Sanctus: 61 mm.
    Sanctus [CM] *non troppo lento.* satb choir; *Benedictus*, SATB soli/satb choir [imitation].
Pie Jesu: 39 mm.
    Pie Jesu [bm] *andante.* SATB soli/satb choir [imitation].
Agnus Dei-Communion: 86 mm.
    Agnus Dei I, II, III [fm] *moderato.* SAT soli/satb choir; *Lux aeterna* [EM/c# m] *molto calmo.* saatb choir; *Requiem aeternam* [as in Introit] saattb choir.
Responsory: 94 mm.
    Libera me [b flat m] *moderato.* saatbb choir; *Requiem aeternam* [b flat m] satb choir [imitation].
In Paradisum: 24 mm.
    In Paradisum [EM] *andante.* saatb choir.

DISCOGRAPHY

Hortus, 009, Les Eléments chamber choir and organ.

MAURICE DURUFLÉ
January 11, 1902–June 16, 1986

Duruflé was a pupil of Charles Tournemire and later became his assistant at St. Clothilde. Further studies were done at the Paris Conservatoire, in composition with Paul Dukas and organ with Eugène Gigout. In 1930, he was appointed organist at St. Etienne-du-Mont and in 1943, professor of harmony at the Conservatoire. He left only a handful of superb compositions that include organ pieces, several orchestral works, and a few choral works that include four motets, the *Requiem*, Op. 9 (1947), and *Missa Cum Jubilo* for baritone, choir, and orchestra, Op. 11 (1966).

The oft-performed *Requiem* of Duruflé is one of the more beautiful choral works of the twentieth century. It possesses a remarkable blend of Gregorian chant style and of French impressionism. Like the *Requiem* of Fauré, it lacks the *Dies irae*; its spiritual outlook is tempered by kindness and belief in a more gentle view of the Last Judgment. Its mood is tender, yet there are powerful, moving climaxes within the work. For example, the *Hosanna* of the *Sanctus*, building ever so slowly and quietly, comes to a thundering, majestic climax before tapering off into quietude.

Although much of the choral texture is four-part homophonic style, Duruflé's mastery of counterpoint and fugue is obvious in the *Kyrie, Dum veneris,* and *Hosanna* passages. Gregorian requiem melodies appear in all of the movements, sometimes as a *cantus firmus* (Introit), but more commonly as the basis from which the newly composed melodies were derived. The subject of the *Kyrie* fugue is based upon the Gregorian original. Chant melodies are quoted in the Introit, *Sanctus, Pie Jesu,* and *In Paradisum.* Another unique feature of the work is the use of choral vocalizations, *"ou"* (*Lux aeterna*) and *"a"* (Introit) in settings in which the choir provides a chordal accompaniment with the vocalise while the sopranos sing the chant melody.

Duruflé made three arrangements of the *Requiem,* one for SATB choir and baritone and mezzo-soprano soloists and full orchestra; a second for SATB choir, SBar soli, and organ; and a third for SATB choir, SBar soli, string quintet, three trumpets, harp, timpani, and organ.

Basic Data

EDITION

Maurice Duruflé
Requiem pour Solo, Choeurs, Orchestre et Orgue

[vocal-organ score]
Durand & Cie, Editeurs Paris
D. & F. 13, 373

DURATION

Nine movements, 718 mm., perf., c. 43′

VOICING AND ORCHESTRATION

Choir: SATB [*divisi*] range: S-B flat 6; B-F # 3
Soloists: mezzo-soprano, baritone
Orchestra: vn. I/II, vla., vc., db., 2 ob., Eh., 2 fl., 2 cl., 2 bsn., 2 tpt., 2 tbn., 2 Fh.,
   timp., tamtam, cymbals, harp, org.

OUTLINE

Introit: 63 mm.
   Requiem aeternam, andante moderato. satb choir (canonic); *Te decet,* s choir; *Exaudi,*
   a choir; *Requiem aeternam,* st choir/satb choir. ABA form. (Introit segue to *Kyrie.*)
Kyrie: 74 mm.
   Kyrie, andante. satb choir (fugue); *Christe,* sa choir (canon); *Kyrie,* satb choir.
Offertory: 169 mm.
   Domine Jesu Christe, andante. a choir/satb choir; *Libera eas,* satb choir; *Sed Sig-
   nifer,* s choir; *Quam olim Abrahae,* sa choir; *Hostias,* Bar sol; *Quam olim Abrahae,*
   sa choir.
Sanctus-Benedictus: 66 mm.
   Sanctus, andantino. ssattb choir; *Hosanna,* sa & tb/ssattb choir; *Benedictus,* ssa
   choir.
Pie Jesu: 60 mm.
   Pie Jesu, andante espressivo. mezzo-soprano solo/cello obbligato.
Agnus Dei: 68 mm.
   Agnus Dei I, andantino. a choir; *Agnus Dei* II, t choir; *Agnus Dei* III, sa choir;
   Agnus Dei IV, satb choir; *Dona eis,* satb choir.
Communion: 59 mm.
   Lux aeterna, moderato. satb choir; *Requiem aeternam,* st choir; *Qui pius est,* satb
   choir; *Requiem aeternam,* ab choir.
Responsory: 129 mm.
   Libera me, andantino. satb choir; *Tremens factus, senza rigore.* Bar solo/satb choir;
   Dies illa, animato. b choir/satb choir; *Requiem aeternam, piu lento.* s choir; *Libera
   me, tempo primo.* satb choir (choral version of opening *Libera.*)
In Paradisum: 30 mm.
   In Paradisum, andante moderato. s choir/satb (saattbb *divisi*).

DISCOGRAPHY

1. Telarc, CD-80135, Atlanta Symphony Chorus & Orchestra, cond. Robert Shaw.
2. Hyperion, CDA66757, The Choir of Westminster Cathedral, cond. James
   O'Donnell.
3. Multiple listings in the Schwann Catalogue.

RENAUD GAGNEUX
May 15, 1947

The *Requiem*, written by Renaud Gagneux, is a masterpiece of late twentieth-century musical composition. The composer became interested in creating such a work in 1975 and, upon receiving a commission by Radio France, completed the music in 1982.

It is a composition rooted in French musical tradition; the scoring developed out of the impressionist tradition. Its colorful and massive orchestration is often filled with serenity and lightness, yet the *instrumentarium* is quite capable of registering great force and violence. The musical language of the *Requiem* comes from diverse sources: impressionism, Gregorian chant, Hebrew chant, Russian Orthodox melody, the Lutheran chorale, and harmonic and rhythmic experiments of the twentieth century avant-garde movement. Gagneux further incorporated into the *Requiem* a number of ecumenical elements characteristic of Judaism, Islam, Christianity (bell carillon), and Shinto (percussion instruments), thereby creating a spirit of universality surrounding the work.

Like Hector Berlioz, Gagneux specified precisely which and how many instruments and choral voices were to be employed in the performance of this music. The vocal choir is occasionally employed in four-part texture, but more often is scored for unison and two-part writing to give greater linear clarity for the text. Texts are not only sung, but are also hissed and spoken. Humming on *"om"* and *"um,"* a soothing, calming technique found in Eastern liturgies, such as Buddhism, is employed in this work.

Tonality and atonality, sustained tone clusters, numerous ostinati passages, pitched and nonpitched sound are intermingled in a grand sonorous *mélange*.

Basic Data

EDITION

Conductor's score: manuscript located in the library of Radio France [Editions Durand]

DURATION

Fourteen movements, 653 mm. + unbarred passages, perf., c. 54'

VOICING AND ORCHESTRATION

Choir: SATB (30 for each part) [*divisi*] and children's choir (30)
Soloists: 2 sopranos
Orchestra: 16 vn. I, 14vn. II, 12 vla., 10 vc., 8 db., 2 pic., 4 fl., 4 ob., 2 Eh., 4 cl., 1
    bcl., 4 bsn., 2 cbsn., 6 Fh., 4 tpt., 4 tbn., 2 btbn., 1 tuba, 2 timp. 3 harps, 1 celesta,
    piano. org. PERC: (4 players) xylophone, marimba, glockenspiel, vibraphone,

bells, handbells, 2 clappers, 3 gongs, 4 bongo drums, 2 temple blocks, pitched drum, bass drum, hand cymbals, suspended cymbals, Chinese gong, 3 tam-tams, 3 triangles, guiro, rattle, fovet, 2 wood-chimes, 2 pairs of maracas.

OUTLINE

Introit: *Requiem aeternam*: 56 mm. + unbarred conclusion, perf., 4'52"

The sonorities of opening movement of the *Requiem* are similar to those of the fourth movement of Alberto Ginastera's *Cantata para America Magica*, for fifty-three percussion instruments and dramatic soprano (1963). The composer employed unpitched sound, tinged with a tinkling, magical, and exotic palette of percussion effects and colors—a nocturne for unpitched tone. *Requiem aeternam* [quarter-note = 50], SSSAAATTTBBB choir (tone clusters/eight-part string ostinato patterns/sixteen ostinato patterns-piano/four ostinato patterns-celesta); *Et lux*, two SS soli; *Te decet*, SSSAAATTTBBB choir; *Exaudi*, S solo (reduced orchestra for middle sections); *Requiem aeternam*, same as opening. ABA form.

Kyrie: barred and unbarred passages, perf., c. 3'

Kyrie [quarter-note = 60] tb choir; *Kyrie*, T solo, unaccompanied; *Christe*, sat choir (spoken-sung); *Christe*, T solo/satb choir, (*eleis*)ON; *Kyrie*, T solo; *Christe*, sat choir (spoken-sung), (*eleis*)ON; *Christe*, sat choir (spoken)/satb choir, (*eleis*)ON. Atonal and unpitched.

Sequence: 384 mm., 6 movements. perf. c. 23'

The orchestration of the first of these movements was inspired by the instruments depicted by Peter Brueghel (c. 1525–69), in a painting, titled *The Triumph of Death*. *Dies irae*: 84 mm., orchestral introduction, piano ostinato, ostinato for three harps, strings, timbales; sa choir (*Dies irae*)/tb choir (ostinato on *la-ilahe-illalah*); *Solvet saeculum*, sa choir; *Quantus tremor*, sa choir; *Cuncta stricte*, ssaa choir; *Dies irae*, sa choir. Instrumental ostinati, tb choir ostinato continue throughout the movement. Brass fanfares are placed throughout the piece. The melodies of the handbells, harp, piano, and women's choir are derived from the Gregorian melody. Trumpets and strings quote the plainsong *Dies irae*. The tenor and bass parts on the Latin word *illa* are used as word-play on the Islamic phrase *la ilahe illallah* ("There is no God but one God.") This word-play, on the same text, was earlier used by Frederic Delius in his setting of the requiem.

Tuba mirum: 33 mm., perf., 2'08"

Tuba mirum [quarter-note = 60] tenor choir; *Coget omnes*, sa choir; *Mors stupebit*, soprano choir; (*To*) *tum continetur*, tenor choir; *Judex ergo*, alto choir; *Quem patronem*, soprano choir. The choir rarely sings in four-parts, rather in solo or duet groupings. The instrumental ensemble employs muted strings, quiet percussion passages along with occasional brass fanfares and trombone *glissandi*. (vv. 3–7).

Rex tremendae: 66 mm., perf., 5'09"

This movement is one of the most unique pieces in the requiem literature. Although other requiem composers have employed the sounds of bells and chimes in their funeral music, Gagneux reproduced the specific sounds of the carillon at the Russian Orthodox Cathedral in Geneva, Switzerland. The faithful

depiction of this carillon is recreated by the bells, hand-bells, celesta, vibraphone, and harp. At the same time, the melody and harmonization of the hymn
text, *Fons pietatis*, is derived from the Russian Orthodox liturgy. The choir is
scored in two modes: satb tone-clusters and sssaaa, tonal, canonic writing. The
orchestra employs lengthy ostinato passages. (v. 8).

Recordare, Jesu Pie: 70 mm., perf., 4'23"

    Recordare [quarter-note = 50] ss children's choir; *Quaerens me*, tttbbb choir;
Ingemisco, ss children's choir; *Qui Mariam-Preces meae*, satb choir; *Inter oves*, satb
choir (spoken). The Lutheran chorale, *Ach Gott, vom Himmel sieh darein*, is
quoted by the children's choir (*Recordare*). Sustained string passages, punctu-
ated by outbursts from the brass and percussion. Atonal and tonal harmonies.
(vv. 9–15)

Confutatis: 60 mm., perf., 4'07"

    Confutatis [quarter-note = 70]; orchestral introduction; *Confutatis*, sat choir (uni-
son recitative); *Oro supplex*, B solo/unison & two-part choir. Atonal impressionism coupled with an amophorous rhythmic complex. Rhythmic orchestral
ostinati. (vv. 17–18).

Lacrimosa: 71 mm., perf., 4'24"

    Lacrimosa [quarter-note = 80] satb choir. The concluding movement of the
Sequence is an apotheosis of various musical elements taken from the Introit
and Sequence. Fragments of the Lutheran hymn, celesta and piano ostinato patterns from the Introit, and string tone-clusters are intermingled.

Offertory: 71 mm. + unbarred passages, 2 movements. perf., c. 7'

    Domine Jesu Christe: 41 mm. + unbarred conclusion [quarter-note = 60] satb
choir, unaccompanied (sung and spoken); Brief orchestral interludes divide the
text. Much of the movement is scored for two sopranos and a two-part men's
choir that hums a variety of "*m*" and "*n*" sounds.

Hostias: 30 mm. + unbarred conclusion, perf., 3'59"

    Hostias, at/tb choir/woodwinds/piano/harp. t/b choir (humming "*on*" &
"*in*")/bell/xylophone/chime accompaniment.

Sanctus: 22 mm. [two movements] perf., c. 1"

    Sanctus [quarter-note = 60/80] SS soli/satb choir (*divisi*)/large orchestra. The
overall texture has a "pointillistic" quality.

Benedictus: 55 mm.[quarter-note = 80] perf. time, 3'22"

    Benedictus, ss children's choir/woodwinds/harps/vibraphone/pizzicato
strings. The choral melody is taken from a Jewish Sabbath chant used in southern France. The instrumentation possesses an "oriental" sonority.

Agnus Dei: 25 mm., perf., 3'47"

    Agnus Dei [quarter-note = 60] children's choir/SS soli/orchestra. Most strings
remain tacit; *Dona eis*, S solo/organ/woodwinds/percussion.

Communion: 40 mm. + unbarred conclusion at *Lux aeterna*, perf., 6'20"

    Communion [quarter-note = 60] satb choir, divided into t/b and s/a groupings.
Temple blocks, gongs, maracas, wood blocks, bongos, and wood chimes recre-
ate the *instrumentarium* employed in the animist religions of the Orient. The
choral parts, especially in the concluding *Lux aeterna*, utilize the "*om*" and "*um*"
sounds that are also associated with eastern religious ceremonies. The text is
unraveled in short phrases.

DISCOGRAPHY

Chambre, CHCD 5632, Nouvel Orchestre Philharmonique de Radio-France, Choeurs de Radio-France, Matrise de Radio France, dir. Jacques Mercier.

KARL HÖLLER
July 25, 1907–April 14, 1987

Höller studied composition with Joseph Haas and Hermann Freiherr von Waltershausen at the Munich Academy of Music. For many years, he taught composition at the Frankfurt am Main Hochschule für Musik. He also played the piano, organ, and cello.

He wrote a number of orchestral works, including an organ concerto (1966), orchestral variations on *Mein jünges Leben hat ein End* (1950–51), the *Hymnen über gregorianische Chorale-melodien* (1932–34), and concertos for the violin, cello, and harpsichord. He also wrote a great deal of chamber music and solo piano music. Among the sacred vocal works are a *Missa brevis* (1929), *Weihnachts und Passionmusik* (1932), a motet for Good Friday (*Tenebrae factae*) (1937), and the *Requiem* (1932).

His musical style has several facets. Although he employed neo-classic techniques in his approach to form and structure, he poured a late-romantic, harmony into those forms. The *Requiem*, Op. 14 is a very fine setting of the text, and is scored for organ and a high and low voice. The organ and choral writing is broad and melodic and employs a post-romantic style harmony that includes many V9 chords (and its inversions), the major V7, and other seventh chords.

The writing between the upper and lower voice is sometimes unison, but more often, canonic. Many of the melodies are chant-like. It is clear that Höller attempted to follow the ideals of the Caecilian Movement when he composed *Opus 14*. It is not only a superior liturgical work with the necessary devotional qualities, but is also an excellent concert piece.

Basic Data

EDITION

Karl Höller
Missa pro defunctis, Op. 14 für Ober- und Unterstimmen mit Orgelbegleitung
Anton Böhm & Sohn, Augsburg (#12582-02) 1994.

DURATION

Eight movements, 489 mm.

VOICING AND ORCHESTRATION

Choir: high voice, low voice range: high voice—F♯ 6; low voice—C 4
Instruments: org.

OUTLINE

Introit-*Kyrie*: 58 mm.

Requiem aeternam [am] *langsam und ausdrucksvoll* [slow, expressive] high-low voice duet (canonic); *Kyrie*, unison high-low voice.

Graduale: 54 mm.

Requiem aeternam [am] *ruhig fliessend* [flowing quietly]. high-low voice, unison; *Et lucis aeternae*, high-low voice (canonic).

Sequence: 138 mm.

Dies irae [f♯ minor-AM] *ziemlich bewegt* [rather moving]. high-low voice (alternating sections of unison or two-part canonic writing) (vv. 1–5, 7–9, 18–19)

Offertory: 85 mm.

Domine Jesu Christe [am-CM] *langsam* [slow]. high-low voice in unison or canon; *Hostias, leicht bewegt* [lightly moving]. high or low voice part scored separately; *Quam olim Abrahae*, high-low voice (canonic).

Sanctus: 32 mm.

Sanctus [EM-BM] *ruhig, gesangvoll* [quiet, song-like]. high-low voice, unison; *Hosanna*, high-low (canonic).

Benedictus: 25 mm.

Benedictus [BM] *etwas fliessend* [somewhat flowing]. high-low voice separate; *Hosanna*, high-low voice (canonic).

Agnus Dei: 54 mm.

Agnus Dei [bm/BM] *langsam, ausdrucksvoll* [slow, expressive]. Canonic writing for the two vocal lines.

Communion: 43 mm.

Lux aeterna [BM-am] *bewegt* [moving]. Canonic and unison writing; *Requiem aeternam, langsam* [slow]. Same material as Introit. Canonic and unison writing between the high and low part.

DISCOGRAPHY

None found.

KARL KOCH
January 29, 1887–September 20, 1971

A native of Tyrol Province, Austria, Koch studied music and religion in Brixen and, later, composition with Joseph Marx at the Vienna Academy of Music. He worked in Innsbruck as a choral conductor from 1924 until he retired in 1967.

Although he wrote some instrumental music, the greater part of his output was sacred music that included six masses, two requiems (1916 and 1955–58), a large choral work, *Psalm Kantate,* and a vocal symphony for solo, vocal quartet, women's chorus, mixed chorus, and orchestra. He also wrote a significant amount of organ music.

The *Requiem for Solo Quartet, Mixed Choir and Orchestra*, Op. 85 took several years to compose. The work, begun in 1955, was completed in 1958. It is dedicated to the Tyrolean Heroes of the 1809 battle against the French, the Bavarian authorities, and their troops.

The tonal vocabulary of the *Requiem* is late romantic harmony, joined to Renaissance polyphonic style. The predominant, four-part imitative texture of the *Kyrie* and *Sanctus* is notable. Koch also employed baroque forms such as the chaconne (*Agnus Dei, Dies irae, Quantus tremor*), canon (*Recordare, Quaerens me, Juste judex*), and fugue (*Quam olim Abrahae*). He made two orchestrations of the *Requiem*: one for brass and woodwinds for outdoor concert performance and one for organ, brass, and woodwinds for church usage. The conservative musical style of *Opus 85* adheres to the ideals of the Caecilian Movement.

Basic Data

EDITION

Karl Koch
Requiem für Soloquartett, gemischten Chor und Orchester, Op. 85
[Organ-Vocal Score]
Doblinger # D. 9721 Vienna, Wiesbaden
1958

DURATION

Seven movements, 679 mm.

VOICING AND ORCHESTRATION

Choir: SATB range: S-A6; B-E3
Soloists: SATB
Orchestra: Orchestra I: fl., 2 ob., 2 cl., 2 bsn. 2 Fh., 2 tpt., 3 tbn., timp.: Orchestra II: fl., 2 cl. 2 Fh., 2 tpt., 2 tbn. string bass, timp., org.

OUTLINE

Introit-*Kyrie*: 93 mm.
  Requiem aeternam [cm-E flat M-cm] *adagio.* satbb choir. ABA form. *Kyrie* [cm] *larghetto.* satbb choir; *Christe* [CM] *andante.* ssatb choir.
Sequence: 260 mm.
  Dies irae [cm] *moderato.* satb choir (canon and ostinato); *Tuba mirum* (Gregorian melody-trumpet) ssaattbb choir; *Mors stupebit-Liber scriptus* (ostinato) satb choir; *Quid sum miser, adagio.* A solo; *Rex tremendae, maestoso.* T solo; *Recordare* [EM] AB duet (canon); *Quaerens me*, TS duet (canon); *Juste judex*, SAATB solo quintet (canon); *Ingemisco*, satbb choir; *Qui Mariam*, ST duet (canon and ostinato); *Preces meae*, satbb choir; *Inter Oves-Confutatis* (canon) satb [*divisi*] choir; *Voca me*, S solo/satbb choir; *Oro supplex* [cm] *langsamer als zu Beginn* [slow as at the beginning] satb choir (ostinato); *Lacrymosa* [am] ssaatbb choir; *Pie Jesu*, SATBB soli/ssaattbb choir [CM].

Offertory: 136 mm.

> *Domine Jesu [adagio]*. satb choir (canon); *Libera animas*, B solo; *de poenis*, satbb; *Sed signifer, andante* [EM] ssatbb choir; *Quam olim Abrahae* [dm] *moderato*. satb *(divisi)* choir (fugue). *Hostias* [dm] *adagio*. satb choir; *Tu suscipe*, ST duet; *Quam olim Abrahae* fugue is repeated.

Sanctus: 30 mm.

> *Sanctus* [CM] *sostenuto*. satbb choir (canon)

Benedictus: 29 mm.

> *Benedictus* [A flat M] ST soli/satb choir; *Hosanna* [CM] satb choir.

Agnus Dei: 87 mm.

> *Agnus Dei* [cm] *grave*. satb-ssaattbb choir (chaconne).

Communion: 44 mm.

> *Lux aeterna* [CM] *sostenuto*. S solo/satbb choir; *Requiem aeternam* [cm] satbb choir/S solo. Same musical material as the Introit.

DISCOGRAPHY

None found.

JOONAS KOKKONEN
November 13, 1921–October 1, 1996

A native of Finland, Kokkonen attended the Sibelius Academy of Helsinki in 1949. Although he was basically self-taught in the field of composition, he became a professor of composition at the Sibelius Academy in 1959; in 1965, he was elected to the chairmanship of the Society of Finnish Composers. His music is firmly rooted in the classical symphonic style and his orchestra music has been described as the continuation of the symphonic style of Sibelius. Kokkonen is particularly noted for his writing for strings. His orchestral music includes four symphonies, music for strings, two operas, string quartets, and other chamber music. Among the choral works are a *Missa a cappella* (1963), *Laudatio Domine* (1966), and *Requiem* (1981).

The *Requiem* was composed in memory of the composer's wife, Maija Kokkonen, who had died in 1979. It is scored for SATB choir, soprano and baritone soloists, and orchestra. The musical language of the *Requiem* is a mixture of triadic harmony, "modern" dissonant harmony, and the serial, twelve-tone technique. The prevailing choral texture is chordal and homophonic with a modest amount of imitative polyphony, only in the *Kyrie* and *Hostias*.

Although the individual movements bear a C major signature, there is no key center in this tonal work (tonal areas are suggested in the Outline). Harmonies are derived from a nonfunctional tonal harmony in which parallel chordal harmonies are used. Chromaticism is employed widely in the melodic lines. Chords similar to the V9 and chords that use only major and minor seconds are also commonly employed.

Strings form the backbone of the orchestral sound, with woodwinds used for melodic and coloristic interest and brass for powerful orchestral *tuttis*. A particularly novel orchestration and sonority is used in the Introit: "flutter-tonguing" of the flutes, accompanied by brushed, suspended cymbals. The same "fluttering" motive reappears in the concluding section of the work, *Lux aeterna*. A unique feature of the vocal writing is the constant dialogue between the soloist and choral parts. Rather than composing big vocal solos, the composer chose to use episodic baritone and soprano solos, interwoven into the choral fabric.

Kokkonen used frequent ostinato techniques. Notable is the repetitious, sixteenth-note motive employed in the *Kyrie* and the two sixteenth–one eighth-note figuration in the *Hostias*.

This work embodies a faith of comfort and serenity in its approach to death. Its mood is devoid of anger and doom, very much like the requiems of Fauré, Duruflé, Desenclos, and Ropartz. With no *Dies irae* in this work, the text of the Tract sets the tone: *"liberate the souls of the deceased from the bonds of sin."* There are no overbearing moments of drama or emotion, only a restrained, controlled movement toward the spiritual eternal light of the concluding movement, *Lux perpetua*.

Basic Data

EDITION

Joonas Kokkonen
Requiem for Soprano & Baritone Solo, Mixed Chorus and Orchestra
Piano Score
Edition Fazer, Helsinki (F. M. 06788-4) 1983

DURATION

Nine movements, 748 mm., perf., c. 35'

VOICING AND ORCHESTRATION

Choir: SATB [*divisi*] range: S-A6; B-F♯3
Soloists: S BAR
Orchestra: vn. I/II, vla., vc., db., pic., 2 fl; alto fl., 2 ob., Eh., 2 cl., bcl., 2 bsn., cbsn., 4 Fh., 3 tpt., 3 tbn. harp. PERC: timp., bells, chimes, vibraphone, large tam-tam, bass drum, large and small suspended cymbals.

OUTLINE

Introit: 107 mm.
Requiem aeternam, andante. satb choir/S Bar soli; *Te decet,* satb-ssatb choir;

Requiem aeternam, satb choir/S solo; *Alleluia* (interpolated). Modified ABA form.
[AM-EM]
Kyrie: 76 mm.
    Kyrie, allegro. satb choir (canonic); *Christe*, S Bar soli; *Kyrie*, satb choir/S Bar. soli.
    [EM, conclusion]
Tract: 140 mm.
    Absolve me, andante. satb choir [B flat]; *Ab omni*, ssaatb choir; *Et lucis*, orchestral
    intro., satb choir [EM, conclusion].
Offertory: 169 mm., two movements.
    Domine Jesu Christe: 87 mm., *moderato*. satb choir/S Bar soli. [AM-A flat M].
Hostias: 82 mm., *allegretto*. satb-ssaattb choir.
Sanctus-Benedictus: 131 mm.
    Sanctus, allegro moderato. ssattb choir/S solo; *Dominus Deus*, S solo; *Pleni sunt
    coeli-Hosanna*. ssattb choir; orchestral interlude; *Benedictus*, Bar solo/ssa-tab
    choir; *Hosanna*, ssa-tab choir/ S Bar soli. [AM, conclusion]
Agnus Dei: 42 mm.
    Agnus Dei I, *moderato*. satb choir; *Agnus Dei* II, satb choir/S, Bar soli; *Agnus Dei*
    III, Bar solo/satb choir. [EM, conclusion]
In Paradisum: 44 mm.
    In Paradisum, andante. satb choir/S, Bar soli, unison chant. [EM, conclusion].

DISCOGRAPHY
Finland, FACD 353, The Academic Choral Society and Helsinki Philharmonic
Orchestra, cond. Ulf Söderblom.

RAFAEL KUBELIK
June 29, 1914–August 11, 1996

Kubelik was the son of Jan Kubelik, a virtuoso violinist. His father provided the earliest musical training. Later he was a composition and conducting student of the Prague Conservatory. Much of his professional
career was spent as conductor with the Prague Philharmonic, Brno
Opera, Chicago Symphony, Covent Garden, and the Bavarian Radio Symphony Orchestra. He was named music director of the Metropolitan
Opera, but resigned before completing one year in the post.
    Kubelik was a composer who left a substantial oeuvre that included
five operas, six string quartets, three symphonies (two with chorus), concerti for cello and violin, chamber music, and three requiems. The
Requiem, Pro Memoria Uxoris, was composed in 1961, in memory of the
composer's wife, and scored for children's choir, SATB choir, baritone
soloist, and orchestra.
    The harmonic language of the work is based upon the twelve-tone,
serial system. The prevailing four-part texture is frequently thinned to a
two-part, three-part, and unison fabric. Atonality gives way to a more tri-

adic, tonal harmony in such passages as *Kyrie* (Responsory), *Sed signifer* (Offertory), *Libera eas* (Offertory), and the unison chant, *Benedictus*. Much of the choral writing is syllabic and chordal, although the text, *Pleni sunt coeli*, is the sole fugue in the work.

Kubelik employed numerous ostinati figures in both the choral and instrumental parts and much of the Sequence contains ostinato-like, eight-note melodic motives that appear simultaneously in original and inverted forms. The fugue on *Pleni sunt coeli* employs original and inverted forms of the fugue subject. Simultaneous heterophonic versions of the themes appear in such passages as *Juste Judex* and *Liber scriptus* and transposition of themes to other pitches is a commonly employed technique.

Basic Data

EDITION

Rafael Kubelik
Partitur
Universal Edition (UE 13475 Z) [1961]

DURATION

Five movements, 322 mm.

VOICING AND ORCHESTRATION

Choir: SATB [*divisi*] range: S-B flat 6; B-F3
Children's choir (2-part)
Soloists: Baritone
Orchestra: vn. I/II, vla., vc., db., 2 ob., Eh., 2 fl., 2 cl., bcl., 2 bsn., 4 Fh., 2 tpt., 3 tbn., tuba, harp. PERC: timp., bass drum, tom-tom, military tambour, triangle, marimba, tam-tam, gong, xylophone, cinelli.

OUTLINE

Introit-*Kyrie*: 26 mm.
  Requiem aeternam [quarter-note = 54] satb choir/2 pt. children; *Te decet* [quarter-note = 72] satb choir/2 pt. children [canonic]; *Requiem aeternam-Exaudi*, satb choir/2-pt. children; *Kyrie* [quarter-note = 60] ssattb choir/children, unison.
Sequence: 101 mm.
  Dies irae [quarter-note = 72] Bar solo; *Quantus tremor*, sat choir; *Tuba mirum* [= 84], Bar solo; *Mors stupebit*, satb choir; *Liber scriptus* [= 72] Bar solo; *Judex ergo* [= 80] satb choir; *Quid sum miser*, Bar/solo/satb choir; *Rex tremendae* [= 76] satb choir/Bar solo; *Recordare* [= 66] sssabbb-satb choir; *Querens me* [= 80], Bar solo/ satb choir; *Juste judex*, satb choir; *Ingemisco*, Bar solo; *Qui Mariam*, sat choir/Bar solo; *Preces meae*, Bar solo; *Confutatis* [= 84] satb choir; *Oro supplex*, satb choir; *Lacrymosa, largamente* [= 60] satb choir; *Pie Jesu, piu tranquillo*. sssattt choir/children's choir.

Offertory: 42 mm.

Domine Jesu Christe, ben misurato. Bar solo/tb choir; *Libera eas* [= 54] ssaattbb choir; *Sed signifer*, three-part children's choir; *Quam olim Abrahae* [= 60] Bar. solo; *Hostias*, Bar solo; *Quam olim Abrahae*, tb choir.

Sanctus: 88 mm.

Sanctus [= 72] satb choir; *Pleni sunt coeli* [half note = 92] satb choir (fugato); *Pleni sunt coeli*, children's choir/satb choir (fugal); *Sanctus* [= 72] satb choir/children's choir; *Benedictus*, Bar solo (chant); *Hosanna* [= 60] satb choir/children's choir.

Agnus Dei-Communion: 66 mm.

Orchestral introduction (violin I-II, *divisi à 3*, viola, *divisi à 3*); *Agnus Dei*, children's choir/ sssaaattbb choir; *Et lux*, Bar solo/saa choir; *Lux perpetua*, Bar solo/ solo violin; *Kyrie, molto tranquillo* [= 54] saatbb choir.

DISCOGRAPHY

None found.

HENRI LE FRANÇOIS
1893–1963

Henri Le François, a minor musical poet, was the organist and choirmaster of Notre Dame de Grace de Passy in Paris. Over a period of at least ten years (1942–1952), he composed three movements of a requiem mass; *Kyrie, Pie Jesu,* and *In Paradisum.* These fragments are scored for SATB choir and organ. The harmonic language preserves the spirit of modal and impressionistic writing and the melodies are suggestive of Gregorian chant. The mood of all three works is one of emotional and spiritual peace.

Basic Data

EDITION

Unpublished, but manuscript photocopy available through: Societé des Auteurs, Compositeurs & Editeurs de Musique. Paris.

DURATION

Three movements, 95 mm.

VOICING AND ORCHESTRATION

Choir: SATB range: S-F6; B-F3
Instruments: org.

OUTLINE

Kyrie: 50 mm.

Kyrie [em] satb choir. ABA form. Composed in 1942.

Pie Jesu: 11 mm.

> *Pie Jesu* [gm] satb choir; *Pie Jesu*, S solo; *Pie Jesu*, satb choir. ABA form. No composition date indicated.

In Paradisum: 34 mm.

> *In Paradisum* [E flat M] sa choir; (Altos repeat a five-note motif as sopranos sing a chant-like melody.); *Chorus angeli*, tb/ssa choir (tb hum a B flat pedalpoint) The tenors repeat the opening five-note motif to close the movement. A mandatory organ accompaniment calls for the *voix celestes* stops. Composed in 1952.

DISCOGRAPHY

None found.

ANDREW LLOYD-WEBBER
March 22, 1948

Lloyd-Webber came from a musical family. His mother was a piano teacher and his father, the director of the London College of Music. He attended Magdalen College, Oxford, and the Royal College of Music in London. At the age of nineteen, he wrote his first famous show, *Joseph and the Amazing Technicolor Dreamcoat*. His first commercially successful show, *Jesus Christ Superstar*, a blend of jazz and rock styles, was composed in 1971. It had a run of 3,357 performances in London alone. His other famous shows include, *Cats*, *Evita*, *Starlight Express*, and *The Phantom of the Opera*.

The *Requiem*, composed in 1984, is scored for soprano and tenor soloists, boy soprano, SATB (*divisi*) choir, and large orchestra. Lloyd-Webber was inspired to write the work from the death of his father in 1982. At the same time, he was moved by the story of a young Cambodian boy who was forced to kill his own brother during the rule of the Khmer Rouge in Cambodia. The choice of employing a boy-soprano was influenced by this tragic story. Without doubt, he might have been also prompted through his familiarity with English boy choirs and their music.

The triadic tonal language of the *Requiem* and its rhythmic sensibilities are more akin to twentieth-century English church music than to Broadway-style show music, except for the *Hosanna* fugue, with its "hot" Hispanic rhythms and instrumentation. Most of the movements are given a C major signature, but because so much of the writing is mildly bi-tonal or chromatically dissonant, the music is rarely in that key.

The principal choral texture is four-part SATB, but the composer frequently thins or augments the fabric to achieve a wide variety of choral sound. With the exception of the *Hosanna* fugue and several other short passages, the choral writing is homophonic and chordal.

The orchestration of the *Requiem* has a number of colorful moments, the dramatic percussion for *Dies irae*; the harp, flute, and glockenspiel for *Rex tremendae*; an instrumental fugue for organ chimes and brass; the solo flute of the *Recordare*; the percussion for *Hosanna*, and the harp for *Pie Jesu*. While some of the orchestrations are "Broadway-show," most of them could be found in liturgical settings, too.

One of the curious features of the work is the intermingling of texts, such as the *Offertory-Sanctus*, *Hosanna-Dies irae*, and *Agnus Dei-Pie Jesu*. This particular mixture of texts is quite rare in the settings of the twentieth century. The overall mood of the work is dramatic and its tone, serious.

Basic Data

EDITION

Andrew Lloyd-Webber
Requiem
Theodore Presser Co. 1985

DURATION

Ten movements, 549 mm., perf., c. 44'

VOICING AND ORCHESTRATION

Choir: SATB [ssaattbb *divisi*] range: S-A flat 6; B-E flat 3
Soloists: boy soprano, soprano, tenor [soprano extends up to D 7]
Orchestra: vla., vc., db., 2 fl. [pic. & alto fl. doubling], 2 ob. [Eh. & ob. d'amore doubling], 2 cl. [E flat cl.& bcl. doubling], 2 sax. [doubling soprano and tenor, alto and baritone], 2 bsn., cbsn., 4 Fh., 3 tpt., 4 tbn. PERC: timp., side & bass drums, cymbals, triangle, small, medium, large & deep suspended cymbals, tambourine, deep military side drum, small ratchet rattle, glockenspiel, xylophone, gong, large gong, small bell, bells, tubular bells, bell tree, wood block, congas, maracas, marimba, high roto tom, drum kit. [4 players] harp, piano [doubling celesta], synthesizer (DX7), org.

OUTLINE

Introit-*Kyrie*: 55 mm.
Requiem aeternam, lento. boy sop./ss choir soli; *Requiem aeternam*; s choir; *Exaudi orationem*, satb choir; *Kyrie-Requiem aeternam*, ST soli/satb choir/ boy sop.; *Requiem aeternam*, satb choir. Variations on a theme format.
Sequence: 219 mm., four movements.
Dies irae: 49 mm. *Dies irae-Quantus tremor, moderato maestoso.* satb choir/ST soli/ boy sop.; *Tuba mirum-Dies irae-Mors stupebit-Dies irae-Liber scriptus-Tuba mirum*, satb choir [*divisi*]; *Judex ergo, andante.* T solo; *Mors stupebit-Liber scriptus*, boy sop./ST soli/satb choir; *Mors stupebit, andante.* boy sop.; *Quid sum miser* and *Tuba mirum*, T solo/satb choir. *Rex tremendae*: 15 mm. *Rex tremendae*, [*molto maestoso*]. stb choir/boy sop. ("motto" theme). A bitonal harmonic style is employed. *Recordare*: 34 mm. *Recordare, moderato.* S solo. *Ingemisco-Lacrimosa*:

121 mm. *Ingemisco, lento,* T solo; *Lacrimosa,* TS solo; *Confutatis, andante militaire.* ttbb choir; *Flammis acribus,* satb choir [*divisi*]; *Lacrimosa, andantino.* satb choir; *Huic ergo,* ST soli/satb choir; *Dona eis, meno mosso.* S solo/ssaattbb choir.

Offertory: 68 mm.

Domine Jesu Christe, moderato. satb choir; instrumental fugue, *moderato animato.* organ/chimes/brass; *Sed signifer, moderato.* satb choir; *Hostias, l'istesso tempo.* satb [*divisi*] choir/ST soli; *Sanctus,* satb choir.

Hosanna: 84 mm.

Hosanna, [B flat M] *moderato.* T solo (over B flat pedalpoint); *Hosanna, allegro.* satb choir/T solo (fugue); *Hosanna, double tempo.* satb choir (fugato) *Hosanna, half tempo.* T solo/satb choir; *Dies irae, declamato e feroce.* S solo; *Exaudi orationem, lento solennemente.* satb choir.

Pie Jesu: 32 mm.

Pie Jesu [A flat M] *andante.* boy sop./S solo/satb choir.

Communion: 9 mm.

Lux aeterna [f # m] *molto andante.* unison choir sopranos. The chant-like movement serves as an introduction for the concluding *Libera me.*

Responsory: 82 mm.

Libera me, l'istesso tempo. five solo sopranos/T solo/satb choir; *Libera me,* TS soli/ssattb choir (fugal); *Dies irae, lento.* ssattb choir; *Requiem aeternam, lento.* unison choir basses; *Requiem aeternam,* boy sop. ("motto" theme).

DISCOGRAPHY

London, 448 616-2, Winchester Cathedral Choir, English Chamber Orchestra, cond. Lorin Maazel.

FRANCO MANNINO
April 25, 1924

Franco Mannino received his musical training in piano at St. Cecila's Academy in Rome (1940). He was a composition pupil of Virgilio Mortari, obtaining a diploma in 1947. Since graduation, he has become a well-known name in the world of Italian opera. In the 1980s, he was appointed director and artistic consultant for the Orchestra of the National Arts Center in Ottawa, Canada.

Among his works are nine operas, twenty-one works for orchestra (including five symphonies), more than a dozen works for soloist and orchestra, and about three-dozen chamber compositions. There remain a few secular vocal works and the *Requiem.* The *Missa pro Defunctis,* Op. 233 was composed in memory of the Russian virtuoso violinist, Leonid Kogan (1924–1982). The work, first published in 1987, is scored for SATB choir, SATB soli, violin solo, and orchestra.

Mannino's harmonic style is tonal, with passages of two-part harmony, unisons, and four-part harmony, employing parallel chords. More static harmonic passages are colored by the addition of chromatic notes and accented passing tones. The prevailing choral texture is homophonic, but there are numerous canonic passages, including the *Kyrie, Liber scriptus,* and *Salva me.* The use of the SATB choir and SATB solo quartet represents a modern expression of an older *concertante* structure (Introit, *Liber scriptus, Quid sum miser, Agnus Dei*).

Opus 233 is similar to the requiem settings of Heinrich Sutermeister and Frank Martin in the sense that although a tonal language is used, it is one that greatly stretches traditional boundaries. The work is notated throughout in C, yet the *Kyrie* ends in A major, the *Sanctus* in G major, the *Benedictus* in G minor, and the *Agnus Dei* in G major.

Special effects are employed for the choir. Speaking is used in the opening and concluding *Requiem aeternam.* The soloists use glissandi on *Mors stupebit.* Recitation passages for the choir are employed on *Judex ergo* and text-less vocalises are used during the *Hostias.* In the passage, *Dies illa* (Responsory) the choir sings two texts simultaneously (*Dies irae* & *Calamitatis et miseriae*). The strings employ glissandi even while the remainder of the orchestration remains colorful and kaleidoscopic. In *Dies irae,* the orchestration is massive and powerful; in *Hostias,* intimate and personal. A steady pulse of orchestral quarter-notes in the Introit suggests a funeral cortege. The Mannino work re-examines the same dramatic device used more than 100 years earlier by Verdi, namely the placement of the violent *Dies Irae* passage at three different places in the Sequence and once in the Responsory.

Solo passages for violin appear in the *Kyrie, Judex ergo,* and *Hostias* as a homage to the great Russian virtuoso, Leonid Kogan. The use of a solo violin is also found in the Sgambati setting of 1895. Both settings appear to be among the few from the twentieth century to utilize a virtuoso, solo part for the instrument.

Special rhythms such as the quasi-tarantella of the *Sanctus* or the 7/4 of the *Dies irae* or the free rhythm of the chant-like sections of the *Libera me* and *Lux aeterna* add enormous rhythmic interest to the work.

Basic Data

EDITION
Franco Mannino
Missa pro defunctis, Op. 233
[full score]
Boccaccini & Spada Editori, [B.S. 1198] Rome. 1987

DURATION
Seven movements, 869 mm.

VOICING AND ORCHESTRATION
Choir: SATB range: S-B flat 6; B-E 3
Soloists: SATB

Orchestra: vn. I/II, vla., vc., db., pic., 2 fl., 2 ob., Eh, 2 cl., bcl., 2 bsn., 4 Fh., 3 tpt., 3 tbn., tuba. PERC: timp, cymbals, temple blocks, bass drum, snare drum, tam-tam.

OUTLINE

Introit-*Kyrie*: 210 mm., two movements.

> *Requiem aeternam*: 113 mm. *adagio.* satb choir; *Te decet*, SATB soli/T solo; *Requiem aeternam.* satb choir. ABA form
>
> *Kyrie*: 97 mm. *andante scorrevole.* satb choir/SATB soli/violin solo.

Sequence: 465 mm.

> *Dies irae, allegro feroce.* satb choir/orchestra/percussion battery; *Quantus tremor, andante, molto moderato.* satb choir; *Tuba mirum*, B solo/SAT soli; *Mors stupebit*, B solo; *Liber scriptus*, SATB solo quartet/satb choir (*Dies irae* text); *Judex ergo*, A solo/violin solo/satb choir (*Dies irae*); *Liber scriptus*, T solo; *Dies irae, allegro feroce.* satb choir; *Quid sum miser, lento.* SATB soli/unison choir/satb choir. *Rex tremendae, maestoso.* orchestral introduction; *Rex tremendae*, B solo/sat choir; *Salva me*, A solo/SATB soli/satb choir. *Recordare-Querens me, andante scorrevole.* SATB soli (solo/duet); *Juste judex*, satb choir (*divisi*). *Ingemisco-Qui Mariam-Preces meae-Inter oves, lento.* T solo; *Confutatis, andante energico.* orchestral introduction; *Confutatis-Oro supplex*, B solo; *Dies irae, allegro feroce.* satb choir (*divisi*); *Lacrimosa, andante, molto moderato.* SATB soli/satb choir; *Huic ergo*, satb choir.

Offertory: 66 mm.

> *Domine Jesu Christe, andante.* SATB solo quartet; *Sed signifer*, S solo; *Hostias, andante.* T solo/satb choir/violin solo.

Sanctus: 38 mm.

> *Sanctus, allegretto giocoso.* satb choir (*divisi*), Canon between voice pairs (sa-tb or tb-satb); *Benedictus*, satb choir (*divisi*).

Agnus Dei: 25 mm.

> *Agnus Dei, lento.* satb choir/SATB soli/unison bass choir.

Communion: 17 mm.

> *Lux aeterna, moderato.* satb choir/unison bass choir/SATB soli; orchestral introduction; satb choir (*divisi*) (chant-unison, fifths, complete chordal harmony).

Responsory: 48 mm.

> *Libera me*, unaccompanied A solo (chant)/ STB unison soli; *Dies irae, allegro feroce.* satb choir. (music from the Sequence) Simultaneous presentation of two texts (*Dies irae* (satb choir) & *Calamitatis et miseriae* (SATB solo quartet) *Requiem aeternam, moderato.* satb choir.

DISCOGRAPHY

None found.

FRANK MARTIN
September 15, 1890–November 21, 1974

Frank Martin, an important twentieth-century Swiss composer, worked with Jacques Dalcroze. He taught at Cologne Conservatory and the Dalcroze Institute in Geneva. One of the organizing founders of the Chamber Music Society (Geneva), he worked as its pianist and harpsichordist. He wrote a number of ballets and operas, works for orchestra, chamber music, and vocal compositions. Among the vocal works are four oratorios on sacred subjects, an *Unaccompanied mass for double chorus* (1922), and a *Requiem* (1971–72).

The *Requiem* is scored for SATB soli, SATB (*divisi*) choir, organ, and orchestra. This work possesses great orchestral variety and harmonic color. The percussion battery plays an important timbral role. The harp gives a feeling of lightness to the opening of the Offertory. Contrasting with the full orchestra and choir is the organ and alto solo (*Agnus Dei*), the strings, organ, harpsichord, and solo woodwind quartet (*In Paradisum*), the tenor solo and oboe obbligato (*Quaerens me*), the spoken chorus (*Dies irae, Quantus tremor*), and the tubular chimes (*Sanctus*). All strings play *divisi* and glissando passages (Introit, Sequence, *Sanctus*).

The solo melodies are arch-like and expansive. The alto and soprano are given major solos in *Agnus Dei* and *In Paradisum*. The choral fabric is dominated by an imitative contrapuntal texture that is variously scored for unison, two-part, and some four-part writing. The imitative sections include *Te decet, Et lux perpetua, Qui salvandos,* and *Pie Jesu*. The *Sanctus* and *Benedictus* employ fugal forms.

His harmonic language, built on thirds and fourths, is the product of a linear conception. Although the composition is notated in C, the tonality of the music hovers on the borders of numerous other tonalities. Chromatic melodic elements contribute further to the harmonic vagueness. He is noted for his study of rhythm problems, which are explored in the orchestral work *Rhythmes* (1926). This interest in rhythm is also very apparent in the *Requiem* written more than forty-five years later, between 1971–72. Frequent changes in rhythm and meter give a free-flowing movement to every text.

Basic Data

EDITION
Frank Martin
Requiem
[full score]
Universal Edition (#15755Z) 1976

DURATION
Eight movements, 879 mm., perf., c. 43'

VOICING AND ORCHESTRATION
Choir: SATB [ssaattbb *divisi*] range: S-B6; B-E3
Soloists: SATB

Orchestra: vn. I/II, vla., vc., db. [*divisi*], pic., 2 fl., 2 ob., 2 cl., 2 bsn., cbsn., 4 Fh., 3 tpt., 3 tbn., tuba, timp., org., cembalo. PERC: glockenspiel, 1 kettledrum, small & large tom-tom, tenor drum, side drum, bass drum, triangle, 2 gongs, tam-tam & bells; harp.

OUTLINE

Introit: 62 mm.

> *Requiem aeternam, molto lento.* ST soli/sa choir; *Te decet*, SATB soli; *Requiem aeternam*, ST soli/satb choir.

Kyrie: 91 mm.

> *Kyrie, andante.* SATB soli/satb choir (canon).

Sequence: 315 mm.

> *Dies irae-Quantus tremor, vivace.* percussion battery/satb choir (speaking); *Tuba mirum-Mors stupebit*, satb choir (unison, two-part); *Liber scriptus*, satb choir (four-part); *Judex ergo*, satb choir (unison).*Quid sum miser-Rex tremendae, andante moderato*, B solo; *Quaerens me*, T solo/oboe obbligato; *Juste Judex*, satb choir (unison); *Ingemisco*, A solo; *Qui Mariam*, sa choir; *Preces meae*, SATB soli; *Confutatis*, SATB soli/satb choir; *Oro supplex*, aatb choir/SATB soli; *Lacrimosa-Huic ergo*, unison SATB soli/satb choir (two-part); *Pie Jesu, piu lento.* satb choir/SATB soli.

Offertory: 49 mm.

> *Domine Jesu Christe, andante con moto.* satb *divisi* choir/cembalo/strings (unison, two-part, four-part); *Hostias*, ssa choir; *Fac eas, un poco piu largamente.* satb choir

Sanctus: 97 mm.

> *Sanctus, largo.* saattb choir *divisi*/SATB soli; quartet with orchestra. *Pleni sunt coeli*, satb choir/SATB soli (canon); *Sanctus, un poco piu mosso.* SATB soli/satb choir (canon); *Osanna. andante con moto.* B solo/SATB soli; *Benedictus, molto piu moderato.* SATB soli/satb choir. *Osanna, animando.* SATB soli/ satb choir.

Agnus Dei: 88 mm.

> *Agnus Dei, largo.* A solo/organ.

In Paradisum: 45 mm.

> *In Paradisum, andante molto moderato.* S solo/sattbb choir/Str., org., cembalo and solo quartet of 2 fl/ob/cl.

Communion: 44 mm.

> *Lux aeterna, con moto.* S solo/s choir-SATB soli/satb choir; *Requiem aeternam, un poco piu lento.* satb choir/SATB soli (unison, two-part, four-part).

DISCOGRAPHY

Jecklin Disco, JD 631-2, Swiss-Italian Orchestra, Union Chorale, Choir of Our Lady of Lausanne, Ars Laeta Vocal Group, cond. Frank Martin.

GEORGES MIGOT
February 27, 1891–January 5, 1976

Migot attended the Paris Conservatoire, where he studied composition with Charles-Marie Widor, organ with Eugene Gigout and Alexandre

Guilmant, and orchestration with Vincent D'Indy. This multitalented individual was also a fine painter, poet, and writer. From 1949 to 1961, he was keeper of the Museum of Instruments in the Paris Conservatoire.

He left a fairly large amount of music and among his works are seven stage pieces, twelve symphonies, chamber music, vocal pieces, keyboard music, and numerous choral works.

The sacred choral pieces include *Psaume CXVII* for choir, wind quartet and timpani (1912), *Psaume XIX* for choir and orchestra (1925), *Le sermon sur la montaigne* for five soloists, choir, string orchestra (1936), *La Passion* for soloists, choir and orchestra (1941–42), *L'Annonciation* for two solo voices, women's choir and string orchestra (1945–46), *La Nativité de Notre Siegneur* for soli, choir and orchestra (1954), and the *Requiem* (1953).

Migot's setting of the requiem was composed in 1953, scored for unaccompanied SATB voices, and dedicated to the memory of his parents. The musical style of this tonal piece is based upon an exacting, linear technique, similar to that used by Renaissance composers. The semi-transparent quality of his diatonic harmony avoids any suggestion of key. Migot called his writing style "permodality." Contrasts to the four-part, polyphonic texture are provided by occasional voice thinning.

The entire work, notated in C, contains diatonic melodic lines and chordal passages contain dissonance created by unusual combinations of sevenths and seconds. The bar lines appear to be almost superfluous since the free-flowing rhythm of the chant-like, melodic lines is derived from the inner rhythm of the text. In the *Requiem*, Migot displays a predeliction for triplet rhythms and the constant contrast between duple and triple rhythms seems to be a hallmark of this work. Tempo indications are not provided.

Basic Data

EDITION

Georges Migot
Requiem a cappella pour Choeur mixte ou quatuor vocal
Les Editions Ouvrières, Paris. 1955

VOICING AND ORCHESTRATION

Choir: SATB, unaccompanied range: S-A6 ; B-F3

DURATION

Nine movements, 506 mm.

OUTLINE

Introit: 45 mm.
  Requiem aeternam, satb choir; *Te decet* (fugato); *Exaudi orationem*; *Requiem aeternam* is repeated. ABCA form.

Kyrie: 50 mm.
   Kyrie (imitation); *Christe*; *Kyrie*, satb choir.
Graduale: 81 mm.
   Requiem aeternam, satb choir.
Tract: 33 mm.
   Absolve me, t/b and s/a (imitative) choir.
Offertory: 49 mm.
   Domine Jesu Christe; *Hostias*; *Quam olim Abrahae*, satb choir.
Sanctus: 55 mm.
   Sanctus, satb choir; *Sanctus*, sab choir (imitative); *Benedictus*, satb choir.
Agnus Dei: 43 mm.
   Agnus Dei I/II; *Agnus Dei* III, satb choir.
Communion: 80 mm.
   Lux aeterna—Requiem aeternam, satb choir. (*Requiescant* included for the Office)
Responsory: 111 mm.
   Libera me (2x); *Tremens factus*; *Dies illa*; *Requiem aeternam*; *Kyrie*, satb choir.

DISCOGRAPHY
None found.

ANTHONY NEWMAN
May 21, 1941

Newman studied composition with Nadia Boulanger (L'Ecole Normale de Musique, Paris) and organ with Pierre Cochereau. He later continued composition studies with William Sydemann (Mannes School), Leon Kirchner (Harvard), and Gardner Read and Luciano Berio (Boston University). He currently directs the graduate music program and teaches music history and composition at Purchase College at the State University of New York.

His compositions include more than two dozen pieces for solo piano, harpsichord, and organ (including several toccatas and fugues, preludes and fugues, as well as two symphonies), numerous solo pieces for strings, woodwinds, and brass, three symphonies, a symphonic poem, and three concertos. The vocal works include one opera, *Nicole and the Trial of the Century* (1998), an oratorio, *Absolute Joy: Lives and Times of Angels* (1997), *Requiem Mass* (2000), and a handful of other pieces. In 1995 he published *How Music Is Composed: A Systematic Approach to the Teaching of Composition*.

Requiem, scored for SATB soli, SATB choir (*divisi*), orchestra, and organ, was commissioned by Frederick Sibley, patron of the arts, in memory of his wife, Elvira Trowbridge Sibley. Newman is currently one of the major interpreters of organ and harpsichord music of Bach. A long association with baroque music has clearly influenced his composing style. The *Requiem* contains many neo-baroque characteristics such as fugue, ostinato, and polyphonic choral writing. A stately, sarabande-like funeral march (*Requiem aeternam*) opens the work, followed by a energetic fugue on *Kyrie*. *Concertante* use of the SATB soli with the SATB choir is found in *Kyrie* and the Offertory. Other fugues are present; *Amen* (*Lacrymosa*) and *Et lux perpetua* (*Agnus Dei*). A harmonic reference to the chorale, "*Komm, süsse Tod*" is employed at the end of the *Kyrie* movement, on the words, *Requiem aeternam dona eis Domine.*

Major vocal solo pieces include *Lacrymosa* and *Pie Jesu* (SA), *Libera me* (Bar), and *Benedictus* (SATB soli). The length and multisyllabic treatment of the melodic lines recalls the ornate disposition of baroque melody construction. Quotes of the Gregorian *Dies Irae* are employed in the opening statement of the sequence hymn and *Ingemisco* (*Rex tremendae* movement). The restless harmonic language and driving rhythm of the *Requiem* recalls that of the baroque era, but coupled with a significant amount of freely introduced dissonance, both melodically and harmonically. A unique feature is the inclusion of a poem, *Ozymandias*, by Percy Bysshe Shelley (1792–1822).

Basic Data

EDITION

T.D. Ellis Music Publishing
Piano-Vocal Score
2000

DURATION

Fourteen movements, 1455 mm. perf. c. 53'

VOICING AND ORCHESTRATION

Choir: SATB [*divisi*]. range: S-C7; B-F3
Soloists: SATB
Orchestra: vn. I/II, vla., vc., db., fl., cl., bsn., tpt. tbn., timp., org.

OUTLINE

Requiem aeternam: 247 mm. (quarter note = 120) [CM]
Kyrie/Christe/Requiem aeternam: 109 mm. (*allegro, grave*) [CM/cm] [3 sections] *concertante* soli/choir. Fugue.
Dies irae: 103 mm. (*molto allegro e furioso*) [b flat m/B flat M]
Rex tremendae: 81 mm. (*maestoso*) [DM]
Confutatis: 48 mm. (*allegro*) [am] A or B solo.
Lacrimosa: 166 mm. (*largo*) [bm] SA duet/satb choir.
Ozymandias: 130 mm. (*allegro*) [B flat M] TB duet.

I met a traveler from an antique land
Who said: Two vast and trunkless legs of stone
Stand in a desert . . . Near them on the sand,
Half sunk, a shattered visage lies, whose frown,
And wrinkled lip, and sneer of cold command
Tell that its sculptor, stamped on these lifeless things,
The hand that mocked them, and the heart that fed.

And on the pedestal these words appear:
"My name is Ozymandias, king of kings:
Look on my works, ye Mighty, and despair!"

Nothing beside remains. Round the decay
Of that colossal wreck, boundless and bare
The lone and level sands stretch far away.

Offertory: Domine Jesu Christe: 47 mm. (*moderato*) [F#M] SATB soli/satb choir.
Sanctus/Hosanna: 106 mm. (quarter note = 126) [B flat M] [2 sections] *Sanctus*
 begins with an organ prelude.
Benedictus/Hosanna: 79 mm. (*largo*) [b flat m] [2 sections]
Pie Jesu: 69 mm. (*andante*) [G] SA duet.
Libera me: 82 mm. (quarter note = 112) [b flat m] Bar solo.
Agnus Dei: 175 mm. (*moderato*) [cm/CM]
In Paradisum: 13 mm. (quarter note = 126) [CM] ssaattbb choir.

DISCOGRAPHY
Khaeton Klassical, KWM600102, Chorus and Orchestra of Bach Works, New York,
cond. Anthony Newman.

KRZYSZTOF PENDERECKI
November 23, 1933

Penderecki began his studies at the Jagellonian University in Cracow,
Poland. He later attended the State Higher School of Music, an institution
with which he maintained a long relationship, first as a student, then as
lecturer (1958) and ultimately as professor and rector (1972). His outstanding musical talent brought him numerous prizes for his compositions.

Penderecki has written four operas, more than three dozen orchestral
works, a dozen pieces for chamber ensemble, and a significant amount of
sacred choral music. The choral works include *The Psalms of David* (1958);
a *Stabat Mater* for three choruses (1962); the *St. Luke Passion* (1962–65), an
oratorio; *Dies Irae* (1966–67); a *Te Deum* (1979–80); and the *Polish Requiem*
(1980–84 and 1993).

The *Polish Requiem* is scored for SATB soli, SATB choir (*divisi*), and orchestra. The work took thirteen years to complete, although many individual movements were performed for special occasions during the course of its ultimate completion. The *Lacrimosa* was composed in 1980 to commemorate the unveiling of the Solidarity monument in Gdansk. In 1983, the *Quid sum miser, Rex tremendae, Recordare,* and *Ingemisco* were written and the *Recordare* dedicated to Father Kolbe, a Franciscan monk who died on behalf of another prisoner in the ovens at Auschwitz. The remainder of the *Dies Irae* was dedicated to the memory of those who died in the Warsaw Uprising of 1944. The *Libera me* was dedicated to the victims of the massacre at Katyn. The *Agnus Dei* was composed for the funeral of Cardinal Wyszynski in May 1981. The *Sanctus,* composed in 1993, completed the *Requiem.*

The name, *Polish Requiem,* comes from a Polish hymn text, *Święty Boże, Święty mocny,* that Penderecki inserted into the *Recordare* text.

The musical style of this work is a mixture of neo-romanticism and twentieth-century expressionism. Polyphonic chromaticism (music without a tonal center), employed in *Libera me,* contrasts with the tonal passages of the neo-romantic *Lacrymosa.* Tone clusters are scored for *Mors stupebit, Lux aeterna,* and *Tremens factus.* The twenty-part choral chord on *peccata* (*Agnus Dei*) is built upon seconds. The choir sings, speaks, hisses, and shrieks the text (*Voca me, Ingemisco*), yet the text is always fairly clear and understandable, regardless of style. Vocal glissandi are employed in *Quantus tremor* and *Oro supplex,* while the strings use the same effect in *Lux aeterna.*

The choral fabric is constantly changed and throughout the work a balance of homophonic and polyphonic writing style is maintained. Fugue and imitative techniques are employed in the *Kyrie, Sanctus,* and *Benedictus.* The melodic style and massive orchestration are a product of the late romantic era. Furthermore, the recurring use of a violent descending melodic passage in the Sequence and repeated tolling of chimes in the *Sanctus* is a modern form of the nineteenth-century, Wagnerian *Leitmotiv.*

The important timbral role played by the percussion battery and the use of numerous asymmetrical rhythms are significant features of this *Requiem.* The *Polish Requiem* requires a large choir, excellent soloists, and large orchestra. The overall mood of the work is dark and moody, yet filled with hope.

Basic Data

EDITIONS

1. Schott (#48050) Rental from European-American Music. 1993 [Partitur]

2. Agnus Dei (1981) Gemischter Chor a Cappella (SSAATTBB) Schott SKR 20002

3. Lacrimosa for soprano solo, mixed
   choir & symphony orchestra
   [full score]
   Polskie Wydawnictwo Musyczne,
      Krakow
   PWM Edition 1980
   B. Schott's Söhne, Mainz ISBN 83-224-1654-7

DURATION

Twelve movements, 1696 mm., perf., c. 105'

VOICING AND ORCHESTRATION

Choir: SATB [*divisi*] range: S-B6; B-F3
Soloists: SATB
Orchestra: vn. I/II, vla., vc., db., pic., 3 fl., 3 ob., 3 cl., bcl., 3 bsn., cbsn., 6 Fh., 4
tpt., 4 tbn., tuba. PERC: 4 timp., xylophone, glockenspiel, vibraphone, tubular
bells, church bells, Sanctus bells, snare drum, bass drum, 2 tam-tams, field
drum, military drum, cymbals, suspended cymbals, 2 triangles, 6 tom-toms, 5
timbales, wood-block, ratchet, whip, rattan stick.

OUTLINE

Introit: 41 mm.
   Requiem aeternam, adagio. satb [*divisi*] choir; *Et lux,* sat (unison) choir; *Te decet-
   Requiem aeternam,* satb choir (unison/two-part).
Kyrie: 63 mm.
   Kyrie, andante. satb choir/SATB soli; *Christe, poco meno mosso.* SATB soli/stb
   choir; *Kyrie,* satb choir/SATB soli.
Sequence: 872 mm., 5 movements. (composed in 1984)
   Dies irae: 313 mm., *allegro molto con fuoco.* orch. introduction; *Dies irae,* tbb choir/
   satb choir; orch. interlude; *Quantus tremor;* satb choir; *Tuba mirum, maestoso,
   meno mosso.* ssaattb choir; *Mors stupebit,* S solo; *Tuba mirum,* B solo/satb choir;
   orch. interlude, *allegro; Liber scriptus,* satb choir (spoken-sung); orch. interlude;
   Judex ergo, ssaattb choir; *Dies irae,* tbb/satb choir; orch. postlude.
Quid sum miser: 111 mm. (composed in 1983)
   Quid sum miser, andante con moto. ssaattb choir/reduced orchestra; *Rex tremendae, adagio.* B solo; *Salva me,* saattb choir (canonic).
Recordare: 123 mm. (composed in 1982–83)
   Święty Boże-Recordare, andante sostenuto. SA soli; *Święty Boże-Recordare-Quaerens
   me,* satb choir; *Redemisti-Święty Boże-Recordare,* SA soli/satb choir; *Święty Boże-
   Recordare,* SA soli; *Juste Judex,* T solo/satb choir; *Juste Judex-Święty Boże,* SATB
   soli/satb choir; *Donum fac-Święty Boże,* BA soli. This movement is the emotional
   heart of the *Polish Requiem*. In setting the Polish Hymn, *Święty Boże, Święty
   mocny* ("Great God, Holy Lord") to the same music as *Recordare Jesu pie*
   ("Think, Kind Jesus on my salvation"), Penderecki gave voice to the collective
   suffering that Poland had experienced during the World War II.

Świętny Boże, świętny mocny	Great God
Świętny a niesmiertelny	Holy, almighty and eternal God
Zmiłuj się nad nami.	Have mercy upon us.

The intermingling of various soloists and satb choir is done in a style not unlike a *sinfonia concertante*. Accompanying the vocal and choral activity is a melodic "lament," most frequently played by the strings.

Ingemisco: 282 mm. (composed in 1983)

Ingemisco, allegro assai. orch. introduction; *Ingemisco,* ssaattbb choir; *Ingemisco,* two satb choirs (spoken); *Qui Mariam, poco meno allegro.* two ssaattbb choirs; *Qui Mariam,* united double SATB choir; orch. interlude, *allegro. Qui Mariam,* satb choir (spoken); orch. interlude; *Mihi quoque,* ssaattb choir; *Preces meae,* SATB soli; orch. interlude; *Inter oves,* T solo; *Confutatis,* ssaattbb choir; orch. interlude; *Confutatis,* ssaattbb choir; *Flammis acribus,* ttbb choir; *Voca me,* satb choir (speaking & singing); *Confutatis,* ssaattbb choir; *Oro supplex, mezza voce quasi recit.,* ssaattb choir.

Lacrymosa: 43 mm. (composed in 1980)

Lacrimosa, lento. S solo/ssaa-satb choir; *Huic ergo-Pie Jesu,* ssaa-tb/satb choir.

Sanctus: 165 mm. (composed in 1993)

orch. introduction, *andante sostenuto; Sanctus,* A solo; *Sanctus,* S solo/satb-ssaattbbb choir; *Benedictus,* ttbb choir; *Pleni sunt coeli,* tb choir; *Benedictus,* T solo; *Sanctus-Benedictus,* AT solo/sab/sa/satbb/sattbb choir; *Benedictus,* ssatb choir. (Clarinet obbligato).

Agnus Dei: 106 mm. (composed in 1981)

Agnus Dei, ssaattbb choir, unaccompanied. The movement begins very quietly, culminating in a massive *fortisissimo* with a twenty-part chord on the word *peccata*. After this climax, there is a dramatic measure of silence. Following the pause, the movement quietly and gradually fades away (the triadic harmony and massive chords are built upon seconds).

Communion: 52 mm. (*Requiem aeternam,* verse not included)

Lux aeterna, lento. ssaattbb choir. (string glissandi and tone clusters) The texture includes triadic harmony and dense chords built on major seconds.

Responsory: 268 mm.

Libera me, allegro moderato. satb choir/reduced orchestra; *Quando movendi-Dum vereris,* S solo/violin tone-clusters/satb choir (spoken); *Quando coeli, agitato,* orch. interlude; *Quando coeli,* aatttbbb/ssaattb/satb choir; orch. interlude (string clusters, violin I/II, viola, cello, divided *a 4,* bass divided *a 3); Tremens factus,* B solo/ reduced orchestra; orchestral "*Leitmotiv*" (from *Dies irae*) *Dies illa,* tb choir; orch. interlude, *Dies irae,* ssaattbb choir (same material as in Sequence, *Dies irae); Quando coeli,* SB soli/16-part strings; *Libera me,* SB soli/satb choir.

Offertory-Finale: 129 mm.

Recordare-Świętny Boże, andante con moto. SATB soli/satb choir in various combinations. (alternating passages for unison violin I/satb choir/SATB soli); *Świętny Boże-Agnus Dei, adagio.* satb choir; *Finale, Libera animas. andante con moto.* (Full orchestra, double choir, and soloists in a massive explosion of sound, the top line ascending to C7 and the lower line descending to C3.) Virtually all important themes and texts are drawn together in a grandiose musical apotheosis.

DISCOGRAPHY

1. Chandos, 9459/60, Royal Stockhom Philharmonic Orchestra & Chorus, cond. Krzysztof Penderecki (complete with *Sanctus*).
2. Deutsche Grammophon, 429 720-2 NDR, Sinfonieorchester, Choir of the Bavarian Radio and the Choir of the North German Radio, cond. Krzysztof Penderecki (missing *Sanctus*).

LORENZO PEROSI
December 20, 1872–November 12, 1956

Perosi was a pupil of the Milan Conservatory. He was appointed to the position of choirmaster at the Cathedral in Imola, but in less than a month's time, received an identical position at St. Mark's in Venice (1895). In 1898, he was appointed to yet another important position, choirmaster of the Sistine Chapel and in 1905, by Papal decree, was given a position as Perpetual Master of the Pontifical Chapel. He continued to work until 1915, when he stopped because of psychological difficulties.

During the productive periods in his career, he wrote twenty-five masses, including two requiems, orchestral music, organ music, eighteen string quartets, and about 350 sacred compositions. His musical style is somewhat of an eclectic nature, employing a mixture of Gregorian chant, sixteenth-century polyphony, and late romantic-era harmony.

The *Messa di Requiem* for two voices is a late work composed in 1950. Scored for soprano and alto voice (s) and organ, it possesses the harmonic and melodic language previously mentioned. It was composed for the first death anniversary of Countess Katie Nasali Rocca di Corneliano. It is a simple work, yet full of charm and elegance.

Basic Data

EDITION

Messa di Requiem a due voci pari.
Edizioni De Santis E.D.S. 836
Rome 1951

DURATION

Ten movements, 519 mm.

VOICING AND ORCHESTRATION

Choir: SA
Instruments: org.

OUTLINE

Introit: 41 mm.
  Requiem aeternam [GM] *moderato.* sa choir; *Te decet* [DM] sa choir; *Requiem aeternam* [GM] sa choir. ABA form.
Kyrie: 27 mm.
  Kyrie [GM] *mosso.* sa choir. ABA form.
Graduale: 36 mm.
  In memoria [GM] *moderato.* alternating sa unison throughout.
Sequence: 156 mm.
  Dies irae, s unison; *Quantus tremor,* a unison; *Tuba mirum,* sa unisons; *Mors stupebit-Liber scriptus-Judex ergo,* alternating sa unisons; *Quid Sum miser-Rex tremendae,* sa choir; *Recordare,* sa choir (canon); *Quarens me-Juste judex,* alternating sa unisons; *Ingemisco,* sa choir; *Qui Mariam,* s unison; *Preces meae,* a unison; *Inter oves,* s unison; *Confutatis,* sa choir; *Oro supplex,* s unison; *Lacrimosa-Huic ergo,* sa choir.
Offertory: 87 mm.
  Domine Jesu Christe, mosso. sa choir; *Hostias, adagio.* s unison; *Quam olim Abrahae,* sa choir.
Sanctus: 27 mm.
  Sanctus [GM] *moderato.* sa choir (canon). The melodic theme of the duet is based upon the chimes of St. Paul 's [St. Paolo].
Benedictus: 12 mm.
  Benedictus, adagio. sa choir. (bell-like organ accompaniment).
Agnus Dei: 24 mm.
  Agnus Dei, moderato. s unison (repeated four note figure on *Agnus Dei*) a unison (chant-like melody)
Communion: 30 mm.
  Lux aeterna, moderato. sa choir (alternating unison lines).
Responsory: 79 mm.
  Libera me, mosso. sa choir; *Tremens factus,* a unison; *Quando coeli,* sa choir; *Dies illa,* s unison/sa choir; *Requiem aeternam,* sa choir; *Kyrie,* sa choir.

DISCOGRAPHY

None found.

The *Messa da Requiem for Three Male Voices* was composed in memory of Perosi's student, Ferruccio Menegazzi. This setting was designed for liturgical usage and its conservative harmonic style and language follow the guidelines of the nineteenth-century Caecilian Movement. Gregorian chant intonations are provided for the Introit, Offertory, and Communion. Occasional imitative polyphonic passages give relief to the prevailing, three-part homophonic texture of the requiem and frequent solo vocal passages are interwoven, *concertante* style, into the three-part choral writing.

A simple accompaniment for organ or harmonium provides support for the voices. There are many lovely melodic and harmonic passages.

Basic Data

EDITION

Messa de Requiem a 3 voci maschili,
con accompagnemento d'organo o armonium.
Ricordi (#101742) [individual parts for tenor I & II and bass are available]
1996

DURATION

Ten movements, 519 mm.

VOICING AND ORCHESTRATION

Choir: T I/II, B range: T-G5; B-F3
Soloists: T I/II, B
Instruments: org. or harmonium

OUTLINE

Introit-*Kyrie*: 72 mm.
  Requiem aeternam [FM] *andante*. ttb choir; *Et tibi*, ttb choir; *Requiem aeternam*, ttb choir (Gregorian intonations); *Kyrie*, ttb choir/T I, B soli.
Graduale: 13 mm.
  Requiem aeternam [dm] *moderato*. b unison; *In memoriam*, tt choir.
Tract: 18 mm.
  Absolve Domine [B flat M] *senza correre*. ttb, *a cappella* trio.
Sequence: 234 mm.
  Dies irae [dm] *vivo*. ttb choir; *Quantus tremor*, b unison; *Tuba mirum*, tt choir; *Mors stupebit*, B solo; *Liber scriptus*. TT soli; *Judex ergo*, ttb choir; *Quid sum miser*, B solo; *Rex tremendae*, ttbb choir (canon); *Recordare*, TT soli; *Quaerens me*, ttb choir/T II-B soli; *Juste judex*, ttb choir; *Ingemisco*, B solo; *Qui Mariam*, B solo; *Preces meae*, ttb choir; *Inter oves*, B solo; *Confutatis*, ttb choir; *Oro supplex*, B solo; *Lacrymosa-Pie Jesu*, ttb choir.
Offertory: 65 mm.
  Jesu Christe [gm-B flat M-E flat M-B flat M] *andante*. ttb choir/TT soli; *Libera eas*, B solo; *Quam olim Abrahae*, ttb choir; *Hostias*, T solo; *Quam Olim Abrahae*, ttb choir. The Gregorian intonation is provided.
Sanctus: 32 mm.
  Sanctus [gm] *andante*. ttb choir.
Benedictus: 24 mm.
  Benedictus [gm] *melodioso con molta espressione*. TT soli; *Hosanna*, TTB soli.
Agnus Dei: 27 mm.
  Agnus Dei [dm] *andante*, ttb choir.

Communion: 18 mm.

Lux aeterna [gm] *come recitativo.* ttb choir/TTB soli. The Gregorian intonation is
provided.

Responsory: 78 mm.

Libera me [gm] *andante.* ttb choir; *Tremens factus,* B solo; *Quando coeli-Dies illa,* ttb
choir; *Requiem aeternam,* T I solo; *Libera me-Kyrie,* ttb choir.

DISCOGRAPHY

SARX, SXAM 2003-2, Coro della Cappella dell'Immacolata di Bergamo, dir. E.
Corbetta.

DANIEL PINKHAM
June 5, 1923–December 18, 2006

Daniel Pinkham graduated from Harvard University in 1944. His compo-
sition teachers were Aaron Copland, Archibald Davison, and Walter Pis-
ton. He studied organ with E. Power Biggs and harpsichord with Wanda
Landowska. Like many American composers, he studied later with Nadia
Boulanger in Paris. In 1958, he became music director of music at King's
Chapel in Boston and has taught at the New England Conservatory of
Music since 1959.

Pinkham has written music of all types, including opera, film, orchestral, and chamber music, as well as a significant amount of sacred vocal
music. There is a *Wedding Cantata* (1956), *Christmas Cantata* (1957), *Easter
Cantata* (1961), and *Advent Cantata* (1991). Other pieces include two settings of the *Stabat Mater* (1964 and 1990) a setting of the *St. Mark Passion*
(1965), *The Passion of Judas* (1975), a *Magnificat* (1968), and two *Requiems*
(1962 and 1992).

The composer's earlier choral works use elements of a neo-classic style,
however after mid-century, he began to explore serial techniques and
electronic tonal sources. Both requiems are tonal and employ a traditional
harmonic language that is colored by a freely dissonant harmonic vocabulary.

The "Big" *Requiem* of 1962 is scored for AT soli, SATB choir, and chamber ensemble. It was composed in memory of his younger brother, William White Pinkham, and commissioned by Leopold Stokowski,
president of the Contemporary Music Society. The premiere of the work
was given in New York City at the Museum of Modern Art by the choir
of King's Chapel of Boston.

Its prevailing two-part writing is a result of a linear conception and construction of the melodic and harmonic materials. This writing allows for
straightforward triadic harmony, as well as a chromatic harmony built on

major and minor seconds. The harmony appears to be a contemporary version of impressionism. The musical lines possess a lyrical, singing quality, and the textures are always spare and delicate in their orchestration. All six movements are notated in C major.

Basic Data

EDITION

Daniel Pinkham
Requiem
C. F. Peters Corp. (#6650) 1963

DURATION

Six movements, 250 mm., perf., 15'

VOICING AND ORCHESTRATION

Choir: SATB range: S-A6; B-A flat 3
Soloists: AT
Instruments: 2 tpt., 2 Fh., 2 tbn., db., org., or piano.

OUTLINE

Introit: 43 mm.
  Requiem aeternam, andante. AT soli; *Te decet,* satb choir (two-part writing); *Requiem aeternam* is repeated. ABA form.
Kyrie: 40 mm.
  Kyrie, maestoso. satb choir (unison/two-part writing); *Christe.* AT soli/satb choir; *Kyrie,* satb choir. ABA form.
Tract: 37 mm
  Absolve me, lento. satb choir (instrumental introduction); *Absolve me, andante.* AT soli; choir. *Absolve me,* satb choir (canonic). ABA form.
Offertory: 73 mm.
  Domine Jesu Christe, andante flessibile. T solo; *Libera eas,* A solo; *Quam olim Abrahae,* ST soli; *Hostias, energico.* satb choir (unison/two-part writing).
Sanctus: 27 mm.
  Sanctus. satb choir (unison/two-part writing)
Agnus Dei: 51 mm.
  Agnus Dei, tranquillo. satb choir (two-part writing).

DISCOGRAPHY

None found.

The *Small Requiem for Solo Medium Voice, Mixed Chorus and Organ* was composed in 1992 and scored for SATB choir, medium voice, and organ. Three movements, *Pie Jesu, Lux aeterna,* and *In Paradisum* were written earlier in October 1991 for colleagues who had sung in the Choir of King's Chapel.

In a conversation with the author, Dr. Pinkham indicated that he "had decided, like Gabriel Fauré, to write the requiem setting just for the pleasure of it."

There exist three versions for the accompaniment of the *Requiem*; (1) for strings (orchestra or quintet) and organ, (2) organ alone, and (3) strings (orchestra or quintet). The first performance of the *Small Requiem* took place on March 29, 1992, at St. Stephen's Church in Providence, Rhode Island.

Basic Data

EDITION

Daniel Pinkham
The Small Requiem for solo medium voice, mixed chorus, and organ.
C. F. Peters Corp.
1991

DURATION

Six movements, 134 mm., perf., c. 15'

VOICING AND ORCHESTRATION

Choir: SATB range: S-A flat 6; B-G 3
Soloists: A
Instruments: (three versions). vn. I/II, vla., vc., db., org.

OUTLINE

Introit-*Kyrie*: 43 mm.
  Requiem aeternam, satb choir (unison/four-part writing); *Te decet*, sa choir; *Kyrie*, satb choir.
Pie Jesu: 24 mm.
  Pie Jesu, A solo (built on an ascending four-note motive).
Sanctus: 12 mm.
  Sanctus. satb choir; *Pleni sunt coeli*, st choir; *Hosanna*, satb choir; *Benedictus*, sa choir (unison); *Hosanna*, satb choir.
Agnus Dei: 16 mm.
  Agnus Dei, unison choral alto sung over repeated two-measure instrumental ostinato.
Communion: 21 mm.
  Lux aeterna, A solo/satb choir [*divisi*].
In Paradisum: 18 mm.
  In Paradisum, sa [*divisi*]; *Chorus angelorum*, sat unison choir/satbb choir.

DISCOGRAPHY
None found.

ILDEBRANDO PIZZETTI
September 20, 1880–Feburary 13, 1968

Pizzetti received his training in composition at the Conservatory of Parma. He was thoroughly acquainted with the choral and instrumental music of the Renaissance. During his career, he held several important teaching positions at the Parma Conservatory, the Florence Conservatory and the Milan Conservatory. After 1930, he became an active conductor in Europe and the Americas. Pizzetti was well-known for his operas, although he wrote a significant amount of instrumental and vocal music. Except for a setting of the *De Profundis* and the *Requiem* (both unaccompanied), he wrote very little sacred choral music.

The *Requiem*, scored for SATB (*divisi*) choir, was composed in 1922 and is one of the outstanding pieces in the unaccompanied choral literature of the early twentieth century. Other works of this genre include the *Mass in G Minor* (1922) of Vaughan-Williams, *Mass in G Major* (1937), *La Figure Humaine* (1943) of Poulenc, *Mass for Unaccompanied Double Choir* (1922) of Martin, *Deutsche Mottette* (1913) of Strauss, and *Friede auf Erden* (1951) of Schönberg.

The choral writing of the *Requiem* recalls the Renaissance idiom with its dramatic polychoral style and its imitative polyphony. Its musical lines possess great lyrical beauty and broad sweep while the harmony tends to be expansive and majestic.

The prevailing texture of the work is imitative polyphony, especially canonic forms. Chordal, homophonic fabric is limited to the *Sanctus* and passages in the *Libera me*. Contrast in the choral mass is achieved by thinning or augmenting the vocal parts. The Sequence movement is constructed around the Gregorian *Dies irae* melody. Pizzetti's work has a broad range of emotional moods, ranging from the forbidding darkness of the *Dies irae* to the luminous quality of the *Sanctus*. Performance of the *Requiem* requires a very good choir.

Basic Data

EDITION

Pizzetti
Messa di Requiem per Sole Voci
G. Ricordi & C. Editori, Milan (#119490) 1966

DURATION

Five movements, 457 mm., perf., c. 27′

VOICING AND ORCHESTRATION

Choir: SATB [SSAATTBB *divisi*] [SSAATTTTBBBB *divisi*]. range: S-A6; B-F3

OUTLINE

Introit: 71 mm.
Requiem aeternam [dm] *largo, non lento*. satbb choir. ABA form; *Kyrie*, sattb choir (Fugue).
Sequence: 196 mm.
Dies irae-Quantus tremor-Tuba mirum-Mors stupebit [dm] *sostenuto, non molto*. ssattb choir (two-part writing); *Liber scriptus*, ssattb choir (two-part, canonic writing); *Judex ergo*, ssattb choir two-part writing); *Quid sum miser*, ssaattbb choir (double canon); *Rex tremendae*, ssaattbb (canon) *Recordare*, ssaattbb choir (canon); *Quaerens me*, ssaattbb choir; *Ingemisco*, ssaattbb choir (canon); *Qui Mariam*, ssaattbb (two-part writing); *Confutatis*, ssaattbb choir (double canon); *Oro supplex*, ssaattbb choir (canon); *Lacrimosa-Huic ergo*, ssaattbb choir (two-part writing). The Gregorian melody is quoted throughout the movement. A counter-theme, set to "*Oh*," depicts lamentation and is used to heighten the textual meaning. This dramatic device, found in the soprano or tenor voice part, is unique among requiem settings.
Sanctus: 101 mm.
Sanctus [FM] *chiaro e spazioso*. ssaa/ttbb/ttbb (three choirs); *Pleni sunt coeli*; *Hosanna* (chordal); *Benedictus* (canon); *Hosanna*.
Agnus Dei: 29 mm.
Agnus Dei [FM] *calmo e dolce*. satb choir (canon).
Responsory: 60 mm.
Libera me [dm] *con fervore profondo*. satbb choir; *Tremens factus*; *Requiem aeternam*; *Libera me*.

DISCOGRAPHY

1. Chandos, CHAN 8964, The Danish National Radio Choir, cond. Stefan Parkman.
2. Hyperion, CDA67017, Choir of Westminister Cathedral, cond. James O'Donnell.

JEAN RIVIER
July 21, 1896–November 6, 1986

Jean Rivier was trained at the Paris Conservatoire after he recovered from injuries inflicted from World War I. Following graduation, he worked with various Parisian musical ensembles devoted to contemporary composition. He taught composition at the Conservatoire from 1948 to 1966.

His musical style is a mixture of French "classic" style and impressionism.

Among his works are an opera, *Venitienne* (1937), eight symphonies (four for strings), and a large number of concertos (*Cello*, 1937; *Viola* or *Alto* Saxophone, 1935 & 1936; two piano concertos, 1940, 1953; *Violin*, 1942; *Alto Saxophone, Trumpet & Strings*, 1945; *Flute & Strings*, 1956; *Clarinet & Strings*, 1958; *Bassoon & Strings*, 1963; *Brass, Timpani & Strings*, 1963; *Oboe & Strings*, 1967; and *Trumpet & Strings*, 1970). Rivier also composed chamber music, solo piano music, and vocal pieces. The sacred works include *Psaume LVI* for soprano, chorus, and orchestra (1937), *Christus Rex*, an oratorio for contralto, chorus, and orchestra (1966), and *Requiem* (1953).

The *Requiem* is scored for mezzo-soprano and bass soli, SATB choir, and orchestra. Its tonal musical language employs impressionistic, parallel triadic harmonies, as well as dissonant chords, chromatic melodic movement, numerous choral and instrumental unisons, and frequent ostinato passages. Although the composer notated the music in C (several brief passages in D flat), the music remains rarely in that tonality. The orchestra provides rhythmic drive and melodic counterpoint for the choral passages.

Although many of the melodic phrases employ chromatic scalar lines, some contain syllabic, repeated-note figures, transposed at various pitch levels. Triadic melodies that suggest key are also used, especially in the *Sanctus*.

The prevailing choral texture is two, three, and four-part unison writing with occasional, three-part, parallel chordal writing that is reminiscent of the impressionist idiom. Complete SATB scoring contrasts with the numerous passages set for single SATB choral lines. This unique form of scoring seems to represent a twentieth-century application of the baroque *concertante* style. A small amount of imitative writing is found in the passages, *Tuba mirum* and *Sed signifer*.

Basic Data

EDITIONS

1. Requiem pour Mezzo-soprano, Basse solo, Choeur mixte et Orchestre. Partition d'Orchestre
Editions Musicales Transatlantique
1956

2. Requiem pour Mezzo-soprano Solo, Baryton solo, Choeur mixte et Orchestre.
[choral score]
Editions Musicale Presses, Inc. [nd]

DURATION

Six movements, 509 mm., perf., 32'

VOICING AND ORCHESTRATION

Choir: SATB [occasional *divisi*] range: S-A6; B-A flat 3
Soloists: mezzo soprano, baritone

Orchestra: vn. I/II, vla., vc., db., pic., 3 fl., 2 ob., Eh., 2 cl., bcl., 2 bsn., cbsn., 4 Fh., 3 tp., tuba. PERC: 3 timp., bass drum, cymbals, tambourine, tam-tam, wood-block, piano.

OUTLINE

Introit-*Kyrie*: 63 mm.

> *Requiem aeternam, molto lento.* satb choir; *Te decet*, satb choir; *Exaudi orationem*, bar.choir/ta unison choir; *Kyrie*, ssaa/ttbb choir. orchestral ostinato on F-F♯-F-F♯.

Sequence: 179 mm.

> *Dies irae, allegro deciso e marcato.* satb choir; *Quantus tremor*, satb choir; *Dies irae*, satb choir; *Tuba mirum*, satb choir (canonic); *Mors stupebit*, satb choir; *Liber scriptus, poco piu vivo.* ab unison choir/satb choir; *Judex ergo*, satb choir; *Dies irae*, satb choir. Rondo-like structure. Orchestral, eighth-note ostinato.

Offertory: 101 mm.

> *Domine Jesu Christe, lento espressivo.* a unison; *Libera eas, poco piu mosso*, b unison/satb choir; *Sed signifer, l'istesso tempo.* mezzo sop. solo; *Hostias, poco piu lento.* sat choir; *Fac eas*, saa choir; *Domine Jesu Christe*, alto/tenor/bass unison choir. ABA form. (G-G♯-A-A♯-B-C-C♯-D ostinato)

Sanctus: 61 mm.

> *Sanctus, moderato affettuoso.* s unison; *Sanctus*, st unison; *Sanctus*, satb choir; *Hosanna*, satb choir; *Benedictus, lento.* Bar. solo; *Sanctus*, st unison; *Hosanna*, satb choir. (melodic ostinato)

Agnus Dei: 42 mm.

> *Agnus Dei I, lent, tres pur.* Mezzo sop. solo; *Agnus Dei* II, ssaa choir/b unison choir; *Agnus Dei* III, Mezzo sop./t unison choir. ABA form.

Responsory: 63 mm.

> *Libera me, lento.* ab unison/satb choir; *Advenisti*, saa choir/t unison; *Requiem aeternam, meno lento.* a unison/satb choir; *Requiem aeternam, poco piu lento.* b unison choir.

DISCOGRAPHY

None found.

JOSEPH GUY ROPARTZ
June 15, 1864–November 22, 1955

Guy Ropartz entered the Paris Conservatoire in 1885 to study with Dubois and Massenet, but left to study with César Franck. He later held the directorships of the conservatories in Nancy and in Strasbourg, where he was active in the promotion of French music. Ropartz composed about 200 works for stage, orchestra, chamber ensemble, and instrumental solo. Among the vocal works are two settings of the mass, two Psalm settings for chorus and orchestra, and the *Requiem*.

Ropartz scored the *Requiem* for SATB choir (ssaattbb *divisi*), soprano and alto soloists, and orchestra. It was composed in 1937–1938. Although much of his musical style was influenced by César Franck, Ropartz's own distinctive personality is wound into the fabric of his music. Traditional triadic harmonies, as well as the sevenths and ninths of French impressionism appear within the tonal language of this requiem. A strong tonic-dominant relationship is blurred by the use of secondary chords.

The rhythmic sense of the *Requiem* is much closer to the spirit of classical French music than to the "dreamy," suspended rhythms of Debussy. The basic SATB choral scoring is continually altered to provide color and variety. Although most of the choral writing is homophonic, there are excursions into imitative polyphony (*Kyrie, Domine Jesu Christe, Quam olim Abrahae, Benedictus,* and *Hosanna*).

The absence of the *Dies irae* text and its gentle tone and mood permit it to be a companion work to the requiem settings of Fauré, Duruflé, and Desenclos. Strings form the basic accompanimental sonority, while brass and timpani are employed sparingly.

Basic Data

EDITION

J. Guy Ropartz
Requiem pour soli, choeur et orchestre
[piano-vocal edition]
Durand & Cie (D & F 12, 944) 1938.

DURATION

Eight movements, 558 mm., perf., c. 36'

VOICING AND ORCHESTRATION

Choir: SATB [ssaattbb *divisi*] range: S-A flat 6; B-E flat 3
Soloists: SA
Orchestra: vn. I/II, vla., vc., db., 2 fl., 2 ob., Eh., 2 cl., 2 bsn., 3 Fh., 2 tpt., tbn., timp.

OUTLINE

Introit: 84 mm.
   Requiem aeternam [gm] *lento.* S solo/saattb choir; *Te decet,* S solo; *Exaudi,* saatb choir; *Requiem aeternam,* satbb/saatb/sattb choir. ABA form.
Kyrie: 59 mm.
   Kyrie [gm] *larghetto.* satbb choir; *Kyrie,* satb choir; *Christe,* satb/ saatb choir; *Kyrie,* saatbb choir; *Kyrie,* satbb choir.
Offertory: 72 mm.
   Domine Jesu Christe [e flat m-E flat M] *largo.* saatb/ssatb/ssatbb/saatb choir; *Sed signifer,* saatbb/sattbb choir; *Hostias,* satbb choir; *Tu suscipe,* satb choir; *Quam olim Abrahae,* sattb choir.

Sanctus-Benedictus: 71 mm.
  Sanctus [BM] *non troppo lento*. satbb choir; *Dominus Deus*, satb choir; *Benedictus*, ssattb; *Benedictus-Hosanna*, ssattbb choir.
Pie Jesu: 28 mm.
  Pie Jesu [DM], *adagio*. S solo/satbb; *Pie Jesu*, S solo/sattbb; *Pie Jesu*, S solo/sattbb choir.
Agnus Dei-Communion: 110 mm.
  Agnus Dei I [B flat M] *andante*. satbb choir; *Agnus Dei* II & III, satb choir; *Lux aeterna, piu mosso*, orchestral introduction; *Lux aeterna*, SA soli (canonic); *Cum Sanctis*, saattb choir; *Requiem aeternam*, ab/saattb choir; *Cum sanctis*, saattbb/satbb choir.
Responsory: 88 mm.
  Libera me [B flat-gm] *poco lento*. satb choir; *Tremens factus*, A solo/satb; *Dies illa*, A solo/satb choir; *Requiem aeternam, piu largamente*, satbb choir; *Libera me*, saatb/satb choir.
In Paradisum: 46 mm.
  In Paradisum [GM] *moderato*. satb/satbb choir.

DISCOGRAPHY

Accord, ACD 205132, Jean-Walter Audoli Instrumental Ensemble, French Vittoria Régional Choir, cond. Michel Piquemal.

ALFRED SCHNITTKE
November 24, 1934–August 3, 1998

Schnittke studied composition with Eugene Golubev (pupil of Miaskovsky) and orchestration with Nikolai Rakov (pupil of Glière) at the Moscow Conservatory from 1953–58. He was subsequently appointed to the staff of the Conservatory, where he taught for ten years (1962–72).

His earliest works were composed in a traditional style, but after visits to Western Europe, he became interested in serial technique and in "sonorism," a style in which the dynamics assume a kind of thematic significance. Schnittke became acknowledged as a bold innovator in modern Russian composition.

He left a large opus of various works, including eight symphonies, concertos, other works for solo instruments (violin, piano, harpsichord, oboe, harp, and cello) and orchestra, and a significant body of chamber music. Among the vocal pieces are secular works and the *Requiem for Three Sopranos, Alto, Tenor, Chorus, and Eight Instrumentalists*. There is also *Communio II*, composed for the collaborative *Requiem of Reconciliation* (1995).

The *Requiem for Three Sopranos* was composed in 1974–75 as stage music for the Frederich Schiller play, *Don Carlos*. This spectacular work, written during the Cold War era, represents a kind of musical miracle. The Soviet government virtually prohibited the production of sacred choral music at this time. The harmonic language of this work embraces triadic tonality (*Kyrie, Quarum hodie, Fac eas*), bi-tonality (sections of the *Credo*), atonality (*Sanctus Michael, Quid sum miser, Dies irae*), unpitched sound (*Tuba mirum, Rex tremendae*), tone clusters (*Quid sum miser*, orchestral accompaniment in *Tuba mirum, Dies irae*), and dissonant chords built upon major/minor seconds (*Quam olim Abrahae, Dies irae*).

To create variety and interest, the basic SATB choral texture is constantly thinned and enlarged from unison to SATB to SSA to SSAATTBB scorings. The texture includes a balance of chordal writing and imitative polyphony (*Requiem aeternam, Mors stupebit, Lacrimosa,* and *Sanctus*). Choral and instrumental ostinati are found in virtually every movement. The downward melodic leap of the seventh and upward leap of the sixth figures prominently throughout the work.

The overall tone of the work is very serious. Every movement possesses an enormous amount of musical interest, from the spectral canonic duet for soprano and tenor of the *Sanctus*, to the crescendo-decrescendo structure of the Introit, to the Orff-like ostinati of the *Rex tremendae*.

The brevity of each movement indicates that the composer conceived this work as a *missa brevis*. Unique in the requiem literature is the inclusion of the Creed, normally omitted from the requiem text. The orchestration of the *Requiem* is also somewhat unusual in its inclusion of electric guitar, electric bass, instruments normally associated with rock and roll.

Basic Data

EDITIONS

1. Alfred Schnittke
Requiem from the stage music for the dramatic production "Don Carlos" by Schiller for soloists, choir and instruments.
Partitur (ed. #2257)
Musikverlag Hans Sikorski, Hamburg

2. Alfred Schnittke
Requiem . . .
Vocal Score
(ed. #2257)
Musikverlag Hans Sikorski
Hamburg [1977]

DURATION

Thirteen movements, 516 mm., perf., c. 35'

VOICING AND ORCHESTRATION

Choir: SATB [SSAATTBB *divisi*] range: S-C7; B-E3
Soloists: 3 Sopranos, Alto, Tenor
Instruments: tpt., tbn., org., piano, celesta, electric guitar, bass guitar, marimba, xylophone, vibraphone, glockenspiel, bells, timpani, flexatone, large drum, tam-tam, drums.

OUTLINE

Introit: 51 mm.

Requiem aeternam, [E] *moderato*. ss/ssa/ssaatt/ssaattbb choir combinations (double canon). E pedalpoint throughout.

Kyrie: 43 mm.

Kyrie, *moderato*. satb/ttbb/ssaattbb choir combinations/SSA soli. Built upon and eighth-note and quarter-note ostinato patterns; *Christe*, SSA soli (fugato)/ ssattb choir; *Kyrie*, ssatb choir. [CM conclusion]

Sequence: 146 mm., 5 movements.

Dies irae: 42 mm., *moderato*. satb choir/ssaattbb choir combinations. Imitation and ostinato patterns. (v. 1). *Tuba mirum*: 50 mm., *lento*. satb choir; *Mors stupebit*, satb choir; *Liber scriptus*, tb choir (sa choir, spoken ostinato "*Tuba mirum*"); *Judex ergo*, satb-sssatttb choir; *Quid sum miser*, sssaaatttb choir. C # pedalpoint throughout the movement. (vv. 3-7). *Rex tremendae*: 27 mm., *maestoso*. satb choir (opening and closing statements sung, middle section is spoken. Orchestral ostinato. (v. 8). *Recordare*: 27 mm., *andante*. satb choir; *Quaerens me*, satb choir. (vv. 9-10). Orchestration reduced to piano, organ, and vibraphone. *Lacrimosa*: 32 mm., *andante*. SA soli/ssaat choir; *Huic ergo*, ssat choir. (melodic ostinato). (vv. 18-19).

Offertory: 72 mm., 2 movements.

Domine Jesu Christe: 32 mm., *risoluto*. satb choir; *Libera eas*, ssaattbb choir. *Hostias*: 24 mm., *maestoso*. ssaattbb choir.

Sanctus: 51 mm.

Sanctus, *lento*. ST soli/ssatb choir (in various scorings). Canon.

Benedictus: 56 mm.

Benedictus, *moderato*. ssaattbb choir (paired and thinned scorings) Orchestra reduced to organ and celesta.

Agnus Dei: 30 mm.

Agnus Dei, *adagio*. A solo/ssaatt choir. Dialogue between soloist and choir.

Credo: 59 mm.

Credo, *largo*. satb choir (*divisi*). Bi-tonal (CM/B flat M) *Requiem aeternam*: the Introit is repeated.

DISCOGRAPHY

Chandos, Chan 9564, Russian State Symphony Orchestra and Cappella, cond. Valeri Polyansky.

HEINRICH SUTERMEISTER
August 12, 1910–November 16, 1995

Sutermeister studied at Hanover Hochschule für Musik. During the 1940s, he received recognition as a composer of opera. Like Carl Orff, one of his teachers, Sutermeister successfully attempted to create a strong rapport between the audience and the performers of his music. He wrote a small amount of chamber music and music for orchestra. There are also ten operas. Among the choral and vocal works are several sacred pieces, including a *Te Deum* (1975), a *Mass in E flat*, and the *Requiem* (1952).

The *Requiem* was scored for soprano and baritone soli, SATB (*divisi*) choir, and orchestra. The primary choral texture is SATB, with contrasting changes in the *divisi* scoring. Much of the writing is homophonic, although there are numerous passages of imitative polyphonic style (*Te decet, Qui salvandos, Pie Jesu*) provided for contrast. Canonic writing is employed for *Benedictus* and the *Sanctus* text is set as a fugue.

Much of the tonal harmony is triadic, although there are numerous unison and two-part passages. Sutermeister uses repeated melodic fragments (*ostinati*), a straightforward rhythm, and broad melodic lines. While every movement bears a C major key signature, the abundant chromatic writing provides many other tonalities. For example, the Introit is composed over an E flat/D♯ pedalpoint for the duration of the movement. Numerous passages of parallel fourths and fifths recall a more ancient harmonic style.

The *Requiem* is a solid, well-written composition, full of effective, dramatic orchestral and vocal writing. The music also possesses the spiritual qualities appropriate for use in the liturgy.

Basic Data

EDITION

Heinrich Sutermeister
Missa da Requiem
[full score]
B. Schott's Söhne, Mainz
1960

DURATION

Six movements, 1054 mm., perf., c. 47′

VOICING AND ORCHESTRATION

Choir: SATB range: S-A6; B-E3
Soloists: S Bar
Orchestra: vn. I/II, vla., vc., db., pic., 3 fl., 2 ob., 1 Eh., 2 cl., bcl., 3 bsn., cbsn., 4 Fh., 3 tpt., 3 tbn., tuba, timp., harp, piano.

OUTLINE

Introit-*Kyrie*: 115 mm.
   Requiem aeternam, andante, pesante. satb [*divisi*] choir; *Kyrie*, SBar duet/satb choir [*divisi*].

Sequence: 343 mm.

Dies irae, allegro deciso. satb choir [*divisi* & various scorings] (verses 1-8). *Recordare, lento, rubato.* S solo; *Quaerens me-Qui Mariam-Preces meae-Inter oves,* S solo/tb [*divisi*] choir; *Confutatis-Oro supplex-Lacrymosa-Huic ergo, allegro.* satbb choir; *Pie Jesu, sostenuto.* sa-tb/ssattb choir; *Amen,* S solo/satbb choir.

Offertory: 237 mm.

Domine Jesu Christe, mosso, ma sostenuto, misterioso. Bar solo; *Sed signifer,* Bar solo; *Hostias,* Bar solo/ssa choir; *Quam olim Abrahae,* Bar solo/satb choir.

Sanctus: 213 mm.

Sanctus, allegro molto e maestoso. ssatbb choir; *Sanctus,* satb choir (fugue); *Benedictus,* S Bar soli/satb choir (*Hosanna*) (fugal); *In nomine,* S Bar soli/satb choir (fugal).

Agnus Dei-Communion: 146 mm.

Agnus Dei I/II/III, *adagio.* S solo/satb/ssaattbb choir; *Agnus Dei* III, S Bar soli/ssatb choir; *Agnus Dei* IV/V, S Bar soli/ssaattbb choir; *Lux aeterna, molto sostenuto.* S solo/satbb choir.

DISCOGRAPHY

Wergo, WER 6294 2, Berlin Rundfunk Orchester und Chor, cond. Heinz Rogner.

JOHN TAVENER
January 21, 1944

Tavener was a student of Lennox Berkeley at the Royal Academy of Music in London from 1961 to 1965. He was appointed to the position of organist at St. John's Church, Kensington, in 1960. He later became professor of music at Trinity College of Music in London (1969). He has composed in a variety of modern styles, including electronic music and the serial technique, as well as more conservative tonal approaches. His conversion to the Greek Orthodox faith has had a profound influence upon the kinds of compositions he has chosen to write.

This composer has written orchestral works, music drama and chamber operas, chamber music, music for piano, one piece for the organ, and an enormous amount of sacred and secular vocal music. The works, *The Great Canon of St. Andrew of Crete* (1981) and *The Orthodox Vigil Service* (1984), the *Liturgy of St. John Crysostom* (1978), and *The Panikhida* (Russian Requiem) of 1986 are but a few of the works composed as a result of his conversion.

His *Little Requiem for Father Malachy Lynch* was composed in 1972 and scored for SATB choir and chamber orchestra. The work was commissioned by the Southern Cathedrals Festival and its first performance took place on July 29, 1972, in Winchester Cathedral. His interest in undertaking the commission came about from his personal contact with Father

Lynch (1899–1972). After attending the latter's funeral, Tavener decided to write a requiem for this outstanding priest and scholar.

He set only three short sections of the *Requiem* text: *Requiem aeternam, Dies irae* (vv.1–2,18–19), and *Libera me*. The harmonic vocabulary employed by the composer borders on the worlds of tonality and atonality. Melodic and rhythmic patterns give a sense of order to the music. Much of the choral texture is unison with occasional four-part chordal writing. Tavener was later encouraged to enlarge the *Requiem* into a complete setting, a task completed in 1978. The overall tone of the piece is one that possesses a great deal of solemnity and spirituality.

Basic Data

EDITION

Contemporary Church Music Series
Little Requiem for Father Malachy Lynch
John Tavener
J. & W. Chester Music 1978

DURATION

Five movements, 48 mm. + *Libera me*, perf., c. 11′

VOICING AND ORCHESTRATION

1. (1972)
Choir: SATB range: S-G6; B-E3
Instruments: vn. I/II, vla., vc., db., 2 fl. tpt., org.
2. (1973)
Choir: 2 countertenors, tenor, 2 baritones, bass.
Orchestra

OUTLINE

Introit: 15 mm.
   Requiem aeternam, quietly. satb choir, unaccompanied. (Unison/octave chant-like passages of seven notes appear six times). Quiet, string chords separate each seven-note passage.
Sequence, *Die irae*: 33 mm.
   Dies irae, satb choir (octave unison). Repeated melodic patterns of five notes, written 3/8 + 5/8 meter. (ostinato for flutes/trumpet); *Lacrymosa*, satb unaccompanied choir. (canonic instrumental interludes); *Dies irae* is repeated.
Responsory: unbarred.
   Libera me, satb choir (*divisi*, sasatbtb-sasasasatbtbtbtb choir). Begins as a unison *parlando* chant, expanding to parallel seconds and ultimately, tone clusters.
Introit: *Requiem aeternam* is repeated.

DISCOGRAPHY

Sony, SK 66613, English Chamber Orchestra, Westminster Abbey Choir, cond. Martin Neary.

VIRGIL THOMSON
November 25, 1896–September 30, 1989

At the age of twelve, Virgil Thomson began to give solo piano and organ concerts. He took lessons in organ, singing, and music theory from local Kansas City teachers and he played organ for Calvary Baptist Church. He enjoyed a prestigious career at Harvard, and, after graduation, became an assistant instructor at Harvard. By 1925, he decided to continue his musical studies in Paris with Nadia Boulanger. While in Paris, he composed his opera, *Four Saints in Three Acts*. It was this work that brought him fame. He continued to make a livelihood through teaching, commissions, and the publication of seven books of musical criticism.

Thomson composed three major operas, several ballets, two dozen works for orchestra, incidental music, film scores, solo piano pieces, many songs, and a number of choral works. Among the latter pieces are Psalm settings, two *missae brevis* (*a cappella* male voices; female voices and percussion), *The Nativity as sung by the Shepherds*, and *Requiem Mass*.

The *Requiem Mass* for men's chorus, women's chorus, and orchestra was composed in 1960 and commissioned by the State College of Education in Potsdam, New York. Its premiere was given by the Crane Chorus on May 14, 1960. It is a fairly difficult work to perform because of the bi-tonal dissonance and whole tone patterns employed by the composer. Thomson, in the performance recommendations, suggests that the two choruses rehearse separately until the notes and intonation are completely secure. In performance, the two groups should stand on opposite sides of the orchestra. He proposed that four clarinets be placed among the women's chorus and four horns or bassoons among the men, to provide harmonic support for the singers.

This requiem is unique among twentieth-century settings because of its exploration of bitonality as well as the whole tone harmony and melody found throughout the work. Thomson frequently employed melodic, chordal, and rhythmic canons. (see Outline). At times, the recurrent parallel chords, moving at the interval of the tenth, sound like the pipe organ. The choral intonation is supported by the orchestral accompaniment. The snare drum is often used to join different sections and movements together.

Basic Data

EDITION

Virgil Thomson
Missa Pro Defunctis for Men's Chorus, Women's Chorus & Orchestra
Piano-Vocal Score
H. W. Gray Co., Inc., New York

DURATION

Eleven movements, 956 mm., perf., c. 45'

VOICING AND ORCHESTRATION

Choir: two choirs, SA [*divisi*], TB [*divisi*] range: S-A 6; B-F♯ 3

Orchestra: vn. I/II, vla., vc., db., pic., 3 fl., 3 ob., Eh., 3 cl., 2 bcl. [double 4th horn part], 2 bsn., 4 Fh., 3 tpt., 3 tbn., tuba, harp, celesta, timp., PERC: snare drum, field drum, glockenspiel, cymbals, bass drum, tam-tam, bells.

OUTLINE

Praeludium: 18 mm., *maestoso*, strings and woodwinds.

Introit: 46 mm.

Requiem aeternam, l'istesso tempo. sa-tb choirs. (parallel major chords); *Te decet, un poco piu mosso*. sa-tb choirs (melodic canon), orchestral postlude.

Kyrie: 58 mm.

Kyrie, andante. saa-tbb choirs (canon of chords); *Christe, un poco piu mosso*. tbb-saa choirs (melodic-chordal canon); *Kyrie*, tbb-saa choirs (canon). orch. postlude. ABA form.

Graduale-Tract: 95 mm.

Requiem aeternam, [*moderato*]. satb choir (parallel major chords moving in 10ths); *In memoria*, st-ab choirs (canon); *Absolve Domine, piu mosso*. tbb-saa choirs (canon of chords). Bi-tonal. *Et lucis aeternae*, satb choir (parallel major chords moving in 10ths).

Sequence: 440 mm.

Dies irae, marzial. satb choir (bi-tonal); *solvet saeclum-Teste David*, ssa-ttb choirs (canon); *Quantus tremor*, ssatbb choir (two sets of octave-unisons moving at different rhythms) Whole tone harmonies; *Tuba mirum*, satb octave-unison/brass; *Mors stupebit*, satb choir (melodic/harmonic arrangement of major thirds/ whole tone chords and triads); *Liber scriptus*, saa-ttb choirs (two separate sets of whole tone triads, bi-tonal effect); *Judex ergo*, ssaattbb choir (massed choral passages on successive C-D flat-D-E flat-F-F♯-G major chords) bi-tonal; orch. postlude; *Quid sum miser*, satb choir. (series of parallel 10ths/major 3ds over a C pedalpoint); *Rex tremendae*, sa-ttbb choirs (two different sets of choral unisons/ octaves, (sa, C pedalpoint. ttbb, contrasting melodic/intervallic line) orchestra plays series of parallel chords. bitonal; *Recordare*, saa-tbb choirs. (two different unison melodies), bitonal. Each melody is based on the whole tone. orchestral postlude; *Quaerens meae*, saa-ttbb choir (ssa choir duet employing parallel major thirds while ttbb choir accompanies with three and four-part minor harmony) bi-tonal; *Juste judex*, sa-tb choirs (sa voices in octaves/unisons, tb voices in octaves move in contrary motion to the sa voices) bi-tonal; *Ingemisco*, ssaatb choir (5/4 meter) bitonal; orch. Interlude for woodwinds/strings (two-part writing), two sets of parallel major thirds. The lower set is an inversion of the upper set; *Qui Mariam*, sa-tb choirs (canonic duet. Inversion used.); *Preces meae*, saatbb choir (chordal, whole-tone harmony); *Inter oves*, sa-tb choirs (two melodies, both written in parallel major thirds/ whole-tone violin obbligato); *Confutatis*, sa-tb choirs (two melodies, both written in parallel major thirds. canon.);

Oro supplex, ssaa-tbb choirs (whole-tone, four/five-part harmonizations. augmented triads); *Lacrimosa*, saa choir (canonic trio); orch. interlude; *Judicandus-Huic ergo*, tbb-ssa choirs (bitonal); *Pie Jesu*, saa-tbb choirs (bitonal, six-part chordal writing).

Offertory: 97 mm.

Domine Jesu Christe, sa-tb (*divisi*) choirs (parallel 10ths, 3ds, canon); *Sed signifer-Quam olim Abrahae*, (canon); *Hostias*, saa-tbb choirs (harmonies built on parallel major third triads and major seconds); *Quam olim Abrahae* is repeated.

Sanctus: 67 mm.

Orch. introduction; *Sanctus*, ttbb choir (four-part imitation); *Pleni sunt coeli*, (parallel chords); *Hosanna* (four-part imitation).

Benedictus: 20 mm.

Benedictus-Hosanna, ssaa choir (four-part imitation)

Agnus Dei: 56 mm.

Agnus Dei I/II/III, sattbb choir (two-part writing); *Agnus Dei* IV (parallel major chords, parallel 10ths).

Communion: 41 mm.

Lux aeterna. saa-ttb choirs (canon of triads). Instrumental postlude: 18 mm. Same thematic materials as the Prelude.

DISCOGRAPHY

None found.

ERNST TITTEL
April 26, 1910–July 28, 1969

Ernst Tittel was trained at the Vienna Academy of Music, the school where he later became lecturer in theory and composition (1936) and ultimately professor (1961). He was also the organist of the Franziskanerkirche in Vienna. Tittel wrote a small amount of secular choral music and some organ works. Among the sacred choral pieces are five masses, one Psalm setting, and two requiems (Op. 34 and Op. 81).

The *Requiem*, Op. 34, was first published in 1949 and scored for SATB choir, and organ. It is a modest, liturgical work, employing a late-romantic vocabulary and style. It is quite suitable for smaller choirs. Adhering to the ideals set forth by the nineteenth-century Caecilian Reform Movement, the composer employed Gregorian melodies, either suggested or stated plainly at various points within the work. The choral textures are a blend of imitative polyphony (*Quid sum miser*, *Voca me*, *Oro supplex*, *Benedictus*, *Agnus Dei*, *Libera me*) and homophonic writing. For the most part, the organ doubles the vocal lines.

Basic Data

EDITION

Ernst Tittel

Op. 34, Requiem mit Libera für vierstimmigen gemischten Chor und Orgel. Styria Steirische Verlagsanstalt. Graz, Vienna. 1949

DURATION

Ten movements, 567 mm.

VOICING AND ORCHESTRATION

Choir: SATB range: S-A flat 6; B-F 3
Instruments: org.

OUTLINE

Introit-*Kyrie*: 89 mm.
  Requiem aeternam [gm] *tranquillo*. satb choir; *Te decet* [gm] satb choir; *Requiem aeternam* [gm] satb choir, ABA form; *Kyrie*, satb choir (fugal).
Graduale: 21 mm.
  Requiem aeternam [FM] *moderato*. satb choir. Gregorian melody is present in the tenor and bass line.
Tract: 34 mm.
  Absolve Domine [FM] *ruhiges Zeitmass* [quiet tempo] satb choir.
Sequence: 138 mm.
  Dies irae [gm] *wuchtig und ernst* [heavy & serious] satb choir; *Quantus tremor*, sat choir; *Tuba mirum*, b unison; *Liber scriptus*, a unison; *Judex ergo*, satb choir; *Quid sum miser*, sat choir; *Rex tremendae*, satb choir; *Recordare*, t unison; *Quaerens me*, sa unison; *Juste judex*, b unison; *Ingemisco*, satb choir; *Qui Mariam*, st unison; *Preces meae*, a unison; *Inter oves*, satb unison; *Confutatis*, satb choir; *Oro supplex*, sat choir; *Lacrimosa-Huic ergo-Jesu Pie*, satb choir.
Offertory: 83 mm.
  Domine Jesu Christe, con moto (canonic) satb choir; *Quam olim Abrahae*, [B flat M] *andante assai*. satb choir; *Hostias, larghetto piu*. satb choir; *Quam olim Abrahae* is repeated.
Sanctus: 37 mm.
  Sanctus [B flat M] *tranquillo*. satb choir; *Hosanna*, satb choir (fugal). The Gregorian melody is present.
Benedictus: 16 mm.
  Benedictus [E flat M] *andante moderato*. satb choir (canonic) *Hosanna* is repeated.
Agnus Dei: 52 mm.
  Agnus Dei [gm] *moderato*. satb choir. (canon).
Communion: 35 mm.
  Lux aeterna-Cum sanctis-Requiem aeternam, satb choir.
Responsory: 62 mm.
  Libera me [gm] *piu grave*. satb choir; *Tremens factus* [cm] *sostenuto*. satb choir; *Quando coeli* [gm] *piu moderato*. satb choir (canon); *Dies illa* [gm] *grave*. unison

satb choir; *Requiem aeternam* [gm] *tranquillo*. satb choir. The Gregorian melody is quoted.

DISCOGRAPHY
None found.

VINCENZO TOMMASINI
September 17, 1878–December 23, 1950

Tommasini is one of the lesser-known, excellent Italian composers of the twentieth century. His musical studies were done at the *Liceo di Sancta Cecilia* in Rome and with Max Bruch at the *Hochschule für Musik* in Berlin. He composed several operas and a significant body of chamber music, yet today he is best remembered for his arrangement of Scarlatti's music, *Le donne di buon umore* (The Good-Humored Ladies).

The *Messa di Requiem* was written in 1944 and is scored for SATB choir and organ. It is one of the many "Caecilian" liturgical requiem settings of the late nineteenth–early twentieth centuries. Its harmonic language is a mixture of chant-like melody, supported by late romantic and impressionist harmony styles. The prevailing chordal harmony is relieved by occasional imitative polyphonic passages (*Kyrie, Ingemisco, Sanctus, Benedictus*, and *Agnus Dei*).

Basic Data

EDITION

Musiche Liturgiche di Autori Moderni a Cura di Bonaventura Somma
Nr. 2
Messa di Requiem per coro a 4 voci miste e organo.
Ediziono De Santis #754 [Full score] Rome. 1949

DURATION

Ten movements, 436 mm.

VOICING AND ORCHESTRATION

Choir: SATB range: S-G flat 6; B-E3
Instruments: org.

OUTLINE

Introitus-*Kyrie*: 88 mm.
  Requiem aeternam, andante. satb choir; *Te decet*, satb choir; *Requiem aeternam*; satb choir. ABA form; *Kyrie*, satb choir (canonic voice pairing)
Graduale: 12 mm.
  Requiem aeternam, moderato. satb choir.

Tract: 20 mm.

Absolve Domine, andante. unison tenor choir.

Sequence: 90 mm.

Dies irae-Quantus tremor-Tuba mirum, mosso. satb choir; *Mors stupebit,* sa choir; *Liber scriptus-Judex ergo-Quid sum miser-Rex tremendae-Recordare,* satb choir; *Quarens me,* atb choir (canonic); *Juste judex,* satb choir; *Ingemisco,* satb choir (canonic); *Qui Mariam-Preces meae-Confutatis,* satb choir; *Oro supplex,* b-t-s-a unison choral lines; *Lacrimosa-Huic ergo-Pie Jesu,* satb choir.

Offertory: 40 mm.

Domine Jesu Christe, moderato ma non troppo. b unison choir; *Libera eas,* ab unison choir; *Sed signifer,* ssattb choir; *Quam olim Abrahae,* b unison choir; *Hostias,* satb choir; *Quam olim Abrahae,* b unison choir.

Sanctus: 68 mm.

Sanctus, allegro. satb choir ("bell-like" imitative melody); *Benedictus,* satb choir (imitative).

Agnus Dei: 36 mm.

Agnus Dei, moderato. tb choir (canon) alternates with sssaaa or tttbbb choir.

Communion: 17 mm.

Luceat eis, moderato. satb choir; *Et lux perpetua,* satb choir. Two Gregorian intonations included.

Responsory: 36 mm.

Libera me, moderato. s/a unison lines; *Tremens factus,* satb choir; *Dies illa,* s/a unison lines. ABA form.

Responsory [*Requiem aeternam*]: 29 mm.

Requiem aeternam, andante. satb choir; *Libera me,* s unison choir; *Kyrie,* satb choir. ABA form.

DISCOGRAPHY

None found.

ERKKI-SVEN TÜÜR
October 16, 1959

Tüür was born in Estonia and studied at the Conservatory in Tallinn. In 1991, he taught composition at the Conservatory, but in 1993, gave up the position in order to devote himself full-time to composing. Although he had begun his musical career as a rock musician, he later went on to produce compositions that included orchestral works, music for the theater, chamber music, solo music, and a number of choral works, including the *Lumen et Cantus Mass* (1989), and a *Requiem*.

His modern works combine both elements from tonality and atonality. He uses elements from the serial techniques, indeterminate sound and tonal sound textures, as well as traditional forms. Tüür has stated that he tried to "connect these two worlds in a single composition so that it is not a mixture but a structurally felt and built musical totality." (see Discography, Notes, CD booklet)

The twenty-eight minute *Requiem*, composed in 1994 in memory of Peeter Lilje, the chief conductor of the Estonian State Symphony Orchestra, is a representative work of this composer. Scored for soprano and tenor soloists, SATB choir (*divisi*), strings, piano, and triangle, it has the distinction of being the only almost-complete setting of the requiem (in this guide) conceived as a one-movement work. Although it has only one movement, the work possesses the feeling and structure of a number of smaller sections joined together that correspond to the text of the traditional requiem canon. The work flows smoothly from section to section.

The text is somewhat truncated, for example, one section of the *Kyrie* is missing, the *Dies irae* setting omits the eleventh through the sixteenth verses, and one statement of the *Agnus Dei* is dropped. The orchestration of the *Requiem,* as well as the requiem text, is vital in setting off the various sections and moods of the composition. All three musical mediums—the mixed choir, the strings, and the piano are scored and played with great variety and ingenuity. The only other instrument present, a triangle, is used briefly and only at the opening, middle, and conclusion of the work.

The strings play a major role in the *Requiem*, and are employed in constantly changing combinations and divisions in the scoring. Violins 1 are scored for a single line up to five-part *divisi* and violins 2—from one part to a four-part *divisi*. Violas and cellos divide up into three-part *divisi*. Basses are limited to only one line. "Glides," glissando passages and trills are frequently used by the strings to create an indefinite tonal sonority. Complex polyrhythms are routinely used in the string writing, thereby creating a seething, roiling accompaniment for the choral parts. Last, the strings are scored for solo as well as ensemble playing.

The piano is employed in a stream of experimental techniques, ranging from serial-like arpeggio figurations, chromatic tone clusters, improvisatory passages, to new techniques of playing upon the keyboard strings. These techniques include: playing on the lowest string register with timpani sticks (to create a dark sonic boom), sweeping over or plucking the piano strings with a plectrum, pressing upon the string with the thumb to create short sounds, beating upon the strings with the hand, and sweeping the strings with a metal drum brush.

The scoring for the chamber choir is somewhat more tonal. At the same time, there is variety in the number of voices used. Parts for the women's voices do not appear until the *Tuba mirum* of the *Dies irae,* and even then they are employed in humming and vowel sounds. There are beautiful melodic passages, reminiscent of Gregorian chant, scored for the men.

Vocal *glissandi* are occasionally used and there are solo lines for the tenor and soprano. A unison chant, sung by the basses, opens and concludes the composition. Homophonic choral texture is used throughout.

This highly original work possesses a wide variety of sonorities and mood contrasts.

Basic Data

EDITION

Requiem
Kammerchor, Klavier und Streicher
[Full Score]
Edition Peters Nr. 8886
Henry Litolff's Verlag. Frankfurt. Leipzig. London. New York 1996.

DURATION

One movement, 505 mm., perf., 28'

VOICING AND ORCHESTRATION

Choir: SATB [*divisi*] range: S-G6; B-D3
Soloists: ST
Instruments: vn. 1 [*divisi à* 5], vn. 2 [*divisi à* 4], vla. [*divisi à* 3], vc. [*divisi à* 3], db., piano, triangle.

OUTLINE

Introit-*Kyrie*:
  Requiem aeternam-Te decet-Exaudi [quarter note = 65] b unison choir; *Requiem aeternam*, tb unison choir; *Requiem aeternam*, b choir; *Kyrie-Christe*, T solo; *Kyrie*, tb unison choir. strings/triangle.
Sequence:
  Dies irae [quarter-note = 80] ttbb choir [ttttbbbbb *divisi*] (Pianist plucks the keyboard strings with a plectrum); *Quantus tremor*, ttttbb choir; As a prelude to the *Tuba mirum-Mors stupebit*, the strings play an improvised set of patterns, moving from the highest to lowest sound register. The ssaa choir hums and sings vowel sounds). The violent mood is enhanced by a quarter-note ostinato figure in the string basses. Choral *glissandi* employed; *Rex tremendae*, satb choir [*divisi*], string ostinati, piano tone-clusters; *Recordare-Quaerens me*. S solo is accompanied by a pianist who sweeps the piano strings with metal brushes. The first violin soloist plays short melodic fragments, in duet with the soprano. *Lacrimosa*, ssaattbb choir. String interludes separate the choral sections.
Offertory:
  Domine Jesu Christe, [quarter note = 80] satb choir. Begins with a few string players on each sustained instrumental part. The pianist separates the choral statements with an arpeggiated, serial figuration. During the final section of the Offertory there is a graduale, yet massive increase in rhythmic activity, volume,

and number of instruments employed as the piece moves into the *Sanctus*. Piano tone clusters. Various ostinati.

Sanctus:

Sanctus, sssaaatttbbb choir. *Divisi* strings play various ostinati patterns. The triangle is used like a *Sanctus* bell, which appears for five short rings as *divisi* strings play a repeated, quiet octuplet figuration. *Benedictus*, satb choir [*divisi*]/ string ostinati.

Agnus Dei:

A quiet instrumental interlude introduces the *Agnus Dei*, ssa/aatb choir. Sung in a chant-like fashion by the women, and full choir. The piano reappears during the *Agnus Dei*, playing yet a different arpeggiated figure.

Communion:

Lux aeterna, ttbb/ssaatb choir; *Cum sanctis*, sssaaab choir; *Requiem aeternam*, bass unison choir/tb choir/ssattbb/sssaaatttb scorings. The strings play an extended, sustained accompaniment during the opening and final sections. The same chant-like melody at the opening of the work is again employed.

DISCOGRAPHY

ECM New Series, ECM 1590, Tallinn Chamber Orchestra, Estonian Philharmonic Chamber Choir, cond. Tõnu Kaljuste.

ERICH URBANNER
March 26, 1938

Urbanner was a student of composition and piano at the Vienna Academy of Music from 1955–1961. He later studied with the avant-garde composers, Wolfgang Fortner, Karlheinz Stockhausen, and Bruno Maderna. In 1968, he was appointed to a professorship in composition and harmony at the Vienna Hochschule für Musik.

He is the author of several stage works and a significant amount of orchestral and chamber music that includes concerti for piano, oboe, flute, violin, double bass, cello, and alto saxophone. There is a *Concertino for Organ and Strings* (1961) and four string quartets. In the area of sacred music is *Missa benedicite gentes* for choir and organ (1958) and the *Requiem* for SATB soli, SATB chorus, and orchestra (1982–83).

The *Requiem* was composed for the celebration of the 175th anniversary year (1984) of the battle for freedom of the Tyrol, an autonomous province in western Austria. The work is dedicated to the Tyrolese. Although his musical pieces seem to follow in the classical tradition, his musical vocabulary and style are atonal. Urbanner created a requiem setting based upon contrapuntal and linear concepts. The resulting vertical sonorities and chords are, therefore, a product of this linear polyphonic construction.

The harmonic vocabulary is determined by twelve-tone technique. The texture appears thick and very dissonant, yet each separate line is written melodically. The prevailing texture of the choral matrix is a four-part fabric and imitative polyphony can be found in the *Kyrie, Absolve* (Tract) *Tremens factus,* and *Libera me* (Responsory). This *Requiem* requires highly skilled singers for performance of both the vocal and choral parts.

Basic Data

EDITION

Erich Urbanner
Requiem für 4 Soli, gemischten Chor, Orgel & Orchester
Klavierauszug [Piano-Vocal Score] #46 071
Doblinger KG, Vienna, Munich

DURATION

Ten movements, 749 mm., perf., c. 60'

VOICING AND ORCHESTRATION

Choir: SATB [some *divisi* passages] range: S-B flat 6; B-E3
Soloists: SATBar
Orchestra: vn. I/II, vla., vc., db., pic., 3 fl., 3 ob., Eh., 3 cl., bcl., 3 bsn., cbsn., 4 Fh., 2 tenor tubas, 2 bass tubas, 3 tpt., 3 tbn., bass tuba, contrabass tuba, 3 timp., harp, org. PERC: small drum, tenor drum, bass drum, cymbals, 2 hand cymbals, gong or tam-tam, ratchet, glockenspiel, tubular bells, triangle, tambourine (4 players).

OUTLINE

Introit: 60 mm.
   Requiem aeternam, andante. satb choir; *Requiem aeternam,* satb choir/ SATBar soli.
Kyrie: 65 mm.
   Kyrie, andante con moto. saatb choir; *Christe,* satb choir/SATBar soli; *Kyrie,* satb choir. Multiple meters: 4/4, 6/4, 3/4, 5/4 and triplet rhythms. Full orchestra.
Graduale: 43 mm.
   Requiem aeternam, andante. satb choir/S solo. Instrumental prelude, interlude & postlude. Strings & woodwinds.
Tract: 45 mm.
   Absolve Domine, adagio. SATBar soli/satb choir. Each group performs separately, as a double choir. Organ, brass, strings.
Sequence: 121 mm.
   Dies irae, allegro assai. satb choir [ssaattb *divisi*] (vv. 1-6); *Quid sum miser,* satb choir, unaccompanied; *Rex tremendae,* satb choir; *Recordare, l'istesso tempo.* tb choir; *Quaerens me,* atb choir; *Juste judex,* satb choir; *Ingemisco-Qui Mariam-Inter oves-Confutatis-Oro supplex,* satb choir; *Lacrimosa-Huic ergo, adagio.* satb choir. (several meters: 5/4, 6/4).

Offertory: 47 mm.

Domine Jesu Christe, [*adagio*]. Bar. solo/full orchestra; *Hostias, religioso.* ttbb choir/Bar. solo.

Sanctus-Benedictus: 65 mm.

Sanctus, allegro con moto. satb choir/SATB soli (double choir); *Benedictus, tran-quillo.* ssaa choir; *Hosanna,* ssaatb choir.

Agnus Dei: 59 mm.

Agnus Dei, andante con moto. satb choir/A solo. (orchestral prelude, postlude, and two interludes)

Communion: 39 mm.

Lux aeterna. Double satb choirs (harp, glockenspiel, string bass, and light per-cussion); *Lux aeterna, tranquillo.* T solo.

Responsory: 205 mm.

Libera me, senza misura. T solo/satb choir; *Quando coeli, piu allegro.* ST soli/satb choir; *Tremens factus, allegro assai.* ST soli/satb choir; *Dies illa,* satb choir (speak-ing and shrieking on pitch); Instrumental intermezzo, *con moto* (57 mm.); *Requiem aeternam, andante.* double satb choir.

DISCOGRAPHY

None found.

ELINOR REMICK WARREN
February 23, 1900–May 27, 1991

Elinor Warren has the distinction of being one of the few women compos-ers to have composed a complete requiem setting. Most of her early musi-cal training was done with private teachers, yet in mid-career (1959), she studied intensively with Nadia Boulanger. In the 1920s, she worked as an accompanist for singers at the Metropolitan Opera. During this period, she began to compose and publish her songs and many of the Met singers with whom she worked performed her music.

Among her compositions is *The Passing of King Arthur*, for tenor and baritone soli, chorus, and orchestra (1940); a tone poem, *The Crystal Lake* (1946); *Suite for Orchestra* (1955); and *Along the Western Shore*, for orchestra (1954). Her late works include *Symphony in One Movement* (1970) and *Requiem* (1966).

The *Requiem*, commissioned by Roger Wagner for the Roger Wagner Chorale, is scored for mezzo-soprano and baritone soli, SATB choir, and orchestra. Its tonal language is a mixture of chromatic, late romantic har-mony and angular, "dissonant," non-triadic chords. Key designations in the Outline are only approximate because of the constantly changing tonal centers. The prevailing four-part, homophonic choral texture is relieved by *divisi* scoring and occasional passages in imitative polyphonic style (*Exaudi, Domine Jesu Christe, Kyrie, Sanctus, Pleni sunt coeli*, and *Quam olim Abrahae*). The orchestral part is fully independent of the choral matrix.

Basic Data

EDITION

Elinor Remick Warren
Requiem for mixed chorus
Lawson-Gould Music Publishers, Inc. New York 1965.
[Latin and English]

DURATION

Six movements, 856 mm., perf., c. 50'

VOICING AND ORCHESTRATION

Choir: SATB [*divisi*] range: S-B flat 6; B-D flat 3
Soloists: Mezzo-Soprano, Baritone
Orchestra: vn. I/II, vla., vc., db., pic., 2 fl., 2 ob., Eh., 2 cl., 2 bsn., 4 Fh., 2 tpt., 3 tbn., tuba. PERC: timp. bass drum, snare drum, cymbals, xylophone, gong. celeste. harp.

OUTLINE

Introit-*Kyrie*: 117 mm.
   Requiem aeternam [dm] *largo.* satb choir; *Te decet*, satb choir; *Requiem aeternam*, satb choir; *Kyrie* [DM] satb choir.
Graduale: 39 mm.
   Requiem aeternam [dm] *largo molto tranquillo.* satb choir; orchestral postlude.
Sequence: 340 mm.
   Orchestral prelude, *ominously*; *Dies irae*, satb choir; *Quantus tremor*, satb choir; orchestral interlude [E flat]; *Tuba mirum*, ssaattbb choir; *Mors stupebit*, satb choir (imitation); *Liber scriptus, faster.* satb choir; *Judex ergo*, Bar solo/b choir; *Quid sum miser* [CM] *andante.* Mezzo-soprano solo; *Rex tremendae* [fm] *moderato, marcato.* ssaattbb choir; *Qui salvandos*, Mezzo soprano solo/satb choir [ABA form]; *Recordare* [bm] *andante.* satb choir; *Quaerens me*, satb choir; *Oro supplex*, [dm] *moderato*, Bar. solo; *Lacrymosa* [D flat], *slower.* sa/tb choir (canonic); *Huic ergo*, satb choir; *Pie Jesu*, satb choir.
Offertory: 123 mm., 2 "movements."
   Domine Jesu Christe: 65 mm. [C-A flat-e flat] *moderato.* satb choir; *Sed signifer*, Mezzo sop solo/satb choir; *Quam olim Abrahae*, satb choir (imitative); segue to *Hostias*: *Hostias*: 57 mm. [F] *with marked rhythm.* Bar. solo; *Quam olim Abrahae*, satb choir.
Sanctus: 121 mm.
   Sanctus [bm] *moderato tranquillo.* ssaa choir/ssaattbb choir (imitation); *Pleni sunt coeli*, Mezzo sop., Bar. soli/ttbb choir (canonic); *Hosanna* [bm] *allegro giocoso.*

ssaattbb choir; segue: *Benedictus* [F] *andante*. Bar. solo/satb choir; *Hosanna* [D]
allegro giocoso. ssaattbb choir.
Agnus Dei-Communion: 116 mm.
   Agnus I, II, III [B flat] *slowly, very tranquilly*. satb choir; *Agnus Dei* IV, sattbb
choir; *Lux aeterna* [dm] *molto tranquillo*. mezzo sop. solo/ssaa choir; *Requiem
aeternam* [gm-GM] satb choir.

DISCOGRAPHY
Cambria, CD 1061, Polish Radio-TV Symphony, Chorus of Cracow, cond. Szymon
Kawallo.

HEALEY WILLAN
October 12, 1880–February 16, 1968

The Canadian, Healey Willan received his earliest musical training at St.
Saviour's Choir School in Eastbourne from 1888 to 1895. At fifteen, he
began his musical career as organist for the St. Cecilia Society in London.
During his teens and twenties, he served a number of churches as organist
and was appointed conductor of several choral societies. In 1913, he emigrated to Canada, settling in Toronto as head of the music theory department at the Conservatory of Music. In 1921, he became organist-
choirmaster of the Anglican Church of St. Mary Magdalene, a position in
which he remained until his death in 1968. He taught composition and
counterpoint at the University of Toronto from 1937 to 1950. During his
tenure in Toronto, he started a number of musical societies and received
many professional honors in recognition of his distinguished service to
music.
   Willan wrote two orchestral symphonies, a piano concerto, and several
other pieces of program music, as well as two operas and a half dozen
radio and ballad operas. The major part of his *oeuvre* was sacred music.
He composed nearly 100 organ chorale preludes and several large organ
works. His choral music includes more than forty anthems, thirty hymn-
anthems, fourteen settings of the *Missa brevis*, eleven liturgical motets,
eight cantatas, eighty fauxbourdons to hymn-tunes, and other miscellaneous works.
   The *Requiem* was composed, though never finished, during the years
1912 to 1918. It is scored for SATB soli, SATB (*divisi*) choir, and orchestra.
His biographer, Frederick Clarke, has suggested that Willan was stimulated to write the work in reaction to his father's death and that a possible
reason for the work remaining unfinished was the upheaval in the composer's life as he moved to Canada.
   Willan completed the Introit, *Kyrie*, *Dies Irae*, *Sanctus*, and *Benedictus*.

The music for *Agnus Dei* and the Communion was taken from Willan's *Communion Service* (1910) and the *Requiem* itself. Clarke completed the work that Willan had begun nearly seventy years earlier. Its first perform-ance took place in 1988. The orchestration was also done by Prof. Clarke, who based his work on other symphonic works already completed by Willan.

The musical language of the work was greatly influenced by the Renais-sance modal system, joined to the late romantic harmonic idiom and the modal, Anglican revival style. The music flows freely from chordal, homophonic sections to passages of imitative contrapuntal style, such as found in *Kyrie, Christe, Inter oves, Confutatis,* and *Dona eis.* There is also a complete fugue on the text, *Pleni sunt coeli.* Although there are a number of significant vocal solos in the *Requiem,* the bulk of the writing treats the soloists as a second choir, *concertante* style.

Basic Data

EDITION

Healey Willan
Requiem
[Organ-Vocal Score]
Completed & Edited by F. R. C. Clarke
Oxford University Press, Inc. 1992

DURATION

Seven movements, 1172 mm, perf., c. 55'

VOICING AND ORCHESTRATION

Choir: SATB [*divisi*] range: S-C7; B-D3
Soloists: SATBar
Orchestra: vn. I/II, vla., vc., cb., pic., 2 fl., 2 ob., 2 cl., 2 bsn., 4 Fh., 2 tpt., 3 tbn., tuba, timp., harp. PERC: bass drum, snare drum, tam-tam, cymbals.

OUTLINE

Introit: 135 mm. [composed in 1914]
   Requiem aeternam [FM] *lento.* ssaattbb choir; *Te decet,* ssaa-ttbb/ssaattbb choir; *Requiem aeternam.* ABA form.
Kyrie: 129 mm. [composed in 1918]
   Kyrie [fm] *largo e solenne.* satb [ssaattbb *divisi*] choir; *Christe* [D flat M] SATBar soli quartet; *Kyrie* [fm] ABA form.
Sequence: 152 mm. [composed before 1914]
   Dies irae [b flat m] *allegro e con terrore.* ttbb choir; *Quantus tremor-Tuba mirum* (*maestoso*)-*Mors stupebit,* satb choir; *Liber scriptus,* alto unison choir; *Judex ergo,* tb unison choir; *Quid sum miser,* soprano unison choir; *Rex tremendae, allegro.* ssattbb choir/S solo; *Recordare,* Bar. solo; *Quaerens me,* S solo; *Juste judex-Inge-*

misco [fm] satb choir; *Preces meae* [fm] *allegro*. T solo; *Inter oves*. satb choir; *Confutatis* [f# m] *allegro*. ssattb choir; *Voca me* [BM] *dolce*. S solo/satb choir; *Lacrymosa* [b flat m] *andante espressivo*. SATBar soli/satb choir; *Judicandus, piu mosso*. ssaattbb choir; *Huic ergo*, satb choir; *Pie Jesu* [B flat M] SATBar soli/ssaattbb choir.

Sanctus: 152 mm. [Choral parts composed in 1914]

    Sanctus [CM] *andante molto maestoso*. double satb choir; *Pleni sunt coeli, allegro moderato*. ssaatb choir (fugue); *Hosanna*, ssaattbb choir (coda).

Benedictus: 85 mm. Willan composed the *Benedictus*; *Hosanna* fugue was adapted by F. R. C. Clarke, from the *Pleni sunt coeli* fugue in the *Sanctus*. *Benedictus* [EM] *lento*. T solo/SATBar soli; *Hosanna* [CM] *allegro moderato*. satb choir (fugue). Concluding *Hosanna* is the same as the *Sanctus*.

Agnus Dei: 47 mm. [The music was taken from Willan's *Communion Service* (1910) by Prof. Clarke, who altered the vocal parts slightly to accommodate the Latin text.] *Agnus Dei* I [E flat M-CM] *larghetto*. T solo/satb choir; *Agnus Dei* II, Bar. solo/satb choir; *Agnus Dei* III [CM] satb choir.

Communion: 95 mm. [The music was arranged by Prof. Clarke, who adapted material from the Introit and *Kyrie*] *Lux aeterna* [FM] *lento*. ssaattbb choir; *Requiem aeternam* [fm] *largo e solenne*. ssaattbb choir/SATBar soli.

DISCOGRAPHY

None found.

PIETRO ALESSANDRO YON
August 8, 1886–November 22, 1943

Yon received his early training in organ and piano at the Milan and Turin Conservatories. An outstanding student, he received important honors in every area of study. He went on for further training at the prestigious Academy of St. Cecilia in Rome. Yon was appointed assistant organist at the Vatican and at the Royal Church of Rome, holding these positions for only two years. Subsequently, he came to New York City, where he was appointed organist at St. Patrick's Cathedral.

He left a small amount of musical works that include a number of pieces for organ (*Sonata cromatica*, two concert studies, and ten divertimenti). Although he composed six masses and ten motets, Yon is best remembered today for his Christmas solo song, *Jesu Bambino*.

His *Missa et Absolutio pro Defunctis*, scored for TTB choir, was first published in 1917 and remained in general use throughout many New York City churches until the 1960s. This liturgical setting is a model of the "Caecilian" style. Its musical vocabulary consists of simple diatonic harmony. Contrasting sections employ the Gregorian melodies and simple, monophonic chant-like passages.

Basic Data

EDITION

Pietro Yon
Missa et Absolutio pro Defunctis
[Organ-Vocal Score]
J. Fischer & Bro. # J. F. & B. 4350-34
New York 1917

DURATION

Ten movements, 317 mm.

VOICING AND ORCHESTRATION

Choir: T I, T II, B
Instruments: org.

OUTLINE

Introit-*Kyrie*: 46 mm.
    Requiem aeternam [fm] *andante*. ttb choir; *Te decet*, accompanied Gregorian chant;
    Requiem aeternam is repeated. ABA form; *Kyrie* [A flat M] ttb choir.
Graduale-Tract: 12 mm.
    Requiem aeternam-Absolve Domine. unison chant.
Sequence: 31 mm.
    Dies irae-Quid sum Miser-Qui Mariam (vv. 1-7-13). Gregorian chant; *Quantus*
    tremor-Rex tremendae-Preces meae, (vv. 2-8-14) chant recitation; *Tuba mirum-*
    Recordare-Inter oves, (vv. 3-9-15) Gregorian chant; *Mors stupebit-Quaerens me-*
    Confutatis, (vv. 4-10-16) three-part harmony; *Liber scriptus-Juste Judex-Oro sup-*
    plex, (vv. 5-11-17) Gregorian chant; *Judex ergo-Ingemisco*, (vv. 6-12) three-part
    imitative writing; *Lacrimosa*, (v. 18) Gregorian chant.
Offertory: 57 mm.
    Domine Jesu Christe [A flat M] *adagio ma non troppo*. T solo; *Quam olim Abrahae*,
    ttb choir; *Hostias* [CM] *poco piu mosso*. ttb choir; *Quam olim Abrahae* repeated.
Sanctus: 18 mm.
    Sanctus [A flat M] *allegro*. ttb choir; *Pleni sunt coeli*, Gregorian chant; *Hosanna*,
    allegro. ttb choir.
Benedictus: 18 mm.
    Benedictus [A flat M] *adagio*. B solo; *Hosanna*, ttb choir.
Agnus Dei: 18 mm.
    Agnus Dei [A flat M] *adagio*. TB soli/ttb choir.
Communion: 20 mm.
    Lux aeterna [FM] *allegro*. ttb choir; *Requiem aeternam*, Gregorian chant; *Cum Sanc-*
    tis, ttb choir.
Responsory: 73 mm.
    Libera me [fm] *allegro moderato*. ttb choir; *Quando coeli, adagio*. ttb choir; *Tremens*
    factus, B solo/unison choir; *Dies illa*, [A flat M] *allegro moderato*. ttb choir;

Requiem aeternam [fm] *andante.* Same material as Introit; *Libera Domine,* repeat of
the beginning of the movement; *Kyrie* [fm] *adagio.* ttb choir (imitation)
Antiphon, *In Paradisum:* 24 mm.

In Paradisum [FM] *allegro maestoso.* ttb choir; *Chorus angelorum.* ttb choir.
Yon includes other pieces in this setting: Psalm: *Benedictus* & *Sub Venite. Amens.*

DISCOGRAPHY

None found.

THOMAS BEVERIDGE
April 6, 1938

Thomas Beveridge studied composition at Harvard (Walter Piston and
Randall Thompson), the Longy School of Music, and Fontainbleau Conservatory (Nadia Boulanger). This multitalented composer is a proficient
organist, pianist, oboist, and singer. He has held such distinguished positions as chorus-master of the Washington Opera, music director of the
Washington Men's Camerata, and music director of the McLean Choral
Society. Beveridge served on the vocal faculty of Longy School and is currently the founder and artistic director of the National Men's Chorus.

He has composed more than 450 works, including three symphonies,
an opera, *Dido and Aeneas,* an oratorio, *Once: In Memoriam Martin Luther
King, Jr.,* numerous songs, a song cycle, *Odysseus,* chamber music such as
the *Serenade for Baritone and String Quartet,* and choral works.

The *Yizkor Requiem,* composed in 1993, is dedicated to memory of his
parents. It is scored for cantor (tenor), soprano and mezzo-soprano soli,
SATB choir, and orchestra. Its premiere took place on April 9, 1994, at St.
Mark's Church, Vienna, Virginia.

In this liturgically based, concert work, Beveridge fused equivalent
liturgical poetry from the texts of the Jewish Yiskor (Memorial) Service
and the traditional Catholic requiem liturgy. Such examples include the
Kadosh/Sanctus (movement VI), the *Requiem aeternam/Or zarua* (movement II), and the *Domine Jesu Christe/Baruch ata, Adonai* (movement IV).
Two other joined texts are the Lord's Prayer and the Mourner's Prayer
(Kaddish). These last texts are said at virtually every religious service of
their respective traditions.

The texts of the Reader's Kaddish (Movement 1), *Eil Maley Rachamim*
(movement VII) are drawn exclusively from the Jewish Memorial Service,
while the Offertory (movement V), *Lux aeterna* (movement VIII), and *Justorum Animae* (movement IX) are taken from the Catholic liturgy. *Psalm 23*
(movement III) is used and beloved by both traditions.

Much of the choral texture is unison or two-part writing. The harmony is often built upon the open sound of parallel fourths and fifths while four-part harmony is reserved for the more dramatic sections. Canonic writing is found in the first movement passage, *Blessed Be His name* and the seventh movement, *May They rest in the Garden of Eden* (fugal).

Many of the cantor's solo lines are syllabic and chant-like. Especially notable passages are found in the fourth (Remember) and concluding movement (Mourner's Kaddish). In the latter piece, the choir provides a background for the chant. This style is commonly employed for the Sabbath service. Quite different is the ornate melodic structure found in the Sanctification and opening movement.

The only other requiem setting listed in this guide that employs a similar ecumenical approach in combining Jewish and Christian texts is James DeMars *An American Requiem* (1993). This work employs portions of the Yizkor (memorial) service, the complete Latin requiem as well as texts by Walt Whitman, Martin Luther King, and Michel Sarda.

Other related works are *Requiem*, Op. 39 (1963) (complete setting of the Kaddish) by Wilfred Josephs, the *Third Symphony "Kaddish"* (1963) by Leonard Bernstein, and the *Holocaust Requiem-Kaddish for Terezin* (1986) by Ronald Senator.

Basic Data

EDITION

Yizkor Requiem. A quest for spiritual roots.
Thomas Beveridge
Piano-Vocal score
Yizkor Press. 1996 [orchestral score and parts available from composer]

DURATION

Ten movements, 914 mm., perf., c. 55′

VOICING AND ORCHESTRATION

Choir: SATB [*divisi*] range: S-A flat 6; B-E3
Soloists: soprano, mezzo-soprano [cantor] tenor
Orchestra: vn. I/II, vla., vc., db., 2 fl.[1 offstage], ob., cl., bsn., 2 tpt., Fh., timp.
  PERC: suspended cymbal, triangle, crotales, cymbals, tambourine, gong, "high hat" cymbal.

OUTLINE

Reader's Kaddish: 91 mm.
  Magnified and exalted, maestoso. cantor/satb choir. (cantor-Hebrew text, satb choir-English translation. Texts are interspersed.)

Magnified and sanctified be His great name.
Great is the name of the Lord.
Throughout the world which He created according to His will.
And great is His glorious creation.
And may his kingdom come during our lives and days,
And during the life of all the House of Israel.
May His kingdom come, His will be done in earth as it is in heaven.
Speedily and soon, and let us say: Amen.
May His great name be blessed.
O praised be His holy name, forever and ever to all eternity.
Blessed and praised and glorified and exalted and extolled,
And honored and magnified and lauded
Be the name of the Holy One, blessed be He.
O blessed be the name of the Lord, O bless His name
Though He be beyond all blessings and songs
And praises and consolations that can be uttered
In this world, and let us say: Amen
Blessed be His name and His glorious creation.
Blessed be the name of the Lord.

Requiem aeternam: 239 mm.
   Orchestral intro.; *Requiem aeternam, largo.* satb choir-Latin text; *Or zarua*, (cantor-Hebrew text, SA soli; English translation); *Te decet*, SA soli/satb choir; *Exaudi orationem* (satb choir-Latin text, cantor/SA soli-Hebrew text); *Kyrie* & *'Slachlanu* (satb choir-Latin text, SA soli/cantor-Hebrew text).

Requiem aeternam-traditional Introit text . . .
Or zarua . . . light is sown for the righteous and
shall shine upon the pure in heart.
All flesh shall return to you.
All flesh shall praise and bless Your name.
Forgive us.

Psalm 23:88 mm.
   The Lord is my shepherd . . . allegro. two-part satb choir.
Remember: 98 mm.
   Baruch ata, Adonai/Domine Jesu Christe (Offertory text). Freely. (Cantor-Hebrew text; SA soli-Latin text); *Baruch ata*, unison choir/satb choir/cantor; *Recordare* (Sequence)/*Zochreynu*, SA soli/cantor/unison choir (English translation).

Blessed art Thou, O Lord,
Our God and God of our fathers;
God of Abraham, God of Isaac
and God of Jacob.
Blessed art Thou . . .
Thou bestowest loving kindness upon
all Thy children.

Thou bringest redemption to their descendants,
for Thy name's sake, out of love.
Remember us unto life.
King, who delightest in the Book of Life,
For Thy sake, O God of Life.
Thou, King, art our helper, saviour and protector.
Blessed art Thou, O Lord, Shield of Abraham.

Offertory: 40 mm.
 Hostias [Offertory], satb [ssaattbb *divisi*] choir/SA soli.
Sanctification: 168 mm.
 Nekadesh/Sanctus (cantor/SA soli-Hebrew text, satb choir-Greek text); *Pleni sunt
 coeli/Melochol* (satb choir-*Pleni sunt coeli*, SA soli/cantor-*Melochol*); *Benedictus/
 Boruch* (satb choir-Latin text, SA soli/cantor-Hebrew text); *Hosanna/Yimloch
 Adonay* (satb choir-Latin text, cantor/SA soli-Hebrew text)

We sanctify, we sanctify, we sanctify.
We sanctify Your Holy Name on earth.
As the heavens on high do glorify You.
And, as did the prophets of old,
We cry out, saying: Holy! Holy! Holy!
Lord God of Hosts!
The whole earth is full of Your glory.
Heaven and earth is full of Your glory.
God our strength, God our Lord,
How excellent is Thy name in all the earth.
Blessed be the glory of the Lord throughout the universe.
Our God is ONE.

He is our Father, He is our King.
He is our Saviour and He will answer our prayers
in the sight of the living

Eil Maley Rachamim (Lord of compassion): 104 mm.
 Eil maley rachamim . . . largo. cantor/satb choir (cantor-Hebrew text, satb choir-
English translation).

Lord, full of compassion, who dwells in heaven,
grant perfect peace.
Lord of mercy, with wings of compassion
enfold our loved ones who have returned to Thy care.
Under the wings of the Divine Presence, among the high places
of the holy and pure ones,
who shine as the brightness of the firmament,
upon the souls of our dear ones who have gone on to their eternity.
May they rest in the Garden of Eden.
O Lord of compassion, grant them eternal peace.

In the Garden of Eden let them find rest, we beseech You,
Lord of compassion, let them find shelter
under Your wings forever.
May their souls be bound up in the bond of life.
The Lord is their inheritance.
And may they rest in peace.
And let us say: Amen.

Lux aeterna: 21 mm.
  Lux aeterna, andante. S solo.
Justorum animae: 32 mm.
  Justorum animae, andante. S solo/satb choir.

The souls of the righteous are in the hand of God
and they shall not be touched by the torment of judgement.
In the eyes of the foolish they appear to no longer exist,
but, actually, they are at peace.

Mourner's Kaddish and Lord's Prayer: 33 mm.
  Our Father/Magnified and sanctified, very slowly. cantor/satb choir. (see text for
  # 1)

May there be abundant peace from Heaven and Life
for us and all Israel. And let us say: Amen.
May He who makes peace in heaven grant peace for us
and for all Israel. And let us say: Amen.
The departed whom we now remember have entered
into the peace of Life Eternal. Amen.
They still live on earth in the acts of goodness they
performed and in the hearts of those who cherish their memory. Amen.
May the beauty of their life abide among us
as a loving benediction. Amen.
May the Father of Peace send peace to all who mourn
and comfort the bereaved among us.
And let us say: Amen.

DISCOGRAPHY
1. New Dominion Chorale, Thomas Beveridge, Director.
2. Naxos, 8.559074, The Chorale Arts Society Orchestra and Chorus of Washington, cond. Norman Scribner.

GAVIN BRYARS
January 16, 1943

The English composer, Gavin Bryars, began to write in the late 1960s,
studying composition with Cyril Ramsey and George Linstead. His activ-

ity with experimental styles, electronic music, indeterminacy, and the creation of a new tonal language constitute the hallmarks of his style. Bryars' compositions often require unusual instrumentations and frequently bear curious, if not whimsical, titles: *Private Music* (1969), *The Ride Cymbal and the Band That Caused the Fire in the Sycamore Tree* (1970), *Serenely Beaming and Leaning on a Five-Barred Gate* (1970), *1-2-3-4* (1971), *Jesus' Blood Never Failed Me Yet* (1971), *One Last Bar, Then Joe Can Sing* (1994), and *Sub Rosa* (1986). Other titles are more traditional: *Quartet No. Two for Strings* (1990), *Cadman Requiem* (1989), and *After the Requiem* (1990).

The *Cadman Requiem*, a more traditional work, scored for ATTB male quartet and string trio (optional quartet), was composed in memory of a friend, William Cadman, who was killed in the Pan-American airplane crash over Lockerbie, Scotland (1989).

The tonal harmonies employed by Bryars evoke, occasionally, the ethereal sonorities of medieval polyphony, and, at other times, the dissonant polyphony of seventeenth-century Russian polyphony. The violas and cello [viols, in the 1997 revision] provide a rich, resonant string sound to complement the intimate choral matrix. The integrated sonorities create a spiritual, other-worldly atmosphere.

The prevailing four-part, homophonic vocal texture is relieved by the presence of unisons, fifths, and voice thinning. Imitative techniques are absent. Passages of quiet, sixteenth notes for the strings, in the second, third, and fourth movements, propel the work forward.

The work's five movements employ two textual sources; the traditional Latin liturgy and the poetry of the earliest-known English poet, Caedmon (fl. 680). Caedmon is known through the writings of the English historian and Benedictine monk, the Venerable Bede (c. 673–735). Bryars chose this poetic text because of a possible ancestral connection of his friend to the medieval shepherd-poet.

In 1997, Bryars revised the orchestration of the *Requiem,* scoring it for six viols and, in 1990, wrote a work, *After the Requiem*, which employs some earlier material from the *Requiem* of 1989. A performance of the *Requiem* calls for professional singers and instrumentalists. This work possesses a powerful, expressive sense of sadness and the small string ensemble summons up a quiet intimacy.

Basic Data

EDITION

Cadman Requiem
[Full score]
Schott. (ED 12475)
Mainz. London 1996

DURATION

Five movements, 380 mm., perf., c. 26′

VOICING AND ORCHESTRATION

Soloists: ATTBAR [male singers]
Instruments: vla. I/II, vc., and optional db.

OUTLINE

Requiem aeternam-Kyrie: 128 mm.
    Requiem aeternam, slow. ATTB soli.
Caedmon Paraphrase: 60 mm.
    Nunc laudare, [*moderato*] T II. The text is a paraphrase, by Bede, of Caedmon's
    Anglo-Saxon original poem.

Nunc laudere debemus auctorem regni caelestis, potentiam Creatoris et consilium
    illius, facta Patris gloriae. Quomodo ille, cum sit aeternus Deus, omnium
miraculorum auctor exitit, qui primo filiis hominum caelum pro culmine tecti,
                              dehinc terram
                custos humani generis omnipotens creavit.

                Now we must praise the Maker of the heavenly kingdom,
                            the power of the Creator
            and his counsel, the deeds of the Father of glory and how He,
                            since He is the eternal
            God, was the author of all marvels and first created the heavens
                        as a roof for the children
    of men and then, the almighty Guardian of the human race, created the earth.

Agnus Dei-Lux aeterna: 82 mm.
    Agnus Dei [*adagio*] ATTB soli. (scored variously for two, three, and four solo
    singers).
Caedmon's Creation Hymn: 56 mm.
    Nu scylun . . . [*moderato*] Bar solo. (alternating *pppp* and *mf* dynamics support
    the dreamlike quality of Caedmon's poetic vision).

Nu scylun hergan	hefaenrices uard
metudaes mecti	end his mogdedanc,
uere wuldurfadur	sue he wundra gihwaes,
eci drynctin	or astelidae;
he aerist scop	aelda barnum
heben til hrofe	haleg scepen,
tha middungeard	moncynnaes uard;
eci dryctin	aefter tiadae
firum foldu	frea allmectig.

(translation in Movement 2)

In Paradisum: 54 mm. [*lento*]
  In paradisum [*lento*] ATTB soli (chant-
  like, unison writing)

> In paradisum deductant Angeli: in tuo adventi suscipiant te Martyres,
>   et perducant te in civitatem sanctam.
> Chorus Angelorum te suscipiat, et cum Lazaro quondam paupere
>   aeternam habeas requiem.
> May the angels receive you in Paradise; may the martyrs receive you as you arrive,
>   and bring you into the holy city, Jerusalem.
> May the angel's choir receive you, and with Lazarus, once a beggar,
>   may you have eternal rest.

DISCOGRAPHY
Point Music, PY 925, Hilliard Ensemble and Fretwork.

JAMES DE MARS
April 17, 1952

James De Mars received his musical training at Macalester College and
the University of Southern California, where he studied composition with
Dominick Argento and Eric Stokes. He is currently a faculty member at
the School of Music at Arizona State University.

De Mars has written a number of works on American themes, including *Far from the Water*, an aria for native American flute and orchestra;
Native Drumming, a concerto for pow-wow drum, orchestra, and singers
(1996); *Seventh Healing Song of John Joseph*, a blues for alto saxophone and
tape (1982); *Two-World Concerto* for native American flute and orchestra
(1993); and *Spirit Horses*, a double concerto for Navaho flute and cello. *An
American Requiem* (1993) was commissioned by Michel F. Sarda, president
of the Art Renaissance Foundation.

An American Requiem is scored for SATBAR soli, SATB choir, and
orchestra. Within the work, the composer has joined several "American"
themes to the traditional Latin requiem text; themes drawn from the
poetry of Walt Whitman, the words of Martin Luther King, Jr., the Yizkor
Prayer (*El Mole*), *The Canticle of the Sky—Homage to Native American*, and
Psalm 39:4–5. The intermarriage of these texts to a Latin requiem text,
with a reduced number of references to Jesus Christ (*Christe eleison* and
Recordare) permits for an ecumenical or civic performance of *An American
Requiem*.

An American Requiem is divided into four principal sections and the
movements within each section are related to and derived from the initial
piece of the given section. The musical language of the work is a tradi-

tional harmonic tonality, with traces of Renaissance modality and polyphony, the spacious sonorities and warm harmonies of Aaron Copland's "Americana" pieces, and, lastly, the rhythmic "feel" of the African-American spiritual.

Musical lines are broad and ample and the orchestration remains supportive of the choral mass without overshadowing it. The composer's melodic approach to the text is lyrical and restrained. The implicit violence and terror of the Last Judgment, so skillfully explored by Verdi and others, is never over-emphasized here, although it is certainly suggested. The general mood of the setting is one of a profound, optimistic spirituality.

The choral texture is a mixture of homophonic and polyphonic style. Imitative polyphony is employed for the *Kyrie* (triple fugue) and the *Sanctus*. The *concertante* choral style also reappears in the *Kyrie* and *Sanctus* movements, as the SATB soli and SATB choir are treated as a double chorus. In the *Sanctus*, each ensemble is assigned a unique role: the soloists sing Martin Luther King's text in gospel style while the choir contrasts the *Sanctus* in hymn-like fashion. This passage is written in eight-part counterpoint.

Basic Data

EDITION

An American Requiem for vocal soloists, chorus and orchestra
Art Renaissance Foundation, Phoenix, Arizona [1994]

DURATION

Fourteen movements, 1574 mm., perf., c. 76'

VOICING AND ORCHESTRATION

Choir: SATB [*divisi*] range: S-A6; B-F3
Soloists: SATBAR
Orchestra: vn. I/II, vla., vc., db., pic., 2 ob., 2 fl., 2 cl., 2 bsn., cbsn., 2 Fh., 2 tpt., 2 tbn, bass tbn., PERC: timp., suspended cymbal, bass drum, snare drums [with yarn mallets], crotales, wind gong, tam-tam, bells, wind chimes.

OUTLINE

SECTION I.
Canticle of the Sky, Homage to Native Americans: 82 mm.
   Open sky . . . [quarter-note = 60] satb choir. (plainsong style)

Open—open sky
Brothers of sorrow, sisters of despair
As the sky is open we share.

Sister of sorrow, brothers of strength
The dreams of fallen children we share
Earth and sky in morning shine
Mourning their fallen children,
Shine blue and deep the water,
Open yourself, open your whole self.
Sisters of hope, brothers of will
As the sky is open and still
Open your whole self,
Dream and pray, dream of angels
The better angels of our nature.
[Michel Sarda]

Introit: 65 mm.
   Requiem aeternam [quarter-note = 48] satb choir; *Te decet* is omitted.
Kyrie: 60 mm.
   Kyrie [quarter-note = 60] satb choir/SATBAR soli. Triple fugue.

SECTION II

Psalm 39, "The measure of my days." 71 mm.
   Lord let me know mine end . . . [quarter-note = 58] T solo/flute.

Lord, let me know my end and the measure of my days,
What is it that I know how frail I am.
Behold, thou hast made my days as an handbreadth,
and mine age is as nothing before thee:
Verily every man in his best state is altogether vanity.
[Psalm 39:4–5]

Sequence, *Dies irae*: 170 mm.
   Dies irae [quarter-note = 70] S solo/satb choir (vv. 1–11). Important role for the percussion.
Sequence, *Tuba mirum*: 255 mm.
   Tuba mirum . . . [dotted quarter-note = 60] satb choir. (vv. 3–4) Brass occupies a prominent role in this movement.
Sequence, *Liber scriptus*: 135 mm.
   Liber scriptus/Quid sum miser, largo doloroso. Bar. solo; *Oro supplex*, TBAR soli/ssatb choir; *Ingemisco*, Bar. solo/satb choir; *Confutatis*, TBar soli. (vv. 7, 17, 5, 16, 12 & 6.)
Sequence, *Recordare*: 97 mm.
   Recordare [quarter-note = 62] SA soli/strings. (vv. 9–11).
Sequence, *Rex tremendae*: 193 mm.
   Rex tremendae, appassionato. satb choir/full orchestra. (v. 8).

SECTION III

Dedication, "*When lilacs last in the dooryard bloom'd*" 93 mm.
   When lilacs . . . [quarter-note = 60] S solo/woodwinds/strings/French horn.

> For the sweetest, wisest soul of all my days and land
> and this for his dear sake
> Lilac, bird and star entwined with the chant of my soul.
> Comrades mine and I in the midst, their memory ever to keep.
> I weep for the ones I loved so well.
> [Walt Whitman]

Sanctus: 137 mm.
   Sanctus, maestoso. SATB soli/satb choir. The *Sanctus* text is "glossed" with lines from Martin Luther King's "*I have a dream*" speech. The soli and choir are treated as two choirs (gospel-style, hymn-style). String/brass sections also treated as two responsorial ensembles. (call and response technique) TB soli are responsible for the King texts; the choir, for the *Sanctus*. (eight-part counterpoint).

> [choir]
> Sanctus, sanctus, sanctus, Lord God of hosts.
> Glory to God in the highest. Glory on earth and in heaven.
> Blessed who comes in the name of the Lord.
> [tenor]
> I have a dream, a dream that one day
> we sit down together and pray like brothers and sisters.
> We join hands together and sit at the table and pray
> [bass]
> Let freedom ring, dark days will pass and we will sing we're free at last,
> Great God, Almighty, we're free at last.
> [choir]
> Hosanna in excelsis. Amen

SECTION IV

Memorial Prayer [*El mole*]: 116 mm.
   O merciful God . . . Bar solo/strings/woodwinds/French horns.

> O merciful God, full spirit of Heaven,
> God of compassion, grant shelter, grant rest.
> Under wings of your presence, grant shelter.
> Your presence which shines as the brightness of day,
> Grant shelter, grant rest, perfect rest.
> God of compassion, master of mercy, full spirit of Heaven,
> Grant rest to the ones we loved so well.
> After them, let us seek sacred living.

Let us seek sacred life and remember
the ones we loved so well.
Bind these souls in life's bonds forever,
under wings of your presence grant shelter.
After them let us seek sacred living,
After them let us seek sacred life
And let us say "Amen."

Communion: 51 mm.
Lux aeterna [quarter-note = 60] ssssaa choir, unaccompanied.
Responsory: 49 mm.
Libera me/El mole [quarter-note = 44] (*recitativo*). SATB soli; *Requiem aeternam*,
satb choir (thematic material taken from movement two).

DISCOGRAPHY

1. BWE, BCD 9601-2 , The Mormon Tabernacle Choir, cond. James De Mars.
2. Art Renaissance Foundation, ARF 94001, Arizona State University Choirs,
   cond. James De Mars.

LUBOŠ FIŠER
September 30, 1935–June 23, 1999

Fišer studied composition at the Prague Conservatory of Music from 1952
to 1956 and at the Prague Academy of Music. He has written a variety of
works including opera, ballet, orchestral and chamber music, music for
piano, and vocal pieces. Perhaps his most famous orchestral piece is the
Fifteen Pages after Dürer's Apocalypse (1964–65), for which the UNESCO
prize was awarded in 1966.

In the same year, he wrote the vocal work, *Caprichos for Vocalists and
Chorus*. This work was inspired by prints of Goya and was the second
part of a planned musical triptych. The last section of the triptych was the
Requiem, completed by November 1968. These three works are unified by
the use of a six-note mode, a tragic-dramatic mood, and the use of a time
element that depends upon aleatoric writing.

Although the first two works were based upon the art of the famous
painters, Dürer and Goya, the *Requiem* was most likely inspired by the
invasion and occupation of Czechoslovakia, by the Russian army, in 1968.
In June 1967, Czech writers and intellectuals unleased an attack upon the
hard-line policies of the Czech Communist government. This led to a lib-
eralization of Czech life that culminated in a period known as the
"Prague Spring." While this period of freedom was short-lived, it paved
the way for ultimate democracy and freedom.

The *Requiem* possesses a point worthy of mention. Namely, that the work is almost surely a political statement. The requiem text has been greatly truncated, using only the Introit text, *Requiem aeternam*, the *Libera eas* from the Offertory and the *Lux aeterna* of the Communion. Four of the seven movements employ the *Libera eas* text, which seems to imply, at least to this writer, a demand for freedom expressed in musical language. The *Requiem* is a painting in music; a canvas of historical events unfolding in the composer's homeland.

The first movement of the *Requiem* employs a baritone soloist who offers a throbbing, sorrowful lament, using the *Requiem aeternam* text. This stunning solo is absolutely unique among all requiem settings mentioned in this study. It is emotionally powerful in both an intellectual and visceral manner.

The second movement is a unique musical painting. It is a depiction of tanks invading the city of Prague and the rage and anger of the crowd as its freedom is robbed from them. The violence comes to an abrupt end with timpani blows, symbolic of tanks firing upon the crowd, and a choral statement that contains the only clearly discernable words sung by the choir during the entire work: *mors* (death). The choral parts of this movement are a modern version of the baroque *turba* (crowd) choruses found in Bach's settings of the *St. Matthew* and *St. John Passions*. This hair-raising movement is one of the great passages in the twentieth-century requiem.

While the very last chord of the *Requiem* is a C major chord, the remaining choral passages are written as tone clusters or atonal chords. There are no key signatures, bar lines, or measures, and virtually all of the rhythm is determined by aleatoric technique. Fišer uses contrasting structures and lines, as well as various vertical groupings (densities) of the voices and instruments. It is a fascinating work that deserves more frequent performance.

Basic Data

EDITION

Luboš Fišer
Requiem pro soprán a baryton sólo, dva smíšené sbory a orchestr
[Requiem for soprano & baritone soloists, two mixed choirs & orchestra]
1968
Partitura (#H 4984)
Editio Supraphon, Praha. 1971

DURATION
Seven movements, perf., c. 19'

VOICING AND ORCHESTRATION
Choir: choir I, SATB; choir II, SATB
Soloists: Soprano, Baritone
Orchestra: vn. I/II, vla., vc., db., 3 fl., 3 ob., 3 bsn., 3 tpt., 3 tbn., 3 Fh., timp.

OUTLINE

Introit: *Requiem aeternam*. unaccompanied baritone solo.
   The solo is built on short chromatic motives (b flat-b-c/c# or c#/c-f#-f-g). The "tonal" baritone melody is a wailing, mournful chant that throbs with overwhelming emotional intensity.
Offertory: *Libera eas*. satb choir I/II.
   Shifting *divisi* sections within each choir. The choral melodies are built upon the same short melodic motives derived from the baritone solo. The choirs are accompanied by db. [*divisi à* 6], vc. [*divisi à* 4], bn. [*divisi á* 3], cl. [*divisi à* 3], vla. [*divisi à* 5], Fh [*divisi à* 3], ob. [*divisi à* 3], fl. [*divisi à* 3], vn. II [*divisi à* 6], vn. I [*divisi à* 7], tbn. [*divisi à* 3], and tp. [*divisi à* 3]; each instrument entering in this order. Three timp. and unison choirs, speaking "*mors*" [death] five times, in a decreasing dynamic level [*ff-f-mf-p-pp*] end the movement. The structure of the movement is a gradual crescendo, culminating in a final explosion of sound, and a quick descent into quietude. The "program" of this movement is a musical depiction of the armed invasion of Prague and the suppression of a growing freedom movement in the Czech nation.

Libera eas de ore leonis ne absorbeat eas tartarus
ne cadant in obscurum. Mors !
Deliver them from the jaws of the lion, lest they fall into darkness
and are swallowed-up in the black gulf. Death!

Offertory: *Libera eas*. choir I, TTBB, choir II, TTBB, accompanied by the timpani, divided into three sections. The choral parts are sung, either in unison or divided into intervals of fourths or fifths. The phrase *Libera eas* is repeated, continuously.
Offertory: *Libera animas*. Soprano solo.
Built on a c-c#-g-f-f# motive) and accompanied by vn. I/II, *divisi*. At the conclusion of the movement, satb choirs I/II and full orchestra, appears. The choir sings the word, *libera*; the orchestral parts play various tone clusters or intervals. Only the French horns play the melodic, six-note motive.
Offertory: *Libera eas de ore leonis*. satb choirs I/II [*divisi*] accompanied by vc. [*divisi à* 8], db [*divisi à* 4], tr. [*divisi à* 3] tbn. [*divisi à* 3]. Gradually vn. I & II and vla. [each *divisi à* 4] enter. At the conclusion, all woodwinds and French horns [each instrument *divisi à* 3] are added to the accompaniment. The coda is scored for soprano solo, accompanied by three timpani.
Communion: *Lux aeterna*. choir I, ssaa, choir II, ssaa, unaccompanied.
Four-part chordal writing for each choir. The chord notes are taken from the melodic motive present in the previous movements. The mood created by the composer is quiet and mysterious.
Communion: *Requiem aeternam*. unaccompanied baritone solo.
This movement is a companion piece to the opening movement. The only tonal moment in the *Requiem* occurs at the very end, as the choir sings a concluding *Amen* on the C major chord.

DISCOGRAPHY
Supraphon, [LP] 1-12-1537, Czech Philharmonic Chorus and The Prague Symphony Orchestra, cond. Antonin Sidlo.

SANDRO GORLI
June 19, 1948

Sandro Gorli received a degree in piano in his native city, Como, Italy. He continued his musical work at the Giuseppe Verdi Conservatory, along with studies in architecture at Milan University. Gorli has been associated with the Divertimento Ensemble, a group dedicated to the performance of modern music and is currently professor of composition at the Giuseppe Verdi Conservatory in Milan.

The composer has written a variety of musical compositions, including *Me-Ti for Orchestra* (1975); *Chimera la Luce* for piano, vocal sextet, chorus, and orchestra (1976); *On a Delphic Reed*, for oboe and seventeen performers (1980); *Il Bambino perduto*, for orchestra (1981); and *Super Flumina* (1989).

In 1989, he composed the *Requiem for fourteen unaccompanied voices*. This work is a virtuoso, nonliturgical concert setting arranged in five movements. Its harmonic language ranges from clear harmonic tonality to atonality and to virtual unpitched tone while the musical sonorities move freely from one style to the next. The choral texture is constantly altered by voice thinning or augmentation. A number of special vocal effects are employed, including diaphragm accents, throat accents, vowel sounds and combinations, shutting the mouth while singing, and sustaining a variety of consonant sounds. Each movement contains evocative poetry composed by Sandro Gorli.

Basic Data
EDITION
Requiem per 14 voci a cappella
Partitura
Casa Ricordi, Milan (# 135081) 1989.

DURATION
Five movements, 193 mm., perf., c. 14'

VOICING
Choir: 4 sopranos, 3 altos, 3 tenors, 4 basses. range: S-G6; B-E3

OUTLINE
Movement One: 25 mm.
   Varying passages for 6-9 vocal lines. Pointillistic texture employed. Tonal areas border on areas nonpitched sound. The movement ends on a B flat chord.

Dead, we are still dying . . .

Movement Two: 62 mm.
   Scored for fourteen voices [ssssaaatttbbbb], an extremely dense texture is created by interlocking sets of intervals.

Child, when I die, let me be a child, the smallest child.
Take me in your arms and carry me into your house.
Cast away my tired human soul and put me in your bed.
And tell me stories to make me fall asleep.
And give me your dreams so I can make them my toys.

Movement Three: 32 mm.
   Scored for fourteen voices, the texture uses dense chordal sonorities, contrasting with lighter cluster groupings. There are several passages of sustained *"N"*
   sounds. Much of the text is unintelligible because of sound clusters. This movement continues directly into the next, on an *"o"* and *"un"* sound.

Take me into your arms, eternal night and call me son.

Movement Four: 22 mm.
   Scored for twelve voices, this short piece consists of slow-moving, sustained
   notes that form a harmony for the faster-moving, first soprano or alto melodic
   line. Dynamic markings range from *ppp* to *pp*.

Gentle, gentle, very gentle, a very gentle wind comes and leaves,
still very gentle.
Come light, bright pallor of the damp evening . . .
Come light, invisible ash, sleepless ennui.

Movement Five: 52 mm.
   Scored for twelve voices, this movement employs canonic writing between several interlocking groups of singers. Gradually, the number of voice parts is
   reduced to six at the conclusion. At measure twenty-nine, the choir sings an *"a"*
   and *"o"* passage. As the work closes, the male voices are retired as the female
   voices sing *abbandona* (forsaken).

Father. Father why hast thou forsaken me?
Requiem.

DISCOGRAPHY

Harmonia Mundi, HMT 7901320, Ensemble Vocal Européen, dir. Philippe Herreweghe.

EDGAR GRANA
April 14, 1944

The American composer, Edgar Grana, studied piano with Furguson Webster at the Sorbonne. He later studied composition with David Diamond and Milton Babbitt at the Juilliard School, from which he graduated in 1983. Currently, he is composer in residence and instructor in music composition in the graduate computer arts department at the School of Visual Arts in New York City.

Among his compositions are three symphonies, two string quartets, chamber music for piano and cello, and a number of vocal songs. A number of works are allied with multimedia expression, including *Qua*, written for the HERE Gallery and *Synaethesia*, composed for the Mary Anthony Gallery, both in Soho, New York City. The choral music includes a *Missa Brevis* and *Stones, Time and Elements: a Humanistic Requiem*.

Stones, Time and Elements was composed in 1991 and scored for SATB choir, SATB soli, chamber orchestra, percussion, and synthesizer. Grana dedicated the work to Ray Evans Harrell, Artistic Director, Magic Circle Opera Repertory Ensemble and a medicine-man for the Cherokee Nation. The rich and colorful, yet spare, intimate orchestration of the requiem was inspired by the work of Ravel. Its tonal harmonic language, polyphonic orchestral texture, and fragmented melodic lines are reminiscent of those same elements found in David Diamond's *Trio for violin, cello and piano* (1951). An intimate, delicate scoring for the percussion recalls Ginastera's *Fantastic Interlude* (*Cantata para América Mágica*, 1960).

The wind-synthesizer (played and fingered like a woodwind instrument) is employed throughout the requiem, and generally colors the orchestral texture, although sometimes it is used in a solo role, such as that at the end of the section, *That day will be one*, and at the conclusion of the requiem. Three significant passages for this instrument (as well as the percussion) are improvised.

Because the orchestral mass is independent of and vastly different from the choral passages, any performance of this work will require trained, experienced singers. Contrast to the prevailing SATB choral texture is provided by choral unisons or two-part writing. Both the orchestral and choral fabric include canonic passages, as well as a sophisticated, rhythmic complexity. Solo vocal parts are interwoven into numerous choral passages, including *Day of Wrath*, *That day will be one*, *I groan*, *Hosanna*, *O Cosmos*, and *Let not eternal light*. *Stones, Time and Elements* is a continuous, one-movement requiem divided into a dozen principal sections.

A unique feature of this requiem setting is an anti-*Dies irae* text, written by Kurt Vonnegut. This poetry, a revised version of the traditional requiem text, is a reinterpretation of the Catholic original. It seeks to counter the harshness and violence of the medieval sequence hymn, *Dies irae*. Inspiration for a "revised" version occurred after Vonnegut heard the premiere of Lloyd-Webber's *Requiem*. In Vonnegut's version, violence is replaced by satire ("Let not light disturb their sleep"), ("When the litiginous have been confounded . . . Count me among the gratified") and anger by compassion (". . . no guilty man or woman or child to be judged. I depend upon you to spare them, O Stones . . . "), (". . . did try to redeem me by suffering . . . on the Cross: Let not such toil have been in vain"). The Latin text, occasionally interspersed with Vonnegut's poetry, comes from a translation made by John F. Collins that was commissioned by the author.

Basic Data

EDITION

Stones, Time and Elements
A Humanist Requiem
Music: Edgar David Grana
Text: Kurt Vonnegut
Available from author
1991

DURATION

Twelve movements, 601 mm. perf. c. 47'

VOICING AND ORCHESTRATION

Choir: S I/II, A (optional), T I/II, Bar. range: S-B6; B-F3
Soloist: SATB
Instruments: vn. I/II, vla., vc., db., (electric bass, optional). Fl., alto fl., ob., Eh., bcl., Fh., tbn., bass tbn., wind synthesizer. PERC: vibraphone, marimba, o-daiko, snare drum, tenor drum, wood blocks, timbale, claves, gong, crotales, bass marimba (optional).

OUTLINE

Part I. The Reading
Part II. Stones, Time and Elements
Rest Eternal: 50 mm. [quarter note = 84]

[choir]
Rest eternal grant them, O Cosmos and let not light disturb their sleep.
A hymn is naught to Thee, O flying stones, nor a vow ungratified
in a dream in Jerusalem.

Yet I pray:

From Thee all flesh did come; Time have mercy upon us;
Elements have mercy upon us.
Rest eternal grant them, O Cosmos, and let not light disturb their sleep.
Day of Wrath: 128 mm. [quarter note = 60]
[Instrumental interlude & postlude]
[choir]
A day of wrath: that day, *Salvemus*
[S/Bar soli]
We shall dissolve the world into glowing ashes, as attested by our weapons for
wars
in the names of gods unknowable.
[choir]
Let not the ashes tremble, though some Judge should come
to examine all in some strict justice!
[S, Mezzo, T soli, sat choir]
Let no trumpet's wondrous call sounding abroad in tombs throughout the world
drive ashes toward any throne.
[S 1, S2, Mezzo, T soli, satb choir]
Let ashes remain as ashes, Though summoned to approach in terror,
as in life, some Judge or Throne.
Must a written book be brought forth in which everything is contained
from which the ashes shall be judged?
Then when some Judge is seated and whatever is hidden is made known,
let him understand that naught hath gone unpunished.
[S1, Mezzo soli, satb choir]
Let Death and Nature say what they will
when ashes sleep as ashes when commanded to give answers to some Judge.
Die irae, die illa.
What shall I, wretch, say at that time?
What advocate shall I entreat when even the righteous have been damned
by wars in the names of gods unknowable?
[29 mm. postlude for orchestra and synthesizer]

Structure of awesome majesty: 29 mm. [*lento*, quarter note = 52]

[S2, Mezzo solo duet]
Structure of awesome majesty,
Donor of sleep or wakefulness,
Thou font of random pain or pity,
Give me the innocence of sleep.

Gambler with flesh: 42 mm. [*allegro*, quarter note = 126]

[satb choir]
Gambler with flesh, thou art the reason for my journey:
Do not cast the dice again on that day.
My wild and loving brother did try to redeem me by suffering on the Cross:
Let not such toil have been in vain.

I groan: 91 mm. [*allegro*, quarter note = 126]

[tb choir]
I groan like one condemned; My face blushes for my sins.
Spare a suppliant from more such wakefulness.
[38 mm interlude for orchestra & synthesizer]
[S 2, Mezzo, satb choir]
Thou who didst neither condemn nor forgive Mary and the robber on the cross
hast given me hope as well.
My prayers are unheard,
but thy sublime indifference will ensure that I burn not in some everlasting fire.
Give me a place among the sheep and the goats, separating none from none,
leaving our mingled ashes where they fall.

That day will be one: 40 mm. [*lento*, half note = 44]

[S2, Mezzo, Bar soli, satb choir,]
That day will be one of comical dissapointment to any who hoped to see rise
again
from the embers the guilty to be judged.
When the litiginous have been confounded and sentenced to comical
disappointment
count me among the gratified.
That day will be one of comical disappointment, on which shall rise again from
the embers
no guilty man or woman or child to be judged.
I depend upon you to spare them, O Stones, O Time, O Elements.
Grant them rest. Amen.

[Major improvised solo for synthesizer]

O Cosmos: 62 mm. [*molto allegro*, quarter note = 132]

[satb choir]
O Cosmos, O structure of awesome majesty,
deliver without exception the souls of the departed
from the pains of hell and from the bottomless pit.
Libera animas omnium ad unum defunctorum de poenis inferni et de profundo lacu.
Libera eas deore leonis ne absorbeat eas tartarus,
ut plane cadant im obscurum tranquillum et suave.
Hostias et preces tibi, Munde, laudis obtulimus in milia annorum.
Dona nos tua perpetua negligentia fatorum, quae sunt
trans mortem earum animarum quas hodie commemoramus.
Save them from the lion's jaws, that hell may not engulf them,
that they may only fall into darkness which is still and sweet.
Dazzle them not with light promised in a dream to Abraham
and his seed.

Sacrifices and prayers of praise to Thee, O Cosmos,
We have offered for millennia. Reward us with
thy continued indifference to the destinies past death
of those souls whom we this day commemorate.
[S 2 solo, satb choir]
Life was sport enough! Allow them to pass from death unto sleep. [quarter
note = 69]
[Mezzo, T, Bar soli]
Holy, holy, holy, Time and the Elements: Heaven and earth are full of Thy Glory.
[quarter note = 88]

Hosanna: 35 mm. [*meno mosso*, quarter note = 50]

[S 2, Mezzo, Bar, satb choir]
Hosanna in the highest.
Humbled and amazed are he and she who have experienced life.
Hosanna in the highest.
Die irae, die illa
A day of wrath, that day:
We shall dissolve the world into glowing ashes,
as attested by our weapons for wars in the names of gods unknowable.
Thus I pray to Thee, from whom all flesh did come.

Merciful time: 34 mm. [half-note = 92]

[satb choir]
Merciful Time, who buries the sins of the world,
Grant them rest.
Merciful Elements, from whom a new world can be constructed, most, blue-green
and fertile,
Grant them eternal rest.

Let not eternal light: 58 mm. [*andante*, quarter note = 69]

[tb choir]
Let not eternal light disturb their sleep, O Cosmos, for Thou art merciful.
[satb choir]
Deliver me, O Cosmos, from everlasting wakefulness on that dread day when
heavens and earth shall quake,
[S1, Mezzo, T, Bar soli]
when we shall dissolve the world into glowing ashes in the names
of gods unknowable.
I am seized with trembling and I am afraid until the day of reckoning shall arrive
and the wrath to come.
[Bar solo, satb choir]
Hence I pray.
Deliver me, O Cosmos, from everlasting wakefulness
on that day of wrath, calamity and misery.

Postlude [Requiem]: 19 mm. [*meno mosso*, quarter note = 52]

[satb choir]
Rest eternal grant them, O Cosmos,
and let not light perpetual disturb their harmless sleep.
[synthesizer-postlude]

DISCOGRAPHY

Newport Classic, LC 8554, The Manhattan Chamber Orchestra, Magic Circle
Opera Ensemble, cond. Richard Clark.

FRANK LEWIN
March 27, 1925

Frank Lewin studied composition with Felix Deyo, Jack Frederick Kil-
patrick, Hans David, and Roy Harris before attending Yale University,
where his teachers were Richard Donovan and Paul Hindemith. He was
later appointed to a professorship in composition, at Yale, a position he
occupied from 1971 to 1992.

Lewin has a significant body of musical compositions, including three
stage works, *It's Cultural* (1958), *Gulliver* (1975), *Burning Bright* (1993), two
concertos (Viola, Harmonica), music for the theatre (incidental music and
vocal solos), scores for television and 200 films, and the song cycles, *Shall
I Compare Thee* (Shakespeare), *Innocence and Experience* (Blake), *Variations
of Greek Themes* (Robinson), *A Musical Nashery* (Nash), *Phoenix* (Williams),
She walks in Beauty (Byron), and *Wedding Music* (Song of Songs). There
remain a number of choral compositions; *Psalm 148* (1949), *Psalm 137*
(1956), *Behold How Good* (1963), *Music of Early America* (1965), and *Mass for
the Dead*, in English (1969).

The *Mass for the Dead* is scored for SATB choir, SATB soli, congregation,
organ, and instruments and dedicated to the memory of Robert F. Kennedy. Its first performance took place during a memorial service in the
Chapel of Princeton University. The idea for such a work came as the
composer observed Kennedy's funeral train passing through Princeton.
In a conversation with the author, the composer indicated that he had also
been greatly moved by the music for the funeral services of President
Kennedy.

His setting of the Latin requiem is one of the very few, and possibly,
first concert requiem settings in English. The choice of language might
reflect the decision of the Second Vatican Council to permit the use of
vernacular languages in the celebration of the liturgy. While this setting
is notated in C, the music moves freely through a series of tonalities, and

at the same time, no sense of a primary "key" is suggested. The harmony appears to be a result of the linear structuring of the melodic strands. The harmonic language is often triadic, but colored by dissonant intervals. The only movement that possesses a clear tonality is the *Lord's Prayer* (D flat M).

The prevailing SATB choral texture is frequently thinned by unison and two-part writing while points of melodic imitation are commonly employed. The writing remains simple and direct, especially in the movements in which congregational participation is expected (*Sanctus, Agnus Dei*).

Basic Data

EDITION

Mass for the Dead (in English)
In Memory of Robert Kennedy
For Mixed Chorus, Solo Voices, Congregation and Organ
Frank Lewin
Demeter Music Inc. [c. 1969]

DURATION

Eleven movements, 570 mm., perf., c. 32'

VOICING AND ORCHESTRATION

Choir: SATB [*divisi*] range: S-B flat 6; B-D3
Soloists: SATB
Instruments: org., 2 tp., 2 tbn., 2 Fh., fl.

OUTLINE

Introit-*Kyrie*: 83 mm.
   Eternal rest [quarter note = 72] satb choir. ABA with *Lord have mercy*, satb choir/ B solo.
Graduale-Tract: 51 mm.
   Eternal rest [quarter note = 72] satb choir; *The just man*, T solo; *Absolve, O Lord*, S solo.
Offertory Antiphon: 87 mm.
   Lord Jesus Christ [quarter-note = 69-72] satb choir; *We offer you*, T solo; *Grant O Lord*, satb choir.
Sanctus: 59 mm.
   Holy, Holy, Holy [quarter-note = 80] satb choir/congregation/brass; *Blessed is He*, satb choir (imitative); *Hosanna*, satb choir/congregation/brass.
Lord's Prayer: 37 mm.
   Our Father [quarter-note = 80] [D flat] satb choir.
Agnus Dei: 42 mm.
   Lamb of God/Agnus Dei [half-note = 56] satb choir/satb congregation (Latin-choir, English-congregation).

Communion Antiphon: 36 mm.

May eternal light [quarter-note = 72] A solo/satb choir.

Libera me: 81 mm.

Deliver me [quarter-note = 72] B solo/satb choir; *I am in fear*, B solo/tb choir; *That day*, B solo/satb choir; *Eternal rest*, satb choir; *Deliver me*, B solo/satb choir; *Lord have mercy*, B solo/satb choir.

Lord's Prayer: 36 mm.

Organ solo.

In Paradisum: 40 mm.

May the angels [quarter-note = 66] satb choir/flute.

Conclusion: 18 mm.

Eternal rest [quarter-note = 72] satb choir.

DISCOGRAPHY

Demeter 102, Stereo Disc (recording of the premiere).

GYÖRGY LIGETI
May 28, 1923

Ligeti was born in Hungary and received his earliest musical training at the Budapest School of Music with Ferenc Farkas. In 1956, he immigrated to Germany, where he studied at the Electronics Studio in Cologne. He later settled in Austria. He has composed a significant body of music for orchestra and various solo instruments such as organ, harpsichord, and cello.

There are a handful of works for chamber ensembles and an unusual work, titled *Poème Symphonique*, scored for 100 metronomes. Much of his music is in the *avant garde* idiom. He has been an experimenter and innovator in the field of orchestral and choral textures and in the concept of aleatoric counterpoint. Ligeti has used these techniques to explore deep spiritual feelings and moods, especially in his setting of the *Requiem*, scored for soprano, mezzo-soprano, double SATB choir, and orchestra. The work took nearly two years to complete; from the spring of 1963 to January 1965. Considered to be a masterpiece of *avant garde* atonal writing, the composition won the Bonn Beethoven Prize in 1967.

The music has several ties to traditional, older historical settings of the requiem text: a traditional text of great antiquity, employed at a time when composers were using ultra-modern poetry and the vocal polyphonic style of the old masters. Even the structure of the *Kyrie* is based upon a much older model, the fugue; and its texture within the greater structure is canonic. Renaissance "word-painting" is employed in the *Dies irae* movement. Yet, for all its obligation to the past, the work remains thoroughly modern.

The *Requiem* uses a super-dense, atonal harmony that borders on unpitched sound and a rhythmic structure so complex that the polyrhythms create a virtually static sense of rhythm. Technical problems, related to the rhythm or the maintenance of accurate choral intonation, are significantly difficult. The range of the jagged, serial melodies for the soprano soloist extends from E flat 7 down to B 4. Perfect pitch is essential for members of any choral ensemble choosing to perform this work.

Basic Data

EDITION

Ligeti
Requiem für Sopran, Mezzosopran, zwei gemischte Chöre und Orchester
Klavierauszug [Vocal Score] made by Zsigmond Szathmáry
Peters Edition #8152
Henry Litolff's Verlag/C. F. Peters 1975.

DURATION

Four movements, 423 mm., perf., c. 27'

VOICING AND ORCHESTRATION

Choir: Choir I: twenty parts. S MS ATB [each *divisi à 4*). Choir II: five parts.
S MS ATB [each *divisi à 2*] range: S-C flat 7; B-C3.
Soloists: soprano, mezzo soprano
Orchestra: vn. I/II, vla., vc., db., 3 fl. (doubling 2 pic.), 2 ob., Eh., 3 cl. (doubling bcl. and contrabass cl.), 2 bsn., cbsn., 4 Fh., 3 tpt., bass tpt., 3 tbn., contrabass tuba. PERC: (3 players) bass drum, side drum, tam-tam, tambour de basque, whip, suspended cymbal, xylophone, glockenspiel, celesta, harpsichord, harp. [Extensive directions are given in the score, regarding the placement of the chorus.]

OUTLINE

Introit: 83 mm.
Requiem aeternam, sostenuto. Choir I/S-MS soli. (atonal harmony-chromaticism-polyphonic choral texture-orchestral tone clusters) employed. Words unintelligible because of the textual density. A gradual transformation from the very dark sound (bbbb choir) into a concluding ssssmmmmaaaa bright tone. The orchestra employs sustained tone clusters.
Kyrie: 120 mm.
Kyrie, molto espressivo. s ms atb choir [each section *divisi à 4*]. The *Kyrie* is a five-part "fugue" in which each section functions as a four-part canon. Orchestral support is very modest.
Sequence, *De Die Judicii Sequentia*: 158 mm.
Dies irae, agitato molto. S MS soli/choir I/II. Vocal lines are extremely jagged and dissonant. Solo lines alternate with violent choral outbursts. Polyrhythmic writing [3 notes against 5 notes and other combinations], abrupt dynamic

changes, the splitting-up of words into syllables, while assigning the syllables to successively different vocal parts and the alternation of measures with rhythm or no rhythm are commonly used techniques.

Sequence, *Lacrimosa*: 62 mm.

Lacrimosa, molto lento. S MS soli. A lament. The mood is one of quietude and simplicity. The orchestral accompaniment is subdued, ranging from *pp* to *ppppp*.

DISCOGRAPHY

Wergo, 60 045-50, Sinfonie-Orchester des Hessischen Rundfunks, Choir of the Bayerischen Rundfunks, dir., Micheal Gielen.

PAUL PATTERSON
June 15, 1947

The English composer Paul Patterson studied at the Royal Academy of Music in London. In 1971, he was appointed a Manson Fellow at the Royal Academy, where he later headed the composition and twentieth-century music program (1985). He was director of twentieth-century studies at the University of Warwick from 1974 to 1985. Patterson developed a composition style that combines a number of modern compositional techniques, such as electronic and aleatoric techniques, with a more traditional approach to composition.

Among his compositions are film scores, orchestral works, chamber music, piano, and organ solos, as well as a significant number of vocal scores. Among the latter works is a *Kyrie* for chorus and piano (1971); *Gloria* for chorus and piano (1972); *Requiem* for chorus, boy's choir, and orchestra (1974); the *Canterbury Psalms* for chorus and orchestra or organ (1981); *Missa Brevis* for chorus (1985); *Stabat Mater* for mezzo-soprano, chorus, and orchestra (1985–86); *Magnificat and Nunc Dimittis* for chorus and organ (1986); and *Te Deum* for soprano, chorus, boy's chorus, and orchestra (1988).

The *Requiem* (1974), scored for SATB chorus, boy's choir, and orchestra, utilizes a number of modern compositional techniques, including aleatoric passages for both chorus and orchestra; instrumental and vocal slides (*glissandi*) of three types (ascending, descending, swirling); modified serial techniques; polytonality; and vocal effects, such as whispering, clapping, hissing, shouting, (gliding up or down $1/2$ tone from the printed note), percussive consonant-vowel sounds, tone clusters, and many other unusual effects (including tonality). The composer asks the player to blow wind through their instruments at various dynamic levels. The sonority of the work presents a kaleidoscope of new sounds. One "instrument," needed throughout the work, is the stop-watch. It is employed for the timing of aleatoric passages that occur in nearly every movement.

The "harmonic" language of the *Requiem* is a mixture of atonality, dissonant tonality, tone clusters, unpitched sound, and aleatoric sound. For performance, this virtuoso piece is best suited to a professional chorus. This setting of the *Requiem* is not designed for liturgical usage, but rather for concert. It includes passages from Ecclesiastes and an early version of the *Dies irae* text as found in Zephaniah I.

Basic Data

EDITION

Paul Patterson
Requiem for Chorus and Orchestra
[vocal score]
Josef Weinberger Ltd. London. 1975

DURATION

Six movements, 696 mm., perf., c. 40'

VOICING AND ORCHESTRATION

Choir: SATB range: S-A6; B-F3; Boy's choir: SA
Orchestra: vn. I/II, vla., vc., db., pic., 2 fl., 2 ob., 2 cl., 2 bsn., 4 Fh., 3 tpt., 2 tenor tbn., bass tbn., tuba. PERC: vibraphone, gongs, cymbals, bass drum, timpani, marimba, wind machine, tam-tam, wood blocks, flexatone.

OUTLINE

Introit: 103 mm.
   Requiem aeternam [quarter-note = 48] satb choir. ABA form.
Kyrie: 108 mm.
   Orchestral introduction [quarter-note = 80]; *Kyrie*, ssaa choir
Sanctus: 144 mm.
   Orchestral introduction [quarter-note = 80] satb chorus. *Hosanna*, ssaatbb choir.
   Benedictus, satb choir (whispered).
Ecclesiastes: 49 mm.
   To everything there is a season, molto legato [quarter-note = 48] satb choir, unaccompanied. (unison/atonal harmony).

To everything there is a season
and a time to every purpose under the heaven.
A time to be born and a time to die,
A time to heal, A time to weep and
A time to laugh. A time to love and a time to hate.
A time of war and a time of peace.

Sequence: 131 mm.
   Dies irae [quarter-note = 48] satb choir [*divisi*]/sa boy's choir.

Dies irae, dies illa calamitatis et miseriae.
Dies magna et amara valde.
(Zephaniah 1:14–16)

In Paradisum: 161 mm.

Orchestral introduction; *In paradisum*, [quarter-note = 60] satb choir [*divisi*]/
boy's choir.

DISCOGRAPHY

None found.

ELIS PEHKONEN
June 22, 1942

Elis Pehkonen was born in England and studied composition with Peter
Racine Fricker at the Royal College of Music. In 1967, he became a music
teacher at the Cirencester School in Gloucestershire, where he became
particularly interested in music for percussion and the voices of young
people.

His music is written in a tonal idiom and style. Among his works are a
Concerto with Orchestra for piano, instrumental quintet, percussion, and
orchestra (1968), *My Cats*, for voices and percussion (1968), *Three Symphonies for 10 Players* for piano and percussion (1968), *Gymels* for piano
and percussion (1969), and *The Music of Paradise* for four choirs, string
ensemble, recorders, nightingale whistle, cymbal, and auto-harp (1971).
Pehkonen's choral works include *Requiem* for soli, choir, orchestra, and
organ (1967, rev. 1982), *Sinfonia Beata Maria Virgine* (1981–83), *Ode to St.
Cecilia* (1991), *The First Coming* (1992), *Gloria* (1993), *Laudate* (1995), and
Russian Requiem.

The *Russian Requiem* was composed in 1986, by commission of the Birmingham Festival Choral Society and Jeremy Patterson. It is scored for SA
soli, SATB choir, and orchestra and the premiere took place on November
1, 1986, in St. Philip's Cathedral, Birmingham. In the creation of the *Russian Requiem*, Pehkonen was inspired by *Stalin's Secret War*, written by
Nikolai Tolstoy. The composer chose to contrast human reality and free
will with divine hope and aspiration. This nonliturgical requiem utilizes
portions of the Latin rite, which are glossed by four other sources: Dante's
Inferno, The Revelation of St. John the Divine, aphorisms by Lenin and,
last, excerpts from Boris Pasternak's evocative "Zhivago's Poems." These
texts, when interpolated with the requiem text, constitute a commentary
upon the text of the liturgical rite, much in the same way as the war
poems of Wilfred Owen comment upon the requiem text in Britten's *War
Requiem*.

Although the prevailing, four-part choral texture is homophonic, there are occasional passages of imitative, polyphonic writing. Much of the texture is reduced to unison and two-part writing—even when expanding the choral texture to eight voice parts. The harmonic language of the *Requiem* is a modern form of tonality, employing a substantial amount of dissonance. Like many other twentieth-century requiems, the *Russian Requiem* is notated in E, though the composer moved freely through many tonal areas, rarely settling in the key of E major.

Basic Data

EDITION

Elis Pehkonen
Russian Requiem for soprano and contralto soloists, chorus and orchestra.
Vocal Score [Full Score]
Oxford University Press, Oxford and New York. 1989

DURATION

Four movements, 971 mm., perf., c. 42′

VOICING AND ORCHESTRATION

Choir: SATB range: S-A6; B-G3
Soloists: SA
Orchestra: vn. I/II, vla., vc., db., ob., Eh., 2 C tpt., timp., org. PERC: snare drum, bass drum, cymbals, suspended cymbal, tam-tam, glockenspiel.

OUTLINE

Introit: 101 mm.
  Requiem aeternam, con moto. satb choir; *Et lux,* satb choir (canonic); *Requiem aeternam,* satb choir. ABA form. [bitonal-am/EM].
Sequence: 487 mm.
  Prologue: *Lasciate, poco adagio.* A solo; *I looked, presto.* S solo/satb choir; *Dies irae* I. (unison) *allegro con spirito.* (*The world must be destroyed/Quantus tremor; Dies irae* II. (two-part), (*We destroy/Per me siva*) satb choir/A solo; *Dies irae* III. (canonic) S solo/satb choir (*I looked/Insult them*); *Dies irae* IV. (canonic) (*Spit on them/ Intensify the revolution*) satb choir; *Dies irae* V. (chordal) satb choir [*divisi*]; Epilogue: *And I saw the souls,* S solo/satb choir [*divisi*]; *Non isperate,* A solo. Rondo form. Pehkonen created an original theme for *Dies irae,* employing it in original, inversion, augmentation, and diminution forms.

Lasciate ogni speranza, voi ch'entrate. Abandon all hope, ye that enter here.
(Dante, *Inferno,* Canto III) alto solo
I looked and beheld a pale horse and the man that sat on him was Death,
and Hell followed with him.
And power was given unto them over the fourth part of the earth,
to kill with the sword, with hunger and with death.
[soprano solo & choir]
The world must be destroyed through fire and iron.

We destroy in order to build better.
Podonki, nasekomi, tuneyadtsi. (Scum, insects, parasites)
Root them out! Slap them down! Trample them underfoot!
[Lenin]
Per me si va nella citta dolente; Through me is the way to the doleful city;
Per me si va nell'eterno dolore; Through me the way to eternal pain;
Per me si va tra la perduta gente. Through me the way amongst the lost
generations.
[Dante, *Inferno*, Canto III]
I looked and beheld another horse that was as red as blood,
and power was given to him that sat thereon to take peace from the earth,
and that they should kill one another.
[St. John]
Insult them! Spit on them! Arrest them all and don't forget your rifles.
Intensify the repression! Long live the Revolution!
We destroy in order to build better!
[Lenin]
And I saw the souls of them that were slain for the word of God,
and they cried with a loud voice saying,
"How long wilt thou wait, O Lord, to avenge our blood?"
[Revelation of St John] soprano solo
Non isperate mai veder lo cielo: Hope not to see heaven:
i'vegno per menarvi all'altra riva, I come to lead you to the other shore,
nelle tenebre eterne, in caldo e in gelo. into eternal darkness, into fire and ice.
[Dante, *Inferno*, Canto III] alto solo

Offertory: 282 mm.
Orchestral introduction (fugal); *Domine Jesu Christe, con moto.* satb choir [*divisi*],
(unaccompanied rhythmic canon); *My soul, poco piu mosso.* S solo/oboe obbligato;

My soul is sorrowful unto death.
Stay here and watch with me!
[Pasternak]

The Night, meno mosso. A solo/satb choir; *Only the garden,* SA soli duet/satb
choir; *Sweating blood, movente.* Satb choir/SA soli; *Ne absorbeat eas,* satb choir;
God has granted, con moto, A solo; *Could not my Father,* S solo/ssaattbb choir.

The night was a kingdom of despair.
The world seemed uninhabited.
Only the garden was a place for the living.
He gazed into the black abyss.
Empty, without beginning or end.
Sweating blood, he prayed to the Father
that the cup of death should pass him by.
[Pasternak]

God has granted you to live in my time.
The hour of the Son of Man has struck,
he will deliver himself into the hands of sinners.
Could not my Father send me a host of winged legions to defend me?
Then would no hair of my head be touched.
I shall go freely, through torment, down to the grave.
And on the third day I shall rise again.
Like rafts down a river, like a convoy of ships,
the centuries will float to me out of the darkness.
[Pasternak]

Agnus Dei: 101 mm.

Agnus Dei/Snow, con moto. SA soli/satb choir. This movement is composed on two levels: a duet with eleven statements of the *Agnus Dei* text as satb choir continuously sings *Snow swept over the world* (Pasternak, *Winter Night* from *Zhivago's Poems*).

DISCOGRAPHY

Corinium Music, CMCD001, Birmingham Festival Choral Society, dir. Jeremy Patterson.

ZBIGNIEW PREISNER
May 20, 1955

Preisner is a Polish composer of film music. Among his better-known contributions to that medium are *Dekalog*, *The Double Life of Veronique*, *Three Colors Blue*, *Three Colors White*, and *Three Colors Red*, all films of Krzysztof Kieslowski. Other films include *At Play in the Fields of the Lord*, *The Secret Garden*, and *When a Man Loves a Woman*. He has won awards for his music from the French Film Academy, the Berlin Film Festival, and the Los Angeles Critics Association Awards. In 1992, he received an important award from the Polish Minister of Foreign Affairs for his efforts in the promotion of Polish culture.

The *Requiem for My Friend*, was composed in 1996 and scored for six soloists (soprano, two countertenors, two tenors, and bass), SATB choir, orchestra, string quartet, organ, and percussion. It was written in memory of his friend Krzysztof Kieslowski, filmmaker. This work is the first large-scale work by the composer and was first performed on October 1, 1998 at the Teatr Wielki, Warsaw. It is divided into two principal sections; Part One: REQUIEM and Part Two: LIFE.

The tonal language of *Requiem for My friend* is traditional harmony, influenced both by "minimalist" approach and popular "New Age" music style. The vocal writing is primarily homophonic and includes many passages of two-part and unison writing. At the same time, the music possesses strong emotions of grief and spirituality. Its overall quality is that of a lament—an outpouring of sorrow.

Basic Data

EDITION

Zbigniew Preisner
Requiem for My Friend
Vocal Score
Chester Music, London 1998.

DURATION

Two Parts, eighteen movements, 447 mm. (Requiem), 1115 complete work, perf., c. 69'

VOICING AND ORCHESTRATION

Part I
Soloists; soprano, 2 countertenors, 2 tenors, bass
Instruments: string quintet [vn. I/II, vla., vc., db.], org., Percussion.

Part II
Soloists: soprano, counter tenor, voice.
Choir: SATB
Orchestra: vn. I/II, vla., vc., db., ob., cl., fl., bsn., Fh., tpt., tbn., PERC: timp., chimes, triangle, bells, side drum, various other drums. org. Solo instruments: piano, alto saxophone, recorder.

OUTLINE

PART I: REQUIEM
Officium [*Requiem aeternam*]: 79 mm.
    Requiem aeternam, misterioso. S C-T TB soli, unaccompanied.
Kyrie: 80 mm.
    Organ introduction (ostinato throughout); *Kyrie* [quarter-note = 58] S-CT-TB soli/S solo.
Sequence: 58 mm.
    Rex tremendae, misterioso. S solo; *Ingemisco*, S-CT soli; *Dies irae*, S solo/S CT TB soli. (vv. 1, 8, 12)
Offertory: 51 mm. (*Hostias* only)
    Major solo for cello. *Hostias*, S solo; *Fac eas*, S-CT soli.
Sanctus: 53 mm.
    Organ prelude; *Sanctus*, S solo/CT-TB soli; *Hosanna*, S solo/S CT TB soli; *Benedictus*, S solo; *Hosanna*, S solo/S-CT-TB soli.
Agnus Dei: 30 mm.
    Agnus Dei, S solo/S-CT soli.

Lux aeterna: 22 mm.

Psalm 130 [v. 1 and v. 2, beginning]. [quarter-note = 76] S solo/S-CT soli (*Swiat-losc Wiekustia. . . . May eternal light*); Psalm 133 S solo/S-CT-TB soli (*Wsrod Swietych . . . Out of the Depths*) Unaccompanied.

Lacrimosa: 40 mm.

Lacrimosa [quarter-note = 54] S solo/S-CT-TB soli. (v.18).

Epitaphium: 34 mm.

Part I ends with a quiet organ solo.

PART II LIFE

The Beginning. Three short instrumental movements.

Meeting: 58 mm.

Discovering the world: 37 mm.

Love: 64 mm.

Destiny: One movement. Kai Kairos, (Ecclesiastes 3:1–8).

Kai Kairos: 185 mm.

Apocalypse: Four movements.

Ascende huc: 66 mm.

> Come up hither and I will show the things
> Which must be hereafter.

Veni et Vidi: 80 mm.

> "Come and see." And I looked, and beheld a pale horse;
> and his name that sat on him was Death,
> and Hell followed him.
> And power was given unto them over the fourth part of the earth,
> to kill with the sword and with Hunger,
> and with death, and with him the beasts of the earth.

Qui erat et qui est: 89 mm. [That which was and is].

> They shall hunger no more, neither thirst any more;
> neither shall the sun light on them, nor any heat.
> For the Lamb which is in the midst of the throne shall feed them,
> and shall lead them unto the fountains of waters;
> and God shall wipe away tears from their eyes.
> That which was and which is and is to come.

Lacrimosa—Day of Tears: 42 mm.

(Sequence vv. 18–19) [*Lacrimosa* & *Huic ergo*]

Postscriptum. one movement.

Prayer: 67 mm.

> Lord, help us to gather our strength in difficult times,
> So that we could go on living,
> believing in the meaning of future days. Be so good to
> give us that hope. Be so good.

DISCOGRAPHY
Erato, 3984-24146-2, Warsaw Chamber Choir and Sinfonia Varsovia.

SÁNDOR SZOKOLAY
March 30, 1931

Szokolay graduated from the Budapest Academy of Music in 1957 and a few years later, in 1966, he joined the Academy staff. His dynamic musical style appears to have been influenced by Orff, Bartok, and Stravinsky.

The bulk of his *oeuvre* is vocal music and includes seven operas and a large number of choral pieces. Among the choral works are the oratorios, *Isthar's Descent into Hell* (*Isthár pokoljárása*), *Fiery March* (*A tüz márciusa*); and the cantatas, *Children's Cantata* (*Vizimesék*), *Apokalipszis* (*Apocalypse*), *Hommage à Kodaly*, *Rivalry of the Worlds* (*Világok vetélkedése*), and *Déploration, à la memoire de Francis Poulenc*. Several of the smaller choral works include *Ten Fragments by Jozsef Attila*, *Revelation*, *Hungarian Christmas Carols* (*Magyar karácsony*), *Gloria*, and *Pastoral Carols* (*Karácsonyi pasztorál*). Szokolay further composed concertos for the piano, violin, and trumpet.

The *Déploration* in memory of Francis Poulenc was composed in 1964 for the second Choir Festival, held in Tours, France. The work is dedicated to the choral group, Ensemble Vocal Jean de Ockeghem. Szokolay scored the music for solo piano, SATB choir, orchestra, and organ. The title, *Déploration*, is taken from the name of a type of lament, more commonly written by members of the fifteenth- and sixteenth-century Franco-Flemish school. A principal difference between the Renaissance *déploration* and that of Szokolay is that the latter work is a setting of the requiem text, while the text of the earlier *déploration* was freely, if not stereotypically, composed.

The *Déploration* is a tonal work employing traditional triadic harmonies but combined with a "modern" dissonant harmony that employs intervals of the ninth and second. Although the work is notated in C, the use of chromatic notes and harmony removes the music far from that tonality.

Rhythmic and melodic ostinati, played by every instrument are utilized as a major structure-building technique, throughout the composition. The ostinati give a sense of tonality to the work. In this respect, *Déploration* superficially resembles Carl Orff's *Carmina Burana*.

Contrasts to the prevailing four-part choral texture are provided by *divisi* writing and thinning of voice parts. Most of the choral fabric is syllabic and chordal, but there are occasional imitative passages (*Libera me, Pleni sunt coeli*). The choir uses several "modern" twentieth-century vocal techniques, such as glissandi on *Dies irae* and the vocalization "*a*" (*amen*) in *Agnus Dei* III and "*a*" (*dona*) in the Introit.

The use of a solo piano and twelve-part *divisi* strings writing (nine-part/cello and three-part/bass) are some of the novel features in the orchestration. The piano occupies an important virtuoso role in every movement, except the *Kyrie*. While the *Déploration* employs the words of the liturgical requiem, the texts have been greatly diminished in length (see Outline) and the usual text sequence has been rearranged (see Outline).

Basic Data

EDITION

Sandor Szokolay
Déploration à la memoire de Francis Poulenc
pour Piano solo, Choeur mixte, Orgue et Orchestre de Chambre
Alphonse Leduc. Paris [1982]

DURATION

Six movements, 413 mm. perf., c. 20′

VOICING AND ORCHESTRATION

Choir: SATB [*divisi*] range: S-A6; B-E3 [D3 rare]
Soloists: SAAB
Orchestra: vc. I/II/III [each *divisi à* 3], db. [*divisi à* 3], 2 fl., ob., cl., bsn., 2 tpt., tbn., timp., piano solo, org., PERC: cymbals, bass drum, small tambour, tam-tam.

OUTLINE

Introit: 150 mm.
   Requiem aeternam, calme. b/t choir; *Requiem aeternam, moderato.* sattbb choir; *Requiem aeternam, calme.* sattbb choir; *Domine, allegro risoluto.* satb choir. Orchestral introduction, interludes and postlude. (text: *Requiem aeternam dona eis Domine et lux perpetua luceat eis.*)
Kyrie: 21 mm.
   Kyrie, andante. ssaa choir, unaccompanied. (full text)
Sequence: 112 mm.
   Orchestral introduction, *allegro*; *Dies irae,* tb choir/satb choir; *Dies irae;* satb choir (*divisi*); orchestral interlude; *Dies irae,* satb choir [*divisi*] (canonic writing); orchestral interlude; *Dies irae,* satb choir. (text: *Dies irae, dies illa . . . calamitatis et miseriae . . . Requiem dona . . . Dies magna et amara valde . . . Dies irae, dies illa*)
Responsory: 34 mm.
   Libera me, adagio. SB soli/sa & tb choir (canonic). (text: *Libera me de morte. Libera me, libera me Domine*)
Sanctus: 24 mm.
   Sanctus, allegro risoluto. ssaattb choir; *Pleni sunt coeli,* ssattbb choir (imitative); *Sanctus,* ssaattbb choir; orchestral interlude; *Sanctus,* ssattbb choir. (text: *Sanctus Dominus Deus Sabaoth. Sanctus. Pleni sunt coeli et terra. Sanctus. Sanctus. Dominius.*)

Agnus Dei: 72 mm.

Agnus Dei I, *andante sostenuto*. S solo/saa choir; *Agnus* II, sa or tb choir; *Agnus* III, *"a"* satb choir; *"Amen"* satb choir.

DISCOGRAPHY

None found.

RANDALL THOMPSON
April 21, 1899–July 9, 1984

The American Randall Thompson earned his fame with instrumental works that included three symphonies, string quartets, an opera, and numerous chamber pieces. He studied composition with Ernest Bloch and later held significant teaching positions at Harvard, Princeton, Wellesley College, and the directorship of Curtis Institute.

Although he was a prolific instrumental composer, his most famous pieces remain those written for the choral repertory. Among the sacred pieces are *Alleluia* (1940), *The Peaceable Kingdom* (1936), *The Last Words of David* (1949), *Mass of the Holy Spirit* (1955–56), *The Nativity According to St. Luke* (1961), and *The Passion According to St. Luke*. The secular works include *Frostiana* (1959), *The Testament of Freedom* (1943), and *Ode to the Virginian Voyage* (1956–57).

The *Requiem for Unaccompanied Double Chorus* was composed in 1957–58, on a commission from the May T. Morrison Music Festival, which was dedicating the Morrison Music Building and the Hertz Concert Hall at the University of California, Berkeley. Scored for double SATB choir, its first performance was given by the University of California Chorus on May 22–23, 1957.

This nonliturgical requiem owes much of its inspiration to the dramatic polychoral style of Gabrieli and Cavalli. The use of free speech rhythms and quasimodal harmonies can be described as derived from the "Anglican Revival" style.

The *Requiem* is scored, variously, for one SATB choir (*Be filled with the spirit*), for two SATB choirs (*Ye were sometimes darkness*), and once, for three SATB choirs (*Lamentations*). Much of the work is set in the form of a dialogue between the choir of the Faithful (choir I) and the choir of the Mourners (choir II). The prevailing choral texture is contrapuntal, polyphonic style with contrasting homophonic passages. Imitative polyphony is employed in several passages: *O let the nations be glad*, *Blessed be the Lord*, and *Alleluia, Amen*.

The choral baritone recitatives of Part Five are, likewise, inspired by similar passages in the late madrigals of Monteverdi. The texts, arranged into five major divisions and compiled by the composer, were extracted from seventeen different books of the Bible (Old/New Testaments and the Apocrypha).

Thompson employed word-painting suggesting wailing (*Lamentations*), joy and leaping (*Praise him all*), and length (*Thou hast given him*).

Basic Data

EDITION

Requiem for Double Chorus of Mixed Voices
Randall Thompson
E. C. Schirmer Music Co. 1958.

DURATION

PARTS ONE to FIVE, eighteen movements, 1032 mm., perf., c. 75'

VOICING AND ORCHESTRATION

Choir: choir I, SATB; choir II, SATB range: S-B flat 6; B-E flat 3

OUTLINE

PART I: Lamentations
   Lamentations, 92 mm. [em-phrygian] *adagio*. satb choirs I/II/III. Texts: Nehemiah, Job, Jeremiah, Lamentations, Ezekiel, Gospel of St. Luke, and Paul's Letters to the Ephesians. Theme: The faithful attempt to console the grieving.

Lamentations and mourning and weeping.
Mourn not, weep not, cry not, grieve not.
The joy of our heart is ceased; our dance is turned into mourning.
Refrain thy voice from weeping and thine eyes from tears.
Mourn.
Neither shalt thou mourn nor weep,
neither shall thy tears run down.
Mourn.
Grieve not, cry not, mourn not, nor weep.

PART II: The Triumph of Faith. 3 movements, 215 mm.
   Why make ye this ado? 38 mm. [phrygian/aeolian] *allegro*. satb choirs I/II. Text: Job 14. (Rondo form, canonic techniques). Theme: a discussion about immortality.

Why do ye make this ado and weep?
Man that is born of woman is of few days and full of trouble.
He cometh forth like a flower and is cut down. He fleeth also
as a shadow and continueth not. All flesh shall perish together
and man shall turn again into dust.

What man is he ? 108 mm. [am-AM] *allegro conciso e lento tranquillo.* satb choirs I/II. Theme: Discord between the mourners and the faithful.

What man is he that liveth and shall not see death?
How is it that ye have no faith?
Behold, we die, we perish, we all perish.
The just shall live by his faith.
Shall we be consumed by dying?
The eternal God is thy refuge and underneath are the everlasting arms.
The righteous perisheth and no man layeth it to heart.
Everlasting joy shall be unto them and merciful men are taken away.
Everlasting joy shall be unto them
By the blast of God they perish and by the breath of his nostrils are they consumed.
Everlasting joy shall be unto them.
How long Lord? Wilt thou hide thyself forever?
Shall thy wrath burn like fire?
His anger endureth but a moment; in his favor is life.
Life?—Stay yourselves and wonder.
Unto you it is given to know the mystery of the kingdom of God.
Stay yourselves and wonder.
O Lord thou hast brought up my soul from the grave.
Thou hast kept me alive.
Behold ye, regard, and wonder marvelously.

Good Tidings to the Meek, 69 mm. [GM] *poco andante.* satb choir I. Text: Isaiah. ABA form.

Good tidings to the meek. He hath sent me to bind up the broken-hearted;
to comfort all that mourn; to give unto them beauty for ashes,
the oil of joy for mourning, the garment of praise for the spirit of heaviness.
Behold ye, regard, and wonder marvelously.

Part III: The Call to Song. 4 movements, 198 mm.
Be filled with the spirit. 31 mm.[CM] *lento e sereno.* ssaa/ttbb choir. Theme: The faithful urge the mourners to sing praise to God.

Be filled with the spirit, singing and making
melody in your heart to the Lord.—None answered.
Be filled . . . But none answered.
Be filled . . . None giveth answer.

O let the nations be glad, 59 mm. [GM] *andante piacevole.* satb choir I. (fugue).

O let the nations be glad and sing for joy.
But they hearkened not.

Sing unto him, 74 mm. [FM-A flat unison] *allegro con spirito*. ssaattbb choir I.

Sing unto him. Talk ye of all his wondrous works.
Sing unto him.

Utter a song, 34 mm. [CM] *andante moderato*. satb choir I/II. *Utter a song*, satb
choir I;
Blessed be the Lord God, allegro giusto. satb choir II. (Fugue)

Utter a song . . .
Can I hear anymore the voice of singing men and singing women?
Blessed be the Lord God, who only doeth wondrous things.
Part IV: The Garment of Praise. 5 movements, 251 mm.
Sing with the spirit. 16 mm. [A flat M] *lento e devoto*. satb choirs I/II. Text: St.
Paul. Prelude to Part IV.

Sing with the spirit.
I will sing with the spirit
and sing with the understanding also.
And I will sing with the understanding also.

Let everything that hath breath. 22 mm. [B flat M] *allegro*. satb choirs I/II. Choral
baritone recitative opens the movement.

Let everything that hath breath praise the Lord.
Let the inhabitants of the rock sing,
Let them shout from the top of the mountains.
Break forth into singing ye mountains,
O forest and every tree therein.

Let them give glory, 81 mm. [D flat M] *andante moderato, senza rigore*. satb choirs
I/II. Choral baritone recitative opens the movement; *Let the earth rejoice, allegro
con brio*. satb choirs I/II. (canon)

Let them give glory unto the Lord and declare his praise in the islands.
Let the earth rejoice; let the multitude of isles be glad thereof.

Praise him all ye stars of light. 102 mm. [FM] *andante*. satb choirs I/II. Text:
Wisdom of Solomon, 19:9. Choral baritone recitative opens the movement. Tone
"painting" and imitation are employed extensively.

Praise him all ye stars of light.
Let the heaven and earth praise him.
The morning stars sang together and all the sons of God shouted for joy.
For they went at large like horses and leaped like lambs,
praising thee, O Lord.

I am their music. 30 mm. [A flat M] *lento.* satb choirs I/II.

> I am their music.
> And now am I their song.
> I will praise the Lord with my whole heart;
> till he fill thy mouth with laughing and thy lips with rejoicing.

Part V: The Leave-Taking. 5 movements, 332 mm.
   Ye were sometimes in darkness. 113 mm. [CM] *lento e cupo.* satb choirs I/II. (canonic writing). Theme: consolation, peace and acceptance.

> Ye were sometimes darkness but now are ye light in the Lord.
> Walk as children of light.

   The Lord shall be unto thee. 16 mm. [FM] *largo.* satb choir II.

> The Lord shall be unto thee an everlasting light
> and thy God, thy glory.

   Return unto thy rest. 35 mm. [am] *poco adagio.* satb choir I. A chorale-like movement in homophonic, chordal style. Neapolitan sixth chords used for modulation and color.

> Return unto thy rest, O my soul;
> for the Lord hath dealt bountifully with thee.
> Return unto thy rest, O my soul.

   Thou hast given him, 33 mm. [em] *lento e tranquillo.* satb choir II.

> Thou hast given him his heart's desire and hast not withholden the request of his lips.
> He asked life of thee and thou gavest him a long life: even for ever and ever.

   Amen and amen. Alleluia. 135 mm.[EM] *allegro moderato.* satb choirs I/II. (Fugue)

> Amen and amen. Alleluia.

DISCOGRAPHY
None found.

GERARD VICTORY
July 24, 1921–March 14, 1995

Victory received his musical training at Belvedere College (Dublin) and Trinity College, University of Dublin. His professional life was spent at the Irish Radio Service, where he worked as a television producer and director of music. He was awarded an honorary doctorate in music from Trinity College in 1972 and elected to the presidency of UNESCO's International Rostrum of Composers (1981–83).

Victory composed a remarkable number of works including ten operas, nearly fifty major orchestral works (four symphonies, two piano concerti, a concerto for accordion), twenty pieces for chamber ensemble, piano music, and a quantity of vocal music. Among the choral works are *Mass of the Resurrection* for chorus and organ (1977); *Mass for Christmas Day* for baritone, choir, and organ; and *Ultima Rerum*, a symphonic requiem. *Ultima Rerum* (translated as "last things") was scored for SATB soli, large SATB choir, small SATB choir, children's chorus, and orchestra (1979–1981).

The first performance of *Ultima Rerum* was given in 1984. This humanistic requiem is a philosophical work that employs the traditional Latin requiem text, as well as other poetry from such sources as the Koran, the Norse *Edda*, Navaho Indian chant, and poetry of William Blake, James Elroy Flecker, Giacomo Leopardi, Alfred Tennyson, and Walt Whitman. It holds the distinction of being the longest requiem setting written by one individual: 2029 measures in ten movements.

This composition is arranged in two *Cantos* (halves) with five movements in each *Canto*. Like the *Czech Requiem* of Vycpálek, the work progresses from initial despair to final hope; using the traditional Christian beliefs, as well as the personal insights of various writers and non-Christian textual sources.

Victory's musical style and language is an eclectic conglomeration of tonal harmony that makes brief excursions into the realm of aleatoric music, medieval harmony, techniques and sonorities, Impressionism, and contemporary atonal chromatic composition. Much of the melodic material was derived from a scale (note row) that contains three motives. These motives are called sequences by the composer. *Ultima Rerum* is notated in C. (F 5-B flat 5; A 5-G♯ 5-F♯ 5-E 5-D 5; Eflat 5-B 4-C 5-C♯ 5-G 5)

The composer employs a wide variety of rhythms, including the free rhythm of chant, recitative, flamenco, and metered passages, thereby giving the music great rhythmic freedom. The basic SATB choral texture is frequently thinned or divided to provide a extensive range of sound. The choirs sing text, as well as effects (such as humming, speaking, and vocalizations). A small choir sings the more meditative passages, while the large choir is used for choral declamation. Both choirs come together for the musical climaxes. A children's choir is used for the Koran verses in the Offertory. The four soloists frequently interchange the dramatic and liturgical narrative roles, although the baritone is frequently used as a narrator.

Because of the complexity of the work, each movement will be described in broad strokes.

Basic Data

EDITION

Gerard Victory
Ultima Rerum: Requiem Cantata for Four soloists, Choirs and Orchestra
Vanderbeek & Imrie Ltd
15 Marvig, Lochs, Isle of Lewis, Scotland. 1988.

DURATION

Ten movements, 2029 mm., perf., c. 101'

VOICING AND ORCHESTRATION

Choirs: large SATB choir [*divisi*]; small SATB choir [*divisi*]; children's choir. range: S-B flat 6; B-E3
Soloists: SATB
Orchestra: vn., I/II, vla., vc., db., pic., 2 fl., 2 ob., 2 cl., bcl., 2 bsn., alto sax., 4 Fh., 3 tpt., 3 tbn., tuba, harp, timp., org., PERC: tam-tam, bass drum, gong, vibraphone, glockenspiel, marimba, tom toms, celesta, triangle, xylophone, chimes, small bells.

OUTLINE

First Canto

Movement I: Kyrie: 223 mm.
    Kyrie, *misterioso tranquillo* [a wide tempo range employed] SATB soli/large satb choir/small ssa choir; *Requiem aeternam*, A solo; *Kyrie*, large satb choir; Flecker's *Hassan* prose, STB soli; Spirit of the Maker of the Fountain, Bar. solo; the two lovers, Rafi and Pervaneh, ST soli. Harmonic language: Impressionism, medieval parallel fifths-fourths. The alto recitative-solo is accompanied flamenco rhythm. A colorful and programmatic orchestral accompaniment illuminates the text. A quasi-aleatoric choral passage is employed on the text, *Life is sweet.*

Requiem aeternam & Kyrie
[baritone]
The trees are moving without a wind.
The flowers are talking, the stars are growing bigger,
The garden to the ghosts.
[small choir]
Ah!
[baritone]
Come forth, new brother and sister
Those that are past shall dance with those who are to come.
[soprano & tenor]

We are here, O Shadow of the Fountain.
Tell us, shall we stay in this Garden and be lovers still
and fly in the air and flit among the leaves?
[baritone]
Ah! You have forgotten you are ghosts.
The memories of the Dead are thinner than their dreams.
I stay here by the fountain which I created.
What have you created in the world?
[soprano]
The story of our lives, the story of our torment—
Oh! May we not stay also?
May I not touch the shadow of his lips and hear the whisper of his love?
Must we be driven from here, O Man of the Garden?
[baritone]
How do I know? Can I foresee?
Why should the Dead be wiser than the Living?
I know only this—you will forget;
You will forget the Fire of Love when the wind blows,
When the Great Wind blows you asunder.
And you are borne like drops on a wave of air,
What do I know of where it shall take you?
I only know that it rushes
I only know it blows through the Garden and drives ten million souls together—
The souls of the Unborn Children that live in the flowers.
They pass like a comet across the midnight skies.
[small choir]
Ah!
[soprano]
I shall be satisfied: I shall be answered!
What of reason?
[baritone]
Ask of the wind!
[soprano]
And what of desire?
[baritone]
Ask of the wind!
[soprano]
And what of Justice, what of Paradise and what of the Stars?
[small choir]
And what of Life?
[soprano]
AH! LIFE IS SWEET, my children!
[small choir]
Life is sweet. Ah—
[baritone]
It is the Wind!

It comes to blow you asunder.
Kyrie & Requiem aeternam

Movement II: Canzone Funebre, 93 mm.
Sola nel mondo eternal . . . (poetry of Giacomo Leopardi), *andantino*. T solo/ttbb choir.

[tenor]
Death ! You alone are eternal in the universe. To you all creation comes—
our fragile nature must rest in you—happily?—
no not at all but securely free from ancient grief.
Darkest night deepens the melancholy thought already lurking confusedly in the mind.
The barren spirit feels its will to hope and to desire failing.
Now free from anxiety and fear it spends the slow void of the ages without tedium.
[male choir]
We lived: just as the troubled memory of terrifying ghosts
and the fevered dream haunts the soul of the infant, so does the memory
of our lives remain with us; but our memory has no hint of fear.
[tenor & ttbb choir]
What were we? What was the bitter brief moment which was called life?
To us life seems now a dark and mysterious thing just as death seems a thing unknown
to the minds of the living.
As our fragile nature shunned death while we lived, so now we shun the flame of life.
Happy? by no means but nonetheless secure.
Happiness is denied by Destiny both to the living and the dead.

Movement III: Dies Irae, 304 mm.
Dies irae [quarter-note = 144] (Latin text) satb choir (speaking-singing); (Vision of the Last Judgement, taken from *The Visionary Books* of William Blake), SATBar soli. Sequence vv. 1-7; *Lacrymosa*, [v. 18] S solo. Aleatoric choral passages.

Dies irae—Quantus tremor—Tuba mirum—Mors stupebit
[mezzo-soprano]
Then fell the fires of Eternity with loud and shrill
Sound of Loud Trumpet thundering along from heaven to heaven.
A mighty sound articulate!
[soprano & tenor]
Awake, awake and come to Judgement.
Liber scriptus
[baritone]
Folding like scrolls of the Enormous volume of Heaven and Earth
With thunderous noise and dreadful shakings rocking to and fro.

The heavens are shaken and the Earth removed from its place,
The foundation of the Eternal hills discovered.
Dies irae
[soprano]
His right hand branching out in fibrous strength
Siez'd the Sun, His left hand like dark roots cover'd the Moon
and tore them down cracking the heavens across from immense to immense.
Tuba mirum
[tenor & mezzo-soprano]
The books of Urizen unroll with dreadful noise.
The folding Serpent of Orc began to consume in fierce raving fire.
His fierce flames issued on all sides,
roaming abroad on all the winds, raging intense reddening,
into resistless pillars of fire!
Judex ergo
[all soloists]
Then fell the fires with loud and shrill
Sound of Loud Trumpet thundering along from heav'n to heav'n.
His fierce flames issued on all sides,
roaming abroad on all the winds, raging intense reddening,
into resistless pillars of fire!
Quid sum miser—Lacrimosa—Dies irae

Movement IV: De Profundis, 81 mm.

De Profundis, tranquillo. A solo/small satb choir [*divisi*] The florid alto solo resembles chant. (canonic choral writing) Some special choral and vocal effects [*parlando* and humming] used to intensify the dramatic presentation.

Movement V: Offertorium, 421 mm.

Orchestral introduction, *allegretto con moto*; *Domine Jesu Christe*, ST soli/large satb choir; *Libera animas*, Bar solo; *Sed signifer*, ST soli; *Quam olim Abrahae*, large satb choir; *Ho-zo-go* (Navaho chant, sung in tri-tone intervals), tb large choir, English trans., large satb choir [*divisi*]; *Ah, the just* (Koran), sa children's choir; Navaho chant, trans., large satb choir; *Libera animas*, ST soli; *Sed signifer*, SATBar soli (canonic); *Quam olim Abrahae*, SATBar soli/large satb choir; *Ho-zo-go*, small satb choir/large satb choir; *Hostias, maestoso con moto.* small satb/large satb choirs; *The just* (Koran), sa children's choir/*Libera eas*, SATBar soli; *In lucem sanctam/Ho-zo-go*, SATBar soli/small satb choir/large satb choir. The harmonic language is derived from medieval polyphony and from twentieth century impressionism.

[large choir]
Domine Jesu Christe
[soprano & baritone]
Libera animas
[soprano, tenor, baritone & choir]
Sed signifer
[large choir]

Hozogo Sokun Sinastlin—a Navaho chant
translation: Heaven is where all things are restored to the Just.
[children's choir]
Ah! The Just.
The Just who stand upon the Right
What's prepared for their delight?
A garden built for them to please
Watered by a crystal stream
With golden fruits upon the trees.
A silken couch of precious cloth
Where angels serve a magic draught
From agate cups so finely wrought (The Koran)
[all choirs]
Hozogo Sokun Sinastlin
[soprano & tenor]
Libera animas
[soloists and choirs]
Sed signifer
[large & small choirs] *Hostias*
[all]
Domine Jesu Christe

Second Canto

Movement VI: Canzone a se stesso (*A Song to One's Self, Giacomo Leopardi*), 66 mm.
Orposerai per sempre . . . tranquillo. A solo. The melodic material is derived from
the "b" and "c" motives of the tone scale devised by Victory. The tri-tone occupies a prominent role in the vocal solo line.

Now you will rest for ever, O my weary heart.
The last illusion has perished—an illusion which I believed eternal.
Yes, it has perished.
I feel that within us not only hope of, but desire for illusion has perished.
Rest now for ever; you have throbbed long enough.
Nothing can repay your striving nor does the earth merit any regrets.
Life is mere bitterness and travail; otherwise it is nothing—the world is merely
clay.
Be tranquil now—despair for the last time.
To humankind Fate has appointed Death as its only gift.
On Nature bestow your contempt.
It is brutal force which rules for the ruin and for the infinite futility of all things.

Movement VII: Sanctus, 258 mm.
Sanctus, tranquillo. S solo; *Ring out wild bells*, Alfred Tennyson, T solo/large satb
choir (various arrangements).

[tenor & large choir]
Ring out wild bells to the wild sky

The flying cloud, the frosty light
The year is dying in the night:
Ring out wild bells and let him die.

So runs my dream: but what am I?
An infant crying in the night
An infant crying for the light:
And with no language but a cry.

Ring out the grief that saps the mind
For those that here we see no more;
Ring out the feud of rich and poor.
Ring in redress to all mankind.

Are God and Nature then at strife
That Nature lends such evil dreams?
So careful of the type she seems
So careless of the single life;

Ring out the want, the care, the sin,
The faithless coldness of the times;
Ring out, ring out my mournful rhymes.
But ring the fuller minstrel in.

So careful of the type? but no,
From scarped cliff and quarried stone
She cries "A thousand types are gone:
I care for nothing, all shall go.

Ring out false pride in place and blood,
The civic slander and the spite
Ring in the love of truth and right
Ring in the common love of good.

Thou makest thine appeal to me:
I bring to life, I bring to death:
The spirit does but mean the breath
I know no more?"

[large choir]
And he shall be Man her last work
[soprano] Who seemed so fair
Such splendid purpose in his eyes
Who rolled the psalm to wintry skies
[baritone]
Who built him fanes of fruitless prayer
Who trusted God was love indeed

and Love Creation's final law—
[soprano]
Tho' Nature red in tooth and claw
With ravine shriek'd against his creed—
[full choir]
Shall he, who loved, who suffer'd countless ills
Who battled for the True, the Just
Be blown about the desert dust
Or seal'd within the iron hills?
[soprano & baritone]
No more? A monster then, a dream. A discord!
[choir]
Ring out wild bells and let him die.
[tenor]
Peace, come away, the song of woe
is after all an earthly song.
Peace, come away, we do him wrong
To sing so wildly; let us go.
Yet is these ears, till hearing dies
One set slow bell will seem to toll
The passing of the sweetest soul
That ever look'd with human eyes.
Come let us go; your cheeks are pale,
But half my life I leave behind:
Methinks my friend is richly shrined
But I shall pass; my work will fail.
[tenor & choir]
I hear it now, and o'er and o'er
Eternal greetings to the dead:
And "Ave, Ave, Ave" said
Adieu, adieu for evermore.

Movement VIII: In Paradisum, 70 mm.
Orchestral prelude; *In paradisum, tranquillo.* small ssaattbb choir/S solo. (*parlando* and humming vocal effects employed).
Movement IX: Benedictus, 223 mm.
Benedictus, vivace. large satb choir; *Sal sek standa* (Norse *Edda*), small tb choir/ small satb choir/small & large unison choirs; *I see a mansion,* (English translation), small satb choir; *Hosanna-There shall dwell,* small satb choir/large satb choir. (Venetian polychoral style).

[large choir]
Benedictus
[small choir]
I see a mansion fairer than the sun, plated gold upon its dome.
There shall dwell the blessed ones, Till the stars their course have run.
And earthly time no more be known.

[large choir]
Benedictus
[small choir] I see a mansion fairer . . .

Movement X: Agnus Dei, 290 mm.
　Agnus Dei, molto tranquillo. SATBar soli/small satb choir/large satb choir; *Kyrie,*
　Mors stupebit and *Dies irae,* small satb choir; *O Night, why should I be afraid ?* [*The*
　Sleepers] and *Away, away O soul* [*Passage to India*], Walt Whitman, SATBar soli;
　the Irish hymn, *Light excelling all light.* small & large satb choirs/SAT soli.

[soprano, mezzo-soprano & tenor]
Agnus Dei
[small choir]
Kyrie, Mors stupebit, Dies irae
[baritone]
O night, why should I be afraid to trust myself to you?
I too pass from night
I stay a while away O night
But I return to you again and love you:
I know not how I came of you
And I know not where I go with you
but I know I came well and shall go well
And rise betimes . . . into the night
[Walt Whitman: *The Sleepers*]
[both choirs]
Light excelling all light!
Joy without grief, youth without age
Peace without quarrel:
Light brighter than all light
City of light eternal.
Vast is the beauty of that City,
Music sweeter than all music,
Wond'rous its serenity
repeat: Light excelling all light!
[baritone]
Away, away O soul!
hoist instantly the anchor!
Cut the hawsers—haul out—shake out every sail
Have we not stood here like trees in the ground long enough?
Have we not grovel'd here long enough eating and drinking like mere brutes?
Have we not darken'd and dazed ourselves with books long enough?
Sail forth—steer for the deep waters only,
Sail forth, sail!
[both choirs]
Sail to the City of Light!
[baritone]
Reckless O soul, exploring, I with thee and thou with me,

For we are bound where mariner has not yet dared to go,
And we will risk the ship, ourselves and all.
[choir]
Light, brighter than all light!
[baritone]
O my brave soul!
O farther farther sail!
O daring joy
[choirs]
Joy!
[baritone]
But safe! Are they not all the seas of God?
[choirs] Joy!
[Walt Whitman: *Passage to India*]
[choirs & soprano, mezzo-soprano and tenor]
Agnus Dei

DISCOGRAPHY

Marco Polo, 8.223532-3, RTE Philharmonic Choir and the National Symphony Orchestra of Ireland, cond. Coleman Pearce.

LADISLAV VYCPÁLEK
February 23, 1882–January 9, 1969

Vycpálek earned a doctorate in Czech literature from Prague University in 1906. He was a member of a vocal society in his youth and played the violin in string quartets during his school and university years. He obtained a post as a librarian at Prague University Library. From 1908 to 1912, Vycpálek studied composition with Viteslav Novak (1870–1949), an important late-romantic Czech composer.

Vycpálek did not compose an enormous amount of music, but left forty-one works of distinction. The great bulk of his music is vocal-choral, although nothing liturgical. There are three important choral works with orchestral accompaniment: the *Cantata of the Last Things of Man*, Op. 16, for soprano & baritone soli with SATB choir (1920–22); *Blessed is This Man* for soprano & baritone soli and SATB choir (1933); and the *Ceské Requiem*, Op. 24, for soprano & baritone soli with SATB choir (1940).

His musical language is that of a nervous post-romanticism. Nonfunctional harmony is wrapped into contrapuntal, polyphonic textures for both orchestra and choir. During the turbulent passages of *Dies irae*, the harmony appears to be close to the border of atonality. The vocal solos are major pieces that possess expansive melodic lines, and are often supported by a large orchestral accompaniment. In this respect, one is reminded of the music of Richard Strauss or Gustav Mahler.

The general mood of the *Czech Requiem* is one of restlessness in the solo sections and turbulence in the choral passages. Vycpálek was careful and sensitive in the word settings, while faithfully illuminating and matching the textual meaning. A flexible sense of rhythm further enhances the music and text. The vocal soloists play a major role in the *Czech Requiem*, occupying almost all of the first movement, all of the third, and more than half of the last movement. The second movement is completely choral.

The SATB choral texture is almost always polyphonic, employing imitation in the passage, *For everything there is a season*, sections of the *Dies irae*, *Mors stupebit* (fugal), *A dead man came out* (fugue), and *Amen* (canonic).

The work is a humanist, nonliturgical requiem, employing numerous passages from the Bible, a Czech translation of the *Dies Irae* text and the text of a Czech hymn from the time of Jan Hus (1369–1415), *Jesus Christ, Thou Generous Knight* (*Jesu Kriste, štědrý kněže*).

The title of the work, incidentally, is derived from the use of the Latin *Dies irae* in Czech translation. This wonderfully restless composition possesses a passionate and moving spiritual atmosphere. It describes four stages on the road from death to life; from despair to belief. Its subtitle *Death and Redemption* (*Smrt a spasení*) is perhaps as fitting as *Requiem*.

Parts I and II are pessimistic in outlook; Part III offers hope whilst discussing the human condition; Part IV is centered around the story of the raising of Lazarus and the words of hope offered by Jesus.

Basic Data

EDITION

Barenreiter Editio/Supraphon
[rental only] [Czech text]

DURATION

Four movements, 1976 mm., perf., c. 97'

VOICING AND ORCHESTRATION

Choir: SATB [*divisi*] range: S-A6; B-F3
Soloists: SABAR
Orchestra: vn. I/II, vla., vc., db., pic., 2 fl., 2 ob., Eh., 2 cl., bcl., 2 bsn., cbsn., 4
    Fh., 3 tpt., 2 tbn. tuba, PERC: triangle, side drum, cymbals, timpani, bass drum,
    tambourine, tam-tam.

OUTLINE

First movement, Vanity of Vanities [*Marnost nad marnostmi*], 484 mm.
    Vanity of vanities . . . moderato non tanto pesante. ABar soli/satb choir. Text: Job

and Ecclesiastes. (pessimistic) Theme: the transitory nature of life and ultimate death that awaits all living beings.

Vanity of vanities; and all is vanity.

What does man gain . . . moderato. A. solo. Theme: the implications of life and death (a soliloquy).

What does man gain by all the toil at which he toils under the sun?
A generation goes and a generation comes, but the earth remains forever.
The sun rises and the sun goes down and hastens to the place where it rises.
All streams run to the sea, but the sea is not full;
to a place where the streams flow, there they flow again.
The wind blows to the south and goes round to the north; round and round goes
the wind.
All things are full of weariness; a man cannot utter it;
the eye is not satisfied with seeing, nor the ear filled with hearing.
What has been will be, and what has been done will be done
and there is nothing new under the sun.
There is no remembrance of former things nor will there be any remembrance
of later things yet to happen among those who come after.
Vanity of vanities and all is vanity.

For everything there is . . . allargando un pochino. satb choir. Text: Ecclesiastes,
Chapter three.

For everything there is a season and a time for every matter under heaven.
A time to plant and a time to harvest.
A time to seed and a time to lose, a time to keep and a time to cast away,
a time to rend and a time to sew.
A time to be silent and a time to speak, a time to weep and a time to laugh,
a time to dance and a time to mourn.
A time to cast away stones and a time to gather them together,
a time to embrace and a time to refrain from embracing,
a time to love, a time to hate.
A time for war and a time for peace, a time to kill and a time to heal,
a time to tear down and a time to build up.
A time to be born and a time to die—a time to die.

And I thought . . . moderato ma enfatico. Bar. solo. Text: Job. Theme: the futility of
life.
(soliloquy).

And I thought the dead who are already dead more fortunate that the living
who are still alive.
But better than both is he who has not yet been and has not seen the evil deeds
that are done under the sun.

For affliction does not come from the dust nor trouble sprout from the ground,
but man is born to trouble, man is born to affliction—
While he lives, his body is subjected to pain and his soul groans within him.
Naked he came and shall go again and he shall take nothing for his toil,
which he may carry away in his hand.
Again this is a grievous evil that the wise die, the fool and the stupid alike must
perish.
Why did you bring me forth from my mother's womb to the pain of the world ?
Would that I had died before any eye had seen me,
would that I had died and were as though I had not been, carried from the womb
to the grave.
If I look for Sheol as my house, if I spread my couch in darkness,
if I say to the pit "you are my father" and to the worm
"my mother" or "my sister" where then is my hope?

My face is red . . . moderato assai. satb choir. Theme: a summation of the human
condition.

My face is red with weeping and on my eyelids is deep darkness;
my eye pours out tears to God.
Has not man a hard lot on earth and are not his days like the days of a hireling?
Behold, thou hast made his days as a few handbreadths
and his lifetime is as nothing in thy sight.
And man is like a breath, even if his steps are secure.
He will come to his grave in ripe age as a shock of grain
comes up to the threshing floor in its season;
and he will carry nothing away, nor will his glory go down after him.
And when man renders his soul, where shall he be?
The eye of him who seeks him, behold him do more.
He weathers away like grass, he vanishes like a cloud, he flees like a shadow.
Vanity of vanity and all is vanity.

My strength is dried up. . . moderato molto quasi lento. A. solo. Theme: the value of
our transitory existence. (soliloquy).

My strength is dried up like a potsherd and my tongue cleaves to my jaws.
Thou dost lay me in the dust of death and thou hast fed me with the tread of bears
and given me tears to drink in full measure.
But I am a worm and no man, scorned by men and despised by the people.
Thou turnest man back to the dust and sayest,
"Turn back, turn back, O children of men!"
For a thousand years in thy sight are but yesterday
when it is past or as a watch in the night.
Even though a man should live a thousand years, twice told,
do not all go to the one place?
There they go, all men go whence they will not return, to the land of gloom

and deep darkness, the land of gloom and chaos where light is as darkness.
Vanity of vanity and all is vanity.

Second movement, The Day of Wrath [*Ten Den hnevu*] 522 mm.
   Dies irae. . . con moto decciso. satb choir. Text: the Sequence hymn, *Dies irae*, in
   Czech translation. *Dies irae-Rex tremendae,* stormy, agitiated; *Mors stupebit*
   (fugal); *Recordare*, music becomes quieter, and builds to a climax at *Oro supplex.*
   The remainder of the movement becomes quieter.
Third movement, A Light in the Darkness [*Svetlo v temnotách*] A Psalm Inter-
mezzo. 324 mm.
   Text: selected Psalm verses, including # 10, 38, 55, 63, 71, 77, 79, 91, 114, 121,
   130, and 142. Structure: an intermezzo of six vocal solos.

How long, O Lord . . . lento, molto serioso. Bar. solo.

How long, O Lord, how long? Wilt thou be angry forever
Will thy jealous wrath burn like fire? Why dost thou stand afar off, O Lord
Why dost thou hide thy face in times of trouble?
Be not far from me when death is near and I have no helper.
Do not forsake me, my strength, haste to help me.

I stretch out my hand . . . moderato, con desiderio. A. solo.

I stretch out my hands to thee, my soul thirsts for thee like a parched land.
For thy name's sake, O God, preserve my life.
In thy righteousness, O Lord, bring my soul out of trouble.
Out of the depths I cry to thee, O Lord! Lord, hear my voice.
Let thine ears be attentive to the voice of my supplications!
If thou, O Lord, should mark iniquities, Lord, who can stand?

If I lift my eyes . . . moderato, semplice. S. solo.

I lift my eyes to the hills. From whence comes my help?
My help comes from the Lord who made heaven and earth.
He will not let my foot be moved, he who keeps me will not slumber.
Behold, he who keeps us all will neither slumber nor sleep.
He will deliver my soul from death, he will deliver my eyes from tears,
my feet from stumbling.
He is my Father, he is my strong God, the rock of my salvation.
Righteousness and justice are the foundation of his throne,
steadfast love and faithfulness go before his face.

How long O Lord . . . poco piu mosso. Bar. solo

How long, O Lord, how long?
I cry aloud to God that he can hear me in the day of trouble,
that he can incline his ears to my prayers.

In the day of trouble, in the time of affliction, I seek the Lord
and in the night my hand is stretched out without wearying.
Will the Lord spurn me forever and never again be favorable?
Has God forgotten to be gracious? Has he—offended by me—shut off his
compassion?
O Lord, consider my members are like a shadow.

Attend to me . . . moderato con desiderio. A. solo

Attend to me, O Lord, attend to me.
Give me thy help and conceal me in the shadow of thy wings.
Satisfy us in the morning with thy steadfast love
and teach us to number our days,
that we may get a heart of wisdom
and that death may not take us in the midst of our days.
Bow thy heavens, O Lord, and come down.
O God, thou hast rejected us,
broken our defenses; Thou hast been angry; O restore us!
Hast thou made the sons of men only to destroy them?

Enter into thy tent . . . moderato, semplice e calmato. S. solo

Enter into thy tent in peace, my soul, thy benefactor is God alone.
The Lord will judge the peoples but he will bless the righteous those who love his
name.
O Lord almighty, Thou hast made the night and day;
Thou hast established the stars and the sun,
Thine are the heavens and the earth.
I know that the Lord has made me in his love.
The hands of the Lord have made me and fashioned me;
The Lord fashioned my body and my soul by his might.
He is my creator, he is my good Lord,
He is my Father, the rock of my salvation.
He who dwells in the shelter of the Most High,
will abide in the shadow of the Almighty for evermore.

Fourth Movement, He came to save [*Přišel, aby spasil*], 646 mm.
SABar soli/satb choir. Texts: Gospel of St. John, Chap. 11, passages from the Gospel of St. Matthew and the medieval Czech hymn, "Jesus Christe, thou generous knight" . . . (*Jesu Kriste, štědrý kněže*). Theme: The raising of Lazarus. Organization: An operatic tableau with soloists and choir. The baritone is assigned the words of Jesus, the contralto sings the words of Martha, the sister of Lazarus, the soprano soloist echoes the words of St. John's Gospel, 4:16–17 and the choir narrates the story. The initial pessimism of the first two movements is replaced by positive faith and a mood of exaltation.

[choir]
Now a certain man was ill, Lazarus of Bethany,
in the village of Mary and her sister, Martha.
And it was Mary who anointed the Lord with ointment
and wiped his feet with her hair.
So the sisters sent for him, saying "Lord, he whom you love is ill."
so he said to his disciples:
[baritone]
"Our friend Lazarus has fallen asleep, but I go to awaken him from sleep."
[choir]
The disciples said to him:
"Lord, if he has fallen asleep, he will recover."
Now Jesus had spoken of his death
but they thought that he meant taking rest in sleep.
Then Jesus said to them plainly;
[baritone]
"Lazarus of Bethany is dead; but let us go to him."
[choir]
And they went and Jesus went with them
and they found that Lazarus had already
been in the tomb for four days.
When Martha, his sister, heard that Jesus was coming, she went and met him.
and so spoke Martha and Jesus:
[alto]
"Lord if you had been here my brother would not have died."
[baritone]
"Your brother will rise again."
[alto]
"I know that he will rise again in the resurrection at the last day."
[baritone]
"I am the resurrection and the life. He who believes in me, though he die, yet
shall he live.
and whoever lives and believes in me shall never die. Do you believe this?"
[alto]
"Yes, Lord, I believe that you are the Christ, the Son of God, who is coming into
the world."
[choir]
When Jesus saw those who came with her weeping, he was deeply moved in spirit
and troubled, and he said:
[baritone]
"Where have you laid him?"
[choir]
They said to him, "Lord, come and see."
And Jesus wept. So they said:
"See, how he loved him."
Then Jesus deeply moved again, came to the tomb.

And he came there, he came to the tomb and it was a cave
and a stone lay upon it.
[baritone]
"Take the stone away."
[alto]
"Lord, he has been dead four days."
[baritone]
"But I told you that if you would believe, you would see the glory of God."
[choir]
So they took away the stone and Jesus lifted up his eyes and
cried with a loud voice:
[baritone]
"Lazarus, come out!"
[choir]
The dead man came out, his hands and feet bound with bandages,
and his face wrapped with a cloth.
(Czech hymn) Blessed are the poor, for theirs is the kingdom of heaven.
Thy largess, our good, by thy blessing. Alleluia. Amen.

DISCOGRAPHY

Supraphon, 11 1933–2, Czech Philharmonic Chorus and Orchestra, cond. Karel
Ancerl.

BENJAMIN BRITTEN
November 22, 1913–December 4, 1976

Benjamin Britten studied composition with Frank Bridge and John Ireland, both of whom were pupils of Charles Villiers Stanford. From 1945
to 1954, he wrote an astonishing series of English operas, including *Peter
Grimes* (1945), *The Rape of Lucretia* (1946), *Albert Herring* (1947), *Billy Budd*
(1951), *Gloriana* (1953), and *The Turn of the Screw* (1954).

Britten's friendship with the tenor, Peter Pears, was an important factor
in determining the kinds of works he wrote. From 1939 to 1965, he turned
out a series of vocal cycles for Pears. Among them are *Les Illuminations*
(1939), *Seven Sonnets of Michelangelo* (1940), *Serenade for Tenor* (1942), *The
Holy Sonnets of John Donne* (1945), *Canticles I & III* (1947–54), *Winter Words*
(poems by Thomas Hardy) (1953), *Nocturne* (1958), and *The Poet's Echo*
(Pushkin) (1965).

Britten produced a number of important orchestral works. Related to
this study is the *Sinfonia da Requiem* of 1940, dedicated to the memory of
his parents. It was Britten's first large-scale orchestral composition and it
was originally dedicated to the Emperor of Japan, who refused the work
at the beginning of World War II.

He was interested in church music and wrote numerous works in this style. Several of the better-known pieces are *A Ceremony of Carols* (1942), *Rejoice in the Lamb* (1943), *Missa Brevis* in D (1959), and *War Requiem* (1961). The *War Requiem*, Op. 66, one of the few requiem settings to bear this title, was composed in 1961 and first performed on May 30, 1962, at the rededication of the Cathedral of St. Michael, Coventry, which had been destroyed by the German Luftwaffe during World War II. It is scored for STB soli, boy's choir, SATB choir, large orchestra, and chamber orchestra.

Britten dedicated the work to four friends he had lost during the war and, in an act of reconciliation, chose for the first performance of the work, three singers; two from England (soprano, Heather Harper, tenor, Peter Pears), and one from Germany (baritone, Dietrich Fischer-Diskau). For the first recorded version, he kept two of the original performers, replacing Harper with Galina Vishnevskaya of Russia.

For this work, Britten used the traditional requiem text, interspersed with the *War Poems* of Wilfrid Owen; poems that were written out of Owen's own World War I experiences. Here, the author's personal plea for eternal peace between nations and peoples is joined to the prayers of the traditional requiem text. It is a setting in which the traditional Latin texts are glossed by the poetic observations of Owen. Although this requiem setting is not liturgical, it closely adheres to the words of the traditional canon.

Britten scored the work for three different ensembles; the first, a large orchestra with soprano soloist and mixed choir. This group sings the requiem text, representing humankind and its desire for peace. The second ensemble is a chamber orchestra with tenor and baritone soloists. These two singers, who sing the poetry of Owen, represent two individual soldiers from opposing sides in the war. Their texts underscore the horror and ugliness of war. A third ensemble employs organ and boy's choir. This group sings some of the requiem text and the scoring for boy's choir obliquely suggests that innocent children will be the raw material for those who wish to make future wars.

The *War Requiem* displays the multifaceted talents of the composer, be they his melodic flair and tonal harmonic language or his sense of drama and broad knowledge of English literature. The musical textures are always transparent, whether massive or delicate. The prevailing four-part, homophonic texture is frequently relieved by thinning or augmentation of the parts and the use of polyphonic style. *Quam olim Abrahae* is set as a fugue and the passages, *Pleni sunt coeli, Quid sum miser, In paradisum, Quando movendi sunt,* and *Let us sleep on* employ canonic writing. His study of baroque music reveals itself in the use of recitative-like melody throughout the work or the intertwining of soloists and chorus in a modern version of the *concertante* technique used by Purcell, Handel, and a score of sixteenth- and seventeenth-century composers.

The *Requiem* is unified by the use of the tritone, sometimes in melodic or harmonic form; at other times in choice of instrumental sound. The tritone appears in the first measures of the *Requiem aeternam* and is used extensively in the *Sanctus* and *Agnus Dei*. It reappears at the very conclusion of the work. This work is one of the great musical masterpieces of the twentieth-century repertory. A performance requires large choral and instrumental forces.

Basic Data

EDITIONS

1. Benjamin Britten
War Requiem, op. 66
Vocal Score by Imogen Holst
Boosey & Hawkes
London. Paris. New York. 1962.

2. Benjamin Britten
War Requiem
Minature Score
Boosey & Hawkes [c. 1962]

DURATION

Six movements, 1485 mm., perf., c. 85'

VOICING AND ORCHESTRATION

Choir: SATB choir; boy's choir, SA range: S-B flat 6; B-E3
Soloists: STBar
Orchestra: two ensembles: large orchestra and chamber orchestra
Large orchestra: vn. I/II, vla., vc., db., pic., 3 fl., 2 ob., Eh., 3 cl., bcl., 2 bsn., cbsn., 6 Fh., 4 tpt., 3 tbn., tuba, Piano, org. timp. PERC: (4 players) 2 side drums, tenor drum, bass drum, tambourine, triangle, cymbals, castanets, whip, Chinese blocks, gong, bells (C & F♯), vibraphone, glockenspiel, antique cymbals (C & F♯). Chamber Orchestra: 2 vn., vla., vc., db., harp, pic., fl., ob., Eh., cl., bsn., Fh., timp., side drum, bass drum, cymbal, gong.

OUTLINE

Introit: 176 mm.
Requiem aeternam, slow and solemn. satb choir (tritone-motif); *Te decet, allegro.* sa boy's choir/strings; *Requiem aeternam*, slow. satb choir (ABA); *What passing bells for these?, allegro molto ed agitato.* T solo/chamber orchestra [tritone-motif]. Text: *Anthem for Doomed Youth.*

What passing-bells for these who die as cattle?
Only the monstrous anger of the guns.
Only the stuttering rifles' rapid rattle
Can patter out their hasty orisons.
No mockeries for them from prayers or bells,

Nor any voice of mourning save the choirs—
The shrill demented choirs of wailing shells;
And bugles calling for them from sad shires.
What candles may be held to speed them all?
Not in the hands of boys but in their eyes
Shall shine the holy glimmers of good-byes.
The pallor of girls' brows shall be their pall;
Their flowers the tenderness of silent minds,
And each slow dusk a drawing-down of blinds.

Kyrie, very slow. bells/ssaattbb choir, unaccompanied.
(tritone-motif resolves into FM)

Sequence: 468 mm.
   Dies irae, allegro. satb choir (*Dies irae-Quantus tremor-Tuba mirum-Mors stupebit*);
   Bugles sang, tranquillo. Bar solo/chamber orchestra. (*Bugles sang* describes the
   horrors of trench warfare.)

Bugles sang, saddening the evening air,
And bugles answered, sorrowful to hear.
Voices of boys were by the river-side.
Sleep mothered them; and left the twilight sad.
The shadow of the morrow weighed on men.
Voices of old despondency resigned,
Bowed by the shadow of the morrow, slept.

Liber scriptus, slow and majestic. S solo/satb choir/large orchestra. *Liberscriptus-
Judex ergo-Quid sum miser.* satb semi-chorus. *Rex tremendae,* S solo/satb choir/
large orchestra. *Out There, allegro e giocoso.* TBar soli/chamber orchestra. Text:
   The Next War. Theme: two soldiers from opposing armies describe their
   companionship with death in a sneering, cynical duet.

Out there, we've walked quite friendly up to Death;
Sat down and eaten with him, cool and bland,
Pardoned his spilling mess-tins in our hand.
We've sniffed the green thick odour of his breath,
Our eyes wept, but our courage didn't writhe.
He's spat at us with bullets and he's coughed
Shrapnel. We chorussed when he sang aloft;
We whistled while he shaved us with his scythe.
Oh, Death was never an enemy of ours!
We laughed with him, we leagued with him, old chum.
No soldier's paid to kick against his powers.
We laughed, knowing that better men would come,
And greater wars; when each proud fighter brags
He wars on Death—for Life; not men—for flags.

Recordare, slow. ssaa choir/large orchestra. (*Recordare-Quaerens me-Ingemisco-Qui Mariam-Inter oves*). *Confutatis, allegro.* ttbb choir/orchestra. (*Confutatis-Oro supplex*) two contrasting melodic ideas. *Be slowly lifted up, molto largamente.* Bar solo/chamber orchestra. Text: *Sonnet on seeing a piece of our artillery brought into action.* Theme: human arrogance and the sin that grows out of it. (tritone motif).

Be slowly lifted up, thou long black arm,
Great gun towering toward Heaven, about to curse;
Reach at that arrogance which needs thy harm,
And beat it down before its sins grow worse;
But when thy spell be cast complete and whole,
May God curse thee, and cut thee from our soul.

Dies irae, allegro. satb choir/large orchestra. Repeat of opening material. *Lacrimosa, molto lento.* S solo/satb choir. (*Lacrimosa-Huic ergo*) *Move him into the sun*, recitative style. T solo/S solo/chamber orchestra. The poem, *Futility*, is interspersed with the previous *Lacrimosa* material.

Move him into the sun—
Gently its touch awoke him once,
At home, whispering of fields unsown.
Always it woke him, even in France,
Until this morning and this snow.
If anything might rouse him now
The kind old sun will know.
Think how it wakes the seeds,
Woke, once, the clays of a cold star.
Are limbs, so dear achieved, are sides,
full-nerved—still warm—too hard to stir?
Was it for this the clay grew tall?
O what made fatuous sunbeams toil
To break earth's sleep at all?

Pie Jesu, very slow. ssaattbb choir, unaccompanied/bells. (tritone motif) Coda.

Offertory: 276 mm.
Domine Jesu Christe, largamente. organ/boy's choir. (choral ostinato and chant-like melody); *Sed signifer* and *Quam olim Abrahae, animato.* satb choir/large orchestra. (This section resembles a choral version of the keyboard prelude and fugue.); *So Abram rose, deliberamente.* TBar soli/chamber orchestra. Text: *The Parable of the Old Man and the Young.* Theme: Owen's interpretation of the story of Abraham and Isaac. (canon). The end of the poem is joined to the *Hostias* verse (boy's choir).

So Abram rose, and clave the wood, and went,
And took the fire with him, and a knife.

And as they sojourned both of them together,
Isaac the first-born spake and said, My Father,
Behold the preparations, fire, and iron,
But where is the lamb for this burnt-offering?
Then Abram bound the youth with belts and straps,
And builded parapets and trenches there,
And stretched forth the knife to slay his son.
When lo! an angel called him out of heaven,
Saying, Lay not thy hand upon the lad,
Neither do anything to him. Behold,
A ram, caught in a thicket by its horns;
Offer the Ram of Pride instead of him.
But the old man would not so, but slew his son,
And half the seed of Europe, one by one.

Quam olim Abrahae, satb choir (theme and dynamics are inverted form).

Sanctus: 195 mm.

Sanctus, liberamente. S solo/percussion [vibraphone, antique cymbals, bells and glockenspiel] Recitative; *Pleni sunt coeli, lento*. ssaattbb choir/large orchestra. Choral recitative; *Hosanna, brilliante*. satb choir [*divisi*]/large orchestra; *Benedictus, molto tranquillo*. S solo/satb choir; *Hosanna, brilliante*. satb choir/large orchestra; *The End, molto lento*. Bar solo/chamber orchestra. Text: *The End*. Theme: despair.

After the blast of lightning from the East,
The flourish of loud clouds, the Chariot Throne;
After the drums of Time have rolled and ceased,
And by the bronze west long retreat is blown,

Shall life renew these bodies? Of a truth
All death will He annul, all tears assuage?
Fill the void veins of Life again with youth,
And wash, with an immortal water, Age?

When I do ask white Age he saith not so:
"My head hangs weighed with snow."
And when I hearken to the Earth, she saith:
"My fiery heart shrinks, aching. It is death.
Mine ancient scars shall not be glorified,
Nor my titanic tears, the sea, be dried."

Agnus Dei: 53 mm.

Agnus Dei/One ever hangs, lento. T solo/satb choir/large orchestra/chamber orchestra. The two texts are intertwined. The tenor sings the text of Owen's *At Calvary near the Ancre*.

One ever hangs where shelled roads part.
In this war He too lost a limb,
But His disciples hide apart:
And now the Soldiers bear with Him.
Near Golgatha strolls many a priest,
And in their faces there is pride
That they were flesh-marked by the Beast
By whom the gentle Christ's denied.
The scribes on all the people shove
And bawl allegiance to the state,
But they who love the greater love
Lay down their life; they do not hate.

Libera me: 317 mm.

Libera me, marcia. satb choir/large orchestra. (an orchestral dirge-choral lamentation); *Tremens factus, piu allegro.* S solo/unison satb choir/large orchestra; *Libera me, molto allegro.* S solo/satb choir/large orchestra; *Dies illa, allegro.* S solo/satb choir; *Libera me, molto largamente.* satb choir/brass/organ; *It seemed that out of battle, lento e tranquillo.* T solo/chamber orchestra.

(accompanied recitative) Text: *Strange meeting; None said the other*, Bar solo/chamber orchestra. (recitative); *Let us sleep now*, brief duet for tenor and baritone. Each man represents a dead soldier from each of the opposing armies. This text is the emotional summit of Owen's poetry.

Tenor
It seemed that out of battle I escaped
Down some profound dull tunnel, long since scooped
Through granites which titanic wars had groined.
Yet also there encumbered sleepers groaned,
Too fast in thought or death to be bestirred.
Then, as I probed them, one sprang up, and stared
With piteous recognition in fixed eyes,
Lifting distressful hands as if to bless.
And no guns thumped, or down the flues made moan.
"Strange friend," I said, "here is no cause to mourn."
Baritone
"None," said the other "save the undone years,
The hopelessness. Whatever hope is yours,
Was my life also; I went hunting wild
After the wildest beauty in the world.
For by my glee might many men have laughed
And of my weeping something had been left
Which must die now. I mean the truth untold,
The pity of war, the pity war distilled.
Now men will go content with what we spoiled.
Or, discontent, boil bloody, and be spilled.
They will be swift with swiftness of the tigress,

None will break ranks, though nations trek from progress.
Miss we the march of this retreating world
Into vain citadels that are not walled.
Then, when much blood had clogged their chariot-wheels
I would go up and wash them from sweet wells,
Even from the wells we sunk too deep for war,
Even the sweetest wells that ever were.
I am the enemy you killed, my friend.
I knew you in this dark; for you so frowned
Yesterday through me as you jabbed and killed.
I parried; but my hands were loathe and cold."
tenor & baritone
"Let us sleep now."

Segue into: In Paradisum, molto tranquillo. STBar soli/boy's choir/satb choir/
organ/chamber orchestra/large orchestra. (*"Let us sleep now,"* TBar duet; *In
Paradisum,* boys choir/satb choir/S solo) All themes are intertwined;
Requieascant in Pace, Amen. satb choir [*divisi*]/bells. (tritone motif)
Ends in F major.

DISCOGRAPHY

1. Telarc, CD-80157, Atlanta Symphony Orchestra and Chorus, cond. Robert Shaw.
2. Multiple listings in the Schwann Catalogue.

FREDERIC DELIUS
January 29, 1862–June 10, 1935

Delius was one of England's great late romantic composers, along with Holst, Elgar, Stanford, and Vaughan-Williams. He was laid to rest in Poet's Corner of Westminster Abbey. Although he was born in England, he moved to Florida in his youth, where he worked in orange groves. From there, he returned to Leipzig, where he received his musical education. He finally settled in the tiny French village of Grez-sur-Loing, remaining there until his death. He produced more than two-dozen tone poems; six stage works; concertos for the piano, violin, and cello; a significant amount of chamber music; and about a dozen works for choir and orchestra. The most famous choral works are *A Mass of Life* (texts by Friedrich Nietzsche) and the *Requiem*.

His musical language is a mixture of chromatic late romanticism and impressionism. The third movement is particularly influenced by the latter style, where medieval quartal and quintal harmonies pepper the first movement. Chromatic harmonies, fluid rhythm (there are eighteen tempo changes in first movement), and fussy dynamics are also important aspects of his style. His orchestral sounds are very rich, sensuous, and poetic. They range from massive, powerful sonorities to the most delicate and intricate, web-like textures. String tremolos are used to create luminous effects (first movement), a clarinet depicts a cuckoo-call (movement six) and six-part *divisi* strings, bells, harp, and celeste make a shimmering, magical benediction for the *Requiem*. The choral texture, be it satb, satb-satb, or saa-ttb scoring is homophonic and chordal. The two vocal soloists are assigned major, virtuoso roles within the work.

Scored for double SATB choirs, soprano and baritone soloists, and orchestra, the *Requiem* is a superior work. It has been neglected for a long time, mainly because of its controversial text; a text written by Heinrich Simon, a friend of the composer. The text is not religious, in fact, Delius referred to this piece as his "Pagan Requiem." Although it was written between 1913 and 1916, its premiere did not take place until 1922.

Early audiences, who had lost family members in the First World War, were probably shocked by the text and its lack of connection to any religious belief, ideology, or institution. The text is a paraphrase of various works by Friedrich Nietzsche and passages from Ecclesiastes. Delius explained the *Requiem* by saying, "This is not a religious work. Its underlying belief is that of a pantheism." It is a work that is decidedly anti-war, and to a great extent, opposed to the principles of institutional religion. Its anti-war stance is similar to the position found in the poems of Wilfrid Owen, used by Benjamin Britten in his *War Requiem*. More in public fashion would have been the sentiments expressed in the *World Requiem* of John Foulds. Delius dedicated his Requiem "To the memory of all young Artists fallen in the War."

Although the work is divided into five movements, one flows into the next, without break. This romantic-impressionistic work contains much beautiful music that deserves to be better-known.

Basic Data

Frederick Delius
Requiem
Full Score
B. & H. 19386 [English & German texts]
Boosey & Hawkes, Ltd. 1952

DURATION
Five movements, 481 mm., perf., c. 31'

VOICING AND ORCHESTRATION
Choir: double SATB choir range: S-B6; B-E flat 3
Soloists: soprano, baritone

Orchestra: vn. I/II, vla., vc., db., pic., 3 fl., 2 ob., Eh., bass ob., 3 cl., bcl., 3 bsn., cbsn., 6 Fh., 3 tpt., 3 tbn., tuba, timp., celesta, harp. PERC: bass drum, cymbals, small drum, triangle, bells.

OUTLINE

Movement I, *Our days here are as one day*: 143 mm.
Our days here [*solemnly*] double satb choir/Bar solo/orchestra. Text: a non-Christian, naturalistic (Darwinian) view of our mortality.

[choir]
Our days here are as one day, for all our days are rounded in
a sleep they die and ne'er come back again.
[baritone]
Why then dissemble we with a tale of falsehoods?
We are e'en as a day that's young at morning and old at
eventide, departs and nevermore returns.
[choir]
We are e'en as a day that's young at morning and old at
eventide, and comes again no more.
[baritone]
At this regard the weaklings waxed sore afraid, and drugged
themselves with dreams and golden visions, and built
themselves a house of lies to live in.
[choir]
They drugged themselves with dreams and golden visions.
[baritone]
Then arose a storm with mighty winds and laid it low.
[choir]
And laid it low.
[baritone]
And out of the storm the voice of truth resounded in
trumpet tones: "Man thou art mortal and needs must thou die."
[choir]
"Man, thou art mortal and needs thou must die."
Our days here are as one day, for all our days are rounded in
a sleep, they die and ne'er come back again.

Movement II, *Hallelujah*: 84 mm.
Halleluja-La, il Allah [*with vigor and fervor*] two satb choirs or ssa-ttb choirs/Bar solo/orchestra. Text: women (Christian *Hallelujah*), men (Islamic, *La, il Allah*) The lengthy baritone solo is a condemnation of holy war and a reference to the underlying religious strife in the Balkans that led to World War I.

[The crowd—female choir & male choir]
Hallelujah . . . (ladies)
La il Allah . . . (men)

[baritone]
And the highways of earth are full of cries, the ways of the
earth bring forth gods and idols.
Who so awhile regards them turns from them, and keeps
apart from all men, for fame and its glories seem but idle nothings.
For all who are living know that Death is coming, but at the
touch of Death we lose knowledge of all things, nor can they
have any part in the ways and doings of men on the earth
where they were.
[choir I]
For all who are living . . .
[choir II]
Ah!
[baritone]
Therefore eat thy bread in gladness and lift up thy heart,
and rejoice in thy wine.
And take to thyself some woman whom thou lovest,
and enjoy life.
What task so e'er be thine, work with a will, for none of
these things shalt thou know, when thou comest to
thy journey's end.
[choir I]
For all who are living . . .

Movement III, *My beloved whom I cherish*: 62 mm.
  My beloved [*moderato*] Bar solo/satb choir/orchestra. Text: Ecclesiastes.

[baritone]
My beloved whom I cherished was like a flower.
Like a flower whose fair buds were folded lightly, and she
Open'd her heart at the call of Love.
Among her fragrant blossoms Love had his dwelling and to
all who longed her love she gave.
[choir]
Among her fragrant blossoms Love had his dwelling.
[baritone]
I praise her above all other women who are poor in their
being and so are poor in giving too.
Were not the world the abode of dissemblers and were not
Men's hearts so impure, then all the world would join me
in praising my beloved.
She gave to many and yet was chaste and pure as a flower.
My beloved whom I cherished was like a flower.

Movement IV, *I honour the man who can love life*: 70 mm.
  I honor [*with energy*] S solo/satb choir/reduced orchestra. Text: a pantheistic
version of Adam and Eve.

[soprano]
I honour the man who can love life, yet without
base fear can die.
He has attained the heights and won the crown of life.
[choir]
The crown!
[soprano]
I honor the man who dies alone and makes no lamentation.
His soul has ascended to the mountain-top, that is like a
throne which towers above the great plains, that roll far
away into the distance.
The sun goes down and the evening spreads its hands in
blessing o'er the world.
Bestowing peace.
And so creeps on the night that whelms and quenches all,
the night that binds our eyes with cloths of darkness,
binds them in a long and dreamless sleep,
thou that art death's twin brother.
[choir]
[Long dreamless sleep.]
[soprano]
And the passing spirit sings but this only: "Farewell, I loved ye all!"
And the voices of nature answer him:
[choir]
"Thou art our brother!"
[soprano]
And so the star of his life sinks down in the darkness
whence it had risen.

Movement V, *The snow lingers yet*: 122 mm.
   The snow [*very slow*] SBar soli/satb choir/orchestra. Theme: a song of ever-
returning spring and the rebirth of life.

[baritone]
The snow lingers yet on in the mountains, but yonder in the valleys
the buds are breaking on the trees and hedges.
[soprano]
Golden the willow branches and red the almond blossoms.
The little full-throated birds have already begun
their singing. But hearken, they cannot cease, for every joy,
from singing a song whose name is Springtime.
[choir]
Springtime!
[baritone]
The woods and forests are full of coolness and silence, and
Silv'ry brooklets prattle round their borders.
[choir]

The woods and forests are full of silence.
[baritone]
The golden corn awaits the hand of the reaper, for ripeness bids, death come.
[choir]
Ripeness bids death come.
[baritone]
Eternal renewing, everything on earth will return again.
[choir]
Eternal renewing . . .
[soprano, baritone, choir]
Springtime, Summer, Autumn, and Winter, and then comes
Springtime. Springtime!
[translated from the German by Philip Heseltine]

DISCOGRAPHY

Chandos CHAN 9515 Bournemouth Symphony Orchestra and Chorus, cond. Richard Hickox.

JOHN FOULDS
November 2, 1880–April 24, 1939

John Foulds, an English composer and conductor, began his career in the Hallé Orchestra. In 1918, he became Director of the London Central YMCA. In 1921, Foulds was named conductor of the University of London Musical Society. Although his name is not well-known today, he left a large opus of orchestral music, some of which has been recorded. In addition to the orchestral works, he wrote chamber music, music for solo piano, and incidental music for a number of plays.

His contribution to the world of requiem music is represented by one very large work: *A World Requiem*, Opus 60. Composed in 1920 (completed August 2), it is scored for SATBAR soli, SATB choir [*divisi*], small boy's (or youth) choir, orchestra, and organ. Like Berlioz, nearly a century earlier, and Gagneux, sixty years later, Foulds specified the exact number of performers required for a performance of this colossal, massive work. The work was premiered on Armistice Day, November 11, 1923. In subsequent years, it was performed annually in London, but seems not to have been performed elsewhere. It appears to have met a need of the English public, namely as a way to remember their soldiers killed during the First World War. Critics called the work too sentimental and banal; after a dozen years, the work faded from public view.

A World Requiem is not a liturgical work; rather an enormous civic oratorio, divided exactly into two halves; each half consisting of ten movements. Present are recitatives, solos, orchestral pieces, and choruses. Although many of the choral passages are scored for SATB choir, there are a number of polychoral settings (*Praise and exalt Him, Lux veritas, Requiem, Hymn of the Redeemed*, and *Blessed Be the King*).

Imitative choral style plays a very small role in *World Requiem* (*A light perpetual* and *But Thou shalt call*), while homophonic choral settings are more commonly used. Fould's late-romantic harmonic vocabulary uses key signatures, but often the music is in other tonal areas than the one indicated because the language is highly chromatic.

Five movements, *Pronuntiatio, Jubilatio, Requiem, Elysium*, and *Laudamus* are built upon ostinato techniques. All movements, except the last ones of Part One and Part Two, are joined together by common tone or common chord.

The text bears only a superficial resemblance to that of the requiem as its first movement contains the words, *Requiem aeternam, Lord grant them rest eternal*. The bulk of the text is drawn from selected passages of the Bible (King James Version) and paraphrases of various commonly used Biblical verses. Some original material, probably by Foulds, dominates the *Audite, Elysium*, and *Consummatus* movements. All textual sources are thoroughly intertwined. The composer wanted the work performed in a cathedral or any other consecrated building, especially on days of national remembrance.

Basic Data

EDITION

A World Requiem, Opus 60
for soprano, contralto, tenor and baritone soli, small chorus of boys and youths, full chorus, orchestra and organ.
W. Paxton & Co. Ltd., London (#15180) [1923]

DURATION

Part One, ten movements; Part Two, ten movements, 1965 mm.

VOICING AND ORCHESTRATION

Choir: SA (at least 100 of each), TB (at least 80 of each) range: S-B flat 6; B-D3
Soloists: SATBar
Chorus of 8 boys & 8 youths (women can substitute for boys, tenors: the youths)
In part I, the boys and youths, together with the harps, celeste, and 4 solo vn., are to be placed in a gallery distant from the main orchestral/vocal forces. In part II, they join the main choral ensemble.
Orchestra: vn. I/II [14 each], 14 vla., 12 vc., 8 db., 3 fl., 2 pic., 2 ob., 1 Eh., 2 cl., bcl.,

2 bsn., cbsn., 4 Fh., 3 tpt., 4 tbn., tuba, 3 timp., bass drum, cymbals, triangle, gong, tubular bells, large bell in A, sistrum, celeste, 2 harps, and pipe organ.

OUTLINE

Part One

Requiem aeternam: 117 mm.

Requiem aeternam [half-note = 44] ssaattbb choir/Bar solo. (BM) Theme: a prayer for all who fought and perished in World War I. It ends with a quotation from Psalm 23.

[choir]
Requiem aeternam. Lord grant them rest eternal. Amen [Requiem text]
[baritone]
(These three dedicatory lines were probably penned by Foulds.)
All those who have fallen in battle—
All those who have perished by pestilence and famine—
Men of all countries who died for their cause—
Yea, though I walk through the valley of the shadow of death,
I will fear no evil; for thou art with me. [Ps. 23]

Pronuntiatio: 141 mm.

The heathen raged [quarter-note = 160] satb choir/Bar solo. [bm-BM] (*Be still*, baritone; is taken from Psalm 46: 10; *But thou shalt call*, ssaattbb choir. (fugal). Theme: a poetic equivalent of the *Dies irae*.

[choir]

The heathen raged; the kingdoms were moved:
He uttered His voice—the earth melted.
He maketh wars to cease unto the ends of the
earth; [Ps. 45:10] He breaketh the bow and cutteth
spear in sunder; He burneth the chariot with fire.
God is our refuge and strength [Ps. 46:1]
[baritone]
He saith: *Be still and know that I am God*. [Ps. 46:10]
[choir]
The earth mourneth; the world languisheth: but the Lord
will destroy the face of the covering cast over all people
and the veil that is spread over all nations.
He will swallow up death in victory. [I Corinthians 15:55]
[baritone]
He saith: *Be still . . .*
[choir]
He has scattered the nations that delight in war. Nation shall not lift up
sword against nation, neither shall they learn war any more. Violence
shall no more
be heard in thy land: wasting nor destruction within thy borders.

[Isaiah 2:4; 60:18]
But thou shalt call thy walls Salvation, and thy gate, Praise.
[baritone]
He saith: *Be still. . .*

Confessio: 93 mm.
Lo, this is God, solemn [quarter-note = 63] Bar solo. [BM-EM]

Lo! This is God. This is the Lord God. Omnipotent, immutable,
omniscient, eternal, Alpha and Omega, creator, almighty!
He is knowledge and wisdom and power: He is justice
and truth; He is faithfulness and mercy. [paraphrase. Revelation 1:8]
God is Light! [I John 1:5]
He is gracious and gentle: the Comforter: He is vision and magic and beauty.
[para. Ps. 112 & Prayer of Azariah 1:68]
God is Love. [I John 4:16]
We have waited for Him. [para. Isa. 25:9]
We have come out of great tribulation, [Rev. 7:14]
and have endured grievous distress. (Many have been led away
captive): many have fallen. For these things, I weep. [para. Ps. 137]
Yet (the Lord delivered us); yea, (the Lord delivered us).
[para. of 2 Samuel 19:9]
He will wipe away tears from all faces. [James 4:9; Rev. 21:4]
We will be glad and rejoice in His salvation. [Isa. 25:3]

Jubilatio: 75 mm.
Praise Him/Blessed art Thou [quarter-note = 100, *allegro*] satb choir I/boy's and
youth choir. [EM] Theme: praise and exaltation. Most of the text is a paraphrase
of the Prayer of Azariah, 1:29–63 (Apocrypha).

[boy's & youth choirs]
Blessed art Thou, O Lord the God of our Fathers.
Blessed is the Holy name of Thy glory.
Blessed art Thou on the throne of thy kingdom, and
exceedingly to be praised, and exceedingly glorious forever.
Thou that beholdest the depths.
Thou that sittest upon the Cherubim. Blessed forever.
[first choir]
Praise Him.
Blessed art Thou in the firmament of heaven.
Blessed the holy name of Thy glory.
Blessed art Thou on the throne of thy kingdom,
and exceedingly glorious forever.
Thou that sittest . . .
[boy's & youth choirs]
Praise Him.

Praise and exalt Him above all forever.
[first choir & boy's & youth choirs]
O ye stars of heaven. O ye spirits. O all ye powers.
O ye angels. O ye sun and moon. Every shower and dew.
Fire and heat. Ice and cold. Light and darkness. Nights and days.
[second choir]
Praise and exalt Him above all forever.
[all choirs]
O ye mountains. O ye rivers. O ye fountains.
O ye priests. O ye servants of the Lord.
Praise Him. Praise Him and exalt Him forever.
(Now proclaim ye His word.) (Cry aloud unto all.) [Jer. 7:2 and Ps. 55:17]
The God of glory thundereth: hear ye His words [para. Ps. 29:3]
and obey. (Make proclamation) unto all His peoples. [2 Chronicles 30:5]
Hear ye His words and do them. [Leviticus 19:37]

Audite: 132 mm.
A theatrical piece scored for baritone solo and orchestra, divided into several sections by brass and timpani fanfares. Each solo section begins with a stentorian call to the nations of the North, South, West, East as well as all four corners of the globe. A lyric melody, accompanied by the strings, represents a plea for peace. (Separate brass and timpani ensembles are placed in the four sides of the performance hall. Theme: call for peace. John Foulds is the probable author of the "fanfare" texts.

[Baritone]
Give ear, all ye nations of the world. Give ear, all ye peoples of the earth.
[fanfare to the North]
Ye people of the North—
You Greenlander, Kamschatkan,
Laplander, you Norwegian, Russian, Icelander—
Let the peace of God rest in your hearts.

[fanfare to the South]
Ye people of the South:—
You Australian, New Zealander, Tasmanian,
you African, Roman, Abyssinian, Greek,
Have peace with one another. Follow peace with all men.

[fanfare to the West]
Ye people of the West:—
You Canadian, Californian, Brazilian,
you Missourian, Texan, Kentuckian, Mexican,
Be of one mind; live in peace, and the God of love
and peace shall be with you.

[fanfare to the East]
Ye people of the East:—

You Hindu, Buddhist, Parsi, Mohammedan,
you Chinaman, Tartar, Armenian, Japanese,
Live peaceably with all men. Keep the unity
of the Spirit in the bond of peace.

[fanfare to the four quarters of the globe]
You men of all continents:—
Be at peace among yourselves. Follow peace with all men;
[I Thessalonians 5:13-14]
for the (Prince of Peace) cometh, and [para. Isaiah 9:6]
He will speak peace to His people. [Ps. 85:8]
He will give the light to them that sit in
darkness and in the shadow of death: He will guide
our feet into the way of peace. [Luke 1:79]

Pax: 238 mm.
Peace I leave with you [quarter-note = 72] unison boy's choir/two harps/four solo violins/celeste/sistrum [C flat M] (placed in an area, distant from the orchestra and choir). Theme: peace.

Peace I leave with you. My peace I give unto you.
Let not your heart be troubled. [St. John 14:27]
Love one another as I have loved you. [St. John 13:34]
And the peace of God which passeth all understanding
shall keep your hearts and minds through Christ Jesus. [Philippians 4:7]

Consolatio: 59 mm.
The Lord is nigh [eighth-note = 84] alto solo/orchestra. [E flat M] A major solo, in 12/8 meter, divided into three smaller passages: two lyrical, outer sections with a middle passage in recitative style.

[alto]
The Lord is nigh unto them that are of a broken heart, [Ps. 34:18]
and none of them that trust in the Lord shall be desolate. [Ps. 34:22]
Blessed are the dead which die in the Lord, for they
shall rest from their labors. [Rev. 14:13]
The Lord gave: the Lord taketh away. Blessed be the name of the Lord. [Job 1:21]
Weeping may endure for a night, but joy cometh in the morning. [Ps. 30:5]
Weep ye not for the dead, neither bemoan him. [Jeremiah 22:10]
Sorrow not concerning them which are asleep; [para. I Thess. 4:13]
for the hour is coming, and now is, when the dead shall hear the voice of the
Son of God, and they that hear shall live. [St. John 5:25]
He saith: I will not leave you comfortless: I will come to you. [St. John 14:18]
Lo I am with you always; even unto the end of the world. [Matt. 28:20]
Yea (the Lord is nigh unto them). O why mourn ye? [para. Ps. 34:18]
(Weep ye not for the dead); sorrow not concerning them.
Weep not. Sorrow not. Lo! [para. Jer. 22:10]

He is with them always, even unto the end of the world. [para. Matthew 28:20]

Refutatio: 12 mm.
   O death [arioso] Bar solo/brass/strings.

O Death! Where is thy sting? O Grave!
Where is thy victory? [I Cor. 15:55]
Awake thou that sleepest; and arise from the dead.
And Christ shall give thee light. [Ephesians 5:14]

Lux Veritas: 29 mm.
I am the light [eighth-note = 100] three-part boy's choir/satb choir. [BM] (*cori spez-zati* technique: harps-celeste-four solo violins accompany the boy's choir; pizzi-cato strings-horns-timpani, the satb choir.

[boy's choir]
I am the Light of the world: [St. John 8:12]
the Light that lighteth every man that cometh into the world: [St. John 1:9]
the Resurrection and the Life. He that believeth in Me, though he were dead,
yet shall he live. [St. John 11:25]
[mixed choir]
Lux veritatis, Light. [Requiem mass]

Requiem: 38 mm.
Thy Light perpetual. ABar soli/boy's choir/satb choir.[BM]

[mixed choir]
Thy light perpetual shine down upon them. *Lux veritatis*.
Lord grant them rest eternal. Amen. [Requiem mass]
[boy's choir]
I am the Light of the world. [St. John 8:12]
I will come to you. Amen [St. John 14:18]
[contralto & baritone]
Blessed are the dead which die in the Lord, for Christ shall give them light.
Though they were dead yet shall they live and rest from their labors. Amen.
[Rev. 14:13]

Part Two

Laudamus: 254 mm.
Orchestral introduction [half note = 152] (includes a "synthetic" chorale-style
   melody); *Compass me about* [DM-B flat M] S solo/satb choir (synthetic melody).
   The text is a loose paraphrase of several biblical Psalms.
[soprano]

Compass me about with songs of deliverance: [Ps. 32:7]
Praise the Lord with a loud noise. Blow upon the trumpet. [Ps. 150:3]

Let the sea make a noise. [Ps. 96:11]
Let the floods clap their hands. [Ps. 98:8]
O let the hills be joyful. [Ps. 96:11]
Praise the Lord with harp and shawm: with tabret and lute. [Ps. 150:4]
[choir]
Alleluia. The Lord God reigneth. Let us be glad and rejoice. [Rev. 19:6–7]
He healeth the broken heart: [Ps. 147:3]
He hath delivered our souls from death and our feet from falling.
[para. PrAzar 1:66]
Great is the Lord our God alike in earth and heaven. [para. Ps. 147:5]
[soprano]
It is like the voice of a great multitude: it is like the sound
of many waters and, as it were, a great thunder. [Rev. 19:6]
Praise Him upon the strings and pipes. Praise Him upon
the loud cymbals. [Ps. 150:4–5]
Sing a new song before the Throne. [Ps. 144:9]
Shout unto God. [Ps. 47:1]
[choir]
Praise ye Him, all ye angels. Praise ye Him, all His hosts. [Ps. 148:2]
(Shout unto God with a voice of triumph), for (He is King of Kings).
Sing (unto God with a voice of triumph), for (He is King of Kings).
[para. Ps. 47:1, Rev. 17:14]

Elysium: 168 mm. [Sanctus]
Holy, Holy, Holy [EM] ssaa choir/ST soli; The women's choir provides an ostinato
motive on the word *holy* during the duet for soprano and tenor. The text is probably a Foulds original.)

[women's choir]
Holy. Holy. Holy. [Isa. 6:3] Elysium.
[tenor]
There is a land where no sorrow nor doubt have rule,
where the terror of death is no more.
[women's choir]
Holy. Holy. Holy.
[soprano & tenor]
There the woods are abloom, and fragrant scent is borne
on the wind. All the gardens and groves are abounding in
blossom. Sorrow is no more. The terror of death is no more.
The sea of blue spreads in the sky: the air breaks forth into
ripples of joy: a million suns are ablaze with light.
[women's choir]
Holy. Holy. Holy. Elysium.
[soprano & tenor]
The fever of life is stilled: all stains are washed away.

[women's choir]
Holy. Holy. Holy. Elysium.
[soprano & tenor]
It is the land of Beulah beyond the Delectable Mountains:
the abode of the blessed—Elysium.
[women's choir]
Holy. Holy. Holy. Holy.

In Pace: 148 mm.
I heard the voice, not slow. T solo; *These are they,* S solo; *The Father hath redeemed*
[Hymn of the redeemed] TS soli/two-part youth choir/two-part boy's choir/ttbb
choir. [C major signature] The tenor and soprano solos are paraphrases built upon
snippets from the Book of Revelation.

[tenor]
I hear the voice of the dead speaking from (before the Throne of God.)
[Rev. 7:15–17]
Their ears are deaf to sounds of earthly sorrow: (from their eyes
the tears are wiped away). They look upon the Throne of God. [Rev. 7:17]
They have stepped into the (sea of glass like unto crystal),
and behold the radiance of a million wings.
They hear the eternal music of a million suns. [para. Rev. 4:6]
Absent from the body, they are present with the Lord; [2 Cor. 5:8]
(for underneath are the Everlasting Arms). [Deuteronomy 33:27]
[soprano]
These are they which came out of great tribulation. They have washed
their robes and made them white in the Blood of the Lamb.
Therefore are they before the Throne of God, and serve Him
day and night in the Temple. [Rev. 7:14–15]
[boy's, youth & men's choir]
The Father hath redeemed us. (He hath delivered us from the power of
darkness and hath translated us into the kingdom of His dear Son).
Jesus our Savior hath ransomed us: we take our rest. [para. Colossians 1:13]
(Be not afraid): (fear not). He giveth His beloved rest; and (underneath
are the Everlasting Arms). [para. St. John 6:20, Luke 1:13, Deut. 33:27]

Angeli: 81 mm.
Behold, under the firmament, not slow. T solo/ssaattbb choir [CM-GM] (The choir
accompanies with vowel sounds and humming.); *They are the angels,* S solo; *And
He giveth,* three-part boy's and youth choir.

[tenor]
Behold. Under the firmament are the Cherubim and the Seraphim.
And the noise of their wings is as the noise of great waters. [Ezekiel 1:22, 24]
And I hear the voice of angels round about the Throne.
And the number of them is ten thousand times ten thousand.
And thousands of thousands. [Rev. 5:11]

[soprano]
They are the angels of the Lord: [PrAzar 1:37] His elect angels: [Timothy 5:21]
stewards of the Mysteries of God: [I Cor. 4:1]
His angels that do His commandments. [Ps. 103:20]
[boy's choir]
And He giveth His angels charge over thee, to keep thee in all thy ways.
[Matt. 4:6]

Vox Dei: 65 mm.
And behold, T solo; *This is the appearance*, S solo; *And behold*, T solo; *This my beloved*,
T solo/satb choir. [CM signature, but BM is actual key] The textual material is a
loose reworking of Ezekiel 1.

[tenor]
And behold! Above the firmament is the likeness of a throne. [Ezek. 1:26]
A brightness as the color of amber and as the appearance of
a rainbow of fire. And a cloud of glory shineth round about within it.
[para. Ezek 1:28]
[soprano]
This is the appearance of the likeness of the glory of the Lord, [Ezek. 1:28]
before Whom the Seraphim ever veil their faces.
[tenor]
And behold! Out of the fiery cloud a voice, saying:
[choir and tenor]
This is my beloved Son, in Whom I am well-pleased.
Hear ye Him [Matt. 17:3]
Hear, O heavens! And give ear, O Earth!
For the Lord hath spoken. [Isa. 1:2]

Adventus: 103 mm.
And behold [chromatic, ends in D flat M], *not slow*. T solo/satb choir/A solo.
(March)

[tenor]
And behold! Hereafter ye shall see heaven open, and the angels of God
ascending and descending upon the Son of Man. [St. John 1:51]
And there shall be signs in the sun and in the moon and in the stars,
and upon earth distress of nations with perplexity and great tribulation,
and the sea and the waves roaring. And the powers of heaven shall be shaken.
[Luke 21:25–26]
[choir]
Then shalt thou see the Son of Man coming in the clouds of the heavens with
power and great glory, and all the holy angels with Him: His holy angels
that excel in strength, that do his commandments. [para. Matt. 24:30]
[alto]
Every eye shall see Him. Yea, thine eyes shall see the King in His beauty.
[Isa. 33:17]

Be ye patient, for the coming of the Lord draweth nigh. [James 5:8]

Vigilate: 25 mm.
Watch ye [BM] *rather free*. Bar solo/French horns/winds/strings. (recitative/arioso style)

[baritone]
Watch ye therefore, lest coming suddenly He find you sleeping.
Watch! [Mark 13:35–36]
For the Son of Man cometh at an hour when ye think not.
Be ye therefore ready: be ye patient. [Matt. 24:44]
Watch!
For blessed are those servants whom the Lord when He cometh
shall find watching. [Matt. 24:46]
Yea, blessed are they. [Luke 11:28]
Watch ye therefore, for the Lord hath said: [Mark 13:35]

Promissio et Invocatio: 125 mm.
Surely, I come quickly [eighth-note = 138] T solo (recitative & aria); *Our Savior*, SATBar soli; *Amen* & *Blessed be the King* (chromatic) SATB soli/satb choir.

[tenor]
Surely I come quickly. [Rev. 22:20]
And thou shalt know that I the Lord am thy Savior and thy Redeemer. [Isa. 49:26]
I am the bright and morning Star. [para. Rev. 22:16]
Behold! I make all things new. [Rev. 21:5]
I will come to you and your hearts shall rejoice.
Your sorrow shall be turned into joy. [para. St. John 16:20]
I will receive you [St. John 14:3]
[soprano, alto and tenor]
Our Savior Christ will receive us. [para. St. John 14:3]
[tenor]
And I, if I be lifted up, will draw all men unto Me. [St. John 12:32]
I will ransom them. I will redeem them. O Grave! I will be thy destruction.
[Hosea 13:14]
[soprano, alto, baritone]
Our Savior hath abolished death. [2 Tim. 1:10]
[tenor]
Yea! Because I live ye shall live also. Ye shall have eternal life, for I
have overcome the world. [St. John 16:33]
I am the Light of the world. [St. John 8:28]
[soprano, alto, baritone, and choir]
Through Him we have eternal life. [para. St. John 6:68]
Out of Zion God hath shined. [para. Ps. 50:2]
Praise the Lord! Praise His holy Name. [Sirach 17:10]
He is the Way, the Truth and the Life: [para. St. John 14:6]

He is the Light of the World. [para. St. John 8:12]
From (out of the) holy chalice of His (heart) wells forth love divine.
(For this is the promise He hath promised us) (from the foundation of the world).
[para. I John 2:25, Rev. 17:8]
[tenor]
I will pour out of My Spirit upon all flesh. [Joel 2:28; Acts 2:17]
[soprano, alto, and baritone]
Amen. This is the promise he hath promised us. [1 John 2:25]
Blessed be the King. [Luke 19:38]
Praise Him. (Praise His holy Name.) [Ps. 145:21]
For He hath said:
[tenor]
Yea, surely I will come to you. [St. John 14:18]
[baritone]
Amen. Even so, come Lord Christ. [Rev. 22:20]

Benedictio: 20 mm.
Full orchestra [A flat m] [half-note = 54] Prelude for the concluding movement.

Consummatus: 42 mm.
He hath blessed us [G sharp M] satb choir/boy's-youth choir/SATB soli. *Concertante* scoring of the three ensembles. The author of the poetry is probably John Foulds.

[choir]
He hath blessed us from Whom all blessing flows: the living,
loving Father, in Whom, with Christ and the Holy Spirit,
we are at peace for evermore.
[soprano, alto, tenor]
Alleluia !
[choir]
He hath poured out His Spirit upon us, He hath blessed us. Amen.
[solo quartet]
Alleluia. Amen. Alleluia.

DISCOGRAPHY
None found.

PAUL HINDEMITH
November 16, 1895–December 28, 1963

Hindemith's earliest musical studies were received at Hoch Conservatory in Frankfurt. He became a superior violinist, violist, and, later, an excellent pianist. Ultimately, he learned to play most of the orchestral instruments, as well as several of the older instruments, including the viol. His knowledge of composition, however, was largely self-acquired.

He was particularly interested in early music (pre-1700) and especially the works of J. S. Bach. His experience with and knowledge of this body of music revealed itself in his compositions. Hindemith created a unique, neo-classic musical idiom by blending the forms and sonorities of the past with those of the present. A glance at his musical *oeuvre* reveals a large body of music, including symphonies, quartets, concertos, vocal, and chamber music. Forms, such as canon, fugue, sonata, and trio, figure large in his output. Each of these forms was common in the seventeenth and eighteenth centuries. His *Kammermusik* is a twentieth-century "version" of Bach's *Brandenburg* concertos.

The poetic imagination of Walt Whitman exercised its influence upon the creativity of a number of American composers. Over a period of nearly forty years, five who made a setting of *When lilacs last in the Dooryard Bloomed* were Normand Lockwood (1931), Herbert Elwell (1946), Paul Hindemith (1948), Roger Hannay (1961), and Roger Sessions (1970).

The Requiem, *When Lilacs Last in the Dooryard Bloomed*, scored for ABar soli, SATB choir and orchestra, was commissioned by Robert Shaw. It was composed between 1946–1948, during the years Hindemith taught at Yale. With this music, Hindemith commemorated the passing of Franklin Roosevelt and those who were killed in battle during the Second World War, just as Whitman's poetry had been a personal tribute to Abraham Lincoln and those who suffered and died during the Civil War.

Whitman used for imagery "Leitmotives" of purple lilac blooms, the star rising in the West, and the grey-brown thrush to represent, respectively, the spirit of love, the martyred president, and the soul of the poet. The poem, a plea for reconciliation and peace, uses important baroque forms and techniques: passacaglia (*Come, lovely* and soothing death), fugue (*Lo, body and soul*), ostinato (*Sing on*), binary form (*O how shall I warble*), and Baroque "affections" (motives that depict sighing-lamentation, *Sing on*).

Furthermore, the quartal sonorities of Hindemith's harmonic system suggest those of the late middle ages. The polyphonic choral textures are similar to those of Renaissance polyphony. Contrast in the prevailing choral matrix is achieved by thinning the vocal parts. The composer never employed *divisi* scoring in the choral parts. A musical, Wagnerian-type of *Leitmotiv* is found throughout the first section of this requiem, while thematic *Leitmotives* appear during the entire work.

This secular requiem is a philosophical work that could even be considered a "war" requiem because both the poetry of Whitman and the death of President Roosevelt are associated with war. It is a superior work with many haunting, elegiac moments and passages of great power and energy.

Basic Data

EDITIONS

1. Paul Hindemith
When Lilacs Last in the Dooryard
  Bloomed: A Requiem "For those we
  love."
Piano-Vocal Score [German & English
  text]
Edition Schott 3800
1948

2. Paul Hindemith
  Sämtliche Werke, Band VII, 2.
When lilacs last in the Dooryard bloom'd.
A Requiem "For those we Love"
Herausgegeben von Charles Jacobs
B. Schott's Söhne, Mainz 1986.

DURATION

Twelve movements, 1323 mm., perf., c. 63'

VOICING AND ORCHESTRATION

Choir: SATB range: S-A6; B-F♯ 3
Soloists: mezzo-soprano, baritone
Orchestra: vn. I/II, vla., vc., db., pic., fl., ob., Eh., cl., bcl., bsn., cbsn., 3 Fh., 2 tpt.,
  2 tbn., tuba, 3 timp., org. offstage bugle. PERC: bass drum, chimes, cymbal,
  glockenspiel, gong, parade drum, snare drum, triangle.

OUTLINE

Introduction, 54 mm.
  Orchestral prelude (built upon note, A-C-F-E, over a C♯ pedalpoint). [*very broad*, quarter-note = 60–66].
When lilacs . . . 39 mm.
  When lilacs . . . [quiet] Bar. solo; *O powerful, western fallen star*, satb choir; *In the dooryard*, Bar. solo. ABA form. Theme: the poet's anger at the death of the "great star," Lincoln. (depicted in the "*Leitmotiv*")

[baritone]
When lilacs last in the dooryard bloom'd,
and the great star early droop'd in the Western sky in the night,
I mourn'd, and yet shall mourn with ever-returning spring.
O ever-returning spring, trinity sure to me you bring,
Lilac blooming perennial and drooping star in the west,
And the thought of him I love.
[choir]
O powerful western fallen star!
O shades of night—O moody, tearful night!
O great star disappear'd—O the black murk that hides the star!
O cruel hands that hold me powerless—O helpless soul of me!

O harsh surrounding cloud that will not free my soul.
[baritone]
In the dooryard fronting an old farm-house near the white-wash'd palings,
Stands the lilac bush tall-growing with heart-shaped leaves of rich green,
With many a pointed blossom rising delicate, with the perfume strong I love,
With every leaf a miracle—and from this bush in the dooryard,
With delicate-color'd blossoms and heart-shaped leaves of rich green,
A sprig with its flower I break.

Arioso, *In the swamp*, 23 mm.

In the swamp [eighth-note = 58-69, *very quiet*] MS solo/English horn/orchestra.
Theme: the grey-brown bird (the soul of Whitman), a haunting lament. "*Leitmo-tiv*" in woodwinds.

In the swamp in secluded recesses,
A shy and hidden bird is warbling a song.
Solitary, the thrush,
The hermit withdrawn to himself, avoiding the settlements,
Sings by himself a song.
Song of the bleeding throat,
Death's outlet song of life (for well dear brother I know
If thou wast not gifted to sing, thou would'st surely die).

March: 171 mm.

Over the breast [half-note = 60, *slow, solemn*] satb choir/Bar. solo/orchestra.
Theme: the train journey made by Lincoln's coffin and those who lined the train-tracks to see the last journey of their slain president. At the end of the choral statement, the baritone appears, in the role of the poet, as he offers his own personal testimony and his sprig of lilac for the coffin. "*Leitmotiv*" employed.

[choir]
Over the breast of the spring, the land, amid cities,
Amid lanes and through old woods, where lately the violets
Peep'd from the ground, spotting the gray debris,
Amid the grass in the fields each side of the lanes,
passing the endless grass,
Passing the yellow-spear'd wheat, every grain from its shroud
in the dark-brown fields uprising,
Passing the apple tree blows of white and pink in the orchards,
Carrying a corpse to where it shall rest in the grave,
Night and day journeys a coffin.
Coffin that passes through lanes and streets,
Through day and night with the great cloud darkening the land,
With the pomp of the inloop'd flags, with the cities drap'd in black,
With the show of the States themselves, as of crepe-veil'd women standing,
With processions long and winding and the flambeaus of the night,

With the countless torches lit, with the silent sea of faces
and the unbared heads,
With the waiting depot, the arriving coffin, and the sombre faces,
With dirges through the night, with the thousand voices
rising strong and solemn,
With all the mournful voices of the dirges pour'd around the coffin,
The dim-lit churches and the shuddering organs—where amid these you journey,
With the tolling bells' perpetual clang,
[baritone]
Here, coffin that slowly passes, I give you my sprig of lilac.
(Not for you, for one alone,
Blossoms and branches green to coffins all I bring,
For fresh as the morning, thus would I carol a song for you,
O sane and sacred death.
All over bouquets of roses,
O death, I cover you over with roses and early lilies,
But mostly and now the lilac that blooms the first,
Copious I break, I break the sprigs from the bushes,
With loaded arms I come, pouring for you,
For you, and the coffins of all of you, O death.)

O western orb: 99 mm.
  O western orb [dotted-half note = 96, *fast*] Bar. solo/sat choir/orchestra. Theme:
Whitman reviews his own reaction to the death of Lincoln.

O western orb, sailing the heaven,
Now I know what you must have meant as a month since we walk'd,
As we walk'd up and down in the dark blue so mystic,
As we walk'd in silence the transparent shadowy night,
As I saw you had something to tell, as you bent to me night after night,
As you droop'd from the sky low down, as if to my side
(while the other stars all look'd on),
As we wander'd together the solemn night (for something, I know not
what, kept me from sleep),
As the night advanced, and I saw on the rim of the west,
ere you went, how full you were of woe,
As I stood on the rising ground in the breeze,
in the cold transparent night,
As I watch'd where you pass'd and was lost in the netherward
black of the night,
As my soul in its trouble dissatisfied sank, as where you, sad orb,
Concluded, dropt in the night, and was gone.

Arioso, *Sing on*: 16 mm.
  Sing on, there [quarter-note = 40, *very slow*] MS solo/orchestra. The orchestral
accompaniment is an ostinato, its melodic shape derived from the *"Leitmotiv."*

Sing on, there in the swamp,
O singer bashful and tender, I hear your notes, I hear your call,
I hear, I come presently, I understand you,
But a moment I linger, for the lustrous star has detain'd me,
The star, my departing comrade, holds and detains me.

Song, *O how shall I warble*: 94 mm.
   O, How shall [quarter-note = 92, *quiet*] Bar. solo/satb choir/orchestra. Binary
   form. (Choir answers the baritone solo.) Theme: the poet's personal response to
   the death of Lincoln.

[baritone]
O how shall I warble myself for the dead one there I loved?
And how shall I deck my song for the large sweet soul that is gone?
And what shall my perfume be for the grave of him I love?
[choir]
Sea-winds, blown from the east and west,
Blown from the Eastern sea, and blown from the Western sea,
till there on the prairies meeting,
[baritone]
These, and with these and the breath of my chant,
I perfume the grave of him I love.
O what shall I hang on the chamber walls?
And what shall the pictures be that I hang on the walls,
To adorn the burial-house of him I love?
[choir]
Pictures of growing spring, and farms, and homes,
With the Fourth-month eve at sundown,
and the gray smoke lucid and bright,
With floods of the yellow gold of the gorgeous, indolent,
sinking sun, burning, expanding the air.

Introduction and fugue: 186 mm.
   With the fresh sweet herbage [dotted half-note = 92-98, *fast*] satb choir/orchestra.
   (Prelude and Fugue) Theme: a hymn for a united country.

[introduction]
With the fresh sweet herbage under foot,
and the pale green leaves of the trees prolific,
In the distance the flowing glaze, the breast of the river,
with a wind-dapple here and there,
With ranging hills on the banks, with many a line against the sky,
and shadows,
And the city at hand, with dwellings so dense, and stacks of chimneys,
And all the scenes of life, and the workshops,
and the workmen homeward returning.
[fugue]

Lo, body and soul!—this land,
Mighty Manhattan with spires, and the sparkling and hurrying tides,
and the ships,
The varied and ample land, the South and the North in the light,
Ohio's shores and flashing Missouri,
And ever the far-spreading prairies, cover'd with grass and corn.
Lo, the most excellent sun, so calm and haughty,
The violet and purple morn with just-felt breezes,
The gentle, soft-born, measureless light,
The miracle, bathing all, the fulfill'd noon,
The coming eve delicious, the welcome night and the stars,
Over my cities shining all, enveloping man and land.

Soli and Duet, *Sing on*: 97 mm.
Sing on [eighth-note = 112–120, *quiet*] MS Bar. soli/orchestra. Theme: an exploration of the poet's deepest feelings about death and the fate that awaits all. An ostinato figure employed depicts sighing and lamentation. Structure: Bar. solo, *Now I sat in the day*, (free recitative) and Hymn *"For those we love."* (duet).

[mezzo-soprano]
Sing on, sing on, you gray-brown bird,
Sing from the swamps, the recesses, pour your chant from the bushes,
Limitless out of the dusk, out of the cedars and pines.
Sing on, dearest brother, warble your reedy song,
Loud human song, with voice of uttermost woe.
O liquid and free and tender!
O wild and loose to my soul—O wondrous singer!
You only I hear—yet the star holds me (but will soon depart),
Yet the lilac with mastering odor holds me.
[baritone recitative]
Now while I sat in the day and look'd forth,
In the close of the day, with its light and the fields of spring,
and the farmer preparing his crops,
In the large unconscious scenery of my land, with its lakes and forests,
In the heavenly, aerial beauty (after the perturb'd winds and the storms),
Under the arching heavens of the afternoon swift passing,
and the voices of children and women,
The many-moving sea tides, and I saw the ships, how they sail'd,
And the summer approaching with richness,
and the fields all busy with labor,
And the infinite separate houses, how they all went on,
each with its meals and minutiae of daily usages,
And the streets, how their throbbings throbb'd, and the cities pent—
lo, then and there,
Falling upon them all and among them all, enveloping me with the rest,
Appear'd the cloud, appear'd the long black trail,
[baritone, Hymn "For those we love"]

And I knew death, its thought, and the sacred knowledge of death.
Then with the knowledge of death as walking one side of me,
And the thought of death close-walking the other side of me,
And I, in the middle, as with companions, and as holding the hands
of companions,
[duet]
I fled forth to the hiding receiving night that talks not,
Down to the shores of the water, the path by the swamp in the dimness,
To the solemn shadowy cedars and ghostly pines so still.
And the singer so shy to the rest received me,
The gray-brown bird I know receiv'd us comrades three,
And he sang what seem'd the carol of death, and a verse for him I love.
From deep secluded recesses,
From the fragrant cedars and the ghostly pines so still,
Came the carol of the bird.
And the charm of the carol rapt me,
As I held, as if by their hands, my comrades in the night,
And the voice of my spirit tallied the song of the bird.

Death Carol, *Come, lovely and soothing death*: 179 mm.
   Come lovely [eight-note = 88, *slow*] satb choir/orchestra. Form: Introduction and
passacaglia (a variation form, in which the melody is in the bass line). Concluding section is the gray-brown bird's death carol.

Come lovely and soothing death,
Undulate round the world, serenely arriving,
In the day, in the night, to all, to each,
Sooner or later, delicate death.

Prais'd be the fathomless universe,
For life and joy, and for objects and knowledge curious,
And for love, sweet love—but praise! praise! praise!
For the sure-enwinding arms of cool-enfolding death.

Dark mother, always gliding near with soft feet,
Have none chanted for thee a chant of fullest welcome?
Then I chant it for thee, I glorify thee above all,
I bring thee a song that when thou must indeed come, come unfalteringly.

Approach, strong deliveress,
When it is so, when thou hast taken them, I joyously sing the dead,
Lost in the loving, floating ocean of thee,
Laved in the flood of thy bliss, O death.

From me to thee, glad serenades,
Dances for thee I propose, saluting thee, adornments
and feastings for thee,

And the sights of the open landscape and the high-spread sky are fitting,
And life and the fields, and the huge and thoughtful night.

The night in silence, under many a star,
The ocean shore and the husky whispering wave whose voice I know,
And the soul turning to thee, O vast and well-veil'd death
And the body gratefully nestling close to thee.
Over the tree-tops I float thee a song,
Over the rising and sinking waves, over the myriad fields
and the prairies wide,
Over the dense-pack'd cities all, and the teeming wharves and ways,
I float this carol with joy to thee, O death.

Solo, *To the tally of my soul*: 254 mm.
   To the tally [dotted quarter-note = 62–66, *slow*] Bar. solo/satb choir/orchestra.
Theme: death is an outcome of wartime battle and slaughter. Whitman sees
those who survive the war as the real victims and sufferers, not the peaceful
dead. Form: The quiet solo gives way to a march passage, along with visions
of violent wartime battle and destruction. An orchestral postlude, in which an
offstage Army bugle plays *Taps*, ends the movement.

[baritone]
To the tally of my soul,
Loud and strong kept up the gray-brown bird,
With deliberate note spreading, filling the night.
Loud in the pines and cedars dim,
Clear in the freshness moist, and the swamp perfume,
And I with my comrades there in the night.
While my sight that was bound in my eyes unclosed,
As long panoramas of visions.
I saw askant the armies,
And I saw, as in noiseless dreams, hundreds of battleflags,
Borne through the smoke of the battles and pierced with missiles,
I saw them,
[choir]
And carried hither and you through the smoke, and torn and bloody,
And last but a few shreds left on the staffs (and all in silence),
And the staffs all splinter'd and broken.
[baritone]
I saw battle-corpses, myriads of them,
And white skeletons of young men, I saw them,
I saw the debris, and the debris of all the dead soldiers of the war,
But I saw they were not as I thought,
[choir]
They themselves were fully at rest, they suffer'd not.
The living remain'd and suffer'd, the mother suffer'd
And the wife and the child and the musing comrade suffer'd
And all the armies that remain'd suffer'd.

Finale: 111 mm.

Passing the visions [eighth-note = 60–66, *very slow*] Bar. MS soli/satb choir/ orchestra. Theme: Whitman takes leave of his symbols of grief, the lilac, star and bird, yet he knows that they will always be with him. The choir recalls the three symbols, *there in the fragrant pines and cedars dusk and dim.* There is a note-worthy line, quite near the end of the poem, *for the dead I loved so well.* This line may have been a paraphrase of a then-popular love song, *Lorena,* well-known by both soldiers and civilians of the Union and Confederacy.

[baritone]
Passing the visions, passing the night,
Passing, unloosing the hold of my comrades' hands,
Passing the song of the hermit bird and the tallying song of my soul,
Victorious song, death's outlet song, yet varying, ever-altering song,
As low and wailing, yet clear the notes, rising and falling, flooding the night,
Sadly sinking and fainting, as warning and warning,
and yet again bursting with joy,
Covering the earth and filling the spread of the heaven,
As that powerful psalm in the night I heard from the recesses,
Passing, I leave thee, lilac with heart-shaped leaves,
I leave thee there in the door-yard, blooming, returning with spring.
I cease from my song for thee,
From my gaze on thee in the west, fronting the west, communing with thee,
O comrades lustrous with silver face in the night.
Yet each I keep, and all, retrievements out of the night,
The song, the wondrous chant of the gray-brown bird,
And the tallying chant, the echo arous'd in my soul,
With the lustrous and drooping star, with the countenance full of woe,
With the lilac tall, and its blossoms of mastering odor,
With the holders holding my hand, nearing the call of the bird,
Comrades mine, and I in the midst, and their memory ever I keep,
for the dead I loved so well.
For the sweetest, wisest soul of all my days and lands—and this for his dear sake,
[choir]
Lilac and star and bird, twined with the chant of my soul,
There in the fragrant pines and the cedars dusk and dim.
[soloists]
When lilacs last in the dooryard bloom'd.

DISCOGRAPHY

1. Berlin Classics, BER 9170, Berlin Radio Orchestra and Chorus, cond. Helmut Koch.
2. Telarc, 80132, Atlanta Symphony Orchestra and Chorus, cond. Robert Shaw.
3. Multiple listings in the Schwann Catalogue.

DMITRY KABALEVSKY
December 3, 1904–February 14, 1987

In 1925, Kabalevsky began his studies in piano and composition at Moscow Conservatory with Alexander Goldenweiser and George Catoire. After the death of Catoire, he continued his work with the composer, Alexander Miaskovsky (1881–1950), who exercised a great influence upon his musical style.

Kabalevsky was a prolific Soviet composer who left a large catalogue that includes seven operas, a ballet, four symphonies, numerous symphonic pieces, seven concertos (piano, cello, violin), solo piano works, chamber music, songs, film scores, and incidental music.

His choral oeuvre includes two large cantatas, *The Mighty Homeland* (1941–42) and *The People's Avengers* (1942). Like the two cantatas, much of his music deals with political and social topics close to the interests of the Soviet government. The *War Requiem*, Opus 72, was written in 1962–63, the years just after Britten had completed his *War Requiem* (1961). Robert Rozhdestvensky (b. 1930) is the poet-author of this humanist requiem text. The text is a model of Soviet socialist realism and conforms to standards acceptable to the Communist authorities. The musical style of the requiem also adheres to the principles of socialist realism. As principal editor for *Soviet Music*, Kabalevsky acted as spokesman for the Communist Party and its musical policies.

The text includes important patriotic elements and themes. *"Eternal Glory to the Heroes"*, *"Motherland"*, *"In the name of the Fatherland, Victory,"* *"We will build,"* *"Red banner,"* and *"Kill off the war"* were catchwords and phrases in the socialist-realist lexicon. An appeal to the worker-peasant society is seen in reference to *"cherries,"* *"poplar trees,"* and *"craftsmen . . . use their clever hands."* Belief in a happy future is depicted by the children's chorus in *"Our Children."* The Great Patriotic War, as World War II is known in Russia, figured greatly in the Russian experience.

Fortunately, much of this humanist requiem text transcends the narrow limits of socialist realism and embraces a wider, more universal viewpoint and appeal. In fact, this work is one of the great "war" requiems of the twentieth century.

Its post-romantic, musical language is derived from the work of Miaskovsky and Alexander Scriabin (1872–1915). While each movement employs a key signature, the tonal center of the music continues to move around from section to section. At the same time, each movement employs a wide variety of tempi in order to illuminate the spirit of the text.

The prevailing, four-part choral texture is homophonic, with contrasts provided in the thinning or *divisi* of the voices employed. Polyphonic choral writing is fairly rare as "formalistic" style was denounced in 1948 by the Soviet musical authorities. Nevertheless, imitative (melodic or rhythmic) writing can be found in the second (*Remember*), sixth (*Black stone*), tenth (*Listen*), and final (*Eternal glory*) movements. The vocal solo roles of the *Requiem* are dramatic and technically demanding.

Basic Data

EDITION

Kabalevsky
War Requiem with Russian and English text
Op. 72
[Full score]
Edwin Kalmus [1974]

DURATION

Thirteen movements, 2459 mm., perf., c. 88'

VOICING AND ORCHESTRATION

Choir: SATB [*divisi*] range: S-B flat 6; B-E flat 3
Soloists: baritone, soprano
Orchestra: vn. I/II, vla., vc., db., pic., fl., ob., Eh., cl., bcl., bsn., cbsn., Fh., tpt., tbn., tuba, timp., bass drum, tam-tam, harp, piano.

OUTLINE

PART ONE
Introduction, *"Remember"*: 27 mm.
  Remember [b flat m] *largo.* SBar soli.

Remember! Through the years, through the centuries—Remember!
Those that will never come!
Cry not! Stifle your bitter sobs in your throat.
The memory of the fallen—be worthy.

Eternal Glory: 332 mm.
  Eternal Glory [b flat m-e flat m] *allegro maestoso.* satb choir/ttbb choir/SBar soli.

[choir]
Eternal glory to the Heroes!
(mezzo-soprano/choir)
Why do the dead need this glory?
For what purpose is glory?
Those who saved the living, not saving themselves.
What is glory to the dead?
[choir]

When clouds are illuminated by lightning,
and the vast sky, by thunder is rent,
If a shout is torn from all people,
not one of the fallen will quiver.
I know: the sun will not blind empty eye-sockets.
I know: a song will not open the deep graves.
But from my heart—in the name of the living,
I shall repeat: Eternal glory to the heroes!
To those who died, to the fallen—
In the name of the living, in the name of the future,
Eternal glory!
[baritone, soprano soli/choir]
Remember them by name,
Let our grief awaken remembrance.
The dead have no need of it—
But the living do!
Remember those proud and unflinching souls who died in battle.
There exists a great privilege: to forget yourself.
There exists a noble privilege: to desire and to dare.
To eternal glory turns instant death!

Homeland: 141 mm.
   Did you will them . . . [e flat m] *lento.* saa/tbb/satb choir.

[choir]
Did you wish them to die, Homeland?
You promised life and love, Homeland.
Are children born only to die, Homeland?
Did you desire their death, Homeland?
Flames rose skyward—do you remember, Homeland?
Quietly it was said "Rise up and help."
Homeland.
No one begged for glory from you. Homeland.
Clearly, the choice was there:
Myself or my Homeland.
The best and most cherished—Homeland.
Your grief is our grief, Homeland.
Your truth is our truth, Homeland.
Your glory is our glory, Homeland.

I will not die: 128 mm.
   I will not die . . . [dm-DM] *moderato assai.* Bar solo/sat/satb choir.

[baritone solo/choir]
I cannot—I will not die.
If I die, I will become grass, leaves, smoke.
Spring earth. The morning star.

I'll become a wave, a frothy wave.
I'll carry my heart afar.
I'll become dew, the first thunder,
Children's laughter, a woodland echo.
Out on the steppe, the grass shall whisper.
A wave will break on the shore.
Give me time to finish!
To fully savor my fate.
If only the trumpet would sound at night-time.
If only the fields would ripen with wheat.
Fate, provide me a lifeline.
Fate, give me a proud death.

The march of the Divisions: 198 mm.
    The crimson banner . . . [b flat m-am] *marcial pesant e sostenuto.* satb/tb choir.

[choir]
The crimson banner fluttered.
The crimson stars brightly shone.
A blinding snowstorm shrouded
a blood-red sunset,
And came the great, firm march of the Divisions.
The distinct march of soldiers.
We went into battle, so pure and determined,
toward the peals of howling thunder.
Our banners bear the word: Victory!
In the name of our Homeland—victory.
In the name of the living—victory.
In the name of the future—victory.
We must destroy War.
No prouder fate existed.
And no honor higher.
While there is the desire to survive,
There is, too, the courage to live.

PART TWO
Black stone: 327 mm.
    Black stone . . . [em] *andante molto sostenuto.* sa/sb/satb choir (choir).

O black stone, why do you keep silent?
Did you want this fate?
Did you ever dream of becoming a tombstone
for the grave of the Unknown Soldier?
Why do you remain silent, black stone?
We searched for you in the mountain peaks.
We shattered solid rock.
Trains echoed throughout the night.

Craftsmen kept vigil,
in order to employ their clever hands at their livelihood,
to turn ordinary stone into a mute gravestone.
Are stones to blame for why—somewhere
buried deep and for too long—soldiers sleep?
Soldiers without name . . .
While above them, grasses wither, stars fade—
the golden eagle circles and the sunflower sways.
Standing over them are pines and the snow settles.
The golden sun colors the sky.
Time moves . . .
But once someone in the world remembers
the name of the Unknown Soldier . . .
Just before death he had so many friends.
For still there lives an old mother.
She was once a bride. Where is she now?
The soldier faced death known.
He died—unknown.

A Mother's Heart: 110 mm.
  O Why . . . [am] *largo. S solo/satb choir.*

[mezzo-soprano solo/choir]
Why my son, do you not return from empty war,
From the peals of howling thunder?
I will save you from calamity,
Fly quickly as a bird . . .
Answer me, my life's blood! My child. My only one . . .
The world is meaningless and I am in pain.
Return to me, my hope.
My grain, my dawn, my grief—where are you?
I cannot find the path to your grave
so that I may weep for you.
I want nothing, only my darling son.
Beyond the forests and huge mountains is
my sweet one.
When tears are drained, the hearts of mothers cry.
The world is bleak.

The Future: 130 mm.
  When do you . . . [BM] *marcial. maestoso. SBar soli/satb choir.*

[baritone & soprano soli/choir]
Future, when will you arrive? Soon?
Replying to what pain?
You see: the proudest came forth to meet you.
Enough for several lives . . . for a thousand lives

would last our suffering . . . our grief.
Enough for a million lives
our strength, our will, would last,
our faith in the future, bright and dear,
will hold no war, no fear.
Our future will hold no suffering, no poverty.
The sky will be clear, huge and dear.
In our future our children will forget tears
and will laugh merrily.
They will preserve in their hearts the glory of their fathers.

Our Children: 172 mm.
This song is about the sunny world . . . [CM] andantino con moto. children's choir/satb choir.

[children's choir/satb choir]
This song is about sunlight . . . about sun in your heart.
This song is about a young planet whose future is just ahead.
In the name of the sun, of the Motherland, we pledge.
In the name of life we solemnly promise the fallen heroes,
what our fathers did not finish building, we shall build.
Shoots reaching towards the heart, you shall grow to the heavens.
We, born in the victory song, begin to live and dream.
What our fathers did not finish singing, we shall sing.
What our fathers did not finish building, we shall build.
Hurry, joyful springs.
We have come to take the place of the dead.
Do not be so proud, distant stars.
Await quests from the earth.

PART THREE
Introduction *"In memory of the Dead:"* 97 mm. (orchestra)

Listen: 266 mm.
Listen . . . [cm] *non troppo allegro.* satb choir.

[choir]
Listen!
We are speaking. The dead. Us.
From the darkness. Listen!
Open your eyes. Listen to the end.
We are speaking. The dead.
We knock at your hearts.
Do not fear.
Once we shall disturb your sleep.
Above the fields our voices carry through the quiet.
We have forgotten, how sweet is the flower's odor.

How the poplar tree murmurs.
We have forgotten the Earth.
What is it like, our earth?
Are the birds singing without us?
Are cherries in blossom without us?
Does the river run clear?
And the clouds above us? Without us.
We have forgotten the grass, the trees.
We are never not to walk the earth.
Never shall we awaken to the orchestra's sorrowful brass.
Birds sing and cherries blossom without us.
Rivers run clear and clouds float above us, without us.
Life goes on. Again day begins.
The rainy season draws close.
Growing wind sways the ripe crops.
This is your fate.
This is our common fate.

Eternal Glory: 101 mm.
Eternal glory . . . [bm] *allegro maestoso.* satb choir [*divisi*].

[choir]
Eternal glory to the heroes!
So what if not all are heroes.
Those who died—the fallen, in the name of their Homeland.
The fallen in the name of the living, in the name of the future,
Eternal glory to the fallen.
All living—who saved themselves not saving.
Eternal glory.

Remember: 430 mm.
Remember. . . [B flat M-b flat m] *adagio sostenuto.* SBar soli/children's choir/satb choir [*divisi*].

[soprano & baritone soli/children's choir/satb choir]
Through years. Through centuries. Remember.
Those that are never to return come. Remember.
Do not cry. Your throat suppresses a bitter wail.
Be eternally worthy of the fallen.
With bread and song in dreams and poem,
in life so full, every second, with every breath, be worthy.
In the name of the sun, the name of the Homeland we pledge.
Be worthy.
In the name of life we make a solemn promise to the fallen heroes:
What our fathers did not finish singing, we shall sing.
What our fathers did not finish building, we shall build.
People! While our hearts beat—Remember.

What price was paid for happiness—Remember.
When sending your song on wings—Remember.
Those, who shall never sing—Remember.
Tell your children about them.
See, they will remember.
Your children's children should know of them,
So they, too, will remember.
At every time remember our immortal.
Flying ships to the shimmering stars—Remember the dead.
Greet the robust spring.
Carry your dream through the years and fill yourself with life.
People of the earth, kill war!
People of the earth, curse war!
But those, who are not to ever return, I appeal to you—Remember!

DISCOGRAPHY

Olympia, OCD 290 A + B, Moscow Symphony Orchestra, Choir of the Artistic
Education Institute, cond. Dimitry Kabalevsky.

ALEXANDER DIMITRI KASTALSKY
November 28, 1856–December 17, 1926

Kastalsky began his studies at the Moscow Conservatory in 1875, where
he studied piano and composition with Tchaikovsky and Taniev. Early
in his professional career, he conducted a number of amateur choirs and
orchestras and gave voice lessons in various schools. His first major
appointment was to the Moscow Synodal Academy in 1887, where he
taught a variety of musical subjects, including Russian singing. By 1910,
he was director of the Synodal Choir, which toured Europe in 1911. In
1923, the Academy was renamed the People's Choral Academy and
absorbed by the Conservatory. During the last decade of the nineteenth
century, he became an important authority on old Russian chant.

Kastalsky was primarily a choral composer, who made numerous settings of native folksongs into concert arrangements and who wrote
church music. He composed the music for Lenin's funeral; a work titled
To Lenin: at his graveside. It was scored for reciter, chorus, and orchestra.

In 1916, he composed one of the earliest "War" requiems, the *Fraternal
Commemoration* (*Bratskoyeh Pominovennie*), in memory of those soldiers of
all nations who died in World War I. Scored for SATB soloists, SATB choir,
and orchestra, it is arranged into fourteen movements. Kastalsky
employed liturgical melodies from a number of European nations as well

as the traditional Gregorian and Orthodox models. The Preface of the score reads:

> The incessantly strengthening brotherhood and union of the allied nations, their accordance and mutual assistance in the present war naturally bring forth the idea of confraternal prayer for the warriors fallen for the common case.
> The author thus pictures himself the solemn religious ceremony of Commemoration: around the divine acting are assembled parts of the allied armies; melodies of the requiem are to be heard, now russian, now catholic, now servian, [serbian] now english; one language replaces the other, betimes signals of horns of different armies, drum-beat and cannonade are audible; at a distance lament and sob the orphan wives and mothers; on the side of the asiatic troops are heard the sounds of Japanese and Indian tunes. At the proclamation of "rest eternal" join the military bands, salutes of cannons are to be heard and the music assumes a bright colour of glorification of the fallen heroes.

Kastalsky's orchestration follows the colorful tradition of the Rimsky-Korsakov style. There are numerous picturesque passages, such as the tolling bells of the first and eighth movements, the martial trumpet solos of the twelfth movement, and the harp-bell-celesta combination of the eighth and eleventh movements. The ninth movement is an instrumental piece that attempts to depict Japanese musical sonorities by use of the pentatonic scale and an instrumental combination of piano, tam-tam, harp, bass drum, and muted strings. The thirteenth movement attempts to capture the sound of Indian music by the use of various percussion instruments, a male choir that sings a nasal *ah* sound and violins that are held like guitars and plucked. The final movement employs a battery of field cannon and other percussion instruments.

The melodic material and harmonic structure have a definite "Russian" sound created by the use of native folk scales and melodic patterns. Kastalsky had spent significant time researching old Russian canticles. These centuries-old pieces borrowed melodic patterns from folksong and, in turn, this folksong tradition became part of Kastalsky's musical vocabulary.

The SATB choral texture is predominantly homophonic and frequently augmented by *divisi* scoring or reduced by thinning the vocal parts. The only notable polyphonic exceptions are the fugue, *Hosanna*, and the canon, *Pie Jesu*. Another unique feature of the *Commémoration Fraternelle* is the ecumenical use of melodies from Gregorian, Russian, English, Serbian liturgies, as well as Japanese and Indian sources. The Gregorian *Dies irae* melody is quoted in the third and twelfth movements.

This composition is one of the few large-scale Russian sacred works for choir and orchestra written in the early twentieth century. Rachmaninoff's *Vigil* (1915) and Gretchaninoff's *Liturgia Domestica* (1917) are several of the notable choral works written prior to the Russian Revolution of 1917. One cannot help but wonder what would have taken place in the development of Russian Orthodox liturgical music had this revolution followed a different direction—one less hostile to the religious and spiritual life.

Nearly all movements include three textual versions: Latin (or Greek), Russian, and English. The first movement includes an Italian text.

Basic Data

EDITION

Commémoration fraternelle
Pour voix seules, choeur et Orchestre
[Full score] [1916]
P[eter] Jurgenson, Moscow

DURATION

Fourteen movements, 789 mm., perf., c. 60′

VOICING AND ORCHESTRATION

Choir: SATB [*divisi*] range: S-A6; B-E3
Soloists: STB
Orchestra: vn. I/II, vla., vc., db., pic., 2 fl., 2 ob., Eh., 2 cl., bcl., 2 bsn., cbsn., 2 Fh., 2 tpt., 3 tbn., 2 tubas, org., piano, celesta, harp. PERC: timp., bass drum, tamtam, triangle, military tambourine, snare drum, chimes, bells, cannon.

OUTLINE

Movement 1, *Requiem aeternam*: 74 mm.
  Comrades, in memory, lugubre. B solo; *Requiem aeternam* [Russian chant] satb choir. A funeral procession. ABA form.
Movement 2, *Kyrie*: 91 mm.
  Kyrie [Catholic chant] *moderato*. orchestra/satb choir [*divisi*]; *Kyrie* [Serbian chant]; *Lord have mercy* [English tune] satb choir; *Kyrie* [Russian chant] satb choir; *Kyrie* [Catholic chant] satb choir.
Movement 3, *Rex tremendae*: 67 mm.
  Rex tremendae [Russian chant] *energico*. satb choir [*divisi*]; *Salva me* [Catholic chant] satb choir; *Think good Jesu* [Russian chant]; *Caused Thy wondrous* [Catholic chant] satb choir [*divisi*]; *Quarens me* [*Dies irae* tune] satb choir; *Juste judex*, B solo; *Alleluia* [Russian chant] satb choir. (vv. 7–11).
Movement 4, *Ingemisco*: 47 mm.
  Ingemisco [English tune], *andante pietoso*. S solo/strings/French horn solo. ABA form. (vv. 12–15).

Movement 5, *Confutatis*: 28 mm.

Confutatis [English tune] *grave e maestoso.* satb choir [*divisi*]. (vv. 16–17).

Movement 6, *Lacrimosa*: 58 mm.

Lacrymosa [Catholic chant] *andantino.* SB soli/satb choir [*divisi*]; *Pie Jesu* [Catholic chant] satb choir. (canonic SB duet). (vv. 18–19).

Movement 7, *Domine Jesu*, 49 mm.

Alleluia [Russian chant] *tranquillo.* satb choir; *Domine Jesu Christe*, B solo.

Movement 8, *Hostias*, 42 mm.

Hostias [Russian chant] *andante.* satb choir; *Tu suscipe* [Catholic chant] satb choir; *Fac eas* [Russian chant] satb choir.

Movement 9, *Interludium*: 28 mm.

An orchestral piece, *andantino.* A depiction of Japanese music. Kastalsky wrote in the heading, *"Du cote des troupes Japonaises ou entend une musique douce."* [From the Japanese troops where one hears a sweet music.] Pentatonic scale and melodies employed in this charming musical cameo.

Movement 10, *Sanctus-Benedictus*, 70 mm.

Sanctus [Catholic chant] *allegro maestoso.* satb choir; *Benedictus* [Serbian chant] *tranquillo.* Satb choir (Organ stops indicated: voix celeste, musette, vox humana); *Hosanna* [Russian chant] *allegro maestoso.* satb choir. Fugue.

Movement 11, *Agnus Dei*: 34 mm.

Agnus Dei [Serbian chant] *andante misterioso.* satb choir.

Movement 12, *Kyrie & Absolve & Kyrie*: 85 mm.

Kyrie [Russian chant] *allegro moderato.* satb choir; *Absolve me* [Catholic chant] satb choir; *Lucis aeternae, andante.* satb choir/trumpet solo; *Kyrie* [English chant] *meno mosso.* satb choir. The Gregorian *Dies irae* is quoted.

Movement 13, *Interludium, L'Hymne a Indra*: 50 mm.

An orchestral piece in which Kastalsky tried to capture the sounds of the Indian soldiers who fought on the side of the Allies during the war. He included the following comment at the beginning of the score:

> Du cote de troupes indoues resonne l'hymne a Indra. Selon les mythes indous, les guerriers tombes au champ du bataille sont recus au sein d'Indra, dieu du firmament.
> [From the side of the troops resounds the hymn to Indra. According to Indian belief, soldiers who have fallen on the field of battle are received into the bosom of Indra, God of Heaven.]

Movement 14, *Requiem aeternam*: 60 mm.

Requiem aeternam [Russian chant] *moderato.* satb choir; *Let light perpetual* [Serbian chant] *adagio tranquillo.* satb choir/small choir of altos/T solo; *Let light perpetual* [Russian chant] *poco meno mosso.* satb choir/small bass choir/T solo; *Shine upon them, Grave alla Marcia funèbre.* satb choir/orchestra/a wide variety of percussion, including cannon. A recollection that recalls the grandeur and pomposity of the military funerals of the post-war era.

DISCOGRAPHY

Russian Disc, RD CD 10 043, USSR Symphony Orchestra and Radio Large Choir, cond. Evgeni Svetlanov.

YURI LEVITIN
December 15[28], 1912–June 27, 1976

Yuri Levitin was a Ukrainian pianist and composer who received his musical education from the Leningrad Conservatory, where he studied with Dimitri Shostakovitch. From 1931 to 1941, he was the pianist for the Leningrad Philharmonic Orchestra. He then worked in the Variety Theatre of Tashkent from 1941–42, after which time he returned to Moscow.

Levitin wrote a great deal of orchestral music, including dance suites, ballet suites, several concerti (piano (1944, 1952), cello (1961), clarinet and harp (1970), oboe and strings (1960), chamber music, piano music, and secular vocal works. His tonal language is a mixture of late-romantic and modern harmony and the programmatic musical style is modeled after the works of Dimitri Shostakovitch and Sergei Prokoviev.

The *Requiem in Memory of Fallen Heroes,* Opus 20, is a secular oratorio that was composed in 1946 during the Stalinist era. It is scored for soprano solo, SATB choir, and orchestra. It is a soviet-realist version of the liturgical requiem and is one of the earliest, if not the first, Russian, twentieth-century war requiems. This setting precedes the most famous Russian work of this type, the *War Requiem* of Kabalevsky, not written until sixteen years later in 1962.

Because the Russians lost so many millions to the Nazi holocaust, the nightmarish events of World War II have loomed large in Soviet memory and history. Although the text is an example of conservative Soviet realism, the music was written in a more modern, non-national style than many other works of this ideological style.

The language of the work is Russian and the poetry is by Vasily Ivanovitch Lebedev-Cumach (1898–1949). Although much of the poetic imagery is horrific, there are passages of great tenderness and spirituality. There are also numerous moments, such as the concluding movement, in which the hand of the Communist Party can be felt. The English translation of the poetry was made by the author of this guide.

The prevailing choral texture is homophonic with occasional polyphonic style. The third movement, *In fierce combat*, is a four-part fugue. The orchestration is particularly colorful and dramatic (strings and French horn in movement four; alto flute and clarinet duos in the first, sixth, and seventh movements, and a percussion battery in the fifth movement). The choral writing includes a number of vocalized passages, such as that in the fifth movement, *Villages ablaze*.

Basic Data

EDITION

Y. Levitin
Requiem in Memory of Fallen Heroes, Op. 20

Partitura [full score]
Izdatelstvo "Sovietskii Compositor" [Publishing Firm: "Soviet Composer"]
Moscow. 1971

DURATION

Eight movements, 972 mm.

VOICING AND ORCHESTRATION

Choir: SATB [*divisi*] range: S-B6; B-E flat 3
Soloists: soprano
Orchestra: vn. I/II, vla., vc., db., pic., fl., alto fl., 2 ob., Eh., pic., cl., 2 cl., bcl., 2
    bsn., cbsn., 6 Fh., 4 tpt., 3 tbn., tuba, timp. PERC: triangle, tambourine, snare
    drum, bass drum, cymbals, tam-tam, bells, little bells, xylophone.

OUTLINE

Movement I: Orchestral Introduction, 100 mm.
    Largo [b flat m] full orchestra/solo alto flute/clarinet. Serious mood.
Movement II: *The Military Banner*, 84 mm.
    The military banner [em] *largo*. S solo/satb choir/orchestra.

[soprano]
The military banners line the rows of sacred graves
Do not forget the selfless national victors . . . heroes all.
[choir]
The living will never forget those who were taken by others.
The field flowers on the grave mounds do not fade.
And passing by a new green grave, children and grandchildren
lovingly remember those souls upon whom they depended.
[soprano]
In silent, deep sorrow their native land receives them.
And resounding over them is the Kremlin's majestic cannon salute.
[choir]
Their holy blood fell like dew upon the fields.
So that the Soviet Land will bloom ever more beautiful and light.
[soprano]
The flag of the Motherland will guard our sleep.
Eternal Glory to the heroes who fell for the Motherland!

Movement III: *In fierce combat*, 138 mm.
    In fierce, deadly combat [fm] *allegro risoluto*. satb choir/orchestra. (fugue).

In fierce deadly combat, the National Hero stood up
for the life and honor of our suffering homeland.

Movement IV: *The Soldier's Grave*, 75 mm.
    The dark blue canopy [f# m] *adagio quasi recitativo*. After an orchestral introduc-

tion of fifteen measures in 10/4 meter, the remainder of the movement is scored unaccompanied satb [*divisi*] choir.

The dark blue canopy of the mountain casts its shadow over the dull water
and covers the sunny spaciousness of the rocky ridge.
Grey waves beat upon the shore and roll back,
They sing of the courage of those whose bravery is without limit.
There is a grave hillock on the shore,
It is fresh and low in height.
This grave is guarded only by the waves and the sand.
The soldier lies there with lead in his chest.
Death overtook him in battle.
The pines rustle, the shore falls silent.
For the honor of the Motherland, he gave up his life.
And the memory of the soldier, like the flag and the way will live forever.
Clouds lie over the water and cover the sunny spaciousness of the rocky ridge.
Clouds flow down from the mountain and hang over the water.

Movement V: *Villages ablaze*, 331 mm.
The villages have been set ablaze [am-AM-am] *allegro*. satb choir. After a fiery orchestral introduction of 124 measures, the choir sings of the terror and devastation that visited much of Russia during the Nazi invasion.

The villages have been set ablaze; fire envelopes the hut.
The guns of war sound like nearby thunder.
A dull glow illuminates the nightly firmament.
The wheels of war roll along every road
and pressing on, bring sadness to every threshold.
The war has trampled over our spacious motherland
and blood has stained Earth's green cover.
Tears fell like rain. Blood flowed like a river.

Movement VI: *Here they sleep*, 66 mm.
There are so many [GM] *moderato*. S solo/strings/woodwind trio.

There are so many of them, some modest and austere,
some are simple and low . . . these grave mounds on former war-fronts.
Our beloved people preserve the memory of past battles.
Here they sleep, enveloped in eternal peace . . .
they have forgotten the noise of battle and the burning wounds . . .
these soldier-heroes, sailor-heros and old, local partisans . . .
Whoever you are, wherever you go, remember that terrible time!
You golden buttercups, ox-eye daisies and fragrant mint
growing in the broad fields.

We remember those years of great suffering, sleepless nights and anxious days,
as we come to kneel quietly on the slopes and pray for you, dear friends.

Movement VII: *Each of them*, 82 mm.
Each of them [b flat m] *largo*. satb choir/orchestra/alto flute-clarinet duet.

> Each of them, killed by the enemy, was our brother.
> Each of them suffered and loved.
> Like us, they smiled in Spring; saw picturesque figures in the snow.
> They looked at little children with kindness.
> Each one of them wanted happiness for himself and the people.
> Just like yourself, each one sang songs and loved flowers.
> The tears of the dead remind us of dew.
> The wind repeats to us their voices.
> We will never forget these heroes,
> like dew, their blood fell upon the fields.

Movement VIII: *Eternal Glory to the Heroes*, 96 mm.
Eternal Glory [b flat m-M] *largo*. unaccompanied sattbb choir. Later the orchestra
begins quietly and along with the choir builds to a triumphant climax.

> Eternal Glory to the heroes who fell for the Homeland!
> The flag of the Motherland will guard their sleep.
> In silent, deep sorrow their native land receives them
> and the Kremlin's stately salute resounds over them.
> The military banners line the rows of sacred graves.
> The nation will not forget these selfless conquering-heroes.
> The living will not forget those taken in battle.
> The field flowers on the grave mounds will never fade.
> Glory to the Heroes!

DISCOGRAPHY
None found.

RUDOLF MAUERSBERGER
January 29, 1889–February 22, 1971

Rudolf Mauersberger was one of the most important German church
musicians in the twentieth century. He studied with Karl Straube at the
Leipzig Conservatory. During his career, he held a number of posts as a
church musician, but the most important one was that of *Kantor* of the
Church of the Holy Cross (Kreuzkirche) in Dresden, where he worked
from 1930 to 1971. His tenure there lasted during two lengthy periods of
political duress and dictatorship, first from the Nazis, then from the com-
munists.

Although his earliest musical compositions were instrumental and symphonic vocal works, it is the church music, written during his tenure at the Kreuzkirche, that is remembered today. Mauersberger was especially interested in the music of Heinrich Schütz and was a strong champion of contemporary church music, particularly the works by Hugo Distler, Ernst Pepping, and Wolfgang Fortner. He composed more than twenty pieces for choir, including *St. Luke Passion* (1947), *Dresdner Requiem* (1948–49), the choral cycle *Dresden* (1945), and a number of motets.

Mauersberger wrote the *Dresdner Requiem* in 1947 and 1948, making a number of revisions and additions to it, up to 1961. It is scored for three unaccompanied SATB choirs and for a small instrumental ensemble that is employed for several of the chorales. The three choirs include a large SATB choir, a smaller SATB "altar" choir that symbolizes Jesus Christ, and an SATB "echo choir" that represents the world of the departed. The *Requiem* is a modern concert version of the Evangelical Lutheran Church memorial service.

Not only is it a German requiem, it is also a genre of "war" requiem. On February 14 and 15, 1945, the American and English Air Force bombed Dresden in a punitive raid, killing tens of thousands of civilians while laying waste to a city known as the "Venice" of northern Europe. It was in memory of this catastrophe that Mauersberger composed the *Dresdner Requiem*. Its premiere took place on St. John's Day, 1948.

The harmonic vocabulary used by Mauersberger is a contemporary version of triadic tonality that borrows upon the quartal and quintal sonorities of the middle ages. The polychoral style of the *Musikalisches Exequien* (Heinrich Schütz) and the *Polyhymnia Caduceatrix and Panegyrica* (Michael Praetorius), with its mixed homophonic-polyphonic textures, is evident in the *Dresdner Requiem*. A number of the pieces are based upon the German chorale melodies of the sixteenth and seventeenth centuries. The ideals of the Caecilian Movement, in terms of unaccompanied choral singing and a devotional presentation of the text, are realized in this work..

The texts, with the exception of the opening, Latin *Requiem aeternam*, are taken from the Bible (Luther's translations of the Old and New Testaments), the Lutheran Hymn Book, and a Catholic prayerbook from Bohemia, in which the liturgical texts are set in paraphrase and free translation. This music and texts of this masterpiece project a profoundly moving spiritual quality. The modern performance edition provides both the original German text and its English translation by Robert Scandrett.

Traditionally, a performance of the *Dresdner Requiem* is preceded by the mourning motet, *Wie liegt die Stadt so wüst* (1945), a text employed earlier by Hugo Kaun in his post-World War I *Deutsches Requiem*. A large choir is needed for the performance of this work. Regrettably, this superb music is not well known outside Germany.

Basic Data

EDITIONS

1. Rudolf Mauersberger

Wie liegt die Stadt so wüst, Trauermotette nach den Klagliedern Jeremiae für vier-
bis siebenstimmigen gemischten Chor a cappella. [Mourning motet with words
from *The Lamentations of Jeremiah,* for mixed choir, four to seven voices, unac-
companied] Text in German & English.
Edition Merseburger #418
Verlag Merseburger, Berlin.1949

2. Rudolph Mauersburger

Dresdner Requiem, nach Worten der Bibel und des Gesangbuches RMWV 10.
Partitur [Full Score]
First Edition edited by Matthias Herrmann [English translation: Robert Scandrett]
Carus Verlag (7.200/01) 1995 [The edition contains extensive notes on the work &
its performance.]

DURATION

Thirty-seven movements, 984 mm., perf., c. 55'

VOICING AND ORCHESTRATION

Choirs: 3 SATB choirs [*divisi*]—large choir, altar choir, echo choir. range: S-B flat
6; B-C3
Soloists: boy soprano
Instruments: 3 tp., 3 tbn., tuba. PERC: timp., bass drum, snare drum, tam-tam,
cymbals, xylophone, bells, glockenspiel, string contrabass, celesta, org.

OUTLINE

Funeral motet: 126mm. *Wie liegt die Stadt so wüst, langsam* [slowly] satb choir
[*divisi*].

How lonely sits the city that was full of people.
All of her gates are desolate. The holy stones lie scattered
at the head of every street. From on high he sent fire;
into my bones he made it descend. Is this the city,
which was called the perfection of beauty, the joy of all the earth?
She took no thought of her doom; therefore her fall is terrible,
She has no comforter. For this our heart has become sick,
for these things our eyes have grown dim.
Why do you forget us forever, why do you so long forsake us?
Restore us to yourself, O Lord, that we may be restored.
Renew our days of old. O Lord, behold my affliction,
O Lord, behold my distress.
[Lamentations 1:1–4, 13; 2:15; 1:9; 5:17, 20–21; 1:9]

Dresden Requiem
Introitus: 135 mm., 4 movements.
Prelude and *Requiem aeternam*: 38 mm. [*adagio*] altar satb choir/instruments.
   Antiphon, *Herr, gib ihnen die ewige Ruhe*: 63 mm. *langsam* [slowly] large satb
   choir/echo satb choir, unaccompanied. Structure: polychoral dialogue between
   the living and the dead.

> Lord , grant unto them rest everlasting
> and may everlasting light shine upon them.

Psalm, *Gott, man lobet dich*: 17 mm. large ssaatb choir, unaccompanied.

> God, we give you praise in the stillness of Zion,
> and unto you, we pay our vows. You who hear prayer,
> to you then shall all flesh come.
> [Psalm 65:2–3]

Antiphon, *Herr gib ihnen die ewig Ruhe*: 17 mm. large satb choir/echo satb choir,
unaccompanied.
Kyrie: 159 mm., 3 movements.
   Kyrie, Incline your ear: 63 mm. large choir [ssaattbb *divisi*]/altar satb choir, unaccompanied.

> Incline your ear to our supplication, O Lord
> and let our cry come unto you.
> God our heavenly Father, you who have created
> the souls of the departed in your own image
> and have called them to eternal fellowship with you,
> have mercy upon us.
> God the Son, Savior of the world, you who for
> them have forsaken the splendor of your throne
> and endured a shameful death on the cross,
> have mercy upon us.
> God, Holy Ghost, who has blessed them with your grace
> and has consecrated them to the temple of the living God,
> have mercy upon us.

Epistle, *I heard a voice*: 50 mm. large satb choir/echo satb choir, unaccompanied.

> I heard a voice from heaven saying, Write this:
> Blessed are the dead who die in the Lord henceforth.
> Blessed indeed, says the Spirit, that they may
> rest from their labors, for their deeds follow them.
> [Revelation 14, 13]

Prayer (Graduale), *Lord grant them rest*: 46 mm. large SATB choir/echo satb choir/
S solo, unaccompanied.
This movement is a variation of the same prayer found in the Introit.

> Lord, grant them eternal rest
> and may perpetual light shine upon them.

The Transitory, Death, *Dies irae*, and Comfort. 17 movements. 376 mm.
Vergänglichkeit "A very short and troublesome thing," 43 mm. large satb choir [*divisi*],
unaccompanied.
The concluding section, *I will therefore*, is scored for ttbb choir.

> A very short and troublesome thing is our life. Our names
> will be forgotten as time passes by, and no one
> will remember what we did. And our life will blow away
> like the last, fleeting vestige of a cloud and dissolve like a mist.
> Thus, who goes to his grave comes back not again,
> comes not ever again. And comes no more to his house,
> and his dwelling is known no more. I will therefore, not restrain
> my mouth from speaking. I will speak in the anguish of my spirit,
> and I will complain in the bitterness of my grieving soul.
> For now shall I lie in the quiet earth and one may
> come to seek me there, but I shall not be.
> [The Wisdom of Solomon 2:1. 4; Job 7:9–11; 9:21]

Gospel, *In the world you have fear*: 14 mm. altar satb choir [*divisi*].

> In the world you have fear. But be of good cheer, the world I have overcome.
> [Gospel of John 16:33]

Chorale, *Ich hab' nun überwunden* [*I have now overcome*]: 8 mm. echo satb choir. (the
first of ten chorales used in the *Requiem*) The tune and text, *Christus der ist mein
Leben* are by Melchior Vulpius, (c. 1560–1615).

> I have now overcome cross, suffering, fear, distress;
> through Christ's redeeming ransom, God's love I now confess.

Tod [*Death*]: 25 mm. large satb choir [*divisi*].

> Who would God instruct, who on the mighty brings judgement.
> This one dies sound, in full health, in all his wealth,
> and full of his worldly things. Yet another dies with a troubled
> spirit and has never happiness tasted; and yet lies each
> with the other in the cold earth.
> [Job 21, 22–23, 25–26]

Gospel, *Ich bin die Auferstehung* [*I am the resurrection*]: 12 mm. altar satb choir [*divisi*], unaccompanied.

> I am the resurrection and the life. He who believes in me,
> shall live, even though he die.
> [Gospel of John 11:25]

Chorale, *Gern will ich folgen* [*Then let us follow Christ*]: 10 mm. echo satb [*divisi*] choir. The second chorale melody [*Mach's mit mir*] was composed by Bartholomaus Gesius (c. 1555–c. 1613) and the text, written by Johann Herman Schein (1586–1630).

> Then let us follow Christ, our Lord,
> and take the cross appointed,
> and firmly clinging to his Word, in suffering
> be undaunted. For those who bear the battle strain
> the crown of heavenly life obtain.

Dies irae I, Er tut grosse Dinge [*He does great things*]: 40 mm. Instrumental ensemble/large satb choir.

> Surely, he does great things which are beyond our knowing.
> He makes some of the people into a great nation, and then,
> his wrath destroys them. He expands another people and then
> he disperses them. The nations fear and tremble before him. All their
> countenances become pale. Before him trembled the earth, the heavens
> shook. Sun and moon were darkened and the starlight could no longer
> be seen. He shook the earth out of its place, and its pillars trembled.
> [Job 9, 10, 12, 23; Joel 2, 6, 18; Job 9, 6]

Choral, *Und ein Buch* [*Lo! The book*]: 14 mm. large satb choir/instrumental ensemble. Third hymn text is based upon a text by Thomas of Celano. The German version of the hymn is better known as *Tag des Zorns, o Tag voll Grauen*.

> Lo! The book, exactly worded, wherein all has been recorded:
> Thence shall judgement be awarded. Low I kneel with heart submission:
> See like ashes, my contrition: Help me in my last condition.

Gospel, *Der Frieden lasse ich euch* [*My peace I leave with you*]: 12 mm. altar satb choir [*divisi*].

> My peace I leave with you, my peace I give unto you.
> Not as the world gives, give I unto you, Let not your
> hearts be troubled, neither let them be afraid.
> [Gospel of John 14:27]

Dies irae II, *Und des Herrn Hand* [*And the Lord's hand*]: 28 mm. instrumental ensemble/large sattbb choir. A march.

> And the Lord's hand was over me and he brought me,
> by the Spirit of the Lord and there in the midst of the valley
> was filled with bones, filled with dry bones.
> And behold, there were very many bones in the valley and the
> bones were very dry. And he said to me: Oh Son of man,
> can you believe, that this field of bones can be brought back
> to life? And I said: All is in your hands.
> [Ezekiel 37:1–3]

Gospel, *Fürchte dich nicht* [*Be not afraid*]: 19 mm. altar ssaattbb choir/organ.

> Be not afraid. I am the first and the last, and he who
> is living still. I was dead, but surely, I am living, from
> eternity to eternity and have the keys of death, the keys of Hades.
> [Revelation 1:17–18]

Chorale, The German "*Dies irae:*" 12 mm. large ssattbb choir/instrumental ensemble. The German text of this chorale is based upon the Latin *Dies irae* and is set to a mid-sixteenth century, German *Lied.*

> The day is surely drawing near when Jesus, God's anointed,
> in all his power shall appear as judge whom God appointed.
> Then fright shall banish idle mirth, and hungry flames shall ravage earth,
> as scripture long has warned us.

Dies irae III, *Der Herr hat seine Hand* [*The Lord has raised His hand*]: 104 mm. large satb [*divisi*] choir/instrumental ensemble. The text, although centuries old, is a direct reference to the Allied bombing of Dresden and its aftermath.

> The Lord has raised his hand against me in his wrath. Terror loosed against me,
> his terrible anger is poured out against me. A fire He kindled, a raging fire He
> kindled, which consumed the city's foundations.
> Lord you have loosed these nations which have trod over us. Smoke went forth
> and an all-consuming fire.
> The earth did tremble and shake. And their corpses lay in the streets and byways
> of the fallen city.
> And I saw a pale horse, and one who rode thereon, whose name was death.
> Then I saw death, and Hades following after him.
> And there followed hail and fire, and the fire with blood was mingled, and which
> fell on the earth.
> And a third part of the trees were burnt and all green grass.

And I saw and heard a bright angel flying in mid-heaven and crying aloud and
saying:
Woe, woe be to you who now on the earth are living.
Now lie in the streets of the city, children and old ones. Each day have you choked
on the bitterness of my wrath.
My spirit you have made desolate, that I daily, sorely must weep.
The towers now have fallen, and the builders grieve with bitterness, for their gates
lie hidden deep in the earth.
All her people groan as they search for bread. They give their dearest treasures
for food.
Ah, why was I born to see this thing, and that I should see the destruction of this
holy place, the crushing of my people. I looked for aid, for help from mankind,
and found nothing.
Then my thoughts turned to you, and I remembered your love,
and how in all things you have been our help.
[Lamentations of Jeremiah 3, 3; 4, 11, 2, 21; 13 8–9; Job 30,15;
Psalm 66, 12; 18, 8–9; Revelation 11, 8; 6, 8; 8, 7, 13;
Maccabees 2, 7; Sirach 51,10–11]

Gospel, *Gott wird abwischen*. [*God will wipe away all tears*]: 25 mm. altar ssaatb choir.

God shall wipe away all tears from their eyes and now
dying shall be no more, neither mourning nor pain, nor
crying shall there be. For the former things have passed away.
See now, I make all things new.
[Revelation 21:4–5]

Chorale, *Du Herberg*.[*You refuge on this journey*]: 11 mm. echo satb choir. The chorale melody comes from the sixteenth century and the text is by C. F. H. Sachse.
The tune is better known as *Wohlauf, wohlan, zum letzen Gang*.

You refuge on this journey long, no more will weep,
your heart be strong.
Lock now the door and peaceful rest;
Why do you mourn? Your guest pursues his joyful quest.

Sanctus: 157 mm., 10 movements. (The first six movements are joined together.)
Prefatio, In der Gewissheit [*In firm conviction*]: 6 mm. large satb choir, unaccompanied.

In firm conviction of God's holy promise through Christ,
we raise our hearts to you, full of joy, and with thanks,
and sing with the choir of the blessed.
[liturgical prayer]

Sanctus, "Heilig, Heilig, Heilig" [*Holy, Holy, Holy*]: 39 mm. large satb choir/satb altar choir/satb echo choir, unaccompanied. The text is a German version of the liturgical *Sanctus.* Style: a conversation among the three choirs.

> Holy, holy, holy is the Lord God of Sabaoth!
> The world is full of thy glory.

Osanna, Hosianna in der Höhe [*Hosanna in the highest*]: 54 mm. three satb choirs, unaccompanied.

> Hosanna in the highest!

Benedictus, Gelobet sei, der da kommt [*Blessed is he*]: 22 mm. large satb choir/smaller satb ensemble/S solo, unaccompanied.

> Blessed is he that comes in the name of the Lord!

Osanna [repeat]: 10 mm. large satb choir/echo satb choir, unaccompanied.
Chorale, *Was für ein Volk* [*What kind of people, this?*]: 14 mm. large satb [*divisi*] choir. The chorale melody and verse was composed by Melchoir Franck in 1633 (*Jerusalem du hochgebaute Stadt*)[*Jerusalem, thou high-built city*].

> What throng is this, what noble troop, that pours, arrayed
> in beauteous guise, out through the city's open doors to greet
> my wondering eyes?
> The host of Christ's elected, the jewels that he bears, in his
> crown selected to wipe away my tears.

Osanna, [repeat]: 8 mm. altar ssaatb choir/echo ssaatb choir, unaccompanied.
Chorale, *Wenn dann zuletzt* [*One more at last*]: 14 mm. altar satb choir. Verse taken from, *Was für ein Volk.*
[see above]

> One more at last arrived they welcome there, to beauteous Paradise;
> where sense can scarce its full fruition bear or tongue for praise suffice:
> Glad hallelujahs ringing with rapturous rebound, and rich hosannas
> singing Eternity's long round.

Prelude-Chorale, *Mit Jubelklang* [*With Jubilee*]: 28 mm. instrumental ensemble/ large unison choir/congregation. The chorale employed is *Was für ein Volk.* [see above].

> Unnumbered choirs before the Lamb's high throne there
> shout the jubilee, with loud resounding peal and sweetest
> tone, in blissful ecstasy: A hundred thousand voices take
> up the wondrous song; Eternity rejoices God's praises to prolong.

Prayer, *Jesu, milder Herrscher*, [*Jesu, gentle Saviour*]: 7 mm. large sa choir/A solo.

> Jesu, gentle Saviour, grant to the dead eternal rest.

Agnus Dei: 157 mm., 5 movements. Chorale, *O du Lamm Gottes* [*O Lamb of God*]: 31 mm. large satb choir/altar satb choir. [both choirs *divisi*] This movement includes three settings of the chorale verse, each one scored for a different unaccompanied vocal combination. The chorale melody is taken from a church songbook of 1545 [*Spangenberg's Kirchengesange*].

> O Lamb of God, you who carries the sins of the world,
> have mercy upon us.
> O Lamb of God, you who carries the sins of the world,
> have mercy upon us.
> O Lamb of God, you who carries the sins of the world,
> grant us your peace.

Closing prayer, *Aus der Tiefe* [*De Profundis*]: 30 mm. large satb choir, unaccompanied/A solo.

> In my deepest need, I cry to you, O Lord.
> O hear my supplication. Let your ears be attentive to the
> voice of my entreaty.
> We pray to you, O Lord, deliver the souls of the departed
> from all their sins, by the hope which is ours through your
> word and through the glorious resurrection of Jesus
> Christ, our Lord. Amen.
> [Psalm 130]

Antiphon, *Gib ihnen die ewige Ruhe* [*Give them eternal peace*]: 36 mm. large satb choir/echo satb choir. The musical and textual material is taken from the opening movement, thereby rounding out the work, thematically and melodically.

> Grant unto them rest everlasting, and may everlasting light shine upon them.
> Grant unto them eternal rest and let light eternal shine upon them. Amen.

Prelude-Chorale, *Seid getrost und hocherfreut.* [*Take comfort and rejoice*]: 22 mm. instrumental ensemble/large satb choir/congregation. The chorale is based upon the melody, *Jesus, meine Zuversicht* [*Jesus, my confidence*], composed in 1653.

> Then take comfort and rejoice, for his members Christ will
> cherish. Fear not, they will hear his voice; dying, they will never
> perish; for the very grave is stirred when the trumpet's blast is heard.

Final chorus, *Lass sie ruhen* [*Let them rest*]: 18 mm. altar satb choir/large ssaattbb choir, unaccompanied.

Let them slumber in peace. Amen.

DISCOGRAPHY

Carus, 83. 116, Dresden Kreutzchor, members of the Dresden Philharmonic, cond. Matthias Jüng.

REQUIEM OF RECONCILIATION

One of the most recent "War" requiems, the *Requiem of Reconciliation* [*Requiem der Versöhnung*], was created by the collaborative effort of fourteen contemporary composers. It is only one of two joint requiems listed in this book; the other one is the Verdi-Rossini Requiem. The work was commissioned by the Internationale Bachakademie Stuttgart for the music festival, Europäisches Musikfest Stuttgart, in 1995. It commemorates the fiftieth anniversary of the end of World War II and is dedicated to memory of its victims. Composers from the countries that greatly suffered from the horrors of the war were chosen to compose the music for one or another section.

The overall work constitutes an anthology, if not encyclopedia, of late-twentieth century compositional techniques and style, much in the same way as the *Messa per Rossini* was for late-nineteenth composition. Apart from a *Prolog*, an *Interludium*, an *Epilog*, and an instrumental *Communio*, the joint work follows the usual liturgical requiem text, although the traditional text is often rearranged. One such example would be the insertion of a portion of the *Libera me* text into the *Kyrie*. Although the *Requiem of Reconciliation* is modern in every sense of the word, movements six, seven, eight, ten, and thirteen employ the ancient Gregorian melodies while the twelfth employs a chant-like melody.

The scoring of the music includes a large SATB [*divisi*] choir that is subdivided in various ways, six vocal soloists (boy treble, two sopranos, alto, tenor, and bass) and a large symphonic orchestra that includes a wide variety of percussion. The orchestra is further supplemented by alto and tenor saxophone, accordion, piano, and electronic organ.

The author would like to be more specific in the description, but the work, which has been published as individual pieces, is very difficult to obtain. (In fact, only one score of the fourteen pieces has been available.) Therefore the description has been made from a careful, listening examination of the work.

Basic Data

EDITION

various publishers [see Outline]
[Rental material from Universal]

DURATION

Fourteen movements, perf., c. 105'

VOICING AND ORCHESTRATION

Choir: SATB [*divisi*]
Soloists: SATBBar.
Instruments: symphonic orchestra & large percussion battery

OUTLINE

Movement 1. *Prologo*, 5'37." Composer: Luciano Berio (b. 24.11.1925), Italy.
Atonal, style. Pitched and unpitched sound employed. Massive sound patches.
satb choir/orchestra. Text: Paul Celano.

Die Posaunenstelle	The trumpet part
tief im gluhenden	deep in the glowing
Leertext	lacuna
in Fackelhohe	at lamp height
im Zeitloch:	in the time hole:
hor dich ein	listen your way in
mit dem Mund.	with your mouth.

Trombone blasts are meant to depict the shofar, a Hebrew ram's horn that is
played on the Jewish High Holidays. The horn is used to symbolically open
hearts and the heavens to attain human reconciliation with God.

The choir sings the text of the Celano poem, but any clear understanding of
the words is not possible because the words are either broken up into separate
syllables, sung in sustained fashion, shouted, shrieked, or spoken. Numerous
vocal glissandi are employed. Colorful percussion effects are numerous and an
accordion can be heard.

The musical texture seems to suggest the cataclysm of World War II,
consequently, a mood of despair and anguish prevails. Score: *"Hor" per coro e
orchestra* (1995), Universal Edition, Vienna.

Movement 2. *Introitus* and *Kyrie*, 9' 16."Composer: Friedrich Cerha (b. 17.2.1926),
Austria.

Scored for satb choir [*divisi*]/orchestra. Employs an atonal harmony that
extends into nontonality (unpitched sound). Frequent instrumental and vocal
glissandi are used. The *Libera me* text is inserted, like a trope, into the *Kyrie* section.
The general mood is one of despair and rage. Score: *Requiem* (*Introitus & Kyrie für
grossen gemischten Chor und Orchester* (1994) Universal Edition, Vienna.

Movement 3. Sequenz: *Dies irae*, 11'02." Composer: Paul Heinz Dittrich (b. 4.12.1930), Germany

Scored for orchestra/satb choir/TS soli. The choir is divided into three groupings [ssssaaaattttbbbb; two separate groups; thirty-two soloists]. The choir executes both pitched and unpitched sound, including whispering, hissing, toneless sound, and glissandi. The soloists sing with definite pitch and tone, sometimes unaccompanied, at other times, with orchestral support. The percussion section is divided into three groups; each group playing about ten various instruments. In addition to the violent percussion effects, the work employs the more delicate sonorities of bells, woodblocks, and vibraphone.

The orchestra employs massive blocks of sound and chamber-like solo lines. In the concluding moments, there are quiet, sustained clusters of string and choral sound. This movement, like the first two, is generally nontonal and its mood, apprehensive. Score: *Dies Irae für Soprano und Tenor Solo, Chor und Orchester*. Deutscher Verlag für Musik, Leipzig.

Movement 4. Sequenz: *Judex ergo*, 7' 53." Composer: Marek Kopelent (b. 28.4.1932), Czech Republic

Scored for large SATB choir/orchestra/Bar. solo. Orchestral introduction for the strings. Gradually woodwinds and trumpets are added. The choir uses trills and, as a sign of fear, whispers the text. The word *Rex* [King], a key word, is used repeatedly by the choir and baritone soloist. The passage, *Quid sum miser* is a dialogue for the baritone soloist and choir. The pitch and rhythm of the baritone solo is precisely notated, although some passages are improvised. The first four movements constitute a group that possesses great similarities in the usage of a musical style employing imprecise sonorities and a mood of fear and apprehension. Score: *Judex ergo . . .* (1955) published by the author, Prague.

Movement 5. *Juste judex*, 5' 48." Composer: John Harbison (b. 20.12.1938), United States

Scored for Bar. MS soli/orchestra. The full orchestral resources are used in smaller, chamber groupings, much like Debussy. This tonal piece has no sonorities created by indeterminate pitch. Stylistically, it is very different from the first four movements. The choir sings only at the conclusion of the piece: a chorale-like *Inter oves*. The mood is quite bright and filled with hope. Score: *Juste judex* from *Requiem of Reconciliation*, Associated Music Publishers, New York.

Movement 6. *Confutatis*, 71 mm., 8'13." Composer: Arne Nordheim (b. 20.6.1931), Norway

Scored for SSAATTBB choir/S solo/orchestra. It is a tonal composition. The Gregorian chant melody is quoted (tenor and bass). At *Flammis acribus*, the strings and woodwinds suggest the flames of Hell. The second half of the work begins at *Oro supplex* with a dialogue between soprano soloist and choir. Closing on a B major chord, the movement ends on a note of hope and redemption. Score: *Requiem der Versöhnung, Confutatis* (1995) *für Solo-Sopran, Chor und grosses Orchester*, Edition Wilhelm Hansen, Copenhagen.

Movement 7. *Interludium*, 11' 36." Composer: Bernard Rands (b. 2.3.1934), England

The tonal *Interludium* is primarily an orchestral work in which the choir functions as one more orchestral voice (as in *Fetes* of Debussy's *Nocturnes*). The choir is assigned a humming part, with the exception of an outburst on the word, *Deus* (God). An instrumental five-bar theme, suggestive of Gregorian melody forms the basis of the melodic content and development of the movement. The harmony, texture, and the melody are suggestive of Impressionist style. Score: *Interludium*. European American Music Corp.

Movement 8. *Offertorium*, 7', 34." Composer: Marc André Dalbavie (b. 10.2.1961), France

Scored for a large orchestra and eight-part male choir. This tonal piece is split into three distinct sections: *Domine Jesu Christe*, the Gregorian melody is sung in unison while some singers sustain the melody as others proceed forward with the tune; *Hostias*, employs massive orchestral chords that include bells. The choir sings the chant in an eight-part canon; *Domine Jesu Christe* is sung in unison and unaccompanied, just as at the beginning. Score: Offertoire pour orchestre symphonique et choeur d'hommes. Gerard Billaudot Editeur, Paris.

Movement 9. *Sanctus*, 6' 37." Composer: Judith Weir (b. 11.5.1954), England

Scored for SMS soli/six-part choir/large orchestra. It is the lightest, most playful movement of the work. The first three choral entries use the Gregorian melody. The remainder of the movement has melodies and rhythmic motives derived from the text. (The word-pairs, *Sanctus Dominus* and *Deus Sabaoth*, each possess five syllables.) A melodic figuration of five notes is derived from the "fiveness," of the text. This figuration is used throughout the first half of the movement. In the last half of the work, the composer adds a five-note motive, that is derived from the string and woodwinds, to the choral parts. The *Benedictus* and *Hosanna* texts are intermingled. Score: *Sanctus*, Chester Music, London.

Movement 10. *Agnus Dei.* 7' 35." Composer: Krzysztof Penderecki (b. 23.11.1933), Poland

This harmonic, neo-romantic setting possesses a mood of sadness and melancholia. Divided into four, continuous sections, it is scored for solo SATB quartet, satb (*divisi*) choir, and orchestra. The Gregorian melody functions as the principal motive throughout the piece. Score: *Agnus Dei*, Musikverlag B. Schotts Söhne, Mainz.

Movement 11. *Communio I.* 4' 49." Composer: Wolfgang Rihm (b.13.3.1952), Germany

The text-less *Communio I* is scored for a unique instrumentation; solo alto, boy soprano, a choir that is variously divided into men's, women's, or mixed voices. Because there is no text in the movement, Rihm employs the choir and soloists as an orchestral voice (vowels or humming). Complementing the choir are four percussion groups, two solo violins, solo double bass, six tutti basses, harp, and timpani. At the very end of the movement, a brass ensemble is added. The moods of this piece range from terror and fear to prayer and serenity. *Communio I* is a tonal work that uses nontonal, indefinte pitched effects, much like the remaining three movements. Score: *Communio (Lux aeterna) für Soli, grossen gemischten Chor und Orchester* (1994), Universal Edition, Vienna.

Movement 12. *Communio II*, 5' 17." Composer: Alfred Schnittke (b. 24.11.1934), Russia

During the composition of the Communion section, Schnittke suffered a stroke, however, the choral parts had been extensively sketched out. Gennady Roschdestwenski, conductor of the Moscow State Symphony Orchestra and the Royal Stockholm Philharmonic Orchestra, orchestrated the movement, with Schnittke's consent and cooperation.

This impressive work is scored for SATB choir, violin I/II, viola, cello (eight each), three double basses, several woodwind instruments, and four French horns. The choral writing, reminiscent of Gregorian chant, is always done in canon and unaccompanied. The four choral sections are separated by quiet horn interludes. An instrumental postlude concludes the movement. Score: *Lux aeterna für gemischten Chor und Orchester*, Musikverlag Hans Sikorski, Hamburg.

Movement 13. *Responsorium*, 12' 26." Joji Yuasa (b. 12.8.1929), Japan

The *Libera me* is scored for SATB solo quartet, choir, and orchestra. The music is developed out of the Gregorian theme. A violent orchestral introduction opens the work. *Libera me* is scored for solo and orchestra; at *Quando coeli*, the choir and strings dominate; *Dies irae*, for soloists and choir is quite violent; *Requiem aeternam* is then sung quietly by the choir; *Libera me* is reintroduced and is sung by each soloist, followed by the choir. The movement ends on a C major chord as all of the nonharmonic tones are slowly cleared away. Score: *Responsorium*. Zen-On Music, Tokyo.

Movement 14. *Epilog*, 3' 15." György Kurtag (b. 19.2.1926), Romania

The opening of the movement uses, as its text, an inscription found on a grave in Cornwall, England. The text is scored for unaccompanied choir.

> We have a building of God
> An house not made with hands
> Eternal in the heavens
> Where the spirit of the Lord is
> There is liberty
> [anon.]

A second section, a kind of orchestral postlude, consists only of chords, two of which are played *fortissimo*; the remainder, *ppppp*. To the regular *instrumentarium*, Kurtag adds tenor recorder and bass traverse flute. The choir then whispers *Ite missa est*, (The mass is over.) concluding the *Requiem of Reconciliation*. Score: *Inscription on a grave in Cornwall*, op. 34, Editio Musica, Budapest.

DISCOGRAPHY

Hanssler Classic, 98.931, Gächinger Kantorei and Krakauer Kammerchor with the Israel Philharmonic Orchestra, cond. Helmuth Rilling.

MAX REGER
March 19, 1873–May 11, 1916

Max Reger received organ instruction from his father and Hugo Riemann. He became organist of the cathedral church in Weiden. Eventually, his talent was recognized by the organ virtuoso, Karl Straube, who became a lifelong friend and champion of Reger's music. Reger held several important positions at the Leipzig Conservatory; as Director (1907–08) and as composition teacher from 1907 until his death. He left a large musical output that includes virtuoso organ music, solo works for string instruments (violin, viola, and cello), many piano pieces, orchestral pieces, chamber works, two concertos (violin and piano), and choral music. His choral music includes motets for voices and orchestra, four choral cantatas, a setting of Psalm 100, and an unfinished requiem.

Reger's compositional style was grounded in the techniques used by eighteenth-century baroque and classic masters, as well as in the polyphonic vocal style of the Renaissance. Like Brahms, he cultivated absolute music forms, such as the concerto, prelude and fugue, quartet, and thematic variations. At the same time, his harmonic language is characteristic of the chromatic, late romantic style. His music is a link between postromantic and contemporary style.

The *Latin Requiem*, Op. 145a was started toward the end of Reger's life, during the First World War. Except for the Introit and *Kyrie*, the work was never fully completed. What exists is scored for SATB choir, SATB soli, and orchestra. A sizeable section of the *Dies irae* exists, yet, it remains incomplete. The choral texture is a mixture of homophonic and polyphonic writing.

The music of the first movement is based upon the music of an earlier work: the so-called *Hebbel Requiem*, op. 144b, a work written in memory of the soldiers who were dying in the "Great War." The text of Op. 144b is taken from Friedrich Hebbel's (1813–1863) poem, *"Requiem."*

REQUIEM

Seele, vergiss sie nicht die Toten,	Forget not, O soul, the dead.
Vergiss sie nicht.	Forget them not.
Sieh, sie umschweben dich,	Look, they float round thee,
schauernd, verlassen.	shivering and forlorn.

und in die heiligen Gluten die den Armen	And in the holy glow which
die Liebe schürt	stirs up love for the poor [ones]
atmen sie auf und erwarmen und	they breathe and warm up,
geniessen zum letzen Mal	as they enjoy their fading life
ihr verglimmendes Leben.	for the last time.
Seele, vergiss sie nicht die Toten,	Forget not, O soul, the dead.
vergiss sie nicht.	Forget them not.
Sieh, sie umschweben dich,	Look, they float round thee,
schauernd, verlassen.	shivering and forlorn.
und wenn du dich erhaltend	and if you, yourself, grow cool
ihnen verschliessest,	they, too, will wear out,
erstarren sie bis hinein in das Tiefste.	benumbed to their utmost depths.
Dann ergreift sie der Sturm der Nacht,	Then they are seized by the Storm of the Night,
dem sie zusammengekrampft	those who are gathered together,
in sich trotzten in Schosse der Liebe,	In the bosom of love, in defiance.
und er jagt sie mit Ungestüm,	Furiously it hunts them down
durch die unendliche Wüste hin,	through the endless desolation
wo nicht Leben ist,	where life no longer is,
nur Kampf losgelassener Kräfte	merely the struggle of released strength
um erneuertes Sein.	striving for renewed Being.
Seele, vergiss sie nicht,	Forget not, O soul,
Seele vergiss nicht die Toten.	Forget not the dead, O soul.
	translation, RAC

Reger reworked the musical material that accompanied Hebbel's poem, using it for the Introit of his *Latin Requiem*, op. 145a. The main mood of the requiem is one of overwhelming grief. The musical orchestration is massive and summons up the sonorities of a colossal requiem procession. The continuous roll of the timpani and the throbbing quarter-note pulse of the string basses highlight the march-like rhythm. This sonorous image is so impressive that it remains in the mind's eye long after the sound has faded. Another spectacular aural image is created by *divisi* upper strings that accompany *Christe*. Strings and choral lines are often scored *divisi*, up to three parts, thereby thickening the musical texture. A very large chorus is needed to perform this music in a manner suitable to the composer's vision.

The first performance of the solitary movement did not take place until 1938 in Berlin.

Basic Data

EDITION
Max Reger
Sämtliche Werke

Band 28
Werke für Soli, Chor und Orchester
Revidiert [re-edited] by Ulrich Haverkampf
Breitkopf & Härtel, Wiesbaden. 1966

DURATION

One completed movement, 267 mm., perf., c. 23'

VOICING AND ORCHESTRATION

Choir: SATB [each part *divisi* 2 & 3]. range: S-A6; B-D3
Soloists: SATB
Orchestra: vn. I/II, vla., vc., db. (*divisi*), pic., 2 fl., 2 ob., Eh., 2 cl., 2 bsn, cbsn., 4
   Fh., 3 tpt., 3 tbn. tuba. 3 timp., org. PERC: percussion battery, bass drum, tam-
   tam, cymbals.

OUTLINE

Introit: 267 mm.
   Requiem aeternam [dm-AM] *molto sostenuto.* satb choir/SATB soli; *Et lux*, S solo/
   SATB soli/satb half-choir-full choir; *Te decet, piu andante.* satb choir/SATB soli;
   Requiem aeternam, satb choir/SATB soli; *Kyrie, allegro.* satb choir/SATB soli.

DISCOGRAPHY

Koch Schwann, CD 313 004 H1, Symphony Orchestra and Choir of the North German Radio, cond. Roland Bader.

HENRI TOMASI
July 17, 1901–January 13, 1971

Tomasi studied at the Paris Conservatoire in 1920 with Paul Vidal. He
won the Prix de Rome (1927) and the *Grand Prix de la Musique Francaise*
(1952). He established his reputation through his stage works and his outstanding work as conductor of L'Orchestre National. In 1938, he decided
to "retire from the world" and entered into a novitiate at the Monastery
of Ste. Baume. However, the horrors of World War II severely eroded his
Christian faith. In 1952, Tomasi had a serious accident that led to deaf-
ness, which remained during the last decade of his life.
   Among his works are concerti for trumpet, saxophone, guitar, flute,
viola, violin, and harp, several symphonic poems, a number of stage
works, and several sacred works, the most significant of which is the
Requiem pour la Paix, composed in 1945. Scored for SATB soli, SATB choir,
and orchestra, it bears the dedication: *à tous les Martyrs de la Resistance et
à tous ceux qui sont morts pour la France* (to all the martyrs of the Resistance

and all those who died for France). This work highlights the relationship between heroism and eternal peace. The premiere took place on April 11, 1946. After the *Requiem* was completed, Tomasi lost all interest in the work.

Its tonal musical language is rooted in impressionism, jazz, and modality, and its *melos* bears the imprint of Gregorian chant. The predominant four-part choral texture frequently reduced to unison, two, and three-part writing. There are numerous passages of parallel chordal writing (*Ingemisco*, *Lacrymosa*, *Pie Jesu*, *Sanctus*, and *Agnus Dei*). The SATBar soloists play an exceptionally important role in the *Requiem pour la Paix* and occasionally occupy an entire movement. Imitative polyphony is employed only in the Sanctus (*Hosanna* and *Benedictus*).

Tomasi's colorful orchestration flows from the tradition of Ravel. This concert-version, liturgical requiem remains a masterful and moving work.

Basic Data

EDITION

Henri Tomasi
Requiem
[full score]
Editions Henri Lemoine [rental only]

DURATION

Ten movements, 576 mm., perf., c. 62'

VOICING AND ORCHESTRATION

Choir: SATB [*divisi*] range: S-A6; B-G3
Soloists: SATB
Orchestra: solo vn. I, vn.I/II, vla., vc., db., fl., ob., cl., bsn., Fh., tpt., tbn., tuba.
  PERC: timp., cymbals, bass drum, snare drum, tam-tam. 2 harps. celesta.

OUTLINE

Introit-Kyrie: 56 mm.
  Requiem aeternam, satb choir; *Kyrie*, satb choir/ABar soli.
Tract: 27 mm.
  Absolve me, Bar. solo/solo violin.
Sequence: 125 mm., 3 movements.
  Dies irae: 70 mm., *Dies irae*, choral unison; *Quantus tremor*, tb choir; *Tuba mirum*, satb choir; *Mors stupebit*, T solo; *Liber scriptus-Judex ergo*, satb choir; *Quid sum miser*, A solo/violin solo; *Rex tremendae*, satb choir.
  Recordare: 28 mm., *Recordare-Quaerens me-Juste judex*, S solo/harps.
  Ingemisco: 48 mm., *Ingemisco-Qui Mariam-Preces meae-Inter oves*, Bar. solo/saa choir; *Oro supplex*, A solo; *Lacrymosa*, sssatttb choir; *Huic ergo*, unison alto choir; *Pie Jesu*, saa choir.

Offertory: 66 mm.

Domine Jesu Christe, T solo; *Libera eas*, satb choir; *Hostias*, unison alto choir; *Quam olim Abrahae*, satb choir.

Sanctus: 133 mm.

Sanctus, satb choir; *Hosanna*, satb choir (fugal); *Benedictus*, satb choir (imitative); *Hosanna*, satb choir (fugal).

Agnus Dei: 26 mm.

Agnus Dei, S solo/satb choir (responsorial structure); instrumental postlude, trumpet solo/snare drum/string tremolo.

Communion: 27 mm.

Lux aeterna, T solo/strings/harp/celesta/violin solo.

Responsory: 95 mm.

Libera me, Bar. solo; *Libera me*, satb choir (fugal); *Quand coeli*, T solo; *Dies illa*, satb unison choir/brass/timpani; *Requiem aeternam*, satb choir; *Libera me*, A solo/violin solo.

DISCOGRAPHY

Naxos 8.554223 Choeur Régional Provence Alpes-Côte d'Azur and Orchestre Philharmonique de Marseille, dir. Michel Piquemal.

ERIC ZEISL
May 18, 1905–February 18, 1959

Austrian-born composer, Eric Zeisl, was a graduate of the Vienna State Academy of Music. A winner of the Austrian State Prize for his *Requiem Concertante* (1933–34), Zeisl abandoned a promising career in his homeland when Austria was annexed to Germany in 1938. He moved to Los Angeles, where he was appointed to a professorship of theory and composition at City College.

Requiem Ebraico (Hebrew Requiem) was composed in 1944–1945. It is a one-movement composition, scored for SAB soli, SATB choir, and organ (or orchestra) and divided into five large, continuous sections. *Requiem Ebraico* is dedicated to the memory of Zeisl's father, who was murdered in Treblinka concentration camp, and all the others who suffered at the hands of the Nazis.

His musical language is influenced by late romantic harmony. Melodic gifts and the ability to create dramatic expression are key elements in his technique. The harmonic vocabulary employs modal scales and melodic figures associated with Hebrew folk music and short melodic motives are used to develop his ideas throughout the work. The prevailing choral style is polyphonic and the composition is capped-off with a vigorous, four-part fugue in its fifth movement, *To show that the Lord is upright*.

Zeisl's orchestrations are rich, sensual, and illuminate the text properly.

This stunning work is passionate; its musical poetry designed to comfort and console. The piece is properly a Mourner's Kaddish, a prayer in which the Lord is glorified and sanctified. The text used is Psalm 92.

Basic Data

EDITION

Requiem Ebraico: The 92nd Psalm for soli, mixed chorus and organ (or orchestra) Transcontinental Music Corporation, New York
TCL No. 266 1955 [Both Hebrew (transliterated) and English texts are included]

DURATION

One movement divided into five principal sections, 409 mm., perf., c. 18'

VOICING AND ORCHESTRATION

Choir: SATB range: S-B flat 6; B-F♯ 3
Soloists: SABar
Orchestra: vn. I/II, vla., vc., db., 2 fl., 2 ob., Eh., 2 cl., 2 bsn., Fh., tpt., tbn., tuba, org., harp. PERC: timp., bass drum, snare drum, xylophone, cymbals, chimes.

OUTLINE

Section I. *Tov l'hodos ladanoy*: mm. 1–68
How good to give thanks. grave moderato. A solo/satb choir/orchestra. (canonic writing) Orchestral postlude.

[Choir]
How good to give thanks unto the Lord and sing praise to thy name,
God supreme.
To show forth thy truth in the morning and thy faithfulness every night.
How good to give thanks unto the Lord.
[Alto solo]
I play on my strings on the psaltery, with solemn sound on the harp.
[Choir]
For thou, O Lord, hast made me glad through thy work;
I will exult in the works of thy hands and I shall triumph.

Section II. *Mah godlu massecho, Adonoy*: mm. 69–132
How great are thy works, Lord, *lento*. Bar solo/satb choir. Elaborate, cantorial passages for the baritone.

[Baritone]
Oh how great are thy works, my God, very deep are thy thoughts.
A brutish man knows not, neither doth a fool understand.

Whenever the wicked spring up like grass and when all the workers
of iniquity flourish, they shall be destroyed forever.
[Choir]
But thou, O Lord, art on high for evermore.

Section III. *Ki kineh oyvecho, Adonoy:* mm. 133–149
Lo, thine enemies, Lord. freely psalmodising. Bar solo/strings.

[Baritone]
Lo, thine enemies, O Lord my God, they shall be dispersed and perish;
but thou wilt exalt my horn, I shall be anointed with fresh oil.
For mine eyes have seen my desire on mine enemies and mine ears
have heard of the wicked who rise up against me.

Section IV. *Tzadik katomor:* mm. 150–246
Like the palm tree, andante. SA duet/orchestra.

[soprano & alto soloists]
Like the palm tree the righteous shall bloom and grow like a cedar in Lebanon.
They are planted in the house of God, they shall flourish in the courts of our Lord.
They shall bring forth fruit in old age and shall be full of richness and sap.

Section V. *L'hagid ki yoshor Adonoy:* mm. 246–409.
To show that the Lord is upright, allegro. satb choir/Bar solo (fugue).

[choir & baritone solo]
To show that the Lord is upright,
He is my rock.
There is no unrighteousness in Him.

DISCOGRAPHY

London, 289 460 211-2, Berlin Rundfunk Sinfonieorchester and Chor, dir. Lawrence Foster.

9

Dies Irae

The sequence, *Dies Irae,* is a Latin poem that has been commonly ascribed to the Franciscan monk, Thomas of Celano (d. c. 1250), but because of the discovery of an earlier twelfth-century version of the poem, his authorship has been opened to question. Furthermore, a part of the text, *Lacrimosa, dies illa,* predates the thirteenth century. It is possible that Thomas of Celano reworked an earlier version of the poem at some point in his life.

The text is divided into nineteen verses, each one possessing three lines of eight syllables, with the exception of the eighteenth verse, which has four octosyllabic lines, and the nineteenth verse, which has two lines of seven syllables. The opening lines of the text seem to be a gloss (commentary) from the prophet Sophonias (Zephaniah) 1:14–16.

The author of the poem clearly drew upon the medieval *Sibyll* tradition. (The *Sibylline Oracles* extend back to the second century before the death of Christ.) In this poem, the Sibyl, a prophetess, is associated with King David, *Teste David cum Sybilla.*

The *Dies irae* text bears similarities with other ancient texts; for example, the Hebrew chant, *Une thane tokef,* a piece that is sung during the festival of Yom Kippur (Day of Repentance) and the seventh century Christian Advent hymn, *Apparebit repentina dies magna Domini* ("There will appear days of repentance on the great day of the Lord").

The author of the melody of *Dies irae,* as well as the exact time of its composition remain unknown. It has been suggested that it is from the time period (if not the pen) of Adam *Praecentor* (cantor) of Notre Dame (an individual formerly known as "Adam of St. Victor"). Adam *Praecentor* died sometime around 1146, and was a well-known writer of *prosae* (sequences).

The melody is divided into six principal melodic lines, of which the first three are further sub-divided into three phrases. (Verses 1–2, 7–8, and 13–14, employ the first melodic line; Verses 3–4, 9–10, and 15–16, the second melody and Verses 5–6, 11–12, and 17, the third melody. The last three verses, 18–20, employ the remaining three melodies). It is the initial phrase of the first melody that has become so well-known because it has been quoted or paraphrased by many later composers. (see Appendix A, example 1).

An interesting arrangement of the *Dies irae* was made by Louis Homet (1700–1777). In this version, the odd-numbered verses are sung in chant while the even-numbered verses employ four-part, chordal harmony. This version was used for several centuries in French parishes. (see Appendix A, example 2).

By the end of the Council of Trent (1563), all but four sequence hymns had been abolished from use in the liturgy, although a fifth sequence, *Stabat Mater*, was later added to the liturgy in 1727. Unlike many of the Gregorian chant texts that possessed multiple musical versions, the *Dies irae* appears to have had only one melody. Yet, there must have existed other alternate melodies. One of those other melodies, rarely used and little-known, comes from Spain. This tune is found in a collection of various chant melodies, *Arte de canto llano* (1610 and 1616) of Francisco de Montano. In this melodic version, virtually every line has its own melody, but with much repetition of melodic phrases. (see Appendix A, example 3).

The *Dies irae* was first introduced into the Roman funeral liturgy during the fourteenth century, but not into the French liturgy until the fifteenth century. It was formally incorporated into the Roman Missal in 1585 by Pope Paul VI and was initially sung in Gregorian chant. The adventuresome Antoine Brumel earlier published the first-known polyphonic setting of the text in 1516. After its incorporation into the Missal, it was not long before other composers began to set the text in polyphony. Almost 500 years later, in an attempt to soften the "hard" message of the *Dies irae*, the Second Vatican Council virtually dropped the text from the liturgy. The commonly used *Order of Christian Funerals* does not include the Sequence, though the Gregorian tune and another newer melody and harmonization by H. Stanley Taylor (b. 1905) are included in the hymnbook, *The Adoremus Hymnal* (Ignatius Press, San Francisco, 1997).

Today, it is rarely sung, though it is still used in Paris and other places.

Numerous settings of the *Dies irae* have already been discussed and outlined in other chapters of this book, yet there is a group of independent compositions, that first appeared in France during the early baroque era, which are devoted exclusively to this poem. These works are not connected to any of the other usual musical pieces associated with the funeral Mass. The reason for this development probably rests in the fact that the

small and large motet forms (*petit* motet and *grand* motet) were more popular at the French court than the traditional requiem and ordinary mass
settings. The earliest group of composers to recognize the musico-dra-
matic possibilities of the *Dies irae* text were the leading luminaries of the
French baroque, Jean Baptiste Lully, Marc Antoine Charpentier, and
Michel-Richard De Lalande. Yet once these composers of independent
Dies irae settings had made their innovative contributions, interest in the
form grew and expanded. The Italians, Giovanni Legrenzi and Antonio
Lotti, made superb arrangements of the text, set in the form of vocal
suites.

Others who wrote independent choral settings of the *Dies irae* include:
Arnold von Bruck (1500?–1554, 4 vv), Antonio Calegari (1757–1828, 3 settings, 3–4 vv, 4 vv), Angelo DiAngeles (d.1825, 4 vv), Victor Dourlen
(1780–1864, 4 vv), Francesco Feo (1691–1791, 2 settings, 4 vv, 5 vv), Luis
Gargallo (c. 1620–82, 2 settings, 4 vv, 8 vv), Johann Christoph Gayer
(1668–1734, 2 choirs), Juan Padilla (1590–1664, 8 vv), and Francesco Vallotti (1692–1780, 3 settings, 2 vv, 4 vv, 5vv). Settings with instruments
include those of Francois Benoist (1794–1878, satb soli, choir, and orch.),
Nicolas Bergiron (1690–1768, grand motet), Ferdenando Bertoni (1725–
1813, satb choir, orch., and b.c.), Ermenegildo Cinque (1690s?–1770, 4 vv
and instruments), Odon Farkas (1851–1912, choir and orchestra), Valentin
Fioravanti (1770–1837, 8 vv and orch.), Bonaventure Furlanetto (1738–
1817, 3–4 vv and orch.), Giovanni Gaiano (1559–1818, 4 vv and orch.),
Fayer-Garcia (1731–1809, 8 vv and orch.), Janos Kajoni (1629–1687, female
vv and organ), Andrea Lucchesi (1741–1801, 4 vv and orch.) Giacomo
Perti (1661–1756, tb vv and strings), Emil Reznicek (1860–1945, 4 vv and
orch.), Federic Ricci (1809–1877, 4 vv and orch.), Francesco Ricci (1732–
1817, 4 vv and orch.), and Anton Schmid (1772, 4 vv and brass). Settings
without scoring indicated include, Jose Arzac (nineteenth-century Uruguay), Alphonse Eve (1666–1727), Giuseppe Ferrata (1865–1928), Charles
Lebelle (1849–1902/3), Honore Langle (1741–1807), Charles Latrobe
(1758–1836), Wenceslas Pichl (1741–1804, Solemn Dies Irae), Nicolo Vaccai (1790–1848), and Charles Weisflog (1780–1828).

During the romantic era, Hector Berlioz, Antonin Dvorak, Giuseppe
Verdi, Alfred Bruneau, and Giuseppe Sgambati created the most picturesque and dramatic settings of the text in the history of the piece. Sgambati, a friend and pupil of Liszt, even quoted the original Gregorian theme
in the *Dies irae* movement in his setting of the requiem (1895). Bruneau
also quoted the theme in his requiem of 1895. Although this was commonly done in the earliest settings of the text, it was not often done by
composers of the romantic era; however, the tune appears in a number of
symphonic works of the era.

Berlioz included the famous *Dies irae* melody in the fifth movement of his programmatic symphony, *Symphonie Fantastique* (1830). Introduced by the sound of bells, the theme is hammered out by the bassoons and tubas in a series of grotesque-sounding notes, while, at the same time, the pizzicato strings, clarinet, and piccolo play a burlesque dance version of the same tune.

Liszt was similarly interested in the tune, for it appears in his half-symphonic poem-half piano concerto, *Totentanz* (1849). This work contains a series of variations on the *Dies irae* theme. Other composers who employed the melody were Camille Saint-Saëns in his *Danse Macabre* (1874) and Sergei Rachmaninoff in his tone-poem *Isle of the Dead* (1909) and the famous, oft-played *Rhapsody on a Theme of Paganini* (1934). (Here, the *Dies irae* theme appears in the seventh and tenth variation, as well as the coda. Rachmaninoff appears to have had a fascination with the melody for it appears in several other of his works, *The Symphonic Dances for Orchestra*, Op. 45 (1940) and the *Etudes Tableaux*, opus 39 (#6), for solo piano (1916).

During the twentieth century, the *Dies irae* melody continued to be of interest to a number of composers. The well-known composer of French *melodies*, Reynaldo Hahn, quoted the theme in the piano accompaniment of his song, *Trois jours de vendage* (Three days of vintaging) Even Debussy, constantly alludes to the incipit of famous Gregorian theme in *Nuages* (Clouds) from his *Trois Nocturnes pour Orchestre*. Arthur Honegger employed the Gregorian melody in his oratorio, *La Danse des Morts* (Dance of the Dead) (1938). Aram Khatchaturian used the melody in the third movement (*Funeral March*) of his *Second Symphony* (1942) and Ildebrando Pizzetti quoted most of the *Dies irae* melody in his unaccompanied choral setting of the *Requiem* (1922) as well as his opera *Assassini Nella Catedrale* (*Murder in the Cathedral*) (1958). Dimitry Kabalevsky employs the melody as background music (unaccompanied choir) during scene 1, Act II of his opera, *Colas Breugnon or The Master of Clamecy* (1937). Igor Stravinsky used the sequence poetry for his *Requiem Canticles* and Arvo Pärt inserted eight verses of the *Dies Irae* into his setting of the *Miserere*, and composed an independent setting of the *Dies irae*.

Penderecki wrote an oratorio, *Dies Irae*, in memory of the victims of Fascism in the notorious death-camp Auschwitz-Birkenau. Neither the melody nor the text of the original sequence are cited in this work, rather the composer created an original music to depict the hellish-nightmare conditions of the Nazi concentration camp. The American, George Crumb, quoted fragments of the *Dies irae* melody in a work inspired by the tragic events of the Vietnam War; *Black Angels: Thirteen Images from the Dark Land*, for electric string quartet (1970). In the fifth movement, *Danse Macabre*, the chant tune can be found in the violin part. The contemporary

Ukrainian composer, Valentin Bibik, composed an extraordinary set of variations for piano, titled, *Dies irae: 39 Variations for piano*. Op. 96 (1993).

A number of other twentieth-century composers, including Miaskovsy, Resphigi, Stevenson, Vaughan-Williams, Dallipiccola, and Bantock, have worked with the Gregorian melody and it has been quoted in a number of twentieth-century requiems: Pizzetti (1922), Calmel (1979), Gagneux (1982), and Guido Guerrini (1943).

During the same period also appeared a number of character pieces for organ that incorporate the Gregorian melody. Some of these pieces are *Dies Irae* (Charles Villiers Stanford), *Fantasie on "Dies Irae"* (Francis Snow, 1890–1961) and *Dorian Prelude on "Dies Irae"* (Bruce Simonds, 1895–1989).

STEFFANO BERNARDI
c. 1585–1636

Bernardi wrote a substantial amount of church music, including mass settings and one known requiem. There exists a separate *Dies Irae* setting for eight voices and was probably composed in the first decades of the seventeenth century. In all likelihood it was part of a larger, more complete requiem setting.

It is written in the style of the Venetian polychoral tradition and scored for two unaccompanied SATB choirs. Much of the text is presented in antiphonal fashion, with occasional massive climaxes employing both ensembles. This setting is divided into five sections and the prevailing texture is homophonic. This exciting work deserves to be performed more often.

Basic Data

EDITION
Denkmäler der Tonkunst in Öesterreich
Vol. XXXIII 1
Steffano Bernardi
Kirchenwerke
ed. Karl August Rosenthal
Universal Edition
1929 Wien [clefs: C (soprano, alto, tenor) & F]

DURATION
One movement, 131 mm., five sections.

VOICING
Choir: double SATB choirs. range: S-E6; B-F3

OUTLINE
Dies irae: 54 mm., satb choirs I/II.
Juste judex: 14 mm. satb choir I. (imitative polyphony)

Ingemisco: 10 mm. satb choirs I/II.
Qui Mariam: 15 mm. satb choir II. (imitative polyphony)
Preces meae: 38 mm. satb choirs I/II.

DISCOGRAPHY

None found.

MARC ANTOINE CHARPENTIER
1645/50–February 24, 1704

Charpentier's setting of *Prose des Morts: Dies Irae* is scored for SSATB soli, SATB choirs I/II, and orchestra. Located in a collection of manuscripts (*Mélanges*, Volume I, along with the *Messe des trépasses*), it was probably composed when Charpentier was in his twenties.

This dramatic work was conceived as a *grand motet* and divided into six movements. In the tradition of the Venetian polychoral writing style, Charpentier employed double SATB choirs in a dialogue convention and frequently used the soloists as a concerto third choir. The predominant choral and instrumental texture is imitative polyphony, with numerous passages of canonic writing. The orchestra is also scored in concerto style.

Basic Data

EDITION

Marc Antoine Charpentier
Miserere des Jesuites, Dies Irae pour soli, choeur et orchestre.
Edités par Roger Blanchard
Editions du Centre Nationale de la Recherche Scientifique
15, Quai Anatole-France, Paris. 1984

DURATION

Six movements, 640 mm., perf., c. 20'

VOICING & ORCHESTRATION

Choir: SATB choirs I/II. range: S-A flat 6; B-F 3
Soloists: SSATB
Orchestra: double string orchestra; vn. I/II, vla., vc., org.

OUTLINE

Dies irae: 76 mm. [cm] ATB soli trio/b.c. (fugal). Gregorian melody: *Quantus tremor*, satb choirs I/II/orch.
Tuba mirum: 37 mm. [CM] SI/II soli duet-BI/I soli duet/strings/b.c. (canon).
Mors stupebit: 71 mm. [cm] satb choirs I/II/double orch.; *Cum resurget* (canonic).

Liber scriptus: 113 mm. [cm] ATB solos/orch. (instrumental ritornelli); (includes: *Judex ergo-Quid sum miser-Rex tremendae*); *Recordare*; ATB trio/b.c. (canon); *Quaerens me*, satb choirs I/II/b.c. (canonic); *Tantus labor*, SSA solo trio/satb choirs I/II/b.c. (canon)

Juste judex: 162 mm. [cm] *Juste judex-Ingemisco-Qui mariam*, S solo/solo string trio; *Preces meae*, SS soli/b.c. (canon); *Inter oves*, A solo/satb choirs I/II; *Confutatis*, satb choirs I/II/double orch. (canonic).

Oro supplex: 181 mm. *Oro supplex*, T solo/string trio/b.c.; *Oro supplex*, TS duet/strings (canon); *Lacrymosa*, B solo/string trio; *Huic ergo*, ATB solo trio/string trio; *Pie Jesu*, satb choirs I/II/double string orch. (Canon).

DISCOGRAPHY

Erato, 4509-97238-2, Choeur Symphonique et Orchestre de la Fondation Gulbenkian de Lisbonne, cond. Michel Corboz.

MICHEL RICHARD DE LALANDE
December 15, 1657–June 18, 1726

De Lalande began his musical education as a choirboy at St. Germain l'Auxerrois and taught himself to play organ, harpsichord, violin, and bass viol. In 1683, he was appointed to the position of Director of the Royal Chapel during the reign of Louis XIV. Although he composed nineteen stage works, today he is remembered chiefly as a composer of sacred music, nearly all of which are *grand* motets for chorus, soloists, and orchestra. There are seventy-eight known motets, of which seven are lost. Most of them are made up of separate, independent movements; a series of vocal solos and choral ensembles. The *grand* motet, *Dies Irae*, is not an exception to this general rule. De Lalande was a gifted melodist and possessed a keen sense of expressive harmony.

The *Prose pour la Messe des Morts: Dies irae* was initially composed for the death of the dauphine (the king's eldest daughter), Princess Marie-Anne-Christine-Victoire de Baviére, who died on May 1, 1690. De Lalande revised the work in 1711, possibly for the death of the dauphin (the king's eldest son) or either of his own two daughters, all of whom died within a six-week period. This elegant work is scored for six soloists, six-part choir, flutes, and strings, arranged in twelve movements.

Typical of the French baroque is the presence of elaborate ornamentation in the vocal and instrumental parts. The choral texture is a mixture of homophonic writing and imitative polyphony (*Tuba mirum*, *Ingemisco*, *Lacrimosa*, and *Pie Jesu*). The seventh movement, *Quaerens me*, is arranged as a canon and sixth and ninth movements (*Recordare* and *Inter oves*) employ the concerto principle between the soloists and choir. It is a work of stunning beauty, drama, and genuine spirituality.

Basic Data

EDITION

A modern, but as yet unpublished, edition was prepared by Lionel Sawkins (London) in 1989. (The writer received a copy of this edition, courtesy of Baronet Sawkins.)

DURATION

Twelve movements, 714 mm., perf., c. 28'

VOICING AND ORCHESTRATION

Choir: SATBarB range: S–A flat 6 ; B–G3
Soloists: SATBarB
Orchestra: vn. I/II, vla., vc., db., viole da gamba, 2 fl., org., therobo.

OUTLINE

Dies irae: 40 mm. [cm] *adagio*. unison choral sopranos/strings. (Gregorian melody) Brief orchestral sinfonia.
Quantus tremor: 32 mm. [fm-gm] *gravement*. satbarb choir/strings.
Tuba mirum: 68 mm. [fm] *allegro*. Bar. solo/strings. Brief orchestral sinfonia.
Mors stupebit: 33 mm. [fm-cm] *adagio*. satbarb choir/strings.
Liber scriptus: 64 mm. *adagio*. A solo (recitative)/b.c.; *Rex tremendae, affectusement*. A solo/b.c.; *Quid sum miser*, A solo (aria)/strings; *Rex tremendae*, A solo (recitative)/flutes/b.c.
Recordare: 55 mm. [cm] *andantino*. ATB-SSB solo trios/satbarb choir/[strings.sb]
Quaerens me: 74 mm. [gm-cm] *andante*. SS soli/b.c. (canon). This duet was composed for the famous castrati, Antonio Bagniera and Antonio Favalli.
Juste judex: 76 mm. *adagio*. Bar. solo/flutes/two violins/b.c. (recitative, solo) [vv. 11–14]
Inter oves: 88 mm. [CM] multiple rhythms. *adagio*. SSA solo trio/ssatbarb choir/strings [vv. 15–16]
Oro supplex: 34 mm. [am] *adagio*. S solo/strings. Brief instrumental sinfonia.
Lacrimosa: 64 mm. [cm] *adagio*. ATB solo trio/b.c. Brief instrumental sinfonia.
Pie Jesu: 80 mm. [cm] *adagio*. satbarb choir/strings. Brief instrumental sinfonia. (Gregorian melody)

DISCOGRAPHY

Harmonia Mundi, 901352, La Chapelle Royale, dir. Philippe Herreweghe.

GIOVANNI LEGRENZI
August 12, 1626–May 27, 1690

Legrenzi worked as assistant conductor (1681) and as *maestro* (1685) at San Marco, Venice, along with Antonio Sartorio (c. 1620–1681). Evidently,

Johann Sebastian Bach held Legrenzi's music in some esteem because he composed a *Fugue in C Minor* (BWV 574) based upon a theme of the latter man. Legrenzi composed nineteen stage works, seven oratorios, a number of instrumental pieces, secular vocal music, and sacred choral pieces. Among the liturgical works are mass settings, psalms, motets, and a setting of the *Dies irae*.

Legrenzi's setting of the *Dies irae* is a suite of eighteen short cameo pieces for two SATB choirs, SSAATB soloists, strings, and organ. The date of composition remains unknown, but Legrenzi performed his own setting of the requiem for Carlo Pallavicino in 1688. Unfortunately, this work seems to have been lost.

The predominant choral texture is a mixture of four- or eight-part polyphonic writing, with occasional imitative passages, especially at the beginning of the piece. The extreme brevity of most movements does not permit any extensive fugal treatment, but canons can be found in the *Quantus tremor, Judex ergo, Quaerens meae, Ingemisco,* and *Confutatis* passages.

Rare chordal passages, such as *Recordare* and *Juste Judex*, tend to stand out from the polyphonic music. Much of the writing for the double choir is structured in dialogue fashion. The orchestra usually supports or doubles the choral ensembles, yet plays an independent role in *Ingemisco* and in the movements for the vocal soloists.

Basic Data

EDITION

Giovanni Legrenzi
Prosa pro mortuis (Dies irae)
ed. Julia De Clerck
Publications d'Histoire de l'Art et d'Archéologie de l'Université Catholique de
    Louvain. XXIV. 1981.

DURATION

Eighteen movements, 519 mm.

VOICING AND ORCHESTRATION

Choir: two SATB choirs. range: S-G6; B-F3
Soloists: SSAATB
Orchestra: vn., vla. I/II , vc., db., org.

OUTLINE

Dies irae: 19 mm. [cm] satb choirs I/II/strings/b.c.
Quantus tremor: 44 mm. [gm] ATB soli/b.c. (fugal).
Tuba mirum: 28 mm. [E flat M] satb choirs I/II/strings/b.c.

Mors stupebit: 24 mm. [cm] S solo/strings/b.c.
Liber scriptus: 23 mm. [cm] satb choirs I/II/strings/b.c.
Judex ergo: 32 mm. [fm] AA solo duet/b.c. (canon).
Quid sum miser: 28 mm. [cm] SSATB soli/b.c.
Rex tremendae: 22 mm. [B flat M] B solo/strings/b.c.
Recordare: 19 mm. [gm] satb choirs I/II/strings/b.c.
Quaerens me: 23 mm. [gm] SS soli duet/b.c. (canon)
Juste judex: 15 mm. [E flat M] satb choirs I/II/ strings/b.c.
Ingemisco: 62 mm. [cm] five-part strings/ssattb choir/b.c. (canon) Opening sinfo-
   nia, independent string part.
Qui Mariam: 15 mm. [FM] strings/satb choirs I/II/b.c.
Preces meae: 15 mm. [dm] ATB soli/b.c.
Inter oves: 18 mm. [B flat M] satb choirs I/II/strings/b.c.
Confutatis: 23 mm. [E flat M] TTBB soli/b.c. (canon).
Oro supplex: 60 mm. [gm] A solo/five-part strings/b.c.
Lacrimosa-Finale: 49 mm. [cm] satb choirs I/II/strings/b.c.

DISCOGRAPHY

None found.

ANTONIO LOTTI
c. 1667–January 5, 1740

Lotti, a pupil of Legrenzi, was first organist of St. Mark's in Venice from
1704 until 1736, when he was appointed to the post of *primo maestro di
cappella*. It is not known precisely when he composed this setting of the
Dies irae nor if it is part of one of the several requiem settings he wrote or
an independent piece. Scored for SATB soli, SATB choir, strings, two
oboes, two trumpets, and organ, it is a suite of choral and vocal pieces
that was probably written for use in Venice. The presence of the ornate
violin solo (*Qui Mariam*), divided violins, muted string playing, and two
obbligato oboes and trumpets (all existed during and some slightly before
Lotti's lifetime), as well as the length of 717 measures, suggest a possible
date of c. 1700–20. One of the salient features of the work is its constantly
changing scoring for voices and instruments. There are obbligati for violin I, two oboes, and two trumpets.
   The predominant choral texture is four-part polyphonic writing, with
numerous passages in imitative style (*Quid sum miser, Judex ergo, Confutatis, Oro supplex*, and *Inter oves*). Canon and ostinato are employed in the
alto-tenor duet, *Liber scriptus*, in the soprano-alto duet, *Lacrymosa*, and in
the obbligato for violin I and II (*Quantus tremor*). Dramatic, instrumental
dotted rhythms are found in *Oro supplex* and *Ingemisco*.

Basic Data

EDITION

Antonio Lotti
Dies Irae per soli, coro, 2 oboe, 2 trombe, organo e archi
21698 Partitura
Carisch, S. p. A. Milano [1965]

DURATION

Nineteen movements, 717 mm.

VOICING & ORCHESTRATION

Choir: SSATB range: S-A flat 6; B-G3
Soloists: SATB
Orchestra: vn. I/II, vla., vc., db., 2 ob., 2 tpt., org.

OUTLINE

Dies irae: 70 mm. [cm] *adagio*. Instrumental sinfonia; ssatb choir/strings/oboes/
    trumpets/b. c.
Quantus tremor: 63 mm. [gm] *andante*. Instrumental sinfonia; sab choir/violins I/
    II/cello/b.c.
Tuba mirum: 31 mm. [CM] *allegro*. ssatb choir/strings/oboe/trumpet/b.c.
Mors stupebit: 60 mm. [E flat M] *allegro*. S solo/muted strings-no bass.
Liber scriptus: 41 mm. [B flat M] *allegretto*. AT soli/violin I/II/viola/organ.
    (canon).
Judex ergo: 25 mm. [gm] *andante*. ssatb choir/strings/organ.
Quid sum miser: 65 mm. [cm] *allegro*. ssatb choir/oboes-obbligato/strings/organ.
Rex tremendae: 24 mm. [E flat M] *largo*. tttbbb choir/viola I/II/cello/bass.
Recordare: 34 mm. [B flat M] *allegro*. S solo/violin I/II/viola.
Quaerens me: 13 mm. [cm] *allegro*. ssatb choir/trumpet solo/strings.
Juste judex: 44 mm. [gm] *andante*. SAB soli/strings.
Ingemisco: 26 mm. [CM] *allegro*. ssatb choir/strings.
Qui Mariam: 29 mm. [FM] *andante*. S solo/violin I solo/organ.
Preces meae: 51 mm. *allegretto*. AT soli/2 oboes/strings/organ.
Inter oves: 32 mm. [gm] *solemn*. ssatb choir/strings/organ.
Confutatis: 56 mm. [E flat M] *allegretto*. A solo/strings/organ.
Oro supplex: 25 mm. [CM] *allegro*. ttbb choir/obbligati for 2 trumpets/strings/
    organ.
Lacrymosa: 28 mm. [fm] *andante*. SA soli/oboe I/strings.
Judicandus: 25 mm. [cm] *solemne*. Satb choir/strings/oboes/trumpets/organ.

DISCOGRAPHY

None found.

JEAN BAPTISTE LULLY
November 28, 1632–March 22, 1687

Lully was responsible for three important musical positions at the court
of Louis XIV, ballet-dancer, composer of ballet music, and violinist in the

Les Petits Violons du Roi. In 1664, he began a collaboration with Moliére in the composition of a number of comedy-ballets. This association led to the development of French opera, a musical form for which he is remembered today. In total, there are about three dozen extant stage works, several orchestral works, and thirty-six sacred choral works, all of which are *petit* and *grand* motets.

The *grand* motet, in structure, is akin to a cantata, with a succession of choral and solo pieces with instrumental accompaniment. Recitative is absent from the *grand* motet. The *grand* motet, *Dies irae,* was composed in 1674 and scored for double choirs; one small and one large SATBarB choir. The work was probably performed for the funeral services of Queen Marie-Thérèse in 1683 and was first published in the following year by Charles Ballard of Paris. It is a one-movement, through-composed piece. Text is rarely repeated and there are numerous rhythm changes, twenty-seven, in total, which are varied according to the mood and poetry of the text.

As in the case of the other two *grand motets,* this work opens with a harmonized statement of the Gregorian *Dies irae* melody sung by the bass soloist. Lully reveals a great musical sensitivity in setting each passage of the text.

Choral passages, solos, and vocal ensembles follow each other without break in a very dramatic setting. The predominant choral texture is declamatory, homophonic style with contrasting passages of imitative polyphony at *Tuba mirum, Ingemisco,* and *Pie Jesu.* Both soloists and choirs are scored in concerto structure.

Basic Data

EDITION

Oeuvres Complètes de J. B. Lully
Les Motets
Tome II
Plaude, Laetare, Gallia, Te Deum Laudamus, Dies Irae, Dies Illa
1664–1677
Edited by Henry Pruniéres
Basse-continue à l'Orgue par Henry Letocart & G. Sazerac De Forge
Edition de la Revue Musicale, Paris. 1935

DURATION

One movement, 390 mm., perf., c. 18′

VOICING AND ORCHESTRATION

Choir: small SATB choir, large SATBarB choir. range: S-G6; B-F3
Soloists: SSATB
Orchestra: vn. I/II, vla. I/II/III, vc., org.

OUTLINE

Symphonie: mm.1–14. [gm] strings/b.c.
Dies irae: mm. 14–21. [gm] B solo/strings. (Gregorian melody)
Quantus tremor: mm. 21–34. [gm] satb-satbarb choirs/strings.
Tuba mirum: mm. 24–56. [gm] satb-satbarb choirs/strings. (imitative polyphony)
Mors stupebit: mm. 56–66. [gm] B solo/b.c.
Liber scriptus: mm. 66–84. satb-satbarb choirs.
Quid sum miser: mm. 85–95. [gm] A solo/b.c.
Rex tremendae: mm. 95–109. [gm] satb-satbarb choir/strings; *Qui salvandos*, B solo; *Salva me*, satb-satbarb choirs/b.c.
Recordare: mm. 109–134. [gm] B solo/violin I/II/b.c.; *Quaerens me*, A solo/b.c.
Juste judex: mm. 134–144. [gm] satb-satbarb choirs/strings.
Ingemisco: mm. 144–156. [gm] SATB soli/b.c. (imitative polyphony)
Qui Mariam: mm. 156–194. [gm] ATB soli/violin I/II/b.c.
Preces meae: mm. 194–204. [gm] T solo/b.c.
Inter oves: mm. 204–227. [gm] SAT soli/b.c.; *Et ab haedis*, satb-satbarb choirs/strings; *Statuens*, A solo/b.c.
Confutatis: mm. 227–294. [B flat M-gm] satb-satbarb choirs/strings; *Voca me* ATB soli/satb-satbarb choirs/b.c.
Oro supplex: mm. 294–296. [gm] B solo/b.c.
Lacrimosa: mm. 296–319. [gm] SATBarB soli; *Judicandus*, satb-satbarb choirs/strings.
Huic ergo: mm. 319–325. [gm] AB soli-b.c./satb-satbarb choirs/strings. Symphonie: mm. 326–346. [gm] strings/b.c.
Pie Jesu: mm. 346–390. [gm] TA soli-b.c./satb-satbarb choirs/strings. (imitative polyphony)

DISCOGRAPHY

Harmonia Mundi, 901 352, Choir and Orchestra of the Royal Chapel, dir. Philippe Herreweghe.

ARVO PÄRT
September 11, 1935

The Estonian composer Arvo Pärt was trained at Tallinn Conservatory, where he studied composition with Heino Eller. A prolific composer, he has written a significant amount of music in various forms, including three orchestral symphonies, chamber music, vocal pieces, and choral works. Among the choral compositions are a *Magnificat* for unaccompanied voices (1989); *Stabat Mater* (1985); *St. John Passion* (1981–82); *Dies irae* (1986); and *Miserere* for vocal quintet, mixed chorus, organ, and instruments (1989).

Much of his music, including the *Miserere*, has been influenced by medieval and early Renaissance style—especially that of the Gregorian chant; the Notre Dame School; and the composers Machaut, Ockeghem, and Josquin. At the same time, the influence of the Eastern Orthodox Church, in which the composer has deep roots, is present in the sense of mystical spirituality felt in his compositions.

One of the guiding principles of his musical composition is a technique that is referred to as *tintinnabuli*, a word that describes the pealing of bells and the rich, sonorous texture that is associated with the lingering overtones, after the bells have been struck. He also understands music as sound that is simultaneously static and in motion. These ideas can be experienced by reading through or by hearing his work, *Miserere*. In this work, the music seems to arise and subside, step by step, from and back into silence. Like Stravinsky's *Requiem Canticles*, the orchestration is almost minimalist, often with only one voice or instrument sounding in a particular moment.

The harmonies of the *Miserere* cover a broad spectrum, extending from a consonant tonality, based on single- and two-part intervallic writing, to dissonant atonality generated by four- to eight-part imitative texture. The insertion of the first seven verses of *Dies irae* into the middle of this composition is one of the unique features of the *Miserere*. Verse eight is placed at the end of the work.

Dies irae is set in eight small sections and the first section is repeated, rondo style, throughout the presentation of the text. Each section is part of a series of three different, three-part, strict mensuration canons in which the same canonic melody is performed simultaneously at a fast and at a slow tempo. The setting of the *Dies irae* is similar to the writing style of Guillaume Machaut and is the most dissonant part of the work as the mensural canons unfold at a ratio of 2:1. Dissonance arises in exactly the same way as in music of the Notre Dame School or other composers of the *Ars Antiqua*: vertical harmony results from the accidental crossing or clashing of separate melodic lines. Other parts of the *Miserere* use a modern version of the medieval hocket technique.

Basic Data

EDITION
Arvo Pärt
Miserere für Soli, Chor, Ensemble und Orgel
(1989 rev.1992)
Partitur [full score]
Universal Edition (UE 30871) 1989

DURATION
Dies irae only: 57 mm. + 15 mm. (entire work) perf. c. 30'

VOICING AND ORCHESTRATION
Choir: SATB
Soloists: SA (contratenor), TTB

Instruments: ob., cl., bcl., bsn., C tpt., tbn., electric guitar, electric bass guitar, org. PERC. (3 players) tubular bells, timpani, triangle, tam-tam, tambourine.

OUTLINE

Dies Irae: 57 mm. eight sections of repeated, three-part mensuration canons. *Dies irae—Quantus tremor—Tuba mirum—Mors stupebit—Liber scriptus—Juste Judex—Quid sum miser—Dies irae*. Scored for satb choir/full ensemble.

Rex tremendae: 15 mm. Concluding section. Canonic writing for satb choir/SA soli/organ/tubular bells/tam-tam/electric bass guitar.

DISCOGRAPHY

ECM Production, ECM 1430, The Hilliard Ensemble, Western Wind Choir, cond. Paul Hiller.

IGOR STRAVINSKY
June 17, 1882–April 6, 1971

Igor Stravinsky was one of the most important composers of the twentieth century. He began piano lessons at age nine and slightly later, harmony and counterpoint. Although he studied formally, much of his learning was self-motivated. This important characteristic stayed with him, even in late life. At the age of twenty, he met and studied orchestration and form with Rimsky-Korsakov. Over a long, productive life, he wrote music for all kinds of mediums and every important style, including that of impressionism, neo-classicism, and serial composition.

In the field of sacred music is the *Symphony of Psalms* (1930), the *Mass* (1944, rev. 1947–48), *Canticum Sacrum* (1955), *The Requiem Canticles* (1966), and a handful of other pieces. *The Requiem Canticles*, scored for alto and bass soli, SATB choir, and orchestra, are included in this chapter because the bulk of its text is taken from the medieval sequence, *Dies irae*.

The first performance of this nonliturgical work took place at Princeton University, the institution that commissioned the work, on October 8, 1966. It is a work of great delicacy in orchestration and transparency in its melodic line and a condensed harmonic texture. Because the harmonic language is based upon a modified serial technique, there is no sense of tonal center.

The same kind of ostinato-like melodies, found in *Rite of Spring* (1913) are employed in the *Canticles*, yet with a more atonal, serial quality. Each movement possesses a fluid, ever-changing meter. The Prelude, for example, has six different, constantly changing meters. It is one of three purely instrumental pieces included in the work. The overall texture of the *Requiem Canticles* was conceived contrapuntally. It is a nonprogrammatic work of pure music that projects a variety of moods.

Basic Data

EDITION

Igor Stravinsky
Requiem Canticles for Contralto & Bass Soli, Chorus and Orchestra.
Vocal Score
Boosey & Hawkes Music Publishers, Ltd.
London. Paris. New York. 1967

DURATION

Nine movements, 305 mm., perf., 15′

VOICING & ORCHESTRATION

Choir: SATB range: S-G6; B-F3
Soloists: alto, bass
Orchestra: 6 vn. I, 5 vn. II, 4 vla., 3 vc., 2 db., 2 fl., 2 bsn., 2 Fh., 4 tpt., 3 tbn., harp,
celesta, piano. PERC: 2 timp., xylophone, vibraphone, bells.

OUTLINE

Prelude: 54 mm. [sixteenth-note = 250] strings/solo string quartet. Staccato osti-
nato-rhythm patterns of sixteenth notes set in various meters, which contrast
with the legato playing of the first and second violins. Multiple rhythms.

Exaudi: 26 mm. [eighth-note = 104] strings/harp/woodwinds/satb choir. Homophonic choral texture, but conceived contrapuntally. Multiple rhythms.

> Exaudi orationem meam, ad te omnis caro veniet.
> [Hear my prayer, all flesh shall come before Thee.]

Dies irae: 22 mm. [eighth-note = 68] full orchestra/satb choir. (verses 1–2) ABA
form. (A sections are sung; B section, spoken) Multiple rhythms.

Tuba mirum: 33 mm. B solo/two trumpets. (verse 3) Thin and crystalline texture.
Wide leaps in bass vocal line.

Interlude: 67 mm. [sixteenth-note = 104] woodwinds/timpani. Two-part writing
with occasional three or four-part chords. Multiple rhythms built on the sixteenth-note unit; 2/16, 3/16, 4/16, 5/16, 7/16 or 9/16.

Rex tremendae: 26 mm. [quarter-note = 104–106] satb choir/woodwinds/trumpet
(polyphonic setting of v. 8).

Lacrimosa: 37 mm. [sixteenth-note = 132] A solo/full orchestra. A delicate, pointillistic sound created. (vv. 18–19).

Libera me: 23 mm. [quarter-note = 170] SATB solo quartet/speaking satb choir.
Accompanied by a sustained, organistic-type of instrumental orchestration.
("modern" version of baroque recitative) The entire text of the *Libera me* is chanted by one ensemble or spoken by the other. Multiple rhythms.

Postlude: 17 mm. [quarter-note = 40] woodwinds/trombone/chimes/piano. Intervallic harmony. Multiple rhythms.

DISCOGRAPHY

Deutsche Grammophone, 447-068-2, London Sinfonietta and New London Chamber Choir, cond. Oliver Knussen.

10

Ein Deutsches Requiem: The German Requiem

The German Requiem is a musical form that constitutes a small part of a vast liturgical repertory that had come to the forefront after the 1526 advent of Martin Luther's *Deutsche Messe* (German Mass). This requiem is identified by a variety of names, such as *Deutsches Requiem*, *Totenmesse*, and *Trauersmesse*. Past and current musical forms include *Deutsche Messe*, *Deutsches Amt*, *Deutsches Hochamt*, *Deutsches Requiem*, *Deutsche Passion*, *Deutsches Ordinarium*, *Deutsches Proprium*, *Deutsche Singmesse*, *Deutsches Magnificat*, *Deutsche Messgesänge*, *Seelenmesse*, and German-language motets.

October 29, 1525, marked the celebration of the first Protestant German mass, a ceremony that has been regularly observed in the Stadt-Kirche of Wittemberg after Christmas of that same year. Luther generously employed the vernacular tongue for the purpose of attracting not only practicing Christians, but also those individuals who might be best described as "unchurched." In its infancy, the Protestant service remained similar, if not identical, to the established Catholic form.

Lutheran Evangelical tradition called for the use of both Latin and German texts, thus Protestant composers that included Praetorius, Hassler, Senfl, Hammerschmidt, among others, created works in both languages. *Marcronic* hymns with texts that intermixed both Latin and German (e.g., *In dulci Jublio* and *Puer natus in Bethlehem*) enjoyed immense popularity during this era. Lutheran Leonhard Lechner (c. 1553–1606) is credited with composing one of the earliest Protestant German requiem settings circa 1606 with his work *Deutsche Sprüch von Leben und Tod*, which by three decades antedates the more widely recognized Heinrich Schütz setting, *Musikalisches Exequien*, composed in 1636. Lutherans continued to adapt and compose anew settings of the Latin mass (*missae brevis*, consisting of the *Kyrie* and *Gloria*), however, a standardized requiem setting never managed to take root, hence these two particular works hold a somewhat unique status in the literature.

Lechner's *Deutsche Sprüch von Leben und Tod* (pub., Bärenreiter) consists of fifteen German aphorisms, which are appropriate for both living and dying. These short polyphonic pieces assume a musical scheme composed in the unaccompanied four-part, motet-style of the Netherlands school. The following is a translation of this exceptionally significant early Protestant requiem:

Alles auf Erden stets mit Gefährden des Falls, sich wendet, hin und her ländet.
(Everything on earth is always in danger of Adam's fall from grace; here and there, a body is brought forth.)

Auch Sonn, Mond, Sterne, Wittrung bewahren samt den Jahrszeiten Unbständigkeiten.
(The sun, moon, stars and weather, prove as true, along with the seasons, this instability.)

Wir Menschen reisen gleich armen Waisen die sind mit Sorgen ungwiss wo morgen.
(We humans travel like poor orphans, burdened with grief, uncertain about tomorrow.)

Heint frisch, wohlmächtig, gsund, schön und prächtig, morgen verdorben und gestorben.
(This night (we are) fresh, powerful, healthy, beautiful and lovely, tomorrow, spoiled and dead.)

In Gottes Handen alls steht zu enden; sein wir geduldig, erwarten schuldig.
(At the end, all is in God's hands, therefore be we patient, expect to be found guilty.)

Gedenke mitnichten, dich bständig zrichten in die Welt gfahrlich, drin nichts beharrlich.
(Do not think, be upright in the dangerous world; therein is nothing constant.)

Wenn sich erschwinget das Gluck, dir glinget, tu nit drauf bauen, ihm zviel vertrauen.
(If good fortune and success arises, don't depend upon it; Do not trust in it too much.)

So uberfallen dich Trübsals Qualen, sei nit kleinmutig, murrend, ungültig.
(So the torment of distress falls upon you, be not faint-hearted, nor grumble, nor take it amiss.)

Was jetzt im Laufen liegt bald zu haufen, das sich schicken all Augenblicken.
(What now, in life's course, is soon to be heaped-up, will come to pass in an instant.)

Weil dann so unstet, dies Schiff der Welt geht, so lasst uns denken wohin zu lenken.
(Because the Ship of the World is so changeable, let us consider where to navigate.)

Wir wöllen kehrten zu Gott dem Herren, uns nach sein Gfallen richten in allem.
(Would we turn to the Lord God, so that we follow His will.)

Ihn fürchten lieben, sein Wort stet üben, er wird erbarmen sich unser Armen.
(Love Him in fear; Follow His word. He will have mercy upon us poor.)

Sein Gnad und Güten wird uns behuten, trösten entbinden von unsern Sünden.
(His mercy and goodness will preserve and console us, it will free us from our sins.)

Sein Hand wird retten aus allen Noten, wir leben, sterben—jetzt nit verderben.
(His hands will save us from all suffering. We live and die—we will not spoil.)

Nach diesem Leiden, er ewig Freuden uns schenkt ohnfehlig. Dann sind wir selig.
(After this suffering, He will send, without fail, eternal joy. Then we are blessed.)

The Shütz work, *Musikalisches Exequien*, adopts a more traditional form of the Protestant *missa brevis* (*Kyrie* and *Gloria*) with the incorporation of Biblical passages drawn from Romans, Job, the Gospel of St. John, Isaiah, Philippians, and the Psalms. Much of the Gloria text was set to the Lutheran chorale melodies *Aus tiefer Not, Nun lasst uns Gott, Est ist das Heil, Nun freut euch,* and *Wenn mein Stündelein.*

Through a gradual transition, the Lutherans eventually replaced the traditional Roman requiem with other musical forms, including the motet, the cantata, the oratorio, and an extensive variety of memorial musical styles. Johan Schein (1586–1630) composed almost fifty funeral motets included in collections published in 1627, 1628, and 1645. *Sie fröhlich meine Seele, Wie lieblich sind deine Wohnungen,* and *Ach Herr nach dir* are the notable pieces cited among these collected works. Gottfried Scheidt (1593–1661) composed *Selig sind die Toten,* a funeral work for Sophie Elisabeth, the Duchess of Saxony, in 1650. This highly recognized text became repeatedly utilized in motet settings by numerous composers, including Heinrich Schütz (1585–1672), Georg Telemann (1681–1767), Gottfried

Homilius (1714–1785), Gustave Jenner (1865–1920), Johannes Weyrauch (1897–1977), Hugo Distler (1903–1942), and Othmar Kist (b. 1932). The piece can also be cited within Johann Sebastian Bach's Cantata 60, *O Ewigkeit du Donnerwort*, the opening chorus to Johannes Brahms' (1833–1897) *Ein deutsches Requiem*, and in the oratorio *Die letzen Dinge* by Ludwig Spohr (1784–1859). Charles Villiers Stanford (1852–1924) utilized an English translation of the text for his motet *Blessed are the Dead*.

Death served as the topic for several church cantatas written by Johann Sebastian Bach between 1707 and 1726, including *Gottes Zeit ist die allerbeste Zeit* ("God's Time is the Best Time"), BWV 106 (1707), *Komm du süsse Todesstunde* ("Come Thou Sweet Hour of Death"), BWV 161 (1715), *Liebster Gott, wann werd' ich sterben* ("Dear God, When I Die"), BWV 8 (1724), and *Wer weiss, wie nahe mir mein Ende* ("Who Knows How Near is My End"), BWV 27 (1726).

George P. Telemann composed a number of cantata-like compositions for the deaths of nine Hamburg mayors during his years of association with that city. The *Schwanengesang 1733* (Swansong), composed for the Mayor (*Burgomeister*) Garlieb Sillem is an exceptionally moving work, consisting of an introductory sinfonia, four chorales; *Ach, wie nichtig* ("O how futile"); *Komm, Sterblicher, betrachte mich* ("Come, mortals, consider me"); *Da meine Kräfte brechen* ("When my strength succumbs"); and *Wenn du an jenem Tag* ("When you raise the dead"); as well as five arias, three dicta, and six recitatives.

At the height of the Enlightenment in 1791, Beethoven, then nineteen years of age, composed funeral music for soloists, choir, and orchestra entitled *Cantata of the Death of Emperor Joseph II*. A year later, the Swedish composer Joseph Martin Kraus developed a similar work of his own, *Funeral Cantata for Gustave III*, in response to the assassination of the Swedish monarch. Other composers contributed to the genre as well, among them Johann Schwanberg (1740–1804) with his *Funeral Cantata for the Death of the Duchess of Brunswick*, Ernst Julius Otto (1804–1842) with his *Funeral Cantata* for choir and orchestra, and Johann Frederick Reichardt (1752–1814) with his *Cantus lugubris in obitum Frederici Magni* (Paris, 1787).

The Protestants had completely discarded the traditional Latin requiem at the beginning of the Reformation, although it remained a significant part of the Roman rites. During the seventeenth and eighteenth centuries, the chasm of differences between the two traditions continued to expand, despite the fact that the Catholic Church had been employing German texts into the Roman rite, drawn from the Cantual of Mainz, as early as 1605. As more such pieces emerged, they served to supplement the Latin liturgy and ultimately transformed into their own unique form referred to as the German *Singmesse* (Song-mass). By the late 1600s, these texts were often substituted for the centuries-old mass ordinary (Fellerer: The *History of Catholic Church Music*).

Luther's setting of the Lied, *Gelobet seist du, Jesu Christ* ("Praise be to thee, Jesus Christ"), surfaced in several Catholic songbooks (1537, Michael Vehe; 1567, Leisenstritt). This development reflected the overall spirit of the Protestant reforms and was likely enticed and coaxed forward by Luther's successful approach. It is presumed that German text-settings were first sung during low mass. New texts generally paralleled those of the original Latin requiem, assuming they were not merely translations of the Latin original. Although it was the duty of the priest to recite the Latin prayers for all celebrations of the mass, the choir was permitted, even encouraged, to sing a German version of the liturgical text, hence creating what could be called a "double" service.

Schubert's *Deutsche Messe* ("Gesange der Messe, nebst einem Anhange: Das Gebet des Herrn") stands as the most celebrated of these works. Composed in 1862 upon commission from the Polytechnic School of Vienna, Schubert conformed to the folk-melody style previously employed by Michael Haydn in 1782 for his *Erstes deutsches Hochamt: Hier liegt vor deiner Majestät* (pub., Böhm). Less well-known is the setting composed by Benedikt Holzinger (1747–1815) for SAB soli, SAB choir, orchestra, and organ. Other early Catholic composers who contributed to the *Singmesse* genre were Ignaz Holzbauer (1711–1783), Nikolaus Betscher (1745–1811), and Johann Amon (1763–1825). During the eighteenth century, steadily increasing nationalistic impulses nurtured and vitalized the use of the German language in these mass settings, mirroring a patriotic pride that eventually culminated in the national Revolution of 1848.

The latter part of the eighteenth century is presumed to be the era when many German translations of the Requiem mass began making their way to the forefront. The first German requiem for the Catholic liturgy recognized in this volume is a setting composed in 1790 by Peter van Winter, scored for soloists, choir, and orchestra, which incorporated both Latin and German texts. In 1808, Georg Vogler composed a concert version of the *Deutsches Requiem* for soloists, SATB choir, and symphonic orchestra that is conceivably the first model of its kind. Other composers credited with developing some of the earliest settings of the *Deutsches Requiem* are Thomas Selle (1599–1663), Johan Friedrich Fasch (1688–1758), Georg Schirm (1768–1833), Adolf Marx (1795–1866), Joseph Ignace Schnabel (1767–1831), and Franz Schubert (1797–1828).

Schubert and Gruber both modeled their requiem settings, *"Hier liegt vor deiner Majestät,"* after Michael Haydn's renowned 1782 work. Also noteworthy is Franz Süssmayr (1766–1803), who not only completed Mozart's unfinished requiem, but penned two original German requiems of his own.

German text settings continued to appear in the late nineteenth century. The most famous *Deutsches Requiem* dates from this era. Brahms' beloved setting is performed regularly in concert halls and churches around the world. Hugo Kaun (1921) followed the romantic musical tradition of the Brahms *German Requiem* with a concert setting for soloist, male choir, and orchestra. Although Kaun and Brahms both utilized Biblical texts, neither demarcated themselves to the traditional requiem format. Both German and Latin texts were provided by Franz Lachner for his monumental, neo-renaissance requiem setting composed in 1872.

Twentieth-century composers who have created German requiems include Gustave Anton (*Requiem quasi una Fantasia*, Anton-Verlag, Gummersbach), Helmut Barbe (*Requiem, 1965*, Hänssler Verlag), Jean Marie Bernard [Jürgen Müller-Bernhardt] (*Ein deutsches Requiem*, 1990, Verlagsgemeinschaft ANARCHE), César Bresgen (*Totenmesse*, 1971–72, pub., Doblinger), Josef Butz (*Deutsche liturgische Messe für die Verstorbenen*, private), Karl Erhard (Totenmesse, 1989, Böhm), Helmut Gärtner (*Kleines deutsches Requiem*, private), Joseph Haas (*Totenmesse. Ein Melodram*, 1955, Schott), Peter Hölzl (*Messe für Verstorbene*, Carus, 1989) Franz Höss (*Deutsches Requiem*, Böhm), Karl Kraft (*Deutsche Totenmesse*-two settings, Böhm), Gerhard Kronberg (*Deutsche Messe für die Verstorbenen*, Musikverlag Coppenrath), Ernst Kutzer (*Deutsches Requiem*, c. 1968, Coppenrath), Fridolin Limbacher (*Deutsches Requiem*, 1976, Böhm), Alfons Mayer (*Deutsches Requiem*, 1966), Paul Metschnabl (*Messe für Verstorbene*, Böhm), Hans Micheelsen (*Tod und Leben: Ein deutsches Requiem*, 1938, Bärenreiter), Egon Nesitka (*Deutsche Seelenmesse*, private), Johann Pretzenberger (*Messe für die Verstorben*, 1971, Bischöflichen Seelsorgeamt, St. Pölten), Sepp Rubenberger (*Seelenmesse*, 1979, Musikverlag Max Hieber, München), Ludwig Scherr (twentieth century), Karl Norbert Schmid (*Deutsches Requiem*, Feuchtinger & Gleichauf, Regensburg), Ernst Tittel (*Deutsches Requiem mit Libera*, 1965, Verlag Doblinger), Max Welcker (*Deutsche Seelenmesse*, Böhm), and Erna Woll (*Requiem: Deutsche Totenmesse*, Verlag UNI-Druck, München). Many of these works emerged after the Second Vatican Council's (1962–1965) attempts to reform the liturgy by promoting the use of vernacular languages for the celebration of mass. As a result, most of these pieces were not designed as concert works, but instead as presentations of functional worship music. Although the majority of these settings are quite simple (and may reflect a larger number of private, never-published pieces), many are much more musically sophisticated. Such settings include those by Bernard, Bresgen, Hass, Hölzl, and Barbe. There are also the unaccompanied, virtuoso choral settings by Micheelsen and Tittel, which can be cited as concert works because of the complexity of the choral arrangements.

One of the more unique settings of the German requiem is the *Alpenlän-*

disches Requiem composed by Johann Zehetbauer (pub., Promultius) in 1981. Based on a native folksong, the work is scored for three voices and zither (or harp, guitar, and dulcimer), as well as wind instruments that separate the instrumental marches from the various vocal movements. All movements of the piece are composed in a major tonality.

There exist several varieties of the German requiem text, however, the one most frequently used appears to be the German translation of the Latin liturgy based upon the words of Schott's *Messbuch*. The translations are as follows:

Introit: *Requiem aeternam* (*Herr gib ihnen ewige Ruhe*)
Kyrie: (*Herr erbarme Dich unser*)
Graduale: *Requiem aeternam* (*Herr gib ihnen die ewig Ruhe*)
Tract: *Absolve Domine* (*Befreie, o Herr* || *Lose, o Herr*)
Sequence: *Dies irae* (*Tag der Rache*)
Offertory: *Domine Jesu Christe* (*Herr Jesus Christus*)
Sanctus: (*Heilig, Heilig, Heilig*)
Agnus Dei: (*Lamm Gottes*)
Communion: *Lux aeterna* (*Das ewige Licht*)
Responsory: *Libera me* (*Rette mich, Herr*)

Portions of this text version are cited in the settings of Tittel, Zehetbauer, and Kutzer. Micheelsen's 1938, *Tod und Leben: ein deutsches Requiem*, incorporates various prayers, such as *In the Midst of Life* (*Mitten wir im Leben*), fragments of Psalm 90, *Lord, hast been our refuge* (verses 1–6, 10, and 12), and Psalm 126, *Those who sow in tears* (verses 5–6), along with First Corinthians 15 (verses 20, 42–43, 52, and 54), and the first verse of the folksong, *Er ist ein Schnitter, der heist Tod* ("There is a reaper, called Death"), composed in 1638. This particular tune, as well as its accompanying text, has been adopted by numerous composers.*

Es ist ein Schnitter heisst der Tod,
hat G'walt vom grossen Gott.
Heut wetzt er das Messer,
es schneidt schon viel besser,
Bald wird er drein schneiden,
Wir müssens schon leiden.
Hüt dich, schöns Blümelein!

There is a Reaper called Death,
this Reaper has the power of a great God.
Today he whets the knife; he can cut much better,
Soon the knife will cut; only we will suffer.
Take care, beautiful flowerlet!

Composed in a modern, post-impressionist musical language, Jean Marie Bernard's *Requiem für Angela*, Opus 28, utilizes a combination of prayers as well as portions of the traditional canonic requiem text. Written for and dedicated to the grandmother of his wife, Angela Wurmdobler, the requiem is scored for SATB choir and organ.

Zum Eingang (Introit)

Herr nimm sie auf in deinem Frieden und lasst sie ruhen in dem Licht deiner Herrlichkeit,	Lord take her into Thy peace and let her rest in the light of Thy splendor.
denn wir glauben und bekennen, dass dein Sohn für uns gestorben und auferstanden ist.	for we believe and know that Thy Son died for us and was resurrected.
So lasse sie durch Christus auferstehen, lass sie die ewig Freude geniessen in deinem Frieden geborgen sein.	So let her arise, through Jesus Christ, let her enjoy eternal joy and be secure in Thy peace.

Kyrie ("troped" version)

Herr Jesus Christus, du hast uns den Weg zum Vater gezeigt.	Lord Jesus Christ, you have pointed out to us, the way to the Father.
Herr, erbarme dich, Herr erbarme dich.	Lord have mercy, Lord have mercy.
Du hast durch deinen Tod, der Welt das Leben geschenkt.	Through Thy death, you gave life to the world.
Christus erbarme dich, Christus erbarme dich.	Christ have mercy, Christ have mercy.
Du hast uns im Hause deines Vaters eine Wohnung bereitet.	Thou hast prepared, for us, a room in Thy Father's house.
Herr erbarme dich, Herr erbarme dich.	Lord have mercy, Lord have mercy.

Nach der Lesung (After the reading)

Der Herr hat das Tor zum Leben aufgetan zur Heimkehr in das Reich wo kein Tod mehr ist, in das Land der ewigen Freude.	The Lord has opened the gateway to life, to return into the kingdom where death no longer is, in a land of eternal joy.
Barmherziger Gott, in dir ist Vollendung. Schenke Verzeihung denen die in Christus entschlafen sind.	Compassionate God, in Thee is completion. Send forgiveness to them who sleep in the Lord.

Zur Opferung (Offertory)

O Herr unser Gott, dein Sohn hat am Kreuz getilgt alle Schuld.	O Lord our God, upon the Cross has Thy Son taken away all guilt.

Wir bitten dich schenke Heil und Erlösung bewahre vor dem ewigen Tod.	We pray Thee send health and redemption, guard against eternal death.
So lasse sie schauen die himmlische Freude.	So let her behold heavenly joy.
Barmherziger Gott, so löse sie aus den Fesseln des Todes und nimm sie auf in die Schar deiner Heiligen ins Reich des Lichts, des ewigen Friedens.	Compassionate God, release her from the bonds of death and take her into the company of the hallowed, into the kingdom of light, of eternal peace.

Heilig, Heilig, Heilig (Sanctus)
(traditional text)

Lamm Gottes [Agnus Dei]
(traditional text)

Nach den Kommunionausteilung (Post Communion)

So sprich der Herr: ich bin die Auferstehung und das Leben.	Thus spake the Lord: I am the Resurrection and the Life.
Wer an mich glaubt wird leben auch wenn er stirbt.	Whoso believes in me, even though he die, and who believes in me will,
Und jeder der an mich glaubt wird in Ewigkeit nicht sterben.	through all eternity, never die.

Requiem für Wilma Heiss, a secular, three-movement setting by Herman Heiss (1897–1966), (pub., Breitkopf and Härtel) is scored for SA soli (or choir) and string quartet (or organ), and also employs the evocative poetry credited to Georg Frauenfelder, actually Heiss's pseudonym (*Die Rose in der Hand* and *Mein Leben, dies ist Gottes Nacht*), and Friedrich Rückert (1788–1866) (*Wer einmal hier*).

I.

Die Rose in der Hand.	A rose in the hand, this life completed,
Dies Leben ist vollkommen,	
das Duft und Farb und drängend Knosp geblieben.	the fragrance and color and pressed bud remain.
O Leben, bleib uns!	O life, stay with us!
Wir sind von Gott dir zugegeben, du füllest uns mit Gottschaft:	We are given over to you by God, fill us with Godliness: with desire,
mit Wollen, Halten, Lieben.	support, love.
Wir wissen um den Tod.	We know about death.
Wir leben ihm entgegen wie Blumgewind	We move toward it, as a garland of flowers in
in seine harten Hande. O Tod, sei gut!	its rude hands.

Wir bringen dir geliebtes Leben,	O death be good!
füll es mit neuen Sein	We bring to you a beloved life,
nach dieser letzten Wende.	fill it with new being,
	after this last turning.

II.

Mein Leben, dies ist Gottes Nacht,	My life, this is God's night,
danach ein Gottesmorgen lacht.	After it, a God's morrow smiles.

III.

Wer einmal hier hat in geliebtem Angesicht	Who has ever seen the blessed face of death
des Todes Bild geseh'n vergisst es ewig nicht.	will never forget it.
Der Schatten legt, wohin fort an dein Auge schaut sich über alles, was dir lieb ist oder traut.	The shadow falls wherever your eyes gaze, upon everything that is dear or trusted.
Wem ein Geliebtes stirbt,	He whose beloved dies,
dem ist es wie ein Traum,	to him it is as a dream,
die ersten Tage kommt	the first days come,
es zu sich selber kaum.	it scarcely seems real.
Wie er's ertragen soll	He cannot ask himself
Kann er sich selbst nicht fragen;	how he should endure,
und wenn er sich besinnt	and if he considers,
so hat er's schon ertragen.	thus has he endured.
Je länger du's gehabt	The longer you have known your beloved,
je länger willst du's haben	the longer will you yearn,
und dein Geliebtes wird dir stets zu früh begraben.	and it will always seem a burial too soon.
Du bildetest dir ein, Es sei auf ewig dein,	You imagine the beloved is always yours,
und solltest Gott, den dir's so langliess dankbar sein.	and you should be thankful to God who let you have your love so long.

Another noteworthy secular variety of the German requiem is associated with the poem simply titled "Requiem" by Friedrich Hebbel (1813–1863). (For a translation of the text, see Max Reger.) A nonliturgical, humanist text, it was never utilized for the church loft, but instead for the choral society. Numerous composers have set this poem to music, among them Gustav Anton (b. 1938), Peter Cornelius (1824–1872), Hans Gebhard (1882–1947), Paul Geilsdorf (1890–1976), Willy Giesen (1911–1981), Hans Peter Haller (b. 1929), Vagn Holmboe (1909–1996), Kurt Lissmann (1902–

1983), Max Reger (1873–1916), Jean Reinartz (1913–1957), Hans Reinhardt (b. 1911), and Fritz Zschiegner (1813–1863).

*Felix Mendelssohn (1809–1847) (*Twelve Songs, Op. 8*, # 4, *Erntelied*, 1828), Robert Schumann (1818–1856) (*Romanzen u. Balladen*, Op. 75, #1, *Schnitter's Tod*, c. 1849), Johannes Brahms (1833–1897) (20 Volkslieder for choir, # 5, *Schnitter's Tod*, c. 1859–62), Paul Hindemith (1895–1963) (*Dance Pieces* for piano, Op. 19, c. 1920), Max Drischner (1891–1971) (organ), Johann Nepomuk David (1895–1977) (*Chaconne for organ*), Hugo Distler (1908–1942) (*Theme and Variations* for flute solo), Kurt Thomas (1904–1973) (*Variations for organ*, Op. 19), Anton Heiller (1923–1979) (*Partita*), Jürgen Gölle (1942–) (*Organ Partita*), and Michael Gees (1953–) (*Piano Variations*, 1997).

HELMUT BARBE
December 28, 1927

Barbe studied composition with Ernst Pepping at the Berlin Kirchenmusikschule. In 1950, he was appointed the choirmaster post at St. Nicholas, Spandau and in 1955, joined the faculty of the Kirchenmusikschule to teach music theory, where he led a seminar in twelve-tone composition.

The main body of Barbe's work is sacred music. Included is *Psalm Eight* (1952), a six-voice motet, *Ich will dem Herren singen* (1955), a Passion motet for five voices (1955), *Magnificat* (1956), *Canticus Simeonis* (1958), *Die Auferweckung des Lazarus* (1959), *Ostergeschichte* (1961), *Missa Brevis* (1961), *Te Deum* (1964), and the *Requiem* (1965).

The *Requiem 1965* is scored for soprano solo and an instrumental, chamber-ensemble. Its harmonic language is based upon an atonal, twelve-tone technique that is notable for its numerous melodic leaps of tenths, ninths, and sevenths. The orchestration is quite light and airy and employs a "pointillistic" type of texture and writing.

Basic Data

EDITION

Helmut Barbe
Requiem 1965 für Sopran, Flote, Oboe, Fagott, Viola, Violincello, und Kontrabass. Hanssler Verlag, Neuhausen-Stuttgart (HE 10.277) [1971]

DURATION

Three movements, 225 mm., perf., c. 13'

VOICING AND ORCHESTRATION

Soloists: soprano
Instruments: fl., ob., bsn., vla., vc., db.

OUTLINE

Introit: 113 mm.

Herr, gib ihnen die ewig Ruhe, und das ewige Licht leuchte ihnen. Wenn den Herr die Gefangenen Zions erlösen wird, so werden wir sein wie die Träumenden. Dann wird unser Mund voll Lachens und unsre Mund voll Ruhmens sein. Dann wird man sagen unter den Heiden Der Herr hat Grosses an ihnen getan. Der Herr hat Grosses an uns getan, des sind wir fröhlich. Herr, führe uns heim aus dem Elend, wie du Wüsten wandelst in grune Auen. Die mit Tränen säen, werden mit Freuden ernten. Sie gehen hin und weinen und tragen edlen Samen. und kommen mit Freuden und bringen ihre Garben. Herr, gib ihnen die ewige Ruhe, und das ewige Licht leuchte ihnen.	Lord, give them eternal peace and let eternal light upon them shine. When the Lord frees Zion's captives, then shall we be like those who dream. Then our mouths be full of laughter and joy. Then it will be said among the heathen, that the Lord performed great things. The Lord has done for us great things. Therefore are we joyful. Lord, lead us from tribulation, as you turned wilderness into green pastures.

Those that sow in tears shall Reap in great joy. They go in weeping and return, bearing their harvest. Lord, give them eternal peace, Let heavenly light shine upon them. |

Apokalypse: 66 mm.

Diese sinds, die gekommen sind aus grosser Trübsal und haben ihre Kleider gewaschen und haben ihre Kleider hell gemacht im Blut des Lammes. Darum sind sie vor dem Thron Gottes und dienen ihm Tag und Nacht in seinem Tempel: und der auf dem Thron sitzt, wird über ihnen wohnen. Sie wird nicht mehr hungern noch dürsten; es wird auch nicht auf sie fallen die Sonne oder irgendeine Hitze: denn das Lamm mitten auf dem Thron wird sie weiden und leiten zu den lebendigen Wasserbrunnen, und Gott wird abwischen all Tränen von ihren Augen.	These are those who have come out of great tribulation and have washed their garments and have made them bright in the blood of the Lamb. Therefore, they are before God's throne, serving Him in the Temple day and night: and He that is seated on the throne, dwells among them. They shall no longer hunger or thirst, nor be stricken by the sun, nor shall any heat burn them; For the Lamb, on the throne, guides and leads them to the living waters. And God shall wipe away all tears from their eyes.

In Paradisum: 46 mm.

Ins Paradies geleite dich der Engel Chor, bei deiner Heimkehr nehme dich auf der Märtyrer Schar, und sie führe dich heim in die heilige Stadt Jerusalem. Der Chor der Engel nehme dich auf, und mit Lazarus gebe dir Gott den ewige Frieden.	May the angelic choirs lead you into Paradise, with the flock of martyrs receive you, and lead you home to holy Jerusalem. The angel's choir will surround you, and with Lazarus, give to you the eternal peace of God.

DISCOGRAPHY

None found.

JOHANNES BRAHMS
May 7, 1833–April 3, 1897

Although Brahms is particularly remembered today for his orchestral works, chamber compositions, and piano music, he remains one of the most significant composers of vocal music of any era in the long history of Western music. Brahms was an active conductor of several choral groups, often writing works for them. Although he wrote secular choral music, there are also many sacred pieces, including Op. 29; *Zwei Motetten*, Op. 110; *Drei Motetten*, Op. 22; *Marienlieder*, Op. 27; *Psalm 13*, Op. 12; *Ave Maria*, Op. 109; *Fest und Gedenksprüche*, Op 37; *Drei geistliche Chore*, and *Ein Deutches Requiem*, Op. 45.

The *German Requiem* is perhaps the most beloved of Brahms' choral works and is possibly the best known requiem by any composer. It is scored for SATB choir, soprano and baritone soloists, and orchestra. Brahms began to compose the requiem in 1861 and completed it by 1868 when he was thirty-five years old. The last movement to be composed was the fifth, *Ihr habt nun Traurigkeit*. It was a memorial to his mother.

Apparently, Brahms was not a religious man in the general sense of the word and there is no evidence that he was a practicing Christian. Yet it is obvious that he drew comfort from the Biblical passages chosen for his music. At the core of the traditional requiem is the *Dies irae*, and its visions of the Divine Judgment, yet it plays no part in the message of Brahms' music. It is also a unique fact that the name of Jesus appears nowhere in this setting of the *German Requiem*. When questioned about whom the work was written for, he replied that he had all humanity in mind. The first full performance took place on Feb. 18, 1869, in Leipzig.

Brahms was very interested in old music, particularly in that of the Renaissance and baroque, and adapted many of the features of these styles into his own instrumental and vocal music. Four of the seven movements (1, 2, 4, 7) are in tri-partite (ABA) form. The baroque spirit is alive in the two double fugues (*But the souls of the Righteous* and *Lord, Thou art worthy*), the four-voiced fugue (*And the ransomed*), and the fugato (*They praise Thy name*). The baroque influence is also heard in the sarabande (here used as a funeral cortege) in the second movement and in the dialogues between the baritone or soprano soloist and the choir (movements three and five). The Renaissance influence appears in Brahms' linear, polyphonic treatment of the choral voices. The *German Requiem* brought him recognition as an important composer.

Basic Data

EDITIONS

1. Brahms	2. Sämtliche Werke, Band 17
Op. 45 Ein deutsches Requiem	Ein Deutsches Requiem, nach
Full score	Worten den heiligen Schriften
Ernst Eulenberg, Ltd	für Soli, Chor und Orchester.
	Op. 45
	Breitkopf und Härtel
	Wiesbaden. 1926.

DURATION

Seven movements, 1479 mm., perf., c. 70'

VOICING AND ORCHESTRATION

Choir: SATB range: S-B flat 6; B-E3
Soloists: soprano, baritone
Orchestra: vn. I/II, vla., vc., db., pic., 2 fl., 2 ob., 2 cl., 2 bsn., 4 Fh., 2 tpt., 3 tbn., tuba, timp., harp (used only in the first & second movements).

OUTLINE

Selig sind: 158 mm. [fm] *ziemlich langsam und mit Ausdruck* [rather slow and with expression] satb choir/orchestra. ABA form [*Blessed are they-They that sow-Blessed are they*].

> Blessed are they that mourn,
> for they shall be comforted.
> [Matthew 5:4]
> They that sow in tears shall reap in joy.
> He that goeth forth and weepeth, bearing precious seed,
> shall doubtless come again with rejoicing,
> bringing his sheaves with him.
> [Psalm 126:5–6]

Denn alles Fleisch: 237 mm. [b flat m] *langsam, marschmassig* [slow, in march tempo] satb choir/orchestra.

The movement is divided into seven sections: *For all flesh is as grass* [1–2]; *Be patient therefore* [3]; *For all flesh is as grass* [4–5]; *But the word of the Lord* [6]; *And the ransomed of the Lord* [7]. Sections 1–5 form an large A-B-A structure in march rhythm (a funeral cortège) that can be described as a monumental Baroque sarabande. Sections 6–8 are a choral version of the baroque keyboard prelude and fugue. The exuberant fugue, *And the ransomed of the Lord,* balances the weightiness of the opening march-like sections.

For all flesh is as the grass, and the glory of man as the flower of grass.
The grass withereth, and the flower therof falleth away.
[I Peter 1:24]
Be patient therefore, brethren, unto the coming of the Lord.
Behold the husbandman waiteth for the precious fruit of the earth,
and hath long patience for it, until he receive
the early and latter rain.
[James 5:7]
But the word of the Lord endureth forever.
[I Peter 1:25]
And the ransomed of the Lord shall return,
and come to Zion with songs and everlasting joy
upon their heads:
They shall obtain joy and gladness,
and sorrow and sighing shall flee away.
[Isaiah 35:10]

Herr, lehre doch mich: 208 mm. [dm-DM] *andante moderato.*
Lord make me to know, Bar solo/satb choir/orchestra; *Now, Lord, what do I wait for?,* Bar solo/satb choir/orchestra; *But the souls of the righteous,* satb choir/ orchestra. (double fugue: theme I is begun by the tenors, theme II by the violins).

Lord, make me to know mine end, and the measure of my days,
what it is; that I may know how frail I am.
Behold thou hast made my days as a handbreadth; and mine age
is as nothing before thee.
Verily, every man at his best state is altogether vanity.
Surely every man walketh in a vain show:
Surely they are disquieted in vain:
He heapeth up riches and knoweth not who shall gather them.
And now Lord, what do I wait for ?
My hope is in thee.
[Psalm 39:4–7]

But the souls of the righteous are in the hand of God,
and there shall no torment touch them.
[Wisdom of Solomon 3:1]

Wie lieblich sind deine Wohnungen: 179 mm. [E flat M] *Con moto moderato.*
  satb choir/orchestra. ABA form, with a short, agitated *fugato* middle section.

> How lovely is thy dwelling place, O Lord of Hosts.
> My soul longeth, yea fainteth for the courts of the Lord:
> My soul and body crieth out for the living God.
> Blessed are they that dwell within Thy house:
> They praise thee forevermore.
> [Psalm 84:1–2, 4]

Ihr habt nun Traurigkeit: 82 mm. [GM] *Langsam* [slow].
  S solo/satb choir/orchestra. The musical form is dictated by the dialogue
  between the soprano soloist and choir.

> Ye now have sorrow, but I will see you again
> and your heart will rejoice and your joy
> shall not be taken away.
> [John 16:22]
> As one whom his own mother comforteth,
> so will I comfort you.
> [Isaiah 66:13]
> Behold with your eyes, how I have labored but little
> and found for myself much rest.
> [Ecclesiastes 51:27]

Denn wir haben: 349 mm. [cm-CM] *andante & allegro.*
  satb choir/Bar solo/orchestra. *For here we have no continuing place* (an anxious
  dialogue between the baritone and choir in which St. Paul's mystery of the Last
  Day is explained); *For the trumpet shall sound*, satb choir/orchestra; *Lord, Thou
  art worthy*. satb choir (double fugue).

> For here we have no continuing place, but we seek one to come.
> [Hebrews 13:14]
> Behold, I tell you a mystery; We shall not all sleep,
> but we shall be changed in a moment, in the twinkling of an eye,
> at the last trumpet call: For the trumpet shall sound,
> and the dead be raised incorruptible, and we shall be changed.
> Then shall be brought to pass the saying that is written,
> Death is swallowed up in victory.
> O death, where is thy sting ? O grave where is thy victory ?
> [I Corinthians: 15:51–2, 54–5]
> Lord, Thou art worthy to receive honor and power:
> for Thou hast created all things, and for thy pleasure
> they are and were created.
> [Revelations 4:11]

Selig sind die Toten: 166 mm. [FM-AM-FM] *maestoso.*

satb choir/orchestra. Tri-partite ABA structure: *Blessed are the Dead; They shall rest; Blessed are the Dead.* Here Brahms confirms the notion that the living will, at the end, attain blessed comfort.

Blessed are the dead which die in the Lord from henceforth:
Yea, saith the Spirit, that they may rest from their labors;
and their works do follow them.
[Revelations 14:13]

DISCOGRAPHY

1. Telarc, 80092, Atlanta Symphony Orchestra and Chorus, dir. Robert Shaw.
2. Multiple listings in the Schwann Catalogue.

CÉSAR BRESGEN
October 16, 1913–April 7, 1988

César Bresgen, an Austrian composer, was trained at the Munich Music Academy. While a student, he went to London, where he worked as a pianist for the Leslie Barrows Dance Studio. This experience helped to nurture an interest in ballet and stage music. In 1939, he was invited to teach composition at the Mozarteum in Salzburg, an organization with which he maintained a life-long association. After World War II, he worked as a choirmaster and organist in Mittersill, a town where he met Anton Webern.

He later studied composition with Paul Hindemith and Ernst Krenek. His compositions won a number of important prizes. Among his compositions are a number of practical pieces that were stimulated by his association with young people. He also composed a large oeuvre of serious art music, including stage pieces, orchestral works, chamber music, and vocal music. There is a *Requiem für Anton Webern* (1945–72), *Surrexit Dominus* (1970) and the *Totenmesse* (Funeral Mass, 1971–72). The *Deutsche Totenmesse* for SATB choir and organ was composed in 1971–1972. Its texts are poetry by Huub Oosterhuis and Psalm texts arranged by Bresgen. The work is notated in C major, but the various movements are in other tonalities and modalities. Bresgen's melodies have a chant-like quality and many choral passages are set in unison. The harmony is modern, modal, and spare in its texture. The music was conceived in a linear, polyphonic manner. The simplicity of the work suggests that the composer wanted to make available a practical work that could be sung in small parishes where large trained choirs were not available.

The constantly changing meter of the music is a special feature of this composition. Reminiscent of *Carmina Burana* by Carl Orff (a close friend of Bresgen), the metered rhythms include 2/4, 3/4, 4/4, 5/4, 6/4, 7/4, 9/

4, 2/2, 3/2, 5/2, 5/8, 7/8, 8/8, as well as free rhythm. This variety of rhythm is designed to suit the flow of the poetry. The choir is scored from one to six voice parts. Several purely instrumental movements are included in this composition. Its premiere took place on November 2, 1973, at the Basilica of the Benedictine Abbey Seckau in Steiermark.

Basic Data

EDITION

Deutsche Totenmesse für gemischten Chor und Orgel
Texte: Huub Oosterhuis & César Bresgen (nach Psalmtexten)
Orgelpartitur
Verlag Doblinger (#45543)

DURATION

Eight movements, 295 mm.

VOICING AND ORCHESTRATION

Choir: SATB [*divisi*] range: S-F6; B-G3
Instruments: org.

OUTLINE

Introit: *Ich steh vor dir*: 32 mm. [dm] *sostenuto* [I stand before Thee]
Brief organ introduction; three-six part choir (saatbb). Chant-like passages alternate with syllabic chordal harmony. The absence of C # gives the harmony a modal (dorian) quality. Text: Oosterhuis. Organ interludes separate the three verses.

1.

Ich steh vor dir in Armut und in Not.	I stand before thee in weakness and in need.
Fremd ist dein Name, dunkel deine Wege.	Unknown is Thy name, dark Thy ways.
Seit Menschen denken, Herr,	Humankind has long thought, Lord, Thou art my
bist du mein Gott. Mein Los ist Tod.	God. My lot is death.
Hast du nicht bessren Segen?	Hast Thou not a better blessing?
Bist du der Gott, der meine Zukunft fugt?	Art Thou the God who ordains my future?
Ich glaube Herr.	I believe Lord.
Was stehst du mir im Wege?	What do you place in my way?

2.

Es uberschätzen Zweifel meinen Tag, mein Unvermogen halt mich ganz gefangen.	Doubt overshadows my day, My lack of power binds me completely.
Mein Name ist in deine Hand gelegt.	My name is placed in Thy hand.

Mein Los ist Tod.	My lot is death.
Braucht mir um dein Erbarmen noch zu bangen?	Need I still be anxious about Thy compassion?
Darf ich dich noch mit neuen Augen sehn?	Am I allowed to see with new eyes?
Darf in dein Land, darf ich noch lebend gelangen?	Allowed in Thy land, will I be permitted to remain alive?

3.

Spricht du das Wort, das mir Befreiung gibt, schenk deinen Tod und nimmt mich auf in Frieden. Tu auf die Welt, die ohne Ende ist, und alle Liebe sei dem Sohn beschieden.	Say the word that will bring me freedom, give Thy death, and take me away in peace. Open up the world that is without end, and all love be given to the Son.

Zwischengesang: *Der Herr hat mich gesehn*: 33 mm. *hell* [bright] [CM]
The Intermezzo begins with a ten-measure organ introduction. Satb choir (unison to five-part). The organ accompaniment doubles the choral lines. Text: Oosterhuis

Der Herr hat mich gesehen und über Nacht gab er mir neues Leben und Gedeihen, aus Finsternis hat er mich licht gemacht, gab mir ein lebend Herz und neue Augen. So kommt er stets in stiller Übermacht und lasst zufrieden seine Schwachheit taugen.	The Lord has seen me and through the night has given to me a new life and vitality, out of the darkness, has he made me light, has given me a living heart and new eyes. Thus he always comes, in quiet strength, and with satisfaction, lets his weakness be of use.

Die mit Tränen säen: 38 mm. *andante*
Brief organ prelude. satb choir (homophonic). Text: Psalm 126, adapted by Bresgen.

Die mit Tränen säen werden in Freuden ernten, denn Gott der Herr hat Grosses für sie getan. Sie gehen hin und weinen, sie tragen edlen Sämen, denn Gott . . . Sie kommen her mit Freuden und wiegen edlen Garben, denn Gott . . . Alleluia!	Those who sow in tears shall reap in joy, for God the Lord has done great things for them. They go forth and weep, they yield noble seeds, for God the Lord . . . They come forth in joy and bring golden sheaves, for God the Lord . . . Alleluia!

Heilig, Heilig: 22 mm. [AM] *lento maestoso* satb choir (unison to six-part). Text: Oosterhuis, poetry derived from the traditional *Sanctus*.

Heilig, Heilig. Mächtiger, Herr Gott, Sabaoth.	Holy, Holy. Almighty One. Lord God of Sabbaoth.

Himmel und Erde sind erfüllt	Heaven and earth are filled
von diener Herrlichkeit.	with Thy glory.
Hosanna, Hosanna in der Höhe.	Hosanna, Hosanna in the Highest.
Hochgelobt sei, der da kommt im	Blessed be He who comes in
Namens des Herrn,	the name of the Lord.
Hosanna, Hosanna in der Höhe.	Hosanna, Hosanna in the Highest.

Mediation: 22 mm. [chromatic, ends in EM] *andante sostenuto.* Organ solo.

Die Seelen der Gerechten [from: *Proprium Missarum de Sanctis*]: 30 mm. [AM] *calmo.*
satb choir (four-part).

Die Seelen der Gerechten sind in Gottes Hand,	The souls of the righteous are in God's hand,
nicht erreicht sie die Folterung des Bosen.	Let not the torture of evil ones touch them.
Sterbende waren sie in den Augen der Toren.	In the eyes of fools they were dying.
Sie aber weilen in Frieden.	They, however, abide in joy.
Alleluia! Wunderbar ist unser Gott in seinen	Alleluia. Wonderful is God in His holiness.
Heiligen. Alleluia	Alleluia.

Niemand lebt fur sich selbst: 79 mm. *sostenuto.* Organ introduction. satb choir. Text:
Oosterhuis.

Niemand lebt für sich selbst,	No one lives only for himself,
niemand stirbt für sich selbst.	no one dies only for himeself.
Ihm sind wir zu eigen.	We belong to Him.
[organ interlude]	
Lasst uns nun gehen in Frieden und ihn,	Now let us depart in peace, as he,
den wir in deiner Stunde zum letzten	that we have in your hour, for the last time,
Mal in unserer Mitte haben,	in your midst, is borne off to
wegtragen zu seines Grab.	his grave.
Wir geben ihn aus den Handen und	pass him from our hands and lay
legen ihn wieder in die Erde,	him again into the earth,
in die Hande des lebendigen Gottes.	into the hands of the living God.
In namen des Vaters und des Sohnes	In the name of the Father and the Son
und die Heiligen Geistes.	and the Holy Ghost.
[organ interlude]	
Niemand lebt für sich selbst . . .	No one lives only for himself . . .
[organ postlude]	

Lasst uns nun gehn in Frieden: 19 mm. *sostenuto.* satb choir (unison to six-part).
Verse form. Text: Ooster-huis (based upon The Song of Solomon)

| Lasst uns nun gehn in Frieden, denn | Let us depart in peace, for behold: |
| sehet: dies ist das Ende nicht. | This is not the end. |

Unser Gott ist ein Gott der Lebenden	Our God is a God of the living,
und seine Güte wahret ewiglich.	and His good endures forever.
Lass uns nun gehn in Frieden, denn	Let us depart in peace, for behold:
sehet: dies ist das Ende nicht.	This is not the end.
Wir richten unsere Augen hin zu dem	We turn our eyes upon the Cross of
Kreutze Jesu Christi.	Jesus Christ.
Lass keine Toten fallen, die du nur	Let none of the dead fall, those that
für das Leben gemacht hast.	Thou made only for life.
So rette unsere Toten, den die lebst,	So save our dead, those that live in
O grosser Gott.	Thee,
	O Great God.

Postludium: 20 mm. [DM] A short, full-*pleno*, written for the organ, concludes the work.

DISCOGRAPHY

Calig, CAL 30426 [LP disk], The a-cappella choir "Chor Zeltweg," cond. Kurt Muthspiel.

FRANZ XAVER GRUBER
November 25, 1787–June 7, 1863

The composer of possibly the most famous melody in the world, *Silent Night, Holy Night*, was born in Hallein, a little village near Salzburg, Austria. By the age of eighteen, Gruber was accompanying church services. He was a school teacher and organist and cantor of St. Nicholas Church in Oberndorf from 1816–29. In 1835, he was appointed the choir director at the Stadpfarrkirche in Hallein, remaining there until his death. He was not a prolific composer, in fact there remain only a handful of pieces: *Deutsche Seelenmesse*, a *Tantum Ergo*, *Silent Night*, and two other liturgical pieces.

The *Deutsche Seelenmesse* was composed in 1836 and is currently published as *Deutsches Requiem*. Gruber originally composed it for soprano and alto duet and organ, but at a later date provided a tenor and bass part for this simple, folksong-like piece. All six movements are quite brief. The texts chosen by Gruber generally parallel those of the Roman Catholic requiem mass and its musical language is made up of simple diatonic harmony with an occasional secondary dominant. The textures are a fabric of homophonic, chordal writing as in *Silent Night*. The piece possesses much charm in its original, duet form, with its numerous parallel thirds and sixths.

Basic Data

EDITION

Denkmäler der Musik in Salzburg
Einzelausgaben, Heft 8
Franz Xaver Gruber
Deutsches Requiem
"Gib den Seelen in der Pein" für zwei (vier) Singstimmen und Orgel
Comes-Verlag. Bad Reichenhall. 1991

DURATION

Six movements, 152 mm.

VOICING AND ORCHESTRATION

Choir: SA (TB) range: S-F6; B-F3
Instruments: org.

OUTLINE

Zum Eingang [Introit]: 20 mm. *Gib den Seelen in der Pein*, [FM] *langsam* [slow].

Gib den Seelen in der Pein	Give the souls in torment,
Die um Hilfe klaglich schrein,	who call out pitifully for help,
Herr, gib ihnen ew'ge Ruh.'	Lord give them eternal rest.
Sieh, wie sie in heissen Flammen	Behold how they, in hot flames,
ringer ihre Hand.	wring their hands.
Fuhr' sie bald dem Himmel zu.	Lead them soon into Heaven.

Dies Irae, 36 mm. *Christen, denkt*, [B flat M] *massig* [measured].

Christen, denkt an jene Stunde	Christian, ponder on the hour, when
da nach des Propheten Munde	according to the words of the
einst der Richter kommen wird.	Prophets, The judge will come.
Sunder, wie wird's dir ergehen,	Sinner, what will become of you?
enn Gerechte kaum bestehen?	Even the Upright can scarce endure.
Denk wie dir zu Mute wird.	Ponder how you will feel.
O wie wirst du beben, zagen	Oh, how thou will'st tremble and fear
wenn das Buch wird aufgeschlagen,	as the Book, wherein your faults are
worin deine Fehler steh'n.	recorded, is opened.
Drum benütze noch die Tage,	So use your days wisely,
scheue weder Muh noch Plage,	fear neither trouble nor misery,
um dereinstens zu besteh'n.	so that you will endure.

Zur Opferung [Offertory]: 31 mm. *Jesus, nimm sie auf* [FM] *sehr langsam* [very slow]

Jesus! Nimm sie auf, die wir dir empfehlen,	Jesus! Receive those we commend, to you all of the new souls, dear to us,

All' die teuren uns entschwinden neu
Seelen sind sie noch im Ort der
Reinigung.
Uns're Väter, Mutter, Schwestern,
Brüder wollen einst wir selig finden
wieder, wo kein Schmerz mehr brennt
der Laüterung.

who now stand in the place of
cleansing. Our Father, Mother, Sister,
Brother, one day we will find, blessed
in that place where there is no more
pain.

Zum Sanctus: 20 mm. *Mit den sel'gen Cherubinen* [CM] *andante.*

Mit den sel'gen Cherubinen
mit dem ganzen Himmelschor
lasst uns heilig, heilig, singen!
Froh steig' unser Lied empor.

With the holy Cherubim,
with the entire Heavenly Choir,
let us sing Holy, Holy,
Joyfully raise up our song!

Lass die Stimmen zu dir dringen,
O du Herr des Herrlichkeit.
Wenn wir heilig, heilig, singen,
sei gelobt, gebenedeit.

Let our voices reach up to you,
O Thou Lord of Glory.
As we sing Holy, Holy,
be Thou praised and blessed.

Nach der Wandlung [Post-Communion]: 23 mm. *Ans Kreuzesholz geschlagen* [FM] *langsam* [slow].

Ans Kreuzesholz geschlagen,
erblick ich, Jesus dich!
Du hast die Schuld getragen
so liebevoll für mich.

Nailed on the wooden Cross,
I see Thee, Jesus.
Thou hast borne my sin
out of love for me.

Du bist für uns gestorben,
O Jesus, wahrer Gott!
Du hast uns Heil erworben,
erlost vom ew'gen Tod.

You died for us,
O Jesus, true God !
You have brought us blessing,
redeemed us from eternal death.

Zum Agnus Dei: 22 mm. *Zum Himmel früh erkoren*: [B flat M] *langsam* [slow].

Zum Himmel früh erkoren,
seid ihr uns nicht verloren,
um die Träne fliesst,
Hier trübten uns're Freuden
doch Sorgen und Leiden,
Wir suchen nur, was ihr geniesst.

To Heaven quickly take them,
Let not those for whom our tears flow,
be lost.
Now, our joy is often troubled
by cares and suffering,
We seek only what pleases you.

DISCOGRAPHY
None found.

HUGO KAUN
March 21, 1863–April 2, 1932

Hugo Kaun studied at the Berlin Hochschule für Musik. He later studied composition with Friedrich Kiel at the Prussian Academy of Arts. His career included teaching, composition, and conducting. In 1886, he moved to Milwaukee, Wisconsin, where he worked with the famous choral society, the Milwaukee Liederkranz. In 1902, he resumed his career in Germany.

Kaun left a significant body of music, including four operas, three symphonies, three piano concertos, three tone poems (two on American subjects: *Hiawatha*, Op. 43, *Minnehaha*, Op. 43), four string quartets, a variety of chamber and orchestral music, and more than 200 choral pieces. The sacred works include a setting of *Psalm 126* and a *Requiem*, Op. 116.

The *Requiem*, Op. 116, was composed after World War I (1921) and scored for TTBB [*divisi*] choir, alto solo, and orchestra. The tonal language of the *Requiem* is a late-romantic, Wagnerian-style chromatic harmony. Keys listed in the Outline are only approximate tonalities because the music is in a constant state of harmonic change.

The prevailing, four-part choral texture is homophonic with occasional passages of imitative polyphony at *Unser Erbe, Herr warum willst du, und meine Zuversicht*. A complete fugue, scored for TTBB choir and boy's choir, is employed for the text, *Denn der Herr*. The alto soloist plays a major role in three movements of the *Requiem* and the third movement, *Alles ist eitel*, is an accompanied vocal solo.

Basic Data

EDITION

Requiem nach Worten der Heiligen Schrift für Mannerchor, Altsolo (Mezzosopran) und Orchester (Orgel ad lib.) Op.116
Hugo Kaun
Leipzig, Verlag F. E. C. Leuckhart (8189) [nd]

DURATION

Seven movements, 831 mm.

VOICING AND ORCHESTRATION

Choir: TTBB [*divisi*] choir. Boy's choir. Range: T-B flat 6; B-C3
Soloists: alto
Instruments: symphonic orchestra. organ.

OUTLINE

Part I
Alles was auf dem Erde kommt: 120 mm.
> *Alles was dem Erde* [cm] *sehr ruhig und innig.* ttbb choir; *Ach, dass ich* . . . , A solo/ ttbb choir; *Leben wir* . . . ttbb choir.

Alles was aus der Erde kommt,	Everything that comes from the earth
muss wieder zur Ende werden.	must again return to the earth.

Ach, dass ich Wasser genug hätte
in meinem Haupte, und meine Augen
Tränenquellen waren, dass ich
Tag und Nacht beweinen möchte
die Erschlagenen in meinem Volke.
Leben wir, so leben wir dem Herrn.
Sterben wir, so sterben wir dem
Herrn.
darum nur leben oder sterben,
so sind wir des Herrn.

O that I would have water enough in
my head, so that my eyes might be a
spring of tears, that I, day and night,
could mourn those of my people
struck dead.
We live, so we live in the Lord.
We die, so we die in the Lord.
Therefore we live or die,
So we are the Lord's.

Herr, sieh an unsere Schmach: 131 mm.
Herr, sieh an. . .[B flat M] sehr bewegt, leidenschaftlich. ttbb choir; *Herr, warum willst du . . . ruhiges Zeitmass.* ttbb choir (fugal).

Herr, sieh an unsere Schmach.
Herr, gedenke wie es uns gehet.
Unser Erbe ist den Fremden,
Zu teil worden und unsere Häuser
den Ausländern.
Wir sind Waisen. Wir haben keine
Vater, unsere Mütter sind wie
Witwen, und
wenn wir schon müde sind,
lasst man uns doch keine Ruhe.
Knechte herrschen über uns.
Herr, warum willst du uns so gar
vergessen? Bringe uns Herr wieder zu
dir,
dass wir wieder heim kommen.

Lord, look upon our disgrace.
Lord, consider our condition.
Our inheritance is shared with
strangers; our homes, with
foreigners.
We are orphans. We have no
father. Our mothers are as
widows and although we are
tired, we are given no peace.
Slaves rule over us.
Lord, why do you want to cast us
off ? Lord, bring us again to Thee
that we may return home.

Alles ist eitel: 46 mm.
Alles ist eitel [f#m] langsam und drangend. A solo.

Alles ist eitel. Was hat der Mensch
von all seiner Mühe?
Ein Geschlecht vergehet, das andere
kommt, die Ende aber bleibt ewiglich.
Die Sonne gehet auf, und gehet unter
und lauft an ihnen Ort, dass sie
wieder daselbst aufgehe.
Alle Wasser laufen ins Meer—und
wird das Meer nicht voller; an den Ort
da sie herfliessen, fliessen sie wieder
hin.
Alles ist eitel was ist's, das geschen
ist, und hernach nicht geschen wird.
Alles ist eitel.

All is vain. What has man for all his
trouble? A race passes away and
another comes. However the end
remains eternal.
The sun rises and sets and runs in its
place, that it again rises in the same
place.
All water flows into the sea—yet the
sea becomes no fuller in that place
since it flows back and forth again.
All is vain that is, that was and that
has not yet been.
All is vain.

Wie liegt dei Stadt: 120 mm.

Wie liegt die Stadt . . . [dm-B flat M] *sehr langsam, unheimlich, duster.* ttbb choir.

Wie liegt die Stadt so wüste, die voll Volks war. Sie ist wie eine Witwe.	How empty lies the city that was full of people. It is like a widow.
Die eine Konigin in den Ländern war, muss nun dienen, es ist niemand von allen ihren Freunden der sie troste.	She, a queen among the lands, must now serve, and is nothing before all of her friends who comfort her.
Das Schmach bricht unser Herz.	The disgrace breaks our hearts.
Der Herr hat zertreten alle unsere Starken, unsere Feinde freuen sich und sprechen:	The Lord has dispersed all of our strength, our enemies rejoice and say:
Heh! Wir habe sie vertilget, das ist der Tag dess wir haben begehet, wir haben's verlangt, wir haben's erlebt.	Hey! We have exterminated you. This is the day to which we have committed ourselves. We have demanded it. We lived to see it.
Wie liegt die Stadt so wüste die voll Volks war. Schauet doch und sehet, ob irgend ein Schmerz sei wie unser Schmerz.	How empty lies the city that was full of people. Behold and see whether there be any sorrow unto our sorrow.

Part II

Meine Zuversicht: 103 mm.

Meine Zuversicht . . . [E flat M] *sehr ruhig und ausdruckvoll.* ttbb choir [*divisi*]; *Der Mensch vom Weibe.* A solo; *Meine Zuversicht,* A solo/ttbb choir.

Meine Zuversicht und meine Burg ist mein Gott auf den ich hoffe.	My confidence and my fortress is my God in whom I place my hope.
Er wird mich mit seinen Fittichen dekken und meine Zuversicht wird sein unter seiner Flügeln.	He will cover me with his pinions and my confidence under his wings.
Der Mensch vom Weibe geboren lebt kurze Zeit, gehet auf—wie eine Blume und fallt ab.	Man that is born of woman lives but a short time—goes forth like a flower and withers away.
Ach Herr, lehre doch mich, dass es ein Ende mit mir haben muss und mein Leben ein Ziel hat und dann muss wie ein Wasser ausläuft aus dem See— und wie ein Strom versieget und vertrocknet, so ist ein Mensch wenn er sich legt und wird nicht aufstehen und aufwachen.	O Lord, let me know my end and the measure of my days, what it is and that I may flow like water from the sea—and like a stream, dry up and withers like a man when he lies down and arises and awakens no more.

Das ist ein kostlich Ding: 188 mm.

Das ist ein köstlich Ding . . . [GM] *bewegt.* ttbb choir [*divisi*]; *Denn der Herr, lebhaft, wuchtig.* ttbb choir/boy's choir (fugue).

Das ist ein köstlich Ding, dem Herrn	It is a precious thing, to thank the

danken und lobsingen seinem
Namen.
Er heilet die zerbrochenen Herezens
sind und verbindet ihre Schmerzen.
Die Güte des Herrn hat kein Ende,
sondern sie ist alle Morgen neu.
Denn der Herr ist gross und von
grosser Kraft.
Jesus meine Zuversicht und mein
Heiland ist im Leben.
Dieses weiss ich, sollt ich nicht darum
mich zufrieden geben.
Was die bange Todesnacht mir auch
für Gedanken macht und ist
unbegreiflich, wie er regieret denn
der Herr ist gross und von grosser
Kraft.

Lord and sing praises to His name.

He heals the broken heart and binds
up your grief.
The goodness of the Lord has no
end, it is new every morning.
For the Lord is great and of great
strength.
Jesus, my confidence and my
Saviour is in life.
These things I know, I ought not be
discontent.
For what the fearful night of death
makes me to think.
and it is unconceivable that it rules
for the Lord is great and of great
strength.

O Tod, wie bitter bist du: 123 mm.
O Tod . . . [CM, end] *sehr ruhig, mit grossem Ausdruck.* A solo; *Fürchte den Tod,*
ttbb choir [*divisi*]/A solo.

O Tod, wie bitter bist du, wenn an
dich gedenkt ein Mensch dem es
wohlgehet in allen Dingen.
O Tod, wie wohl tust du dem
Dürftigen,
Der nichts zu hoffen noch zu
erwarten hat,
Herr Gott, du bist unsere Zuflucht für
und für.
Der du die Menschen lässest sterben
und
spricht: Kommet wieder
Menschenkinder.

Du lässest sie dahinfahren wie einen
Strom und sind wie ein Schlaf.
Fürchte den Tod nicht.
Gedenke, das also geordnet ist vom
Herrn über alles Fleisch beide derer,
die vor dir gewesen sind, und nach
dir kommen werden. Und Christus
spricht: Ich bin die Tür—so jemand
durch mich eingehet, der wird selig
werden und ich gebe ihm da ewige
Leben.

O Death, how bitter art Thou,
when I consider a man that is
well in all things.
O Death, how well doest Thou
for the needy, who hope for and

expect nothing.
Lord God, you have been our
refuge for ever and ever.

You, who permits mankind to die,
and says: Come again, Children of
Man.
Thou who orders them to travel
like a stream and as in a sleep.

Fear not death.
Remember that both are ordered
by thee and will return unto thee.
And Christ said: I am the Gate and
whosoever goes through me will
become holy and I will give them
eternal life.

FRANZ SCHUBERT
January 31, 1797–November 19, 1828

This composer, famous for nine symphonies (especially the *"Unfinished"*), numerous piano compositions, more than 600 Lieder, and chamber music, left an impressive amount of sacred music. There are six masses for soloists, SATB choir, organ, and orchestra: F major (1814), G major (1815), B flat major (1815), C major (1816), composed in his teenage years, while the A flat major (1819–22) and E flat major (1828) were written in his twenties. There are other works: *Psalm 92* for SATB choir (1828), *Psalm 23* for female voices (1820), a *Stabat Mater* for STB soloists, choir, and orchestra (1816), *Salve Regina* for soprano and strings (1819), *Kyrie* for unaccompanied choir (1813), *Magnificat* for SATB soloists, organ, choir, and orchestra (1815), two settings of *Tantum Ergo* (1814 & 1828), a *German Mass* for choir, woodwinds, and organ (1827), and the *German Requiem* (*Deutsche Trauermesse*) of August 1818. There remains an unfinished setting of the requiem mass, consisting of the Introit and *Kyrie*, completed.

The *Deutsche Trauermesse*, a short work, scored for SATB choir, SATB soli, and organ, was misattributed to his brother, Ferdinand. As is the case with most of Schubert's music, the spirit of the Lied is present, even though some of the movements are as brief as eight measures in length. Its first performance date cannot be discovered, but it is probable that it took place in 1818 at The Home for Orphans, in the Alsergrund District, of Vienna.

The choral writing is homophonic throughout and the organ provides a modest support for the choral parts. Many movements possess sections for solo singers, usually in duet form. These quartet/duet sections alternate with the full choral passages. Each movement functions as a choral response to the prayers and readings.

Basic Data

EDITION

Deutsche Trauermesse (German Requiem) für gemischten Chor und Orgel
Franz Schubert, Hitherto ascribed to Ferdinand Schubert
Schubert-Erstdrucke II
Publisher: Otto Erich Deutsch 1928.
[includes extensive notes by Otto Deutsch]

DURATION

Ten movements, 140 mm.

VOICING AND ORCHESTRATION

Choir: SATB range: S-F6; B-E flat 3
Soloists: SATB
Instruments: org.

OUTLINE

Zum Eingang [Introit]: 14 mm. [gm] *langsam* [slow] satb choir/SA soli.

Bei des Entschlafnen Trauerbahre versammeln wir uns am Altare; sieh mitleidsvoll, O Herr! auf uns herab.	At the mourning-bier we are all gathered at the altar; look with sympathy upon us, O Lord.
Voll des Vertraums zu deiner Gute, erheben wir uns im Gemüte zu dir, O du, der in den Tod für uns sich gab.	Full of mourning for Thy good, brought up in our hearts, for Thee, who gave Himself in death for us.

Nach der Epistel [Epistle]: 12 mm. [B flat M] *etwas bewegter* [more movement] satb choir/SATB soli.

Der Tod ruckt Seelen vor's Gericht, wo Jesus thront im reinsten Licht. Da wird, was hier verborgen war, den Augen aller offenbar.	Death moves all souls toward Judgement, where Jesus is enthroned in purest light. What has been concealed here on earth, will be made plain before all eyes.

Zum Evangelium [Gospel]: 8 mm. [gm] *massig* [measured] satb choir.

Wie tröstlich ist, was Jesus lehrt: "Wer an mich glaubt und mich verehrt, der lebt, komm nicht in das Gericht, und sieht den Tod auf ewig nicht."	How comforting is that, which Jesus taught: "Whoever believes in me and honors me, that one will live, not in Judgement, and will not behold Death as eternal."

Zum Offertorium [Offertory]: 18 mm. [E flat M] *langsam* [slow] satb choir/SA soli.

Dir, Vater! weihen wir hier Gaben von reinem Brot und reinem Wein. Du bist's von dem wir alles haben; lass sie dir wohl gefallig sein! Mit ihnen steige unser Flehen für die Entschlafenen empor;	To Thee, Father, we here consecrate gifts of pure bread and pure wine. That is all we have of You; let them be well-pleasing to You. With them ascends our plea for the deceased;

lass sie in Herrlichkeit dich sehen,   let them, in splendor, behold Thee,
umgeben von der Engel Chor.   surrounded by the Angel's Choir.

Zum Sanctus [Sanctus]: 25 mm. [E flat M] *feierlich* [solemn] satb choir/SATBsoli duet.

Droben nur ist wahres Leben!   Only above is the true Life!
Millionen stehen schon,   Millions stand there already,
ihren Retter zu erheben,   praising their Saviour,
selig da vor seinem Thron.   blessed, before Thy Throne.
Engel und Verklärte singen,   Angels and the Blessed sing,
Lob und Dank ihm darzubringen: Praise and thanks, to You they bring:
Heilig! Heilig! Heilig ist   Holy! Holy!
der Erbarmer Jesus Christ !   Holy is the God of Mercy, Jesus
                                               Christ!

Zur Wandlung [Transubstantiation]: 8 mm. [B flat M-GM] *massig* [measured] satb choir.

Jesu! dir leb' ich; Jesu! dir sterb' ich;   Jesu! I live in Thee; Jesu! I die in Thee;
Jesu! dein bin ich im Leben und Tod.   Jesu! I am Thine in life and death.

Zum Memento für die Abgestorbenen [Memorial for the Deceased]: 17 mm. [GM] *langsam* [slow] SA soli.

Der Frommen abgeschiedene Seelen,   The devout, departed souls,
Gott! deiner Vaterlieb emphehlen: God! To Thy Fatherly-love are
dies ist der Hinter lassne Trost und   commended:
Pflicht.   This is the last part left for comfort
Drum hoffen wir, du wirst das   and duty.
Flehender   With everything, we hope that You
Bruderliebe nicht verschmahen,   will not let languish the pleas for
die hoffnungsvoll für teure Seelen   brotherly love, that
spricht.   You will speak for those, hopeful, for
                                               the be-loved souls.

Zum Agnus Dei [Agnus Dei]: 14 mm. [dm] *sehr langsam* [very slow] satb choir/SA soli.

Lamm Gottes! Gnade, Heil, und   O Lamb of God ! Grace, health and life
Leben hast du erbarmend mir   hast Thou compassionately given me,
gegeben, du starbst, um mich vom   You died to free me from death.
Tode zu befrei'n.
Ermattet gingst du, mich zu suchen.   You went, exhausted, to seek me.
Du liessest dir am Kreuze fluchen!   You allowed Yourself to pledge it, on
                                               the Cross.
Herr! Soll dein Blut an mir verloren   Lord! Let not Your Blood be lost on
sein.   me.

Zur Kommunion [Communion]: 12 mm. [B flat M] *langsam* [slow] satb choir/SA soli.

O hohes Glück, vor dir zu steh'n!	O highest happiness, to stand before Thee!
O Freude, Jesu! dich zu seh'n!	O joy, Jesu! to see Thee!
Dich herrlich Haupt der Glieder!	The magnificent Head of the elect.
Zu sehen dich in deinem Licht,	To see Thee in Thy light,
von Angesicht zu Angesicht!	face to face,
Dich ersten aller Bruder.	Thou first of all Brothers.

Am Ende der Messe [the end of the Mass]: 12 mm. [gm] *langsam* [slow] satb choir.

Euch, die von uns geschieden,	To you who are from us separated,
verlieh Gott seinen Frieden,	grant God His peace,
bis wir nach dieser Pilgerzeit	until, after this Pilgrim's-time,
mit euch in Gottes Herrlichkeit	are united with you, for all eternity,
vereinigt ewig leben.	in God's splendor.

DISCOGRAPHY

Kirchenmusik St. Augustin #2 KSA 27002 Chor, Solisten und Orchester von St. Augustin-Wien, dir. Alois Glassner.

HEINRICH SCHÜTZ
October 8, 1585–November 6, 1672

Schütz was one of the most important church musicians of the seventeenth century. His main achievement was the introduction of, into German music, important features of Italian musical style. After his study in Venice with Giovanni Gabrieli, he brought back with him the dramatic style of monody so popular in Italy. He also imported into German music the Italian polychoral technique that used double choirs and various solo voices or combinations of voices (or instruments) in contrasting and complementary scorings. These elements, when mixed with the Germanic polyphonic traditions, helped to create a new type of music now known as baroque.

Schütz was a prolific choral composer whose collected works occupy seventeen volumes. There are four Passion settings, a *Christmas Oratorio*, the *Psalms & Motets* (1619), the *Cantiones Sacrae* (1625), *Symphoniae Sacrae*, Parts I, II, & III (1629, 1647, 1630), *Geistliche Konzert* (1636 and 1639), *Musicalia ad chorum sacrum* (1648), the Italian Madrigals (1611), and other works.

Published in 1636, *Musikalische Exequien*, Opus 7, was composed in 1635 at the request of Heinrich Reus Posthumus, the Lord of Gera, Schleiz, and Lobenstein. This work is the first known setting of a Lutheran, German requiem and one of the very few Protestant requiems. The music, scored for SSATTBB soli, two SATB choirs, and *basso continuo* instruments, is arranged into three movements. Its texts are taken from the Bible and verses from church hymns.

The prevailing choral texture is a mixture of imitative polyphony and expressive homophonic passages. The concerto form, with its *tutti* and *soli* passages, is the organizing principle of the first two movements.

Basic Data

EDITIONS

1. Heinrich Schütz
Musikalische Exequien für
Solostimmen, Chor und Basso Continuo

Edited by Friedrich Schoneich
Bärenreiter Kassel. Basel. Paris,
London. New York (BA 250)
[German only]1956

2. Neue Ausgabe. Samtliche Werke. Band 4.
Musikalische Exequien . . . praktischen Gebrauch.
Herausgegeben von Friedrich Schoneich
Bärenreiter Verlag
Kassel und Basel. 1956

DURATION

Three movements, 402 mm., perf., c. 35'

VOICING AND ORCHESTRATION

Choir: SATB choirs I/II range: S-F♯ 6; B-D3
Soloists: SSATTTBB
Instruments: organ, therobo, cello, violone

OUTLINE

Movement I: Concerto in the Form of A German Mass for the Dead, 293 mm.
Scored for 2–6 voices [ssattb], the "tutti" sections are hymn verses; soloist sections, Bible verses. The first movement is a Lutheran form of the *Kyrie* and *Gloria*.

KYRIE
[intonation]
Naked came I from my mother's womb.
[TT, B 1 soli]
Naked shall I return thither. The Lord gave and the Lord taketh away,
Blessed be the name of the Lord. [Job 1:21]
[ssattb choir]
Lord God, Son of God, have mercy on us.

CHRISTE
[SS, T 1 soli]
For me to live is Christ, to die is gain. Behold the Lamb of God,
who takes away the sins of the world. [Phil. 1:21; John 1:29]
[ssattb choir]

Jesus Christ, Son of God, have mercy on us.
KYRIE
[A 1, B 1 soli]
If we live, we live in the Lord; if we die, we die unto the Lord;
and so, if we live or die, we are the Lord's. [Romans 14:8]
[ssattb choir]
Lord God, Holy Spirit, have mercy on us.

GLORIA, *Gloria in Excelsis Deo*
[intonation]
For God so loved the world, that He gave his only begotten Son,
[SSATTB soli]
That whosoever believeth in him should not perish, but have
life everlasting. [John 3:16]
[ssattb choir]
He spoke to his beloved Son: The time is ripe to be merciful;
go forth then, treasure of my own heart and redeem weak humankind,
save Man from the misery of sin, overcome for him the sharpness
of death and suffer him to dwell with Thee. Martin Luther:
Set to the hymn-tune, *Nun freut euch* [Now rejoice].

GLORIA, *Domine Fili unigenite, Jesu Christe*
[S 2, T 2]
The blood of Jesus Christ, the Son of God, cleanses us from all sin. [John 1:7]
[ssattb choir]
Through Him all our sins are forgiven, life bestowed. In Heaven
we shall receive, O Lord, such great gifts. Ludwig Helmbod, 1575:
Set to the hymn-tune, *Nun lasst uns Gott* [Now let us to God].
[S 1, B 1]
For our conversation is in Heaven; from whence we also seek the Savior,
the Lord Jesus Christ: who shall change our base body, that it may be
fashioned like unto his glorious body. [Phil. 3:20–21]
[ssattb choir]
Life is a vale of woe, fear, misery, distress everywhere; our life-span
is short, full of bitter hardship, and who heeds it is in strife.
Johann Leon, 1582: Set to the hymn-tune, *Aus tiefer Not* [Out of the Depths].

GLORIA, *Qui tollis peccata mundi*
[TT soli]
Though your sins be as scarlet, they shall be white as snow; though they be red
as crimson, they shall be as wool. [Isaiah 1:18]
[ssattb choir]
His Word, his Baptism, his Communion, preserve us from all evil; the
Holy Spirit, by faith, teaches us to trust in Him. Ludwig Helmbold, 1575:
Set to the hymn-tune, *Nun lasst uns Gott* [Now let us to God].

GLORIA, *Suscipe deprecationem nostram*
[A solo]

Come my people, enter into my chamber, and shut the door after Thee;
Hide Thyself as it were for a little time, until the indignation be past.
[Isaiah 26:20]
[SS, B 2 soli]
But the souls of the righteous are in the hand of God, and there shall be no
torment to touch them. In the sight of the unwise they seemed to die; and their
departure is taken for misery, and their going from us as utter destruction;
but they are in peace. [Wisdom 3:1–3]
[A, T1, T2, B 1 soli]
Lord, there is none upon the earth that I desire but thee. My flesh and my heart
faileth, but God is the strength of my heart and my portion forever.
[Psalm 73:25–26]
[ssattb choir]
He is the salvation and blessed light of the Gentiles, to enlighten those who know
Him not and lead them unto Him; He is the jewel, the glory, joy and
delight of His people Israel. Martin Luther, 1524:
Set to the hymn-tune, *Es ist das Heil* [Salvation now is come].
[B 1 & 2 soli]
The days of our years are threescore and ten; and if by reason of strength
they be fourscore, yet is their strength labor and sorrow. [Psalm 90:10]
[ssattb choir]
O how wretched is our time here on earth. As soon mankind shall come
to nothing, so must we all perish; Here, throughout this vale of woe is
toil and trouble everywhere, even when all things prosper.
Set to the hymn-tune, *Aus tiefer Not* [Out of the depths].

GLORIA, *Qui sedes ad dexteram Patris*
[T 1 solo]
I know that my redeemer liveth, and that He shall stand at the latter day
upon the earth; and though worms destroy this body, yet in my
flesh shall I see God. [Job 19:25–26]
[ssattb choir]
Since thou hast risen from the dead, the grave shall not contain me; thy
rising is my greatest comfort, thou canst disperse all fear of death;
for where thou art, there shall I be, that I always may live with thee. Therefore
I die with joy. Nikolaus Hermann, 1562: set to the hymn-tune, *Wenn mein
Stundelein* [When my last hour]

GLORIA, *Quoniam tu solus sanctus*
[SSATTB soli]
Lord, I will not let thee go, except thou bless me. [I Moses, 32:37]
[ssattb choir]
He saith unto me: Be true to me, so shall thy fortunes prosper. I gave my
whole self up to thee; my own life has overcome death, my innocence bears
thy sins that thou mayest be saved. Martin Luther, 1523:
Set to the hymn-tune, *Nun freut euch* [Now Rejoice].

Movement II: Motet, *Herr, wenn ich nur Dich habe*. 48 mm.
  Scored for two satb choirs/continuo. Form: choral dialogue in homophonic texture.

> Whom have I in heaven but thee? There is none upon earth that I desire besides thee. My flesh and my heart fail, but God is the strength of my heart and my portion forever. [Psalm 73:25–26]

Movement III: *The Song of Simeon*, 61 mm.
  Scored for two choirs: sattb & ssbar. The three-part ssbar choir, designated as the "seraphim" choir should be placed some distance from the five-part ensemble, which Schütz requested be placed next to the organ. The movement begins with an intonation on the words, *Lord, lettest now Thy servant*.

> Lord, now lettest thou thy servant depart in peace, according to thy words; for mine eyes have seen thy salvation, which thou hast prepared before the face of all people; a light to lighten the Gentiles, and the glory of thy people Israel. [Luke 2:29–32]

DISCOGRAPHY
1. Harmonia Mundi, HMD 941261, La Chapelle Royale, dir. Philippe Herreweghe.
2. Multiple listings in The Schwann Catalogue.

GEORG JOSEPH VOGLER
June 15, 1749–May 6, 1814

Abbé Vogler was a German music theorist, teacher, organist, pianist, and composer. In 1763, he enrolled at Wurzburg University; by 1772, he was appointed court chaplain at the Mannheim Court. Vogler possessed an insatiable curiosity, traveling widely throughout Europe to undertake a comprehensive study of music theory and practice. In 1784, he was appointed to the position of first *Kapellmeister* at the Munich Court. Two years later, he resigned this position to enter into the service of Gustavus Adolphus of Sweden. In 1792–93, he trekked to Spain, North Africa, and Greece in order to trace the origins of Gregorian chant. Over the course of an active career, he became involved in theory and composition, producing a number of theoretical works.

He was also interested in the organ and gave more than 2,000 recitals during his career. Although he had a fine reputation as a pianist, Mozart declared him a charlatan; a label that has stuck to the Abbé for several centuries, even coloring opinions today. Among his numerous students were Carl Maria von Weber, Giacomo Meyerbeer, and the Swedish composer, Joseph Kraus.

Although Vogler composed fifteen stage works, orchestral symphonies, concertos, chamber music, vocal and choral music, little of it became well-known. The sacred pieces include nine mass settings, seven requiems, settings of the *Miserere, Te Deum,* and numerous single mass movements.

The *Deutsches Requiem* was first published in Munich in 1808. It consists of nine movements and the vernacular texts parallel those of the Roman Rite. The harmonic vocabulary and musical style is that of late Viennese classicism. Scored for SATB choir, SATB soli, organ, and orchestra, the prevailing four-part choral texture is written in an elaborate homophonic style. Occasional imitative polyphonic passages can be found on the texts, *Amen, Wir preisen dich, Noch hebt ers Kreutz, Er nimmt hinweg,* and *die uns den gottlichen.* The SATB solo quartet is employed, in *concertante* fashion, with the SATB choir in the fourth, sixth, and eight movements.

Basic Data

EDITION

Deutsche Kirchenmusik . . .
Arrangement dedicated to His Royal Highness, the Grand Duke of Hessen, Duke of Westphalia, etc. etc.
Senefelder & Gleissner [Steindruckerung]
Munich 1808 [C [soprano, alto, tenor] & F clefs]
[microfilm copy at the University of Virginia]

ORIGINAL TITLE-PAGE

In: Deutche Kirchenmusik mit einer Zergliederung
die vorlaufig die Inaugural Frage beantwortete
Hat die Musik seit 30 Jahren gewonnen oder verloren
Umarbeitung
Seiner Konigl. Hoheit
Dem Grossherzog von Hessen
Herzog von Westphalen, etc. etc.
Unterhangst gewidmet vom grossherzogl. Hoffischen geistlichen geheimer Rathe
ABT VOGLER
Munich 1808
In der Konigl Baierisch allein privil.
Steindruckerung von Senefelder und Gleissner

DURATION

Nine movements, 562 mm.

VOICING AND ORCHESTRATION

Choir: SATB range: S-G6; B-F3
Soloists: SATB

Ochestra: vn. I/II, vla., vc., db., 2 fl., 2 ob., 2 cl., 2 bsn. 2 Fh., 2 tpt., 3 tbn., timp., org.

OUTLINE

Kyrie: 64 mm.

Hier liegt [am] *adagio molto.* satb choir.

Hier liegt im Staub vor dir vor deiner Majestät, die Christen Schaar, das Herz zu dir, O Gott! Erhöht die Augen zum Altar.	Here lying in the dust before Thee before Thy majesty, your Christian flock. Its heart ready for Thee, O God, Eyes raised to the altar.
O Vater shenk uns deine Huld die wir bekennen unsre Schuld, die Sünden Schuld. Wir weinen hier vor deinen Thron, und flehn wie der verlohrne Sohn.	O Father send us Thy favor, That we recognize our guilt, the guilt of sinners. We cry here, before Thy throne and plead like the Lost Son.
Herziger, sieh gnadig her auf unsern Schmerz, verwirf nicht ein zerknirschtes Herz. O Gott vor deinem Angesicht verstoss uns arme Sunder nicht!	Blessed One, look graciously upon our pain, Reject not a contrite heart. O God, before Thy presence Do not disown us poor sinners!

Gloria: 135 mm.

Gott soll gepriesen [DM] *allegro vivace.* satb choir/orchestra. *Amen* (fugal).

Gott soll gepriesen werden der Herr der Herrlichkeit in Himmel und auf Erden jetzt und in Ewigkeit. Wir preisen dich O Gott und Herr Wir loben dich Allmachtiger.	God be praised, the Lord of Splendor, in Heaven and Earth, now and forevermore. We praise Thee, O God and Lord, We extoll Thee, Almighty-One.
Du sendest uns den Frieden her. unendlich ist dein Gnaden Meer. Lam Gottes, nun sitzest du dem Vater gleich zur Rechten in dem Himmelreich.	Thou sendest peace to us here, Unending is Thy sea of grace, Lamb of God, who sittest at the right hand of the Father in heaven.
Lam Gottes, erbarme dich über uns. Huld flies und Heil auf uns Vom Gnaden Meer, von deinem Gnaden Meer.	Lamb of God, have mercy upon us. Grace and holiness flow over us, from the sea of grace, Thy sea of grace.
Gott du bist Herr und heilig, Nur du allein bist heilig.	God, Thou art Lord and holy, Thou only art holy.

Herr wir preisen dich!	Lord, we praise Thee.
O Gott und Herr wir loben dich,	O God and Lord, we extol Thee,
O Gott allmachtiger!	O God and Lord almighty.
Durch Himmel, Erd und Meer	Through heaven, earth and sea,
erschalle Preis und Ehre.	resounds praise and honor.
Lob den Dreyeinigkeit.	Praise to the Trinity,
Wir preisen deinen Namen,	We praise Thy name,
die Engel sprechen Amen	Angels say "Amen"
mit deiner Christenheit.	with all Thy Christiandom.

Graduale: 44 mm.

Sich Vater von den höchsten Thron [GM] *andantino.* satb choir/orchestra.

Sich Vater von den höchsten Thron	The Father, himself, on highest throne,
sieh gnadig auf den Altar.	looks graciously upon the altar.
Wir bringen dir in deinem Sohne	We bring Thee, in Thy Son,
ein wohlgefallig Opfer dar.	a well-pleasing offering.
Wir flehn durch ihn, wir deine Kinder	We plead through Him, we Thy children,
und stellen dir sein Leiden vor.	and place his suffering before Thee.
Er starb aus Liebe für uns Sünder	He died, out of love, for us sinners,
noch hebt er's Kreuz für uns empor.	still, we raise the Cross high.

Credo: 85 mm.

Allmachtiger [FM] *adagio.* satb choir/SATB soli/orchestra.

Allmächtiger, vor dir in Staube,	Almighty One, before Thee in the dust,
Kent dich deine Creatur.	your creatures know Thee.
Gott und Vater, Ja, ich glaube	God and Father. Yes ! I believe
an dich du Schopfer der Natur	in Thee, Creator of Nature,
auch an das Wort.	also in the Word.
so du gebohren, das Licht das ewig	And Thy birth, the Eternal Light,
war der Sohn durch den wir Heil	the Son through whom we are saved,
erlangen und den vom heilgen Geist	was conceived of the Holy Spirit.
empfangen und Jesus ist zu uns	and Jesus, born of The purest Virgin,
gekommen die reinste Jungfrau uns	has come to us, that we might be
gebohr dass er versöhne uns mit Gott.	reconciled, through Him, with God.
Er hat die Schuld auf sich genommen	He took the sins upon Himself.
er litt für uns der Kreutzes	He suffered death upon the Cross for
Toddadurch besiegt er Tod und Holle.	us, and triumphed over Death and
Fohrt zu des Vaters Rechten aufer	Hell.
wird als Richter jeder Seele zum Lohn	He is seated at the right-hand of God,
des Himels oder Holle	and will be the Judge of each soul,
einst prüfen unsern Lebenslauf	and will give Heaven or Hell as a
des heilig Geist dies Licht regieret	

die wahre Kirch und Christenheit	reward, on that day when our life's
ein bussen Schaf das sich verirret	record is examined.
bey Gott lässt er uns finden	The Holy Spirit rules the Light,
den Frieden seine Huld.	the one True Church and all
	Christiandom.
	He bore all our guilt.
	With God, He lets us find peace,
	the peace of His favor.

Agnus Dei: 31 mm.

O Herr [AM] *andante*. satb choir/SATB soli/full orchestra. Structured in two sections: *O Herr ich bin* and *O stille mein Verlangen*.

O Herr ich bin nicht würdig zu	O Lord, I am not worthy to go to Thy
deinen Tisch zu gehn	Table, but Thou, hast made me worthy
Du aber mach mich würdig deinem	to go.
Tisch zu gehn.	Hear my child-like plea,
erhor mein Kindlich Flehn	Quiet my requests, Thou Bridegroom
O stille mein Verlangen du Seelen	of my soul.
Braütigen	Receive me into Thy Holy Spirit,
in Geist dich zu empfangen	Thou true Lamb of God.
dich wahres Gottes Lamm.	

Nach den *Ite Missa Est* [the mass is finished]: 59 mm.

Nun ist das Lamm [CM] *allegro maestoso*. satb choir/orchestra.

Nun ist das Lamm geschlachtet	Now is the Lamb sacrificed,
das Opfer ist vollbracht	the offering is completed,
wir haben jetzt betrachtet	we have now observed
Gott deine Lieb und Macht	God, Thy Love and Power.
das uns den göttlichen Frieden	God's peace to us, that has been
hergebracht,	brought us,
die uns den göttlichen Frieden so	that peace that has been so lovingly
liebreich hergebracht.	brought to us.

DISCOGRAPHY

None found.

11

The Anglican Requiem

The Anglican Requiem is an English-language work based upon the texts of the *English Book of Prayer* of 1552 and it subsequent editions. The *First Prayerbook of Edward VI*, believed to be the first English prayer-book, was originally engaged by the Act of Uniformity of 1549. Since its initial inception, the *Book of Prayer* has undergone numerous revisions, the most recent occurring in 1976. The Anglican Church was not alone in its adoption of this particular prayer book. The American Episcopal Church embraced it as well. The general outline of the memorial service is as follows:

Opening Prayers & Sentences
I am the resurrection and the life, saith the Lord;
He that believeth in me, though he were dead, yet shall he live;
And whosoever liveth and believeth in me shall never die.
Or:
Blessed are the dead who die in the Lord;
Even so saith the Spirit, for they rest from their labors.
Or:
I know that my Redeemer liveth,
And that he shall stand upon the latter day upon the earth.

Readings from the Old Testament (Isaiah, Lamentations, Wisdom)

Followed by a *canticle* (one choice)

Psalm 42 (*Like as the Hart*), Psalm 46 (*God is our hope and strength*)
Psalm 90 (*Lord, Thou hast been our refuge*), Psalm 121 (*I will lift mine eyes*)
Psalm 130 (*Out of the deep*), Psalm 139 (*O Lord, Thou hast searched me out*)

567

Readings from the New Testament (Romans, Corinthians, Revelations)

Followed by a *canticle* (one choice)

Psalm 23 (*The Lord is my Shepherd*), Psalm 27 (*The Lord is my light*)
Psalm 106 (*O give thanks unto the Lord*), Psalm 116 (*My delight is in the Lord*)

Reading from the Gospel of St. John

Homily

Eucharist (optional)

Commemoration Prayers

Committal Prayers

In the midst of life we are in death;
Of whom may we seek for succor,
But of Thee O Lord,
Who for our sins art justly displeased?
Yet, O Lord God most holy, O Lord most mighty,
O holy and most merciful Savior,
Deliver us not into the bitter pains of eternal death.

Thou knowest, Lord the secrets of our hearts;
Shut not Thy merciful ears to our prayer;
But spare us, Lord most holy, O God most mighty
O holy and merciful Savior,
Thou most worthy judge eternal.
Suffer us not, at our last hour,
Through any pains of death, to fall from Thee.

Concluding Prayers

Lord's Prayer

Throughout the past three centuries, the most commonly used texts set to music for the burial are: *Man that is born of woman, Thou knowest Lord,* and *I heard a voice from heaven.*

Man that is born of woman hath but a short time to live and is full of misery.
He cometh up and is cut down, like a flower; he fleeth as it were a shadow
And never continueth in one stay.
In the midst of life we are in death; of whom may we seek for succor,
But of thee, O Lord, who for our sins art justly displeased?

Yet, O Lord God most holy, O Lord most mighty, O holy and
Most merciful Saviour, deliver us not into the bitter pains of eternal death.
(Job 14)

Thou knowest Lord, the secrets of our hearts;
Shut not thy merciful ears unto our prayer; but spare us Lord most holy,
O God most mighty, O holy and most merciful Saviour,
Thou most worthy Judge eternal, suffer us not,
At our last hour, for any pains of death, to fall from Thee. Amen.

I heard a voice from heaven, saying unto me,
Write, from henceforth blessed are the dead which die in the Lord.
Even so saith the Spirit, for they rest from their labors. Amen
(Revelation 14:2–3)

John Merbecke (c. 1505–c. 1585) is credited with composing the first musical setting of the Anglican burial service. The monographic arrangement of the funeral text is detailed in *The Book of Common Praier Noted* (1550). Thomas Morley (c. 1557–1603) is recognized as composing one of the earliest polyphonic settings of the Burial Service, as is William Tye (c. 1500–1572/73), although in some circles the authorship of his particular setting remains in dispute.

The Latin mass and requiem were once again brought into use during the reign of Mary Tudor. With the ascension of her successor, Elizabeth I, came the reinstatement of the Anglican forms. Two very important extant settings created during the eighteenth century were the works of Henry Purcell (1659–1695) and William Croft (1678–1727). Later works were composed by Henry Stephen Cutler (1824–1902) and Dennis Fitzpatrick (*Music for Absolution and Burial*, 1955.)

Noteworthy funeral texts from the burial service (*Man that is born of woman*) were contributed by Samuel Sebastian Wesley (1810–1876), Charles Southgate (17—18—) (SATB choir, pub. 1818), Oliver Holden (1765–1844), Abraham Wood (1752–1804) (*Brevity*, SATB choir), Ralph Vaughan-Williams (1872–1958) (1891), Carlisle Floyd (1926–) (*Pilgrimage*, pub. 1959), and Gary Daverne (1939–) (*Three Songs for Choir and Orchestra*). The text was also adopted by Arthur Honegger for his oratorio, *King David*.

I heard a great voice, was employed by William Billings (1746–1800) (*Funeral Anthem*, 1778), Ernest MacMillan (1893–1973) (SSAA choir, mid 1920s), Jacob Kendall (1761–1826), and John Goss (1800–1880) (*Requiem Motet*, 1827).

The text, *Lord let me know mine end*, taken from Psalm 39, served as a resource for funeral anthems by Maurice Greene (c. 1695–1755), Thomas

Tompkins (1572–1656), Hubert Parry (1848–1918) (Songs of Farewell), and Matthew Locke (1621/22–1677).

English Catholics, from the fifteenth century and on through the eighteenth century, remained a small, and often persecuted, religious minority. It was not until the legislation of the Relief Act in 1791 that Catholics were allowed to register sites of public worship. The Catholic Emancipation Act, enacted in 1829, served to restore extensive religious freedom for Catholic worshippers. Early settings for use in Catholic worship, although closely modeled after the Anglican service, were composed by Henry Harington (1727–1816) (*Requiem, "I heard a voice from Heaven,"* c. 1775) and John Ferrabosco, organist of Ely Cathedral (d. 1682), (*Burial Service* in G minor).

It was apparently not until the nineteenth and twentieth centuries when the Latin settings in the Roman tradition began to reemerge. Recognized composers of those works included Samuel Webbe (1740–1816) (gm and em requiems for 3 vv), Robert Pearsall (1795–1856) (*Requiem* for 4 vv, winds and organ, 1853–56), Richard Runciman Terry (1865–1938) (*Requiem Mass*, 1916), Frederic d'Erlanger (1868–1943) (*Requiem* for SATB soli, SATB choir, and orchestra, 1931), Havergall Brian (1876–1972) (*Requiem* for baritone solo, choir and orchestra, c. 1896), Ian Hamilton (b. 1922) (*Requiem* for SATB choir), Leighton Lucas (b. 1903) (*Missa pro defunctis*, 1934), Douglas Coombes (b. 1930) (*Requiem* for SATB soli, SATB choir, organ, and orchestra, 1997), and Robert Hugill (twentieth) century (*Requiem for Butti*, 2000).

The 1940 *Hymnbook of the Episcopal Church* contains numerous *canticles*, short pieces (four to six measures in length) with four-part harmonizations, used for the chanting of the Psalms. Although the *Hymnbook* notes a vast selection of these pieces, composed by a diverse array of composers, such as Winifred Douglas, John Blow, Francis Snow, and William T. Best, common practice involves the singing of two Psalm settings, the first performed after the readings from the Old Testament and the second performed after the readings from the New. These harmonized chant versions, being quite simple, are often replaced by more complex and elaborate musical settings, hundreds of which are in existence.

Included in the 1940 hymnal are Psalm 39, *Lord let me know mine end*; Psalm 90, *Lord, thou hast been our refuge*; Psalm 27, *The Lord is my light and my salvation*; Psalm 46, *God is our hope and strength*; Psalm 121, *I will lift up mine eyes*; Psalm 132, *Out of the depths*; and Psalm 23, *The Lord is my shepherd*.

Thomas Morley appears to have created one of the earliest, if not the very first, polyphonic settings of the Burial Service. Among the musical settings heard within this piece are *Man that is born of woman* (Job 14:1–2), *Thou knowest Lord*, and *I heard a voice from Heaven*.

Of the early polyphonic versions of the Burial Service, the most widely recognized was written by Henry Purcell. Truly a landmark achievement in musical composition, the *Funeral Music for Queen Mary* employs prayer-book texts and instrumental pieces for brass and timpani, as well as the three choral anthems, *Man that is born of woman, In the midst of life, Thou knowest, Lord, the secrets of our hearts,* which is written with two distinct settings. Although much of the music was composed as early as 1677, the latter anthem was specifically designed for performance at the funeral of Queen Mary in December 1694.

Composed for the funeral of Queen Anne in 1714, William Croft's *Burial Service* contains such pieces as *Souls of the Righteous, Man that is born of woman, I heard a voice from Heaven,* along with Purcell's music for *Thou knowest, Lord, the secrets of our hearts.* Croft was apparently of the opinion that Purcell's setting could not be improved upon, and therefore saw no reason to replace it.

An extensive variety of Anglican funeral musical pieces were contributed to the canon by a diverse collection of composers, including George Frederick Händel (Funeral Anthem, *The ways of Zion do mourn,* 1737) for Queen Caroline, William Boyce (1710–1779) (Funeral Anthem, *Souls of the Righteous,* 1760), Charles Villiers Stanford (*Blessed are the dead which die in the Lord,* 1886) for the funeral of Henry Bradshaw, who held the positions of Librarian and Antiquarian at Cambridge University. Later, in 1910, Stanford composed another funeral anthem, *I heard a voice from heaven.*

Displaying a more ecumenical spirit, many twentieth-century composers expanded the scope of their settings with an integration of both the Roman Catholic and Anglican requiem texts. The most prominently included Latin texts are *Requiem aeternam, Pie Jesu, Sanctus,* and *Kyrie.*

In 1915, Walford-Davies published his setting, *Short Requiem in D Major,* scored for soloist and choir, and dedicated, "In Sacred Memory of all those who have fallen in war," the combat in question being World War I. Herbert Howell's work and John Rutter's popular setting, both entitled *Requiem,* serve as examples of other works derived from the English tradition. Less renowned, but worthy of significant attention, is the beautiful 1999 setting composed by James Bingham, a piece scored for orchestra, SATB choir, soprano, and baritone soloists. (A second version designed for organ and instruments also exists.) The setting is comprised of eight distinct movements: *Requiem Aeternam, Out of the deep, Pie Jesu, Sanctus, Agnus Dei, Laudate Dominum, I heard a voice,* and *Lux aeterna.*

Wilmer Welsh (b. 1932), an American composer, created his Anglican requiem in 1954. With its texts derived from the *Book of Common Prayer,* the setting is scored for soprano and baritone soloists, SATB choir, and organ. As of the writing of this volume, it remains unpublished in the library of Davidson College.

JAMES BINGHAM
July 27, 1945

James Bingham received his first musical training in Geelong, Australia. He later emigrated to the United States, where he received a degree in music from Andrews University, Michigan. For ten years, he was director of the choirs and chairman of the music department at Kingsway College, Canada. Later, returning to the United States, he held a series of positions, including chairman of the music departments at Atlantic Union College and Columbia Union College.

The Requiem was composed between 1998 and 1999 and scored for SATB (*divisi*) choir, soprano and baritone soli, and orchestra. A second version of the work, made by the composer, replaced the orchestra with organ and nine instruments. Bingham states in his program notes for the premiere concert that the work "was inspired by the gentle lyricism, memorable tunes, and simple beauty of Rutter's *Requiem.*"

The harmonic language of the *Requiem* is triadic and tonal with added dissonance, thereby giving the work an impressionist "harmonic" quality. The most chromatic movement, *I heard a voice*, appears to be without a specific key center. The prevailing four-part choral texture is frequently scored *divisi* or thinned down to two-part and unison writing for contrast. Occasional imitative polyphonic passages occur on *For there is no mercy*, *Sanctus*, *Hosanna*, and *Requiem*.

Except for the text by Augustine of Hippo, the texts employed by the composer are those found in the *Book of Common Prayer* and the Latin requiem mass.

Basic Data

EDITION

Requiem
James Bingham
Mark Willey Music Press [1999]

DURATION

Eight movements, 1152 mm., perf., c. 62'

VOICING AND ORCHESTRATION

I.
Choir: SATB range: S-B flat 6; B-D3
Soloists: S, Bar.
Orchestra: vn. I/II, vla., vc., db., 2 fl., 2 ob., 2 cl., Eh., 2 bsn, 2 Fh., 2 tpt., 3 tbn., 4 timp., triangle, chimes, tam-tam, cymbals, bass drum, harp.

II.
Same vocal ensemble. Fl., ob., Eh., 4 timp., bass drum, triangle, harp,. vc., org.

OUTLINE

Requiem aeternam: 164 mm.
> *Requiem aeternam* [dm] *grave*; *Te decet,* [DM] *animato*; *Kyrie* [GM-cm-GM] satb choir.

Out of the Deep: 186 mm.
> (Psalm 130) [dm] *grave*. Bar solo/satb choir.

Pie Jesu: 128 mm.
> *Pie Jesu* [E flat M] *andante cantabile*. S solo/satb choir.

Sanctus: 129 mm.
> *Sanctus* [GM-E flat M] *allegretto e un poco scherznado*. satb choir; *Pleni sunt coeli* [DM] satb choir; *Benedictus* [E flat M] sa/tb, satb choir; *Hosanna* [GM] satb choir.

Agnus Dei: 263 mm.
> *Agnus Dei* [em] *lamentoso*. satb choir; *Qui tollis/Man that is born* [b flat m] satb choir; *Agnus Dei/Whom may we s*eek [em] satb choir; *I am the resurrection, misterioso*. Bar solo; *You have called* [b flat] *andante teneramente*. satb choir.

> All flesh is as the grass and all its loveliness is like the flower
> of the grass; the grass withers and the flower fades away.
> Isaiah 40:6–7
> Man that is born of woman has but a short time to live
> and is full of misery. He cometh up and is cut down like a flower;
> he fleeth as it were a shadow.
> Job 14:1–2
> In the midst of life we are in death:
> Whom may we seek for succour?
> [1662 Book of Common Prayer]
> I am the resurrection and the life, saith the Lord:
> He that believeth in me, though he were dead,
> Yet shall he live:
> And whosoever liveth and believeth in me shall never die.
> John 11:25–26
> You have called, You have cried out,
> And you have pierced my deafness.
> You have radiated forth and have shined out brightly,
> And you have dispelled my blindness.
> You have sent forth your fragrance
> And I have breathed it in,
> And I have longed for you.
> I have tasted you and I have hungered and thirsted for you.
> You have touched me and I ardently desire your peace.
> Augustine of Hippo (354–430 A.D.)

Laudate Dominum: 82 mm.
   Laudate Dominum [GM] *andante con moto.* S solo; *Laudate Dominum*, satb choir;
      Gloria Patri/Laudate Dominum, S solo/satb choir. (Psalm 117 and Doxolgy)
I heard a voice: 69 mm.
   I heard a voice, misterioso. Bar solo/satb choir; *Write*; SBar soli/satb choir.

> I heard a voice from heaven saying unto me, Write:
> Blessed are the dead who die in the Lord, for they
> Rest from their labors: even so saith the spirit.
> Revelation 14:13

Lux aeterna: 131 mm.
   Lux aeterna [DM] *andante tranquillo.* satb choir; *Requiem aeternam*, SBar soli/satb
      choir.

DISCOGRAPHY

Ethereal Recordings, ER 124, Columbia Collegiate Chorale, cond. Dr. James
   Bingham.

HENRY WALFORD DAVIES
October 6, 1869–March 11, 1941

Davies was a pupil of Hubert Parry and Charles Villiers Stanford at the
Royal College of Music. After receiving a Doctorate at Cambridge, he was
called to the Temple Church (London) as organist and choirmaster. In
1927, he was appointed organist at St. George's Chapel, Windsor. His last
important appointment was Master of the King's Musik, succeeding Sir
Edward Elgar.

Davies was a productive composer, writing works for orchestra, chamber music, thirteen cantatas, and sacred choral music. Among the sacred
choral pieces is the *Short Requiem* in D Major for solo and unaccompanied
SATB choir. This music was first published in 1915 and dedicated "In
Sacred Memory of all those who have fallen in the war."

The texts for this setting were taken from the *Book of Common Prayer* and
the Catholic requiem mass (*Requiem aeternam*). Two of the movements, *De
profundis* and *Levavi oculos*, are set as canticles and scored in four-part
Anglican chant style. *Mors ultra non erit* is arranged as a hymn and the
remainder of the movements are written as short, homophonic motets.
All are in the key of D major.

Basic Data
EDITION
Walford Davies
A Short Requiem in D major for solo and Chorus
The Royal School of Church Music (WD41)

DURATION

Nine movements, 185 mm.

VOICING

Choir: SATB [*divisi*] range: S-G6; B-D3
Soloist: soprano
Instruments: optional organ

OUTLINE

Salvator Mundi: 24 mm.
O Saviour of the World, andante. ssattbb choir/satb choir soli/S solo.

> O Saviour of the World, who by Thy cross and precious blood
> hast redeemed us: Save us and help us, we humbly beseech Thee,
> O Lord.

De Profundis: 14 mm. (Psalm 130)
   Out of the deep, very solemnly. satb choir.
Requiem aeternam (1): 18 mm.
   Requiem aeternam, ssatbb choir.
Levavi Oculos: 14 mm. (Psalm 121)
   I will lift mine eyes, gently. satbb choir.
Requiem aeternam (2): 31 MM.
   Requiem aeternam, sattbb choir.
Audi Vocem: 23 mm.
   I heard a voice, B solo/saatb choir.

> I heard a voice from heaven, saying unto me:
> Write, from henceforth, Blessed are the dead
> Which die in the Lord.
> Even so saith the Spirit, for they rest from their labors.

Hymn: *Mors ultra non erit*: 16 mm.
   No more to sigh, satb choir.

> No more to sigh, no more to weep,
> The faithful dead in Jesus sleep:
> Unfading, let their memory bloom,
> while rest their bodies in the tomb;
> nor will the Lord their love distrust
> that strews its garlands o'er their dust.
>
> Though in the grave their clay is cold
> they have not left the Christian fold;
> Still we are sharers of their joy,
> Companions of their blest employ;

> and Thee in them O Lord most high
> and them in Thee we magnify.
> An angel sings that they are blest;
> Yea saith the Spirit sweet their rest;
> In bowers of Paradise they meet
> secure beneath their Saviour's feet,
> nor fear the trump that soon shall all
> before the throne of judgement call.

Gloria Patri: 19 mm.
Glory to the Father, lento. ssattbb choir.

> Glory to the Father and the Son and to the Holy Ghost.
> As it was in the beginning, is now and ever shall be.
> World without end. Amen

Vox ultima Crucis: 26 mm.
Tarry no longer, S solo/satb choir/atb choir trio.

> Tarry no longer; toward thine heritage haste on thy way
> And be of good cheer.
> Go each day onward on the pilgrimage.
> Think how short time thou shalt abide thee here.
> Thy place is built above the starre's clear;
> None earthly palace wrought in so stately wise.
> Come on my friend, my brother most dear.
> For thee I offered my blood in sacrifice.
> Tarry no longer.
> (John Lydgate)

DISCOGRAPHY
None found.

HERBERT HOWELLS
October 17, 1892–February 24, 1983

This distinguished English composer was trained at the Royal College of Music in London, where he studied composition with Charles Villiers Stanford. In 1920, he was appointed to an instructor's position at the Royal College, a position that he held for forty years. In 1936, he was appointed music director at St. Paul's Girls School. Ultimately, he was a professor of music at the University of London.

He wrote all types of music, except opera and oratorio, and his musical style was derived from the rendition of Elgar and Stanford. Among the choral works are three masses, a *Stabat Mater*, motets, and a *Requiem*. He wrote a special funeral motet for the death of President Kennedy, *Take him, Earth, for cherishing*, in 1964.

The *Requiem*, composed in 1936, for unaccompanied SATB choir follows the Anglican rite, drawing upon the texts of the *Rite of Common Prayer*. The *Requiem aeternam* text is taken from the Latin rite. Howells wrote the work to commemorate the death of his only son, Michael, who died in 1935. He did not release the work for publication until 1980. Howells preferred that the music be performed unaccompanied, although he provided a modest organ accompaniment that can be used when absolutely necessary. It is a very moving, personal work. The choral texture is predominantly polyphonic, with passages of imitative style. Contrast in the texture is accomplished by augmenting the basic four- or eight-part choral fabric.

Basic Data

EDITION

Herbert Howells
Requiem for SATB, unaccompanied
Novello (#NOV 29 0491) 1981.

DURATION

Six movements, 216 mm., perf., c. 20'

VOICINGAND ORCHESTRATION

Choir: Choir I, SATB; Choir II, SATB range: S-A6; B-D3
Soloists: SATBAR
Instrument: org. [optional accompaniment]

OUTLINE

Salvator Mundi: 30 mm. [DM-dm] *slowly, but with flexible rhythm.* satb choirs I/II.

O Saviour of the World, who by thy Cross and precious Blood hast redeemed us,
    Help us. Save us. We humbly beseech thee, O Lord.

Psalm 23:21 mm. [dm] *moderato.* SAT soli/satb choir.
    Unmetered rhythm follows the text.

Requiem aeternam (I): 40 mm. [bm-DM] satb choirs I/II.

Psalm 121:22 mm. [em] TBar soli/satb choir

    I will lift up mine eyes unto the hills: from whence cometh my help.
    My help cometh even from the Lord: who made Heaven and earth.

He will not suffer thy foot to be moved: and he that keepeth thee will not sleep.
Behold, he that keepeth Israel shall neither slumber nor sleep.

The Lord himself is thy keeper: he is thy defense upon thy right hand;
So that the sun shall not burn thee by day: neither the moon by night.
The Lord shall preserve thee from all evil: yea, it is even he that
shall keep thy soul.
The Lord shall preserve thy going out and thy coming in:
from this time forth and for evermore.

Requiem aeternam (II): 45 mm. [AM] *quasi lento*. satb choir [*divisi*]

Hymnus Paradisi [I heard a voice from Heaven]: 58 mm. [DM] *slowly and evenly*.
TBar soli/satb choir [*divisi*]; Blessed are the dead, S solo/ssatbb choir.

I heard a voice from heaven, saying unto me, Write,
From henceforth blessed are the dead which die in the Lord.
Even so saith the Spirit; For they rest from their labors.

DISCOGRAPHY

Hyperion, CDA 66076, Corydon Singers, cond. Matthew Best.

JOHN RUTTER
September 24, 1945

Rutter was trained at Clare College, Cambridge; for four years, he was
director of music at Clare College. He has brought out several choral
anthologies, including three volumes in the *Carols for Choirs* series. From
1975 to 1988, he taught at the Open University; in 1981, founded the Cambridge Singers. Rutter remains a prolific composer of choral music. He
composed short anthems and a number of larger works, such as the *Gloria*
for Chorus, Brass Ensemble, Percussion, and Organ (1974), *Te Deum* for
Chorus (1985), and the *Magnificat* for Soprano, Chorus, and Instrumental
Ensemble (1990).

The *Requiem* for soprano, SATB choir, and orchestra was composed in
1985. Unlike other Anglican requiem settings, this one employs more
texts from the Latin requiem mass (*Requiem aeternam, Kyrie, Pie Jesu, Sanctus, Agnus Dei,* and *Lux aeterna*) than the 1662 *Book of Common Prayer* (*Out
of the Deep, The Lord is my shepherd, I am the resurrection, I heard a voice from
Heaven*). The third and fifth movements are personal prayers; second and
fifth are psalms, and the first and seventh are prayers for all humankind.
The central movement, the *Sanctus* is a reaffirmation of God's greatness.

His harmonic style is completely tonal and the melodic style is notable for its sheer beauty and quiet spiritual quality. The prevailing four-part choral texture is laced with two-part and unison writing. Traces of popular and jazz style rhythms are evident.

Basic Data

EDITION

Requiem
John Rutter
Hinshaw Music Inc. (#HMB 164) 1986

DURATION

Seven movements, 605 mm., perf., c. 40'

VOICING AND ORCHESTRATION

1.
Choir: SATB [*divisi*]
Soloists: soprano
Instruments: fl., ob., 3 pedal timp., glockenspiel, harp, vc., org.

2.
Choir: SATB [*divisi*] range: S-A6; B-E3
Soloists: soprano
Orchestra: vn. I/II, vla., vc., db., 2 fl., ob., 2 cl., bsn., 2 Fh., 3 pedal timp., glockenspiel, harp.

OUTLINE

Introit: *Requiem aeternam*, 111 mm.
  Requiem aeternam [GM] *slow and solemn*. satb choir [*divisi*] Steady quarter-note ostinato suggests a funeral procession; *Requiem aeternam*, satb choir. A "motto" theme is presented for the first time. *Te decet, piu animato; Kyrie*, satb choir. ("motto" theme).
Psalm 130: 76 mm.
  Out of the deep [CM] *slow, with some rubato*. satb choir/cello obbligato.

Out of the deep I have called unto thee, O Lord.
Lord hear my voice.
O let thy ears consider well the voice of my complaint.

If thou, Lord, wilt be extreme to mark what is done amiss,
O Lord, who may abide it?
For there is mercy with thee, therefore shalt thou be feared.
I look for the Lord; my soul doth wait for him. In his word is my trust.
My soul fleeth unto the Lord; before the morning watch,

I say, before the morning watch.
O Israel, trust in the Lord, for with the Lord there is mercy,
and with him is plenteous redemption.
And he shall redeem Israel from all his sins.

Pie Jesu: 61 mm.
   Pie Jesu: [FM] *andante e dolce.* S solo/satb choir. (canonic writing) A second notable melodic theme (a variant of the "motto") appears in the solo and choral
   parts.
Sanctus-Benedictus: 49 mm.
   Sanctus [CM] *andante maestoso.* satb choir.(canonic writing); *Benedictus*, satb
   choir (canonic).
Agnus Dei: 89 mm.
   Agnus Dei [CM] *slow and solemn.* satb choir (quarter-note ostinato, suggestive of
   a cortege); A gloss of the three statements of the Latin text with English texts
   taken from the *1662 Book of Prayer* (*Man that is born* and *I am the resurrection
   and the life*). A curious feature of this movement is the insertion of the Gregorian melody, *Victimae paschalis*, during the passage, *I am the resurrection.*

Agnus Dei
Man that is born of woman hath but a short time to live, and is full of misery.
He cometh up and is cut down like a flower, he fleeth as if it were a shadow.
Agnus Dei
In the midst of life we are in death. Of whom may we seek for succor?
Agnus Dei
I am the resurrection and the life, saith the Lord. He that believeth in me,
though he were dead, yet shall he live. And whosoever
believeth in me shall never die.

Psalm 23: 100 mm.
   The Lord is my shepherd [CM] *slow but flowing.* satb choir/oboe obbligato. (com-
   posed in 1978 and added later to the *Requiem*).
Communion: 119 mm.
   I heard a voice [GM] S solo/satb choir; *Lux aeterna, andante tranquillo.* unison-four
   part satb choir. ("motto" theme).

DISCOGRAPHY

1. Collegium Records, COLCD 103, The Cambridge Singers, The City of London
   Sinfonietta, cond. John Rutter.
2. Multiple listings in the Schwann Catalogue.

12

The Byzantine-Greek Requiem

Beginning as early as the early fourth century, the Byzantine liturgy began to flourish and continued to develop until the Turkish conquest in 1453. The Greek rite was adopted by all of the Eastern Christian churches, including the Syrian, Coptic (Egyptian), Armenian, Georgian, Serbian, Ukrainian, and Russian liturgies. Today, it remains the principal rite observed in Eastern Europe and its influence extends further east into Georgia and Armenia.

The musical repertory of this branch of Christianity is enormous, yet it remains poorly known by musicians in the West. The reasons for this condition are several; both principal forms of its musical notation, lectionary and melodic, are vastly different from that of Western staff notation, thereby isolating the Greek repertory from the Gregorian repertory. Even the currently used system, "Middle Byzantine" notation, remains a stranger to most Western musicians. It first appeared about 1300. Unlike the Gregorian melodies, Greek chants employ microtones and a style of melodic ornamentation that is difficult, if not impossible, to render in traditional Western staff notation.

Paralleling the system of eight Gregorian modes is the eight Greek modes called *oktoechos*. The chants of the Greek tradition have remained monophonic, similar to the Gregorian melodies of the West, with one notable difference; the presence of an accompanimental drone, called an *ison*. It is a type of simple parallel polyphony that seems to have originated by the beginning of the fifteenth century, possibly earlier.

The current requiem melodies used in the Greek liturgy date back to the eighteenth century and are based upon earlier traditional tunes and have employed Middle Byzantine notation; that is, until very recently. A *Sacraments and Services Music Book* edited by the Rev. Spencer Kezios in

1995, includes the tunes for the Funeral Service and the Office of Supplication. Not only are the tunes notated in Western notation, but also an accurate English translation of the texts has been made. Great care was exercised to ensure that the translations match the traditional tunes. This task was undertaken and achieved by Father Michael Pallad. The *ison* (drone) is not, unfortunately, included in the musical score.

There appears to be no parallel in the development of concert or polyphonic forms of the Greek requiem (*Parastasos*), except for the setting of Mikis Theorodakis. Greek funeral music has remained strictly liturgical in function and purpose. As is the case with the Orthodox funeral, there are a variety of services, including the service said at home, the service said in church, a funeral service for Renewal Week, a service for the clergy, the service for a child, the memorial service, a memorial service at Saturday of the souls, and a funeral service for nonorthodox Christians.

The music of the Greek Funeral can be divided into five major sections: The *Trisagion*; Funeral Hymns, the *Idiomela, Prokeimenon,* and the *Prosomia.* The *Trisagion* is the hymn, *Holy God, Holy Mighty.* It is sung three times and is one of the most important hymns of the Eastern liturgy.

HYMNS OF THE TRISAGION

Among the spirits of the righteous made perfect,
Give rest to the soul O Saviour, to the soul of your servant.
Keeping it in that blessed life which is with You,
Lover of mankind.

In your place of rest, O Lord, where all your saints repose,
Give rest also to the soul of your servant,
for You alone are the Immortal One.
Glory be to the Father and the Son and the Holy Spirit . . .

You are our God, who went down into Hades,
and there, loosed the bonds of those who were held captive,
give rest also to the soul of your servant, O Saviour.
Now and always and forever and ever, Amen

O Virgin alone, pure and undefiled, who gave birth to God
in a manner beyond describing,
Intercede that the soul of Your servant may be saved.

DISMISSAL
Eternal Memory

Eternal memory be his (her) memory [2 x]
May his (her) memory be eternal.

The Funeral hymns are made up from verses taken from Psalm 118 (119). The verses are interspersed with the *Gloria Patri* ("Glory to the Father . . ."), *Alleluia*, and the *Kyrie* ("Lord have mercy").

Stanza 1

Blessed are those whose way is blameless, Alleluia.
Blessed are You, O Lord, teach me Your commandments. Alleluia.
[vs. 12]

My soul has always longed for Your judgements, Alleluia
My soul has grown weary from sorrow, strengthen me with Your words. Alleluia.
Incline my heart to Your revelations, and not to greed. Alleluia
[vs. 20, 28, 31]

Despair took hold of me because of the sinners who spurn Your law. Alleluia.
I am a companion of all who fear You,
and of those who keep Your commands. Alleluia
Glory be to the Father . . . Alleluia.
[vs. 53, 55]

Stanza 2

Your hands have made me and formed me;
enlighten me that I may learn Your commandments.
Have mercy on me, O Lord.
[vs. 73]

For I have shriveled like a wineskin in the frost,
yet I have not forgotten Your just decrees.
Have mercy on me, O Lord.
[vs. 83]

I am Your own. Save me, for I have sought Your commandments.
Have mercy on me, O Lord.
[vs. 94]

I have not spurned Your judgements, for You have instructed me.
Have mercy on me, O Lord.
[vs. 102]

In return for Your mercies my heart is set on following Your
commandments until the ages of ages.
Have mercy on me, O Lord.
[vs. 112]

It is time for the Lord to act: for they have broken Your law.
Have mercy upon me, O Lord.
[vs. 126]

Glory be to the Father . . .
Have mercy . . .

Stanza 3

And have mercy on me, Alleluia.
Look upon me and be gracious to me,
as those who love Your name. Alleluia
[vs. 132]

I am young and despised, but have not forgotten Your commandments, Alleluia.
[vs. 141]
Hear my voice, O Lord, in Your steadfast love,
quicken me in Your justice, Alleluia.
[vs. 149]
Princes have pursued me without cause, but my heart stands in awe
of Your words, Alleluia.
[vs. 161]
My soul shall live and praise You, and Your law shall be my support.
[vs. 175]
Like a lost sheep I have gone astray.
Seek Your servant, for I have not forgotten Your commandments.
[vs. 176]

The Funeral *Evlogitaria.* The *Evlogitaria* are hymns preceded by the refrain:

[Refrain]
Blessed are You, O Lord, teach me Your commandments.
[Psalm 119:12]
1. The choir of the Saints has found the source of life,
and the Gateway to Paradise. May I also find the
way through repentance. I am the sheep that was lost, O Saviour,
call me back and save me. (Refrain)

2. In the beginning You formed me out of nothing, honoring me
with Your divine image; but when I disobeyed Your commands,
You returned me to the earth from which I was taken. Restore me to
that likeness, that the ancient beauty may be formed anew. (Refrain)

3. I am an image of Your indescribable glory, though I bear the scars of my sins.
Master take pity on the work of Your hands, and in Your loving kindness
cleanse me. Grant me the homeland for which I yearn, making me
once again a citizen of Paradise. (Refrain)

4. Give rest, O God, to Your departed servant and assign him (her)
a place in Paradise, where the ranks of the Saints and the righteous, O Lord,
will shine forth as lights. To Your servant now asleep will You grant rest,
overlooking all of his (her) offenses.
Glory be to the Father . . . (Refrain)

5. Let us devoutly praise the one Godhead as radiant Trinity,
singing Holy are You, everlasting Father, co-eternal Son
and Holy Spirit. Illumine us as we worship You in faith,
and deliver us from the eternal fire.
Now and always and forever and ever. Amen (Refrain)

6. Hail, majestic Lady, who for universal salvation gave birth to God
in the flesh. Through you humankind has found redemption,
through you may we find Paradise, pure and blessed Theotokos.
Alleluia, alleluia, alleluia, glory to You, O God [3 x]

CONCLUDING HYMN OF THE FUNERAL SERVICE
Among the Saints

Give rest, O Christ, give rest among the saints, to the soul of
Your servant, where there is no pain, no sorrow, no grieving,
but life everlasting.

The *Ideomela* are a group of hymns (*troparia*) composed by St. John of Damascus.

[first tone]
1. What pleasure in life is not accompanied by sorrow?
What glory remains unchanged on earth?
All things are flimsier than shadows, more deceptive than dreams.
In but an instant death displaces everything.
But in the light of Your countenance, O Christ,
in the sweetness of Your beauty, give rest to him (her)
whom You have chosen, for You love mankind.
[second tone]
2. Every mortal life is like a flower that withers,
a passing dream that vanishes.
Yet when the trumpet sounds, all the dead will rise up
as in an earthquake to meet You, Christ, our God.
Will You then, master, assign a place where Your saints
abide for the soul of him (her) whom You have
summoned from our midst.
[third tone]
3. All human pursuits are vain, they have no being after death,
wealth does not remain, glory does not accompany along the way.
Once death befalls all these vanish utterly.
So let us cry to the immortal Christ:
Give rest to those who have left our company
in the dwelling place of all who rejoice.
[fourth tone]
4. Where is all our attachment to worldly pursuits?
Where is all the vain display of passing things?
Where is the gold, where the silver?
The hustle and bustle of household servants?
Everything is dust, ashes, shadow.
Let us cry out to the immortal king,
"Lord, deem worthy of everlasting blessings
those who have departed from us,
and give them rest in ageless blessedness."
[fifth tone]

5. I called to mid the prophet, crying, I am but
dust and ashes. And I studied the tombs once more,
considered the naked bones, and asked myself:
Now which of these was king, and which the common soldier,
which was the rich man; which the indigent;
which man was upright, and which a sinner.
But Lord, in Your compassion, to Your servant
give rest among the righteous.
[sixth tone]
6. Your creating command became my beginning and my being.
For it was Your will to bring together visible and invisible
nature to fashion me a living creature. You shaped my body from the earth,
then gave me a spirit by Your divine and quickening breath.
Wherefore O Saviour give rest to Your servant
in the land of the living where the righteous dwell.
[seventh tone]
7. When in the beginning, You created man in Your own image and
likeness, You placed him in Paradise to have dominion
over all Your creation.
But beguiled by the Devil's envy, he tasted of the fruit
becoming a violator of your commandments.
Thus You sentenced him, O Lord, to return to the earth
from which he was taken, and to plead for repose.
[eighth tone]
8. I weep and lament when I ponder death,
when I see our beauty formed in God's image,
laying in the tombs, bereft of form, disfigured without glory.
O the wonder of it!
How did this mystery befall us. How were we given over
to decay. How were we paired with death.
Surely as it is written by the command of God,
who gives rest to the departed.
[Gloria Patri and final hymn in same tone]
Glory to the Father and the Son and the Holy Spirit . . .
Your death, O Lord, became the cause of immortality.
For had You not lain in the tomb, then Paradise
would not have been opened.
Wherefore as loving God, give rest to him (her)
who is now parted from us.
Now and always and forever and ever, Amen
Pure Virgin, Gateway for the Word, Mother of God,
intercede that his (her) soul may know mercy.

The *Prokeimenon*: The Blessed Way

The *prokeimenon* is a form of responsorial singing in which there is a
psalm-verse refrain. In ancient Constantinople, the *prokeimenon* was sung

before the psalm text was sung. In the Greek tradition, the *prokeimenon* is sung before the singing or reading of the Epistle (Paul's First Epistle to the Thessalonians, I Thess. 4:13–17).

PROKEIMENON

Blessed ever be the way, the way on which you walk this day;
for there is prepared for you a place of everlasting rest.

The *Prosomia* (hymn concerning the farewell kiss) is sung during the Dismissal.

Come, brethren, let us give one final sign of affection
to the departed even as we thank God.
For he (she) has now left his (her) kin and hastens toward the grave,
no longer troubled about vain things or the toilsome body.
Where now, where are the family and friends?
Even now we take leave of him (her), asking the Lord to grant rest.
Brethren, what is this parting, this wailing, this grieving at life's
turning point? Come now, let us greet him (her) who was
but now one of us. For he (she) is consigned to the tomb, to be covered
with a stone. Darkness is his (her) abode and the dead his (her)
companions. All of us, family and loved ones are now parted from
him (her) whom we entreat the Lord to repose.

The *Theotokion* Hymn is a hymn in honor of the Mother of God, Mary. It is the concluding hymn of the funeral service.

Mother of the unwaning Sun, birth-giver of God,
save those who hope in you.
We ask that by your prayers, you will entreat the all-gracious
One to give rest to the departed one where all souls of the just repose.
As an everlasting memorial, all pure one, declare him (her) an heir
to divine blessings in the courts of the righteous.

Basic Data

EDITION

Sacraments and Services, Music Book
Rev. Spencer T. Kezios
Narthex Press, Northridge, CA 1995

DISCOGRAPHY

Companion tape to the *Sacraments & Services Music Book*. Narthex Press. 1995

MIKIS THEODORAKIS
July 29, 1925

Theodorakis, the composer and politician, was one of the most important figures in twentieth-century Greek musical life. He was active in the anti-nazi resistance movement, but was deported from Greece during the Civil War that followed World War II. He went to Paris, where he studied composition with Olivier Messiaen in 1953. In the following year, he was admitted into the Paris Conservatoire. In 1961, he returned to Greece. His membership in the Communist Party and United Left Movement led to his arrest by the military junta that took over the Greek government in the 1960s. Freed from prison by international pressure, he went on to become Minister without portfolio for the government (1990–1992) and director of The Greek State Radio Orchestra and Chorus (1993).

Theodorakis composed an enormous body of music that includes almost 800 vocal songs, seven symphonies, music for radio, forty orchestral works (many which include choral and vocal forces), seven operas, three-dozen film scores, ten ballets, piano music, and several liturgical pieces; *Holy Liturgy-Missa Greca* for mixed choir (1982–83), and the *Requiem* (1982–83).

The *Requiem*, scored for SATB choir, children's choir, SABarB soli, and orchestra, was composed in 1984. It memorialized the Greeks who were massacred in the battle at Kalavrita (1944). Orchestrated by Nikos Platyarch in 1993, this moving concert work is quite unique in the repertory of the Greek requiem. Apart from the fact that it is possibly the only concert setting of the liturgy, it includes orchestra, soprano soloist, and children's choir, voices never heard in the usual liturgical setting. Greek services are normally sung only by unaccompanied male voices.

The melodic and harmonic language is based upon modes, peculiar to the Greek Orthodox service and the folk music of Crete. The music is divided into eight major parts with seventy-four smaller subsections. Its prevailing, four-part, SATB choral texture contrasts with unison and two-part writing. The eighth and ninth movements, in particular, employ a wide variety in vocal scoring: TTBB, ATB, SSAA, SAT, ATT, SSATBB, and SAATTBB.

The requiem employs the regular meters (3/4, 6/8, and 4/4) of western European music, as well as the irregular meters of the Balkan region (9/8, 5/8, 7/8, 14/8, and 10/4). The traditional texts are taken from the Orthodox liturgy and from John of Damascus (680–754).

Basic Data

EDITION

Mikis Theodorakis
Requiem [Full score]
Oratorio for Soprano, Alto, Baritone, Bass
Mixed Chorus, Children's Chorus and Orchestra.
Editions Romanos [1996]

DURATION

Eight parts, seventy-four pieces, 987 mm., perf.,

VOICING AND ORCHESTRATION

Choir: SATB [*divisi*], Children's choir. range: S-A6; B-D3
Soloists: SATBarB
Orchestra: vn. I/II, vla., vc., bass. 2 fl., 2 ob., 2 cl., 2 bsn. 4 Fh., tpt., 3 tbn. Timp.
   harp. piano. PERC: tubular bells, glockenspiel, triangle, maracas, 3 tom-toms,
   tam-tam, cymbals, suspended cymbals, bass drum.

OUTLINE

PART 1. Opening exclamation:
   Bless, Master [*andante*] satb choir/children's choir.

PART 2. First stanza (tone 6):
   The blameless in the way [*allegro*] satb choir/children's choir.
   My soul has slumbered [*allegro*] satb choir.
   Incline my heart [*allegro*] satb choir.
   Despair took hold of me [*allegro*] satb choir.
   I am a partaker [*allegro*] satb choir.
   Doxology [*andante*] satb choir.
   Have mercy upon us [*adagio*] Bar solo/satb choir.
   We also pray [quarter-note = 63] A solo/satb choir.
   Let the Lord our God establish [*in stesso tempo*] A solo/satb choir.
   Let us pray to the Lord [*in stesso tempo*] Bar solo/satb choir.
   For you art the resurrection [*in stesso tempo*] Bar solo/satb choir.

PART 3. Second stanza (plagal first tone):
   Your hands have made me [*andante*] children's choir/satb choir.
   Though I have become [*lento*] S solo/satb choir.
   From your judgements [*allegretto*] satb choir.
   I have inclined my heart [*poco piu mosso*] Bar solo/satb choir.
   It is time for the Lord [*andante*] A solo/satb choir.
   Doxology [*in stesso tempo*] satb choir.
   Let us pray unto the Lord [*in stesso tempo*] satb choir.

PART 4. Third stanza:
   Look upon me [*allegro moderato*] satb choir.
   I am young [*in stesso tempo*] satb choir.
   Hear my voice [*in stesso tempo*] satb choir.
   Men in power [*in stesso tempo*] satb choir.
   Let my soul live [*in stesso tempo*] satb choir.
   I have gone astray [quarter-note = 60] saattbb choir.
   Let us pray to the Lord, Bar solo/satb choir.

PART 5. Evoglitaria for the dead:
   Blessed is our Lord God [*andante*] Bar solo/satb choir.
   The choir of the saints [*in stesso tempo*] Bar solo/satb choir.

Blessed are you [*in stesso tempo*] A solo/satb choir.
You have made me [*in stesso tempo*] A solo/satb choir.
Blessed are you [*in stesso tempo*] satb choir.
I am the image [*lento*] S solo/satb choir.
Blessed are you [*andante*] satb choir.
Give rest to your servant [*mosso*] A solo/satb choir.

PART 6. Doxology:
Glory be to the Father [*andante*] children's choir/satb choir.

PART 7. Now and Forever, Amen:
Hail O modest Virgin [*andante*] children's choir/satb choir.
Alleluia [quarter-note = 92] satb choir, unison.
Give rest with the saints [quarter-note = 58] A solo/children's choir/satb choir.

PART 8. The Ideomela [Troparia] by John of Damascus (first tone):
Where is the pleasure? [quarter-note = 100] children's choir/satb choir.
Like a blossom [quarter-note = 80] Bar solo/children's choir/satb choir.
Alas! What a battle [*andante*] A solo/satb choir.
Vanity are all the works of man [quarter-note = 50] Bar solo/satb choir.
Indeed the mystery [quarter-note = 100] satb choir/children's choir.
Where is the desire of the world? [quarter-note = 66] children's choir/satb choir.
I remembered the prophet [quarter-note = 54] Bar solo/ttbb choir.
My begging [quarter-note = 60] A solo/ssaa choir.
Bring to his rest [quarter-note = 56] atb choir.
In your image [quarter-note = 104] children's choir/satb choir (various scorings).
I weep and wail [quarter-note = 56] A solo/sat choir.
What an amazing thing [quarter-note = 69] A solo/satb choir.
Doxology [quarter-note = 76] B solo/satb choir.
Now and forever [quarter-note = 63] children's choir.

PART 9. The Beatitudes:
Blessed are the poor in spirit [quarter-note = 56] A solo/satb choir.
Blessed are those who mourn [*in stesso tempo*] B solo/satb choir.
Blessed are the meek [*in stesso tempo*] S solo/satb choir.
Blessed are the merciful [*in stesso tempo*] S solo/satb choir.
Blessed are they who hunger [*in stesso tempo*] alto solo/satb choir.
Christ, turn the malefactor [quarter-note = 72] children's choir/satb choir.
Blessed are the pure in heart [quarter-note = 72] S solo/satb choir.
Lord of our life [quarter-note = 72] children's choir/atb choir.
Blessed are the peacemakers [*in stesso tempo*] B solo/atb choir.
Lord over body and soul [quarter-note = 72] satb choir.
Blessed are those who have been persecuted [*in stesso tempo*] S solo/satb choir.
May Christ redeem you [quarter-note = 66] att choir.
Blessed are you when men reproach you [quarter-note = 60] Bar solo/satb choir.
Let us go forth to the tombs [quarter-note = 88] children's choir/satb choir.
Be joyful and rejoice [quarter-note = 66] A solo/ssatbb choir.

Let us listen [quarter-note = 63] Bar solo/tb choir.
Doxology [quarter-note = 66] satb choir.
How can milk flow? [quarter-note = 66] ttbb choir/A solo/at choir.
Blessed is the path [quarter-note = 60] children's choir/alto choir.
As it was in the beginning [quarter-note = 50] Bar solo.
Amen [quarter-note = 60] SATBar soli/children's choir/satb choir.
Among the saints [quarter-note = 48] SATBar soli/children's choir/satb choir.

DISCOGRAPHY

Intuition Classics, INT 3292 2, St. Petersburg State Academic Capella Choir and Symphony Orchestra, cond. Mikis Theorodakis.

13

The Russian Orthodox Panikhida Панихйда

The Russian Orthodox Church has several different forms of the funeral mass: The Order of Burial for Laymen, for a Priest, and for a Child. The burial services are done for the burial; it is a distinctly different service from the Roman Catholic Requiem mass, which may or may not be performed just prior to the burial. Last is the Requiem Office for the Dead, called the *Panikhida*. It is similar to the Catholic Requiem mass because it is a memorial service and a part of the Divine Office. The music and prayers of this memorial, like the Roman requiem, are for the remission of sins and eternal rest for the deceased.

The *Panikhida* is not sung as a mass for the burial service. Rather, it can be sung at the internment and on the third day; the latter date patterned after Christ's resurrection on the third day. It can also be sung on the ninth and fortieth days. These days are based upon a vision experienced by Macarius of Alexandria—a vision in which he saw the ninth and fortieth days as moments of personal judgment. Finally, the *Panikhida* is sung on the Ecumenical Saturdays before Meat-Fast Week (during the second week of Lent), at Pentecost, and on the individual's death anniversary.

The two principal ideas associated with the *Panikhida* are sorrow and illumination. There is sorrow at the death of the individual; more importantly is the transformation (illumination) of that sorrow into spiritual joy and glorification of God.

The structure of the *Panikhida* is believed to have been established by Ivan the Terrible in 1548. The service is divided into three major sections:

593

the opening canticles (songs), the Canon, and the canticles sung after the Canon.

Russia converted to Christianity in 988, in the present capital of the Ukraine, Kiev. At this time, the Christian musical tradition was nearly a millennium old in both the Roman and Byzantine world while Russian sacred musical tradition was in its infancy. For several centuries, the Russians borrowed the music of the Byzantine Church, but in the late 1400s, a native, monophonic church music, in the guise of an ornate elaboration of the Byzantine melodies, began to flourish. By the beginning of the seventeenth century, polyphony made its first appearance in western Russia; later spreading to Moscow, Novogorod, and other musical centers.

In the 1700s, a number of Italian composers arrived in Russia, bringing the musical language of Western Europe with them, but by the mid-1800s, Russian composers of sacred music were trying to replace that style and eliminate its influence by the revival of a native musical style. Note that Western music historians were, at the same time, making serious investigations into the origin of Gregorian chant. Unfortunately, research in Russian sacred music came to a virtual end with the 1917 Revolution. After a seventy-year hiatus, this research has been resumed.

Of the handful of *Panikhidi*, mentioned in this study, only one comes from the earliest years of polyphonic writing; the late seventeenth century. The remaining works date from 1860 into the early years of the twentieth century, a period in which Russian Church music flourished. There are undoubtedly other settings of the *Panikhida*, especially the old monophonic versions and the seventeenth- and eighteenth-century polyphonic settings. They await transcription into modern notation, or, in the case of the oldest pieces, knowledge of how to accurately decipher the neumes.

Melodies from the older *Panikhida* chant repertory have made their way into the area of secular and nonliturgical sacred music. The liturgical melody, *With the Saints give rest*, can be found in Tchaikovsky's *Sixth Symphony* (1893) and his opera, *The Queen of Spades* (1890). Taniev used the same theme in Opus 1, *John of Damascus* (1884), and Kastalsky in *Commemeration Fraternelle* (1916).

Modest Mussorgsky used the melody, *Foreasmuch as I behold the sea of life*, in *Boris Godunov* (1874). Because of the 1917 Russian Revolution and the virtual replacement of the Orthodox religion with communist ideology, the flourishing church music in the late nineteenth century came to an abrupt end. However, new life in Russian church music is glimpsed in works such as John Tavener's *Funeral Ikos* (1981), *Panikhida* (1986), *Akhmatova Requiem* (1979–80).

Recent choral compositions, for memorial use, include the *Concert in Memory of Alexander Yurlov* (b. 1927) by Gregory Sviridov. This work, composed in memory of the famous Russian choral-conductor, Alexander Yurlov. It is scored for four-part choir and was originally published in 1975. It consists of three movements, *Weeping, Parting & Choral* (reprinted by *Musica*, Moscow, 1989).

The Byelorussian composer, Viktor Copytsko (b. 1956), composed and published *Two Sacred Chants in Memory of Alexander Men*, scored for unaccompanied SATB (*divisi*) choir and soloists. This modern choral work employs the *Panikhida* hymn, *With the Saints give rest*. Nikolai Lebedev (1947–2000) made a complete setting of the traditional *Panikhida*, which employs an unaccompanied, four-part choir that closely follows the harmonic idiom of the early twentieth century.

Although the *Panikhida* has a basic text, translations of the text from the original Slavonic into foreign languages have led to a number of minor variations in the text, but these changes have not altered the basic essence of the original text. Most of the service can be chanted, but many composers chose certain portions for choral treatment. The model of texts, set to music, which has been used here is found in Seymon Panchenko's Opus 48. All of the composers, with the exception of Kastalsky, followed, with some very minor exceptions, the musical settings as found in this work.

The texts, not set to music as a part of the polyphonic *Panikhida*, are indicated with an asterisk (*). These sections can be chanted, but were not set by the composers listed in this work. Any masculine references in the prayer texts can be replaced by feminine forms; singular pronouns, by plural forms. The following is an outline of the service:

Opening Prayers and Hymns

Opening prayers *
The *Trisagion*.* This hymn begins with the words, *Holy God, Holy Mighty, Holy Immortal One*, a text common to all Orthodox traditions.
Psalm 91 * "*He that dwells in the secret place of the most High. . . .*"
The Great Litany for Peace. The Litany is a series of prayers sung or said by the Priest or deacon and to which the choir responds either *Lord have mercy* or *Amen* or *To Thee O God*. All composers have set this text to music for choir and bass or tenor soloist.

In peace let us pray to the Lord.
R. *Lord have mercy.*
For the peace that is from heaven and for the salvation of our souls:
let us pray to the Lord. R.
For the forgiveness of sins, for the blessed memory of the departed one:
let us pray . . . R.
For the servant of God, worthy of perpetual remembrance,
for the peace of his soul

for his blessed memory: let us pray . . . R.
That all his sins, committed with or without his knowledge may be forgiven:
let us pray . . . R.
For all the sorrowing and the sick who have set their hope in the consolation
of Christ: let us pray . . . R.
That our Lord may take his soul to that place full of light, bliss and
refreshment where the saints rest: let us pray . . . R.
That we will be spared need, affliction and wrath: let us pray . . . R.
Hasten to our aid, save us and have pity, O God, through thy grace. R.
Having implored for him the mercies of God, the Kingdom of Heaven,
and the remission of sins let us commend ourselves, and each other,
and to all our life unto Christ our God: *To Thee O God.*
For thou art the Resurrection, the Life and the peace of thy departed servant,
of our fathers and brothers resting here and elsewhere, orthodox Christians.
O Christ our God, and unto thee we ascribe glory, together with the Father
who is from everlasting, and thine all-holy and good and life-giving Spirit,
now and for ever and evermore. *Amen.*

The Alleluia on the Eighth Tone. * This movement is sung by the priest,
who chants the text and the choir, which responds with *Alleluia.* The Alleluia is divided into four sections: the opening Alleluia with its three
verses (*stikhi*), a hymn (*troparion*) *O Thou, who with profound wisdom*, the
Gloria Patri, and concluding Hymn to the Birth-Giver of God (*Bogoroditchen*).

Alleluia [3x]
Blessed are those who are chosen by God and called to Him.
Alleluia [3x]
Their memory endures from generation to generation.
Alleluia [3x]
Their souls shall dwell with the blessed.
Alleluia [3x]
[*Troparion*]
O Thou who, with wisdom profound, mercifully orders all things,
and provides all our needs, thou Only Creator:
Give rest to the soul of thy servant who has fallen asleep;
For he has set his hope on Thee, our Maker, our Teacher, our God.
[Gloria Patri]
Glory be to the Father . . .
Hymn to the Birth Giver of God [*Bogoroditchen*]
Mary, our shield, our refuge, you who mercifully intercede for us with God,
you gave birth to Him, unwedded Bride: You are the salvation of the faithful.

Psalm 119 * The psalm is sung or said and is divided into two portions:
verses 1–131; verses 132–176.
The *Troparion* (hymn), for rest, *The Company of Saints*, opens with the

refrain, *Blessed art thou, O Lord: teach me thy statutes.* Usually, six refrains accompany the six verses of text. The Gloria Patri, which is split into two sections by the hymn, *Devoutly do we hymn,* follows the opening troparion. This "movement" concludes with a version of the Hymn to the Birth-Giver of God and a final *Alleluia.*

> R. Blessed art thou, O Lord: teach me thy statutes.
> The Choir of Saints has found the Fountain of Life and the Door of Paradise.
> May I also find the right way, through repentance. Call me and save me,
> O Savior.
> R. Blessed art thou . . .
> Ye who preached the Lamb of God, and like unto lambs were slain,
> and are translated unto the life eternal, which waxeth not old;
> ye holy Martyrs, pray ye unto him that he will vouchsafe us remission
> of our sins.
> R. Blessed art thou . . .
> Ye who have trod the narrow way most sad; all ye who, in life, have
> taken upon you the Cross as a yoke, and have followed Me through
> faith, draw near: Enjoy ye the honors and the crowns which I have
> prepared for you.
> R. Blessed art thou . . .
> I am an image of thy glory ineffable, though I bear the brands of
> transgressions: Show thy compassion upon thy creature, O Master,
> and purify him by thy loving-kindness; and grant unto me the
> home-country of my heart's desire, making me again a citizen of Paradise.
> R. Blessed art thou . . .
> S. O thou who of old who didst call me into being from nothingness, and
> didst honor me with thine divine image, but because I had transgressed thy
> commandments hast returned me again unto the earth from which I was
> taken: Restore thou me to that image and to my pristine beauty.
> R. Blessed art thou . . .
> Give rest, O Lord, to the soul of thy servant, and establish him in Paradise.
> Where the choirs of the Saints, O Lord, and of the Just, shine like the stars of
> heaven,
> give rest to thy servant who hath fallen asleep, regarding not all his
> transgressions.
> [Gloria Patri]
> Glory be to the Father and to the Son and to the Holy Spirit.
> [hymn]
> Devoutly do we hymn the triune Effulgence of the one Godhead, crying aloud:
> Holy art thou, O Father, who art from everlasting, O Son co-eternal, and
> Spirit divine. Illumine us who, with faith, do worship thee; and
> rescue us from fire eternal.
> [Gloria Patri]
> Now and ever, and unto ages of ages.
> [hymn to the Birth-giver of God]

Hail, O August One, who for the salvation of all men didst bring forth God
in the flesh; through whom, also, mankind hath found salvation.
Through thee have we found Paradise, O pure, most blessed Birth-giver of God.
Alleluia.

The Lesser Litany for the deceased, *Again and again* (sung by choir and priest).

Lord have mercy.
Let us pray for the peace of soul of your departed servant,
O God, that all his known and unknown sins shall be forgiven.
Lord have mercy.
May the Lord take his soul into the Kingdom where the righteous rest.
Lord have mercy.
Let us beg God's mercy, the Kingdom of Heaven and the forgiveness
of all his sins of Christ, our immortal king and God.
Let us pray to the Lord.
Lord have mercy.
For you are the Resurrection and the life and the peace of your servant,
Christ, our God. We praise you with the your Father and your
merciful life-granting Holy Spirit.
Now and forevermore, world without end.
Amen.

Sitting Hymn (*Sedalen*), *Give Rest.* This hymn is divided into two sections: the
hymn and Gloria Patri, which is split by an inserted hymn.

Give rest with the Just, O our Saviour, unto thy servant, and
establish him in thy courts, as it is written: Regarding not, in that
thou art good, his sins, whether voluntary or involuntary, and all
things committed either with knowledge or in ignorance,
O Thou who lovest mankind.

Glory be to the Father and to the Son and to the Holy Spirit
And all things committed either with knowledge or in ignorance,
O Thou who lovest mankind.
As it was in the beginning, it is now and ever shall be,
world without end. Amen

The Canon

Refrains for the First and Third Canticles and Gloria Patri.

Give rest, O Lord, to the soul of thy servant.

THE *IRMOS* OF THE THIRD CANTICLE

Within the Canon, there is a lengthy hymn of eight or nine odes (canticles) which relate to the occasion that is being memorialized, in this case,

the deceased person. The odes are called canticles in the Russian Orthodox Service Book and each canticle has an opening theme song which is called the *Irmos*. All of the *Panikhida* settings in this chapter have a musical arrangement of the *Irmos* to the third and sixth canticles.

O Lord, Creator of the vault of heaven, and founder of the Church,
strengthen me in thy love, for this security is the crown of the longings
of the faithful. Thou alone art our Lord who loves mankind.

The Lesser Litany.
The refrain for the fourth, fifth and sixth canticles.
Irmos to the sixth canticle, *I pour out my prayers.*

I pour out my prayers before the Lord and call on him in my grief.
For my soul is full of wickedness and my life draws near to Hell,
and I call to you like Jonah: Deliver me, O God, from the abyss.

The Lesser Litany is again repeated.
The Collect Hymn (*Kondak*), *With the souls*. This hymn is divided into several sections: the opening *Kondak*, an *Ikos* (a special verse, thematically related to the idea expressed in the *Kondak*), the *Gloria Patri*, and a concluding prayer to Mary. This collect hymn is sung after the Sixth Canticle of the Canon.

[kondak]
With the souls of the righteous, give rest, O Saviour, to the soul
of thy servant, where there is no more illness or sorrow nor sighing but only
eternal life.
[Ikos]
Thou only art immortal, who hast created and fashioned man. For out of the earth
were we mortals made, and unto the earth shall we return, as thou didst
command when
thou madest me: For earth thou art and unto the earth shall thou return.
Whither also all we mortals wend our way, making our funeral dirge the song:
Alleluia.
[Gloria Patri]
Glory be to the Father and to the Son and to the Holy Spirit . . .
[hymn to Mary]
Holy Mother of God and Mother of the Light, we praise you with our songs.
And the souls of the saints will praise you, O Lord.

Refrains for the seventh, eighth and ninth canticles.
The *Irmos* (theme song) of the 9th Canticle (Hymn) of the Canon.

Heaven and earth are amazed and all the ends of the earth are astonished,
for God has been made flesh and has become man, and thy womb contained more
than the heavens: therefore we praise thee, Mother of God,
the angels and all the orders of mankind.

The Lord's Prayer *

Concluding Prayers and Hymns

The *Troparion* (hymn) *With the souls of the saints.* The *Troparion* is divided into three sections: two opening verses, the *Gloria Patri*, and a Hymn to the Birth-Giver of God.

Let the soul of your departed servant rest with the souls of the saints, O God, and preserve them in the life of the spirit which is with you, O gracious friend of mankind. In your place of rest, where all your saints rest, grant peace also to the soul
of your servant, for you alone are the gracious friend of mankind.

Glory be to the Father . . .

You, Virgin, pure and unspotted, who gave birth to the God without seed, pray for the redemption of his soul.

The Fervent Litany.

Have mercy upon us, O God, according to thy great mercy, we beseech thee: hearken and have mercy
Lord have mercy. [3x]
Again we pray for the repose of his soul, the servant of God, departed this life, and that he may be pardoned all his sins, both voluntary and involuntary.
Lord have mercy. [3x]
That the Lord God will establish his soul where the Just repose.
Lord have mercy. [3x]
Let us pray to Christ, our immortal King and God, for the mercy of God, for the Kingdom of Heaven and the forgiveness of his sins. Grant it O Lord.
Let us pray to the Lord.
Lord have mercy.
For thou art the resurrection and the life and the peace of thy departed servant, of our fathers and brothers and all orthodox Christians who rest here and elsewhere, Christ and our God.
We praise thee and thy Father from the beginning of time and thy all-holy, merciful and life-giving Spirit, now and forever and forevermore. Amen

Dismissal and Benediction.

Wisdom, all holy mother of God, grant us thy salvation.
[opening hymn]
For thou art more venerable than the Cherubim and incomparably more glorious than the Seraphim, thou who, undefiled, gave birth to the Word: O true Mother of God, we praise thee.
[Gloria Patri]

Glory be to the Father . . .
Lord have mercy [3x]. Bless
[Benediction]
Bless us, O Lord.
Thou hast power over the living and the dead, thou Christ, through the intercession
of thy undefiled Mother and of the holy and glorious Apostles,
our venerable fathers who spread the word of God and all the saints,
take the soul of thy servant to the place where the saints rest, let him rest in among
thy saints; let him be numbered among thy saints; and have mercy upon us,
for thou art merciful and living to mankind.

Eternal Memory (Eternal Remembrance) is the concluding prayer of the *Panikhida*.

O Lord, in the life after death grant thy departed servant
eternal peace and grant him eternal remembrance,
eternal remembrance, eternal remembrance.

Basic Data

EDITION

Sputnik Psalomshchika [СПУТНИКЪ ПСАЛОМЩИКА]
Third Edition
Petrograd. 1916 (A photocopy of the edition, printed at Holy Trinity Monastery, Jordanville, NY. 1959, exists.)
[The monophonic chant for the Panikhida is included in this volume.]
[Knowledge of Slavonic and square notation needed.]

DISCOGRAPHY

1. Koch, 3-1217-2, Russian Requiem. Novo-Spasskij Monastery Choir (no indication of composers).
2. Saison Russe, CDM RUS 288 099, Orthodox Requiem (various composers).
3. EMI Classics, 569455 2, Chants Liturgiques Orthodoxes, Choeurs Feodor Potorjonsky.

ANONYMOUS SEVENTEENTH-CENTURY PANIKHIDA

In some settings of the *Panikhida*, the authorship remains unknown. One of the earliest polyphonic settings, recently transcribed, is located in the State History Museum, Moscow. The seventeenth century witnessed the birth of a native polyphonic style. 1668 is a watershed year in the history of Russian sacred polyphonic style; it received official recognition and approval for performance during the worship of Divine Liturgy.

The Russian orthodox polyphonic style consisted of two or three independent melodic lines, all of which were based upon the older monophonic chant. The usual procedure was to begin the lines in unison and
gradually moved them apart, thereby creating a texture of two or three
independent melodic lines.

This linear style was called "triple line style," and was commonly used
from the middle 1600s onward. The characteristic melodic series of parallel seconds and sevenths, as well as dissonant cadence chords, which typ-
ify this "triple line style" produced a unique and somewhat otherworldly
sonority; a sonority not typically found in Western European choral literature. Some scholars believe that the current interpretation, which allows
for such dissonance, is incorrect and that seventeenth century musicians
would have interpreted the notation in a more consonant fashion.

This anonymous *Panikhida* is a magnificent example of "triple line"
composition. Regrettably, no musical score was available for study. The
text format and structure of this sixteenth century work is virtually the
same as those of the late nineteenth–early twentieth century. The composer included settings of several additional pieces that are associated
with the service, but do not appear to be set polyphonically in more
recently composed works. Such pieces include the *Trisagion*, a hymn of
Greek origin, *Holy God, Holy Mighty, Holy Immortal, have mercy on us.* This
hymn is normally sung before the reading of the Epistle and Gospel. In
addition, the settings of the fourth, fifth, sixth, and seventh canticles are
also somewhat special because they are the alternate canticle settings,
reserved to commemorate the death of Orthodox warriors.

Basic Data

EDITION
None available.

DURATION
Twenty-five sections

VOICING
Choir: TBarB

OUTLINE
Opening prayer: *King of Heaven* (unison, melismatic chant).

> King of Heaven, Consoler, Spirit of truth,
> Thou who art everywhere and who fillest all,
> Treasure of grace, Giver of Life, come and live with us.
> From all stains, save our souls, Thou who art goodness.

Trisagion and The Lord's Prayer (solo chant).

O Holy God, Holy Mighty, Holy Immortal One,
Have mercy upon us. [3 times]

[Lord's Prayer]
Our Father, who art in heaven . . .

Alleluia: sung three times after Psalm 91. (three-part polyphony/unison chant).
The Great Litany (three-part polyphony).

Blessed, Lord, are those thou choosest and callest.
R. Lord, have mercy upon us.
Their memory will live forever.
R. Lord have mercy upon us.
Their souls will dwell with the Righteous.
R. Lord, have mercy upon us.

Troparion: *O Thou who, with wisdom profound.* (unison chant and three-part polyphony).

O Thou who, with wisdom profound, mercifully orderest all things,
and givest that which is expedient unto all men, thou Only Creator:
Grant rest, O Lord, to the soul of thy servant, who has fallen asleep;
For he has set his hope on thee, our Maker, the Author of our being
and our God.
[Gloria Patri]
Glory be to the Father . . .

[Hymn to the Birth-Giver of God]
Thee have we as a Wall and a Refuge, and a Mediatrix well-pleasing
unto God whom thou hast borne, O Virgin Birth-Giver of God,
the salvation of mankind.

Psalm 119: (first section) *Blessed are the undefiled in the way.* (three-part polyphony/solo chant).
The Lesser Litany: *Lord have mercy* [3 times] (three-part polyphony).
Psalm 119: (second section) *I am thine, save me* (three-part polyphony/solo chant).
Requiem hymn (*troparion*): *Blessed art Thou, O Lord, teach me Thy statutes.* (three-part polyphony).
The Lesser Litany: *Lord have mercy* [3 times] (three-part polyphony).
The Sitting (*Sedalen*) Hymn: *Grant with the Righteous* unison chant/three-part polyphony).

Grant rest with the righteous, O Saviour, to thy servant
and make him to dwell in Thy courts,
as it is written: As Thou art good, regard not all his sins,

voluntary and involuntary, knowingly or unknowingly committed,
O Lover of mankind.
[Gloria Patri]
Glory be to the Father . . .

The Canon

Irmos (theme song) and Hymn: Canticle One (for Orthodox warriors).
The Canticles set in this version of the Panikhida are those used for soldiers,
seamen, airmen (warriors), and others who died in battle for the Homeland or
the Faith. They differ somewhat from the "usual" settings. (unison chant).

[Irmos]
When Israel had passed through the water as it had been dry land,
and had escaped from the malice of the Egyptians, they cried:
Let us sing praises unto our deliverer and our God.

[verse]
Grant rest, O Lord, to the souls of thy servants who
have fallen asleep.

[hymn]
Having opened my mouth, O Saviour, give me speech to pray,
O Compassionate One, for those who have wrought valiant deeds
of the Faith and the Fatherland; and give rest to their souls, O Master.

[Gloria Patri]
Glory be to the Father, and to the Son, and to the Holy Spirit.
Now and ever and unto ages of ages. Amen

Irmos (theme song) and Hymn: Canticle Three (for Orthodox warriors.) unison
chant.

[Irmos]
O Master and Creator of the vault of heaven, and Founder of the Church,
establish thou me in thy love, O Thou who alone lovest mankind;
the Summit of desire, the Confirmation of the faithful.

[verse]
Grant rest, O Lord . . .

[hymn]
In a place of verdure, a place of repose, where the company of the Saints
rejoice, give rest, O Christ, to the souls of thy servants who have
valiantly wrought for the Holy Church and their Fatherland,
O only, Merciful One.

[Gloria Patri]
Glory be to the Father . . .

Irmos (theme song) and Hymn: Canticle Four (for Orthodox warriors) (unison chant/solo chant).

[Irmos]
I have heard the mystery of thy providence, O Lord;
I have understood thy deeds and have glorified thy Divinity.

[verse]
Grant rest, O Lord . . .

[hymn]
When thou had descended into the nethermost depths, O Christ,
thou didst raise up again with thee all those who were dead.
Grant rest also to him who hath passed away from us,
O generous Saviour.

[Gloria Patri]
Glory be to the Father . . .

Irmos (theme song) and Hymn: Canticle Five (for Orthodox warriors) (unison chant).

[Irmos]
Enlighten us with thy precepts, O Lord, and with thy lofty arm
give us thy peace, O Merciful One.

[verse]
Grant rest, O Lord . . .

[hymn]
O Christ our God, who hast power over life and death,
grant rest to him who hath been taken from among us,
For thou, O Saviour, art the Repose and the Life of all.

[Gloria Patri]
Glory be to the Father . . .

Irmos (theme song) and Hymn: Canticle Six (for Orthodox warriors) (unison chant, solo passage on the Gloria Patri).

[Irmos]
I pour out my prayers unto the Lord, and unto Him do I declare
my grief; for my soul is filled with woe, and my life has drawn me
toward Hell. Yet like Jonah, I implore thee: Raise me up from
corruption, my God.

[verse]
Grant rest, O Lord . . .

[hymn]

Thou didst overthrow Hell, O Lord, thou didst raise up those who lay
dead from all the ages. Those who died for thy Holy Church establish
thou in Abraham's bosom, O Lord, remitting all their transgressions;
forasmuch as thou art of tender compassion.

[Gloria Patri]
Glory to the Father . . .

Kondak: *With the saints, give rest.* (three-part polyphony/unison chant & three-part
polyphony for the *Oikos*) *Ikos*: *Thou only art immortal.* unison chant/solo chant).

Irmos (theme song) and Hymn: Canticle Seven for Orthodox warriors. (unison
chant, solo passage on Gloria Patri).

[Irmos]
The Holy Children, sprung from the Jews of yore, in Babylon,
through the faith of the Trinity did trample under foot the fiery
furnace, singing: O God of our fathers, blessed be thou.

[verse]
Grant rest, O Lord . . .

[Hymn]
O Master, Christ our God, when thou shalt come to judge the world,
spare thou the souls of thy servants who have suffered for Thy Holy Church
and the Fatherland, and whom thou hast taken from us, crying:
O God of our fathers, blessed art thou.

[Gloria Patri]
Glory to the Father . . .

Irmos (theme song) and Hymn: Canticle Eight (for Orthodox warriors) (unison
chant/three-part polyphony).

[Irmos]
With a furnace seven times heated did the Chaldean tormentor
fiercely scorn the God-fearing Ones; but when he beheld the same
saved by a better power, unto their Maker and Deliverer he cried:
Ye Children, bless; Ye Priests, sing praises; Ye People, magnify
forevermore.

[verse]
Grant rest, O Lord . . .

[Hymn]
They who have finished their course and have fled for refuge unto thee,
O Lord, and have suffered for thy Holy Church, now cry aloud unto thee:

Pardon our iniquities, O Christ our God, and condemn not when thou shalt come
to judge all men, us who with faith have cried unto thee: O all ye works of the
Lord,
praise ye the Lord and glorify him evermore.

[Gloria Patri]

Irmos (theme song) and Hymn: Canticle Nine (for Orthodox warriors) (three-part
polyphony).

[Irmos]
The heavens marvelled and the ends of the earth were amazed, when God
manifested to men himself incarnate; and thy womb was more spacious than
the heavens; wherefore, O Mother of God, the leaders of angels and men
glorify thee.

[verse]
Grant rest, O Lord . . .

[hymn]
O Jesus, God and Saviour, thou didst take upon thee Adam's
sin and didst taste death, that thou mightest deliver men
therefrom, O Compassionate One.
wherefore we implore thee:
Grant rest to the deceased in thy holy courts, as thou alone
art most good and compassionate.

[Gloria Patri]
Glory to the Father . . .

Concluding Prayers and Hymns

The *Trisagion*
  Troparion: *With the souls of the just* (unison chant)
  The Fervent Litany (three-part polyphony)
  Memory Eternal (three-part polyphony)
  The *Trisagion* & Lord's Prayer

DISCOGRAPHY

Opus 111, OPS 30-97, Panikhida. Russian Orthodox Requiem 17th Century. Russian Orthodox Patriarchate Choir, dir. Anatoly Grindenko.

ALEXANDER ARKHANGELSKY
October 11 [23], 1846–November 16, 1924

Arkhangelsky was a choral conductor and composer. He received his
training from Penza Theological Seminary. In 1872, he passed the exami-

nations for precentor at the Imperial Court Chapel in St. Petersburg. In 1880, he established a mixed choir that gained an excellent reputation by making a number of highly successful tours throughout Russia and Europe. Although he was an active choral conductor, he made a number of significant contributions to the repertory of Russian church music. His nearly 300 compositions include complete settings of the Divine Liturgy, the All-Night Vigil, the Memorial Service, and many single compositions.

The *Memorial Service*, scored for SATB choir, was composed around 1890 and first published in March 1891. Its chordal, four-part harmonies and metrical rhythm were clearly influenced by Western European style, with the exception of several nonmetrical, intoned passages in the Troparion, *Blessed art thou* and the Dismissal.

The score includes no passages for soloists and the text is arranged in a sequence of musical pieces, as they occur in the order of the Divine Liturgy. The four-part texture is homophonic, enriched by occasional suspensions and passing tones.

Basic Data

EDITION

Panikhida for Four Mixed Voices
G. Schmidt, St. Petersburg (#A 42) March 12, 1891

DURATION

Nineteen sections

VOICING

Choir: SATB range: S-G6; B-E flat 3

OUTLINE

The Great Litany
Alleluia & *Troparion, Deep Wisdom.*
Troparion, Blessed art Thou.
The Lesser Litany
Troparion, Give rest.
Refrain for the 3rd Canticle
Irmos for the 3rd Canticle
The Lesser Litany [see #4]
Refrain for the 6th Canticle
Irmos for the 6th Canticle
The Lesser Litany [see #4]
Kondak, With the saints.
Ikos, Thou only art immortal.
Refrain for the 7th, 8th, 9th Canticles
Irmos to the 9th Canticle

Troparion, With the souls.
The Fervent Litany
Dismissal
Eternal Memory

DISCOGRAPHY
None found.

PAVEL CHESNOKOV
November 24, 1877–March 14, 1944

Pavel Chesnokov attended the most important school for the training of Russian church musicians, the Moscow Synodal School, from 1885 to 1895. After graduation, he studied composition with Taniev and Ippolitov-Ivanov. He later taught at the Synodal School from 1895 to 1920, exerting a significant influence upon a generation of church musicians. From 1920 to 1944, he was a professor of choral conducting at the Moscow Conservatory, an institution that had absorbed the Synodal School into its own organization.

He composed more than 400 choral works for the Orthodox Service, as well as a number of songs and stage works. Among the sacred works are a *Funeral Service* and a setting of the *Panikhida, Op. 39 # 2*. The work was composed sometime about 1910 and dedicated to his good friend and teacher, Stepan Smolensky.

Chesnokov made two arrangements of *Opus 39*: one for SATB choir and another, for TTBB choir (*Opus 39a*). This extraordinarily beautiful work, possesses a mood of grief and great solemnity; a fact that led to criticism by his colleagues, who felt that the work needed lightness and celebration, rooted in the affirmation and hope promised by Christ's resurrection.

Chesnokov used the older Russian chants, imbedding them within his own harmonic language; a language influenced by late romanticism. As is typical with all of the *Panikhida* settings, the tenor and bass soloists sing the portions of the service that are normally chanted or intoned. The choir is responsible for the responses, refrains and occasionally, the hymn texts.

The published edition of his *Panikhida* setting contains only the choral parts and selected portions of the solo chant lines, which cue the choir when to sing. The *Troparion for Rest* is greatly abbreviated and a number of "movements" flow directly, one into another, an innovation that differs slightly from the established structure of the bulk of *Panikhida* settings mentioned in this study. The traditional chant melodies of the themesongs (*Irmos, heirmoi*, pl.) of the canticles in the canon are abandoned, though the chant melodies are preserved in other sections of the *Panikhida*. The four-part choral writing is always homophonic and syllabic, with occasional passing-tones.

Basic Data

EDITIONS

1. P. Chesnokov
Panikhida [No. 2], for Mixed Choir, Op. 39
P[yotr] Jurgenson [Publishers], #33608 Moscow, Warsaw, Kiev
[clefs: C (soprano, alto, tenor) & F]

1a. P. Chesnokov
Panikhida [No. 2], for Male Choir [TTBB], Op. 39a
P[yotr] Jurgenson [Publishers], #36622 Moscow, Warsaw, Kiev
[Both editions out of print]

DURATION

Eleven movements.

VOICING

Choir: SATB or TTBB range: S-A6; B-D3

OUTLINE

1. Great Litany
2. Alleluia
3. *Troparion* for Rest
4. Lesser Litany, including refrain for the third canticle.
5. *Irmos* for the third canticle including Lesser Litany and refrain for the sixth canticle.
6. *Irmos* for the sixth canticle, including the Lesser Litany.
7. *Troparion*, *With the Saints give rest*, including refrain for the ninth canticle.
8. *Irmos* for the ninth canticle
9. *Troparion*, *With the souls of the righteous*
10. Fervent Litany, including Dismissal
11. Eternal Memory

DISCOGRAPHY

1. Koch-Schwann, 3-1750-2 G1, Philharmonic Choir of Ekaterinberg, cond. W. Kopanev.
2. Olympia, OCD 482, Cantus Sacred Music Ensemble, dir. Ludmila Arshavskaya.

Composed in the early years of the twentieth century, the *Funeral Service* is somewhat different from the *Panikhida*. The Orthodox funeral service is the service for burial of the body of the deceased, not a memorial service in the sense of the *Panikhida*. The structure and texts of this service are somewhat different than the latter memorial service. The musical settings of *Op. 30, No. 1* are short choral settings of the funeral texts, with occasional solo lines for the bass or tenor.

The bulk of the work is written in homophonic, syllabic style; the prevailing mood of *Opus 30* is somber and sad. Occasional commentary from the composer indicates that other texts, not set specifically for this work, can be drawn from other sources. Such pieces include the Great and Lesser Litanies.

Basic Data

EDITION

Funeral Service, Op. 30, No. 1
P[yotr] Jurgenson Publisher, #34122 Moscow
no date given [out of print][clefs: C (soprano, alto, tenor) and F]

DURATION

Six movements

VOICING

Choir: SATB [*divisi*] range: S-A6; B-C3

OUTLINE

Beginning of the funeral service, *Blessed be God* [abbreviated form]. Two verses with the refrain, *Alleluia*, a Gloria Patri, and Litany. (choir/soloist).

> Amen. Blessed are the undefiled in the way,
> who walk in the law of the Lord.
> R. Alleluia
> Blessed are they who keep his testimonies,
> and seek Him with their whole heart.
> R. Alleluia
>
> [Gloria Patri]
> Glory be to the Father and to the Son and to the Holy Spirit,
> R. Alleluia
> Now and ever and unto ages of ages. Amen
> R. Alleluia
>
> [Litany]
> I opened my mouth and drew in my breath,
> for my delight was in] thy commandments.
> R. Have mercy upon thy servant.
> Thy hands have made and fashioned me,

R. Have mercy upon thy servant.
I opened my mouth and drew in my breath,
for my delight was in thy commandments.
R. Have mercy upon thy servant.

[Gloria Patri]
Glory to the Father . . .
R. Have mercy upon thy servant.
Look upon me and have mercy upon me,
according to the judgement of them that love thy Name.
Consider me and have mercy upon me.
Blessed be thy holy name. Alleluia.

Seating hymn, *Rest, Our Saviour.* This text is taken from the order of Burial of the
Dead (Laymen). Included are the Seating Hymn and the Hymn to the Birth-Giver
of God (*Bogoroditchen*).

Give rest with the Just, O our Savior, unto thy servant,
and establish him in thy courts, as it is written:
Regarding not, in that thou art good, his sins,
whether voluntary or involuntary, and all things
committed either with knowledge or in ignorance,
O thou who lovest mankind.

[Hymn to the Birth-Giver of God]
O Christ-God, who from a Virgin didst shine forth upon the world,
through her, making us sons of the light, have mercy upon us.

The *Ikos, Thou only art immortal.* (tenor solo (chant)/choir).

Thou only art immortal, who hast created and fashioned man.
For out of the earth were we fashioned and unto the earth shall we return,
as thou didst command when thou madest me, saying unto me:
For earth thou art, and unto earth shalt thou return. Whither, also,
all we mortals wend our way, making of our funeral dirge the song: Alleluia.

The anthem, *What earthly sweetness remains, unmixed with grief?* (John of Damascus) A long poem reflecting upon human mortality. Chesnokov set only a small
portion of this long poem to music.

I weep and I wail when I think upon death, and behold our beauty,
fashioned by God, lying in the tomb disfigured, dishonored,
bereft of form. O marvel! What is this mystery which befalls us?
Why have we been given over to corruption and why have we been wedded
unto death? Of a truth, as it is written, by the command of God,
who giveth the departed rest.

The hymn, *As ye behold me* is taken from the Order of Burial for the Dead (Priests). It represents the prayer and thoughts of the deceased soul, as it is being observed by the living.

As ye behold me lie before you all speechless and bereft of breath, weep for me,
O friends and brethren, O kinsfolk and acquaintance.
For but yesterday I talked with you, and suddenly there came upon me the
dread hour of death. But come, all ye who loved me, and
kiss me with the last kiss. For nevermore shall I walk or talk with you.
For I go hence unto the Judge with whom is no respect of persons. For slave and
master stand together before him, king and warrior, the rich and the poor,
in honor equal. For according to his deeds shall every man receive glory
or be put to shame. But I beg and implore you all, that ye will pray without
ceasing to the Christ-God, that I be not doomed according to my sins, unto
a place of torment; but that he will appoint unto me a place where there is the
light of life.

The Hymn to the Birth-Giver of God, *Through the prayers* is taken from the Order of Burial (Laymen). Through the prayers of her who gave thee birth, O Christ: and of thy Forerunner; of the Apostles, Prophets, Heirarchs, Holy Ones, of the Just, and of all the Saints:

Give rest unto thy servant who is fallen asleep.

DISCOGRAPHY

None found.

ALEXANDER KASTALSKY
November 16 [28], 1856–December 17, 1926

Kastalsky received his musical training at Moscow Conservatory from Tchaikovsky and Taniev. In 1887, he began a long professional career with the Moscow Synodal School of Church Singing that lasted until 1917. (For further biographical details, see the section "The War Requiem").

Kastalsky's arrangement of the *Panikhida*, scored for SAATTBB, is somewhat different from other settings by his contemporaries. Some of the unusual features include the settings of texts in a contrapuntal musical texture; a metrical rhythm; the omission of some of texts regularly scored for the choir; and the use of Russian chants; the Serbian chant, *Eternal Memory*; and the Roman Catholic chant melody, *Dies irae*. Soloists and choir are called for in this setting, making this work suitable for concert hall, yet the deletion of the solo parts and the shortening of textual passages render the setting suitable for singing at the liturgy.

An additional novel feature utilized in the *Panikhida* is the use of a folk-singing tradition in which singers embellish the principal melody with their own variants of the tune. Such passages can be heard in the fifth and the seventh movements. Another folk tune characteristic, strings of melodic parallel thirds, can be found in the sixth and tenth movements. These traits give a traditional "Russian" sonority to the musical fabric, particularly in movements two, three, and six.

Kastalsky's setting of the *Panikhida* was composed in 1917 and is titled *Eternal Memory to the Heros*. It is a rearrangement of some of the passages in his requiem-oratorio, *Fraternal Remembrance*, composed earlier in 1915 and dedicated to those who lost their lives in World War I.

Basic Data

EDITION

Eternal Memory to the Heros, a selection of songs from the Panikhida
P[yotr] Jurgenson, Publisher Moscow, Warsaw, Kiev. 1917

DURATION

Eleven movements

VOICING

Choir: SAATTBB range: S-A6; B-B2
Soloists: TB

OUTLINE

The Great Litany: uses Greek (*Kyrie*) and Russian (*Gospodin pomuldi*) texts. Alleluia and *Profound Wisdom* (theme song for the Troparion): B solo/choir.
Give Rest (from the Troparion): choir.
Rest, Lord (from the refrain of the 1st and 3rd Canticle).
Purge me (Irmos of the 6th Canticle): choir/tenor I.
Kondak, With the Saints: choir.
Oikos (stanza for the *Kondak*), *Thou only art immortal*: choir. Gregorian Dies irae. This movement is divided into two principal sections: *Thou only art immortal* and *Making our funeral dirge*.
Troparion, Thou art God: choir.
Troparion, Give rest to thy servants: choir, Kastalsky employs a Serbian chant.
The Fervent Litany: This movement contains passages that may be deleted so that the music can be used for the liturgy. Scored for choir only, there are numerous stops in the music so that prayers and petitions for the deceased can be added.
Eternal Memory: T solo/several bass soli/choir. This movement uses a traditional Serbian chant as its melodic basis.

DISCOGRAPHY

None found.

There exists a separate setting of the Kondak, *With the saints . . .* and the Ikos, *Only thou art immortal. . . .* The *Kondak*, based upon a Kievan chant, is arranged for SSAATT. This nineteen-measure piece is written in a mixture of homophonic and polyphonic textures. The accompanying Ikos is scored for mixed SSAATTBB choir and possesses a polyphonic texture. The texts of both pieces are set in a metered rhythm. Published in 1898.

Basic Data

EDITION

Kondak & Ikos from the Panikhida
[Piano accompaniment]
Published by V. Gross Milnikov, Moscow
October 15, 1898 [clefs: C (soprano, alto, tenor) & F

VOICING

Choir: [for *Kondak*] SSAATT [for *Ikos*] SSAATTBB range: S-A flat 6; B-C3

DISCOGRAPHY

None found.

ALEXEY LVOV
May 25, [June 5] 1798–December 16[28], 1870

Like Rimsky-Korsakov and Cesar Cui, Lvov began his professional career in the military. In 1833, he composed the Russian national anthem, *God save the Tsar*. From 1837 to 1861, he worked for the Romanov family as the Director of the Imperial Court Chapel. During his tenure in this position, he exercised a powerful influence upon the performance of sacred music in all Orthodox churches and chapels throughout Russia. His personal approval was required for any and all sacred repertory used in the Divine Service. He was further responsible for a system of training and testing of candidates who applied for the position of church precentor.

One of the significant contributions to the repertory of the Church was the *Obichod notnovo peniya*, a liturgical chant book that contains the Ordinary hymns for Vespers, Matins, and the Divine Service, as well as the principal Proper hymns. Lvov's settings were published in 1848 and were part of a long tradition of such liturgical books; books that had first appeared in the middle of the 1400s. The polyphonic setting of the *Panikhida* is among the numerous works found in the 1848 edition.

An important feature of these settings is the four-part SATB harmony, more typical of Western European than of Russian modal style, used to harmonize the older Russian liturgical chants. The texture remains homophonic throughout. Lvov employed free rhythm for the *Panikhida* chants; one determined by poetic accent, rather than fixed meter. In addition to the *Obichod*, Lvov composed about fifty other sacred works. In 1869, Nikolai Bakhmetev (1807–1891) made an arrangement of Lvov's *Obichod* that was commonly used throughout the Russian Orthodox Church.

Basic Data

EDITION
Panikhida
Arranged in four-voices, for use at the Imperial Chapel by A. Lvov.
Partitura with piano accompaniment [no date]
[clefs: C (soprano, alto, tenor) & F]

DURATION
Nineteen sections without any movement indication. [choral parts only]

VOICING
Choir: SATB [*divisi*] range: S-G6; B-G3

OUTLINE
Great Litany
Alleluia
Troparion for peace, *Blessed art thou.*
Lesser Litany
Troparion, Give rest.
Refrain for the third canticle, *Give rest.*
Irmos for the third Canticle, *Vault of heaven.*
Lesser Litany
Refrain for the sixth canticle [see # 6]
Irmos for the sixth canticle
Lesser Litany [see # 4]
Kondak, With the Saints.
Ikos, conclusion only
Refrain for the ninth canticle [see # 6]
Irmos for the ninth canticle
Troparion, With the souls.
Fervent Litany
Dismissal
Eternal memory

DISCOGRAPHY
None found.

SEMYON PANCHENKO
1867–1937

Biographical data concerning Panchenko and his music is, at the moment, scanty. He studied composition with Anatol Liadov (1855–1914). In the early years of the twentieth century, he had a private music school in St. Petersburg. He also worked as a symphony conductor.

There are about 125 published works, including complete settings of the Divine Liturgy, the All-Night Vigil, and the Memorial Service. Many of these works are arrangements (six to eight parts) of the SATB Court chant settings originally composed by Lvov in 1848.

In his setting of the *Panikhida, Opus 48,* Panchenko utilized an SATB homophonic texture. This music was published sometime around 1910 and is the only setting of the Memorial Service, listed in this study, in which the composer wrote a "big" and a "little" version of the same pieces. Such pieces include the Great Litany, the Alleluia, the *Kondak,* and many others. This assured that his arrangements would be accessible to both professional and amateur church choirs.

Unlike the original Lvov setting, this setting employs both free and metered rhythms. The concluding phrases of the hymns, such as the *Bogoroditchen,* use Renaissance-style, polyphonic cadence patterns.

Basic Data

EDITION

Panikhida, Op. 48, for Four Voices
Piano accompaniment
P[yotr] Jurgenson, Publisher, Moscow [no date]

DURATION

Twenty-one movements

VOICING

Choir: SATB range: S-A6; B-D3 [occasional A, G & F♯2]

OUTLINE

Great Litany [4 versions] metrical rhythm
Alleluia [2 versions, including last lines of the Troparion & *Bogoroditchen*] free rhythm
Troparion for rest [2 versions] free rhythm
Lesser Litany [2 versions] metrical rhythm
Concluding line of the *Seydala* [sitting hymn] and *Bogoroditchen* [2 versions] chordal and polyphonic texture
Refrains for the 1st and 3rd Canticles [2 versions]
Irmos for the 3rd Canticle [1 version]
Lesser Litany [see # 4]
Refrains for the 4th, 5th, and 6th Canticles [see # 6]
Irmos for the 6th Canticle [1 version]
Lesser Litany [see # 4]
Kondak [2 versions: SAT; SATB]

Concluding line of the Ikos [2 versions]
Ikos [1 version] nonmetrical rhythm
Refrains for the 7th, 8th, and 9th Canticles [see # 6]
Irmos & Refrain to the 9th Canticle
Troparion, With the souls [1 version]
Fervent Litany [2 versions] Mixture of free and metrical rhythm
Dismissal [2 versions]
Eternal Memory [2 versions: free rhythm; metrical rhythm]
Thrice Holy [2 versions, SAT; SATB]

> Holy God, Holy Strong One, Holy Immortal, Have mercy on us.

DISCOGRAPHY

None found.

STEPAN SMOLENSKY
October 20, 1848–August 2, 1909

Smolensky was trained as a lawyer and philologist, but his primary intellectual interest was church music. He taught at the Theological Seminary (Kazan) from 1875 to 1889. His specialty was the music of the Old Believers, a sect that held onto the old ways of worship and refused to accept the reforms of 1650 instituted by the Patriarch, Nikon. They did not accept polyphony, using only the traditional unison chants carried down from the earliest days of the Russian Church.

In 1889, Smolensky received a professorship in church music at the Moscow Conservatory. At the same time, he became director of the Synodal School of Church Music in Moscow, a position he held until 1901. At the end of his life, he held the position of director of the Imperial Court in St. Petersburg (1901–03). During his years in Moscow and St. Petersburg, he was constantly involved in researching the history of Russian chant.

He left very little music, but among his compositions are a Memorial Service, Paschal Verses, and Litany settings. All works were published privately. The *Memorial Service* was composed in 1904 and scored for TTBB choir. The four-part harmonizations of the chants employed in this service are based upon the traditional modes of Russian sacred chant. The composer chose to set the text in a free rhythm; one determined by the accent of the text, rather than forcing the words into a metered rhythmic pattern, in Western European style. The prevailing, four-part texture is homophonic, with the exception of passages, such as the alternate *Amen* section of the Great Litany, that lapse into a more florid polyphonic style.

Basic Data

EDITION

Panikhida for Men's Voices
Published [privately] by the composer on June 22, 1904.
Approved by the Censor, Archbishop Filaret

DURATION

Nineteen sections

VOICING

Choir: TTBB range: T-A5; B-C3

OUTLINE

The Great Litany
Alleluia
Troparion, Blessed art thou. [a reduced number of verses in this version]
The Lesser Litany
Troparion, Give rest.
Refrain for the 3rd Canticle
Irmos for the 3rd Canticle
The Lesser Litany [see # 4]
Refrain for the 6th Canticle
Irmos for the 6th Canticle
The Lesser Litany [see # 4]
Kondak, With the saints.
Ikos, concluding line only
Refrain for the 9th Canticle
Irmos for the 9th Canticle
Troparion, With the souls.
The Fervent Litany
The Dismissal
Eternal Memory

DISCOGRAPHY

None found.

SERGEY TANIEV
November 25, 1856–June 19, 1915

Taniev, one of the most distinguished Russian composers of the late romantic era, entered the Moscow Conservatory in 1866. He studied piano with Nicolai Rubenstein and composition with Peter Tchaikovsky. By 1875, he made his debut as a concert pianist, performing the *D Minor Con-*

certo for piano by Brahms. In 1883, he taught the piano classes of the Moscow Conservatory. By 1885, he was appointed to the directorship of the Conservatory, a position that he relinquished within five years.

Taniev was an individual of great intellectual curiosity as well as a gifted teacher. During his years at the Conservatory, he authored an important treatise (possibly the most significant ever written) on the art of double-counterpoint. He was also the piano teacher for such pupils as Reinhold Glière (1875–1956), Sergei Rachmaninoff (1873–1943), and Alexander Scriabin (1872–1915).

The general musical style of Taniev is oriented to the classical forms of Western Europe, more so than the other "nationalist" Russian composers of that era. This is clearly seen in his use of abstract musical forms and advanced contrapuntal techniques. Taniev wrote in many musical mediums, including chamber music, orchestral works, music for the keyboard, as well as vocal and choral music. It is the latter two categories that Taniev displays his interest in Russian poetry.

Although he wrote very little sacred music, there are two major cantatas, *John of Damascus*, Op. 1 and *At the Reading of a Psalm*, Opus 15. The former work is included in this study for several reasons: there are few sacred works with orchestral accompaniment that come from late nineteenth-century Russia. The few that do exist are rarely performed. The development of this style was cut short by the 1917 Revolution.

John of Damascus embodies the spirit of the *Panikhida* and should be included in such a study, especially as John of Damascus was one of the known writers of the Orthodox requiem text, and, further, because Taniev quoted a well-known *Panikhida* melody, *With the Saints*, in the cantata. *John of Damascus* was composed in 1884 for the unveiling of a monument to Alexander Pushkin, one of Russia's greatest and most beloved poets. Its premiere, however, was given at a concert in memory of his piano teacher, Nikolai Rubenstein, on March 11, 1884. The cantata text was written by Leo Tolstoy (1828–1910) and the score was first published by Pyotr Jurgenson (Moscow) in 1904.

This composition is a remarkable synthesis of the lyrical and dramatic Tchaikovsky style and the contrapuntal writing of German baroque polyphony. The opening passage of the second movement and coda of the last are strongly suggestive of the Russian liturgical style.

Basic Data

EDITIONS

1. John of Damascus, Opus 1
Cantata for mixed choir and
symphony orchestra.
[full score]

2. Johannes Damascenus
Kantate für vierstimmigen
gemischten Chor und Orchester.
[German text by Enns Fried]

State Publishers Music [Izdatelstvo
"*Musica*"]
Moscow 1971

Klavierauszug [piano score]
Musikverlag Hans Sikorski, Hamburg.
1969

DURATION

Three movements, 485 mm., perf., c. 27'

VOICING AND ORCHESTRATION

Choir: SATB range: S-A6; B-F♯ 3
Orchestra: vn. I/II, vla., vc., db., 2 fl., 2 ob., 2 cl., 2 bsn., 4 Fh., 2 tpt., 3 tbn., tuba,
   timp.

OUTLINE

I walk along a path unknown: 182 mm.
   I walk . . . [f♯ m] *adagio, ma non troppo*; orchestral introduction. satb choir. The
   Znamenny chant melody, *With the Saints give rest*, is employed in tuba/trom-
   bone.

I walk along a path unknown to me,
I walk between fear and hope;
The light of my eye is extinguished, my breast is cold,
I lie mute and motionless,
I do not hear the sobbing of my brethren,
and the blue smoke from the censer
does not waft its sweet perfume over me.

For now I sleep the eternal sleep: 46 mm.
   For now I sleep . . . [D flat M] *andante sostenuto*. satb choir.

For now I sleep the eternal sleep
but my love does not die.
And through it, brothers, I implore you,
each to call out to the Lord:
O Lord!

And on that day: 257 mm.
   And on that day [f♯ m] *allegro*. satb choir. Two sections; A four-part fugue, followed by a slow, unaccompanied choral coda. The Znammeny chant melody,
   With the Saints give rest, appears in the French horn line as well as the choral
   lines. Fugue.

And on that day when the trumpet
announces the passing of this world,
[unaccompanied choral passage]
accept Thy departed servant
into Thy heavenly home.

DISCOGRAPHY

Chandos, CHAN 9608, Russian State Symphonic Orchestra and Cappella, dir. Valeri Polyansky.

JOHN TAVENER
January 28, 1944

John Tavener converted to the Greek Orthodox faith in 1976 and after that date, composed a significant number of choral works related to the Orthodox liturgy. Among those pieces are: *Canticle to the Mother of God* (1976), *The Liturgy of St. John Chrysostom* (1978), *The Great Canon of St. Andrew of Crete* (1981), *Funeral Ikos* (1981), *Doxa* (1982), *Orthodox Vigil Service* (1984), *Two Hymns for the Mother of God* (1985), *Akathist for Thanksgiving* (1986–87), *Apolytikion for St. Nicolas* (1988), and *Ikon the Trinity* (1990).

The *Panikhida* was composed in 1986. It is a somewhat unusual work because it possesses an English text. It appears to be, in fact, the first English setting of the Russian *panikhida*. Tavener kept an outline of the original Russian tones throughout the work. He further suggested that the music be sung quietly, like a sacred lullaby. The music is scored for a priest (chanter), who sings on a reciting tone and an SATB choir. Included are the *Great Litany*, the *Troparion*, the *Alleluia, Refrain for the 3rd Canticle*, *Irmos of the 6th Canticle*, the *Ikos*, *The Lord's Prayer*, *Troparion "With the souls*," the *Fervent Litany*, and *Eternal Memory*. The four-part choral writing is nearly always syllabic and homophonic, while the harmonic language is a mixture of traditional and modern, dissonant harmony, for example, as employed in the *Irmos of the 6th Canticle*.

Tavener makes it clear from his instructions that the work may be used not only in a liturgical setting, but also in concerts.

Basic Data

EDITION

John Tavener
Funeral Service
Chester Music, London

DURATION

Unbarred sections, 46 pp.

VOICING

Choir: SATB range: S-F6; B-F3
Soloist: priest (bass)

OUTLINE

The Litany
Blessed are those whom thou hast chosen
Give rest, O Lord
Irmos of the Sixth Canticle, Forasmuch as I behold
Ikos, Thou only are immortal
Lord's Prayer
Troparia, With the spirits
The Litany
Eternal Remembrance

DISCOGRAPHY

None found.

The *Funeral Ikos* were composed in 1981 and scored for unaccompanied SATB choir. The sopranos and basses are often written *divisi*. The harmonic vocabulary is made up of unisons, parallel chords, and occasional mildly dissonant chords. The choral texture remains declamatory and syllabic throughout the work. An *ikos* is a special stanza that is normally sung along with the *Kontakion* [hymn] after the 6th ode of the *Kanon* and usually develops the ideas expressed in the *Kontakion*.

Basic Data

EDITION

John Tavener
Funeral Ikos for unaccompanied Choir ssatbb
Chester Music, CH 55676
London

DURATION

Six sections, 112 mm., perf., c. 10'

VOICING

Choir: SSATBBB range: S-C6; B-F3

OUTLINE

The work is divided into six sections, all of which end with *alleluia*. Section 1: TBB

> Why these bitter words of the dying, O brethren, which they utter
> as they go hence? I am parted from my brethren. All my friends do
> I abandon and go hence. But whither I go, that understand I not, neither
> what shall become of me yonder; only God, who has summoned me
> knoweth. But make commemoration of me with the song: Alleluia.

Section 2: SSA

> But whither now go the souls? How dwell they now together there?
> This mystery have I desired to learn, but none can impart it aright.
> Do they call to mind their own people, as we do them? Or have they forgotten
> all those who mourn them and make the song: Alleluia.

Section 3: SATB

> We go forth on the path eternal, and as condemned, with downcast
> faces, present ourselves before the only God eternal. Where then
> is comeliness? Where then is wealth? Where then is the glory of
> this world? There shall none of these things aid us,
> but only say oft the psalm: Alleluia.

Section 4: TBB

> If thou hast shown mercy unto man, O man, that same mercy shall be
> shown thee there; and if on an orphan thou hast shown compassion, the
> same shall there deliver thee from want. If in this life the naked thou hast
> clothed, the same shall give thee shelter there, and sing the psalm: Alleluia.

Section 5: SSA

> Youth and the beauty of the body fade at the hour of our death, and the
> tongue then burneth fiercely, and the parched throat is inflamed. The
> beauty of the eyes is quenched then, the comeliness of the face all altered,
> the shapeliness of the neck destroyed; and the other parts have become numb,
> nor often say: Alleluia.

Section 6: SATB

> With ecstasy are we inflamed if we but hear that there is light eternal
> yonder; that there is Paradise, wherein every soul of the Righteous Ones
> rejoiceth. Let us all, also, enter into Christ, that all we may aloud
> thus unto God: Alleluia.

DISCOGRAPHY

Gimell, 454 905-2, The Tallis Scholars.

DIMITRY YAICHKOV
1869–December 30, 1953

The biographical details of Yaichkov's career and work are not well known. He graduated from St. Petersburg Conservatory and subsequently worked in Riga (Latvia) and Tiflis (Azerbaijian). By 1909, he worked as a singing teacher at the Teacher's Seminary in Volsk.

Yaichkov is known to have published twenty-one sacred works, including The Order for Prayer Service of Thanksgiving and a setting of the *Panikhida*. The first edition of the *Memorial Service*, scored for SATB choir, appeared in 1900. Its music themes are derived from Znammeny chants (a style of chant dating from the earliest period of Russian church music) the Kievan chants, and the Greek chants, all of which were borrowed from the *Notated Ordinary* and the *Cycle of Church Hymns* of the Kiev-Pechery Lavra. A second fully harmonized edition appeared in 1951.

The chants used are harmonized in a way that the original melodies are present throughout. The harmony employed by Yaichkov is a modal-diatonic style. This version was an early, widely used, popular setting of the *Panikhida* hymns. Since this century-old edition appeared, there have been numerous other "popular" versions of the *Panikhida* composed.

The author of this study had only an arrangement (for three equal voices) of the original mixed choir version with which to work. The edition of this arrangement appeared in 1901. The fabric of the work is in two and three-part homophonic texture, with occasional pedalpoints.

Basic Data

EDITION

Panikhida arranged for three equal voices.
Publisher, P[yotr] Jurgenson, Moscow, Petrograd, Warsaw, Kiev. 1901

DURATION

Nineteen sections

VOICING

Choir: SSA or TTB

OUTLINE

The Great Litany
Alleluia
Troparion, Blessed art thou.
The Lesser Litany
Troparion, Give rest.
Refrain for the 3rd Canticle
Irmos for the 3rd Canticle
The Lesser Litany [see # 4]
Refrain for the 4th, 5th and 6th Canticles
Irmos for the 6th Canticle
The Lesser Litany [see # 4]

Kondak, With the Saints.
Ikos, Only thou art immortal.
Refrain for the 7th, 8th & 9th Canticles
Irmos to the 9th Canticle
Troparion, With the souls.
The Fervent Litany
Dismissal
Eternal Memory

DISCOGRAPHY

None found.

14

The Serbian Orthodox
Requiem: *Opelo*
ОПЕЛО

The Serbian *Opelo* is, in all essential aspects, the same as the *Panikhida* of the Russian Orthodox Church. A notable difference between the two rites appears to be that although the composers of the Russian service tended to set the same pieces (just as in the Roman Rite) over and over, Serbian composers seemed to exhibit more freedom of choice in selecting the texts set in polyphonic style.

Three of the four works discussed in this chapter (Stevan Hristič, Stevan St. Mokranjac, Nenad Barački, and Milos Raickovich) were composed in the twentieth century. The *Opelo* in F sharp minor (St. Mokranjac) was written in 1888. All settings reveal differences in musical style and texture; Barački left only a unison version of the chant melodies while Hristič did not choose to employ any of the traditional chant tunes in the four-part choral texture. St. Mokranjac widely employed folk song elements and Raickovich followed tradition quite closely, blending Orthodox melodies with a measure of tangy twentieth-century dissonance.

Other settings of the *Opelo* include those of Stanislav Binički and Vojislav Kostic's *Opelo Pesniku Poginulom od Bombardovanja* ("Requiem in Memory of a Poet Killed by Bombing"), a cantata for tenor soloist, mixed choir, children's choir, and chamber orchestra, 1964.

Translations of most *Opelo* texts can be found in the chapter on the *Panikhida*.

Outline of the service:
The Great Litany: *The choir of the saints . . .*

627

The choir of the saints has found the fountain of life and the gate to Paradise.
May I also find the way through repentance.
I am a lost sheep; call me back, O Savior, and save me.
Grant rest, O God, to thy servant, and place . . . in Paradise, where the choirs of
the saints and the righteous shine like stars of heaven. Give rest, O Lord
to thy servant who has fallen asleep, overlooking all transgressions.
Let us devoutly praise the Threefold splendor of the One Divinity by
crying out: Holy art thou, O Father without beginning,

O co-eternal Son, and Divine Spirit.
Enlighten us who serve Thee with faith and deliver us from fire eternal.
Rejoice, O Pure One, who gave birth to God according to the flesh
for the redemption of all. Through you the human race has found salvation.
Through you may we also find paradise, Birthgiver of God, pure and blessed.
Alleluia. Alleluia. Alleluia.

Tone 5: *Give rest to thy servants. . . .*

Give rest with the just, O our Savior, to thy servant and establish . . . in thy courts
as it is written. Since thou art good and lovest mankind, forgive all sins, both
voluntary and involuntary, and all those committed knowingly and unknowingly.

The Canon, Ode Three: *There is none as holy . . .*

There is none so holy as thou, O Lord my God, who exalts the power
of the faithful, O blessed One, and has established us upon the rock of
thy confession.

Sedalion (Seating) Hymn: *Truly all things are vanity . . .*

Truly all things are vanity, and life is but a shadow and a dream.
For everyone born of earth strives in vain, as the Scriptures say.
For when we have acquired the world, then do we take up our abode in the grave,
where kings and beggars lie down together. Therefore, O Christ, God,
grant rest to thy servant departed this life, as the Lover of mankind.

O all-holy Birthgiver of God, do not forsake me all the days of my life, and
do not abandon me to the help of mortal men. But do you, yourself
help me and show mercy on me.

Ode Six: *I behold the sea of life . . .*

I behold the sea of life, surging high with the storm of temptations.
And taking refuge in thy calm harbor, I cry out to thee: Deliver my
life from corruption, O greatly merciful One.

The *Kontakion*: *With the saints . . .*

> With the saints give rest, O Christ, to the soul of thy servant,
> where there is neither sickness nor sorrow nor sighing, but life everlasting.

Irmos to Ode Nine: *The spirits and souls . . .*

> Preserve the spirits and souls of the faithful, Holy God.

Ode nine: *Is it not possible for man to see God . . .*

> It is not possible for man to see God, upon whom the
> ranks of angel dare not gaze.
> But through you, O all-pure One, the Word Incarnate revealed Himself unto men:
> and so as we magnify Him, together with the heavenly hosts, we call you blessed.

Hymns of St. John of Damascus: *What earthly joy remains . . .*

> What earthly joy remains unmixed with grief? What earthly glory remains
> immutable? All things are less than shadows, more deluding than dreams.
> In a single moment all are effaced by death. But in the light of thy countenance,
> O Christ, and in the enjoyment of thy beauty, grant rest to the one whom
> Thou hast chosen, as the Lover of mankind.

Hymns of St. John: *I weep and lament as I contemplate . . .*

> I weep and lament as I contemplate death, and behold our beauty created in
> the image of God, lying in the tomb, disfigured, deprived of glory and expression.
> Oh! What a wonder! What is this mystery concerning us? Why have we been
> delivered to corruption? And why subjected to death? Indeed as it is written,
> by the command of God, who grants rest to the departed.

The Beatitudes
Prokeimenon: *Blessed is the way . . .*

> Blessed is the way in which you walk today, O soul,
> for a place of rest has been prepared for you.

The Epistle and Gospel
The Last Kiss: *Come let us give thanks to God . . .*

> Come let us give thanks to God and give a last kiss to the departed,
> is leaving relatives and hastening to the grave, no longer concerned about vanities
> and passions
> of the flesh. Where now are relatives and friends? Behold, we are parted.
> Let us beseech the Lord that He will give rest.

Glory to the Father . . . Amen: *Brothers and friends, relatives and neighbors . . .*

Brothers and friends, relative and neighbors, weep for me as you see me lying
here
speechless and lifeless; for only yesterday I spoke with you, and suddenly the
terrible hour of death came upon me. But come, all you who loved me, and give
me
your last kiss. For I shall no longer walk with you or talk with you. I go to the
Judge who has no favorites. All will stand before Him, equal in his eyes: master
and slave,
king and soldier, rich and poor. Each will be praised or condemned according to
his deeds.
Therefore, I beseech you all, that you will pray unceasing to Christ God, that I
not be sent to a place of torment because of my sins, but to the place of the light
of life.

Troparion: *With the souls of the righteous departed . . .*

With the souls of the righteous departed, O Savior, give rest also to the soul
of thy servant: preserving . . . in the blessed life that is with Thee, O Lover of
mankind.
In the place of rest, O Lord, where all thy saints repose, give rest also to the
soul of thy servant, for Thou only lovest mankind.
(Glory to the Father . . . Now and ever . . .)
Thou art the God who descended into Hell and loosed the bonds of the captives
held there. Grant rest also to the soul of thy servant.
O only pure and immaculate Virgin, who gave birth to God without ever
knowing man, intercede that the soul of your servant may be saved.

Litany of the Departed
The Dismissal: *Memory eternal!*

Memory eternal [3 times]

Processional Hymn: *Holy God . . .*

Basic Data

EDITION

Barački
Notny zbornik spiskov narodov tsrkvennov
pojana po Karlovackom napevo.
[Chants of the Karlovac Tradition]
Photocopy edition, ed. Danitsa Petrovich
Novi Sad, Serbia. 1995.

VOICING
Choir: Unaccompanied monophonic chant

DISCOGRAPHY
None found.

NENAD BARAČKI
November 25, 1878–1939

In 1923, Barački edited an anthology of traditional Serbian folk-melodies. This edition put into modern notation, for the first time, material that existed in oral tradition. Included are the melodies for the *Opelo* from the Karlovac tradition (northern Serbia).

These melodies constitute one of the several Serbian melodic versions employed for the *Opelo* texts. The current edition includes only the unaccompanied melodies and all texts are in Serbian. No translations are provided. Most of the monophonic melodies are syllabic with occasional florid passages inserted for interest and color.

Basic Data

EDITION
Notny zbornik spiskov narodnov tsrkvennov pojana po Karlovackom napevo.
[Collection of Serbian Traditional Church Chants of the Karlovac Tradition]
Photocopy Edition, Ed. by Dr. Danitsa Petrovich
Novi Sad, Serbia, 1995
[photocopy of the 1923 edition]

VOICING
Choir: Unison or solo voice [monophonic chant]

OUTLINE
The edition includes all of the items mentioned in the introductory comments. There are, in addition, several other pieces that include:
1. Two versions of the processional hymn, *Holy God* (the Karlovac and Somborsk traditions).
2. Several pieces for the burial service.
3. Two additional hymns of St. John of Damascus.

DISCOGRAPHY
None found.

STEVAN HRISTIČ
June 19, 1885–August 21, 1958

The Serbian composer, Stevan Hristič, studied theory and conducting at Leipzig Conservatory (1908). Further studies in sacred music were done in Moscow, Rome, and Paris. He was appointed conductor at the Belgrade National Theater in 1912 and chief conductor of the Belgrade Philharmonic Orchestra in 1923. Later, he was appointed professor and rector of the Academy of Music in Belgrade (1937–1944).

He left a small, but significant list of compositions that include opera and ballet. The sacred works comprise an oratorio, *Resurrection,* and two requiem settings—one in C minor and another in B flat minor. The latter work was composed and published in 1915.

The *Opelo* in B flat minor, scored for SATB choir, was dedicated to those who died in defense of their country during World War I. This exceptionally moving work does not employ any of the traditional orthodox requiem chants, rather it is a totally original composition. The harmony is colored by an old-fashioned modal quality, inspired by the composer's acquaintance with the sacred works of Tchaikovsky, Gretchaninoff, and Taniev. The texture is a mixture of four-part homophonic and polyphonic writing, with some imitative passages. Great rhythmic flexibility is facilitated by constantly changing meters.

Basic Data

EDITION

Opelo for Mixed Choir
No publisher listed, but publication date is 1915, Belgrade.
[includes only the choral responses]

DURATION

Thirteen movements, 370 mm., perf., c. 32'

VOICING

Choir: SATB [*divisi*] range: S-A flat 6; B-D3

OUTLINE

Opening Hymn, *Holy God* [Trisagion]: 44 mm.
   satb choir [b flat m] *molto sostenuto.*
Great Litany: 31 mm.
   satb choir [b flat m] *moderato.* (imitation) The movement is divided into seven
     short responsorial sections.
Gospodi pomuldi [Lord have mercy]: 32 mm.
   satb choir [b flat m] *molto moderato.* Divided into five short responsorial sections.
The Canon, Ode Three, *There is none as holy*: 36 mm.
   satb choir [b flat m] *sostenuto.* A dialogue between the upper and lower voices
     is found in the opening section. (imitative passages).
The Lesser Litany, *Gospodi pomuldi* [Lord have mercy]: 25 mm.
   satb choir. *sostenuto.* Divided into five short responsorial sections.

Ode Six, *I behold the sea of life*: 32 mm
   satb choir [fm] *moderato*.
The Lesser Litany, *Gospodi pomuldi* [Lord have mercy]: 17 mm.
   satb choir [b flat m] Linear homophonic writing, divided into four short,
   responsorial sections.
The *Kontakion, With the saints*: 26 mm.
   satb choir [A flat M—C # M] *sostenuto*.
Irmos to Ode Nine, *The spirits and souls*: 15 mm.
   satb choir [A flat M] *moderato*
Responses, *And with thy spirit & Glory to Thee*: 12 mm.
   satb choir [B flat M/m] *moderato*.
Ode Nine, *It is not possible for man to see God*: 46 mm.
   satb choir [fm] *sostenuto*. (choral fugato).
The Fervent Litany, *Gospodi pomuldi*: 39 mm.
   satb choir [b flat m] *poco piu mosso*. Divided into six responsorial sections.
Dismissal, *Eternal Memory*: 15 mm.
   satb choir [b flat m] *andante sostenuto*.

DISCOGRAPHY

Alleluia, 45061-2, Requiem Orthodoxe Choir of Belgrade Radio-Television, dir.
Mladen Jagust.

STEVAN ST. MOKRANJAC
January 9, 1856–September 28, 1914

St. Mokranjac received his musical education at the Munich Conservatory
where he studied composition with Joseph Rheinberger and theory with
Curt Sachs. In 1887, he was made conductor of the Serbian Choral Society,
a position that he held for life. He founded the Belgrade String Quartet
and the Serbian School of Music. With his choral society, he toured
throughout Europe. He was an avid ethno-musicologist and was greatly
influenced by the folk songs he collected, notated, and studied.

Among his more famous compositions are the folksong arrangements,
the fifteen choral rhapsodies, titled *Rukoveti* [Song Wreaths]. His sacred
pieces include two settings of the requiem (*Opelo*), a setting of the Holy
Liturgy (*Bozestvenaja sluzba*) (1894–95), and a manual of Orthodox church
singing (1935).

Of his two settings of the *Opelo*, only one seems to have been published;
his *Second Requiem* in F sharp minor, scored for SATB choir and composed
in 1888. Although most of his secular and sacred music is permeated with
elements of folk music, the *Opelo* is an original work with very little
influence from that source. His harmonic and contrapuntal language
(canonic imitation and fugato) is much more oriented to the classical tra-

dition. The four-part texture is a mixture of homophonic and polyphonic styles. This excellent work deserves to be better known.

Basic Data

EDITION

Dukhovna Musika [Sacred Music]
[Opelo (1888)]
edited by Milan Baishansky & Voislav Ilich
Prosveta. Belgrade, 1964
[In: Serbian, Cyrillic letters and transliteration into Roman letters]
(includes only the choral responses)

DURATION

Six movements, 118 mm., perf., c. 12′

VOICING

Choir: SATB [TB *divisi*] range: S-A6; B-C3

OUTLINE

Litany: *Gospodi pomuluj*: 24 mm.
　satb choir [f # m] *andante con moto.* Divided into three sections.

Lord have mercy, grant mercy, O Lord. Amen

Canon, Ode Three, *There is none as holy*: 27 mm.
　satb choir [c # m-D flat M] *adagio.* Divided into two sections. Folk melody in
　　the bass line.
Kontakion, With the Saints: 37 mm.
　satb choir [gm] *adagio.* (fugato)
Two brief responses: *With the Holy Spirit* & *Glory to God*: 5 mm.
　satb choir [cm] *moderato-maestoso.*
Irmos to Ode Nine, *The spirits and souls*: 16 mm.
　satb choir [B flat M] *recitando-andante*
Dismissal: *Memory eternal*: 9 mm.
　satb choir [f # m] *Adagio ma non troppo.*

DISCOGRAPHY

Jade, 021/12 19.06, Belgrade Radio-Television Choir, dir. Mladen Jagust.

MILOS RAICKOVICH
July 16, 1956

Milos Raickovich received his musical training in Belgrade and later studied composition with Olivier Messiaen in Paris. He helped to establish the

Belgrade Youth Philharmonic. Later in his career, he moved to New York where he studied with David Del Tredici and received a doctorate from New York University.

His musical style is described as a new classicism, a blend of minimalism and eighteenth-century classical style. Among his orchestral compositions are the *First Symphony* (1992), *Happy Overture* (1987), and *Three Romances* for violin and orchestra. There is a *Dream Quartet* for strings (1986), and the sacred choral work, *Parastos* (Eastern Orthodox Requiem, 1984–85). The latter work was dedicated to the memory of his teacher, Borislav Pascan, a conductor.

The music of the *Parastos*, scored for SATB choir, is very moving and possesses intense spiritual qualities. It adheres closely to the Orthodox musical tradition. Most of the four-part writing is homophonic and the harmonic style is a blend of the traditional orthodox harmonies with a modest amount of dissonant twentieth-century harmony. One of the unique features of *Parastos* is the setting of *Our Father* in a choral recitation.

Basic Data

EDITION

Parastos for Mixed Chorus
Boosey and Hawkes LCB0292
1997 [Serbian in Cyrillic letters and transliteration into Roman letters]
[The solo parts for the priest or chanter are also included.]

DURATION

Seven movements, 121 mm., perf., c. 12′

VOICING

Choir: SATB range: S-G6; B-E flat 3

OUTLINE

Opening Hymn, *Holy God* [Trisagion]: 8 mm.
    satb choir [FM-dm] *adagio maestoso.*
The Lord's Prayer: 21 mm.
    satb choir [GM] *recitando.*
Litany, *Gospodi pomuldi*: 27 mm.
    satb choir [dm,gm] *largo maestoso.* Divided into six sections.
The Canon, Ode Three, *There is none as holy*: 16 mm.
    satb choir [E flat M] *andante.*
The *Kontakion, With the Saints*: 31 mm.
    satb choir [dm] *grave.*

Irmos to Ode Nine, *The spirits and souls*: 9 mm.
   satb choir [am] *andante and largo.*
The Dismissal, *Memory Eternal*: 9 mm.
   satb choir [FM] *largo maestoso.*

DISCOGRAPHY

Personal tape of the composer. Performance by the Russian Chamber Choir "Soboryane," cond. Alexander Zemzerov.

15

The Armenian
Orthodox Requiem

The state of Armenia was the first country to accept Christianity. In 301 A.D., King Tiridates III was converted to Christianity by St. Gregory the Illuminator. Gregory subsequently became the head (*Catholicos*) of the Armenian Church. During the following two centuries, the Syrian and Byzantine Church exercised a major influence upon the Armenian Church. In 404 A.D., the monk, Mesrop-Mashtots, created an alphabet for the Armenian language and by 552 A.D., the Church in Armenia began to enjoy its own autonomy.

Like all other branches of the Christian Church, Armenian liturgical music employed a series of eight modes, to which the chants were sung. Today, there are more than 5,000 liturgical chants; many of them quite ancient. The melodies of the present-day requiem service (*The Service for the Repose of Souls*), date back to the fifth or sixth century. The opening hymn of the requiem liturgy, *O Thou . . . God the Word*, is believed to be one of these pieces. The requiem melodies were sung in monophonic fashion for more than 1,500 years until the Armenian composer-priest, Komitas, made the first polyphonic arrangements in the early twentieth century. The present structure of the service dates back to the fifteenth century.

Unlike most of the other Orthodox liturgies, which preserve the notion that church music should be rendered in a purely vocal fashion, the Armenian Church has accepted the use of the organ to accompany the service music. The Armenian Memorial Office has, by custom, been performed at the end of the Divine Liturgy, and on days when a request has been made by relatives or friends of the deceased to hold a special memorial service. The structure of the service is as follows:

637

INTROIT
[Deacon]
Again in peace let us beseech the Lord:
Receive, save and have mercy.
[Priest]
Blessing and glory to the Father and to the Son and to the Holy Spirit,
now and always and unto ages of ages. Amen.

OPENING HYMNS

Clerks [choir]
MIDDAY HYMN [tone IV]
1. O thou God the Word who art, together with the Father, the creator of beings
out of nothing; grant forgiveness to thy servants who have fallen asleep, when
thou comest to judge those whom thou didst create with spotless hands.
2. O thou who wast sent from the Father and wast incarnate of the holy Virgin;
grant forgiveness . . .
3. O thou who didst give up the ghost on the cross and loosed the power of death;
grant forgiveness . . .
4. O thou who dost crown thy saints and distributest everlasting bounties;
grant forgiveness . . .

MAGNIFICAT [tone IV]
Mother of the Light, unespoused Mary, thou blessed among women.
The Light without a shadow thou didst bear in thy womb, thou blessed . . .
Do not cease to intercede for us, thou blessed . . .

HYMN OF THE CROSS [tone IV]
Upon the rock of faith thou didst build, O Lord, thy holy Church;
keep her in peace.
Thou who didst grant mercy in this inhabitation of angels and the house of
expiation of men; give her unshaken peace.
In the temple of the glory of thy holiness, thy servants sing unto thee;
give them thine abundant mercy.

THE GOSPEL

PRE-GOSPEL PSALM: PSALM 130, Out of the depths . . .
PRE-GOSPEL RESPONSES: Alleluia orthi; Peace unto all . . .
GOSPEL—chosen according to the tone of the day.

Matthew XI: 25–30 [tones IV & VIII]
Mark IV: 26–34 [tones III & VII]
Luke XII: 32–40 [tones II & VI]
John XII: 24–26 [tones I & V]

POST-GOSPEL VARIABLE HYMNS
[tones IV & VIII]
Dispenser of the higher graces to the heavenly and earthly . . .
[tones III & VII]
O thou Life from Life and Light from Light . . .
[tones II & VI]
In gladness did the heavenly hosts come down from heaven onto the earth . . .
[tones I & V]
We priests and people, entreat thee, O merciful and good Lord,
With those who have fallen asleep in faith, receive us who have the same hope,
Into the heavenly city, Jerusalem, in which the just are assembled,
To sing and glorify the three persons of the Trinity.

HYMN FOR SUNDAYS AND DAYS OF RESURRECTION
All the nations of mankind rejoiced when they heard of the resurrection.
With new feathers were they adorned at thy resurrection, O holy Only-begotten.
Merciful Lord, have mercy on the souls of us who have fallen asleep.

PRAYER

[Priest]
To the souls that are at rest, O Christ God, grant rest and mercy,
and to us, sinners, vouchsafe forgiveness of our transgressions.
[Deacon]
Again in peace let us beseech the Lord. For the souls of those who are at rest,
let us beseech Christ our Savior, that he may reckon them with the just and may
save us by the grace of his mercy.
Almighty Lord our God, save us and have mercy.
[Priest]
Lord, have mercy, [3 times]
O Christ, Son of God, forebearing and compassionate, have compassion,
in thy love as our creator, upon the souls of thy servant . . . for whom we
are offering these prayers. Be mindful of them in the great day of the coming of
thy kingdom. Make them worthy of mercy, of expiation and forgiveness of sins.
Glorify them and reckon them with the company of thy saints at thy right hand.
For thou art Lord and creator of all, judge of the living and of the dead.
And to thee is befitting glory, dominion and honor, now and unto ages of ages.
Amen.

DISMISSAL

DIACONAL PROCLAMATION
By the holy cross let us beseech the Lord, that he may thereby deliver us
from our sins and save us by the grace of his mercy.
Almighty Lord, our God, save and have mercy.

PRIESTLY PRAYER
Guard us, O Christ our God, under the shadow of thy holy and venerable
cross in peace. Deliver us from the enemy visible and invisible.
Make us worthy to give thee thanks and to glorify thee together with
the Father and the Holy Spirit, now and always and unto ages of ages. Amen.

THE LORD'S PRAYER

INVITATION FOR THE BLESSING OF DISMISSAL
I will bless the Lord at all times: his praise shall at all times be in my mouth.

THE DISMISSAL
Be blessed by the grace of the Holy Spirit.
Depart in peace and the Lord be with you all. Amen.

DISCOGRAPHY

The Requiem Service of the Armenian Church, sung by Archbishop Arsen Berberian, Primate of St. Sarkis Cathedral of Yerevan, Armenia.

KOMITAS [SOGOMON SOGHOMONIAN]
October 8, 1869–October 22, 1935

Komitas Vartapet (Komitas the monk) occupies a special position in the
history of Armenian music. Komitas went to Berlin for three years (1896–
99) to receive his musical training. He later went on to transcribe more
than 3,000 Armenian songs into modern notation, including the chants of
the Armenian liturgy. He created a unique three- and four-part contrapuntal harmony, ideally suited to the liturgical chants.

After the genocide committed by the Turks against the Armenian people on April 24, 1915, Komitas ceased composing and writing. He fell into
a severe depression, although he did not die until twenty years later.
Komitas' harmonization of the ancient chants represented the fourth
attempt to adapt Armenian liturgical melodies to European notation. The
first three were made by Pietro Bianchini (1877), Amy Apcar (1896), and
Makar Ekmalian (1896). The homophonic texture of Komitas' arrangements was conceived in a linear, polyphonic fashion. The choral soprano
line is generally an elaborate version of the original, ornate chant melody.
Polyphonic points of imitation are employed throughout.

Basic Data
EDITIONS

1. Chants of the Divine Liturgy of the Armenian Apostolic Orthodox Church,
written down in modern notation and harmonized by Komitas Vartapet.

Adapted for mixed choirs by Wardan Sarxian
Diocese of the Armenian Church of America. 1974

2. Sacred Music of the Armenian Church
Two volumes, Volume II
Diocese of the Armenian Church of America, 630 Second Ave, New York City.
1966

DURATION

Eight compositions, not including short responses.

VOICING AND ORCHESTRATION

Choir: SAT & SATB range: S-G6 ; B-F3
Instruments: org.

OUTLINE

O thou God the Word (*Vor haneyitz*): 59 mm. SAT choir.

Alleluia: 5 mm. unison
We the priests (*Kahanayk*): 18 mm. SATTB choir.
In the supernal Jerusalem (*Ee ve rin*): 21 mm. SAT choir.

> In the supernal Jerusalem, in the dwellings of the angels,
> Where Enoch and Elijah live old in age like doves,
> Worthily glorified in the garden of Eden,
> Merciful Lord, have mercy on the souls of us who have fallen asleep.

All nations of mankind rejoiced (*Oo rakhatzan*): 21 mm. SAT choir.
Have compassion Lord (*A Kuta der*): 70 mm. SATB choir/organ.

> From glory to glory (*Paratz i pars*): 17 mm. SATB choir.
> From glory to glory arise those at thy right hand,
> They ascend when they hear thee sound thy blessed voice of benediction,
> Make our faithful who sleep to hear thy divine words,
> Number them with those who sing praises with the angels.

O way of the lost (*Janabarh*): 18 mm. SATB choir/organ.

> O way of the lost and light for those in darkness, thou hast
> called the sons of light unto thy heavenly nuptual feast.
> Thou hast made them worthy to be assembled with the angels.
> With full lamps thou hast made them to enter the feast with the wise virgins.

A mighty sacerdotal mystery (*Ahegh khorhoort*): 29 mm. SAT choir/organ.

> A mighty sacerdotal mystery is enthroned upon the bema,
> Before the Holy Table fire descends, darkness is removed,

sorrowing souls rejoice, for the forgiveness of sins takes place.
Forgiving Lord, have mercy on the souls of our faithful who sleep.

DISCOGRAPHY

Requiem Service of the Armenian Church. Archbishop Arsen Berberian, Primate
of St. Sarkis Cathedral of Yerevan, Armenia (1982) [Available through St. Vartan
Armenian Cathedral, NYC, NY.]

The contemporary Armenian composer, Alexander Haratunian (b. 1920)
composed a four-part, SATB polyphonic setting of the *Kuta der* hymn (#5)
in 1965 to commemorate the fiftieth anniversary of the genocide against
the Armenian people. The original chant melody is found throughout this
sixty-eight measure choral piece. The composer created an independent
thematic motive, derived from the requiem chant, to depict sorrow and
lamentation. Originally scored for chorus and organ, Father Oshagan
Minassian has made an orchestration for this piece, employing strings,
woodwinds, French horns, and organ (unpublished).

Kuta der [Have compassion, Lord]
Have compassion Lord, on those souls, of our faith, at rest.
And remember them in mercy,
For we are the price of your holy blood.
When, by the wondrous sound of the trumpet, the dead will rise
and stand before your terrible tribunal.

EDITION

New Sacred Music of the Former USSR Countries.
Publishing & Creative Laboratory BK, Ltd.
Minsk, Republic of Belarus 1994.
[P.O. Box 241, Minsk, 220071]
(arrangement for choir and organ)

LORIS TJEKNAVORIAN
October 13, 1937

Tjeknavorian received his musical training at Tehran Conservatory and
the Vienna Academy of Music. From 1989 until 2000, he was the principal
conductor and artistic director of the Armenian Philharmonic Orchestra.

He has composed a wide variety of music: ballet, piano pieces, three
operas, chamber music, and concertos for the violin, piano, cello, pi'pa,
and guitar. Numerous orchestral works include three symphonies, as well
as several symphonic suites. Among the sacred compositions are Op. 33,
God is Love (five SATB motets), Op. 40, *In Memoriam* (choir & chamber

orchestra), Op. 32, *Book of Revelations* (SATB soli, SATB choir, and orchestra), and Op. 29, *Armenian Requiem* (ST soli, SATB choir, and orchestra).

The *Armenian Requiem* appears to be the only symphonic, concert setting of the traditional text. Scored for soprano and tenor soli, SATB choir, and orchestra, this work was commissioned by the Gulbenkian Foundation (Lisbon, Portugal) and was given its premiere by the choir and orchestra of the Gulbenkian Foundation on May 15, 1985.

The work, dedicated to the memory of the composer's father, Haykaz Tjeknavorian, is divided into three principal sections: Creation, Betrayal, and Resurrection. The thematic material of the requiem is based upon the ancient, traditional Armenian requiem melodies (fifth-tenth centuries).

Basic Data

EDITION

Score exists. [English]

DURATION

Twelve movements, perf. c. 40'

VOICING AND ORCHESTRATION

Choir: SATB range: S- B
Soloists: Soprano, Tenor
Orchestra: fl., ob., cl., db., 2 Fh., tpt., tbn., perc.

OUTLINE

Creation
O Mystery Deep
The Holy Trinity
Betrayal
Judas' love of silver
Jesus' lament on the Cross to Mary
Mary's lament to the dying Christ
Kyrie eleison
Hymn of Repose of the Soul
Amen
Resurrection
Christ has been revealed & Glory to God
Sanctus
Glory to the Lord
The Lord's Prayer

DISCOGRAPHY

CD exists.

Appendix A

Dies Irae Melodies

Ex. 1

645

Ex. 2

vs 2, 4, 6, 8, 10, 12, 14, 16 18 (phrase 1 and 3)

L. HOMET (1700-1777)

2. Quan-tus tre-mor est fu-tú-rus, Quan-do Ju-dex est ven-tú-rus, Cun-cta-stric - te dis-cus - sú-rus!

20. Pi - e Je - su Dó - mi - ne, do - na e - is ré - qui - em. A-men.

Ex. 3

Ex.4

In-gem-is-co tam-quam re-us, Cul-pa ru-bet vul-tus me-us, Sup-pli-can-ti par-ce, De-us.

Qui Ma-ri-am ab-sol-vis-ti Et la-tro-hem ex-au-di-sti, Mi-hi quo-que spem de-dis-ti.

Pre-ces me-ae non sunt dig-nae, Sed tu bon-us fac be-nig-ne, Ne per-en-ni crem-er ig-ne.

In-ter ov-es lo-cum prae-sta, Et ad hae-dis me se-ques-tra, Sta-tu-ens in par-te dex-tra.

Con-fu-ta-tis mal-e-dict-is Flam-mis a-cri-bus ad-dict-is, Vo-ca me cum be-ne-dict-us.

O-ro sup-plex et ac-cli-nis, Cor con-tri-tum qua-si ci-nis, Ge-re cu-ram me-i fin-is.

La-cri-mo-sa di-es il-la Qua re-sur-get ex fa-vil-la

Ju-di-can-dus ho-mo re-us. Hu-ic er-go par-ce, De-us.

Appendix B

More Liturgical Requiems

The following liturgical requiems are not listed/described in the main body of the book.

Abbreviation Key: R = requiem; MDR = messe de (da) requiem; MPD = missa pro defunctis; vv = voices

A

AAVIK, Juhan. 1884–1982 (EST) Requiem aeternam, Op. 70, mixed choir (1959).

ABBA-CORNAGLIA, Pietro. 1851–1894 (ITA) Requiem in memoriam Carlo Alberto (1876).

ADLGASSER, Anton. 1729–1777 (GER) R.

AIBLINGER, Johann Kaspar. 1779–1867 (GER) R [dm], 4 vv, str., 2 Fh., [tpt. and timp., ad lib.] and org. [pub. Falter c. 1840]; 2 other R.

AICHINGER, Gregor. 1564/65–1628 (GER) Officium pro defunctis, 4–5 vv, and b.c. (Augsburg 1615).

AIGNER, Sebastian. [19th cent.] (GER) 3 R.

ALALEONA, Domenico. 1881–1928 (ITA) R, 4 vv (1927).

ALBERGONI, Angelo. [19th–20th] (ITA) MDR [dm], 2 vv, and organ. [San Marco, Cat. #D.91/1–28].

ALBRECHTSBERGER, Johann Georg. 1736–1809 (AUS) 3 R.

ALLMENDINGER, Carl. [19th–20th cent.] (GER) R, Op. 34, 1, 2 or 4 mixed vv [Böhm, Augsburg] 1906].

ALMEIDA, Ignacio. 1760–1825 (ITA) R.

ALSLEBEN, Julius. 1832–1894 (GER) several R, 6-part and 8-part, a cappella choir.

AMATUCCI, Paolo. 1868–1935 (ITA) MPD, unison choir [Edizioni Musicali Carrara, Bergamo].

AMFITHEATROF, Daniele. 1901–1983 (ITA/RUS) MDR (1930); R., soli, choir, and orch. (1962).

649

AMMANN, Benno. 1904–1986 (FRA) MPD [Editions musicales de la Schola Cantorum, Paris].

AMMON, Blasius. 1763–1825 (GER) R.

AMON, Johann. 1763–1825 (GER) MPD, 5 vv [to be performed at composer's own funeral].

ANDREA, Carolus. d. 1627 (GER) Kyrie from MPD, 5 vv.

ANDREANI, Eveline. [20th cent.] (ITA) Requiem corse (1994).

ANDREN, Francesco. 1786–1853 (ITA?) R (1834).

ANDREVI-Y-CASTELLAR, Francisco. 1786–1853 (SPA) Office and Mass for the Dead.

ANDROT, Albert Auguste. 1781–1804 (FRA?) R.

ANERIO, Giovanni. c. 1567–1630 (ITA) MPD.

ANICHINI, Francesco. 1830–1901 (ITA) MDR, 4 vv, and grand orch. (c. 1850).

ANNECCHINO, Arturo. b. 1954– (VENEZ) Piccolo Requiem (1983) [Edizioni Musacali Carrara, Bergamo].

ANONYMOUS. [Baroque Era] (FRA) MDR d'Aix, trans. Guy Laurent [Editions du Centre de Musique Baroque de Versailles].

ANONYMOUS. [16th cent.] (Valladolid, SPA) R.

ANONYMOUS. [15th cent.] (ENG) [source: Bodelian Library, Oxford Add. C. 87].

ANONYMOUS. (ITA) MDR [am], SATB choir; MDR [dm], SATB choir [San Marco, cat. #B. 1330/1–4 and B. [1329/1–5].

ANSORGE, Konrad. 1862–1930 (GER) R, choir, and orch.

ANTON, Gustave. b. 1938 (GER) Requiem quasi una fantasia, TTBB, and solo vn. [Anton-Verlag, Gummersbach]

ANTONELLI, Abundio. c. 1575–c. 1629 (ITA) MDR.

ANTONELLI, Armando. 1886–1960 (ITA) MDR [gm], ATB, and org. [San Marco, cat. #D. 87/1–56].

ARAUJO, Damaio Barbosa de 1778–1856 BRA—MDR, 4 vv, and orch.

ARCHER, Malcom. b. 1952– (ENG) R.

ARNOLD, Georg. 1621–1676 (AUS) 3 MPD, Op. 6 (1665), 4 , 5, and 7 vv, 3 viols, b.c., and org.

ARNOLD, György. 1781–1848 (HUN) Hungarian Requiem.

ARRIGO, Giuseppe. 1838–1913 (ITA) MDR, Op. 194, TTB and org. (18—).

ARRIU, Claude. b. 1903– (FRA) R.

ARTYMOV, Vyacheslav. b. 1940– (RUS) R (1989).

ARZAC, Jose Maria de. [19th cent.] (URUG) Dies Irae c. 1832–36.

ASSALY, Edmund Phillip. 1920–1983 (CAN) R [ms].

ASSMAYER, Ignaz. 1790–1862 (GER) 2 R.

ATTERBERG, Kurt. 1887–1974 (SWED) R, Op. 8, solo vv, choir, and orch. (1914).

AUER, Joseph. 1855–1911 (GER) R, 4 vv, mixed choir [Augsburg, Böhm 1887]; MDR, Op. 17, TTBB [Regensburg, Coppenrath 1896; R, Op. 19, 2 equal vv, and org. [Regensburg, Feuchtinger and Gleichauf 1896].

AUFSCHNAITER, Benedict. 1885–1942 (AUS) several R.

AULETTA, Domenico. 1723–1753 (ITA) Requiem aeternam: soprano, 2 horns, str., and org.

AUMANN, Franz. 1728–1797 (AUS) 12 R.

B

BABAN, Gracian. c.1620–1675 (SPA) R, 8 vv.

BACCILIERI, Jean. [second half of 16th cent.] (ITA) Totum defunctorum officium quinque vocibus, Op. 3 (1619) [Venetiis apud Barthol. Magni].

BACH, Otto. 1833–1893 (GER) R.

BACHSCHMIDT, Johann 1728–1797 GER—R

BAHAMANTE, Julije. 1744–1800 (ITA/CROATIA) R, SAB choir, and org.

BALASSA, Sandor. b. 1935– (HUN) Requiem for Lajos Kassak, Op. 15, STBar soli, choir, and orch. (1969).

BALBI, Ludovico. c. 1545–1604 (ITA) Missa defunctorum , 5 vv (1595).

BALBI, Melchiore. 1796–1879 (ITA) A Requiem for Rossini (1868).

BALDAN, Carlo. c. 1753–1803 (ITA) R, choir, and orch. (1789).

BALIANI, Carlo. c. 1680–1747 (ITA) R, 8 vv, and orch.

BALLADORI, Angelo. 1865–1919 (ITA) MDR, TTB, and org.

BARGES, Antonio. fl. 1547–65 (ITA) R, 4 vv.

BARONCHELLI, Luigi. 1858–1924 (ITA) R, unison vv [Edizioni Musicali Carrara, Bergamo].

BARRAGA, Franz. 1825–1899 (GER) MPD, Op. 23, voice, and org. [Böhm]

BARTEI, Girolamo. c. 1565–c. 1618 (ITA) Messa di morti.

BARTOLINI, Orindi. c. 1580–1640 (ITA) Messa per li morti (1633).

BARTULIS, Vidmantas. b. 1954– (LITH) R, STB soli, symphony, and wind orch., SATB, and boy's choirs (1989).

BASILI, Francesco. 1767–1850 (ITA) Gran MDR, 4 vv, and orch.; MDR pour des Couvents de religieuses, 3 vv (SSA) and organ: 2 other R.

BASSANI, Giovanni. c. 1657–1716 (ITA) Messa per li defonti concertati, 4 solo vv, choir 4 vv, 2 vn., vla., therobo, and org. (1698); Missa concertata, Op. 20a, 4 vv (1710).

BASURTO, Juan Garcia. d. 1547 (SPA) MPD.

BAUER, Aloys. b. 1854– (GER) MDR, Op. 5, 3 vv, orch., and org. (also arr. for 4 vv, org.).

BAUER, Josef. 1847–1910 (GER) MPD, Op. 7, baritone and org., MPD, Op. 8, solo voice, and org. [Böhm]

BAUERLE, Hermann. 1869–1936 (AUS) R w/Libera, Op. 22, SATB choir; MPD II w/Libera, Op. 64, medium voice or unison [Coppenrath, 1903 and 1917].

BAUMANN, Max. b. 1934– (GER) MPD, Op. 46a, 8-vv choir (1998).

BAUMGARTNER, August. 1814–1862 (GER) R.

BEAULIEU, Desire. 1791–1863 (FRA) MDR, 4 solo vv, and choir (1818 or 1819) [memory of Méhul].

BECK, Conrad. 1901–1989 (SWIS) R (1930) [Schott].

BELLA, Rudolph. b. 1890 (SWIS) R, Op. 84, SA soli, men's choir, and orch.

BELLI, Domenico. d. 1627 (ITA) Officum defunctorum, 4 vv, and b.c. (1616).

BELLI, Guilio. c. 1560–1621 (ITA) 3 R.

BELLONI, Giuseppe. c. 1575–c.1606 (ITA) MPD, 5 vv, and b.c. (org.) (1603).

BELTJENS, Matthias. 1820–1909 (BELG) R.

BENN, Johann. c. 1590–c. 1660 (SWIS) MPD, TTB soli, 4 vv.

BENNER, Paul. 1877–1953 (SWIS) R.

BENNIGER, Josef. [17th–18th cent.] (SWIS) 2 R.

BENOIST, Francois. 1794–1878 (FRA) Dies irae, 4 vv (1842).

BENOIT, Pierre. 1834–1901 (BELG) R (1863).

BERARDI, Angelo. c. 1636–1694 (ITA) MPD, 5 vv [apud Ign. de Lazaris, 1663]; Missa Brevis Defunctorum, SATB, str., b.c.

BERGAMINI, Giovanni Battista. b. 1858 (ITA) MDR, soli, TBB choir, and pianoforte.

BERGAMO, Antonio. c. 1725–1802 (ITA) MDR [dm], TTB, b.c. (1761) [San Marco, cat. #B. 800/1–11].

BERGIRON, Nicolas Antoine. 1690–1768 (FRA) Grand-motet: Dies irae (lost).

BERGMAN, Anton. 1833–1896 (GER) R, Op. 3, tenor (or SA), bass and org. [Coppenrath, 1884].

BERNABEI, Gioseffo. 1620–1687 (ITA) R, 4 vv, 2 vn., vla, and cb.

BERNARD, Jean-Marie. b. 1937– (GER) Ein Deutsches Requiem, Op. 28, 4 vv choir, and org. [Anarche, Munich, 1990]; R, Op. 24, soli, SATB choir, str., and org.

BERTALI, Antonio. 1605–1669 (AUS) 8 R.

BERTELMAN, Jan George. 1782–1854 (NETH) R: MPD, 3 vv, and org./pianoforte [Theune, 1835].

BERTHIER, Jacques. 1923–1994 (FRA) Requiem 1951, soli, choir, org., and orch. [rec: Studio SM D 2703].

BERTINI, Salvator. 1721–1794 (ITA) R [memory of King Charles III, 1790].

BERTON, Henri Montan. 1727–1844 (FRA) R.

BERTONI, Ferdinando. 1725–1813 (ITA) R [gml], arr. TTB by Rova; MDR, SATB choir, str., and b.c. (1758) [San Marco, cat. #A. 152/1–39; MDR: Dies irae [gml], SATB choir, orch., and b.c. (1792) [San Marco, cat. #A. 126/1–8]; MDR: Offertory, SATB soli, SATB choir, orch., and b.c. [San Marco cat. #A. 68/1–33].

BETSCHER, Nikolaus. 1745–1811 (GER) R (cm), soli, choir, and orch. [rec. DA Music, CD 77331], R (gm), soli, choir, and orch. [rec. DA Music, CD 77340].

BETTINELLI, Bruno. b. 1913– (ITA) 2 R (1943, 1945, unaccompanied choir).

BIAGI, Alamanno. [19th cent.] (ITA) MDR, 4 vv [SATB].

BIANCHI, Antonio. c. 1750–1816 (ITA) MPD, 4 vv.

BIBL, Andreas. 1807–1878 (AUS) R.

BICCHIERAI, Luigi. 1846–1923 (ITA) Graduale from MDR.

BIECHTELER von GRIEFFENTHAL, Matthias. c. 1670–c. 1744 (AUS) 4 R.

BIEGER, Franz. 1833–1907 (GER) R, Op. 9, SATB choir, 3 tpt., tbn., and org. [Schwann].

BILL, Josef. 1830–1900 (Ger) R, org., and voice [Max Hirmer, Straubing].

BINDER, Abraham. 1895–1967 (USA) Requiem-Yiskor, SATB choir, and baritone solo [Transcontinental].

BINICKI, Stanislav. 1872–1942 (YUGO) Opelo-Serbian Orthodox Requiem (1912).

BLACHER, Boris. 1903–1975 (GER) R, soprano/baritone soli, mixed choir, and orch. (1958) [Bote].

BLANCO, Guillermo. [20th cent.] (CHILE) MDR (1960) [Alerce, Santiago].

BOCHSA, Nicolas. 1789–1856 (FRA) R (12 Jan. 1816).

BOGENBERGER, Max. [20th cent.] (GER) R, op. 20, SATB choir.

BON, Willem. b. 1940– (NETH) R, Op. 15, mixed chorus, str. orch. and piano [Donemus, Amsterdam 1957].

BONNEFOND, Simon de. fl. 1551–1557 (FRA) R.

BONNO, Guiseppe. 1711–1788 (AUS) 2 R [cm, E flat M].

BONVIN, Ludwig. 1850–1939 (SWIS/USA) MPD [A flat M], 3 male vv, and org. [Coppenrath]; R w/Libera, Op. 153, one voice or unison choir and org. [Gregorian melody] [Coppenrath].

BORDESE, Luigi. 1815–1886 (ITA) R.

BORODIN, Alexander. 1833–1887 (RUS) Requiem aeternam (1877), tenor solo, male choir.

BOSSI, Marco Enrico. 1861–1925 (ITA) MDR, Op 83, choir and org., MDR, Op 90, 4-part male vv, str., harp and harmonium/org. (1892–93) [Zanibon].

BOTTAZZO, Luigi. 1854–1924 (ITA) MDR.

BOTTIGLIERO, Edeoardo. 1864–1937 (ITA) Requiem Mass for unison choir [G. Schwann].

BOURNONVILLE, Jean de. c. 1585–1632 (FRA) MPD, 6 vv (1619).

BOUTELLIER, Pierre. c. 1645—early 18th cent (FRA) Messe des Morts, 5 vv, and b.c. [Editions du Centre de Musique Baroque de Versailles].

BOYER, C. d. 1964 (FRA) MPD.

BOZZA, Eugene. 1905–91 (FRA) R, STB (1950); MDR, choir, and orch. (1971).

BRACESCO, Renzo. 1888–after 1948 (PERU) De profundis e requiem (1920).

BRAGO-SANTOS, Joly. b. 1924– (PORT) R, solo vv, choir, and orch. (1964).

BREE, Johann Bernardus van. 1801–1857 (NETH) MPD, 3 vv, and org. (1848).

BRÉHY, Hercule. 1673–1737 (FRA) R, vv, and inst.

BRETAN, Nicolae. 1887–1968 (HUN) R, soprano/baritone soli and org. (1932) [rec. Nimbus, N15584].

BRETTNER, Joseph. [19th–20th cent.] (GER) R w/Libera, 2–3 vv, [unequal] and org. [Coppenrath, 1917].

BREUER, Bernard. 1808–1877 (GER) R.

BRIAN, Havergal. 1876–1972 (ENG) R, baritone solo, choir, and orch. (c. 1896) lost.

BRINDLE, Reginald. b. 1917– (ENG) Cantata da Requiem.

BRIXI, Frantisek Xaver. 1732–1771 (CZE) 11 R, 4 vv.

BRIZIO, Petrucci. 1737–1825 (ITA) MDR (c. 1762).

BROS, D. Juan. 1776–1852 (SPA) Office des morts.

BRUCK, Arnold von. 1500?–1554 (AUS) Dies irae, 4 vv.

BRUN, Fritz. 1878–1959 (SWIS) MPD [Janta Fréres, Lyon. c. 1912].

BRUNEAU, Alfred. 1857–1934 (FRA) R, solo vv, choir, and orch. (1884–88).

BRUNELLI, Antonio. c. 1575–1630 (ITA) 3 MPD, Op. 14, 4–7 vv, and b.c. (1619); 2 other R.

BRUNNER, Eduard. 1843–1903 (GER) R w/Libera, Op. 3, SA vv, and org.; R II, Op. 8, SATB choir and org. [or woodwind quartet] (1892); R III, Op. 11, SA vv, and org. (1892); R IV w/Libera, Op. 187, medium male or female voice and org. (1903) [all Coppenrath].

BRZOWSKI, Josef. 1803–1888 (POL) R (1845).

BUCHTGER, Fritz. 1903–after 1970 (GER) R, op. 7, men's choir [Leuckart].

BÚHLER, Franz. 1755–1824 (AUS) R, Op. 5, 4 missae et Libera, 4-part choir, str., 2 fl., 2 cl., 2 Fh., 2 tpt., tbn., timp. and org. [Lotter, 1818].

BURGON, Geoffrey. b. 1941– (ENG) R (1976).

BURIAN, Emil. 1904–1959 (CZE) R, chorus, Jazzband (1927).

BUSI, Alessandro. 1833–1895 (ITA) MDR, tenor/bass soli, and grand orch.

BUSONI, Ferrucio. 1886–1924 (ITA) R, soli, choir, and orch. (c. 1881).

BUSOTTI, Sylvano. b. 1931– (ITA) R (1971).

BUSTAMENTE, Jose Maria. 1777–1861 (MEX) Missa de defuntos.

BUTZ, Josef. 1891–1989 (GER) Deutsche liturgische Messe. Op. 65, SATB unaccompanied. [pub. private].

C

CADOW, Paul. b. 1908– (GER) Ein kleines Requiem.

CAFARO, Pasquale. 1716 ?–1787 (ITA) R, 4 vv.

CAGNONI, Antonio. 1828–1896 (ITA) R, 4 vv, and pianoforte/org.

CALDARA, Antonio. c.1670–1736 (ITA) R.

CALEGARI, Antonio. 1757–1828 (ITA) 2 R, 3–4 vv; 4 vv; 2 Dies irae, 3-4 vv; Dies irae, 4 vv.

CALVO, Jose. [1700's] (URUG) Misa brève de Requiem, 2 vv, and org.; MDR, 2 vv, and org.

CAMILLIERI, Charles. b. 1931 (MALTA) Requiem [1 movement], ssaa choir, unaccompanied (1993) [Roberton Pub. 75403].

CAMPIONI, Carlo. 1720–1788 (ITA) R.

CANAL, Marguerite. 1890–1978 (FRA) R, solo vv, choir, and orch. (1921 unpub.).

CANALI, Floriano. c. 1550–c. 1603 (ITA) Missa Mortuorum, 4 vv.

CANNETI, Francesco. 1807–1884 (ITA) MDR.

CAPUANA, Mario. fl. 1645–1707 (ITA) Missa di defonti, Op. 4, 4 vv, and b.c. (1650).

CARAFA, Marzio Gaetano. 1798– (ITA) MDR, 12 vv, and orch. (1821) [based upon the plainchant-canons, ricercari, fugues].

CARATELLI, Lorenzo. 1841–1908 (ITA) MDR, unison choir, and org.

CARESANA, Christophoro. 1655–1713 (ITA) Missa defunctorum in funeribus Alexandri Pape VII, 8 vv, viole, bn, and b.c. (1667); 2 other R.

CARNICER, Ramon. 1789–1855 (SPA) 2 R, 4 vv, and orch. (1829 and 1842 [for King Ferdinand VII]).

CAROLI, Angelo. 1701–1778 (ITA) Messa da morto, 4 vv.

CARON, Joseph Charles Eugene. b. 1900– (CAN) Messe des Morts, choir, and org. [ms].

CARRASCO, Alfredo. 1875–1945 (MEX) Gran Misa de Requiem (1943).

CARRILLIO, Julian. 1875–1965 (MEX) R, Op. 1, choir, and orch. (1900).

CARUSO, Luigi. 1754–1822 (ITA) R, 4 vv, orch., and org.

CASCIATINI [CASCIOLINI], Claudio. 1697–1760 (ITA) MDR, 3 vv.

CASTELLAZZI, Giuseppe. [?] (ITA) MDR [am], TTB choir, and org. [San Marco, cat. #D. 126/1–50].

CATELANI, Angelo. 1811–1866 (ITA) R.

CAVACCIO, Giovanni. c. 1556–1626 (ITA) 4 MPD, Pars II (1593); Messe per i defunti, 4–5 vv (Milan, 1611).

CAZZATI, Maurizio. c. 1620–1677 (ITA) R (1663) [rec. Accord 205082].

CELESTINO da Laterina. [nd] (ITA) MDR, TB choir, and org.

CELLAVERRIA, Francesco. fl. 1538–63 (ITA) Office for the Dead, 5 vv.

CERTON, Pierre. c. 1510–1752 (FRA) MPD, 4 vv (1558).

CHAYNEE, Jean de. c. 1540–1577 (FRA) Officum pro defunctis, 4 vv.

CHION, Michel. b. 1947– (FRA) R (1973).

CHURCHES, Richard. b. 1966– (ENG) SATBAR soli and SATB choir. (1994).

CINQUE, Ermenegildo. [end of 1600s–1770] (ITA) Dies irae, 4 vv, and inst.

CLARI, Giovanni. 1677–1754 (ITA) R, 5 vv; MDR, 9 vv, 2 vn., vla., and org.

CLEMENT, Johann Georg. c. 1710–1794 (GER) 2 R.

CLEREAU, Pierre. fl. 1539–67 (FRA) Missae pro mortuis . . . (1554).

COCCIA, Carlo. 1782–1873 (ITA) Requiem for ex-King Carlo Alberte, SATB choir, and orch.

COCCON, Nicolo. 1826–1903 (ITA) Messa breve da requiem, Op. 538 [FM], TTB choir, and org. [San Marco, cat. #B. 303/1–17]; 7 other R.

COFERATI, Matteo. 1638–1703 (ITA) Officum defunctorum (1727).

COLIN, Jean. 1620–1694 (FRA) R (1688).

COLLINGWOOD, Arthur. 1880–1952 (CAN) R, mixed vv.; R, male vv [Paterson].

COLONNA, Giovanni. 1637–1695 (ITA) Kyrie and Sequence, 5 vv (1676); Messe e Responsori per i defunti, double choir; R, 8 vv; Invitatorio da morti, 8 vv.

COMA, Antonio. 1569–1629 (ITA) MPD.

CONTI, Carlo. 1796–1868 (ITA) 2 R.

CONTINO, Giovanni. c. 1513–c. 1574 (ITA) MPD, 5 vv (1573).

COOMBES, Douglas. b. 1930– (ENG) Requiem, SATB soli, SATB choir, orch., and org. (1997).

COOPER, Timothy. [20th cent.] (CAN) R (1994–96), SATB soli, SATB choir, and orch.

COSACCHI, Stephan. b. 1903– (HUN) R.

COTUMACCI, Carlo. c. 1709–1785 [1698–1775] (ITA) MDR, soprano/bass, and org. (Oct. 20, 1727); R, 5–8 vv, and inst.; Messa Funèbre, 5 vv, and inst.

COUTURE, Guillaume. 1851–1915 (CAN) R, 4 vv, and orch. (1906).

CRESTON, Paul. 1906–1985 (USA) R, Op. 15, tenor, bass vv, and org. (1938).

D

DACCIA, Giusto. 1840–1915 (ITA) MDR [dm] 4 vv, and org.

DACHS, Michael. 1876–1940 (GER)—R #1, medium voice and org. (1900 and 1910); R #2, medium voice and org. (1913) [both Coppenrath].

DALEY, Patrick. R w/Libera, unison choir, and org.

DALLA BELLA Dominique. [early 1700s] (ITA) MDR, TTBBar; Messe Funebre, 4 vv, and org.

DANKOWSKI, Wojciech. b.c. 1760– (POL) R [EM], SATB choir, vn. 1/2, cl. 1/2, Fh. 1/2, and org. [Pro Musica Camerata Edit.].

DAPREDA, Iginio. 1903–1988 (ITA) MDR, choir, and org.

D'ARGENTIL, Charles. fl. 1528–1536 (FRA) MPD, 4 vv, mixed [Corpus Menusurabilis Musicae #95. Early Sixteenth Century Sacred Music from the Papal Chapel. 1982].

DAVICO, Vincenzo. 1889–1969 (ITA) R, soli, choir, and orch. (1950).

D'AVOLA, Marco. b. 1959– (ITA) MDR, Op. 16, for chorus, org., and orch. (1987).

DE ANGELIS, Angelo. d. c. 1825 (ITA) 3 R: 2 for 4 vv; 1 for 5 vv; Dies irae 4 vv; Libera me 4 vv.

DE GIOVANNI, Nicola. 1802–1856 (ITA) MDR, Op. 58, 4 vv, and orch.

DELDEVEZ, Edouard. 1817–1897 (FRA) 2 R.

DEMUTH, Norman. 1898–1968 (ENG) R, a cappella choir (1954).

DENEFRE, Jules. 1814–1877 (FRA) R.

DE RANSE, Marc. 1881–1957 (FRA) Petite Messe Funèbre STB vv, and org. (1939) [Presses Musicales de la Schola Cantorum].

DESAUGIERS, Marc Antoine. 1742–1793 (FRA) R for Sacchini (1786).

DESCONOCIDO. [18th cent. ?] (URUG) Misa de Requiem.

DESPORTES, Yvonne. b. 1907– (FRA) R, soli, choir, and orch. (1951).

DETHIER, Gaston. 1875–1958 (BELG) R, 3 male vv, and org. [Dessain].

DE VAL, Antonio. 1803–1878 (ITA) Messa Funèbre, 4 soli (6 soli vv—SATTBB and 5 vv choir SATTB) (1847) [San Marco, cat., B. 597/1.

DIEBOLD, Johann. 1842–1929 (GER) R, Op. 42, 4-part male vv [Coppenrath].

DIETSCH, Louis. 1808–1865 (FRA) 2 R (one in memory of Adolphe Adam).

DIETZ, Max. 1857–1928 (AUS) R [memory of Emperor Leopold I.

DI GIOSA, Nicola. 1819–1885 (ITA) R for Donizetti (1848 ?).

DIVITIS, Antonius. c. 1470–1515/34 (FLEMISH) MPD, 3–4 vv.

DONATI, Ignazio. c. 1570/75–1638 (ITA) MPD, 4 vv.

DONBERGER, Georg Joseph. 1709–1786 (AUS) 17 R.

DONINI, Agostino. 1874–1937 (ITA) MDR (Rito Ambrosiano), 3 vv, a cappella (unpub.); Piccola MDR (Introit, Kyrie), 3 vv, w/acc. (unpub); Missa defunct-orum "Filiis patris inclinitis," 4 vv (unpub); MDR "Patri pauperium," 4 vv, org. [Musica Sacra]; MDR, 4–5–6–7–8 vv (unpub).

DONOSTIA, Jose Antonio de. 1886–1956 (SPA) MPD, 4 vv choir, and org. (1945).

DORN, Heinrich. 1804–1892 (GER) R.

DOURLEN, Victor. 1780–1864 (FRA) Dies Irae, 4 vv (1808).

DOYAGUE, D. Manuel-Jose. 1755–1842 (SPA) Office des Morts [FM], 4 vv, 2 vn., vla., cb.

DRAGOI, Sabin. 1894–1968 (ROMANIA) Reqviem Romanesc (1943).

DRESCHLER, Joseph. 1782–1852 (BOH) R.

DREYER, Johann Melchior. 1745–1824 (AUS) Opus 20, 6 R, SATB choir, 2 vn., 2 Fh., vc. and org. (1792) (VI breves ac rurales missae pro defunctis, cum 3 Libera).

DROBISCH, Karl Ludwig. 1803–1854 (GER) 3 R.

DUBOIS, Theodore. 1837–1924 (FRA) MDR, solo vv, choir, and orch.; Petite Messe pour les Morts.

DU PLESSIS, Hubert. b. 1922– (SOUTH AFRICA) Requiem Aeternam, Op. 39, choir (1975).

DURANTE, Francesco. 1684–1755 (ITA) 5 R: [am] (SSB); [cm]; [gm], 4 vv, (1738); [FM] (4 vv); [GM] (5 vv); Messa piccola di requie (no Dies irae) [gm] recorded on Bongiovanni GB 2152–2].

DURON, Sebastian. 1660–1716 (SPA) Misa de difuntos, three choirs, and orch. [8 vv].

DUSAPIN, Pascal. b. 1955– (FRA) Requiems: Granum sinapis; Umbrae motris; Dona eis (1998).

E

ECCHER, Celestino. 12.VI.1892–1970 (ITA) Requiem: Messa e Assoluzione, 2 vv, and org. [Ricordi].

EDENHOFER, Aloys. 1820–1896 (GER) R w/Libera, 1 voice and org. [Coppenrath, 1887].

EHLERT, Ludwig. 1825–1884 (GER) R.

EILERS, Albert. 1830–1896 (GER) R.

EKLUND Hans. b. 1927– (SWED) R, soli, orch., and choir [rec. Phono Sueica PSCD 18].

ELSNER, Joseph. 1769–1854 (GER) Requiem dedicatum manibus Alexandri I, 4 vv, inst.

ENNELIN, Sebastian. c. 1660–1747 (GER) R, 5 vv. (1709).

ERBACH, Christian. c. 1570–1635 (GER) Officium pro fidelis defunctis, 5 vv.

ERHARD, Karl. b. 1928– (GER) Totenmesse, sab, and org.; R and Libera, SATB choir, unaccompanied; R and Libera, SATB choir, 2 tbn., 2 tpt., org. [A. Böhm].

ERLANGER, Camille. 1863–1919 (FRA) R, double choir.

ERLANGER, Frederic d'. 1868–1943 (ENG) R, solo vv, choir, and orch. (1931).

ERPF, Hermann. 1891–1969 (GER) R, six-part mixed choir [Möseler].

ESCOBAR, Pedro. 1465–1535 (SPA) Missa pro defunctis (1504).

ESNAOLA, Juan Pedro. 1808–1878 (ARG) Misa de Requiem (1825).

ESPLA, Oscar. 1886–1976 (SPA) R (1949).

EST, L. B. [STEFAN STOCKER]. 1795–1882 (GER) 4 short and easy R, 2 and 3 vv, org.

ESTEVE, Jose Mauri. 1856–1937 (CUBA) Misa de Requiem, 2 vv (T/S or Bar/B), choir, and orch.

ETT, Caspar. 1788–1847 (GER) R [E flat M], 4 vv [pub. Coppenrath, 1892]; 1 other R.

EVE, Alphonse d'. 1666–1727 (BELG) Dies Irae.

EYCHENNE, Marc. b. 1933– (FRA) R, mixed choir, and orch. [rec. Valois V 4626].

F

FAGO, Nicola. 1677–1745 (ITA) R [cm], 10 vv, and inst.

FALCHI, Stanislao. 1851–1922 (ITA) R.

FANTA, Robert. 1901–1974 (GER) R [CM], three-part choir [3 soli], 2 Fh., and org. [Universal].

FARKAS, Odon. 1851–1912 (HUN) Dies Irae, choir, and orch.; R, mixed choir, and orch. [Houten, Ascolta Music, c. 1996].

FASCH, Karl. 1763–1800 (GER) R, 8 vv in: Sammtliche Werke. [Singakademie in Berlin, Trautwein c. 1840].

FASSLER, Guido. 1913–1945 (GER) Missa "Requiem aeternam," 2 or 4 vv, and org. (pub. 1959).

FENAROLI, Fedele. 1730–1818 (ITA) Messa de defunti, 4 vv (1770).

FEO, Francisco. 1691–1761(ITA) 2 Oratorio pro defunctis, 4 vv, and inst. (1723 and 1725); 2 Oratorio pro fidelium defunctorum, 4 vv, and inst. (1731 and 1728);

Missa defunctorum [dm], 5 vv, vns, and b.c. (1718); Dies irae [cm], 5 vv; Dies irae [gm], 4 vv: Juste judex [gm]; Oro supplex [fm]; 2 Tuba mirum [E flat M].

FEROCI, Francesco. 1673–1750 (ITA) MDR; MDR (organ versets)

FERRABOSCO, John. 1626–1682 (ENG) Burial Service [gm], 4 vv.

FERRARI, Carlotta. 1837–1907 (ITA) R.

FERRARI, Giovanni. 1763–1842 (ITA) R.

FERRATA, Giuseppe. 1865–1928 (USA) R; Dies Irae, Op. 35.

FERREIRA, Come-Baena. [?] (PORT) Responsories de officio de defuntos.

FERTA, Domingo. b. 1866– (ARG) Misa de Requiem.

FÉTIS, Francois, Joseph. 1784–1871 (BELG) Requiem en expiation de la mort de Louis XVI, 4 soli vv, 4 vv, 6 Fh., 4 tpt., 3 tbn., sax-horn, bombardon, org., vc., db., and timp. (1850) lost.

FIBICH, Zdenek. 1850–1900 (CZE) R [fragment] (1874).

FIOCCO, Antonio. c. 1650–1714 (BELG) MPD, 4 vv., 2 vn., b.c. and 2 Fh.; 2 other R.

FIORAVANTI, Valentine. 1770–1837 (ITA) Dies irae, 8 vv, orch.

FIORE, Andrea. 1686–1732 (ITA) Vespro pro defunti, 8 vv, and inst.

FIORELLO, Ignazio. 1715–1787 (ITA) R.

FIORONI, Giovanni. 1704 ?–1778 (ITA) 2 R; 4 vv, 8 vv.

FOERSTER, JOSEF. 1833–1907 (CZE) 3 R, chorus and orch., Op. 33 (c. 1880); Op. 34 (c. 1880); Op. 37, 2 equal vv [S/A or T/B] and org. (c. 1890).

FOSCHINI, Gaetano. 1836–1908 (ITA) MDR.

FRANCES DE IRIBARREN, Juan. 1698–1767 (SPA) R, 7 vv; Offices for the Dead.

FREI, Joseph. 1872–1945 (GER) R, Op. 74, 4 mixed vv, and org. [Coppenrath].

FUCIK, Julius. 1872–1916 (CZE) R, Op. 283.

FÚHRER, Robert. 1807–1861 (CZE) R [GM] (1846); 19 other R.

FUMAGALLI, Polibio. 1830–1900 (ITA) MDR, Op. 270, TTB, and org.

FUMET, Dynam-Victor. 1867–1949 (FRA) R (1948), a cappella.

FURLANETTO, Bonaventure. 1738–1817 (ITA) 3 R, 3 vv; 2 Dies irae, 3–4 vv, and orch.; MPD [FM], 3 vv. (ATB) and b.c. [San Marco, cat. #C. 51/1–17]; MDR (Requiem and Kyrie) [dm], SATB choir, orch., and b.c. (1795) [San Marco, cat. #C. 68/1–111]; Dies irae:Sequenza [dm], SATB choir, orch., and b.c. (1794) [San Marco, cat. #C. 69/1–72].

FURLOTTI, Arnuldo. 1880–1958 (ITA) MDR, choir, and org./harmonium (c. 1910).

FÚRST, Konrad. [19th cent.] (GER) MPD, Op. 2; MPD, Op. 56, both for solo voice and org.

G

GAGLIANO, Giovanni. 1582–1643 (ITA) Officum defunctorum, 4 vv–8 vv (1607/8).

GAIANI, Giovanni. 1757–1818 (ITA) Dies irae, 4 vv, and orch.

GALLERANO, Leandro. fl. 1615–1632 (ITA) Missa Defunctorum, 5 vv, b.c. (1615).

GALLO, Domenico [and Anselmo Marsand]. [?] (ITA) Messa da morto, 3 vv, [concertata] and org. [San Marco, cat. #542].

GALLOTTI, Salvatore. 1856–1928 (ITA) MPD, 6 vv [G. Schirmer].

GALUPPI, Baldassare. 1706–1785 (ITA) 5 R.

GANSBACHER, Johann. 1778–1844 (AUS) Op 15 [cm] (1811); Op. 38, [dm] (1834); 5 other unpub. R.

GANZ, Maurizio. [19th–20th cent.] (ITA) Messa da requiem [gm], TTB choir, orch., and org. (1913) [San Marco cat. #B. 1093/1–39].

GARCIA, Gary, [?] R.

GARCIA DE BASORTO, Juan. c. 1477–1547 (SPA) R.

GARCIA-FAJER, Francisco. 1731–1809 (SPA) Officum Defunctorum, 8 vv; MPD, 8 vv, and orch.; Dies irae, 8 vv, and orch.

GARCIA-ROBLES, Jose. 1835–1910 (SPA) R, chorus, and orch.

GARGALLO, Luis. c. 1620/30–1682 ? (SPA) R, 8 vv; R, double choir; 2 Dies irae, 4 vv, 8 vv.

GÄRTNER, Helmut. [20th cent.] (GER) Kleines deutsches Requiem, 4/3 mixed voices, and org. [pub. private].

GASPARINI, Quirino. 1721–1778 (ITA) 3 R.

GASTOLDI, Giovanni. 1550?–1622 ? (ITA) Officum defunctorum integrum, 4 vv (1607).

GATTI, Luigi. 1740–1817 (ITA) 2 R.

GAUSS, Otto. 1877–1970 (GER) MPD, Op. 33, 4 vv [unequal] [Coppenrath].

GAVAERT, Francois. 1828–1908 (BELG) MPD, TTBB, instruments, org.

GAYER, Johann Christoph. 1668?–1734 (BOH) R [cm]; R [FM]; Dies irae [gm], two choirs.

GAZZANIGA, Giuseppe. 1743–1818 (ITA) MPD, 4 vv, and inst.

GAZZOTTI, Luigi. 1886–1923 (ITA) MDR, TB Bar soli, chorus, and orch. (1900).

GEISSLER, Benedict. 1696–1772 (GER) MPD, SATB (1738).

GENERALI, Pietro. 1773–1832 (ITA) R.

GERBER, Jack Sydney. 1902–1979 (SOUTH AFRICA) R, soloists, choir, and chamber orch. (1958–59) [Sparta Florida Music Group] [rec. Prestige Records, PRC-DSP 100].

GEREMIA, Giuseppe. 1732–1814 (ITA) MPD, 4 soli, SATB choir, and orch. (1809) [rec. Classic, CD 225].

GHEERKIN (GHERARDESCA), Philippe. 1738–1808 (ITA) MDR (c. 1805); 1 other R.

GHIZZOLO, Giovanni. d. 1625 (ITA) R.

GIACOMETTI, Bartolomeo. 1741–1809 (ITA) R, 4 vv, and b.c.; Messa di Morti, 3 vv, and b.c.

GIAI, Giovanni. c. 1690–1764 (ITA) R.

GIANNINI, Vittorio. 1903–1966 (USA) R, soli, choir, and orch. (1937) [Universal].

GIGLI, Alfeo. 1907–1994 (ITA) MDR, satb choir, str., 2 tpt, and tuba.

GIGOUT, Eugène. 1844–1925 (FRA) Messe Funèbre.

GILANA, Sister. b. 1898– (?) MPD, unison vv, and org.

GILARDI, Gilardo. 1889–1963 (ARG) Misa de Requiem (1914–18), soli, choir, and orch.

GILLE, Jacob Edvard. 1814–1880 (SWE) R [cm], choir, 3 vv, and orch. (1851).

GINER Y VIDAL, Salvador. 1832–1911 (SPA) 8 R, unaccompanied or with orch.

GIRELLI, Santino. fl. 1620–27 (ITA) R.

GIROLAMI, Giovan. 1702–1786 (ITA) MDR, soli, SATB choir, and orch. [rec. Kicco Classic, KC062.1CD].

GIROUST, Francis. 1737–1799 (FRA) R, satb choir, and orch. (1760–71).

GLEISSNER, Franz. 1761–1818 (GER) 2 R (dm and cm) pub. 1798.

GLOCK, Max. [19th–20th cent.] (GER ?) R, Op. 5, SB [or AT], org., vn. I/II and Fh. [Coppenrath, 1908]; R w/Libera, 3 male vv [TbarB] [Coppenrath, 1907].

GNOCCHI, Pietro. 1677–1771 (ITA) R, 4–8 vv; 6 R, 2–4 vv; 2 settings of Vespers for the Office of the Dead.

GOLDMARK, Rubin. 1872–1936 (USA) R (1919).

GOLLER, Vincenzo. 1873–1953 (GER) MDR, Op. 70 [Anton Böhm, c. 1911]; Opus 10, MPD, 2 equal vv or 4 mixed vv [J. Fischer]; MPD, Op. 13, 2 male vv, and org. [Coppenrath, 1901]; R w/Libera, Op. 26, 4 mixed vv, and org. [Coppenrath, 1904]; MPD, Op. 52, unison high or low vv, and org. [Coppenrath, [1907]; MPD w/Libera and Responsories [Coppenrath, 1908].

GOSS, John Sir. 1800–1880 (ENG) Requiem Motet [em] 6 vv (1827).

GRABNER, Hermann. 1886–1969 (GER) R, solo vv, choir, orch., and org.

GRAU, Theodor. 1886–1952 (GER) MPD w/Libera, Op. 10, one voice, and org. [Coppenrath, 1916].

GREEN-JENSEN, Bo. b. 1955– (DEN) R and Messe [1981].

GREGORA, Frantisek. 1819–1887 (CZE) R.

GREITH, Karl. 1828–1887 (GER) R.

GRELL, Eduard. 1800–1886 (GER) R.

GRETRY, Andre. 1741–1813 (BELG) MDR.

GRIESBACH, Jean Henri. b. 1798– (GER ?) R.

GRIESBACHER, Peter. 1864–1933 (GER) R, Op. 31, 3 high vv, and org. [Coppenrath, 1903]; MDR, Op. 73, SATB choir and org. [Coppenrath, 1906]; MPD, Op. 91, 3 or 4 equal vv, and Org. [Coppenrath, 1907]; MPD, Op. 131, 4 vv, and org. [Coppenrath, 1912]; R, Op. 139, one voice or unison choir and org. [Coppenrath, 1909]; Missa Choralis [Gregorian], Op. 177, for 1 voice and org. [Coppenrath, 1915] ; MDR, Op. 150b, one voice and org. [Coppenrath, c. 1910].

GRIFFEN, D. G. [19th–20th cent.] (?) Requiem Mass #7 [pub. c. 1928].

GRIFONI, Giovanni Battista. [19th] (ITA) MDR, obbligato org. (189–).

GRIPPE, Ragnar. b. 1951– (SWE) R, soprano and synthesizer (1994–95) [rec. Bis CD–820].

GROENEWEG, Henk. 1923–1995 (NETH) R.

GROSS, Paul. b. 1898– (GER) 2 R, unaccompanied (1952, 1956).

GRUA, Franz Paul. 1753–1833 (GER) 4 R, 4 vv, and orch.

GRUBER, Joseph. 1855–1933 (AUS) R [E FlatM], 4 vv, str., 2 Fh., and org. [Urbanek c. 1920]; R w/Libera, Opus 206, 4-part male choir [Coppenrath, 1910]; R [dm], Op. 145, 1–2 voices and org./harmonium or: SAB choir, org., str., and 2 Fh. [Coppenrath, c. 1905]; R (dm), Op. 20, choir, org.; 8 other R.

GUERRINI, Guido. 1890–1965 (ITA) MPR [alla memoria di G. Marconi], solo vv, chorus and orch. (1938–39) [Suvini Zerboni, 1943].

GUTIERREZ Y ESPINOSA, Felipe. 1825–1899 (PUERTO RICO) 2 R.

H

HAAS, Joseph. 1879–1960 (GER) Totenmesse, Op. 105 (1955), congregation, organ, and orch. [text: Weichert, Deutsches Requiem].

HAESER, August Ferdinand. 1779–1844 (GER) MPR.

HAHN, Georg. c. 1690–1769 (GER) 6 missa with 2 R, 2 vv, 8 inst.

HALLER, Michael. 1840–1915 (GER) Missa Quinta (Requiem), Op. 9, SA choir.

HALLER, Michael. 1840–1915 (GER) MPD, Op. 74, 2 voices [ABar] and org. [Coppenrath, 1899].

HAMAL, Henri. 1744–1820 (BELG) 3 R.

HAMAL, Jean-Noel. 1709–1778 (BELG) 5 R, all 4 vv, inst. and b.c.

HAMEL, Coelestin. 1662–1734 (GER) 2 R.

HAMEL, Peter Michael. 1947– (GER) Dies Irae, TTBB choir, 8 vv., bells, timp., and org. (1989/90).

HAMERIK, Asger. 1843–1923 (DEN) R, Op 34, alto solo, chorus, and orch. (1887).

HAMILTON, Ian. b. 1922– (ENG) R, SATB chorus, unaccompanied [Theodore Presser].

HAMM, Benedict. [18th cent.] (GER) R.

HAMMA, Benjamin. 1831–after 1888 (GER/USA) MPD, mixed choir and org. or orch.

HAMPEL, Hans. 1822–1884 (CZE) R.

HANDEL, George Frederick. 1685–1759 (ENG) Funeral Anthem for Queen Caroline (1737).

HANSSENS, Charles Louis. 1802–1871 (BELG) MDR (1837).

HARDOUIN, Henri. 1727–1808 (FRA) 5 R.

HARINGTON, Henry. 1727–1816 (ENG) A Requiem: "I heard a voice from heaven," 3 vv (c. 1775).

HARRISON, Julius. 1885–1963 (ENG) R (1957), SATB choir, soli, and orch. [Lengnick]; Requiem of Archangels (1919).

HAUDIMONT, Joseph Meunier. c. 1756–c. 1790 (GER) Oratorio pro defunctis; Carmen pro defunctis (Dies irae); R.

HAYDN, Michael. 1737–1806 (AUS) German Requiem.

HAYNE, Gilles. 1590–1650 (BEL) MPD, 6 vv (1646).

HEGMANN, Karl. [19th–20th cent.] (GER) R w/Libera, Op. 31, one voice and org./harmonium [Coppenrath, c. 1912].

HEILLER, Anton. 1923–1979 (AUS) R, 3 female vv, a cappella [Universal].

HEINICHEN, Johann David. 1683–1729 (GER) R [E Flat M], SATB soli, choir, and orch. [rec. Capriccio 10570]; 1 other R.

HELLER, Joachim. c. 1518–c. 1590 (GER) R.

HELLWIG, Karl Ludwig. 1773–1838 (GER) R.

HELMONT, Adrien-Joseph. 1747–1830 (BELG) R, 5 vv.

HELMUT, Charles Joseph van. 1715–1790 (BELG) MDR (1739).

HEREDIA, Pedro de. d. 1648 (ITA) R, 5 vv, and org. (1646); R, 4 vv.

HERZOGENBERG, Heinrich. 1843–1900 (AUS) R, Op. 72, chorus and orch. (1891).

HIDAS, Frigges. b. 1928– (HUN) R (1973).

HIGGINSON, Vincent. b. 1896– (USA?) R.

HIRBLINGER, Michael. [19th cent.] (GER?) MPD [am], 3 male voices and org. [Coppenrath, 1894?].

HOCHREITER, Emil. 1871–1934 (AUS) MPD, Op. 38, unison choir and org. ["in memoria militum caesorum annis belli 1914–1915"] [Coppenrath, 1915].

HOFFMANN, Ernst Theodore Amadeus. 1776–1822 (GER) R.

HOFMANN, Leopold. 1738–1793 (AUS) MPD.

HÖHNERLEIN, Max. [19th–20th] (GER?) Requiem w/Libera, Op. 54, one voice and org./harmonium [Coppenrath, c. 1908].

HOLAN ROVENSKY, Václav. 1644–1718 (CZE) Ceské Reqviem, solo church cantatas w/accompaniment.

HOLLANDRE, Charles Felix. 16—?–1750 (BELG) MDR.

HÖLZL, Peter. b. 1920– (GER) Messe für Verstorbene, TTBB choir, tpt. 1/2, tbn. 1/2, org. [Carus, CV 40. 491/01, 1989].

HORAK, Václav. 1800–1871 (CZE) 3 R: Hymni in sacris pro defunctis for chorus and orch.

HORVATH, Joseph Maria. b. 1931– (AUS) R, 6–8 mixed vv., a cappella [Doblinger].

HÖSS, Franz. 1897–1979 (GER) Deutsches Requiem, Op. 26, satb choir, congregation, org.

HOUDARD, Georges. 1860–1913 (FRA) R.

HUBER, Heinrich. 1879–1916 (GER) R, Op. 5, [without Dies irae], mixed choir and org. [Coppenrath, 1913]; R and Libera, Op. 21, satb choir, org.

HUBER, Klaus. b. 1924– (SWIS) R.

HUBER, Paul b. 1918– (SWIS) R (1956).

HUBERT, Johannes Evangelista. 1833–1896 (GER) R.

HUFF, David. b. 1954– (USA) R, STB soli, SATB choir, organ and str. quartet. [Hinshaw Music, 1999].

HUGILL, Robert. [20th cent.] (ENG) Requiem for Butti: In memoriam Robert Buttimore (2000).

HUNT, John Eric. 1903–1958 (ENG) Requiem Mass, SATB choir [Novello].

HÚTTENBRENNER, Anselm. 1794–1868 (AUS) 4 R (one lost).

I

ILINSKI, Stanislav. 1795–1860 (POL) R [em]; 2 R [cm].

INGHELBRECHT, Désire Emile. 1880–1965 (FRA) R, soli, choir, org., and orch. (1940–41). [rec. Editions André Charlin AMS 88-2] [Durand et Fils, #138. 1959].

ISNARDI, Paolo. 1536–1596 (ITA) R.

IVANOFF, Michael. 1849–1927 (RUS) R.

J

JACOB, Gunther. 1685–1734 (BOH) R [am], 4 vv, 2 vn. and org.; R [GM], 4 vv, 2 vn., 2 tpt., 3 tbn., and org.

JADIN, Louis Emmanuel. 1768–1853 (FRA) R, 3 vv, 3 tbn. and db.

JAMES, Joseph. [20th cent.] (Francis JAMES Brown, Stanley JOSEPH Seeger) (ENG)—Requiem after J. S. Bach, orch., choir, and soloists [rec.Black Box, BBM 1023].

JANACONI, Giuseppe. 1741–1816 (ITA) MDR, 4 vv, and org. (CM).

JEREMIAS, Bohuslav. 1859–1918 (CZE) Ceské requiem, chorus and org. (1893).

JERUSALEM, Ignacio. c. 1710–1769 (MEX) Missa "Resquiescat in pace."

JIRAK, Karel. 1891–1972 (CZE) R, Op. 70, solo vv, choir, orch. (1951–52).

JOHANSSON, Bengt. b. 1914– (FIN) R, baritone solo, 2 choirs, 3 instrumental groups (1967).

JOOS, Oswald. [19th–20th cent.] (GER) MPD #9, Op. 9 [J. Fischer]; MPD w/Libera, Op. 21, SATB choir [Coppenrath, 1903].
JOSEPH (Pater Joseph Keinz). 1738–1810 (AUS) 2 R (1775).
JOSEPHSON, Jacob. 1818–1880 (SWED ?) R [Nordiska].
JUMENTIER, Bernard. 1749–1829 (FRA) 4 vv, choir, orch.
JUVINIS, Engarandus. [late 16th–early 17th cent.] (?) MPD.

K

KAFFKA, Johann Christoph. 1759–after 1803 (GER) R.
KAGERER, Markus. 1878–1932 (GER) R, Op. 49, SAB and org. [Coppenrath].
KAINTZ, Joseph. [19th cent.] (GER?) R.
KAISER (KAYSER), P. L. b. 1736- (GER) MPD w/Libera, SAB choir and org.
KAJONI, Janos. 1629–1687 (HUN) Dies Irae: Prosa pro defunctis, female vv, and org.
KALIK, Václav. 1891–1951 (CZE) Male Reqviem (Little Requiem), female vv (1946).
KALOIAN, Alexander. b. 1962– (?) MDR (c. 1996).
KALOUS, Václav. 1715–1786 (CZE) R.
KARCZYNSKI, Alexander. b. 1882– (POL) MPD, 4-part male choir [Zalewski, 1925].
KARG-ELERT, Sigfried. 1877–1933 (GER) Requiem aeternam, Op. 109, 8–12 vv (1913).
KAUER, Ferdinand. 1751–1831 (AUS) 3 R (lost).
KAZANLI, Nikolay. 1869–1916 (RUS) Velikaya panikhida, choir.
KELDORFER, Max. b. 1864– (AUS) R.
KENNIS, Guillaume. 1717–1789 (BELG) Responsorio pro defunctis (lost).
KIMMERLING, Robert. 1737–1799 (AUS) 2 R, 4 vv, inst., and org.
KIRCHNER, Volker David. b. 1942– (GER) R (Messa da Pace), soli, mixed choir, and orch. (1988).
KITTL, Jan Bedrich. 1806–1868 (CZE) R (lost).
KOBECK, Paul. 1891–1974 (GER) Introitus, Requiem und Kyrie, mixed choir [Dulman, Lauman, c. 1984]; R, mixed choir, unaccompanied: In memory of the Fallen [Coppenrath, 1917].
KOBRICH, Johann Anton. 1748–1791 (GER) 8 R.
KOCH, Markus. 1879–1948 (GER) R, Op. 12, mixed choir, str. quartet, 2 cl., 2 Fh., tbn., and org. [Coppenrath, 1908].
KOERPPEN, Alfred. b. 1926– (GER) Missa in commemoratione defunctorum (1976).
KOGOJ, Marij. 1895–1956 (SLOVENIA) R, male choir (1922).
KÖHLER, Alois. b. 1867– (GER) MPD w/Libera, Op. 13, 1 voice and org./harmonium [Coppenrath, 1905].
KÖNIG, Thaddaeus. 1846–1923 (GER) R [am], Op. 5, SATB and org. [or 2 vn., vla., vc., db., 2 Fh., 2 tpt. and timp.] [Coppenrath, 1900]; R w/Libera [FM], Op. 6, SAB choir and org. [or tenor, 2 vn., db. and 2 Fh.] [Coppenrath, c. 1890].
KÖNIGSPERGER, Marianus. 1708–1769 (GER) R, Op. 23, 4 vv, 2 vn., vla., 2 tpt./ Fh., timp., and b.c. (1764); 3 other R.

KOPP, Georg. d. 1666 (GER) R, 10 vv.

KOPPEL, Herman. 1908–1998 (DEN) R, Op. 78, solo vv, choir, and orch. (1965–66).

KOPRIVA, Karel. 1756–1785 (CZE) R [cm].

KORMAN, James. [20th cent.?] (USA) R [McLaughlin and Reilly, c. 1920].

KORNMÜLLER, Utto. 1824–1907 (GER) R [E flat M], SA and organ [Coppenrath].

KÓSA, György. 1897–1984 (HUN) Dies Irae (1937); R (1949); R (1966).

KOUTNIK, Tomas Norbert. 1698–1775 (CZE) R [E Flat M], mixed choir, strings, and two tpt. [Bärenreiter Editio Supraphon 1120983].

KOŽELUCH, Johann. 1738–1814 (BOH) 5 R.

KOZLOWSKY, Joseph. 1757–1831 (POL) R (1798) [Breitkopf, 1798].

KRACHNER, Joseph Matthias. 1752–1827/30 (AUS) 4 R [only one is extant].

KRAFFT, Jozef. 1727–1795 (BELG) MDR [rec. Arion, ARN 55393].

KRAFT, Karl. 1903–1978 (GER) Requiem w/Libera, Op. 91, 4 vv, mixed choir, and org. [Coppenrath]; R, [gm] 3 vv, a cappella (1957); Deutsche Totenmesse, sab, unaccompanied or sa, organ; Die Totenmesse, Op. 101, choir, congregation and organ [A. Böhm].

KRAK, Egon. b. 1958– (SLOVAKIA) MPD, soli, boy's choir, mixed choir, orch., and org.

KRAUS, Joseph Martin. 1765–1792 (GER) R (1776) [rec. Hungaroton, HCD 31782].

KREEK, Cyrillius. 1889–2000 (ESTONIA) R (1927).

KRICKA, Jaroslav. 1882–1969 (CZE) R (1949).

KRIKOVSKÝ, Pavel. 1820–1885 (CZE) R, male vv (1878).

KROGULSKI, Jozef Wladyslaw. 1815–1842 (POL) R.

KRONBERG, Gerhard. b. 1913– (GER) Deutsche Messe für die Verstorbenen, mixed choir, singer, and org. [Coppenrath].

KROTTENDORFER, Joseph. c. 1741–1798 (AUS) R.

KULJERIC, Igor. b. 1938– (CROATIA) Hravatski glagolski rekviem [Croatian Glagolitic Requiem], soli, choir, and orch. (1996).

KUTZER, Ernst. b. 1918– (GER) Deutsches Requiem, Op. 57, congregation, choir, and org. [liturgical texts] [Coppenrath, c. 1968].

L

LABELLE, Charles. 1849–1902 or 1903 (CAN) Messe Funèbre; Dies Irae.

LACÉPÈDE, Bernard. 1751–1825 (FRA) R.

LAGKNER, Daniel. [early 17th cent.] (GER/FRA?) Melodia funèbres, 6 vv (1601).

LAMAS, Giuseppe. 1775–1814 (VENEZUELA) 3 Lessons for the Office of the Dead.

LANDI, Giuseppe. [late 18th – early 19th cent.] (ITA) Requiem e Kyrie da morto, 4 vv.

LANDRE, Willem. 1874–1948 (NETH) Requiem in memoriam uxoris (1931), mixed choir, SATB Soli, and orch. [Donemus].

LANGLE, Honore. 1741–1807 (FRA) Dies Irae (1774–76).

LARIVIERE, Romo C. [20th cent. ?] (?) MPD, 2 or 3 equal vv. (1941).

LATROBE, Christian. 1758–1836 (ENG) Dies Irae (1823).

LAUCHER, Joseph Anton. 1737–1813 (GER) R (1792).

LAURIDSEN, Morten. b. 1943– (USA) Lux Aeterna (1997), SATB choir, and orch. [Peer Music 0044444].

LAUVERJAT, Pierre. d. after 1625 (FRA) MPD, 4 vv (1623).

LAVALLE-GARCIA, Armando. b. 1924– (MEX) Requiem y canto de tristeza, mixed choir, orch., and perc. (1968).

LECHNER, Konrad. b. 1911– (GER) R, chorus and orch. (1952).

LEIFS, Jon. 1899–1968 (ICE) R, Op. 33b, chorus.

LEMACHER, Heinrich. 1891–1966 (GER) R, Op. 132, 2 high vv, org. [A. Böhm].

LEMIEUX, Joseph-Leopold. b. 1908– (CAN) R, male vv [ms].

LENEPVEU, Charles. 1840–1910 (FRA) 2 R (1871, 1893).

LEONCAVALLO, Ruggero. 1857–1919 (ITA) Requiem for King Umberto I (1900).

LESCOT, Francois. c. 1720–c. 1801 (FRA) R (1766).

LESSEL, Franciszek. c. 1780–1838 (POL) R (1837); another R is lost.

LEVENS, Charles. c. 1689–1764 (FRA) 2 MDR.

LEWKOVITCH, Bernhard. b. 1927– (DEN) R, baritone solo, mixed choir, and orch. (1981) [Hansen #2983].

LICHIUS, Santiago. b. 1877– (ARG) 10 R.

LICKL, Johann Georg. 1769–1843 (HUN) R, soli, choir, and orch. (1830); 4 other R [rec. Koch 3-1296-2].

LIMBACHER, Fridolin. 1914–1990 (GER) Deutsches Requiem, 1–4 part choir and org. [Böhm, 1976].

LINDBERG, Nils. b. 1933– (SWE) R, big band, mixed chorus, and three soloists (1993) [Gehrmans Musikförl., Stockholm] [rec. Phono Suecia, PSCD 78].

LINDBERG, Oskar. 1887–1955 (SWE) R, Op. 21, soli, chorus, and orch. (1920–22) [rec. Sterling CDS 1013–2] [Musikal].

LIVERATI, Jean. 1772–after 1817 (ITA) MDR, 4 vv, orch.

LOBMILLER, Theodor. [19th–20th cent.] (GER) R, Op. 5, SABar choir, and org. [Coppenrath].

LOBO de MESQUITA, Jose Joachim. d. 1805 (BRAZ) Officum defunctorum.

LONGO, Achille. 1900–1954 (ITA) MDR (1933).

LOPEZ, Melchior. 1759–1822 (SPA) MDR (El requiem en la música Espanola. Trans. Intro. y notas de Jose Calo y Joan Trillo. Música en Compostella. Ed. Jose Lopez Calo. Santiago de Compostella, 1987).

LOPEZ DE VELASCO, Sebastian. c. 1584–1659 (SPA) Missa defunctorum.

LORENZINI, Raimondo. d. 1806 (ITA) R, 4–8 vv.

LOUET, Alexandre. c. 1735–c. 1817 (FRA) Dies Irae, choir (1770); Dies irae.

LUCAS, Clarence. 1866–1947 (CAN) Requiem Mass [cm], choir and org. (1939).

LUCAS, Leighton. b. 1903– (ENG) MPD, solo vv, choir, and orch. (1934).

LUCCHESI, Andrea. 1741–1801 (ITA) Requiem for the Duke of Monte Allegro (c. 1768); Dies Irae, 4 vv, and orch.

LUCIDI, Achille. 1847–1901 (ITA) MDR, for the 20th anniversary of the death of Victor Emanuele (c. 1898).

LUDFORD, Nicolas. 1485–1557 (ENG) Missa Requiem Aeternam [not surviving].

LUTOSLAWSKI, Witold. 1913–1994 (POL) Requiem fragments (1937) Sop. solo, choir, orch.; Lacrimosa (1937).

M

MABELLINI, Teodulo. 1817–1897 (ITA) R [cm], 4 solo vv, choir, orch., and org. (1851).

MACCHI, Egisto. b. 1928– (ITA) R (1940).

MACIEJEWSKI, Roman. 1910–1998 (POL) MPD, SATB choir, and orch. (1946–49) [rec. PNCD 039 A and B].

MADERNA, Bruno. 1920–1973 (ITA) R (before 1946).

MADERNA, Francisco de. b. 1907– (ARG) Misa de Requiem, choir and org.

MAGGIO, Giuseppe. 1866–1930 (ITA) R, 3 vv mixed [Edizioni Musicali Carrara, Bergamo].

MAGRI, Pietro. 1873–1937 (ITA) Messa "Defunctorum Simplex," TB choir [Edizioni Musicali Carrara, Bergamo].

MAICHELBECK, Franz Anton. 1702–1750 (GER) R for two choirs (Denkmäler der Musik in Baden. Württemberg). Vol. 9 ed. Manfred Herman Schmidt. [Strube Verlag, Munich. 1993].

MAIER, Anton. [19th–20th cent.] (GER?) MPD, Op. 6, 4-part male choir and org. [Coppenrath, c. 1880].

MAIER, Julius-Joseph. 1821–1889 (GER) Requiem aeternam, men's choir [Ed. Ferrimontana, c. 1990].

MAILLARD, Jean. fl. c. 1538–1570 (FRA) R.

MAILMAN, Martin. b. 1932– (USA) R, Op. 51, Belwin Mills c. 1978.

MALIPIERO, Gian. 1882–1973 (ITA) Missa pro Mortuis, baritone solo, chorus, and orch. (1938).

MALISZEWSKI, Witold. 1873–1939 (POL) R, Op. 27, soli, chorus, and orch. (1930).

MALZAT, Johann Michel. 1745–87 (AUS) several R.

MANDL, Johann. b. 1862– (GER) R w/Libera, Op. 18, 1v. and org./harmonium [Coppenrath, 1903].

MANFREDINI, Francesco. 1680–1748 (ITA) Messe Funèbre.

MANFREDINI, Vincenzo. 1737–1799 (ITA) Requiem for Empress Elizabeth (1762); Messe Funèbre, 4 vv and inst.

MANGON, Johannes. c. 1525–1578 (GER) R.

MANNA, Ruggero. 1808–1864 (ITA) MDR, 4 vv, inst.

MARABINI, Giovanni Battista. b. 1873– (ITA) MPD.

MARCKHL, Erich. 1902–1980 (AUS) R, mixed choir, SATB soli, fl., 2 cl., 2 ob., 2 bsn., 2 tpt., 2 tbn., str., and perc. (1965) [Möseler].

MARIANI, Angelo. 1821–1873 (ITA) R (unpub.).

MARIER, Theodore. 1912–2001 (USA) Requiem Mass and Burial Service, people's choir and org. [pub. c. 1965].

MARINUZZI, Gino. 1882–1945 (ITA) MDR.

MARRACO Y FERRER, Jose. 1835–1913 (SPA) R.

MARSAND, Anselmo. 1749–1841 (ITA) MDR, tenor and bass vv (C major) [San Marco, cat. #B. 354]; MDR, two solo vv (TB) and two-part choir (TB) [FM] [San Marco, cat. #349].

MARTIN D'ANGERS. b. 1808– (FRA) MDR (c. 1846).

MARTINI, Giovanni. 1706–1784 (ITA) 3 R.

MARTINI, Jean-Paul. 1741–1816 (FRA/GER) several R.

MARTINI, Johann. 1741–1816 (GER) R, 4 vv, and orch.; R (1816).

MARTTINEN, Tauno. b. 1912– (FIN) R, solists, choir, and orch. (1973).

MASCAGNI, Pietro. 1863–1945 (ITA) R (1887, unpub.).

MASCHERONI, Edouardo. 1852–1941 (ITA) R.

MASI, Giovanni. [second half of 1700s] (ITA) MDR, 5 vv, orch.

MASSENET, Jules. 1842–1912 (ITA) R, 4–8 vv, bass, and organ (c. 1863).

MASSONNEAU, Louis. 1766–1848 (GER) R (1825).

MATONS, Laureano Fuentes. 1825–1898 (CUBA) Misa de Difuntos, 3 vv., and orch. (1856).

MATTIOLI, Andrea. c. 1620–1679 (ITA) R for Marchese Guido Villa (1649) lost.

MATTONI, Filippo. 1848–1922 (ITA) MDR, 3 vv (TTB), and harmonium.

MAUDIT, Simon. 1557–1627 (FRA) Requiem aeternam (mass from Ronsard's funeral), 5 vv (1585).

MAUGERI, Antonio. b. 1918– (ITA) Messa dei defunti: per coro populare all'unisono ed organo [Carrara, Bergamo 1992] [Italian text].

MAURO, Antonio. [19th–20th cent.] (ITA?) MPD, 2 equal vv, and organ [Jumnickel, c. 1916].

MAWBY, Colin. 1936– (IRE) R, Soprano solo, SATB choir andorgan (1989); Pie Jesu, SATB *divisi* (1993).

MAYER, Alfons. 1889–1986 (GER) Deutsches Requiem w/Libera, one voice [Böhm, 1966].

MAYR, Simon. 1763–1845 (GER) 6 R: Gran Messa di Requiem, STB vv, and orch. (1819); R [dm]; 20 requiem movements; 111 movements for the Office of the Dead.

MAZZONI, Antonio Maria. 1717–1785 (ITA) 2 R.

MC CABE, John. b. 1939– (ENG) Requiem Sequence, soprano and piano [Novello].

MEI, Orazio. 1731–1788 (ITA) 2 R, 4 vv, and orch.

MEILCZEWSKI, Marcin. d. 1651 (POL) R.

MELANI, Allesandro. 1639–1703 (ITA) 3 R.

MELNGAILIS, Emilis. 1874–1954 (LATVIA) Latvju rekviema, a cappella choir.

MENDES, Manuel. c. 1547–1605 (PORT) MPD, 4 vv [M. Joaquin, Lisbon, 1951].

MENGEL, Martin-Joseph. 1784–1851 (BELG) R.

MENGELBERG, Rudolph. 1892–1959 (GER) R, solo vv, choir, and orch. (1924).

MENSCHICK, Wolfram. b. 1937– (GER) Dies irae: Lied zum Requiem, 3-part mixed choir and 3-part, equal vv [Eichstatt, Bischoflichen Ordinäriat 1992].

MERCADANTE, Saverio. 1795–1870 (ITA) Requiem Brève (1836).

MERKU, Pavle. b. 1927– (SLOVENIA) MDR "Pro felici mei transitu."

MESQUITA, Jose Joachin Emerico Lobo de. 1746–1805 (BRAZ) Oficio de defuntos.

METSCHNABL, Paul. [20th cent.] (GER) Messe für Verstorbene, satb choir [A. Böhm].

MEURER, Johann. 1871–1955 (GER) MPD w/Libera, Op. 31, SATB choir and org. [or: 3 tbn., tpt.] [or: str.quartet, 2 cl. and 2 Fh.] [Coppenrath, 1907]; MDR w/ Libera, Op. 62, one voice and org./harmonium [Coppenrath, 1910]; R [cm] w/ Sequence and Libera, Op. 66, SATB choir and org. [or: obligatory org., 2 vn., db., and 2 Fh. or: 2 tpt. and timp. or: 2 tpt., 2 tbn., and org.] [Coppenrath, 1915].

MEYERBEER, Giacomo. 1791–1864 (GER) R.

MICHEELSEN, Hans Friedrich. 1902–1973 (GER) Tod und Leben: ein deutches Requiem, 5-part choir, unaccompanied [Kassel, Bärenreiter 1970].

MICHELI, Domenico. c. 1540–c. 1590 (ITA) MPD.

MICHL, Joseph Willibald. 1745–1816 (GER) 2 R (1815).

MIELSZEWSKI, Marcin. c. 1590–1651 (POL) Missa "Pro defuncto fundatore."

MIGAULT, Alfred. 1895–1961 (CAN) MDR, brève, 4 equal vv, and organ (1944) [ms].

MIKI, Minoru. b. 1930– (JAP) R (1963).

MINCHEJMER, Adam. 1830–1904 (POL) R.

MINOJA, Ambrogio. 1732–1825 (ITA) R.

MIRAMONTES, Arnulfo. 1882–1960 (MEX) Misa de Requiem (1917).

MITTERER, Ignaz. 1850–1924 (AUS) MPD, Op. 53, 4 male vv [Coppenrath, c. 1895]; MPD, Op. 69, 2 vv and org. [Coppenrath, 1900]; MPD, Op. 69b, 4 mixed vv, and org. [Coppenrath, 1901]; MPD, Op. 155, unison choir and org. [Coppenrath, 1908].

MIZUNO, Shuko. b. 1934– (JAP) Dies Irae, choir, electronic (1972).

MOLITOR, Alexius. 1730–1773 (GER) 3 R.

MONDO, Michele. [?] (ITA) MDR, Op. 64 [am], 2 vv (TB) and org. [San Marco, cat. #D. 187/1–17].

MONESTEL, Alejandro. 1865–1950 (COSTA RICA) Requiem Mass, 3 male vv [Hamilton Gordon, c. 1919).

MONETA, Giuseppe. 1761– (ITA) R.

MONIUSZKO, Stanislaw. 1818–1872 (POL) 2 Funeral masses [dm] (1850). [gm] (1873); Requiem aeternam, solo vv, choir, and orch. (1890).

MONN, Matthis Georg. 1717–1750 (AUS) R, 4 vv, 2 vn., and org.

MONNIKENDAM, Marius. 1896–1977 (NETH) MPD, alto solo, chorus, perc., and org. (1961) [Donemus].

MONTERO, Jose Angel. 1839–1881 (VENEZ) R w/response, 4 vv (1880); R, 1 voice and org.

MONTES, Juan de. [19th cent.] (SPA) R.

MOOR, Emanuel. 1863–1931 (HUN) R, 4 solo vv, choir, and orch. (1916).

MORALT, Joseph. 1775–1855 (GER) R.

MORLUCCHI, Francois. 1784–1841 (ITA) MDR (1827) [composed for Frederic Auguste I, King of Saxony (written in 10 days)].

MORO, Giacomo. fl. 1581–1610 (ITA) Officum et missa defunctorum, 8 vv (1599).

MORTARI, Virgilio. 1902–1993 (ITA) Requiem de morte transire ad vitam (1959), soprano and alto soli, mixed choir, and orch. (1959) [Universal].

MORTARO, Antonio. c. 1565–c. 1620 (ITA) 1 R (1595).

MOSSO, Giuseppe. b. 1833– (ITA) MPD, two vv (TB) and organ [dm] [San Marco, cat. #159/1–25].

MOULINIE, Etienne. c. 1600–1676 (FRA) MPD, 5 vv [Heugel].

MOZART, Leopold. 1719–1787 (AUS) R.

MUENCH, Gerhart. 1907–1988 (GER/MEX) Missa defunctorum para voces a cappella (1956–59) [La Loma Edition Conal Moreliana].

MUFFAT, Georg. 1653–1704 (GER) Missa "In labore requies," 8 vv, 12 inst. (Schriftenreihe des Salzburg Konsistorialarchivs, Vol. 3. Denkmäler der Music in Salzburg. Selkeverlag, Salzburg 1995).

MULDER, Ernest. 1898–1959 (NETH) R, MPD, SATB soli, chorus, and orch. [Donemus].

MÚLLER, Donat. 1804–1879 (GER) Mass for the Dead in F Major, 4-voice choir, str., 2 cl., 2 tpt., tbn., timp., and org. (1830); an arrangement of this work exists for STB choir and org. [In: *Peters Catholic Harmonist: A collection of sacred music appropriate for Morning and Evening Service . . .* W. C. Peters 1852].

MÚLLER, Franz Xavier. 1870–1948 (AUS) R, 4 mixed vv, unaccompanied.

MULLER, Joseph. [19th–20th cent.] (?) MPD, 3 male vv [Hamilton Gordon, c. 1930].

MURPHY, Edward. [19th–20th] (?) Requiem Mass [c. 1915].

N

NACCIARONE, Nicola. 1802–1876 (ITA) R.

NADAL, Jaime. 1789–1844 (SPA) R.

NAUJALIS, Juozas. 1869–1934 (LITHUANIA) R, 4 vv, and org.

NEBAUER, Franz. c. 1760–1795 (BOH) R, chorus and orch.

NEBRA, Jose. 1702–1768 (SPA) MPD for Maria Barbara's exequies (1758), 8 vv, str., ob, Fh., and tpt.; Misa de difuntos, 8 vv, str., ob., Fh., and trp.

NEGREA, Martian. 1893–1973 (ROMANIA) R, soli, mixed choir, and orch., Op. 25 (1957) [1959].

NEMMER, Michael Ludwig. 1855–1929 (GER?) R and Libera w/Pie Jesu, 1, 2, or 3 vv.

NESITKA, Egon. B. 1902– (AUS) Deutsche Seelenmesse, 2 female voices or choir and org. [pub. private].

NESVERA, Josef. 1842–1914 (CZE) 2 R (Op. 13, Op. 38).

NEUKOMM, Sigismund. 1778–1858 (AUS) MPD, in memory of Louis XVI [1814] [Peters c. 1815].

NEUMANN, Mathieu. 1867–1928 (GER?) R. Op. 93 (1917).

NICHELMANN, Christoph. 1717–1761/2 (GER) R, 4 vv, 2 fl., ob., vn., vla., and db.

NICOLAI, Carl. 1810–1849 (GER) R.

NICOLINI, Giuseppe. 1762–1842 (ITA) 2 R.

NIETO, Miguel. 1844–1915 (SPA) R.

NINI, Alessandro. 1805–1880 (ITA) R.

NORDAL, Jon. b. 1926– (ICE) R, unaccompanied choir and soprano and baritone soli. (1995) [rec. ITM, 7-09].

O

O'BRIEN, Oscar (Rev.). 1892–1958 (CAN) Requiem Mass, 4-part male vv, a cappella [ms] (1934–35).

OCHS, Traugott. 1854–1919 (GER) R.

OELSCHLEGEL, Johann Lobelius. 1724–1788 (BOH) R, 4 vv, and org.

OERTZEN, Rudolph. 1910–1990 (GER) Requiem de morte ad vitam, 4 mixed vv choir, 4 soli, and str. orch., Op. 55.

ORTLIEB, Edouard. 1807– after 1860 (GER) R, 3 vv and org.

OSWALD, Henrique. 1852–1931 (BRAZ) MDR [em] 4 vv.

OTTO, Ernst Jules. 1804–1877 (GER) Cantati funèbre, choir, and orch.

P

PACCHIONI, Antonio. 1654–1738 (ITA) MDR, 8 vv, and org.

PACHSCHMIDT, Carolomannus. 1700–1734 (AUS) R.

PACINI, Giovanni. 1796–1867 (ITA) R [cm], 4 vv, orch., and org. (1843); Requiem for Michelle Puccini, 1864; Requiem for the proposed transfer of Bellini's remains (1864).

PADILLA, Juan Gutierrez. c. 1590–1664 (MEX) Dies Irae, 8 vv.

PAER, Fernando. 1771–1839 (ITA) Offertoire pour la mort du Duc de Berry.

PAGANI, Francesco [20th cent.] (ITA) MDR, TTB, and org., according to the Ambrosian Rite.

PAGELLA, Giovanni 1872–1944 (ITA) Messa Terza da requiem, Op. 23, 2 equal vv, and org. (1902); Messa 14 de Requiem, 2 vv, and org./harmonium, Op. 104 [late 1800s].

PALAZUELO, Jose Maria. 1867–1946 (ARG) Misa de Requiem.

PALESTER, Roman. b. 1907– (ROMANIA) R, solo vv, chorus, and orch. (1945).

PALSSON, Pail. b. 1928– (ICE) R, mixed chorus [Iceland].

PANEBIANCO, Angelo. [?] (ITA) MDR.

PANIAGUA y VASQUES, Cenobio. 1821–1882 (MEX) R (1882).

PANNAIN, Guido. 1891–1977 (ITA) R (1912).

PANNY, Joseph. 1794–1838 (GER) R, 3 vv, 2 vn., db., org.

PAOLETTI, Natale. [19th cent.] (ITA) MDR breve, TB, and org. (c. 1885).

PAQUE, Desire. 1867–1939 (BELG) R.

PAQUET, Raoul. 1892–1946 (CAN) Messe des Morts.

PARISE, Gennaro. [late 1700s–after 1851] (ITA) MDR, large orchestra.

PARTENIO, Giovanni. before 1650–1701 (ITA) MPD [FM], SATB choir and b.c. (1696).

PASINO, Stefano. early 17th cent.–1679 (ITA) R.

PASSANI, Emile. b. 1905– (FRA) Requiem-Symphonia, soli, choir, org., and orch. (1968).

PASTERWIZ, Georg. 1730–1803 (AUS) R.

PAUSCH, Eugen. 1758–1838 (GER) R, Op 4; R, Op. 5; R, 4 vv, 2 vn., 2 Fh., db., org.

PEACAN, DEL SAR, Rafael. 1884–1960 (ARG) Misa de Requiem.

PEARSALL, Robert. 1795–1856 (ENG) R, 4 vv, wind inst., and org. (1853/6).

PEDEMONTI, Giuseppe. b. 1910– (ITA) Rito dei defunti: canti per un servico completo liturgico: per coro 1–4 voci ed organo. [Carrara, Bergamo, 1996].

PEDRELL, Felipe. 1841–1922 (SPA) R.

PEISSNER, Karl. 1890–1952 (GER) Missa "Requiem aeternam," choir and org .

PELLARIN, Giuseppe. 1815–1865 (ITA) MDR, TTB soli, TTB choir, and b.c. [GM] [San Marco, cat. #B. 601/1–17].

PELLEGRIN, Claude Mathieu. 1682–1763 (FRA) Messe des morts.

PELLETIER, Frederick. 1870–1944 (CAN) Requiem Mass.

PEMBAUER, Joseph. 1848–1923 (AUS) R.

PENDER, Scott. b. 1959– (CAN) R.

PEPIN, Rodolphe. [?] (?) MPD, unison, SAB, STB, or TTB choir [McGloughlin and Reilly].

PERALTA-ESCUDERO, Bernardo de. d. 1617 (SPA) MPD, 8 vv.

PEREIRA, Domingos Nunes. d. 1729 (PORT) Lessons for the Office of the Dead, 4 vv; Lessons for The Office of the Dead, 8 vv.

PEREZ, Juan Gines. 1548–1612 (SPA) Music for the Office of the Dead.

PEREZ-ROLDAN, Juan. c. 1610–after 1671 (SPA) MPD, 8 vv.

PERLA, Michel. [mid. 1700s] (ITA) several R.

PERREAULT, Joseph Julien. 1826–1866 (CAN) Messe des Morts [A. J. Boucher].

PERROTI, Giovanni. [19th cent.] (ITA) MDR [FM], SATB soli, SATB choir, and b.c. (1829) [San Marco, cat. #A. 187/1–16]; Messa brevis tribus vocibus, STBB soli, STBB choir, and b.c. (1824).

PERTI, Giacomo. 1661–1756 (ITA) R; Dies irae, TTB, and str.

PETRELLA, Errico. 1813–1877 (ITA) Messe Funèbre per la morte de Angelo Mariani (1873).

PETRUCCI, Brizio. 1737–1828 (ITA) R (1822).

PHILIDOR, Francois-Andre. 1726–1795 (ENG) Requiem in memory of Rameau, 1764 (lost).

PICCHI, Luigi. 1899–1970 (ITA) MDR, ATB choir, and org. [San Marco, cat. #B. 1292/1–63].

PICHL, Wenceslas. 1741–1804 (BOH) MDR; Solemn Dies Irae.

PIER, Battista da Falconara (Padre). (?) (ITA) MDR, breve e facilissimi, SA choir.

PIETKIN, Lambert-Jean. 1613–1696 (BELG) R (lost).

PIETROBONO, Benedetto. [19th–20th cent.] (ITA) MDR, SA or TB, and org.

PIGLIA, Enrico. b. 1885– (ITA) MPD.

PINEDA-DUQUE, Roberto. 1910–1977 (COL) Misa de requiem (1941).

PIPER, Sam. b. 1977– (NEW ZEALAND) R, (1994) SATB choir.

PIZZI, Emilio. 1861–1940 (ITA) Requiem Mass, 4 vv, choir, and org.

PLANTADE, Charles Henri. 1764–1839 (FRA) MDR.

PLANTANIA, Pietro. 1828–1907 (ITA) Requiem [for Vittorio Emanuele], 4 solo vv, choir, and org.

PLATTI, Giovanni. c. 1700–1763 (ITA) Messa Concertata da Requiem per soli, coro e orchestre [Revisione di Luciano Bettarini, Rome 1979–1988].

PLATTNER, Augustin. fl. 1613–1624 (GER) MPD.

PLAZA-ALFONZO, Eduardo. b. 1911– (COL) Misa de requiem (1965).

PLAZA-ALFONZO, Juan-Battista. 1898–1965 (VENEZ) R, unison vv, and org. (1926); R, TTBB choir, and orch. (1933); MDR (1965).

POGLIETTI, Alessandro. 1641–1683 (AUS) Requiem aeternam.

POLL, Josef. 1873–1953 (GER) R, 4 equal vv. [Coppenrath, 1905].

POLLAROLI, Orazio. [18th cent.] (ITA) R.

POLLERI, Giovanni. 1855–1923 (ITA) MDR, 3 male vv, and org. (1899); several other R.

PONCHARD, Antoine. 1758–1827 (FRA) MDR, 4 vv, and orch.

PONTIO, Pietro. 1532–1595 (ITA) Missa Mortuorum (1585).

PONZILACQUA, Aureliano. 1855–c. 1928? (ITA) MDR [dm], SATB choir, and orch. [San Marco, cat. #938/1–68]; MDR [dm], SATB choir, and orch. [San Marco, cat. #B. 940/1–6]; MDR [dm], SATB choir, and orch. [San Marco, cat. #B. 939/1–68]; MDR [am], ATTB soli, ATTB choir, and orch. [San Marco, cat. #B. 941/1–66].

POPPER, David. 1843–1913 (AUS) R, Op 66, 3-part choir, orch. (1892).

PORPORA, Nicola. 1686–1768 (ITA) 3 Notturni de defonti.

PORRO, Giovanni. c. 1590–1656 (GER) R.

PORTUGAL, Marcos. 1762–1830 (PORT?) R.

POSER, Hans. 1917–1970 (GER) R, 4–12 part mixed choir (1968) [Möseler, 1967].

PRADAS-GALLEN, Jose. 1689–1757 (SPA) R.

PRADI, G. (?) Mass for the Dead [nd].

PREDMORE, George. b. 1880–alive 1953 (USA) R w/Libera, unison choir, and org.

PREINDL, Josef. 1756–1823 (AUS) 2 R [E flat M], vv, and orch.; Op. 50.

PREITZ, Franz. 1856–1916 (GER) R, unaccompanied voices [pub.].

PREMRL, Stanko. 1880–1965 (SLOVENIA) R.

PRETZENBERGER, Johann. b. 1897– (AUS) Messe für die Verstorbenen, SATB choir and org. [Bischöflichen Seelsorgeamt St. Pölten, 1971].

PROVENZALE, Francesco. c. 1626–1704 (ITA) Missa defunctorum, 4 vv, 2 vn., and b.c.

PUCCINI, Antonio. 1747–1832 (ITA) Introit: Kyrie for the mass of the Dead, 4 vv, and orch.; Sequence, 3 vv, and small orch.

PUSA-TERI, Cosimo Roosevelt. b. 1908– (USA) R.

PUSCHMANN, Josef. c. 1740–1794 (CZE) R.

Q

QUARENTE, Valentino. (?) (ITA) MDR [dm], SSTBB choir, orch., and org. [San Marco, cat. #1169/1–64].

R

RAAB, Franz de Paulo. 1763–1804 (AUS) R [em], 4 vv, and org.

RAIMONDI, Pietro. 1786–1853 (ITA) 2 R with large orch.; MDR, 8 vv, and 16 vv; 1 other R.

RAMIREZ, Jose Maria Ponce de Leon. 1846–1932 (COL) Misa de requiem.

RAMPINI, Domenico. c. 1765–1816 (ITA) R, 3 vv, orch., and org. (1808).

RAMPINI, Giacomo. 1680–1760 (ITA) R, 4 vv (1756).

RAPHAEL, Günter. 1903–1960 (GER) R, Op. 20, 4 solo vv, 8 vv choir, orch., and org. (1927–28). [Breitkopf]; Sequenz Dies Irae, Op 73, 8 vv choir (1951).

RATHAUS, Karol. 1895–1954 (GER) R, SATB choir [Boosey].

RATHGEBER, Valentin. c. 1690–1744 (FRA) 2 R, 4 vv, 2 vn., b.c., Op. 1; 6 MDR and 2 w/Libera, 4 vv, inst., Op. 8; 2 R, 1 and 2 vv, inst. (ad lib), Op. 12; 2 MDR, 4 vv, and inst., Op. 21 (11 R total).

RAUZZINI, Venanzio. 1746–1840 (ITA) R (1801).

RAVANELLO, Oreste. 1871–1938 (ITA) 2 R.

RAVNIK, Janko. b. 1891– (SLOVENIA) R [bm], Bar solo, men's choir, and org. (1916).

RAYOL, Antonio. 1855–1905 (BRAZ) MDR.

REBBORA, Antonio. [19th cent.] (ITA) MDR, breve, Op. 10, TTB, and org. (18—).

REBELO, Joao-Soares. 1610–1661 (PORT) R w/Dies irae (lost).

REBOITIER, Jacques. b. 1937– (FRA) R (1995).

REDA, Siegfried. 1916–1968 (GER) Requiem Vel Vivorum Consolatio, SATB choir, soprano and baritone soli, and orch. [Bärenreiter].

REDI, Tommaso. c. 1675–1738 (ITA) R, 2 choirs: 4 vv each, strings, and b.c. (1713).

REGEL, Wolfgang. [20th cent.] (GER) Requiem à la Mémoire de César Geoffray (1901–72), mixed choir, soli, and orch. (1974) [Editions à Coeur Joie].

REICHARDT, Johann Friedrich. 1752–1814 (GER) R, 6 vv (lost) (Cantus lugubris in obitam Frederici Magni. Paris, 1787).

REIMANN, Aribert. b. 1936– (GER) R, soprano, mezzo-soprano and baritone soli, mixed choir, and orch.

REIMANN, Ignaz. 1820–1885 (GER) 24 R.

REINECKE, Carl. 1824–1910 (GER) R.

REINHARDT, Johann Georg. c. 1676–1742 (AUS) 3 R.

REISSIGER, Friedrich August. 1809–1883 (GER) R.

REISSIGER, Karl. 1798–1859 (GER) R.

REITER, Josef. 1862–1939 (AUS) R, Op. 60.

REITER, Leopold. b. 1871– (AUS) Deutsche Trauermesse (1924).

REMOUCHAMPS, Henri de. c. 1600–1639 (NETH) R, 8 vv, and continuo (lost).

RENNER, Joseph, Jr. 1868–1938 (GER) Third Requiem, Op. 49, one voice and org. or: SATB choir with or without org. [Coppenrath]; Fourth Requiem, Op. 51, medium voice or unison choir and org./harmonium [Coppenrath, 1904].

RENNER, Joseph, Sr. 1832–1895 (GER) Second Requiem, Op. 45, one voice and org. or: SAB choir and optional org. [Coppenrath, c. 1895]; MPD [FM], 1–3 vv, and org. [Coppenrath, 1883]

REUTTER, Hermann. 1900–1985 (GER) Ein kleines Requiem, bass, cello, clarinet (1961).

REZNICEK, Emil. 1860–1945 (ITA) Dies Irae, 4 vv, and orch.

RICCI, Federic. 1809–1877 (ITA) R; Dies Irae, 4 vv, and orch.

RICCI, Francesco. 1732–1817 (ITA) Dies Irae, Op. 7, 4 vv, and orch.

RICCI, Luigi. 1805–1859 (ITA) R.

RICHTER, Ferdinand. 1651–1711 (AUS) R, 4 vv, and inst.

RICHTER, Franz. 1709–1789 (GER) 3 R.

RIEDER, Ambrosius. 1771–1855 (AUS) several R; R, 4 vv, vn., Fh., tbn., db., org., Op 39 [Haslinger, Vienna].

RIEGEL, Friedrich. [19th cent.] (GER?) Requiem aeternam, Op. 18, 3 male vv, and org. [Coppenrath, c. 1879].

RIES, Ferdinand. 1784–1838 (GER) R, 4 vv, and orch. (1815).

RIHOVSKY, Vojtech. 1871–1950 (CZE) 5 R.

RIMONTI, Pedro. c. 1570– after 1618 (SPA) R (1607).

RINCK, Johann Christian Heinrich. 1770–1846 (GER) R, TTBB choir, and org. (1836) [in: Mason Lowell Collection at Yale University].

RISPOLI, Salvatore. c. 1736/45–1812 (ITA) R, 4 vv, and orch.

RISTORI, Giovanni. 1692–1753 (ITA) 3 R (DM, FM, [1730], fm).

RITTLER, Philipp Jacob. c. 1637–1690 (GER) R.

ROESKE, Ferdinand J. [20th cent.] (BELG) R, men's choir [Alsbach] [conductor].

ROFF, Joseph. 1910–1993 (CAN) Requiem Mass (1949), choir and org.; R, choir and piano (1948) [ms].

ROGISTER, Jean. 1879–1964 (BELG) R, solo vv, choir, and orch. (1944).

ROLDAN, Juan Perez. d. 1722 (SPA) R.

ROSENMÚLLER, Johann. 1619–1684 (GER) MPD, SATB choir, and inst. [rec. Vivarte, S2K 89470].

ROSES, Jose. 1791–1856 (SPA) several R.

ROSETTE, Antonio. c. 1750–1792 (BOH) R [E flat M] (1776); R [dm]; R for Mozart (1791).

ROSSI, Francesco. c. 1645 (ITA) R.

ROSSI, Giovanni. 1828–1886 (ITA) R.

ROSSI, Giuseppe de. [mid. 1600s–1719/20] (ITA) R.

ROSSI, Luigi-Felice. 1805–1863 (ITA) R, male vv, orch. [Ricordi, Milan].

ROSSI, M. Enrico. [19th–20th cent.] (ITA?) MPD, Op. 83 [Reiter-Biedermann, c. 1907).

ROSSINI, Carlo. 1839–1890 ? (ITA?) Requiem Mass, 3 male vv, and org. [Fischer, c. 1922].

ROSSLER Franz Anton. 1750–1792 (GER) R (1791).

ROUMEFORT, R. de. [?] (FRA?) Requiem aeternam, choir, optional solo, optional org. [Lemoine].

ROUSSEAU, Jean Marie. d. 1784 (FRA) 3 R, one for the death of Louis XVI.

ROUWYZER, Francois. 1737–1827 (NETH) 2 R, 4 vv, str., and b.c.

ROVETTA, Jean. [late 1500s–1667] (ITA) R, two choirs.

RUBENBERGER, Sepp [20th cent.] Seelenmesse, 3 or 4 mixed voices and org./ inst. ad lib. [Musikverlag Max Hieber, Munich,. MH 2089].

RUFFO, Vincenzo. c. 1510–1587 (ITA) MPD.

RUHN, Gerhard. b. 1930– (GER) R (1985).

RUZITSKA, Gyorgy. 1789–1869 (HUN) R (1829).

RYBA, Jakub Jan. 1765–1815 (BOH) 7 R.

RZEPKO, Adolf. 1825–1892 (POL) Requiem Polskie, 4 vv, str. orch., and org. (1868).

RZEPKO, Wladyslaw. 1854–1932 (POL) R, baritone and tenor chorus, org. (1905).

RZEWSKI, Frederic. b. 1938– (USA) R, choir and ensemble (1963–67).

S

SABBATINI, Luigi. 1732–1809 (ITA) 2 R, 4 vv, and org.; 2 Messi per defunti, 8 vv, str., and org.; 4 requiem movements, 4 vv, strings, and org.

SALAZAR, Antonio de. c. 1650–1715 (MEX) Oficio de defuntos.

SALONEN, Salo. 1899–1976 (FIN) R, solo vv, choir, and orch. Op. 32 (1962) [1963].

SALVA, Tadeas. b. 1937– (SLOVAKIA) Requiem aeternam, reciter, choir, and orch. (1967).

SALVATORE, Giovanni. d. 1688? (ITA) Messa defunctorum, 4 vv, and org.

SALVOLINI, Alessandro. c. 1700–c. 1770 (ITA) Missa Defunctorum, satb choir.

SALVETTI, Renzo. b. 1906– (ITA/VENEZ) MDR (1943).

SAMINSKY, Lazare. 1882–1959 (USA) Requiem IV, Op. 54, chorus and orch. (1946).

SANCES, Giovanni. c. 1600–1679 (ITA) 3 R.

SANCHO-MARRACO, Jose. 1879–1960 (SPA) R, 4 vv, org., and string orch.

SANDSTROM, Sven David. b. 1942– (SWED) R (1979).

SANTINI, Fortunato. 1778–1862 (ITA) R.

SANTUCCI, Marc. 1762–after 1828 (ITA) Paraphrases of the Dies Irae, 4 vv and orch.

SARTI, Giuseppe. 1729–1802 (ITA) R, 4 vv, and orch.; R, 4 solo vv, 4 choirs—5 vv, orch., and org. for Louis XVI (1793); R for the Grand Duke of Württemberg (1798); MPD [FM], 5 vv, unaccompanied; Dies Irae, 4 vv, and orch.

SASNAUSKAS, Ceslovas. 1867–1916 (LITHUANIA) R, soli, mixed choir, org. (1915).

SAUGET, Henri. 1901–1989 (FRA) Requiem aeternam, chorus and org. (1954); Pie Jesu, choir and org. (1957); Requiem aeternam [from film score: Tu es Petrus], choir, 4 vv (1959).

SCALETTA, Orazio. [2nd half of 1500s–1650] (ITA) Messa breve di morti, 4 vv.

SCARLATTI, Alessandro. 1660–1725 (ITA) MPD, satb choir (1717).

SCHACHT, Theodore. 1748–1823 (GER) R.

SCHAEUBLE, Hans. 1906–1988 (SWIS) R, Op. 6, chorus and orch. (1929).

SCHAK, Benedikt. 1758–1826 (AUS) 2 R.

SCHAUENSEE, Francois Joseph de. d. after 1790 (SWIS) R (1720).

SCHEHL, Alfred. b. 1882– (USA) MPD, Op. 35, unison choir and org.

SCHERR, L. [20th cent.?] (GER?) Deutsches Requiem, SATB choir, org., 2 Fh., and tbn. [Falter, München].

SCHIDLOWSKY, Leon. b. 1931– (CHILE/ISRAEL) R, 12 solo vv (1968).

SCHIEDERMAYER, Joseph Bernard. b. 1840– (AUS) R, Op. 46 [em], 4 vv, 2 vn., 2 Fh., db. and org.

SCHILLING, Vincenz. [19th cent.] (GER) Seelenmesse, SATB and org., Op. 8.

SCHIRM, Georg. 1768–1833 (GER) German Requiem, 4 vv.

SCHLENSONG, Martin. b. 1897– (GER) R (1960).

SCHMID, Anton. b. 1772– (GER) Dies irae, 4 vv, 2 Fh., 2 tpt. w/mutes, tbn.; R w/ Libera, 4 vv, 2 Fh., 2 tpt. w/mutes, db., org.; Chant funèbre, 1 or 2 vv, and org.

SCHMID, Karl Norbert. 1926–1995 (GER) Deutsches Requiem, SAB choir and org. [Verlag Feuchtinger and Gleichauf, Regensburg].

SCHMIDT, Ernst. 1904–1960 (GER) 14 R.

SCHMITT, Aloys. 1788–1866 (GER) R, 4 vv, and org. [German text] [in: Lowell Mason Collection, Yale University].

SCHMITT, Joseph. 1734–1791 (GER) R.

SCHNABEL, Joseph Ignace. 1767–1831 (GER) R and Dies irae, 4 vv, and orch.; Little Requiem.

SCHNEIDER, Franz 1737–1812 (AUS) 15 R.

SCHNEIDER-TRNAVSKY, Mikuláš. 1881–1958 (SLOVAKIA) MPD [c m], Op. 41, ATB soli, satb choir, org. (c. 1922).

SCHNEITZHOEFFER, Jean Madeleine. 1785–1852 (FRA) R.

SCHOLZ, Bernhard. 1835–1916 (GER) R, soli, choir, and orch., Op. 16 [Breitkopf and Härtel, c. 1865].

SCHREIBER, Johann. 1716–1800 (SWIS) 2 R, Op. 2, solo vv, choir: 4 vv, str., tpt. [or Fh.], b.c. and org.

SCHROEDER, Hermann. 1904–1984 (GER) R, 4 mixed vv, a capella (1952) [Ed. Schwann].

SCHUBERT, Franz 1797–1828 (AUS) R [fragment] D. 453.

SCHULZ-BEUTHEN, Heinrich. 1838–1915 (GER) R, chorus, and orch.

SCHWANBERG, Jean. 1740–1804 (SWIS) Cantata Funèbre sur la mort de la duchesse de Brunswick.

SECHTER, Simon. 1788–1867 (AUS) 2 R.

SEIDEL, Frederic Ludwig. b. 1765– (GER) MPD (1819); Fugue funeraire pour les obséquies de l'abbé Stadler, op. 55.

SELLE, Thomas. 1599–1663 (GER) German Requiem.

SERRA, Jean. b. 1787– (ITA) MDR.

SERRA, Michelangelo. 1571–c. 1628 (ITA) MPD Clementis non Papae, 4 vv (1606) lost.

SERRAO, Paolo. 1830–1907 (ITA) R.

SETACCIOLI, Giacomo. 1868–1925 (ITA) Requiem in memory of King Humbert I.

SEYDELMANN, Franz. 1748–1806 (GER) R.

SEYFRIED, Ignaz-Xaver. 1776–1841 (AUS) Grand Requiem, 4 vv soli/choir, 3 vc., db., 2 tpt., timp., Org.; 2 R in MSS; Libera, TTBB [composed for Beethoven's obsequies].

SEŸLER, Carl. 1815–1880 (GER) R (fm), R (cm), R (em), R (E flat M); all for voice and org. [Böhm].

SEYLER, Josef Anton. 1778–1860 (BOH) R.

SHERWOOD, Percy. 1866–1939 (ENG/GER) R.

SHORE, Samuel. 1856–1946 (ENG) R.

SILVA, Francisco. 1795–1865 (BRAZ) MPD; R [B flat M] (1828).

SILVA, Jose de Santa Rita Marques. c. 1778–1837 (PORT) R; Officum Defunctorum.

SINGER, Peter. 1810–1882 (AUS) 13 R.

SKROUP, Dominik Josef. 1811–1892 (BOH) R.

SNEL, Joseph Francois. 1793–1861 (BELG) MDR, 4 vv, org., db.

SOJO, Vincente. 1887–1974 (VENEZ) Requiem in memoriam patris patriae, male vv, orch. and org. (1929) [Ediciones del Congreso de la Republica, Instituto Latinamericano de Investigaciones y Estudios Músicales "Vicente Emilio Sojo" Caracas, Venezuela 1987. Series Collecion Músicos venezolanos contemporaneous, M. V. C. 9].

SOLER, Antonio. 1729–1783 (CATALAN) 5 R; lessons for Officium defunctorum.

SOLER, Francesco. c. 1625–1688 (SPA) 2 R, 6 vv, and b.c.; 8 vv.

SOMMA, Bonaventura. 1893–1960 (ITA) MPD, 5,6, and 8 vv [De Santis, 1942].

SONNINEN, Ahti. b. 1914– (FIN) Landstrassen Requiem, soli, choir, and orch. (1970).

SORIANO-Fuertes, Mariano. b. 1817– (SPA) Misa de Requiem (c. 1844).

SPASSOV, Ivan. b. 1934– (BUL) Holy Bulgarian Liturgy (1991), female choir [rec. Labor LAB 7014-2]; Little Requiem, soprano, 24 vv choir, speaker, 6 inst. (1967).

SPATH, Andreas. 1790–1876 (GER) MPD.

SPEISS, Meinrad. 1683–1761 (GER) 2 R, Op. 4, 4 vv, 2 vn., 2 vc., and org.

SPOHR, Ludwig. 1784–1859 (GER) R, soli, choir, and orchestra (1857–58).

SPRANGER, Jorg. b. 1911– (GER) R and Libera, sab choir, org. [A. Böhm].

SPRINGER, Max. 1877–1954 (GER) MPD.

STACHOWICZ, Damian. 1658–1699 (POL) MDR , 5 vv [SSATB], 2 vn., 2 tpt., and b.c.

STADLER, Maximillian. 1748–1833 (GER) R [cm] (1820); R [FM] (1821), mixed choir, org., 2vn., 2 Fh., and db. [Weinberger].

STANDFORD, Patric. b. 1939– (ENG) Christus Requiem, solo vv, chorus, orch., Op. 41 (1972).

STARCK, Johann Franz. 1742–1799 (GER) R [am], SATB choir, vn. 1/2, vla., Fh. 1/2, and org.

STATTLER, Paul (19th cent.) (GER) MPD, voice, and org. [Böhm].

STEFFANI, Jozef. 1800–1876 (POL) R, 3 male vv, and brass band (org.).

STEHLE, Johann Gustav Eduard. 1839–1915 (GER) R, Op. 52, 1, 2, or 4 vv, and org. (1882). [Böhm].

STEIN, Bruno. 1873–1915 (GER) MPD, Op. 35, 2 equal vv, and organ [pub. Coppenrath, 1907]; MPD, Op. 4, one voice and org. [Coppenrath].

STEIN, Josef. 1845–1915 (GER) MPD, Op. 33, male choir [Coppenrath, 1886]; MPD, Op. 45, one voice or unison choir, and org. [pub. Coppenrath, 1887].

STEKL, Konrad. b. 1901– (JUGO) R, soli, mixed choir, boy's choir, and orch., Op. 45 (1957 Austrian State Prize).

STEPAN, Josef. 1726–1797 (CZE) R.

STERNBERG, Hans. [20th cent.] (GER) R, 4-part, mixed vv choir, and wind inst. [Sternberg, Coburg 1986].

STEWART, Humphrey. 1856–1958 (ENG) MPD, solo quartet, choir, and orch. [J. Fischer].

STIBILJ, Milan. b. 1929– (YUGO) Apokatastasis, Slovene Requiem, tenor, choir, and orch. (1967).

STOEGER, Anton. 1727–1798 (GER) 2 R.

STOGBAUER, Isidor. 1898–1986 (GER) MPD, Op. 14, one voice or unison choir, and org./harmonium [Coppenrath, 1915]; one other R.

STRASSENBERGER, Georg. b. 1898– (GER) Easy R w/Libera, SAB choir, and org. [Coppenrath].

STRATEGIER, Herman. 1912–1987 (NETH) Requiem in Memoriam Matris et Fratris (1961), mixed choir, fl., ob., cl., bsn., Fh., and str. [Donemus].

STUNTZ, Joseph Hartmann. 1793–1859 (GER) R.

STURMER, Bruno. 1892–1958 (GER) R, mixed voices, four soli, orch., and org. [Köln, 1936].

SURZYNSKI, Jozef. 1851–1919 (POL) 4 R.

SÚSSMAYR, Franz. 1766–1803 (AUS) 2 German Requiems (one dated 1786).

SYCHRA, Josef. 1859–1935 (CZE) R.

T

TABART, Pierre. mid. 1600s–d. after 1711] (FRA) MDR [Editions du Centre de Musique Baroque de Versailles CMBV 026e].

TACCHINARDI, Guido. 1840–1917 (ITA) Requiem lirico, soli, chorus and orch.

TADINI, Cesare. [19th cent.] (ITA) MDR, 4 vv, and org. or orch. (18—).

TAGLIAPIETRA, Gino. 1887–1954 (ITA) R (1924).

TAMBURINI, Pietro. 1589–1635 (ITA) R.

TARP, Svend. 1908–1994 (DEN) R, Op. 83 (1980).

TAUWITZ, Julius. 1826–1898 (GER) MPD, solo voice and org. [Böhm].

TELLER, Marcus. fl. 1715–27 (NETH) MDR, Op. 2, 2 vv, and 4 inst. [cm] (1725); R, (c. 1730); MPDs, 10 vv.

TELLO-ROJAS, Rafael. 1872–1961(MEX) 2 R.

TERRABUGIN, Giuseppe. 1842–1933 (ITA) MDR, Op. 65, 2 vv, and org. (18—).

TERRY, Richard Runciman. 1865–1938 (ENG) Requiem Mass [pub. J and W Chester, 1916].

TERZIANI, Eugenio. 1824–1889 (ITA) Requiem in Memory of King Victor Emmanuel.

TERZIANI, Raffaele. 1860–1928 (ITA) Requiem in Memory of King Humbert.

TEYBER, Anton. 1756–1822 (AUS) Requiem pro defuncta Imperatrice Ludovica, 4 vv, and org.

THALLER, Johann. 1872–1952 (GER) MPD, [E flat M], choir, org., and brass (1902); MPD II, 2 equal vv, and org. [Coppenrath, 1900]; R [dm], choir, orch., and org. (unpub.).

THERMIGAN, Delfino. 1861–1944 (ITA) MDR, tenor solo, SATB choir, orch., and org. (April–May 1914) [FM] [B. 1632/1–65].

THIELEN, Peter. 1839–1908 (GER) MPD, Op. 186, 4-part, male choir [or alto, 3-part male] [Coppenrath, 1906].

THOMAS, Ambroise. 1811–1896 (FRA) Requiem Mass, choir, and orch. (1. 1840).

TIBURTIUS VAN BRUSSEL. c. 1605–1669 (BELG) Den Bluden Requiem (1631).

TIEL, Ernst. [20th cent.] (NETH) R, Op. 34.

TINAZZOLI, Agostino. d. c. 1723 (ITA) Messa da Morti, 4 vv; other requiem movements.

TITTEL, Ernst. 1910–1969 (AUS) Deutsches Requiem mit Libera, Op. 81, mixed choir, a cappella (1969) [Wien and München, Doblinger, 1965].

TOLLIS, DE LA ROCA, Matheo. c. 1710–1781 (MEX) R, 8 vv, instruments (1759).

TOMAŠEK, Václav. 1774–1850 (BOHEMIA) R, solo voice, org.

TONASSI, Pietro. 1800–1877 (ITA) MDR, ATTB soli, ATTB choir, and orch. [FM] [San Marco, cat. #B. 591]; Dies Irae [Sequence], ATTB soli, ATTB choir, and orch. [cm] (1876) [San Marco, cat. #B. 592/1–5].

TOPMAN, August. b. 1918– (ESTONIA) R.

TORNE, Bengt von. 1891–1967 (FIN) R.

TORRES, Domenico. [?] (ITA) MDR [dm], ATB choir, and orch. [San Marco, cat. #B. 1192/1–60]; MDR [em], TTB soli, TTB choir, and orch. [San Marco, cat. #B. 1193/1–46].

TORRES Y MARTINEZ BRAVO, Jose de. 1665–1738 (SPA) R.

TORRI, Pietro. c. 1650–1737 (ITA) MPD [FM], 5 vv, 6 inst. (1726).

TOSI, Matteo. 1884–1954 (ITA) MDR [dm], TTB choir and org. (1937) [San Marco, Cat. #1213/1–18]; Messe funèbre, 2 vv (children or mixed); 3 other R.

TOULMONDE, Antoine. 1901–2000. (BELG) R, 2 equal vv, and org. [Musica Sacra].

TREMBLAY, Pierre Joseph Amadee. 1876–1949 (CAN) R.

TREMMEL, Max. 1902–1980 (GER) MPD, Op. 24, SABar choir and org. [Coppenrath].

TRITTO, Jacques. 1732–1824 (ITA) MDR, 4 vv, and orch.

TUCEK, Vincenz. 1773–c. 1821 (CZE) R.

TÚMA, Frantisek. 1704–1774 (BOHEMIA) R.

U

UBEDA, Fray Manuel. 1760–1823 (URUG) Misa para dia de difuntos, 4 vv., db, fl. or cl. (1802).

UBERLEE, Adalbert. 1837–1897 (GER) R.

ULLINGER, Agustin. 1746–1781 (GER) R (lost).

URBAITIS, Mindaugas. B. 1952– (LITH) Lacrimosa, Mixed Choir, unaccompanied (1991–94).

URIBE-HOLGUIN, Guillermo. 1880–1971 (COL) R.

V

VACCAI, Nicola. 1790–1848 (ITA) Dies Irae.

VACHAR, Tomas. 1945–1963 (CZE) R, unfinished.

VALLE, Antonio. 1825–1876 (MEX) Misa de Requiem (1863).

VALLE-RIESTRA, Jose. 1859–1925 (PERU) R.

VALLOTTI, Francesco. 1697–1780 (ITA) Requiem mass movements; Introit 2vv, 4 vv; Sequence 2 vv, 4 vv, 5 vv; other movements, 4 vv, 8 vv; Vespers for the Dead, 8 vv; Esequie per i teologi defunti, 4 vv.

VANHAL, Johann Baptist. 1739–1813 (CZE) 2 R.

VAVRINECZ, Mauritius. 1858–1913 (HUN) R.

VAYNBERG, Moyssey. b. 1919– (POL/RUS) R, Op. 96.

VERDICKT, Benoit. 1884–1970 (CAN) MPD, 3 vv, and org. (1941) [Verdickt].

VERHEY, Theodore. 1848–1929 (NETH) R, Op. 38.

VERHEYEN, Pierre René. 1750–1819 (BELG) MDR (1810) [memory of Haydn].

VERHULST, Johannes. 1816–1891 (BELG) R, Op. 51, soli, mixed choir, and org. [or orch. ad lib, 2 trp., althorn, tbn., and tuba] [Coppenrath]; R, Op. 55, male vv, and winds.

VERRIMST, Victor. 1825–1893 (FRA) MDR, Op. 17 [Richault, Paris].

VEYVANOVSKY, Pavel. c. 1633–1693 (CZE) 4 R (lost).

VIERA, Amaral. b. 1952 (BRAZ) MPD, Op. 187, satb unaccompanied choir (1984); Requiem in Memoriam, Op. 203, satb choir, and orch. (1985).

VIOTTA, Jean Joseph. 1814–1859 (NETH) R, 3 vv; R, 4 vv [performed at composer's funeral].

VITASEK, Jan. 1770–1839 (CZE) 7 R.

VITTADINI, Franco. 1884–1948 (ITA) MDR, TTB choir and org. [cm] [San Marco, cat. #228/1–42].

VIVIANCO, Sebastian de. c. 1550–1622 (SPA) R.

VOGEL, Cajetan. c. 1750–1794 (BOHEMIA) 7 R.

VOGEL, Johann Christoph. 1756–1788 (GER) R.

VOGT, Hans. 1909–1978 (GER) R, mixed choir, soprano and baritone soli, and perc. (1970) [Breitkopf].

VOLANEK, Antonin. 1761–1817 (CZE) R.

VOLPI, Edoardo. [19th cent.] (ITA) Requiem aeternam (Pei Defunts), 2 equal vv, a capella [Zanibon].

VRANKEN, D. J. Joseph. 1870–1948 (NETH) MPD, 4 vv, and org. [Fischer, c. 1909].

W

WALKIEWICZ, Eugenejusz. 1880–1946 (POL) MPD, 3 equal vv, and org.

WALLMAN, Johannes. b. 1952– (GER) R (1995).

WEBBE, Samuel. 1742–1816 (ENG) R [gml], 3 vv (1864); R [em], 3 vv (1864).

WEBER, Gottfried. 1779–1839 (GER) R.

WEIGEL, Eugene. b. 1910 (USA) R, choir, and orch. (1956).

WEIMER, Hubertus. [nd] (GER?) R, mixed chorus [Ed. Ferrimontana].

WEINRAUCH, Ernest. 1730–1793 (GER) R (cm), soli, choir, and orch. [rec. DA music, CD 77334].

WEISSFLOG, Charles. 1780–1828 (GER) Dies irae.

WELCKER, Max. 1878–1954 (GER) Deutsch Seelenmesse, Op. 134a, SATB unaccompanied [Böhm].

WELSH, Wilmer. b. 1932– (USA) R, satb choir, soprano and baritone soli, and org. (1954). Text: *Book of Common Prayer* (1929) [location: Davidson College].

WENZEL, Eberhard. 1896–1982 (GER) R, Media vita in morte sumus, choir and org. (1968), choir and chamber orch. (1969).

WERT, Giaches de. 1535–1956 (FLEMISH) Missa defunctorum, 4 vv.

WESLEY, Samuel. 1766–1837 (ENG) Missa defunctorum, plainsong, b.c.; Requiem (Introit only), 4 vv (1800).

WETZ, Richard. 1875–1935 (GER) R, Op. 50, soprano and baritone soli, chorus, and orch.

WHITE, John. 1855–1943 (USA/GER) R.

WIDEEN, Ivar. 1871–1951(SWED) R, mixed choir, solo, and org. or piano [Nordiska].

WIDMER, Ernst. b. 1927– (SWIS) R (Trilogie, Part I, Op. 71) (1966).

WIESEHAHN, Willem. 1914–1998 (NETH) R, soli, choir, and orch. (1917) [Donemus].

WIGGINS, Christopher. b. 1956 (ENG) R, mixed voices and orch.; Op. 3 (1973–75), SATB choir, brass, org., and str.

WINDSPERGER, Lothar. 1885–1935 (GER) R, Op. 47, solo vv, choir, orch., and org. (1929).

WITT, Franz. 1834–1888 (GER) MPD, Op. 25a, 2 vv, and org. [Coppenrath, 1876].

WITTINGER, Robert. b. 1945– (HUN) Malador Requiem, Op. 42, mixed choir, narrator, and large orchestra [Moeck 1986][rec. Cadenza, CAD 800889].

WOLL, Erna. B. 1917– (GER) Requiem Deutsche Totenmesse, 1or 2 voices, and org. [Verlag UNIK-Druck, Munich].

WOLLANCK, Frederic. 1782–1831 (GER) R.

WOLPERT, Franz. 1917–1978 (GER) R, soprano, choir, and org.

WÖSS, Josef Venantius. 1863–1943 (AUS) Requiem breve, Op. 3F, mixed choir and org. [Coppenrath].

Y

YOSSIFOV, Alexander. b. 1940– (BUL) R (1973).

YSÄYE, Theophile. 1865–1918 (BELG) R, solo vv, choir, and orch. (c.1906).

Z

ZACHER, Johann Michael. 1651–1712 (AUS) R, 4 vv.

ZAGAGNONI, Francesco. 1767–1844 (ITA) MDR, 4 vv, and orch.

ZAJC, Ivan. 1832–1914 (CROATIA) 4 R, inc. "Jelacic" [B flat M], Op. 244, tenor and bass soli, male choir, str., and org. (1870) [rec. Chorus Spalatensis]; "Preradovic" requiem [A flat M], op. 471, mixed choir, and orch.; Op. 471a is the same work, arranged for 2 sopranos, 2 altos, 2 tenors, 2 basses, mixed choir, and orch. (1872); Novi Requiem [New Requiem], op. 947, 2 tenors, 2 basses, male choir and string orch. (1901); Two other, unfinished requiems exist.

ZAMORANO, Antonio Maria Valencia. 1902–1952 (COL) Misa de requiem.

ZANATA, Domenico. c. 1665–1748 (ITA) R.

ZANDONAI, Riccardo. 1883–1944 (ITA) MDR, choir (1915).

ZANELLA, Amilcare. 1873–1949 (ITA) R.

ZANNETTI, Francesco. 1737–1788 (ITA) 2 R.

ZECHER, Johann Georg. 1716–1778 (AUS) 6 R.

ZEHETBAUER, Johann. 1928–1989 (GER) Alpenländische Requiem für dreigesang und Zither [Promultis, 1981].

ZELENKA, Istvan. b. 1936– (AUS) Requiem pro viventibus, soprano, and string-trio (1957).

ZELTER, Carl Friedrich. 1758–1832 (GER) Ein kurzes Requiem, 4 vv (1823); Requiem für Fasch, 4 vv, choir (1802, lost).

ZERLETT, Johann B. 1859–1935 (GER) R, choir, orch.

ZIANI, Marc Antonio. c. 1653–1715 (ITA) 3 R.

ZINGARELLI, Niccolo. 1752–1837 (ITA) 15 R (5 for vv, and orch.); many separate sections.

ZINTL, Georg. [19th–20th cent.] (GER?) MPD, Op. 10 [DM], 4 mixed vv, and org. [Coppenrath, 1914].

ZOLLER, Georg. 1852–1922 (GER) MPD, Op. 38, 3 male vv, and org. [Coppenrath, 1900].

ZORNOSA, Guillermo Quevado. 1886–1964 ? (COL) Misa de requiem, soli, choir, and orch.

ZORZI, Juan Carlols. b. 1936– (ARG) Requiem, soloists, choir, and orch. (1957).

ZUCCHINI, Gregorio. c. 1540–after 1616 (ITA) MPD, 4 vv (1616).

NONLITURGICAL CHORAL REQUIEMS

ANTON, Gustav. b. 1938– (GER) Requiem: *"Seele vergiss sie nicht."*

APOSTEL, Hans Erich. 1901–1972 (GER) Requiem, Op. 4 (1933), mixed choir (minimum 160 vv) and orch. Text: Rilke [Universal].

BADINGS, Henk. 1907–1987 (BELG/NETH) Burying Friends (Hommage to Francis Poulenc), voice and piano (1963).

BANK, Jacques. b. 1943– (NETH) Requiem voor een levende (1985) [Donemus].

BEDFORD, David. b. 1937– (ENG) Requiem (1980), soprano solo, SSAB choir, and orch. Text: R. L. Stevenson [Universal].

BERGMAN, Erik. b. 1911– (SWE) Requiem over en dod diktane, Op. 67, baritone solo, bass, perc., and organ (1970).

BERTOUILLE, Gerard. 1898–1981 (FRA) Requiem des hommes d'aujourd'hui, soli, choir, and orch.

BETTS, Lorne. 1918–1985 (CAN) A St. Paul Requiem (1960) [text from various sources].

BEURDEN, Bernard van. b. 1933– (NETH) Requiem van het volk (1995), women's chorus, men's chorus, accordion and wind orch. [Donemus, 1995].

BINKERD, Gordon. b. 1936– (USA) Requiem for soldiers lost in ocean transports (1984), SATB chorus [text: Herman Melville] [Boosey and Hawkes].

BISSELL, Keith. 1912–1992 (CAN) Requiem, SSA voices (1967) [text: Robert Louis Stevenson].

BOBROWITZ, David. b. 1945– (USA) Requiem for a Friend (Steven Porter), SATB choir, optional brass, drums, and guitar [Walton].

BROD, Max. 1884–1968 (CZE/ISRAEL) Requiem hebraicum, Op. 20, baritone, piano and orch.

BURKHARDT, Soll. b. 1944– (GER) Kleines Requiem: Korczak und seine Kinder (1991), for voice, flute, clarinet, bass clarinet, contra-bass, and percussion [Tonos Musikverlag, 1994].

CERHA, Friedrich. b. 1926– (CZE) Requiem für Hollenstein (1983), speaker, baritone solo, mixed chorus and orch. Text: Thomas Bernhard; Requiem for Rilke 1989), tenor solo and orch. Text: Carl Zuckmeyer.

CHAILLY, Luciano. b. 1920– (ITA) Kinder-requiem: per 4 voci soliste, voce infantile, coro mista, coro di voci bianche e orchestra. [Ricordi, Milano, 1979].

CORAL, Giampolo. b. 1941– (TRIESTE) Requiem per Jan Palach e altri.

CORNELIUS, Peter. 1824–1874 (GER) Requiem, *"Seele vergiss sie nicht,"* 6-part, unaccompanied, mixed choir (1872).

DALBY, Martin. b. 1942– (ENG) Requiem for Philip Sparrow, mezzo-soprano, choir, 3 oboes and strings. (1967).

DANIELPOUR, Richard. b. 1956– (USA) An American Requiem (2001), Mz,TB soli, SATB choir, and orch. [text: Catholic requiem, Whitman, Ralph Waldo Emerson, Michael Harper, Hilda Dolittle, anon].

DAVID, Johann Nepomuk. 1895–1977 (AUS) Requiem Chorale, solo vv, choir, and orch. (1956).

DE JONG, Marinus. 1891–1984 (BELG) *"Flemish Requiem"* Kerkhofblommen, Op. 108. 1957).

DENISOV, Edison. 1929–1996 (RUS) Requiem, soprano and tenor soli, mixed choir, and orch. (1963) [Edition Sirkorski 876].

DESSAU, Paul. 1894–1979 (GER) Requiem für Lumumba, soprano and baritone soli, speaker, chorus, and instruments (1963).

DUSAPIN, Pascal. B. 1955 (FRA) Requiem[s], satb choir, woodwinds, and brass.

EINFELDT, Dieter. b. 1935– (GER) Gomorrha: ein Requiem für Hamburg [Peer c. 1986].

EISLER, Hanns. 1898–1962 (GER) Lenin: Requiem for alto and baritone soli, choir, and orch. (1958, 1st perf.) [Deutscher Verlag für Musik] [rec. Berlin Classics 0092342BC].

ELWELL, Herbert. 1898–1974 (USA) Lincoln: Requiem aeternam, baritone solo, chorus, and orch. (1946).

ETTINGER, Max. 1874–1951 (GER) Jiddisch Requiem (1947).

FELLAGARA, Vittorii. b. 1927– (ITA) Requiem di Madrid (Lorca), chorus and orch. (1958); Dies Irae (Lorca), chorus, 6 trumpets, timpani and percussion (1958).

FINZI, Gerald. 1901–1956 (ENG) Requiem da Camera, baritone solo, choir, and orch.

GAGNEBIN, Henri. 1886–1977 (FRA/SWIS) Requiem des vanities du monde, soli, choir, and orch. (1938–39).

GÁL, Hans. 1890–1987 (AUS) Requiem für Mignon, choir, and orch. (1923).

GIESEN, Willy. 1911–1981 (GER) Requiem: *"Vergiss sie nicht."*

GNESSIN, Michael. 1883–1957 (RUS) Requiem (piano quintet) (1912–13).

GUIDI-DREI, Claudio. 1927–1995 (ARG) Requiem sin palabras, Op. 52.

HALLBERG, Bjorn Wilho. b. 1938– (SWE) Missa pro defunctis for soprano solo, choir, orch., and electronics. Text: Dag Hammarskjold [Sveriges Radio 1969].

HALLEN, Andreas. 1864–1925 (SWE) Requiescat, solo vv, chorus, and piano (1910).

HAMBRAEUS, Bengt. 1928–2000 (SWE) Cantata pro defunctis, baritone, and organ (1951).

HANNAY, Roger. b. 1930– (USA) Requiem (Whitman), chorus and orch. (1961).

HOLMBOE, Vagn. 1909–1996 (DEN) Requiem (Hebbel), boy's vv, and chamber orch. (1931).

HUBER, Klaus. b. 1924– (SWIS) Kleines Requiem für Heinrich Boll, a cappella choir and bass-baritone solo [Ricordi, 1994].

IMBRIE, Matthew. b. 1921– (USA) Requiem in Memoriam John H. Imbrie (1984) for SATB choir, soprano solo and orch. [unpub. score at Columbia University].

JERGENSON, Dale. b. 1935– (USA) Requiem for a city, 6 choirs, and pre-recorded tape.

JOSEPHS, Wilfred. 1927–97 (ENG) Requiem for baritone soloist, double choir, string quartet, and orch. (1963) [Weinberger].

KALLSTENIUS, Edvin. 1887–1967 (SWE) Nar vi do [When we are dying], Op. 11 (1919).

KASEMETS, Udo. b. 1919– (CAN) [Estonia] Little Requiem, Op. 15 (1949) for soprano and alto speaker, SSAA choir [text: Udo Kasemets]; Requiem (1992).

KELEMEN, Milko. b. 1924– (CROATIA) Requiem for Vukovar, Osijek, Dubrovnik, Sarajevo (1995).

KOECHLIN, Charles. 1867–1950 (FRA) Requiem des pauvres bougnes (1937, inc.).

KOMEDER, Krzysztof. 1931–1969 (POL) Daytime Requiem.

KOSTITSYN, Evgeni. (RUS) American Requiem, mixed choir, and orch. [Texts: A. Lincoln, G. Washington, Nostradamus, Kostitsyn-English/Latin.].

KOX, Hans. b. 1930– (NETH) Requiem for Europe, four spatialized choirs with instrumental groups, 2 organs and orch. (1971).

KRUSE, Bjørn. b. 1946– (NOR) Vindsalme for dei døde: Missa pro defunctis bello secundo mundi. SBAR soli, satbchoir, timpani [text: Paal-Helge Haugen] (1995).

LADISLAV, Simon. B. 1929– (CZECH) Requiem [for the Dead, for Those to Whom Music was Their Life]: Oratorio for soli, mixed choir, 2 Jazz Bands and organ.

LAU, Heinz. 1925–1975 (GER) Requiem für eine Verfolgte—in memoriam Anne Frank, tenor and string quartet (1961).

LAVALLE-GARCIA, Armando. b. 1924– (MEX) R. y canto de tristeza, mixed choir, orch., and percussion (1968).

LAZAR, Simon. b. 1948– (BUL) Holocaust: A Requiem for the Fate of the Jews (1993–95), choir and electronic media [rec. Gega, GD 104].

LEITNER, Ernst Ludwig. b. 1943– (GER) Requiem 1991 in memoriam Leonard Bernstein for soprano solo, satb choir, brass quartet, organ, harp and percussion battery [Doblinger, 1993].

LENS, Nicholas. b. 1957– (BELG) Flamma, The Fire Requiem, for choir, soloists and instruments (1994).

LISSMANN, Kurt. 1902–1983 (GER) Requiem: *"Seele, vergiss sie nicht."*

LLOYD, David. 1883–1948 (WALES) Requiem cymraeg (Welsh Requiem), solo vv, and choir (1941).

LOCKWOOD, Normand. b. 1906– (USA) Requiem: *"When lilacs last in the dooryard bloomed,"* tenor solo, choir, and orch. (1931).

LUYTENS, Elisabeth. 1906–1983 (ENG) Requiem for the living (1948).

MARX, Adolf. 1795–1866 (GER) Gebet für die Verstorbenen (Requiem), Op. 7 (1841).

MASSEUS, Jan. b. 1913–1999? (NETH) In memoriam Lucia, Op. 78 (1987?).

MATTSSON, Jack. b.1954– (FIN) Aland Requiem (1990), S, Bar soli, mixed choir, and orch. [text: Valdemar Nyman].

MC CABE, John. b. 1939– (ENG) Requiem sequence, sop and piano (1971).

MILLS, Richard. b. 1949– (AUSTRALIA) Requiem Diptych (1996).

MONK, Meredith. b. 1942– (USA) New York Requiem for voice and piano [rec. ECM, New Series 78118-21589-2].

MÚLLER-ZÚRICH, Paul. 1898–1993 (SWIS) Chor der Toten, Op. 16, chorus, wind orch., double-bass, and organ.

NIELSEN, Riccardo. 1908–1982 (ITA) Requiem nella miniera, solo vv, choir, and orch. (1958).

O'RIADA, Sean. 1931–1971 (IRE) Requiem for a Soldier, soprano, tenor, baritone soli, choir, and organ (1968).

PASHCHENKO, Andrey. 1885–1972 (RUS) Requiem in Memory of the Heroic Warrior, solo vv, chorus, and orch. (1942) For the blockade of Leningrad in 1942.

PETKOV, Dimiter. b. 1919– (BUL) Reqviem sa matrosa [Sailor's Requiem] (1968).

PFLUGER, Hans Georg. b. 1944– (GER) Memento Mori (1995) A Requiem according to the texts of Georg Trackl and the Missa pro defunctis. Bass solo, choir, and orch. [rec. Cadenza 800910].

PINTO, Alejandro. b. 1922– (ARG) Requiem para Alejandra.

PITTON, Robert. b. 1921– (USA) Requiem: A cantata for the Dead and the Living Dead (1983), Text: the Bible, Marcus Aurelius Antonius, Mother Goose, and the Catholic Mass for the Dead. Unpublished. 3 solo voices altered electronically.

PLUISTER, Simon. 1913–1995 (NETH) Requiem for alto solo, mixed choir, string orch., brass, and organ [Donemus, 1995].

POLIFRONE, Jon. b. 1938– (USA) Requiem: For those we love (c. 1993).

PUSZTAI, Tibor. b. 1946– (HUN) Requiem Profana for solo voices and chamber orch.

RAINIER, Priaulx. 1903–1986 (SOUTH AFRICA) Requiem for tenor solo and choir (1955/6) Text by David Gascoigne) [rec. Redcliffe Recordings, RR 011].

RAZDOLINA, Zlata. b. 1959– (RUS/ISRAEL) Holocaust Requiem: The song of the murdered Jewish People [poetry of Itzhak Katzenelson].

REINARTZ, Jean. 1813–1857 (GER) Requiem: *"Seele, vergiss sie nicht"*.

REINHARDT, Hans. b. 1911– (GER) Requiem: *"Seele, vergiss sie nicht"* (1987).

REUTTER, Hermann. 1900–1985 (GER) Ein kleines Requiem für Bass, Cello, and Clarinet (1961).

RIBARI, Antal. b. 1924– (HUN) Requiem for the Lover for alto and tenor soli, chamber choir, and small orch. [poetry of Swinburne, Shelley and Blake].

RIEMANN, Aribert. b. 1936– (GER) Requiem for baritone, cello, and orch. (1974) Text: Otfried Bathe.

RUBENSTEIN, Anton. 1829–1894 (RUS) Requiem für Mignon.

SALMENHAARA, Erkki. b. 1941– (FIN) Requiem Profanum (Beaudlaire, Espiru, The Declaration of Human Rights), soprano, alto and baritone soli, organ, piano, and strings (1968–69).

SAUSENG, Wolfgang. b. 1956– (GER) Requiem, speaker, 12 singers, piano, organ, bass, and percussion. (1984).

SCHAUENSEE, Francois Joseph de. 1720–after 1790 (SWIS) requiem.

SCHEDLICH, David. 1607–1687 (GER) 15 Funeral Lieder, 1–4 vv.

SCHEIDT, Gottfried. 1593–1661 (GER) *Selig sind die Toten*, Funeral music for Sophie Elisabeth, Duchess of Saxony (1650); Funeral Work, 8 vv (1620).

SCHERER, Sebastian. 1631–1712 (GER) Trauer und Klaggesang, 5 vv, and b.c. (1664).

SCHIDLOWSKY, Leon. b. 1931– (ISRAEL) Requiem, 12 solo vv (1968); Requiem (Rilke) soprano solo and orch. (1954).

SCHUBERT, Heino. b. 1928– (GER) Kleines Requiem (*Keiner weiss, wie arm er ist*).

SCHUMANN, Robert. 1810–1856 (GER) Requiem für Mignon.

SCHWEIZER Rolf. b. 1936– (GER) Requiem, 23.02.1945; für Tote und Lebende (1995).

SEBASTIANI, Johann. 1622–1683 (GER) Funeral Songs.

SENATOR, Ronald. b. 1926– (ENG) Holocaust Requiem (1981).

SESSIONS, Roger. 1896–1985 (USA) "When lilacs last in the door-yard bloomed" (1970), soprano, alto and baritone soli, chorus, and orch.

SIMON, Hermann. 1896–1948 (GER) Requiem in bello for strings, soprano, choir, and organ.

SIMPOLI, Giuseppe. b. 1946– (ITA) Requiem Hashirim, unaccompanied (1976).

STREICHER, Theodor. 1874–1940 (AUS) Mignons Exequien, chorus, children's choir, and orch.

SZERVANSKY, Endre. 1911–1977 (HUN) Requiem (Dark Heaven), Pilinszky, oratorio (1963).

TAPKOV, Dimiter. b. 1929– (BUL) Requiem for Song Mi (1970).

TATE, Phyllis. 1911–1987 (ENG) Secular Requiem for chorus and orch. (1967).

TUBIN, Eduard. 1905–1982 (GER) Requiem for fallen soldiers (1979).

VASS, Lajos. b. 1927– (HUN) Requiem a hosok emlekere [Requiem in memory of the heroes] (1963), chorus and orch.

VERIKIVSKY, Mykhaylo. 1896–1962 (UKRAINE) Requiem for Lysenko (1922).

VON EINEM, Gottfried. 1918–1996 (AUS) Tier-Requiem, Op. 104. Text: Lotte Ingrisch [Doblinger, 1997].

WEHRLI, Werner. 1892–1944 (SWIS) Ein Weltliches Requiem, Op. 25, 4 solo vv, chorus, children's choir, and orch. (1928).

WEILL, Kurt. 1900–1950 (GER) Das Berliner Requiem (Brecht), tenor, baritone and bass soloists, chorus, and 15 instruments (1928).

WOLFURT, Kurt. 1880–1957 (GER) Requiem für die Gefallen, Op. 38, solo vv, chorus, orch., and organ.

WUSTIN, Alexander. b. 1943– (GER) Kleines Requiem, for soprano and string quartet [Frankfurt am Main, Belaieff, c. 1998].

ZEISL, Eric. 1905–1959 (USA) Requiem Concertante, satb soli, satb choir, and orch. (1933–34).

ZIMMERMANN, Bernd Alois. 1918–1970 (GER) Requiem für einen jungen Dichter, speaker, soprano, baritone, 3 choirs, orchestra, jazz ensemble, organ, and tape (1967–69).

ZOLL, Paul. 1907–1978 (GER) Requiem for alto and tenor soli, mixed choir, and orch. Text from the Totenmesse of Ernst Weichert].

ZOLLNER, Heinrich. 1854–1941 (GER) Helden-Requiem (Hero's Requiem).

ZSCHIEGNER, Fritz. 1813–1863 (GER) Requiem: *"Seele, vergiss sie nicht"* (1888).

REQUIEMS FOR SOLO VOICE(S)

GILSE, Jan van. 1881–1954 (NETH) R.

HALLER, Hans Peter. b. 1929– (GER) R, alto solo and viola [Hanssler].

HEISS, Herman. 1897–1966 (GER) R, SA soli, strings [Breitkopf].

LECHNER, Konrad. 1911–1989 (GER) R, Alto solo, instruments [Peters].

ROOT, George. 1820–1895 (USA) A Requiem (1852).

SCHMID, Reinhold. 1902–1980 (GER) R, A/BAR solo, piano [Doblinger].

ORCHESTRAL AND INSTRUMENTAL WORKS

BIBIK, Valentin. b. 1940– (UKRAINE) Dies Irae: 39 variations for piano (1993).

BOUSTED, Donald. b. 1957– (ENG) A Woldgate Requiem (1993), solo organ.

BOŽIČ, Darijan. b. 1933– (CROATIA) Requiem spominu umorjenega vojaka mojega oceta (Requiem of a killed soldier, my father) (1969), electronic media, (text by Robert Rozdestvenski).

BRANT, Henry. b. 1913– (CAN) A Requiem in Summer (1934) chamber orch.
BRITTEN, Benjamin. 1913–1976 (ENG) Sinfonia da requiem (1941).
CHELIUS, Oskar von. 1859–1923 (GER) Requiem for Orchestra.
COURTER, John. b. 1941– (USA) Gregorian Triptych: requiem mass for carillon.
HANSON, Howard. 1896–1981 (USA) Symphony #4, Op. 311 "Requiem" (1943).
HENZE, Hans-Werner. b. 1926– (GER) Requiem: Nine Sacred Concertos (1993).
HOVHANESS, Alan. 1911–1999 (USA) Requiem and Resurrection for brass choir and percussion, Op. 224 (1968).
FUKUSHIMA, Kazuo. b. 1930– (JAP) Requiem for a flute (1956).
GORECKI, Henryk. b. 1933– (POL) Kleines Requiem für eine Polka (1993).
JONES, Samuel. b. 1935– (USA) A Symphonic Requiem (Variations on a theme of Howard Hanson) (1983).
JORDANOVA, Victoria. [20th cent.] (YUGO) Requiem for Bosnia (1994), piano, harp.
KILAR, Wojciech. b. 1932– (POL) Requiem Father Kolbe.
KOSTITSYN, Evgeni. b. (RUS) Requiem, violin and orch.
NYSTEDT, Kurt. b. 1915– (NOR) Requiem pia memoria, 9 wind instruments (1972).
PERRY, Julia. 1924–1959 (USA?) Requiem for orchestra (1959).
PIRONHOFF, Simeon. b. 1927– (GER) Requiem for an Unknown Young Man (1968) 13 Strings.
PORCELIJN, David. b. 1947 ? (NETH) Symphonisch Requiem: voor orkest, Op. 1.
RAPF, Kurt. b. 1922– (GER) Requiem für Orgel, Blechblaser und Schlagzeug (1976) [pub. Wien and München, Doblinger, 1981].
RAUTAVAARA, Einojuhani. b. 1928– (FIN) A Requiem in Our Time, Op. 3. orch. (1953).
RAYKI, Gyorgy. b. 1921– (HUN/ECUADOR) Concert Requiem for V and 36 players (1965).
RICHTER, Marga. b. 1926– (USA) Requiem for piano.
SANTUCCI, Marco. 1762–1843 (ITA) Dies irae melodies with orch.
SCHAFER, R. Murray. b. 1933– (CAN) Requiem for the party girl (1966).
SCULTHORPE, Peter. b. 1929– (AUSTRALIA) Requiem (for cello).
SHOSTAKOVICH, Dimitry. 1906–1975 (RUS) Requiem for strings, Op. 1146.
SMITH, Cyril. 1909–1974 (ENG) Requiem for Violin and Orch. (1939).
SORABJI, Kaikhosru. 1892–1988 (JAP) Variations and Fugue on the Dies irae, for piano.
TAKEMITSU, Toru. 1930–1996 (JAP) Requiem for strings (1957).
TJEKNAVORIAN, Loris. b. 1937– (IRAN/ARMENIA) Symphony #1, Op. 20a (Requiem for the Massacred), trumpet, percussion; Symphony #1, Op. 20b (Requiem for the Massacred), chorus and orch.
VEHAR, Persis Parshall. b. 1937– (USA) Requiem for heroes, full orchestra.
WADDLE, P. Kellach. b. 1967– (USA) Requiem for bass trombone and chamber orch. (1998).
WAGEMANS, Peter-Jan. b. 1952– (BELG) Requiem, string orchestra and percussion.

Bibliography

ENCYLOPEDIAS, LEXICONS, CATALOGUES, AND DICTIONARIES

Arizaga, Rodolfo. *Enciclopedia de la música argentina*. Buenos Aires: Fondo Nacional de las Artes, 1971.

Blume, Friedrich, ed. *Die Musik in Geschichte und Gegenwart. Allgemeine Enzyklopädie der Musik unter Mitarbeit zahlreicher Musikforscher des In und Auslandes. . . .* 17 vols. Kassel und Basel: Bärenreiter, 1949–1968.

Clugnet, Leon. *Dictionnaire Grèc-Francais des noms liturgiques en usage dans l'église grècque*. Paris: Alphonse Picard & Fils, Editeurs, 1895.

Contemporary Hungarian Composers. 4th Ed. Budapest: Editio Musica, 1979.

Corte, Andrea della and G. M. Gatti. *Dizionario di musica*, 6th Ed. Torino: G. B. Paravia, 1959.

DeAngelis, Alberto. *L'Italia musicale d'oggi. Dizionario dei musicisti, compositori, direttori d'orchestra, conartisti, insegnanti, liutai, cantanti, scrittori musicali, librettisti, editori musicali, ecc.* 3. Ed., corredata di un appendice. Roma: 1928.

Encyclopédie de la Musique. 3 vols. Paris: Fasquelle, 1958–61.

Eitner, Robert. *Biographisch-bibliographisches Quellenlexicon der Musiker und Musikgelehrten der christlichen Zeitrechnung bis zur Mitte des 19. Jahrhunderts*. 10 Bde. Leipzig: Breitkopf und Härtel, 1900–1904.

Fétis, Francois Joseph. *Biographie universelle des musiciens et bibliographie générale de la musique*. 8 vols. in 4. Paris: Firmin Diderot Fréres et Cie., 1868–70.

Gebhard, Hans, ed. *Harenberg Chormusikführer vom Kammerchor bis zum Oratorium*. Harenberg, 1999.

Günther, Bernhard, ed. *Lexikon zeitgenossischen Musik aus Österreich. Komponisten und Komponistinnen des 20. Jahrhunderts*. Music Information Center Austria, 1997.

Honneger, Marc and Paul Prevost. *Dictionnaire des oeuvres de l'art vocal*. Paris: Bordas, 1991.

———. *Dictionnaire de la Musique*. 6 Vols. Paris: Bordas, 1970.

International Biographischer Index der Musik. Komponisten, Dirigenten, Instrumentalisten und Sänger. 2 Bde. Munich, New Providence, London, Paris: Saur, 1995.

Kallman, Helmut. *Catalogue of Canadian Composers*. Canadian Broadcasting Service, 1952.

Komponisten der Gegenwart in deutschen Komponisten-Verband. Ein Handbuch. Berlin, 1985.

Kovačevic, Krešimir. *Leksikon Jugoslavenski Muzike.* 2 vols. Zagreb: Jugoslavenski Leksikografski Zavod "Miroslav Krleza," 1984.

Kuhn, Laura, ed. [Nicolas Slonmisky]. *Baker's Biographical Dictionary of 20th Century Classical Musicians.* New York: Schirmer Books, 1997.

Oelmann, Werner and Alexander Wagner. *Reclams Chormusik und Oratorien Führer.* Stuttgart: Philipp Reclam, 1999.

Orovio, Helio. *Diccionario de la música cubana.* Havana: Editorial Letras Cubanas, 1981.

Pareyon, Gabriel. *Diccionario de Música en Mexico.* Guadalajara: Secretaria de Cultura de Jalisco, 1995.

Sadie, Stanley, ed. *The New Grove Dictionary of Music and Musicians,* 20 vols. London: Macmillan Publishers Limited, 1980.

Schellert, Peter and Verena Schellert. *Die Messe in der Musik. Ein Lexikon* 3. Bde. Ulm: Fritz Speigel Buch GmbH, 1999.

Thompson, Oscar. *The International Cyclopedia of Music and Musicians.* Eleventh Ed. New York: Dodd, Mead & Company, 1985.

MONOGRAPHS

Albrecht, Christoph. *Einführung in die Liturgik.* Göttingen: Vandenhoeck & Ruprecht, 1995.

Anthony, James R. *French Baroque Music from Beaujoyeulx to Rameau.* Portland, Oregon: Amadeus Press, 1997.

Aries, Philippe. *The Hour of Our Death.* New York: Alfred A. Knopf, 1981. Originally published in 1977 as *L'Homme devant la Mort.*

Ayestarán, Lauro. *La Música en el Paraguay.* 2 Vols. Montevideo: Servico oficial de difusión radio electrica, 1953.

Blum, Klaus. *Hundert Jahre ein deutsches Requiem von Johannes Brahms: Entstehung, Uraufführung, Interpretation, Würdigung.* Tutzing: H. Schneider, 1971.

Blume, Friedrich. *Geschichte der Evangelischen Kirchenmusik.* Kassel, Basel: Bärenreiter, 1965.

———. translated as: *Protestant Church Music. A History.* New York: W. W. Norton, 1974.

Bulletin de la Societe de l'histoire de Paris, XXXIII, 1906 [an anonymous account of the funeral of Francis I] pub: H. Omont.

Bussi, Francesco. *Storia, tradizione e arte nel "Requiem" di Cavalli.* Milano: Suvini Zerboni, 1978.

Capelle, Dom B. *"L'Antienne In Paradisum."* LouvaTravaux Liturgiques de doctrine et d'histoire. 1967. 252ff.

Cessac, Catherine. *Marc Antoine Charpentier.* Portland, Oregon: Amadeus Press, 1995.

Chang, Chi-ren. *An Hwun Chu Tsung Lwun* [A discussion of the requiem]. Taipei: Chung Li Hwei, 1999.

Clerval, M. l'Abbe. *L'Ancienne Maitrise de Notre Dame de Chartres du Ve siecle à la Révolution.* Paris: Alphonse Picard et Fils, 1899.

Cooke, Mervyn. *Britten: War Requiem*. Cambridge: Cambridge University Press, 1996.

Cormican, Brendan. *Mozart's Death: Mozart's Requiem*. Belfast: Amadeus Press, 1991.

Cuyler, Louise. *The Emperor Maximillian I and Music*. Oxford Univ. Press: New York, 1973.

Decker, Harold and Julius Herford. *Choral Conducting: A Symposium*. Englewood Cliffs, NJ: Prentice-Hall Inc., 1973.

De la Espriella Ossio, Alfonso. *Historia de la música en Colombia*. Santa Fe de Bogota: Grupo Editorial Norma, 1997.

DeVenny, David. *American Masses and Requiem: A descriptive guide*. Berkeley, California: Fallen Leaf Press, 1990.

Dix, Dom Gregory. *The Shape of the Liturgy*. London: Dacre Press, Adam & Charles Black, 1964.

Duffy, Eamon. *The Stripping of the Altars: Traditional Religion in England, c. 1400–1580*. New Haven, London: Yale University Press, 1992.

Fabris, Dinko. *Naples. City of Celebrations from the 14th to 19th Centuries*. Paris: Opus 111, 1999.

Fellerer, Karl Gustav. *Geschichte der katholischen Kirchenmusik*. Düsseldorf: Musikverlag Schwann, 1949.

———. *The History of Catholic Church Music*. [translated by Francis A. Benner, C. S. S. R.] Baltimore: Helicon Press, 1961.

Gartner, Heinz. *Mozarts Requiem und die Geschäfte der Constanze Mozart*. München: Langen Müller, 1986.

Giesey, Ralph. *The Royal Funeral Ceremony in Renaissance France*. Geneve: Libraire E. Droz, 1960.

Girard, Sharon. *Funeral Music and Customs in Venezuela*. Special Studies no. 20, Center for Latin American Studies, Tempe, Arizona: Arizona State University, 1980.

Girardi, Michele and Pierluigi Petrobelli. *Messa per Rossini: la storia, il testo, la musica*. Milano, Parma: Istituto di studi verdiani. Ricordi, 1988. [Quaderni dell'istituto di studi verdiani, 5]

Heinemann, Michael. *Johannes Brahms, ein deutsches Requiem: nach Worten der Heiligen Schrift, Op. 45; eine Einführung*. Göttingen und Braunschweig: Hainholz, 1998.

Hesbert, R. J. "*Les Pieces de chant des messes pro defunti dans la tradition manuscrite.*" Actes du Congres international de musicque sacrée, Rome, 1959 (Tournai, 1952).

Jungmann, Joseph. *The Mass of the Roman Rite: Its Origins and Development*. 2 vols. New York, Boston (and others): Benziger Brothers, Inc., 1950.

Kuhlmann, Jürgen. *Requiem: Sinn der Liturgie: Hinweise für Sänger und Hörer der lateinischen Totenmesse*. Nürnberg: Unitas Verlag, 1993.

Mann, Alfred, ed. *Randall Thompson. A Choral Legacy*. Boston: E. C. Schirmer, 1983.

Maunder, Richard. *Mozart's Requiem: On preparing a new edition*. Oxford: Clarendon Press, 1992.

Minear, Paul. *Death Set to Music*. Louisville, Kentucky: John Knox Press, 1987.

Morosan, Vladimir. *Choral Performance in Pre-Revolutionary Russia*. Ann Arbor, Michigan: UMI Press, 1986.

————. *Monuments of Russian Sacred Music. One Thousand Years of Russian Church Music, 988–1988.* Series I, vol. I. Washington, D. C.: Musica Russica, 1991.

Moser, Hans Joachim. [trans. by Carl Pfatteicher] *Heinrich Schütz: His Life and Work.* St. Louis: Concordia Publishing House, 1959.

Murray, Dom Gregory. *The Choral Chants of the Mass.* Lillington, UK: The Society of St. Gregory no. 7, n.d.

Musgrave, Michael. *Brahms: A German Requiem.* Cambridge: Cambridge University Press, 1996.

Noone, Michael. *Music and Musicians in the Escorial Liturgy under the Habsburgs 1563–1700.* Rochester, New York: Rochester University Press, 1999.

Ormond, John. *Requiem and Celebration.* Swansea, UK: Davis, 1969.

Pahlen, Kurt. *The World of the Oratorio.* Portland, Oregon: Amadeus Press, 1985.

Passadore, Francesco and Franco Rossi. *San Marco: Vitalita di una tradizione, Il fondo musicale e la Cappella del Settecento ad oggo.* 4 vols. Venezia: Edizioni Fondazione Levi, 1994.

Perez-Sanjurjo, Elena. *Historia de la Música Cubana.* Miami, Florida: La Moderna Poesia, Inc., 1986.

Prosperi, Virgilio. *La Messa da Requiem di Giuseppe Verdi: guida all'ascolto.* Cortona: Calossci, 1994.

Robertson, Alec. *Requiem: Music of Mourning & Consolation.* New York: F. Praeger, 1967.

Robinson, Michael. *Naples and Neapolitan Opera.* Oxford, UK: Clarendon Press of Oxford University Press, 1972.

Rosen, David. *Verdi: Requiem.* Cambridge: Cambridge University Press, 1995.

Rowell, Geoffrey. *The Liturgy of Christian Burial.* London: Alcuin Club, 1977.

Rush, Alfred C. *Death and Burial in Christian Antiquity.* No. 1 of the Catholic University of America Studies in Chrisitian Antiquity. Edited by Johannes Quasten. Washington, D.C.: The Catholic University of America Press, 1957.

Schnerich, Alfred. *Messe und Requiem seit Haydn und Mozart.* Wien & Leipzig: Stern, 1909.

Srawley, J. H. *The Early History of the Liturgy.* Second Ed., Cambridge: Cambridge University Press, 1957.

Stevenson, Robert. *Spanish Cathedral Music in the Golden Age.* Berkeley and Los Angeles: University of California, 1961.

Taft, Robert. *The Byzantine Rite: A Short History.* Collegeville, Minnesota: The Liturgical Press, 1992.

Thoinan, Er. *Déploration de Guillaume Crétin sur le trépas de Jean Okeghem.* Paris: A. Claudin, Libraire-Editeur, 1884.

Thompson, Bard, ed. *Liturgies of the Western Church.* Cleveland, New York: Meredian Books, The World Publishing Co., 1961.

Thomson, Virgil. *Music With Words.* New Haven: Yale University Press, 1989.

Unverricht, Hubert, ed. *Der Caecilianismus, Anfange-Grundlagen-Wirkungen.* Internationales Symposium zur Kirchenmusik des 19. Jahrhunderts. Tutzing: Hans Schneider, 1988.

Ursprung, Otto. *Die Katholische Kirchenmusik.* Potsdam: Akademische Verlagsgesellschaft Athenaion, 1931.

Volek, Tomislav and Stanislav Jares. *Dejiny Ceské Hudby v Obrazech*. [The History of Czech Music in Pictures] Prague: Edition Supraphon, 1977.

Wagner, Peter. *Geschichte der Messe*, [History of the Mass]. Hildesheim: Georg Olms Verlagsbuchhandlung, 1963. [reprint of the 1913 Breitkopf & Härtel edition]

Weinandt, Elwyn A. *Choral Music of the Church*. New York: The Free Press, 1965.

Wolff, Christoph. *Mozart's Requiem: Historical & Analytical Studies, Documents and Score*. Berkeley, California: University of California Press, 1993.

Wright, Craig. *Music and Ceremony at Notre Dame of Paris 500–1550*. New York: Cambridge University Press, 1989.

BIOGRAPHIES

Glover, Jane. *Cavalli*. New York: St. Martin's Press, 1978.

Henschel, Sir George. *Musings & Memories of a Musician*. London: Macmillan and Co., 1918.

Hitchcock, H. Wiley. *Marc Antoine Charpentier*. Oxford, New York: Oxford University Press, 1990.

Hunt, Jon Leland. *Giovanni Paisello*. [NOA Monograph Series, Vol. II] National Opera Association, 1975.

Klauwell, Otto. *Theodor Gouvy*. Berlin: BerlHarmonie Verlagsgesellschaft für Literatur und Kunst, 1902.

Krenek, Ernst. *Johann Ockegem*. New York: Sheed and Ward, 1953.

Reinecke, Erich. *Friedrich Kiel: Sein Leben und sein Werke*. [Phd. Diss, Univ. of Köln, 1936] Hagen, 1976.

Steinhardt, Milton. *Jacobus Vaet. Motets*. East Lansing: Michigan State College Press, 1951.

Wellesz, Egon. *Fux*. [Oxford Studies of Composers no. 1] New York, Toronto: Oxford University Press, 1965.

MUSIC SCORES AND SERVICE BOOKS

All music scores used by the author are listed with the appropriate composition. [Most scholarly editions contain useful historical and biographical data.]

The Armenian Church of America, ed. *Divine Liturgy of the Armenian Apostolic Church*. Fifth Ed. London: St. Sarkis Church, 1984.

The Book of Common Prayer [proposed] . . . according to the use of the Episcopal Church. New York: The Church Hymnal Corporation & The Seabury Press, 1977.

Gates of Prayer: The New Union Prayer Book. New York. Central Conference of American Rabbis. 1975.

Hapgood, Isabel. *Service Book of the Holy Orthodox-Catholic Apostolic Church*. Seventh Ed. Englewood, New Jersey: Antiochian Christian Archdiocese, 1996.

Hatzopoylos, Harry. *Funeral Services, According to the rite of the Greek Orthodox Church*. Boston, Massachussetts. [n.d.].

The Liber Usualis, ed. by the Benedictines of Solesmes. Tournai and New York: Desclee & Cie, [1956].

Lopez-Calo, Jose (1840–1899). *Obras Musicales de Juan Montes.* Vol. II Oficio y misa de Difuntos [para voces y orquesta u organo] Xunta de Galicia. Santiago de Compostella: Conselleria de Cultura e Xuventude, 1992.

Order of Christian Funerals. [Approved for use in the dioceses of the USA by the National Conference of Catholic Bishops and confirmed by the Holy See] New York: Catholic Book Publishing Co., 1989.

Sputnik Psalomshchika. Third Ed. Petrograd, 1916 [Contains the monophonic chants used for the *Panikhida* service, as well as the chants for all services during the liturgical year.]

Veselinovitch, Rev. Svetozar, comp. *The Funeral Service of the Orthodox Church.* Carmichaels, Pennsylvania: St. George Serbian Orthodox Church of Masontown, 1995.

DISSERTATIONS

Abercrombie, E. Wayne. *A Conductor's analysis of Johannes Brahms Ein Deutsches Requiem, Opus 45.* [Indiana Univ., 1974].

Adamski-Störmer, Ursula. *Requiem aeternam: Tod und Trauer in 19. Jahrhundert im Spiegel einer musikalischen Gattung.* Frankfurt am Main, Lang, 1991. [Reihe: Europäische Hochschuleschriften: Reihe 36, Musikwissenschaft; 66 Münster. [Univ. Diss. 1991].

Auerbach, Johanna Maria. *Die Messen des Francesco Durante. 1684–1755. Ein Beitrag zur Geschichte der neapolitanischen Kirchenmusik.* [Univ. of Munich, 1954].

Bauer, Hans-Günther. *Requiem Kompositionen in neuer Musik: vergleichende Untersuchen zum Verhaltnis von Sprache der Liturgie und Musik.* [Tübingen Univ., 1984]

Carlson, Jon Olaf. *Selected Masses of Niccolo Jommelli.* [DMA treatise, Univ. of Illinois at Urbana-Champaign, 1974].

Cole, Vincent Lewis. *Analyses of "Symphony of Psalms" (1930, rev. 1948) and "Requiem Canticles" (1966) by Igor Stravinsky and "Canticle for large chorus and orchestra on a text from Walt Whitman"* (original composition). [Univ. of California, Los Angeles, 1980]. Ann Arbor, Michigan: UMI.

Eaton, Robert P. Maurice Duruflé's Requiem, Op. 9: An analysis for performance. [Univ. of Hartford, 1991] Ann Arbor, Michigan: UMI.

Ebel, Beatrice. *Die Salzburger Requiemtradition im 18. Jahrhundert: Untersuchen zu den Voraussetzungen im Mozarts Requiem.* München, [Univ. Diss., 1996].

Eberle, Gottfried. *Unterrichtsmaterial zu Johannes Brahms: ein deutsches Requiem.* BerlUrsula Meier Bond, 1983. [Reihe Arbeiterspapiere].

Freund, Anna Katharina. *Benjamin Britten: War Requiem, Op. 66.* Hochschuleschrift, Wien. Hochschule für Musik und darst. Kunst, Dipl. Arbeit. 1995.

Girard, Sharon. *The Requiem Mass and Music for the Dead in Venezuela.* [Univ. of California, Los Angeles, 1975].

Green, Daniel J. *A Study of Andrew Lloyd-Webber's Requiem.* [Univ. of Miami, Coral Gables, 1988] Ann Arbor, Michigan: UMI.

Hall, William Dawson. *The Requiem Mass: A study of performance practices from the Baroque Era to the present day as related to four settings by Gilles, Mozart, Verdi and Britten.* [DMA. Univ. of Southern California, 1970.] Ann Arbor, Michigan: UMI.

Harwood, Gregory. *The genesis of Robert Schumann's liturgical works and a study of compositional process in the Requiem, Op. 148.* [New York Univ., 1991] Ann Arbor, Mich: UMI.

Hausfäter, Dominique. *Les "Requiem" en musique de 1789 á 1840.* [Université de Paris-Sorbonne, Paris, 1995] [Mikrofiche-Ausgaben; Lille, Atelier de Reproduction des Thèses de l'Univ. de Lille 3. 1996].

Jarjisian, Peter. *The influence of Gregorian chant on Maurice Duruflé's Requiem Op. 9.* [Univ. of Wisconsin, Madison, 1991] Ann Arbor, Michigan: UMI.

Kaltenecker, Martin. *Théodore Gouvy.* Thèse de 3e cycle preparée sous la direction de Mme. Daniele Pistone. Université de Paris-Sorbonne, 1986.

Korten, Matthais. *Mozarts Requiem und seine Bearbeitungen.* Essen, [Univ. Gesamthochschule, Diss., 1998].

Kovalenko, Susin Chaffin. *The Twentieth-century Requiem: An emerging concept.* [Washington Univ. Doctoral Thesis, 1971] Ann Arbor, Michigan: UMI, 1998.

Leong, Jeremy. *A comparative analysis of the "Dies irae" in Mozart's Requiem and Cherubini's Requiem in D minor.* [Univ. of North Texas, Denton, 1997].

Luce, H. *The Requiem Mass from its Plainsong Beginnings to 1600.* [Florida State Univ., 1958].

Lundergan, Edward J. *Benjamin Britten's War Requiem: Stylistic and technical sources.* [Univ. of Texas, 1991] Ann Arbor, Michigan: UMI.

MacDonald, J. A. *The Sacred Vocal Music of Giovanni Legrenzi.* [Univ. of Michigan, 1964].

Mattes, Andrea. *Das "Dies irae" im Requiem von W. A. Mozart: mit didaktischen Hinweisen für den Unterricht.* Hochschulschrift, Weingarten, PH Zulassungarbeit, 1985.

Merkle, Josef. *Die Entwicklung des Requiems anhand der Sequenz "Dies Irae": aufgezeigt an den Beispielen Gregorianisches Choralrequiem, Cherubini: D moll Requiem, Benjamin Britten: War Requiem.* Hochschulschrift: Weingarten, PH, Zulassungsarbeit.

Miecke, Andreas. *Das Requiem in ausgehenden 18. und im 19. Jahrhundert: Dargestellt anhand von Introitussatzen ausgewählter Vertonungen.* Bayreuth, [Univ. Schriftliche Hausarb., 1989].

Moberg, Carl-Allan. *Åkthetsfrågor i Mozarts Reqviem.* Uppsala: Lundequist, 1960. Series: Uppsala Universitets årsskrift, 1960.

Page, Gordon. *Melodic unification in Benjamin Britten's "War Requiem."* [Texas Univ., Fort Worth, 1991] Ann Arbor, Michigan: UMI.

Poland, Jeffrey. *Michael Haydn's masses and requiem mass composition.* [Univ. of Cincinnati, 1984] Ann Arbor, Michigan: UMI.

Queen, James Lowell. *The Requiem Masses of Friedrich Kiel: Structure and Style.* [Univ. of Iowa Dissertation, 1991] Ann Arbor, Michigan: UMI.

Reinecke, Erich. *Friedrich Kiel: Sein Leben und sein Werk.* [Univ. Köln, Phd. Diss., 1936] Hagen, Germany, 1976.

Roeckle, Charles Albert. *Eighteenth Century Neapolitan Settings of the Requiem Mass: Structure and Style.* [Univ. of Texas, Austin, 1978] Ann Arbor, Michigan: UMI.

Rosen, David. *The Genesis of Verdi's Requiem* [University of California, Berkeley. 1976].

Salmenhaara, Erkki and Sander Helke. *Das musikalische Material und seine Behandlung in den Werken "Apparitions," "Aventures" und Requiem von György Ligeti.* Regensburg, Germany: Bosse, 1969. Series: Forschungsbeitrage zur Musikwissenschaft; 19 [Helsinki Univ. Dissertation, 1969].

Schaffer, R. J. *A Comparative Study of Seven Polyphonic Requiem Masses.* [New York Univ., 1952].

Schnobelen, M. *The Concerted Mass at San Petronio in Bologna: ca. 1660–1730: A Documentary and Analytical Study.* [Univ. of Illinois, 1966].

Sonnenberger, Johannes. *Das Requiem (mit Beispielen für den Unterricht).* [Hochschule Mozarteum, Salzburg, Hausarb., 1979].

Sopena-Ibanez, Federico. *"El requiem en la música romantica."* Madrid: Ediciones Rialp, 1965.

Wagstaff, George Grayson. *Music for the dead: Polyphonic settings of the of the Missa pro defunctis by Spanish and Latin American composers before 1630.* [Univ. of Texas, Austin, 1995] Ann Arbor, Michigan: UMI.

Wanninger, F. *Dies irae: Its use in non-liturgical music from the beginning of the Nineteenth Century.* Northwestern Univ., 1962].

Westfater, Walter. *Overall unity and contrast in Brahms' German Requiem.* [Univ. of North Carolina, 1973].

Würzwallner, Christian. *Requiem-Vertonungen in Wien zwischen 1750 und 1820.* [Univ. Dipl. Arbeit., Wien, 1990].

Zwick, Gabriel. *Les Proses en usage à l'église de Saint-Nicolas à Fribourg jusqu'au dix-huitième siècle.* Thèse [Doctoral], Univ. of Fribourg, 1950 [pub. Imprimerie et maison d'edition Calendaria S. A. Immensee.] [1 Vol. and Annexe: 19 proses inédites].

ARTICLES

Abercrombie, Wayne. "What's in a label?: Structure and emotion in Brahms's Requiem, movement Six, Finale." *The Choral Journal* 38, no. 2 (Sept. 1997): 17.

Arnold, Denis. "The Significance of 'cori spezzati.'" *Music & Letters* XL (1959): 4.

Barraud, Henry. "La spiritualité du Requiem." *Revue de Musicologie* LXIII, no. 1–2 (1977): 123 [Berlioz Requiem].

Bauman, Thomas. "Requiem, but no Piece." *19th Century Music* XV, no. 20 (Fall 1991): [New Maunder edition of the Mozart Requiem].

Beahrs, Virginia Oakley. "Antonio Salieri: Demon or Demigod." *The Music Review* 51, no. 4 (Nov. 1990): 268.

Beckman-Collier, Aimee. "Performance practices of sacred polyphony in Rome and Madrid at the time of Tomas Luis de Victoria." *The Choral Journal* XXVIII, no. 7 (Feb. 1988): 13.

———. "Sacred choral music in the classical era." *The Choral Journal* XXXI, no. 6 (April 1991): 5.

Beller-McKenna, Daniel. "How *deutsch* a Requiem? Absolute Music, Universality and the Reception of Brahms's *Ein deutsches Requiem*, Op. 45." *19th Century Music* XXII, no. 1, (Summer 1998): 3.

Boyd, Malcom. " 'Dies irae': Some recent manifestations." *Music and Letters*, XLIX (1968): 347–56.

Breden, Sharon. "Brahms on death and destiny: Philospohical, theological and musical Implications." *The Choral Journal* 38, no. 2 (Sept. 1997): 9.

Bruyr, J. "Les grandes requiems et leur message." *Journal musical francais musica disques*, no. 116 (Nov. 1963): 4.

Cabrol, F. "L'offertoire de la messe de morts." *Revue Gregorienne*. 6 (1921): 165–170 and 205–207.

Cassella, Alfredo. "Giovanni Sgambati." *Music & Letters* 6 (1925): 304.

"Charles Villiers Stanford" by some of his pupils. *Music & Letters* V (1924): 193.

Churgin, Bathia. "Beethoven and Mozart's Requiem." *Journal of Musicology* V, no. 4 (1987): 457.

Clarke, Bruce Cooper. "From little seeds." [Mozart Requiem] *The Musical Times* CXXXVII (Dec. 1996): 13.

Cone, Edward. "Berlioz's Divine Comedy: The Grande Messe des Morts." *Nineteenth Century Music*, IV, No. 1 (Summer 1980): 3.

Cook, Larry. " Form and style in the Musikalische Exequien by Heinrich Schütz." *The Choral Journal*, Vol. XIX, no. 2 (Sept. 1988): 5.

Delisi, Daniel. "Penderecki's Polish Requiem. Some notes on texture and form." *American Choral Review* XXXI, no. 1 (Winter 1988).

Dietz, Hanns Berthold. "A Chronology of Maestri and Organisti at the Capella Reale in Naples, 1745–1800." Journal of the American Musicological Society no. 25 (Fall 1972): 379–406.

Dixon, Graham. "The Capella of S. Maria in Trastevere (1605–45): An archival study." *Music & Letters*, Vol. 62 (1981): 30.

Elby, J. "Music in the *Ancien Régime*. A requiem mass for Louis XV: Charles d'Helfer, Francois Giroust and the Missa pro defunctis of 1775." *Early Music* 29, Issue 2, 218–233.

Evans, Peter. "Britten's 'War Requiem.' " *Tempo* (spring/summer 1962): 20–39.

Fassler, Margot. "Who was Adam of St. Victor? The Evidence of the Sequence Manuscripts." *Journal of the American Musicological Society* XXXVII, no. 2 (1984): 233.

Fisher, Gary. "The use of voices and instruments at a sixteenth-century wedding feast." *The Choral Journal* 35, no. 1 (Aug. 1994).

Fox, Charles Warren. "The Polyphonic requiem before about 1615." *Bulletin of the American Musicological Society*, VII (1943): 6–7.

Frank, H. "Der älteste erhaltene ordo defunctorum . . . . " *Archiv für Liturgiewissenschaft*, VIII (1962): 360–415.

Ganus, Clifton. "Renaissance and Baroque music for voices and winds." *The Choral Journal* XVII, no. 4 (Dec. 1976): 5.

Gmeinwieser, Siegfried. "Giuseppi Ottavio Pitoni. 1657–1743." *Archiv für Musikwissenschaft*, no. 32 (1975): 298.

Gregory, Robin. "Dies irae." *Music & Letters*, XXXIV (1953): 133–39.

Gunther, S. "Das säkularisierte Requiem." *Musica*, XVIII (1964):185.

Haenni, G. "Un ordo defunctorum du Xe siècle." *Ephemerides Liturgicae*, LXXIII (1959): 431–434.

Hoorickx, Reinhard van. "Franz and Ferdinand Schubert." *The Music Review* 52, no. 2 (May 1991): 83.

Howie, A. C. "Traditional and novel elements in Bruckner's sacred music." *The Music Quarterly* LXVVII, no. 4 (Oct. 1981): 544 .

Hucke, Helmut. "G. O. Pitoni und seine Messen in Archiv der Capella Giulia: Ein Beitrag zur Geschichte für romischen Messenkomposition im 17/18. Jahrhundert." *Kirchenmusikalisches Jahrbuch*, 39 (1955): 70.

Huntington, Robert. " The "real" Fauré Requiem? The search continues." *The Choral Journal* 37, no. 3 (Oct. 1996): 9.

Husman, Heinrich. "Die Gesange der armenischen Liturgie." *Geschichte der Katholische Kirchenmusik I* [ed. K. G. Fellerer] Kassel, Basel, London. 1972.

Jacobson, Joshua. "Music in the Holocaust." *The Choral Journal* 36, no. 5 (Dec. 1995): 9.

Janower, David. "Berlioz Requiem: Editions." *The Choral Journal* XX, no. 4 (Dec. 1979): 8.

———. "Tonal unity in Berlioz's Requiem." *The Choral Journal* XXVI, no. 8 (March 1986): 31.

———. "Tutti or not Tutti?" The use of concertists in Bach's Mass in B Minor." *The Choral Journal*, Vol. XXV, no. 1 (Sept. 1984): 13.

John, Michael. "Auf dem Wege zu einen neuen Geistigkeit?": Requiem-Vertonungen in der Sowjetunion 1963–1988." *Studia slavica musicological*, Band 9 [E. Kühn, Berlin 1996]

Kowalke, Kim H. "For Those We Love: Hindemith, Whitman, and "An American Requiem." *Journal of the American Musicological Society* 50, no. 1, (1997): 133.

Lang, Paul Henry. "The Symphonic Mass." *American Choral Review* XVIII, no. 2 (1976): 7–12. [Concert Reviews].

Liebergen, Patrick. "Cecilian Movement in the nineteenth century." *The Choral Journal* XXI, no. 9 (May 1981): 13.

Locke, Benjamin. "Christiani: Cryptography in Brahms's Ein deutches Requiem." *The Choral Journal*, Vol. 39, no. 2 (Sept. 1998): 9.

Lundergan, Edward. "Musical metaphor: Cyclic-Intervallic structuring in Britten's War Requiem." *The Choral Journal* 38, no. 7 (Feb. 1998): 9.

Lutterotti, Nikolaus. "Missae pro defunctis quae modio aevo per diocesim Wratislaviensem (Breslau) dicebatur," *Ephemerides Liturgicae* XLI (1927): 445–449.

McClymonds, Marita P. "The Evolution of Jommelli's Operatic Style." *Journal of the American Musicological Society* XXXIII, no. 2 (1980): 326.

Morosan, Vladimir. "Alexander Kastalsky—Requiem: Eternal Memory to the Fallen War Heros." unpub. essay.

Matoni, Charles Rev. "A prayer for peace now: Britten's War Requiem revisited." *The Choral Journal*, Vol. XXIV, no. 2 (Oct. 1983): 21.

Mellers, Wilfrid. "Life, War and Death." Choir & Organ 9, no. 6 (Nov./Dec., 2001): & Vol. 10, no. 1, 72 (Jan./Feb. 2002, 48). [Britten War Requiem].

Musgrave, Michael. "Historical influences on the growth of Brahms' Requiem." *Music & Letters* LIII (1972): 3.

Noske, Frits. "Ritual scenes in Verdi's operas." *Music & Letters* LIV (1973): 415.

Nosow, Robert. "Song and the art of dying." *The Music Quarterly* 82, no. 3/4 (1988): 537.

O'Neal, Melina. "An introduction to performance practice considerations for the Mozart Requiem." *The Choral Journal* XXI, no. 9 (April 1991): 47.

Opfermann, B. "Notizen zur Missa defunctorum in der zweiten Hälften des Mittelalters." *Liturgische Zeitschrift*, IV (1932).

Philippeau, H. R. "Textes et rubriques des Agenda Mortuorum." *Archiv für Liturgie-Wissenschaft*, IV, Regensburg. 1955.

Planchart, Alejandro. "Guillaume Dufay's Masses: Notes and Revisions." *Music Quarterly*, LVIII (1971): 20.

Poland, Jeffrey. "Michael Haydn and Mozart: Two requiem settings." *American Choral Review* XXIX, no. 1 (Winter 1987): 3.

Reynolds, Barbara. "Verdi and Manzoni: An attempted explanation." *Music & Letters* XXIX (1948): 31.

Robinson, Ray. "A new Mozart Requiem." *The Choral Journal* XXVI, no. 1 (Aug. 1985): 5.

———. The Polish Requiem by Krzysztof Penderecki." *The Choral Journal* XXVI, no. 4 (1985): 5.

Roche, Jerome. "Giovanni Antonio Rigatti and the Development of Venetian Music in the 1640s." *Music & Letters*, Vol. LVII (1976): 256.

———. "Music at S. Maria Maggiore, Bergamo 1614–1643." *Music & Letters*, XLVII, 1966, pp. 296–314.

Roland, Jackson. "Polarities, Sound-masses and Intermodulations: A view of recent music." *The Music Review* 41 (1980): 127.

Roccasalvo, Joan. "The Znamenny chant." *The Music Quarterly* 74, no. 2 (1990): 217.

Scherbeck, Lyn. "Discovering the choral music of Estonian composer Arvo Pärt." *The Choral Journal*, Vol. 34, no. 1 (Aug. 1993): 13.

Sheets, Thomas. "Antonin Dvorak's Requiem: An introduction." *The Choral Journal* XXXII, no. 3 (Oct. 1991): 17.

Slotterback, Floyd. "Mozart's Requiem: History and Performance." *American Choral Review* 26 (1984): 2.

Snow, R. "Requiem Mass, Music of" *New Catholic Encyclopedia*, New York, 1967.

Spice, Gordon. "John Rutter speaks about his requiem." *The Choral Journal* 34, no. 7 (Feb. 1994): 23.

Studebaker, Donald. "The Liszt Requiem." *The Choral Journal* XXIII, no. 9 (May 1983): 19.

Suderman, Mark. "Comparisons between the requiems of Florian Gassman and Wolfgang Amadeus Mozart." *The Choral Journal* XXXI, no. 9 (April 1991): 33.

Thompson, Randall. "The choral music of Randall Thompson." *American Choral Review* XVI, no. 4 (Oct. 1974): 16–32.

Wagstaff, Grayson. "Music for the dead and the control of ritual behavior in Spain 1450–1550." *The Music Quarterly* 82, no. 3/4 (1998): 551.

Weinert, William. "A new edition of Ein deutsches Requiem: Implications for future research and Performance." *The Choral Journal* XXXI, no. 10 (May 1991): 35.

Wright, Craig. "Dufay at Cambrai: Discoveries and Revisions." *Journal of the American Musicological Society* XXVIII, no. 2 (1975): 175.

——. "Performance practices at the Cathedral of Cambrai 1475–1550." *The Musical Quarterly* LXIV, no. 3 (July 1978): 295.

Zeileis, Friedrich. "Two Manuscript Sources of Brahms' German Requiem." *Music & Letters* 60. (1979): 149.

Composer Index

Alain, Jehan [1938] 313
Anerio, Giovanni Francesco [1614] 44
Arkhangelsky, Alexander [c. 1890] 464
Asola, Giovanni Matteo [1586] 47
Aube, Lucien-Marie [1947–48] 314

Bach, Johann Christian [c. 1757] 138
Baracki, Nenad [c. 1923] 631
Barbe, Helmut [1965] 537
Berlioz, Hector [1837] 244
Bernardi, Steffano [c. 1600–36] 98;
    [8vv] 513
Beveridge, Thomas [1996] 384
Biber, Heinrich [15vv, 1687; 5vv, c.
    1690] 100
Bingham, James [1998–99] 435
Bomtempo, João [1818] 247
Bottesini, Giovanni [1880] 249
Brahms, Johannes [1861–68] 539
Bresgen, César [1971–72] 543
Brito, Estevao de [after 1600] 48
Britten, Benjamin [1961] 440
Bruckner, Anton [1849] 251
Brudieu, Joan [4 vv] 50
Brumel, Antoine [1516] 20
Brusa, Francesco [1767] 140
Bryars, Gavin [1989] 293

Calmel, Roger [1979; Marie Antoinette,
    1993] 317

Campra, André [c. 1722] 141
Cardoso, Manuel [1625] 51
Casciolini, Claudio [1740?] 144
Caurroy, Eustache du [c. 1606] 53
Cavalli, Francesco [1675] 105
Cererols, Joan [4vv, 7vv, c. 1650–51]
    108
Charpentier, Marc Antoine [4vv/inst.,
    1697–98; 4vv, c. 1690; Trépasses, c.
    1690] 111; [c. 1690] 514
Chein, Louis [1690] 145
Cherubini, Luigi [C minor, 1816; D
    minor, 1834–36] 191
Chesnokov, Pavel [Op. 39, c. 1910; Op.
    30, early twentieth cent.] 609
Cimarosa, Domenico [1787] 146
Clemens non Papa [1580] 55
Clucas, Humphrey [1988] 320
Cordans, Bartolomeo [1738] 149

Davies, Henry [1915] 437
De Lange, Daniel [1868] 253
Delius, Frederic [1913–16] 447
De Mars, James [1993] 391
Desenclos, Alfred [1963] 322
Dittersdorf, Carl Ditters von [before
    1787] 194
Donizetti, Gaetano [1870] 255
Draeseke, Felix [1876–80] 257

About the Author

Robert Chase is a professor of music at Pace University in White Plains, New York. He is also a faculty member of Iona Preparatory School in New Rochelle, New York; the director of music of the Church in the Highlands in White Plains; and the organist, Scarsdale Synagogue-Tremont Temple in Scarsdale, New York. A private lecturer and performing musician, Chase is also the dean of the Westchester Chapter of the American Guild of Organists.

The author's other publications include *Jules Van Nuffel, Eighteenth-century Czech Organ Composers, Free Harmonizations of Hymn Tunes by Fifty American Composers, Jules Van Nuffel and His Music*. He also translated *The History of the Organ in Russian Musical Culture* by Leonid Roisman (from Russian to English).

He is married to Jenny Wei-Liang Kao, professional singer, and has one son, Wayne.